international business

AN INTEGRATED APPROACH

JOHN J. WILD

UNIVERSITY OF WISCONSIN, MADISON

KENNETH L. WILD

UNIVERSITY OF LONDON, ENGLAND

JERRY C. Y. HAN

STATE UNIVERSITY OF NEW YORK, BUFFALO
UNIVERSITY OF HONG KONG

E-Business
UPDATED EDITION

With contributions by Melanie Treviño

Prentice Hall

UPPER SADDLE RIVER, NEW JERSEY 07458

E-Business Update

Beacon

A Look at This Section

This update discusses how the explosion in electronic business is affecting important international business issues. It explores the World Wide Web, the Internet, and different types of electronic business transactions. It then explores several key areas of international electronic business.

For those who were skeptical about its eventual impact, there can no longer be any doubt: The Internet is changing the way the world does business. Every industry, from fast moving consumer goods to industrial products, is being affected by the dissemination and use of Internet technology to conduct business transactions. Companies at every stage in the value chain including manufacturers, distributors, and retailers are being forced to rethink their strategies in the context of Internet commerce. Managers are discovering that they must devise new tactics for competing in a business world that moves at Internet time. New ways of conducting business are threatening the viability of companies and industries slow to adapt to the new realities of Internet commerce. The Internet is further breaking down barriers to international competition, bringing more and more companies in distant locations into direct competition with one another.

What does this mean for companies in different regions of the world? Because the Internet was developed in the United States, it is there that Internet commerce is most advanced. Companies began using the Internet as simply one more broadcast medium to advertise their products. But today, many U.S. companies have woven Internet strategies into their traditional strategies. For these companies, attention is now turning to other geographic markets to get a jump on competition. Thus the markets of Asia, Europe, and Latin America are already seeing dramatic changes in the way their industries conduct business. The Internet revolution will land on every shore, and companies everywhere are planning for its arrival.

Develop Students' Basic Geographic Skills

GLOBE

(Global Landscape of the Business Environment)

helps students develop basic geographic skills and allows them to explore the political, cultural, economic, and physical geography of the world. Students can use this highly interactive CD-ROM to draw their own thematic maps, analyze country or regional economic data, and review how geography impacts business decisions.

In addition, GLOBE contains a full digital reference atlas of the world.

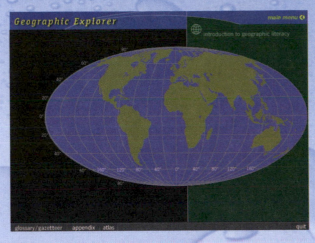

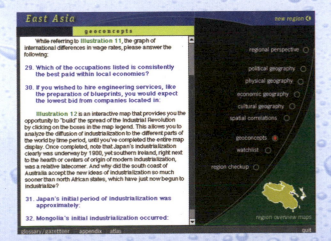

Economic Geography

Using the appendix of statistical data (GNP, birthrate, etc.) students can create regional and country profiles that affect business decisions.

CONTENTS

- *The United States and Canada*
- *Latin America*
- *Africa South of the Sahara*
- *The Middle East and North Africa*
- *Europe*
- *Russia, Central Asia, and Transcauasia*
- *East Asia*
- *South Asia*
- *Southeast Asia*
- *Australia, New Zealand, and the Pacific Islands*

Geo Concepts

These exercises help students identify major concepts and respond to specific situations that managers often confront.

This update discusses how the explosion in electronic business is affecting important international business issues. We begin by explaining the nature of the World Wide Web and the Internet. Then we explore the scope of electronic business and important distinctions between different types of e-business transactions. We conclude this update by discussing how e-business is affecting important international business issues covered in various chapters throughout the remainder of the book.

THE INTERNET AND THE WORLD WIDE WEB

The **Internet** is the integrated global network of telecommunication equipment that provides for the electronic exchange of products and information. The Internet is often referred to as the "information superhighway" because of the enormous amount of information available through it. Access to the Internet typically requires the use of a personal computer, a modem, and physical connection to a computer server via telephone lines. Today, however, we can access the Internet with just a cellular phone—although only a limited amount of information is available this way.

The Internet supports what is called the **World Wide Web**—a user-friendly service operating on the Internet that displays information in what are called Web pages. The "Web" consists of individual Web sites run by organizations (companies, governments, special interest groups, etc.) and individuals. Every day, nearly 4,500 new Web sites are showing up and almost 2 million new Web pages appear. In 2002, there is likely to be about 8 billion Web pages on the Internet. Information is placed on a Web site using a computer programming language called hypertext markup language (html). Individual computers receive information from a specific Web site using what is called the hypertext transfer protocol (http). Receiving information from a Web site on a personal computer requires the use of a Web browser such as Netscape's "Navigator" or Microsoft's "Internet Explorer."

Figure E.1 shows a comparison of the number of years it took the World Wide Web versus several other innovations to reach a base of 50 million users. Thus we see that the Web grew faster than any other major technological introduction in history.

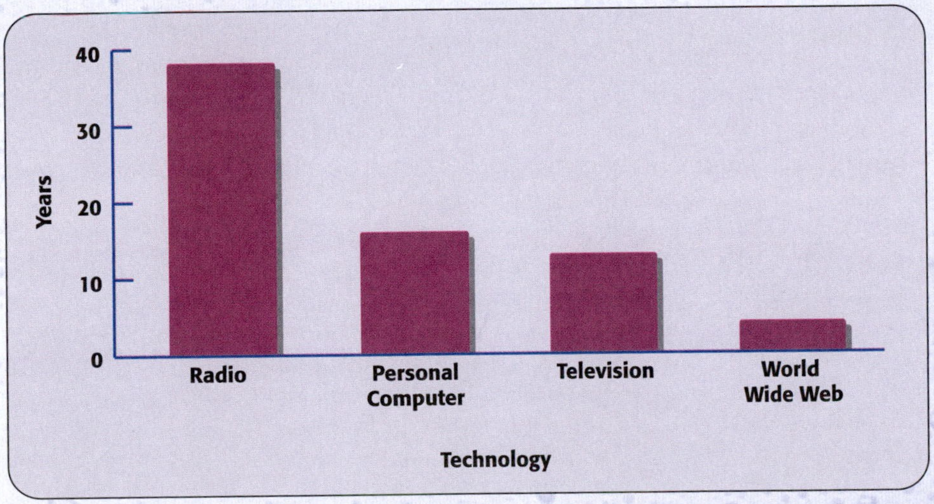

Internet
Integrated global network of telecommunication equipment that provides for the electronic exchange of products and information.

World Wide Web
User-friendly service operating on the Internet that displays information in what are called Web pages.

FIGURE E.1

YEARS TO REACH 50 MILLION USERS

The Internet has existed in various forms since 1969. However, until the World Wide Web was developed in 1995, the Internet was used primarily for e-mail and transferring large computer files. In fact, the number of Internet users doubled in each of its first three years of the Web's existence.

WEB SITE ADDRESSING SYSTEM

Every Web site has an address on the World Wide Web called a Uniform Resource Locator (URL). If you haven't already done so, visit this book's Web site ⟨http://www.prenhall.com/wild⟩. Notice the address begins with "http" and contains "www" which refers to the World Wide Web (today it is common to omit the "http" prefix when referencing an address because it is standard for every Web site). When a specific Web page is then accessed at the site, the "html" suffix appears at the end of the URL. Finally, the "com" portion of the URL indicates that the Web site is that of a company—in this case it designates this book's publisher Prentice Hall (abbreviated "prenhall"). Table E.1 lists the suffixes added to different organizations.

Because the Internet was created in the United States, the Web site addresses of U.S. organizations end with a ".com" or ".edu" suffix. The Web site of an organization located on a computer outside the United States adds a suffix that distinguishes its national origin. For example, the Web site of a company in Mexico adds ".mx" to the end of its address and one in Japan adds ".jp" to its address. Table E.2 lists the suffixes that are added to Web site addresses of a sample of nations.

This system of registering URL addresses (also called domain names) has created some major headaches for some of the world's best-known brands. So-called cyber-squatters register global brand names in the domain designation of their home country. For example, registering your company's domain name in the U.S. ⟨www.yourcompany.com⟩ does not preclude someone from registering the same company name in the United Kingdom following that country's domain registration convention ⟨www.yourcompany.co.uk⟩—companies in the United Kingdom use ".co" in place of the ".com" designation for a company. International law still is not entirely clear on how to resolve such matters for many reasons, not least of which is which country's legal system has jurisdiction. One recent study looked into whether global companies are protecting their brand names worldwide. Curiously, the study found that 6 of the 10 least vigilant companies are in high-tech. For example, Gateway, Inc. ⟨www.gateway.com⟩ owns just

TABLE E.1	The URLs of Organizations
.com	Companies
.edu	Educational institutions
.gov	Governments and their agencies
.org	Non-profits and other organizations
.net	Internet companies

TABLE E.2	The URLs of Countries		
.de	Germany	.dk	Denmark
.uk	United Kingdom	.it	Italy
.ar	Argentina	.at	Austria
.kr	South Korea	.jp	Japan
.nl	Netherlands	.br	Brazil
.au	Australia	.za	South Africa
.ch	Switzerland	.fr	France

three Web addresses worldwide and has allowed 39 derivations of this domain name to be registered—for example, see the Web site of Gateway Computing, Ltd. ⟨www.gateway.co.uk⟩. Texas Instruments ⟨www.ti.com⟩ owns just two domain names globally and has allowed 31 derivations of this address to be registered.[1]

WHAT IS ELECTRONIC BUSINESS?

The purchase, sale, or exchange of goods, services, or information over telecommunication networks is called **electronic business** (or **e-business**). E-business includes many types of activities including on-line advertising, distribution, billing, payment, and service. But e-business (also referred to as e-commerce) involves not only business transactions, but includes all types of electronic exchanges related to business (or commercial) activity.

People often take part in electronic commerce when traveling—whether or not they realize it. For instance, many people no longer rely on traveler's checks when abroad on business because of the wide availability of Automated Teller Machines (ATMs) in industrialized countries. They simply place their credit card into the ATM's card reader and punch in their personal identification number (PIN). The ATM sends the PIN number and the account information it read from the credit card to the credit card company's computers for authorization. This is done via satellite transmission. When the transaction is authorized, cash is dispensed to the person at the ATM and his or her account in the home country is credited for the amount of the cash advance. This entire e-business transaction takes place in mere seconds.

> **electronic business** (or **e-business**)
> Purchase, sale, or exchange of goods, services, or information over telecommunication networks.

BUSINESS-TO-CONSUMER TRANSACTIONS

Most consumers access the World Wide Web through what is called an Internet Service Provider (ISP). The largest and best known is America Online ⟨www.aol.com⟩. AOL does more than simply provide access to the Internet. It channels its customers (Web "surfers") to the Web sites of companies either affiliated with AOL or those advertising on its Web site. Many of these companies have sites that are capable of selling goods and services directly to visitors over the Internet using a credit card. These transactions (called business-to-consumer transactions) account for a relatively small portion of total spending on the Internet. However, for most people it is the most visible type of transaction because either they are not personally involved in business transactions on the Internet or it is the type of transaction covered most by the media.

Figure E.2 shows the growth in the total value of on-line U.S. consumer spending in recent years. As we see, consumer purchases on the Internet did not really occur prior to the introduction of the World Wide Web, which made on-line shopping a fairly easy chore. The figure also shows the expected sharp rise in on-line spending in 2003 and 2004 that could approach $180 billion. The expected increase is due mostly to more households becoming comfortable with on-line shopping and the increasing user-friendliness of the on-line shopping experience. Experts anticipate seeing the same pattern emerge in other industrialized countries in coming years. Outside the United States, on-line sales are expanding most rapidly in Europe. Total on-line spending by businesses and consumers in Europe is expected to jump to $430 billion in 2003, up from $5.6 billion in 1998. Of the European countries, the United Kingdom should be the hottest market, with on-line spending expected to reach $50 million in 2002.[2]

The New Marketspace Traditionally, business transactions took place only between buyers and sellers in the marketplace—the physical environment consisting of stores, offices, and involving contact between individuals. However, e-business transactions take place (at least in part) in the so-called **marketspace**—the electronic environ-

> **marketspace**
> Electronic environment made up of telecommunication technologies in which electronic business activities occur.

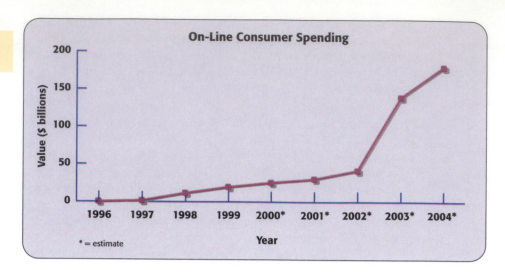

ment made up of telecommunication technologies in which electronic business activities occur. For example, a consumer in Germany purchasing a book on-line at the German Web site of Amazon.com ⟨www.amazon.de⟩ is a transaction that takes place (only in part) in the marketspace. Just part of this transaction takes place in the marketspace because the book itself must still be physically delivered to the customer with the help of a delivery service. On the other hand, purchasing the music of your favorite musical artist from MP3.com ⟨www.mp3.com⟩ is a pure e-business transaction. All that is required is for you to enter your credit card information and download the music directly onto your personal computer. The transaction takes place only in the new marketspace without any involvement of the traditional marketplace.

BUSINESS-TO-BUSINESS TRANSACTIONS

Transactions occurring between two or more businesses that do not involve consumers are called business-to-business transactions. These business-to-business transactions (commonly referred to as B2B transactions) account for around 80 percent of all e-business—totaling more than $150 billion in 1999 and possibly close to $3 trillion by 2004. Today companies in many industries are creating on-line markets to make the purchase and sale of component parts more efficient. For example, leading computer makers and their component suppliers made an important announcement on May 1, 2000. They announced a plan to create an on-line market where members can buy and sell computer components. "This will transform the way our business manages and optimizes its very complex supply chain," said Carly Fiorina, chief executive officer of Hewlett-Packard ⟨www.hp.com⟩. Executives involved in the deal believe that the new market could allow computer makers to trim 5 to 7 percent from manufacturing costs within the next few years.[3]

Figure E.3 shows the actual and estimated total value of U.S. business-to-business transactions between 1996 and 2004. As shown, the value of such transactions is expected to balloon in coming years as more companies move to performing many activities electronically to reduce costs. It is expected that this pattern will be repeated in other countries as the Internet becomes more accepted around the globe. Let's now take a look at how companies have used technology to carry out their transactions and how the Internet is changing the rules of the game.

Electronic Data Interchange There are several ways companies can carry out their e-business transactions in the business-to-business market.[4] First, they can use what is

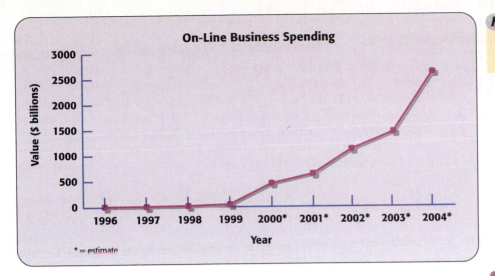

On-Line Business Spending

Value ($ billions) vs. Year (1996, 1997, 1998, 1999, 2000*, 2001*, 2002*, 2003*, 2004*)

* = estimate

called an **Electronic Data Interchange (EDI)**—a telecommunication network that businesses use to exchange information such as purchase orders, invoices, and electronic payments. Let's discuss the two main types of EDI—*traditional* and *Internet-based*.

Traditional EDI A telecommunication network used to translate information created on different computer platforms into a globally understood language is referred to as a traditional EDI. For nearly 30 years until roughly 1996, it was the most efficient and effective way for companies (manufacturers, wholesalers, and retailers) to exchange information with one another. Procter & Gamble ⟨www.pg.com⟩, Toys "R" Us ⟨www.toysrus.com⟩, and Wal-Mart ⟨www.walmart.com⟩ are three companies that were instrumental in spurring the development of traditional EDI. One major innovation that traditional EDI launched was Just In Time (JIT) production scheduling.

Unfortunately, because of the large expense and complexity of setting up a traditional EDI system, only the world's largest companies benefited from its implementation. In fact, because of this high cost, many companies could only connect with the top 20 percent of its business partners—only those who could afford to make the investment.

Internet-based EDI In the mid 1990s, large and small firms alike benefited from the development of Internet-based EDI, often called an **extranet**—a telecommunication network that operates on a single platform that allows for the easy exchange of information between companies. Extranets use the Internet and World Wide Web to link together an unlimited number of business partners (such as suppliers, buyers, and even joint venture partners) at very low cost relative to traditional EDI. Because it makes use of the Internet, even small companies can afford to connect with business partners anywhere in the world. John J. Fontanella, director of supply-chain research at market-watcher AMR Research ⟨www.amrresearch.com⟩ in Boston, estimates that as much as 90 percent of all manufacturing could soon be done through the Internet.[5]

One company applying the new economics of the Internet to its manufacturing is Cisco Systems ⟨www.cisco.com⟩. Cisco outsources production of its computers to 37 factories with which it links through the Internet. These suppliers manufacture all components, do all subassembly work, and perform more than half of all final assembly work. In addition, they often ship the finished product directly to customers with no physical involvement by Cisco. Moreover, by generating 80 percent of its sales on-line, Cisco also needs fewer salespeople, technicians, and paper-shufflers. Using this model,

Electronic Data Interchange (EDI)
Telecommunication network that businesses use to exchange information such as purchase orders, invoices, and electronic payments.

extranet
Telecommunication network that operates on a single platform that allows for the easy exchange of information between companies.

as opposed to owning and operating such component manufacturing operations itself, Cisco saved $500–$800 million in 1999 alone.[6]

A related technological innovation that companies employ in their internal communications is called an **intranet**—a network of computers within an organization that are linked to one another with Internet/Web-based technologies. Companies restrict access to their intranets because it resides on their main computers that contain a great deal of sensitive information. They do this to keep out both competitors and/or "hackers" who can be one and the same. Information commonly accessed on a typical firm's intranet is marketing and sales data. For example, salespeople in distant locations often use their laptop computers to access customer files on the company's central computer through its intranet.

intranet
Network of computers within an organization that are linked to one another with Internet/Web-based technologies.

KEY ISSUES IN E-BUSINESS

Now that we understand the fundamentals of e-business, let's explore how the explosion in e-business is affecting several prominent international business issues. Specifically, we examine language, buyer behavior, Internet censorship, Internet taxation, consumer protection, credit card fraud, e-trading, cybermarkets, and e-business strategy and structure.

CULTURE

The Internet allows companies to access markets they could never before reach in a cost-effective manner. Because the Internet was created in the United States, U.S. companies were first in using the Web to reach a worldwide market. Many companies believed all that was needed to appeal to a global audience was to launch their English-language, U.S.-based Web site. But cultural differences are as important in international e-business as they are in traditional forms of international business. Attention to cultural differences will become even more important as more people outside North America gain access to the Internet.

Figure E.4 shows Internet access by people in different regions of the world. However, this is a static picture. By 2004, more than 110 million Europeans will have Internet access—accounting for about one-third of all Internet users. Germany, the Scandinavian countries, and the United Kingdom will lead the way while Greece, Italy, and Spain will be laggards. The Asia Pacific region is expected to have nearly one-fourth of all Internet users by 2004. Today, 96 percent of all e-business is conducted in English.

FIGURE E.4

INTERNET ACCESS BY REGION

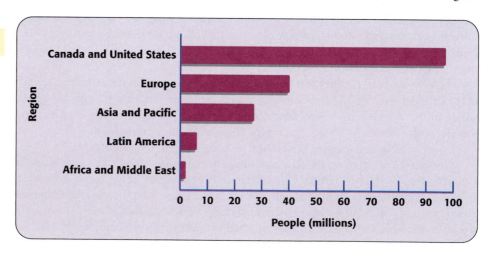

However, this will change drastically as the makeup of Net users shifts and begins to represent a more even distribution worldwide.[7]

Language We discuss the importance of language in international business in Chapter 2 and mention problems related to language translations on the Web (see page 43). Although many tech-savvy people around the world can and do speak English, there remains the possibility that Web site content can be misunderstood. Ideally, a company that does a great deal of retail business globally should have a local-language Web site based in each country in which it does business. Why? Imagine you are a consumer in Australia and wish to purchase an item from a German company. You would need to go to the company's Germany-based Web site, read through material in German, purchase the product, and have it shipped to Australia. This is a cumbersome process that could kill a sale before it begins. The shopping experience would likely be more pleasant and less risky for the consumer if the site were in English and the shipment initiated from within Australia. In addition, having a Web site in each local market can speed up download times for Web site content such as photos and graphics.

It is often the case that only the largest companies, or those that do a great deal of retail business in a country can afford separate Web sites in different countries. But smaller companies and those doing little retail business abroad should at least translate their Web site into the languages of those countries from which buyers are coming to the site. In fact, it has been reported that people are three times more likely to buy a product if a Web site is in their own language. "Every day that our site is not up and running in the customer's local language, we're losing business," says Bill Bass, vice-president of e-commerce at Lands' End ⟨www.landsend.com⟩.[8] Today, translation services are widely available and software to assist in such tasks is constantly improving and will make developing local-language sites a less difficult procedure. SDL International ⟨www.sdlintl.com⟩ is one company that supplies translation assistance and other localization services for companies involved in international e-business.

Buyer Behavior We cover buyer behavior issues in-depth throughout Chapter 2 and in Chapter 15 (for example, page 515). Consumers in different countries do not purchase things in exactly the same way. For example, while people in the United States generally are quite comfortable making on-line purchases with credit cards, the same is not true in Japan. In fact, less than 10 percent of on-line purchases in Japan are made with credit cards. Instead, Japanese buyers rely on bank transfers and cash-on-delivery (COD). Also, many Japanese consumers already go to their local 7-Eleven ⟨www.sej.co.jp⟩ store to pay utility and other bills—7-Eleven's Web site for the U.S. home market is ⟨www.7eleven.com⟩. Therefore, many Web merchants include "Payment at a 7-Eleven Store" as an option on their Japan-based Web sites. Following an on-line purchase, customers simply print out a payment slip and take it to their local 7-Eleven shop. Recently, 7-Eleven launched a new venture ⟨www.7dream.com⟩ that allows Japanese buyers to not only pay for their on-line purchases at one of 7-Eleven's 8,000 shops in Japan, but to pick them up there as well. Thus 7-Eleven shops in Japan could become e-business kiosks in Japan, acting as both payment and fulfillment centers.[9]

Also, the way products are described and the detail to which descriptions go should be tailored to the way consumers shop in different cultures. Some cultures may be quite familiar with a product, a Palm Pilot ⟨www.palm.com⟩ for example, and need little more than pricing information. People in other cultures may be less knowledgeable and require details on how a product actually functions and each of its components. Companies that lack knowledge of local customers are often wise to partner with a local firm that can supply in-depth cultural understanding.

INTERNET CENSORSHIP

Government regulation of all types of international business activity is nothing new. In Chapter 3 we explain that nations can have very different political and legal systems and that this affects the extent to which they regulate business activity. The same holds true for international e-business activity.

The people of some countries (such as Germany, Sweden, the United Kingdom, and the United States) are inundated with "dot.com" advertisements daily and have access to practically any Web site they desire. Meanwhile, the people of other countries (such as Libya, North Korea, and Turkmenistan) probably don't know what the Internet is and are lucky if they have even been exposed to it. People of still other nations (such as Burma and China) have access to the Net but are restricted in its use and are severely punished if they stray from the law. For instance, software engineer Li Hai of Shanghai, China, received a two-year jail sentence for passing a list of Chinese e-mail addresses to a U.S.-based pro-democracy group in 1999.

Some governments block access to certain information in their conventional media but are dismayed when they see people easily accessing it on the Internet. One example is Saudi Arabia's restrictions on the Internet because of the presence of sites offering pornography and gambling—both clearly against Islamic values. The governments of other countries stifle free speech because of fears that it could undermine their authoritarian regimes. These nations restrict Internet access to reduce people's access to criticism of the political leadership by sources outside the country.

Although governments have a number of tools at their disposal to restrict Internet access, citizens have all sorts of ways to evade the watchful eye of big brother. "In Syria, for example, people go to Lebanon for the weekend to retrieve their e-mail," says Virginie Locussol, RSF's desk officer for the Middle East and Africa specialist. Web surfers can also get around government restrictions by dialing up an ISP in their own country and then connecting to a server outside the country that has no restrictions placed on

In the early years of the Web's introduction into Malaysia, the government restricted its use severely. However, it recently relaxed its controls on Internet access, in part, to lure global, high-tech firms into its new Multimedia Corridor. Students at Malaysia's Muslim University also benefited from fewer Internet restrictions by being able to access materials to complete assignments.

Source: (c)Tara Sosrowardoyo/ Indopix 1998.

it.[10] Internet service providers are also doing their part to get around government restrictions. For example, it takes two months on average for Chinese authorities to track down the relay server of a site and block access to it, according to Zhang Weiguo, editor of the U.S.-based Chinese-language Web site New Century Net ⟨www.ncn.org⟩. All a blacklisted site must do is simply change its address and go on with business as usual until caught and filtered out once again. Even if censors are somewhat successful in their efforts, censored pages are sometimes distributed by e-mail—similar to the way underground newspapers are photocopied and passed around secretly.[11]

One organization that reports on the methods governments use to restrict Internet access is Reporters Without Borders (RSF) ⟨www.rsf.fr⟩ based in Paris, France. According to RSF, 45 countries restrict their citizens from freely accessing the Net. The organization calls 20 countries "enemies of the Internet" because they control Internet access totally or partially, censor Web sites, or take actions against Internet users. Table E.3 on page E-12 lists these 20 countries and describes how each one restricts access.

Among other things, the RSF calls on the governments of these nations to:[12]

➡ Abolish state monopoly on Internet access and stop controlling private ISPs

➡ Not oblige citizens to register with the government before obtaining Internet access

➡ Abolish the use of censorship filters and stop blocking access to sites maintained abroad

➡ Protect the confidentiality of Internet exchanges, particularly by lifting controls on e-mail

➡ Cancel legal action against Internet users that exercised their right to free expression

INTERNET TAXATION

In the text, issues related to government taxation of commerce are covered in Chapter 3 (pages 105–107). The regulation objectives of governments of industrialized countries are relatively less invasive. These nations realize the potential boost that e-business can give their economies in increasing efficiency and creating customer value. Light government regulation—especially in the area of taxation—has been shown to have a positive influence on e-business activity. For example, in the United States the volume of e-business skyrocketed in part because of a moratorium on the levying of sales taxes on Internet purchases. This also has certainly been one factor in U.S. companies gaining a leadership position in many industries that are moving to the Net. But this moratorium will not remain in place indefinitely. One reason is that individual state governments are losing revenues that they would otherwise be receiving on sales at brick-and-mortar stores. Second, brick-and-mortar retailers are lobbying their public officials, making the case that e-retailers have an unfair advantage because they attract customers wishing to avoid sales taxes.[13]

CONSUMER PROTECTION

Subjects of controversy that many governments are vigorously pursuing on the Net are hate speech, child pornography, and the protection of consumer privacy (regarding financial and other types of personal data). Authorities often work side-by-side with legitimate businesses to devise reasonable sets of regulations. For instance, a meeting was held in Germany in September 1999 by the Bertelsmann Foundation, a public

TABLE E.3   Enemies of the Net

Belarus	Single, government-owned ISP (Belpak) restricts Internet access.
Burma	State monopoly on Internet access. Anyone owning a computer must declare it to the government (failure to comply may result in a 15-year prison term).
Tajikistan	Single, government-owned ISP (Telecom Technologies) restricts Web access.
Turkmenistan	A black hole of information—more restricted than Tajikistan.
Uzbekistan and Azerbaijan	Privately owned ISPs exist but are controlled by the telecommunications ministry (which chastises those who speak out against the government).
Kazakhstan and Kyrgyzstan	Authorities charge private ISPs extremely high usage and connection fees.
China	Government keeps pressure on users who are closely monitored and supposed to register with the authorities.
Cuba	Government-controlled Internet access. Independent (and illegal) news agencies such as Cubanet and Cuba Free Press phone reports to news organizations in Miami who publish them on the Web—Cuban government punishes offenders when found.
Iran	Censorship includes blocking sites containing/discussing sexuality, religion, criticism of the Islamic Republic, and mentions of Israel and the United States. Filters ban access to some sites—for example, medical students are denied access to Web pages that deal with anatomy.
Iraq	No direct access to the Internet—very few people own computers. Web sites of official press and some ministries are maintained on servers in Jordan.
Libya	Internet access impossible in Libya.
North Korea	Internet access impossible in North Korea. The few official sites aimed at foreigners are maintained on servers in Japan.
Saudi Arabia	Traffic of private ISPs passes through servers of Science and Technology Center—a public body that filters sites that provide "information contrary to Islamic values." Internet is officially regarded as "a harmful force for westernizing people's minds."
Sierra Leone	Authorities crack down on opposition press—including on-line newspaper "Ninjas" which is maintained on a server abroad 〈www.sierra-leone.cc〉.
Sudan	Government-owned ISP (Sudanet) restricts access to the Internet.
Syria	Internet access officially banned to individuals—offenders may face prison sentence. Government provides Internet access to state-owned news agencies and ministries.
Tunisia	The two privately owned ISPs are controlled by the government—one run by the president's daughter and the other by a person close to the government.
Vietnam	Permission required to access the Internet and use is restricted to one of two state-owned ISPs. Access blocked to sites maintained by Vietnamese organizations based abroad and international human rights organizations.

Source: Adapted from Reporters Without Borders, "The Twenty Enemies of the Internet" Press Release, August 9, 1999, Available World Wide Web 〈www.rsf.fr/indexuk.html〉.

policy research organization run by media giant Bertelsmann Corporation 〈www.bertels mann.de〉. The meeting resulted in a call to act upon several measures including:[14]

➡ Broader use of rating and filtering mechanisms at the user end, as opposed to the source

➡ Development of a system consisting of international hot lines to speed detection of subjects such as child pornography

➡ Expansion of industry self-regulatory measures such as codes of conduct

Despite national efforts by industry and government, international agreements regarding privacy issues can be far more elusive. One high-profile disagreement is currently taking place between the United States and the European Union (EU). The EU wants stronger consumer privacy in e-business transactions than U.S. companies can presently provide. The EU is protesting the export of personal data gathered in the course of e-business transactions between European consumers and U.S. businesses. At present, a solution to the problem is very expensive. To satisfy EU demands, U.S. companies would need to establish separate computer systems within Europe that would store personal information on EU customers.[15] Government regulation issues are covered in the text in Chapter 3 (pages 99–107).

Credit Card Fraud Another hot issue in cyberspace is the real and potential abuse of credit card information by individual hackers and organized crime. Credit card fraud is certainly nothing new. Consumers have seen personal credit card information abused for years when there existed only brick-and-mortar stores. Many consumers believe that they are responsible for all Internet purchases made on their account. But if the credit information of an on-line buyer is stolen and put to fraudulent use, credit card companies limit the personal liability to $50, with the companies assuming the remaining liability. In fact, they often forgive even the consumer's initial $50 liability. But help may be on the way in deterring cybercrime. It is likely that rating agencies will be formed to certify Web sites that are deemed safe for conducting e-business. Such ratings would be based on an e-merchant's ability to provide privacy regarding a customer's financial or health-related information.[16]

FINANCIAL MARKETS

The text covers financial markets thoroughly in Chapters 9 and 14—here we discuss only those issues related to the Internet and these markets. The Internet's raw power to effect change is perhaps being felt more strongly in financial markets than in any other realm of international business. Information is the lifeblood of financial markets— lenders and borrowers rely on information to make informed financial decisions. The "information superhighway," as the Internet is often referred to, is forcing fundamental changes in the global financial system. The Internet is altering several key aspects of international financial markets:[17]

➡ Markets will be more efficient and liquid as markets remain open 24 hours a day and investors may buy shares directly from companies. Trading volume on stock exchanges will rise as the cost of trading shares falls drastically.

➡ Risk taking and risk management will change as financial institutions design more sophisticated risk-management tools.

➡ Economic growth will continue worldwide as technological innovation and economic activity increase in efficient capital markets.

➡ Investors will become increasingly savvy at Internet investing, causing the volume of on-line transactions to soar despite a steep learning curve.

➡ Management of financial institutions will reduce costs by building a direct pipeline to customers.

➡ Governments will be pressured to increase the transparency of their financial institutions, but financial and regional financial meltdowns will likely continue.

E-Trading We see the impact of several of these elements at work in the brokerage industry. Moving financial transactions onto the Internet is threatening many long-established stock brokerage firms. In fact, by many estimates, as much as one-half of all retail stock trades could soon be conducted on-line. New, on-line financial intermediaries (or e-brokers) with lower cost structures allow investors to buy and sell shares of stock at far less cost than making trades through a broker at a brick-and-mortar institution.

For instance, e-broker Ameritrade ⟨www.ameritrade.com⟩ charges just $8 for a stock trade regardless of the number of shares traded. Meanwhile, a traditional broker-assisted trade through long-established broker Charles Schwab ⟨www.schwab.com⟩ is $144 for 1,000 shares and $375 for 10,000 shares. Ameritrade, on the other hand, charges just $18 for a broker-assisted trade (regardless of the volume of shares traded). Charles Schwab has responded to the threat posed by e-brokers by aggressively promoting Internet trades. However, Schwab's prices tend to be significantly higher—it charges $29.95 for on-line trades of 1,000 shares and $299.95 for on-line trades of 10,000 shares. Two other e-brokers making inroads on the turf of traditional brokers are Datek ⟨www.datek.com⟩ and E*Trade ⟨www.etrade.com⟩. Datek charges $9.99 and E*Trade charges $14.95 for low-volume trades but both charge higher fees for larger volume trades.[18]

Cybermarkets We discuss how so-called cybermarkets (electronic stock markets) are helping spur growth in the international equity market in Chapter 14 (page 304). Cybermarkets pose a real threat to long-established financial institutions such as NASDAQ ⟨www.nasdaq.com⟩ in the United States. The introduction of Germany's Neuer Markt ⟨www.neuermarkt.com⟩ illustrates the kinds of changes ushered in by cybermarkets. Another less successful on-line exchange based in Europe is Easdaq ⟨www.easdaq.com⟩ based in Brussels. Although Neuer Markt began in 1997 with two listed companies, in early 2000 it boasted more than 200 listed firms with a market valuation of more than $80 billion. Neuer Markt's rapid growth was driven by general excitement about the Internet, a trend toward greater equity investment in Europe, and its own relaxed listing requirements.

Similar to NASDAQ, Neuer Markt lists primarily fast-growing startup companies in the technology sector—the so-called new economy companies. But while trades are executed electronically on Neuer Markt, trades are still executed over fax machines and telephones by human market makers at NASDAQ. This older way of executing orders will surely be phased out soon. As NASDAQ's president Al Berkeley says, "traditionally,

Traditional stock exchanges require a physical location where a large number of brokers and intermediaries make the market function. The Stock Exchange of Hong Kong ⟨www.sehk.com.hk⟩ is a large facility on an island where rents are very expensive. The Internet can reduce or eliminate many of the costs associated with large, physical, stock exchanges by replacing them with entirely electronic exchanges (or cybermarkets).

Source: Photo Researchers, Inc./(c)Rick Browne.

the financial markets are full of intermediaries and intermediaries' intermediaries. It will be disintermediated."[19]

E-BUSINESS STRATEGY & STRUCTURE

In Chapter 5 (page 174) we explain the importance of the so-called first-mover advantage—the economic and strategic advantage gained by being the first company to enter an industry. Companies doing business on the Internet also covet the first-mover advantage. So far, evidence from the development of the Internet shows that those who do not move quickly on the Web will lose out to the nimble. One company taking an aggressive approach to international expansion is California-based eToys ⟨www.etoys.com⟩. The company is launching a retail site in the United Kingdom ⟨www.etoys.co.uk⟩ as a beachhead for future international expansion. "The first-mover advantage is significant," says James Bidwell, eToys director of marketing for Europe. But eToys is utilizing a partnering strategy in its international e-business activities, not going it alone. In the United Kingdom, eToys is partnering with local companies for activities including Web site management, marketing, merchandising, purchasing, and public relations and advertising. "Across all areas of our business. . . We are coupling local knowledge with our U.S. track record," says Bidwell of the firm's strategy.[20]

In Chapter 12 (pages 427–429), we discuss the issues surrounding the centralization versus decentralization decision. The key issues of concern in this decision reflect the desire of companies to "think globally and act locally." They want to increase efficiency and effectiveness by centralizing those activities that do not require local expertise and decentralize those that do. We've already discussed the operations of companies whose storefronts exist only on the Internet. Such e-businesses are not immune to the need to consider the centralization versus decentralization question. E-corporations must also consider the structure of their businesses, just as traditional brick-and-mortar companies do.

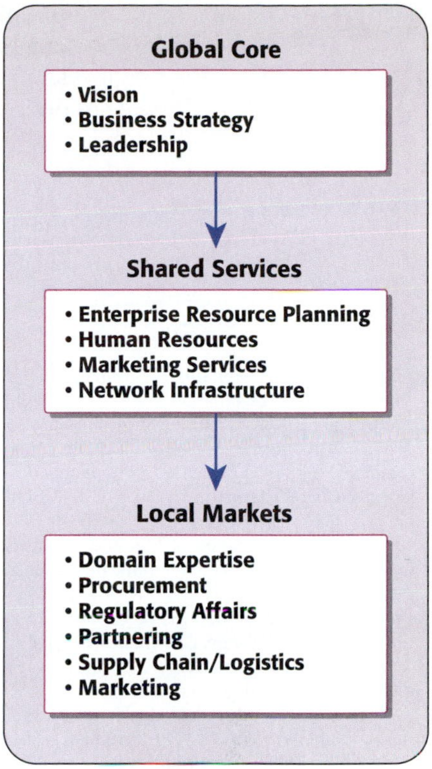

Figure E.5 shows an emerging three-layer model for global e-corporations. In this model, the global e-corporation consists of a global core of activities that includes corporate vision, leadership, and strategy. It is in this core that top executives decide how it will approach international expansion and provide leadership in corporate-wide marketing efforts and administration. The second layer consists of a set of shared services that each regional market unit obtains from the global core. These include enterprise resource planning (procurement), human resource management, marketing, and network infrastructure (partner management) services. The third layer is at the level of local markets and includes those business activities that require knowledge of the local market to be effective. Activities here require an understanding of local domain expertise, local customer nuances, regulatory issues, supply-chain management, and management of local partnerships. The model illustrates a way for companies to balance the efficiencies of centralizing certain activities while being responsive to local market needs.[21]

Global Core
- Vision
- Business Strategy
- Leadership

Shared Services
- Enterprise Resource Planning
- Human Resources
- Marketing Services
- Network Infrastructure

Local Markets
- Domain Expertise
- Procurement
- Regulatory Affairs
- Partnering
- Supply Chain/Logistics
- Marketing

FIGURE E.5

GLOBAL E-CORPORATION

Source: Adapted from Mohanbir Sawhney and Suant Mandal, "Go Global," *Business 2.0*, May 2000, pp. 180–181.

A FINAL WORD

The Internet is changing the way the world does business in many ways. Every company, industry, and nation is being affected by the widespread use of the Internet and World Wide Web. As such, the Internet is continuing to break down barriers to international competition and bringing companies in distant locations into direct competition with one another. The Internet revolution is landing on every shore, and companies, industries, and entire nations must rise to meet the challenge. Companies must consider important cultural, legal, political, and financial issues that are being altered by the World Wide Web. They also must address how the Web is affecting their decisions related to corporate strategies and structure.

 There is a variety of additional e-business material available on the companion Web site that accompanies this text. You can access this information by visiting the Web site at ⟨**www.prenhall.com/wild**⟩.

Notes

1 "Master of Their Domains?," *Business Week*, *E-Business Supplement*, April 3, 2000, p. EB14.

2 Evantheia Schibsted, "All the World in Stages," *Business 2.0*, November 1999, pp. 45–49.

3 Martin Wolk, "Top PC Makers, Suppliers Form Company to Simplify Supply Chain," From the Web site of MSNBC ⟨www.msnbc.com⟩, May 2, 2000.

4 The following discussion of EDI and the distinction between its two main types draws largely upon the discussion contained within Efraim Turban, Jae Lee, David King, and H. Michael Chung, *Electronic Commerce: A Managerial Perspective* (Upper Saddle River, NJ: Prentice Hall, 2000), pp. 222–225.

5 Otis Port, "Customers Move into the Driver's Seat," *Business Week*, October 4, 1999, pp. 103–106.

6 Port, "Customers Move into the Driver's Seat," pp. 103–106.

7 James Daly, "A World of Opportunity," *Business 2.0*, Editor's Note, November 1999, p. 1; Erika Rasmusson, "Targeting Global E-Customers," *Sales & Marketing Management*, January 2000, p. 78.

8 From the Web site of International Translation & Publishing ⟨www.itp.ie⟩, May 1, 2000.

9 Mohanbir Sawhney and Suant Mandal, "What Should Your International Organization Look Like?," *Business 2.0*, May 2000, p. 213.

10 Stewart Taggart, "Censor Census," *Business 2.0*, March 2000, pp. 358–364.

11 Reporters Without Borders, "The Twenty Enemies of the Internet" Press Release, August 9, 1999, Available World Wide Web ⟨www.rsf.fr/indexuk.html⟩.

12 Reporters Without Borders, "The Twenty Enemies of the Internet" Available World Wide Web ⟨www.rsf.fr/indexuk.html⟩.

13 First America, Then the World," *Economist: E-Commerce Survey*, February 26, 2000, pp. 49–53.

14 Taggart, "Censor Census," pp. 358–364.

15 Stephen Baker, "Taming the Wild, Wild Web," *Business Week*, October 4, 1999, pp. 154–160.

16 Baker, "Taming the Wild, Wild Web," pp. 154-160.

17 Adapted from Christopher Farrell, "All the World's an Auction," *Business Week*, October 4, 1999, pp. 120–128.

18 Data obtained from the Web site of Ameritrade ⟨www.ameritrade.com⟩, May 1, 2000.

19 Mark Halper, "The Next NASDAQ," *Business 2.0*, March 2000, pp. 294–304.

20 Schibsted, "All the World in Stages," pp. 45–49.

21 Sawhney and Mandal, "What Should Your International Organization Look Like?," p. 213.

international
business
AN INTEGRATED APPROACH

JOHN J. WILD
UNIVERSITY OF WISCONSIN, MADISON

KENNETH L. WILD
UNIVERSITY OF LONDON, ENGLAND

JERRY C. Y. HAN
STATE UNIVERSITY OF NEW YORK, BUFFALO
UNIVERSITY OF HONG KONG

With contributions by Melanie Treviño

PRENTICE HALL UPPER SADDLE RIVER, NEW JERSEY 07458

Library of Congress Cataloging-in-Publication Data

Wild, John J.
   International business : an integrated approach / John J. Wild,
Kenneth L. Wild, Jerry C. Y. Han.
     p.   cm.
   Includes bibliographical references and index.
   ISBN 0-13-862186-1
   1. International business enterprises—Management.
   2. International trade.   I. Wild, Kenneth L. II. Han, Jerry C. Y.
III. Title.
HD62.4.W586   1999
658′.049—dc21   99-13078
                                CIP

Senior Editor: David Shafer
Managing Editor (Editorial): Jennifer Glennon
Editorial Assistant: Kim Marsden
Assistant Editor: Michele Foresta
Media Project Manager: Michele Faranda
Development Editor: Ron Librach
Executive Marketing Manager: Michael Campbell
Managing Editor (Production): Judy Leale
Production Assistant: Keri Jean
Associate Director, Manufacturing: Vincent Scelta
Production Manager: Arnold Vila/Paul Smolenski
Senior Designer: Cheryl Asherman
Design Manager: Pat Smythe
Interior Design: Lee Goldstein
Photo Researcher: Melinda Alexander
Cover Design: Cheryl Asherman/John Romer
Cover Photo:KAN Photography, Inc.
Associate Director, Multimedia Production: Karen Goldsmith
Manager, Print Production: Christy Mahon
Formatter: Ashley Scattergood
Composition: UG/GGS Information Services, Inc.

Copyright ©2001 by Prentice-Hall, Inc., Upper Saddle River, New Jersey, 07458. All rights reserved. Printed in the United States of America. This publication is protected by Copyright, and permission should be obtained from the publisher prior to any prohibited reproduction, storage in a retrieval system, or transmission in any form or by any means, electronic, mechanical, photocopying, recording, or likewise. For information regarding permission(s), write to: Rights and Permissions Department.

10 9 8 7 6 5 4 3 2 1
ISBN 0-13-031674-1

To Our Parents

BRIEF CONTENTS

CONTENTS

part three
INTERNATIONAL TRADE AND
INVESTMENT, 154

PLANNING AND ORGANIZING INTERNATIONAL OPERATIONS, 406

SELECTING AND MANAGING ENTRY MODES, 442

Welcome to the premier edition of *International Business: An Integrated Approach*. This book is the result of extensive market surveys, chapter reviews, and personal correspondence with instructors and students at a wide range of institutions. We are delighted that an overwhelming majority agrees with our ideas for a fresh approach to international business. This book forges a new path for international business, one which responds to the requests and needs of both instructors and students. From the outset, a main goal in writing *International Business: An Integrated Approach* was to respond to these market needs by developing the most progressive, accessible, current, and customer-driven textbook on the market.

We know that international business is rich in people, culture, geography, politics, economics, and other human and environmental factors. This book exploits this richness to present international business as it genuinely is—as a dynamic and exciting subject. This book goes beyond a "functional approach" to present international business activities in an *integrated framework*. It goes beyond a "U.S.-centric" perspective and takes an *inclusive view* of international business. While it is appropriate for use in the introductory course at either the undergraduate or graduate level, *International Business* is written to give the instructor maximum flexibility in fitting different teaching styles and incorporating outside readings and cases—thereby increasing its scope and breadth as desired.

HOW STUDENTS WILL BENEFIT FROM *INTERNATIONAL BUSINESS*

This book's unique approach to international business benefits students in several ways.

INTEGRATIVE The limitations of the functional approach to international business are apparent to both instructors and students. International business is much more than a simple collection of separate business functions, such as international marketing or international financial management. Rather, it is the extension of business activities across national borders and involves the simultaneous consideration of all business functions. This book rejects the notion that international business is simply a collection of distinct functional "silos" in favor of an approach that views international business as a natural extension of business activities into the global marketplace (see Chapters 11–15). Not surprisingly, feedback tells us that students benefit greatly by studying international business as it is in the real world.

INCLUSIVE Appreciating the dynamic nature of the global marketplace requires an unbiased approach to international business. This is the *only* international business book written from a truly global perspective. This global perspective was accomplished by an author team that has collective expertise in three major economic regions of the world—Asia, Europe, and North America. This book is written from a non-provincial viewpoint: that is, rather than "takes sides" in key debates, it presents the viewpoints of each group or culture involved (see Chapters 2–4).

ACCESSIBLE A successful book for the first course in international business must be accessible to all students. This book describes conceptual material and specialized business activities in concrete, straightforward terms and illustrates them appropriately (see Chapters 5, 9, and 10). Our goal of presenting complex material in an accessible manner is reflected throughout the book. We are convinced that students who use the most readable international business book will master such material most readily.

TOPICAL This book strives to capture the contemporary, topical aspects of international business. Topical coverage is developed to foster enthusiasm and to motivate students to go beyond the classroom to see how concepts relate to the real world. Many fun and interesting examples allow students to reflect upon the experiences of real companies—to see both what worked and what didn't. This book's comprehensive Web site contains updates of important events that keep the book continuously current. To visit our Web site, go to **www.prenhall.com/wild**.

INNOVATIVE FEATURES: THE PEDAGOGY OF *INTERNATIONAL BUSINESS*

We firmly believe that students are motivated to learn when a book effectively demonstrates how concepts are applied. To emphasize the practical side of international business we have integrated the following innovative features into this book.

ENTREPRENEURIAL FOCUS Each chapter contains an *Entrepreneurial Focus* box to underscore the various ways in which chapter topics affect entrepreneurs and small businesses. Entrepreneurial and small business issues are also woven into the content of each chapter and illustrated with current, often colorful examples. These examples, both in the text and in feature boxes, highlight the activities of entrepreneurs and small businesses from countries around the world.

GLOBAL MANAGER Each chapter features a *Global Manager* box that shows how key issues actually affect the daily duties of managers working in the international business arena. This feature expands on issues discussed in the text and delves into those that pose special problems for international managers. In Chapter 14, for instance, we show how managers cope with the effects of culture shock when relocating to unfamiliar cultures. This feature drives home relevant, down-to-earth lessons learned by veterans of international business management.

WORLD BUSINESS SURVEY Each chapter contains a *World Business Survey* to highlight the attitudes of consumers, workers, managers, and policy makers toward important chapter topics. Underscored in these *Surveys* is the importance of culture in forming people's attitudes. This feature is designed to help students recognize the important role of people from other cultures in international business.

FULL-COLOR WORLD ATLAS Our experiences and those of many international business instructors tell us that far too many students are inadequately prepared in geography for their first course in international business. In response, this book includes, as a primer and reference, a full-color world atlas as an appendix to Chapter 1. Students are able to test their knowledge of the global landscape by completing 20 questions accompanying the atlas, which is also broken into several detailed maps for closer study. Important issues regarding world geography and their impact on international business are integrated throughout the book and its assignment materials.

BEACONS Students learn better when they are provided with a "roadmap" to show them how chapters and topics relate to one another. This book contains *Beacons* at the start of each chapter to reinforce the interrelatedness of topics across chapters. Titled "A Look Back," "A Look at This Chapter," and "A Look Ahead," these beacons provide a structure for students as they read through the book.

LEARNING OBJECTIVES WITH CORRESPONDING SUMMARIES Learning objectives are designed to focus on the main lessons students should learn from their reading of the chapter. Each chapter includes summaries that correspond *exactly* to the chapter's learning objectives.

CHAPTER-OPENING VIGNETTES Opening vignettes launch each chapter with brief, informative introductions. These vignettes are designed to pique students' interest in chapter material—not bog them down in fine details to be discussed within the chapter. We find students are motivated to turn the page and read on when given short, interesting, relevant introductions to the material they are about to study.

Tools for Active Learning

This book has more—and more useful—end-of-chapter assignment material than any other international business book. Well-planned assignment materials span the full range of complexity to test students' knowledge and ability to apply key principles.

➡ *Questions for Review* help students check that they understand each chapter's key terms and important concepts.

➡ *Questions for Discussion* raise important issues confronting entrepreneurs, international managers, policymakers, and others. They can be used as a basis for in-class discussion, as in-class team activities, or as homework assignments.

➡ *In Practice* exercises ask students to consider actual scenarios taken from the international business press.

➡ *Projects* take students beyond the text, engaging them in classroom debates or presentations, library or Web-based research, and interviews with local managers. An on-going project called the *Investment Opportunity Notebook* asks students to apply what they've learned in each chapter to an investment opportunity in a specific country. Students gradually develop a report on this opportunity as they proceed through the course.

➡ *A Question of Ethics* exercises allow students to consider the ethical dimensions of important managerial decisions in international business scenarios.

➡ *Business Cases* let students analyze the responses of real-world companies to the issues, problems, and opportunities discussed in each chapter.

➡ Five end-of-part *Integrative Video Cases* bring to life concepts covered in a set of chapters and demonstrate their relevance to the activities of companies actually operating in the international business arena.

SPECIAL FEATURES OF *INTERNATIONAL BUSINESS*

Support for On-Line Study

The World Wide Web site accompanying this text is the most comprehensive of all international business textbooks. Updated every two weeks, current-events articles keep the book continuously up-to-date. A faculty chat room allows instructors to communicate with one another, share teaching ideas, and gain from the experiences of colleagues.

Dynamic Art and Maps

This text contains a variety of **colorful maps** that convey and reinforce the knowledge of where important places are located. They also supplement concepts and data with visual learning aids. A **map index** assists instructors and students in quickly locating every map in the book. Highly **colorful charts** and **figures** help students grasp important information. Numerous **color photos** are strategically placed to add value to the text and provide students with a look at life and work around the world; informative, detailed captions tie photos to chapter material. We underscore **important terms** by boldfacing them in the text, defining them in the margin, and collecting them in a comprehensive glossary at the end of the book.

THE PLAN OF *INTERNATIONAL BUSINESS*

Part I of this book discusses how the world's national economies are increasingly linked. We learn that as globalization penetrates further into national business environments, managers everywhere must take a *global perspective* on business activities.

In **Part II**, we explore *national business environments*, showing how people's attitudes, values, beliefs, and institutions differ from one culture to another. We also explain how companies modify business practices and strategies when operating under different political, legal, and economic systems.

We discuss the major components of the *international business environment* in **Parts III and IV**. We learn why trade and investment flow across borders and why governments try to encourage or discourage them. We explore the process of regional economic integration sweeping the global economy and outline its implications for international companies. We also explain how global financial markets and the global monetary system function and show how they affect international business activities.

In **Part V**, we describe the ways in which *international business management* differs from management of a purely domestic firm. We show how a company analyzes and decides upon the markets in which it will sell or manufacture its products. We explain the strategies and structures companies use for their international operations and explore why companies choose to enter markets in different ways. We wrap up our study of international business by learning how companies acquire and manage their business resources.

SUPPLEMENTS

This text is supported with a comprehensive supplement package that includes the following:

For the Professor

➡ *Instructor's Manual* The *Instructor's Manual* is designed to guide instructors through the text. It includes *chapter summaries, lecture outlines, critical thinking ex-*

ercises, geography activities, additional student projects, lecture enhancements, further readings, and guidance answers to all end-of-chapter assignment material. The IM is available either in print or electronic form.

➡ **Test Item File** The *Test Item File* contains a wide variety of questions, including 50 true/false, 50 multiple-choice, 25 fill-in-the-blank, 25 short-answer/essay, and 10 situation-based questions. Questions are of varying levels of difficulty and are provided in both print and electronic versions.

➡ **PHLIP/CW Web Site** The Prentice Hall Learning on the Internet Partnership (PHLIP) is the most advanced text-specific site on the World Wide Web. Resources are updated every two weeks by professors from around the world. Features of interest to instructors include *bimonthly news articles* relevant to the text with *accompanying discussion questions* and *group exercises*. There is also on-line delivery of *PowerPoint slides* and additional instructor's material. *Sample syllabi* and *teaching suggestions* are posted on a faculty community chat room (see ⟨**www.prenhall.com/wild**⟩).

➡ **Color Transparencies** Over 100 full-color transparencies, all based on key exhibits and concepts from the text, are provided for the instructor. These transparencies are designed to be ideal in-class teaching tools. They are bold, easy-to-read, and clutter-free, and each has accompanying teaching notes to further enhance their ease of use.

➡ **PowerPoint Electronic Transparencies** A set of PowerPoint slides contains every figure in the text and is designed to aid the educator in supplementing in-class lectures.

➡ **Test Manager 4.0** The Windows-based Prentice Hall *Test Manager 4.0* is a comprehensive suite of tools for testing and assessment. The *TM* contains all of the questions found in the *Test Item File* and makes it easy for instructors to create and distribute tests either by printing and distributing them or by delivering them on-line over a Local Area Network (LAN) server.

➡ **On Location! Videos** Part-ending *International Business Video Cases* are provided for each of the five parts of the text. These videos, drawn from Prentice Hall's custom *On Location!* video series, feature experts discussing a wide range of issues in the global marketplace. By focusing on the ways in which well-known companies (including Yahoo!, MTV Europe, Sebago Shoes, and Nivea) became successful beyond their home markets, these videos bring to life chapter concepts and terms, tying them together in a real-world context. Accompanying *discussion questions* and *exercises* allow students to go beyond the textbook and apply what they've learned. A video guide is included to aid the instructor.

For the Student

➡ **PHLIP/CW Web Site** In addition to *bimonthly news articles* relevant to the text, the PHLIP/CW (Prentice Hall Learning on the Internet Partnership) Web site features *Internet resources* for in-depth research on selected topics, *on-line testing with immediate grading and feedback*, and additional *resources for improving study and writing skills* (see ⟨**www.prenhall.com/wild**⟩).

➡ **GLOBE CD-ROM** *GLOBE (Global Landscape of the Business Environment)* CD-ROM features an *extensive atlas and exercises* integrating cultural, geographic, political and economic data. See your Prentice Hall sales representative for information about how to purchase this inexpensive CD-ROM.

- **Free Study Guide** Designed to aid student comprehension of the concepts presented in the text, this *free* study guide contains chapter objectives; chapter outlines; and review, discussion, and study questions.
- **WebCT** This on-line distance learning course offers a WebCT program with preloaded content, communication, and testing features.

ACKNOWLEDGEMENTS

We are grateful for the encouragement, suggestions, and counsel provided by many instructors, professionals, and students in preparing the first edition of *International Business*. This book reflects the innovative ideas and pedagogical needs of both instructors and students. We especially thank those individuals who provided valuable comments and suggestions to further improve this first edition:

Wendell Armstrong, Central Virginia Community College

Robert T. Aubey, University of Wisconsin at Madison

Tope A. Bello, East Carolina University

Fred Burton, University of Manchester (UMIST), England

Derrick Chong, Royal Holloway, University of London, England

Randy Cray, University of Wisconsin at Stevens Point

John W. Eichenseher, University of Wisconsin at Madison

Herbert B. Epstein, University of Texas at Tyler

Carolina Gomez, University of Houston

James Gunn, Berkeley College

James Halteman, Wheaton College

Charles Harvey, University of the West of England

James S. Lawson Jr., Mississippi State University

Carol Lopilato, California State University at Dominguez Hills

Donna Weaver McCloskey, Widener University

C. Richard Scott, Metropolitan State College of Denver

Ali Al-Shamali, Arab Research Center, Middle East Business Review

Coral R. Snodgrass, Canisius College

Kenneth R. Tillery, Middle Tennessee State University

David C. Wyld, Southeastern Louisiana University

Mo Yamin, University of Manchester (UMIST), England

It takes a dedicated group of individuals to take a textbook from rough draft to final manuscript. We would like to thank our partners at Prentice Hall for their tireless efforts in bringing this book to fruition. Special thanks on this project go to Senior Acquisitions Editor, David Shafer and Senior Development Editor, Ron Librach; Associate Managing Editor for Production, Judy Leale; Senior Designer, Cheryl Asherman; Editor-in-Chief, Natalie Anderson; Development Director, Stephen Deitmer; Editorial Director, Jim Boyd; Managing Editor for Editorial, Jennifer Glennon; Director of Marketing, Brian Kibby; Executive Marketing Manager, Michael Campbell; Development Editors Steven Rigolosi and Audrey Regan; Assistant Editor, Michele Foresta; Permissions Coordinator, Monica Stipanov; and Photo Researcher, Melinda Alexander.

We also wish to thank Nancy Brandwein, Mark Green, Elisa Adams, and especially Costas Hadjiyiannis and Sri Raghavan for valuable assistance at various stages of this book's development.

A Final Word

We believe that international business is a rich and dynamic subject. As instructors, one of our challenges is to instill in our students a passion for international business. Another is to give our students every advantage possible in the global marketplace. As authors, our primary mission in writing *International Business: An Integrated Approach* is to equip today's student with the passion, skills, and knowledge necessary to compete in this marketplace. Quality instructional materials, including this textbook, help us all to achieve this mission.

John J. Wild

Kenneth L. Wild

Jerry C.Y. Han

ABOUT THE AUTHORS

As a team, John Wild, Kenneth Wild, and Jerry Han provide a blend of skills uniquely suited to writing an international business textbook. They combine award-winning teaching and research with a global view of business gained through years of living and working in cultures around the world. Together, they make the topic of international business practical, accessible, and enjoyable.

JOHN J. WILD John J. Wild is Professor of Business and Vilas Research Scholar at the University of Wisconsin at Madison. He previously held appointments at the University of Manchester in England and Michigan State University. He received his Ph.D., M.S., and B.B.A. degrees from the University of Wisconsin.

Teaching business courses at both the undergraduate and graduate levels, Professor Wild has received several teaching honors, including the Chipman Excellence in Teaching Award and the Beta Alpha Psi Excellence in Teaching Award. He is a prior recipient of national research fellowships from KPMG Peat Marwick and the Ernst and Young Foundation. He is also a frequent speaker at universities and at national and international conferences.

The author of more than 50 publications and three best-selling textbooks, Professor Wild conducts research on a wide range of topics, including corporate governance, capital markets, and financial analysis and forecasting. He is an active member of several national and international organizations, including the Academy of International Business, and has served as Associate Editor or editorial board member for several respected journals.

KENNETH L. WILD Kenneth L. Wild is with the School of Management at Royal Holloway, University of London, England. He previously taught at Pennsylvania State University. He received his Ph.D. from the University of Manchester (UMIST) in England and his B.S. and M.S. degrees from the University of Wisconsin. Dr. Wild also undertook postgraduate work at École des Affairs Internationale in Marseilles, France.

Having taught students of international business, marketing, and management at both the undergraduate and graduate levels, Dr. Wild is a dedicated contributor to international business education and a distinguished instructor. An active member of several national and international organizations, including the Academy of International Business and the European International Business Association, he has spoken at major universities and at national and international conferences in Austria, Britain, Kuwait, Portugal, and the United States.

Dr. Wild's research, on a range of international business topics including market entry modes, country risk, and international expansion strategies, have taken him into more than 20 countries spanning the globe. He serves as Associate Editor of the *Middle East Business Review* (MBR) and as a board member of the *Arab Research Center*.

JERRY C.Y. HAN Jerry C.Y. Han is an Associate Professor at the University of Buffalo School of Management, where he is also Director of the School's China Management Programs. He also holds appointments at several Chinese Universities, including the University of Hong Kong, Beijing University, and Renmin University. Professor Han previously held appointments at the Hong Kong University of Science and Technology

(HKUST), Michigan State University, and National Chung Hsing University. He received his Bachelors degree from National Chung Hsing University, Masters degree from National Chengchi University, and Ph.D. from the University of Buffalo.

Teaching at both the undergraduate and graduate levels, Professor Han is a highly recognized teacher, known for his commitment and creativity in business education. He is a prior recipient of research fellowships from the government of Hong Kong, HKUST, Price Waterhouse, and National Chengchi University. Dr. Han is actively involved in several national and international organizations, including previously serving as President of the North American Chinese Association.

The author of more than 40 publications on various business topics, including international regulatory and disclosure issues, Professor Han serves on the editorial boards of several prestigious journals. He also consults with international companies and government agencies, as well as teaching business courses for international companies in a number of industries.

SPECIAL FEATURES

Global Manager   These boxes show how key issues affect the daily duties of managers working in the international business arena.

World Business Survey   These boxes highlight the attitudes of consumers, workers, managers, and policy makers toward important chapter topics.

Entrepreneurial Focus   These boxes underscore the various ways in which chapter topics affect entrepreneurs and small businesses all around the world.

international
business
AN INTEGRATED APPROACH

1 the global perspective

Beacons

A Look at This Chapter

This chapter presents a global view of business activities. We begin by describing the forces behind globalization, explaining why companies "go international," and showing what types of companies are involved. We then discuss the main elements of the global perspective on business. We close by briefly discussing the importance of ethics and social responsibility.

A Look Ahead

PART II, covering Chapters 2 to 4, introduces us to different national business environments. Chapter 2 describes important cultural differences among nations. Chapter 3 examines different political and legal systems. Chapter 4 shows how nations differ in economic systems and stages of development and explains how companies adapt to these differences.

Learning Objectives

After studying this chapter, you should be able to

1. Describe *international business* and the process of *globalization*.
2. Explain why companies pursue *international business activity*.
3. Identify the *types of companies* that participate in international business.
4. Explain the *global perspective* on business and identify its three main elements.

Hari Darmawan is an entrepreneur who is concerned about the future of the company he founded, PT Matahari Putra Prima. "Wal-Mart," he laments, "must play fair. That is the Indonesian Way. Indonesians do not try to put one another out of business. It's just not done." With annual sales of $600 million, Matahari Putra Prima is Indonesia's largest retailer. But today the company is preparing to do battle with the world's largest companies.

Competitors from France and the United States are storming into Indonesia's market to challenge Matahari. French retail giant Carrefour expects to have six stores in Indonesia by the early 2000s. Price Venture and JCPenney, both of the United States, will soon open Indonesian outlets. Wal-Mart, with the global muscle of 3,000 stores and annual sales of $300 billion, poses the greatest threat. Wal-Mart will soon have nine stores in the capital of Jakarta and sees Matahari as a strong competitor. Accordingly, it has proceeded cautiously, recently delaying one store opening for fear that staff members weren't quite ready.

"Conventional wisdom," reports one local retail analyst, "has it that Matahari will be crushed by the stampede. But that stance ignores Matahari's intimate knowledge of local conditions." Although large international companies

have the marketing muscle and low prices to make inroads in Indonesia, Mata-hari's managers understand how to operate in the local market. Matahari will need its firsthand knowledge of Indonesian consumers and business practices to survive this competitive onslaught. Indeed, even for companies that consider their business purely domestic, international competition is the rule rather than the exception today.[1]

Although PT Matahari Putra Prima operates only in Indonesia, it is discovering the global nature of the retailing industry. Even though the company does not currently compete in other markets, international business is coming to Matahari.

International business affects the activities of every consumer, worker, company, and government. Falling trade barriers, increasing competition, and converging consumer tastes are creating global markets for many products. *Consumers* enjoy greater product selection at better prices than ever before. *Workers* often find themselves competing for jobs against workers in another country thousands of miles away. *Companies* directly involved in international production or marketing confront cultures, political systems, and economic systems that can differ greatly from their own. Local, regional, and national *governments* work to attract jobs by offering incentives for companies to locate in specific places. As PT Matahari Putra Prima has learned, domestic companies are not isolated from international business. More and more international companies are invading home markets everywhere.

In this chapter, we develop a global perspective on business activity. We investigate important issues currently facing consumers, workers, and international companies. The world atlas at the end of the chapter provides a reference for our discussion of international business as we proceed through the book.

WHY STUDY INTERNATIONAL BUSINESS?

Each of us experiences the result of dozens of international business transactions every day. Your radio-alarm clock was probably made in China. The news broadcast buzzing in your ears comes from Britain's BBC radio. You slip into a Gap T-shirt made in Egypt, Levi's made in Bangladesh, and Nikes assembled in Vietnam from components made in several other countries. You get into your Japanese Toyota (which was made in Kentucky) and pop in a Dutch-made CD of music performed by a Swedish band. At the local espresso bar, you charge up with coffee brewed from beans harvested in Colombia or Kenya.

You don't even have to set foot out of a small town to be affected by international business. No matter where you live, you'll be surrounded by **imports**—all the goods and services brought into a country that were purchased from organizations located in other countries. Your counterparts around the world will undoubtedly spend the day using your nation's **exports**—all the goods and services sent from one country to other nations.

But international business is not just about companies selling their products to customers in other countries. It is also about crossing borders to get products made in the first place. This is particularly true in the information age. Say you're an IBM computer programmer based in Seattle. You may never leave the state of Washington, but you'll be working with colleagues in places such as central Europe and India. Consider the following actual example:

imports
All goods and services brought into a country that were purchased from organizations located in other countries.

exports
All goods and services sent from one country to other nations.

➡ A team of computer programmers at Beijing's Tsignhua University writes software using Java technology for IBM. At the end of each day, they send their work over the Internet to an IBM facility in Seattle. There, programmers build on it before zapping it 5,000 miles to the Institute of Computer Science in Belarus and the Software House Group in Latvia. From there, the work goes to India's Tata Group, which passes the software back to Tsignhua by the next morning. The process repeats itself until the project is done.[2]

IBM's vice president for Internet technology calls this global relay race "Java around the Clock," and it is fast becoming the way things are done. Even a traditional manufacturer such as General Motors is considering reorganizing around a single global auto-development team. It stands to reason, then, that skills in international business—from cross-cultural understanding and communication to a knowledge of international monetary systems and distribution practices—is crucial if you want to become a more valuable player on your global team.

Already, firms like Solid State Measurements Inc., a Pittsburgh-based company with over 65 percent of its sales going abroad, are finding it hard to locate executives with adequate international experience.[3] As more and more companies locate operations beyond their borders, they will hire people who are best equipped to manage their international operations, regardless of citizenship. In Tokyo, for example, Sony Corporation is on the verge of becoming an "un-Japanese" company. Already, Sony's worldwide workforce is split roughly 50/50 between Japanese and non-Japanese. As Sony continues to relocate many of its factories to Mexico, a substantial majority of its workforce will be outside Japan.[4]

INTERNATIONAL BUSINESS AND GLOBALIZATION

As we've seen, international business affects many aspects of our lives. Let's begin, therefore, by explaining just what *international business* is and then describing in greater detail the impact of *globalization*.

WHAT IS INTERNATIONAL BUSINESS?

International business is the total of all business transactions that cross the borders of two or more nations. Consumers, companies, financial institutions, and governments are all important to international business activity. Consumers demand quality products from the international companies that sell and service them. Financial institutions help companies engaging in international business to finance investments, exchange currencies, and transfer money around the globe. Governments regulate flows of goods, services, people, and capital across national borders. Here are just a handful of typical international business transactions:

> **international business**
> Total of all business transactions that cross the borders of two or more nations.

➡ Italian media firm AGB conducts market research in Hungary to identify the television shows that people watch there.

➡ To provide financing for companies entering the Polish market, Daiwa Securities of Japan opens an office in Warsaw, Poland.

➡ American Honda Motor Corporation sends cars from the United States to Honda Motor Corporation in Japan.

➡ Three young entrepreneurs import premium coffee into China to serve urban customers in Beijing and Tianjin.

Map 1.1 shows the total value of goods and services, including both imports and exports, now crossing each nation's borders. The annual total value is a staggering

MAP 1.1

INTERNATIONAL TRADE VOLUME (MILLIONS OF U.S. DOLLARS)

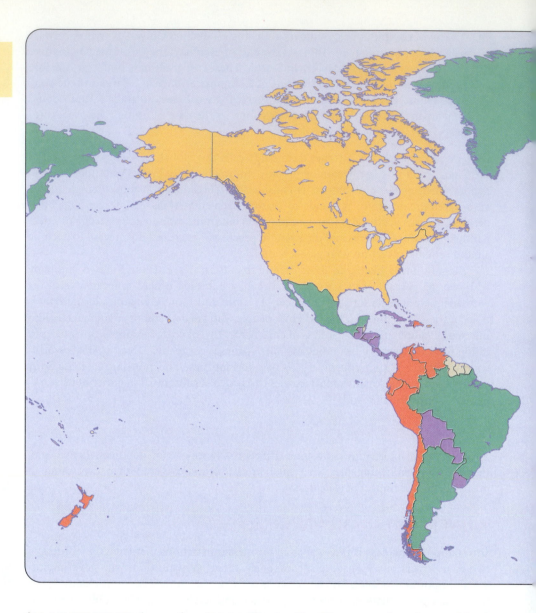

$13,649,858,000,000 (more than $13.6 trillion)—$2 trillion more than the combined annual revenues of the *Fortune Global 500* (the 500 largest companies in the world). This value of trade is more than 76 times the annual revenue of the world's largest company, General Motors.

WHAT IS GLOBALIZATION?

globalization
Process involving the integration of national economies.

Although national governments retain ultimate control over the products, people, and capital passing through their markets, the global economy is becoming increasingly intertwined. The process involving the integration of national economies is called **globalization**. Let's now examine globalization in detail.

Globalized Markets   Globalization of *markets* (places where buyers and sellers meet to exchange goods and services) is very important to our study of international business. For instance, consumer preferences for some products are converging around the world. Sony, L.L. Bean, Nike, The Gap, Calvin Klein, Coca-Cola, and McDonald's

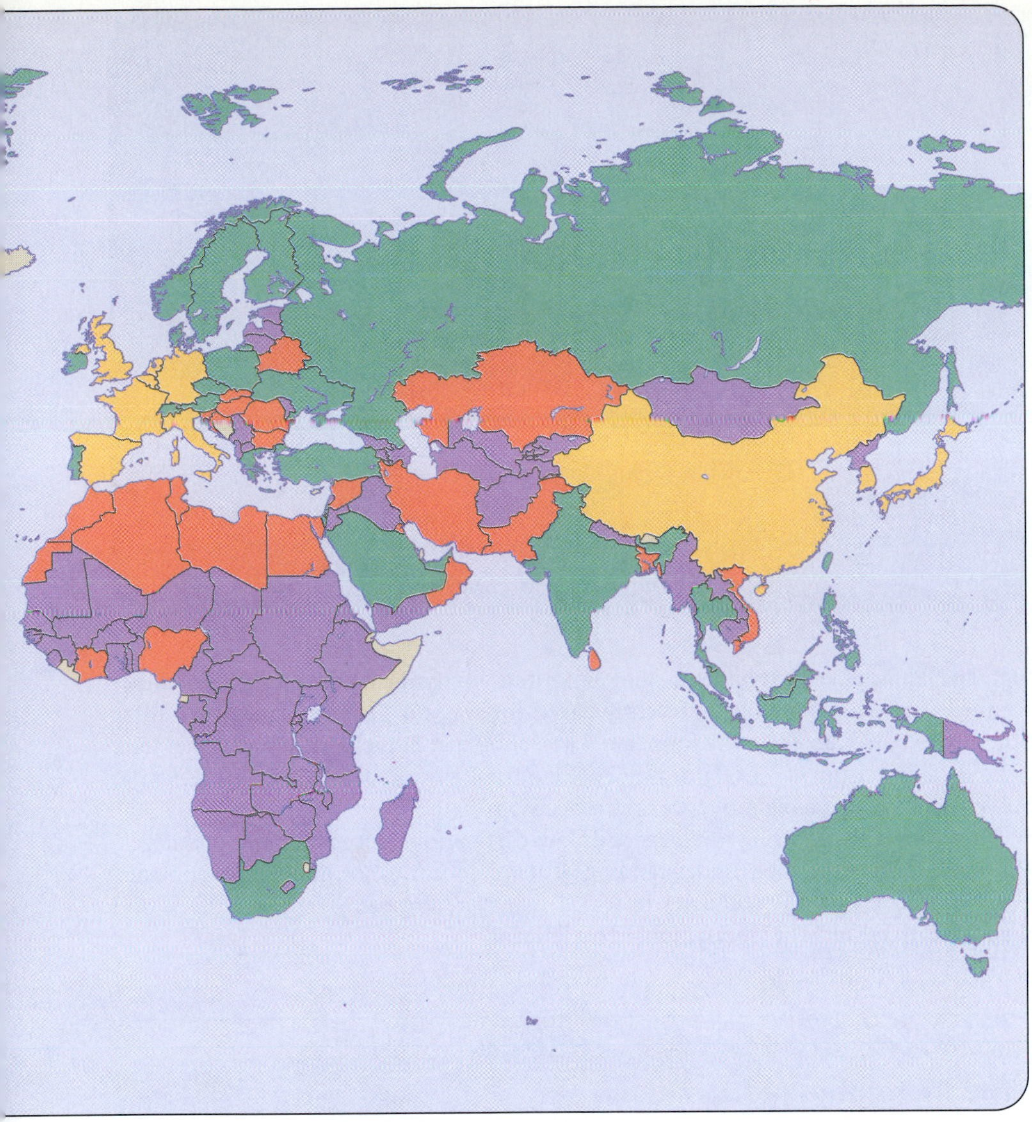

TRADE VOLUME (millions of U.S. dollars)

- $220,000 and up
- 40,000–219,999
- 10,000–39,999
- 0–9,999
- No data

Top Fourteen

United States	1,777,826
Germany	1,167,470
Japan	955,663
France	718,384
United Kingdom	690,263
Italy	590,981
Canada	433,620
Netherlands	432,849
Belgium	396,006
Hong Kong, China	379,287
China	333,066
South Korea	330,088
Singapore	304,647
Spain	292,975

are just a few companies that sell so-called *global products*—products marketed in all countries essentially without any changes. Sometimes they make small modifications to suit local tastes. In southern Japan, for example, Coca-Cola sweetened its traditional formula to compete with sweeter-tasting Pepsi.[5] In India, where cows are sacred and the consumption of beef taboo, McDonald's markets the "Maharaja Mac"—two all-mutton patties on a sesame-seed bun with all the usual toppings.[6]

Globalized Production Activities Today, many production activities are also becoming global. Technology allows any product to be made practically anywhere it is cheapest to do so.[7] Local, regional, and national governments offer firms various incentives to construct factories in their regions or countries. This strategy brings jobs to the country that wins the factory, but can bring unemployment to another if, as a consequence, a factory in that location is closed.

For example, competing business hubs in Asia—such as Kuala Lumpur (Malaysia), Singapore, Shanghai (China), and the Philippines' Subic Bay—routinely entice global companies with favorable tax deals and subsidized rents and worker train-

Despite recent economic turmoil, the Philippines slowly strengthened its economy over the past decade, making it an attractive trade hub to international companies such as Intel and Seagate. Subic Bay, which lies at the southern tip of the Philippine island of Luzon, has become attractive to international investors because it is a free port with few trade restrictions, and because the local people have an affinity for speaking English. Acer, Taiwan's biggest computer maker, plans to make Subic Bay the home of its Central Asian operations facility.

ing. The Philippine government, once notorious for tying up investors from other countries in reams of red tape, recently paved the way for Federal Express and three other carriers to transform the former U.S. naval base at Subic Bay into an Asian hub. "The local government," explains one FedEx official, "wanted to make us a tenant at Subic Bay. That had a big influence on the decision."[8]

Because of the growing importance of low-cost nations, more and more managers will need to increase their understanding of these countries' business environments. For more details on the countries to which managers are being sent, see the World Business Survey on "The International Top Fifteen."

World Business Survey

The International Top Fifteen

A recent survey uncovered the top international destinations of U.S. managers. Asian countries ranked lower in the most recent poll because financial crises there since 1997 have reduced relocations to the region. However, as economies in Asia recover, they will once again move higher in the rankings. Here are the top 15 destinations:

Top 15 Destinations		
1. United Kingdom	6. Mexico	11. Singapore
2. Germany	7. Brazil	12. Thailand
3. Australia	8. Saudi Arabia	13. Switzerland
4. Japan	9. Puerto Rico	14. China
5. France	10. Netherlands	15. Peru

Forces Spurring Globalization   Two main forces are spurring the globalization of markets and production: *lower trade and investment barriers* and *increased innovation*. Let's take a look at each of these factors in greater detail.

Lower Trade and Investment Barriers: GATT   In 1947, 23 nations made history when they created the *General Agreement on Tariffs and Trade (GATT)*. The GATT is an international treaty setting specific rules for international trade designed to pry open national markets by reducing *tariffs* (taxes on traded goods) and *nontariff barriers* such as quotas (restrictions on the volume of goods allowed into a country). Today, GATT has 133 members.

Because merchandise accounted for the majority of total world trade at the time, the 1947 GATT agreement focused on *merchandise* trade. The treaty was quite successful: In 1988, world merchandise trade was 20 times larger than in 1947, and average tariffs dropped from 40 percent to 5 percent. But by the late 1980s, trade conflicts had caused nontariff barriers to increase 45 percent. In addition, service industries grew increasingly important, accounting for 25 percent to 30 percent of total world trade. A 1994 revision of GATT modified the original treaty in several important ways:[9]

- ➡ Average tariffs on merchandise trade were to be reduced further.
- ➡ Subsidies (price supports) for agricultural products were to be reduced significantly.
- ➡ *Intellectual property rights* were clearly defined, giving protection to copyrights (including computer programs, databases, sound records, films), trademarks and service marks, and patents (including trade secrets and know-how).
- ➡ The *World Trade Organization* (*WTO*) was established with power to enforce the new GATT—an agency that the 1947 GATT lacked.

Role of Trade Blocs   Nations are integrating their economies as never before. For example, the *North American Free Trade Agreement (NAFTA)* groups three nations (Canada, Mexico, and the United States) into a free-trade bloc. The even more ambitious *European Union (EU)* combines 15 countries. The *Asia Pacific Economic Cooperation (APEC)* forum consists of 18 nations committed to creating a free-trade zone around the Pacific. All these agreements aim to lower trade barriers. As a result of such initiatives, growth in international trade now outpaces growth in worldwide production. Map 1.2 identifies the countries belonging to these and other free-trade blocs.

Innovation in Information Technology   As lower barriers to trade and investment encourage globalization, increased innovation is accelerating the process. Advancements in information technology and transportation are making it easier, faster, and less costly to move data, goods, equipment, and people around the world.

Business activities, such as managing employees and scheduling production in several locations, are more difficult and costly when conducted across borders and time zones. But new computer technologies are speeding up the flow of information, making coordination and control easier and cheaper. With electronic mail (e-mail), for instance, managers can stay in contact with international operations and respond quickly to important matters. Videoconferencing allows lawyers to meet while still in different branch offices, and engineers to collaborate on designs from remote locations. Consistent with this, worldwide sales of videoconferencing equipment were about $7 billion in 1998—up from $1.6 billion in 1996.[10]

e·biz

Internets, Intranets, and Extranets   Companies also use the Internet and World Wide Web to stay in touch with international production and distribution activities. A recent study revealed that 61 percent of executives feel that knowledge of the Internet will make them more marketable managers; 76 percent believe that being Net-savvy will advance their careers within five years.[11]

e·biz

MAP 1.2

FREE TRADE BLOCS OF THE WORLD
Note: Chile and Bolivia are associate members of MERCOSUR.

Private networks of internal company Web sites and other information sources (called *intranets*) allow employees to access their company's information from distant locations with desktop computers and modems. Microsoft reports that sales-analysis data have been accessed five times more often since becoming available on the company intranet.[12] Today, so-called *extranets* are being developed to give distributors and suppliers access to a company's database so that they can place orders or restock inventories electronically and automatically. All these new technologies permit managers to respond to both internal and external conditions more quickly than ever before.[13]

Technology and Small Business   Computer technologies can also increase the competitiveness of small companies by reducing the costs of reaching an international customer base. In fact, small companies were among the first to use the Web as a global marketing tool, and many are still able to respond faster than large companies to shifting market conditions.

These "webpreneurs" are increasingly gaining a leg up on larger competitors who are neither as nimble nor as Net-savvy. "I think we're fairly typical," says Jim Macintyre

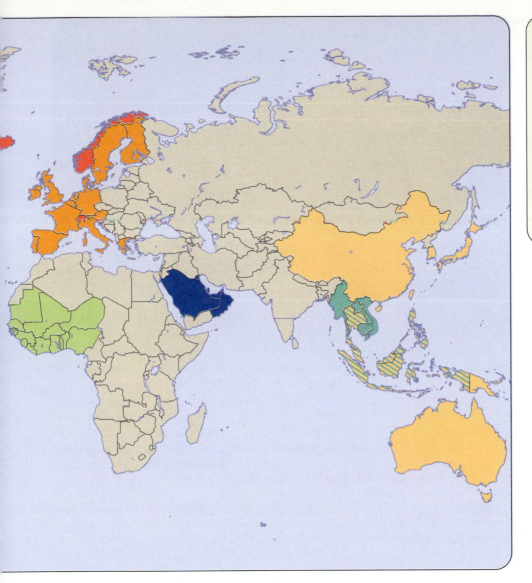

	EU
	EFTA
	NAFTA
	Andean Community
	MERCOSUR
	CARICOM
	CACM
	APEC
	ASEAN
	GCC
	ECOWAS

of Tropical Jim's Remake Shop, a Web designer located in Caracas, Venezuela. "Our firm was in the red until we started selling to the American market. Now 90 percent of our customers are Americans." For Jonathan Strum, a Tropical Jim's customer based in Los Angeles, the Web makes Caracas seem like next-door. "Not long ago," he admits, "I would have thought depending on a firm in Caracas for the services we need for our business was outlandish. Now I am importing all my graphic design and most of my programming from overseas."[14]

Some Pros and Cons of Technology　Some businesses are finding it hard to survive on the Internet. Most Internet sites suffer losses for at least three years before they turn profits—much too long for the majority of small companies. Those who do survive tend to sell the sort of low-priced goods that have broad appeal. But even the hottest-selling items can be hard to peddle on the Internet, especially when buyers are still hesitant about sending credit card information through cyberspace. One recent survey found that only 15 percent of Internet users had actually bought anything on-line.[15] Apparently "window shopping" and information gathering are more common activities.

e·biz

Videoconferencing, which allows for "face-to-face" communication in real time, is helping to ease communications in the global community. The World Economic Forum, a global nonprofit organization with 2,000 members from government, academia, business, and the media, recently embraced videoconferencing as a means to communicate quickly and easily with members across the globe. Likewise, doctors at two children's hospitals, Sri Ramachandra Medical College in India and Toronto's Hospital for Sick Children, use videoconferencing to share visual data instantly—a need that e-mail and telephones can't meet.

With the number of Internet sites growing daily, a company without a partner in cyberspace might be disappointed with traffic in its cyberstore. On-line intermediaries (called portals), such as America Online (AOL), Yahoo, and Excite, offer to funnel Web surfers to your site for a fee. However, the cost of such a partnership can be enormous. Recently, three securities firms—DLJ-direct, E*Trade Securities, and Waterhouse Securities—each paid AOL $25 million for its services over a two-year period. Thus generating traffic in an online store is more difficult than originally imagined. As one expert noted, "Launching an e-commerce site without a portal partner is like opening a retail store in the desert. Sure, it's cheap, but does anybody stop there?"[16]

Technology and the Business of Distribution   Some Internet-based companies pose a threat to competitors who rely solely on traditional distribution methods. On average, for example, 62 percent of a product's cost results from *activities occurring after the production process.*[17] Using sites on the World Wide Web to bypass intermediaries like wholesalers and retailers, companies can enter global markets, cut postproduction costs, and pass on savings to customers.

This strategy is best suited to firms offering products such as music, books, computer software, and travel services. In fact, travel services are expected to receive the biggest jump in on-line revenue by the year 2003 (see Figure 1.1). Amazon.com is a bookseller whose "store" exists only on the Internet. Now slugging it out with long-established booksellers Borders Books and Barnes & Noble, Amazon.com calls itself "Earth's Biggest Bookstore" (playing off B&N's billing as "The World's Biggest Bookstore") and offers more than 2.5 million titles. Brisk sales at Amazon.com prompted Barnes & Noble to create its own Web-based bookstore, barnesandnoble.com.

Innovation in Transportation Technology   Like advances in computer technology, advances in transportation methods are helping to globalize both markets and production activities. Advances in air travel allow managers to travel more quickly and cheaply to locations in other countries. As incomes rise and travel grows more affordable, more and more consumers take international vacations. As a result, consumer tastes become more global as travelers encounter products in other countries and create demand for them at home.

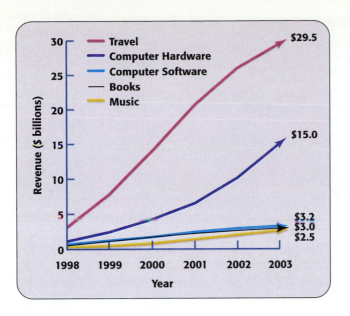

FIGURE 1.1

MAJOR ON-LINE RETAIL SECTORS BY 2003

Advances in shipping methods have also spurred globalization. The development of huge freighters that carry an enormous amount of goods on a single trip has greatly lowered the cost of overseas shipping. Container-shipment methods are becoming popular as well. Because the same containers can now be placed on trucks, trains, and ships, shipping is faster and costs associated with using two or more means to transport a shipment are lower.

WHY DO COMPANIES GO INTERNATIONAL?

Why do companies choose to engage in international business? Basically, they do so for the same reasons that they decide to expand in the domestic market: to *increase sales* and to *access resources*.

INCREASE SALES

The goal of increasing sales is attractive when a firm must deal with either of two conditions: *international sales growth opportunities* or *excess production capacity*.

International Sales Growth Opportunities   As PT Matahari Putra Prima discovered in this chapter's opening example, companies often go international to increase sales. Saturated home markets or an economic slowdown there often forces companies to explore international sales opportunities.

Another impetus for companies to seek international sales is uneven income. Companies might be able to level off their income stream by supplementing domestic sales with international sales. This also helps avoid wild production swings characterized by cycles of overwork and slack capacity. In particular, firms take the leap into international markets when they're confident that buyers in other cultures are receptive to a product and can afford it. Consider the current strategy of McDonald's. Although there is one McDonald's outlet for every 29,000 people in the United States, there is only one for every 40 million people in China. Not surprisingly, McDonald's is aggressively expanding in China (indeed, all across Asia), where long-term growth potential is enormous.[18]

Consider another example. Though nearly as large in area as the United States, Australia has only 17.7 million people, compared to 260 million in the United States.

Thus the Australian Trade Commission is helping small to medium-size companies reach their potential by providing export assistance. Some small exporters have met remarkable success. Duncan MacGillivray of Adelaide developed Two Dogs alcoholic lemonade by using surplus lemons from his neighbor's orchard, adding sugar, and fermenting the mix with yeast. After quickly reaching its potential in Australia, Two Dogs expanded into Hong Kong, New Zealand, Singapore, South Africa, the United Kingdom, and the United States. Asian consumers have received the drink enthusiastically because lemons are a popular source of vitamin C to fight the common cold there. Two Dogs is now made on four continents and sold in 44 countries. Annual revenue now exceeds $39 million, with overseas sales making up most of this figure.[19]

Excess Production Capacity Sometimes companies produce more goods and services than the market can absorb. When that happens, resources sit idle. But if the firm can find new international sources of demand, it can spread its costs over a greater number of units produced, thereby lowering the cost per unit and increasing profits. If it passes on these benefits to consumers in the form of lower prices, the firm might also capture market share from competitors. A dominant market position means greater market power, providing the firm with greater leverage in negotiating with both suppliers and buyers.

ACCESS RESOURCES

natural resources
Products from nature that are economically or technologically useful.

Companies also go international to access resources that are unavailable or more costly at home. What commonly draws companies into international markets is the quest for **natural resources**—products from nature that are economically or technologically useful. Japan, for example, is a small, densely populated island nation with very few natural resources of its own, especially forests. Thus Japan's largest paper company, Nippon Seishi, must do more than simply import wood pulp. It owns huge forests and corresponding processing facilities in Australia, Canada, and the United States. By controlling earlier stages in the papermaking process, the company guarantees a steady flow of an important input (wood pulp) that is less subject to the uncertainties associated with buying pulp on the open market. Likewise, to access cheaper energy resources used in other manufacturing industries, a variety of Japanese firms are locating in China, Mexico, Taiwan, and Vietnam where energy costs are lower.

Labor markets also draw companies into international business. One way firms try to keep their prices internationally competitive is by locating production in countries with low-cost labor. But if low-cost labor were the only reason a nation attracted international companies, businesses would stampede into places like Afghanistan and Somalia. In order to be attractive, a location must offer low-cost, adequately skilled workers in an environment with acceptable levels of social, political, and economic stability. When these conditions exist, the long-term investment necessary for economic development will flow into a country. We discuss the factors that attract international business to different countries more fully in Part II of this book.

WHO PARTICIPATES IN INTERNATIONAL BUSINESS?

Companies of all types and sizes, and in all sorts of industries, enter into international business activities. Manufacturing companies, service companies, and retail companies all search for customers beyond their borders. An **international company** is a business that engages directly in any form of international business activity such as exporting, importing, or international production. Thus companies vary in the extent to which they get involved in international business. For instance, although an importer only purchases from its supplier(s) abroad, it is considered an international company. Likewise, a large company with factories scattered around the world is an international company but is also called a **multinational corporation** (MNC)—a business that has direct investments (in the form of marketing or manufacturing subsidiaries) abroad in several or more countries. Thus although *all* companies involved in some aspect of international trade or investment are considered international companies, only those with direct investments abroad are called multinationals. These multinationals are also sometimes called *global* companies when they operate in practically all countries around the world. However, the *strategies* companies employ in their international business activities is another matter—we discuss *multinational* versus *global strategies* in Chapter 12. Let's now take a closer look at the different types of international companies.

international company
Business that engages directly in any form of international business activity.

multinational corporation (MNC)
Business that has direct investments abroad in several or more countries.

ENTREPRENEURS AND SMALL BUSINESSES

Small companies are becoming increasingly active in international trade and investment. One recent study reports that companies are exporting earlier and growing faster as a result.[20] As noted earlier, technology has toppled some real barriers to exporting for small businesses.

Whereas traditional distribution channels often gave only large companies access to distant markets, electronic distribution is a cheap and effective alternative for many small businesses.[21] Some small companies reside exclusively in cyberspace, reaching out to customers around the world solely through the World Wide Web. For instance, Alessandro Naldi's *Weekend a Firenze* (*Weekend in Florence*) Web site at **www.waf.it/mall** offers global villagers more authentic Florentine products than they'll find in the scores of overpriced tourist shops crowded into downtown Florence. A Florentine himself, Naldi established his site to sell high-quality, authentic Italian merchandise made only in the many small factories of Tuscany. Currently, Weekend a Firenze averages 20,000 visitors each month, with 40 percent of its "guests" coming from Japan, 30 percent from the United States, and the remainder from Greece, Australia, Canada, Mexico, Saudi Arabia, and Italy.[22]

Unfortunately, many small businesses that are capable of exporting have not yet begun to do so. For example, in one recent year only 10 percent of companies in the United States with fewer than 100 employees were exporting compared to 18 percent of companies of all sizes. Although there are certain real obstacles to exporting for small businesses—lack of investment capital, for example—some common myths create artificial obstacles. To explore some of these myths and the facts that dispute them, see the Entrepreneurial Focus "Untapped Potential: Four Myths That Keep Small Businesses from Export Success."

MULTINATIONAL CORPORATIONS

Multinational corporations vary widely in size, being as small as the security firm Pinkerton, with about $900 million in annual revenue, and as large as Mitsubishi Corporation, with revenue of more than $128 billion. Other well-known multinationals are Boeing (U.S.), Sony (Japan), Volvo (Sweden), Coca-Cola (U.S.), and Samsung Electronics (South Korea).

The units of large international companies can function either rather independently or as parts of a tightly integrated global network. Independent operations tend to have a good understanding of local culture and are often able to adapt quickly to changing local market conditions. On the other hand, firms that operate as global networks often find it easier to respond to changing conditions by shifting production, marketing, and other activities among national units. Depending on the type of business, either structure can be appropriate. As stated earlier, we discuss these alternative strategies and structures more fully in Chapter 12.

Untapped Potential: Four Myths That Keep Small Businesses from Export Success

MYTH 1: ONLY LARGE COMPANIES CAN EXPORT SUCCESSFULLY.

Fact: Exporting increases sales and profitability for small firms and can make both manufacturers and distributors less dependent on the health of the domestic economy. It can also help businesses avoid seasonal fluctuations in sales. In addition, selling abroad gives small businesses the advantage of competing with companies from other countries *before* they enter the domestic market.

MYTH 2: SMALL BUSINESSES HAVE NO PLACE TO TURN FOR EXPORT ADVICE.

Fact: Whether a company is just starting out or is already exporting profitably, the federal government has an assistance program to meet its needs. The Trade Information Center (TIC) of the U.S. Department of Commerce is a comprehensive resource for information on all federal export-assistance programs. Firms can get advice from international trade specialists on how to locate and use federal, state, local, and private-sector programs. They also receive free information on sources of market research, trade leads, financing, and trade events.

MYTH 3: THE LICENSING REQUIREMENTS NEEDED FOR EXPORTING ARE NOT WORTH THE EFFORT.

Fact: "Most products," according to international trade specialist Linda Jones, "don't need export licenses. Exporters simply write 'NLR' for 'no license required' on their Shipper's Export Declaration. There is no onerous paperwork involved." A license is needed only when exporting certain restricted commodities (such as high technology or defense-related goods) or when shipping to a country currently under U.S. trade embargo or other restriction. To find out about license requirements, companies can call the Commerce Department's Bureau of Export Administration (BXA).

MYTH 4: THERE IS NO EXPORT FINANCING AVAILABLE FOR SMALL BUSINESS.

Fact: In 1995, the Small Business Administration (SBA) and the Export-Import Bank joined forces to lend money to small businesses. Whereas the SBA is responsible for loan requests below $750,000, Ex-Im Bank handles transactions above $750,000. The Overseas Private Investment Corporation and the Trade and Development Agency also help small and medium-size firms obtain financing for international projects.

Economic Importance of Multinationals If, as we have seen, small and medium-size firms are so important to a country's economy, why do business headlines focus so sharply on large international companies? There are two main reasons:

1. *Their economic and political muscle makes them highly visible.* Large companies generate a large number of jobs, greater investment, and significant tax revenue for the areas in which they operate. Likewise, announced factory closings of large international companies make headlines because of the hundreds, perhaps thousands, of lost jobs.

2. *Their dealings involve large sums of money.* It is common for the income and dealings of large companies, such as mergers and acquisitions, to be valued in the hundreds of millions, sometimes billions, of dollars. In 1998, Germany's Daimler-Benz announced a merger with Chrysler Corporation valued at $40 billion; in December that year two global petroleum companies, Exxon and Mobil, agreed to create a merged company worth $86 billion.

Multinationals and GDP We can see the enormous economic clout of multinational corporations when we compare the revenues of companies in the *Fortune*

Global 500 to the value of goods and services generated by various countries. In Table 1.1, we inserted the nine multinationals with the highest annual revenues into a list of nations ranked from twenty-fourth to thirty-fourth in terms of national output. Our measure of national output is **gross domestic product (GDP)**—the total market value of all goods and services produced during a one-year period with resources located within a country. This means that if General Motors were a country, it would weigh in as a rich nation and rank ahead of both Denmark and Norway. Even the five hundredth largest firm in the world, Sun of the United States, has revenues larger than the GDPs of many countries. The government-owned U.S. Postal Service has 898,384 employees—the most of any company in the *Global 500*. Wal-Mart Stores is second, with 825,000 employees, General Motors third, with 608,000. All types of industries are represented in the *Global 500*, ranging from food and beverages to mining and crude oil production.[23]

Table 1.2 augments the listing of the MNCs with the highest annual revenues (from tenth to twenty-ninth), and Table 1.3 shows the international distribution of the Global 500.[24]

Merger Mania Not only do the largest multinationals dwarf the total economic output of some nations, but the biggest companies are getting bigger. In 1998 alone, the world's largest firms were involved in $1.6 *trillion* worth of mergers; this figure was up from $1 trillion in 1997.[25] But as the chairman of the Federal Trade Commission points out, "More and more deals . . . should be judged on a global-market scale. . . .

> **gross domestic product (GDP)**
> *Total market value of all goods and services produced during a one-year period with resources located within a country.*

TABLE 1.1 **Comparing the Global 500 with Selected Countries**

Country/Company	GDP/Revenue (millions of U.S. Dollars)
24. Turkey	181,464
General Motors	178,174
25. Denmark	174,247
26. Norway	157,802
27. Hong Kong, China	154,767
Ford Motor	153,627
Mitsui	142,688
28. Poland	134,477
Mitsubishi	128,922
Royal Dutch/Shell Group	128,142
Itochu	126,632
29. South Africa	126,301
30. Saudi Arabia	126,266
31. Finland	123,966
32. Greece	122,946
Wal-Mart Stores	122,379
Marubeni	111,121
33. Portugal	104,000
Sumitomo	102,395
34. Malaysia	99,213

TABLE 1.2 — More of the Global 500

Company	Revenue (millions of U.S. Dollars)
10. Toyota Motor	95,137
11. General Electric	90,840
12. Nissho Iwai	81,894
13. International Business Machines (IBM)	78,508
14. Nippon Telegraph & Telephone	76,984
15. AXA	76,874
16. Daimler-Benz	71,561
17. Daewoo	71,526
18. Nippon Life Insurance	71,388
19. British Petroleum	71,194
20. Hitachi	68,567
21. Volkswagen	65,328
22. Matsushita Electric Industrial	64,281
23. Siemens	63,755
24. Chrysler	61,147
25. Mobil	59,978
26. U.S. Postal Service	58,216
27. Allianz	56,785
28. Philip Morris	56,114
29. Sony	55,033

TABLE 1.3 — Distribution of the Global 500

Country	Number of Companies
United States	172
Japan	112
Germany	42
France	38
Britain	35
Italy	13
South Korea	12
Switzerland	12
Netherlands	9
Canada	8
All others	47

Mergers go through now that would have been challenged just 10 years ago because competition now comes from all corners of the world."[26]

Figure 1.2 highlights the rapid growth in mergers and acquisitions since 1980. It shows that international acquisitions by U.S. firms and acquisition of U.S. firms by non-U.S. buyers played a big role in the recent wave of mergers, especially between 1991 and 1997.

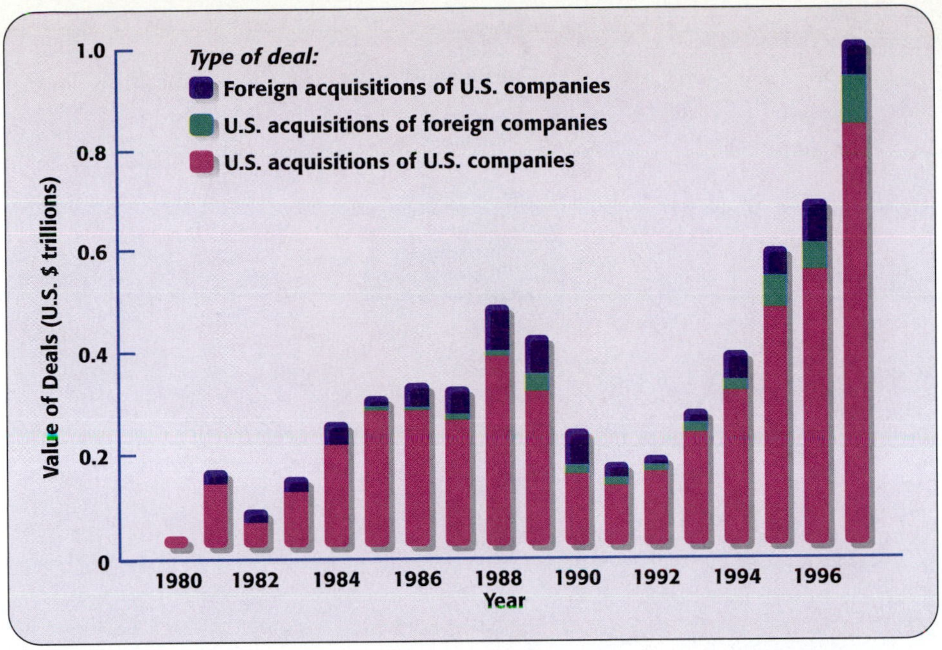

FIGURE 1.2

THE GROWING VALUE OF MERGERS AND ACQUISITIONS

Type of deal:
- Foreign acquisitions of U.S. companies
- U.S. acquisitions of foreign companies
- U.S. acquisitions of U.S. companies

Value of Deals (U.S. $ trillions)

Year

BUSINESS: THE GLOBAL PERSPECTIVE

Some people regard international business as an us-against-them proposition. This defensive mentality causes nations to barricade their markets, cutting off one another from both potential markets and investment opportunities. Following the First World War, countries tried to reduce the outflow of their wealth in the form of gold by discouraging imports and protecting domestic industries. By the early 1930s, this mode of thinking was one factor contributing to the worldwide Great Depression. Thinking globally helps reduce the potential danger associated with this way of thinking.

Businesspeople must try to break out of the boundaries placed upon them by years of living and working within their respective cultures. They must strive to view the global marketplace through the eyes of others with different cultural backgrounds. Today, more and more companies want their managers to think from a global perspective, unhindered by the blinders of nationalism. As we saw earlier in this chapter, for instance, Sony Corporation is in the process of creating a dual-headquarters organization. Global activities in the financial, legal, and business strategy areas that were previously performed only in Tokyo will now be shared with Sony's New York office. "If our headquarters remains in regulation-bound Japan," explains one high-ranking executive, "our managers' thinking will be skewed in a way which limits the development of strategies with a global perspective." At the same time, however, all top executives remain Japanese. Observers argue that for Sony to develop a "truly global" company and culture, top management must include executives with different cultural backgrounds.[27]

Figure 1.3 displays the three elements of the global perspective:

1. Many *national business environments*
2. The *international business environment*
3. The *international business management* of companies

Figure 1.3 also implies that both the national and international business environments influence international business management. Let's examine these three components.

FIGURE 1.3

A GLOBAL PERSPECTIVE ON BUSINESS

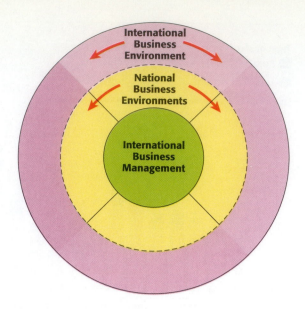

NATIONAL BUSINESS ENVIRONMENTS

Although globalization is drawing the world's economies closer together, many differences among countries remain. Each *national business environment* includes all the elements that are external to a company but that can potentially affect its performance. Each of these elements belongs to one of four external environmental forces: *cultural, political and legal, economic,* and *competitive.*

Four Environmental Forces   Following are the key features of these four forces:

➡ *Cultural forces* reflect a people's aesthetics, values and attitudes, manners and customs, social structure, religion, personal communication, education, and physical and material environments. Understanding national culture helps managers to be more effective at managing their sales and production activities.

➡ *Political and legal forces* are matters of governmental and regulatory importance that concern the management of businesses. Political forces include the stability of government, the level of corruption in the political system, and the political processes that influence economic policies. Legal forces include laws governing the payment of minimum wages, the safety of workers, the protection of the environment and consumers, and what is ruled legal or illegal competitive behavior.

➡ *Economic forces* include financial and economic variables, such as interest and tax rates, consumption patterns, productivity levels, and output levels. They also include infrastructure variables, such as telecommunications, physical distribution networks (roads, highways, airports, and so forth), and the availability and cost of energy.

➡ *Competitive forces* include factors such as the numbers of a company's competitors and their strategies, cost structures, and product quality. It also includes how competition affects the cost and availability of resources such as labor, financial capital, and raw materials. Finally, it involves customers' characteristics, behaviors, and preferences toward the products of a company and its competitors.

These four groups of external forces influence the way all companies operate in any nation's business environment. Entrepreneurs and small to medium-size businesses not involved in international activities can be particularly affected. They must typically employ labor and acquire financial resources in their national or regional market where a limited supply can increase costs.

INTERNATIONAL BUSINESS ENVIRONMENT

Managers of domestic companies are concerned mainly with how external forces *in that one national environment* affect performance. In contrast, managers of international companies must be concerned with external forces in *all of the national business environments in which the company is involved.*

International institutions and processes help shape international business activity. In the *international business environment*, the activities of consumers, workers, companies, financial institutions and governments from different countries converge. The international environment, therefore, links the world's national business environments and is the conduit by which external forces in one country affect companies in others.

Five Influential Groups   Information, capital, people, and products all move about in the international business environment. Five groups account for such movements:

e·biz

➡ *Consumers* around the world are beginning to develop similar wants and needs, especially in such product categories as personal computers, stereos, music, and movies. In addition, they are increasingly knowledgeable about the value of products available in the global marketplace. Today, such merchandise may be purchased directly from manufacturers or retailers over the World Wide Web (and delivered electronically or by conventional means) no matter where either party is physically located.

➡ *Workers* relocate when employment opportunities dwindle in home countries. The formation of free trade areas (such as the European Union) can greatly enhance the mobility of workers among member nations.

➡ *Companies* sell goods and services around the world and acquire investment capital through international financial markets. Multinational corporations transfer employees, information, and capital between their national subsidiaries and compete head-to-head in one another's markets.

➡ *Governments* procure products from international suppliers to accomplish social, economic, and military goals. They also regulate international flows of products, labor, information, and capital. Whereas the global economy benefits from laws that protect consumers and the environment, it can be harmed by laws that are simply barriers to trade and investment.

➡ *Financial institutions* play several important roles in the international business environment. First, they supply companies with the currencies of other countries in order to pay for needed imports. They also buy the currencies of other nations on behalf of companies when managers want to reduce the risk of an international deal. Finally, financial institutions help companies raise capital and invest excess cash in world financial markets.

INTERNATIONAL BUSINESS MANAGEMENT

When a business decides to go international, it faces many challenges. At that point, a firm's internal forces encounter new cultural, political and legal, economic, and competitive external forces. Companies' *internal forces* are those elements within a company over which it has a large degree of control and include:

➡ Human resource staffing policies and employee training and development programs

➡ Organizational culture and the strength with which shared values are emphasized

- The acquisition and allocation of financial resources
- Production methods and scheduling
- Marketing decisions regarding products, pricing, promotion, and distribution
- Policies regarding the evaluation of managers and company performance

Standardization versus Adaptation   International business management is usually subject to the two opposing forces of standardization and adaptation. These forces usually entail a basic decision about doing business abroad. On the one hand, companies can obtain cost savings by *standardizing* various elements of their activities, including production methods, marketing strategy, and corporate policy. On the other hand, they may achieve greater success by *adapting* activities to satisfy the needs of buyers in each local culture—a practice that normally raises costs. Companies must balance the need to cut costs against the special needs of local consumers.

To meet these and other challenges, many companies are working to dissolve the divisions between *business functions* (marketing, production, finance, research and development, and so forth). They are organizing themselves around the processes that create value for their customers, contribute to quality or competitive advantage, or help win new sales contracts. Others are turning to *cross-functional teams* to solve common problems. Teams that cut across functional and cultural boundaries often work to create innovative solutions to problems facing the company in different national markets. We discuss these topics fully in part V of this book.

Ethics and Social Responsibility   When companies venture into international business activities, managers are exposed to different cultures and, therefore, to different ideas about how employees should be treated, different conceptions of ethical behavior, and different guidelines for socially responsible behavior. Firms are often forced to alter their products, advertising, human resource practices, company-wide strategies, and even their organizational structures. Confronting and adapting to such unfamiliar elements presents companies with both tremendous opportunities and potential pitfalls.

Issues such as plant closings, the use of child labor, human rights abuses, and protecting the environment increasingly invade debates on international trade. Whereas ethics pertain to the behavior of individuals, social responsibility relates to the actions of organizations. Let's take a brief look at each of these.

Ethical Behavior   Personal behavior that is in accordance with rules or standards for right conduct or morality is called **ethical behavior**. Ethical dilemmas are not legal questions. When a law exists to guide a manager toward a legally correct action, the legally correct path must necessarily be followed. But in ethical dilemmas there are no right or wrong decisions but alternative choices, each of which may be equally valid, depending on one's perspective.

Ethical questions often arise when managers attempt to either abide by local management practices or import their own practices from the home country. One viewpoint agrees with the old saying "When in Rome, do as the Romans do." This philosophy, however, often runs into trouble when large international companies from developed nations do business in developing nations. Consider one case publicized by human rights and labor groups investigating charges of worker abuse at the factory of one of Nike's Vietnamese suppliers. Twelve of 56 female employees reportedly fainted when a supervisor forced them to run around the factory as punishment for not wearing regulation shoes. Nike confirmed the report and, in suspending the

ethical behavior
Personal behavior that is in accordance with rules or standards for right conduct or morality.

supervisor, took steps to implement practices more in keeping with the company's home-country ethics.[28]

Another viewpoint believes that home-country policies should be implemented wherever a company operates. However, this policy can also create ethical questions. Home-country practice initially won out in 1996 at a Mitsubishi Motors plant in Normal, Illinois. But 30 women later filed a civil suit charging that plant managers fostered an atmosphere conducive to sexual harassment because they let offensive behavior go unpunished. The Equal Employment Opportunity Commission also filed a lawsuit, and Mitsubishi eventually instituted company-wide changes in its human resource policies. Some experts observed that cultural differences and the practices of Mitsubishi that were implemented in the United States from Japan may have contributed to a tolerance of sexual harassment at the Normal plant.

Social Responsibility In addition to individual managers behaving ethically, corporations are expected to exercise **social responsibility**—the practice of going beyond legal obligations to actively balance commitments to investors, customers, other companies, and communities. In recent years governments, labor unions, consumer groups, and human rights activists have combined to drive apparel companies from developed nations to implement codes of conduct and monitoring principles in their international production activities. Pertinent issues include trade initiatives with developing nations (a government issue), the relocation of home-country factories to locations abroad (a labor issue), and the treatment of workers by local contractors abroad (a human rights issue).

> **social responsibility**
> *Practice of companies going beyond legal obligations to actively balance commitments to investors, customers, other companies, and communities.*

Today, companies often don't wait for governments to pressure them before undertaking policy changes. Most business leaders realize that the future of their companies rests on healthy workforces and environments worldwide. Thus some companies have introduced codes of conduct that set standards for working conditions in manufacturing facilities abroad. Starbucks, for instance, introduced a Framework for a Code of Conduct for coffee-exporting countries from which it obtains its coffee beans. This code reflects a larger effort to initiate an industry-wide dialogue among coffee retailers, exporters, and growers to encourage social responsibility.

Levi-Strauss pioneered the use of guidelines in 1992, and company-wide policies have evolved into a set of practical codes. Levi-Strauss relies on these codes both to control working conditions at contractors' facilities and to assess countries as potential locations for doing business. A global staff of about 50 people monitors working conditions in the factories of Levi's contractors abroad.[29] Figure 1.4 summarizes Levi's "Guidelines for Country Selection."

As globalization continues, companies acting in socially irresponsible ways anywhere in the world will come under increasing pressure. The reason is simple: Labor unions, consumer groups, and human rights organizations are also transforming themselves into global organizations. Labor activists in the United States have been instrumental in helping Mexican unions free themselves from decades-long control by a government-backed union that has been accused of not truly supporting workers' rights. For instance, although union leaders in the United States oppose policies that encourage home-based companies to relocate to countries like Mexico, they are now forging closer ties with their Mexican counterparts. Why are they assisting Mexican labor unions in this way? Improved wages and working conditions in Mexico help workers in the United States by reducing the incentive for U.S. firms to move to Mexico.[30]

For some insight into traits (in addition to behaving ethically and acting in a socially responsible manner) that can help managers and their companies succeed in the international marketplace, see the Global Manager "The Keys to Success."

FIGURE 1.4

LEVI STRAUSS & CO. GUIDELINES FOR COUNTRY SELECTION

1. **Brand Image**
   We will not initiate or renew contractual relationships in countries where sourcing would have an adverse effect on our global brand image.

2. **Health & Safety**
   We will not initiate or renew contractual relationships in locations where there is evidence that Company employees or representatives would be exposed to unreasonable risk.

3. **Human Rights**
   We should not initiate or renew contractual relationships in countries where there are pervasive violations of basic human rights.

4. **Legal Requirements**
   We will not initiate or renew contractual relationships in countries where the legal environment creates unreasonable risk to our trademarks or to other important commercial interests or seriously impedes our ability to implement these guidelines.

5. **Political or Social Stability**
   We will not initiate or renew contractual relationships in countries where political or social turmoil unreasonably threatens our commercial interests.

Global Manager

The Keys to Success

Despite the difficulties of managing internationally, many companies prosper when competing beyond their domestic market. Although they assemble everything from 99-cent hamburgers (McDonald's) to $150 million jumbo jets (Boeing), their executives acknowledge certain common threads in their management styles. The most successful global managers offer the following advice:

➡ **Know the Customer** The successful manager has detailed knowledge of what different international customers want and ensures that the company is flexible enough to customize products to meet those needs.

➡ **Emphasize Global Awareness** Good global managers ensure that the company designs and builds products and services for export from the beginning, not as an afterthought following the conquest of domestic markets.

➡ **Market a World-Class Product** Successful managers insist on high-quality products; they know that customers everywhere demand reliability.

➡ **Give Workers a Stake in the Company** The best global companies provide special incentives for employees who perform well.

➡ **Know How to Analyze Problems** Successful managers rarely start out with solutions. Instead, they tackle problems one piece at a time by experimenting and taking risks as necessary.

➡ **Understand Technology** The best managers find ways to match technology with the customer's environment. They do not, for example, make changes out of love for technology but will build new product lines using new, cheaper material when it becomes available.

➡ **Keep an Eye on Exchange Rates** The increasing popularity of using exchange rates to control trade means that global managers must constantly deal with shifts in currency values. In short, they must understand how exchange rates function.

The main theme of this chapter is that the world's national economies are becoming increasingly intertwined. Cultural, political, legal, and economic events in one nation are increasingly affecting business activities in others. As globalization strengthens the bonds among national economies, this trend will continue. By the same token, as globalization penetrates further into national business environments, managers everywhere should take a global perspective on their business activities.

Figure 1.5 shows the path this book takes through the study of international business. Notice that each of the three rings in Figure 1.5 corresponds to the three main elements of Figure 1.3—*the international business environment*, *national business environments*, and *international business management*. In addition, each component of Figure 1.5 corresponds to a chapter in this book.

In Part II, we explore *national business environments*, showing how people's attitudes, values, beliefs, and institutions differ from one culture to another. We also explain how companies modify business practices and strategies when operating under different political, legal, and economic systems.

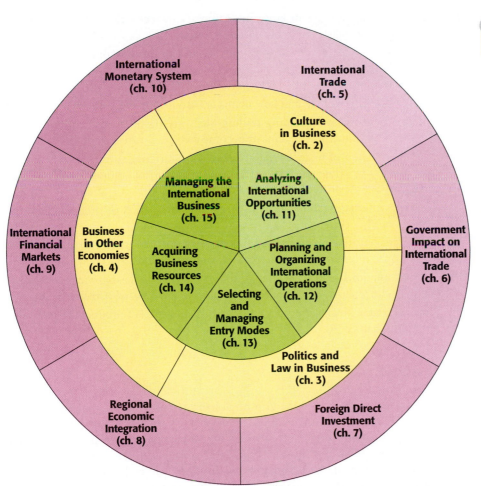

FIGURE 1.5

THE PLAN OF THIS BOOK

- **Outer Ring: International Business Environment** • **Middle Ring: National Business Environments**
- **Core: International Business Management**

We discuss the major components of the *international business environment* in Parts III and IV. We learn why trade and investment flow across borders and why governments try to encourage or discourage their movement. We also explore the process of regional economic integration sweeping the global economy and outline its implications for international companies. Finally, we explain how global financial markets and the global monetary system function and show how they influence companies' international business activities.

In Part V, we describe the ways in which *international business management* is different from managing a purely domestic firm. We discuss how a company analyzes and decides on the markets in which it will sell or manufacture its products. We explain how a company plans and organizes itself for international operations. We explore why different companies choose to enter markets in different ways, and how they acquire and manage their business resources. Among the coming attractions in later chapters, we will explore:

➡ How companies can make marketing and production blunders when they fail to fully understand a people's culture (Chapter 2).

➡ The political and legal obstacles international businesses must overcome, including industrial espionage and terrorism (Chapter 3).

➡ The continuing struggle of emerging countries in recovering from communism and its costly socialist economic policies (Chapter 4).

➡ Why international trade occurs, its positive and negative economic and social benefits, and why and how governments intervene in trade (Chapters 5 and 6).

➡ Why foreign direct investment occurs, why governments insist on interfering with international investment, and how managers can respond (Chapter 7).

➡ Whether continually expanding trading blocs are destined to become fortresses that exclude nonmember nations or become vehicles for freer trade (Chapter 8).

➡ The globalization of financial markets and how currency speculators become extremely wealthy while wreaking havoc with national economies—such as during the 1997–1998 Asian currency crisis (Chapters 9 and 10).

➡ The tools international managers use to select one market or production site instead of another (Chapter 11).

➡ How managers develop an international strategy and choose an entry mode for the leap into the international marketplace (Chapters 12 and 13).

➡ How international managers selected for an international assignment can fall victim to "culture shock" if appropriate precautions are ignored (Chapter 14).

➡ How companies manage production facilities and market products in unfamiliar cultures (Chapter 15).

A FINAL WORD

No business today can escape the grip of globalization—it will breathe new life into some companies and force others into bankruptcy. By thoroughly understanding the dynamics of the international marketplace, you will increase your own chances for success. Whether you work for a global firm in a large cosmopolitan city or for a small business in a rural town, the information in this book will make you a more valuable employee, a more effective manager, or a more successful entrepreneur. This chapter has simply introduced you to the study of international business. We hope you enjoy the rest of your journey as you continue to discover the truly rich and dynamic nature of international business!

There is a variety of additional material available on the companion Web site that accompanies this text. You can access this information by visiting the Web site at ⟨**www.prenhall.com/wild**⟩.

summary

❶ Describe *international business* and the process of *globalization*. *International business* is the total of all business transactions crossing the borders of two or more nations. By means of international business, more and more nations are integrating their national economies into the global economy. This process of integration is called *globalization*. Two main forces behind the increasing globalization of business are (1) *lower trade and investment barriers* and (2) *increased innovation*, particularly in the areas of information and transportation technology.

❷ Explain why companies pursue *international business activity*. Companies engage in international business for two main reasons: (1) to *increase sales* and (2) to *access resources*. Increasing sales is an attractive option when a firm is presented with either of two conditions: (1) an international sales growth opportunity or (2) excess production capacity. Firms try to access both *natural resources* (products supplied by nature) and *labor markets* in countries where low-cost labor helps them to be more competitive.

❸ Identify the *types of companies* that participate in international business. Almost any company can participate in international business. Thanks to the Internet and other technologies that permit them to surmount such obstacles as prohibitively high advertising and distribution costs, many small businesses have become increasingly active in international trade and investment. However, large *multinational*

corporations (MNCs) conduct most international business transactions. Multinationals dominate the international business news for two reasons: (1) They are highly visible because they have so much economic muscle; (2) their mergers and acquisitions are often valued in the billions of dollars.

❹ Explain the *global perspective* on business and identify its three main elements. Adopting a *global perspective* means breaking out of the boundaries placed on us by years of living within our respective cultures. The consideration of three elements goes into the global perspective on business: (a) Separate *national business environments*, which include all the elements that are external to a company but that can affect its performance. These elements belong to one of four external environmental forces: *cultural, political/legal, economic,* and *competitive*. (b) The *international business environment*, which refers to the institutions and processes that shape international business activity. It links national environments by conducting the flow of information, capital, people, and products. In turn, five groups account for these flows: consumers, workers, companies, governments, and financial institutions. (c) *International business management* involves (among other things) balancing a firm's internal forces (human resource policies, organizational culture, production methods, and so forth) with external environmental forces (cultural, political/legal, economic, and competitive).

questions **for review**

1. What is *international business*? Give several examples of international business transactions (other than those included in the chapter).

2. What two major factors have led to greater *globalization* in markets and production? Explain each briefly.

3. For what two main reasons do companies "go international"?

4. What types of companies get involved in international business activities? Explain why large companies capture so much of the international business headlines.

5. What do we mean by "the *global perspective* on business?" Explain how its three main elements interact.

6. What is the *national business environment*? Identify the four external forces that comprise it.

7. What is the *international business environment*? Identify the five groups that account for the international flow of information, capital, people, and products.

8. How does managing an international business differ from managing a domestic company?

9. Why do the issues of *ethical behavior* and *social responsibility* arise in the international marketplace? Explain how these two concepts differ from one another.

questions for discussion

1. International businesspeople must think globally about production and sales opportunities. The World Business Survey "The International Top Fifteen" on page 8 reveals the nations that are expected to attract managers in the future. What can companies do now to prepare themselves for these new markets? What can entrepreneurs and small businesses with limited resources do?

2. In the past, national governments greatly affected the pace of globalization through agreements to lower barriers to international trade and investment. Is the pace of change now outpacing the ability of governments to manage the global economy? Will national governments become more or less important to international business in the future? Explain your answer.

3. Information and communication technologies are developing at a faster rate than ever before. How have these technologies affected globalization? Give specific examples. Do you think globalization will continue until we all live in one "global village"? Why or why not?

4. Consider the following statement: "Globalization and the resulting increase in competition harm people as international companies play one government against another to get the best deal possible. Meanwhile, governments continually ask for greater concessions from their citizens, demanding that they work harder and longer for less pay." Do you agree? Why or why not?

in practice

This chapter discussed the reasons why companies expand into international markets. Read the brief article below and answer the questions that follow.

BMW, VW Expand in Russsia

Two German carmakers—BMW and Volkswagen—have announced plans to build assembly plants in Russia. BMW said it has closely studied the projected long-term growth of the Russian auto market and decided to construct the facility in the Baltic city of Kaliningrad. BMW sales in Russia have declined by about 10 percent over the past several years. The German company has 19 dealerships in Russia, five of which are also licensed to sell Land Rovers produced by its British off-road division. Volkswagen AG's future plans call for the construction of a plant this year at an as-yet undisclosed location in Russia.

1. Given that sales of BMWs in Russia are in decline, why do you think the company is building an assembly plant there? Identify as many possible reasons as you can.

2. Go to the Web site of BMW ⟨**www.bmw.com**⟩ and access its most recent annual report. In what other locations does BMW produce auto parts or assemble cars? Based on the information at the Web site, report on one aspect of the company that interests you.

3. Why does the article refer to Kaliningrad as a "Baltic city?" *Hint:* You might want to take a look at the world atlas that follows this chapter.

projects

1. Imagine that you own a company that manufactures cheap sunglasses. To lower production costs, you want to move your factory from your developed country to a low-wage country. Choose a prospective country to which you will move. What elements of the national business environment will affect your move? Are there any obstacles to overcome in the international business environment? How will managing your company be different when you undertake international activities? What challenges will you face in managing your new employees?

2. With a group of classmates, select a country that interests you. What does its flag look like? What do the various colors and symbols, if any, represent? Identify any neighbors with which it shares borders. Give some important facts about the country, including its population, population density, land area, topography, climate, natural resources, and the locations of main industries. What products are produced there? Do any aspects of the natural environment help explain why it produces what it does? Present your findings to the class.

Perhaps no company exemplifies the maxim "Think globally, act locally" better than MTV. The company beams its irreverent and brash mix of music, news, and entertainment to 281 million homes in over 64 countries, including Brazil, Singapore, India, and 36 countries in Europe. Although style and format are largely driven by the U.S. youth culture, content is tailored to local markets.

In 1987, MTV commanded an audience of 61 million in the United States. But because demand was leveling off, the company took the music revolution global by starting MTV Europe and MTV Australia. Through its experiences in Europe, MTV refined its mix of programming to become a global national brand with local variations. At first, it took a pan-European approach, marketing the same product to all European countries. MTV broadcast primarily British and U.S. music (both of which were topping the charts throughout Europe) and used European "veejays" who spoke English. The European network was a huge overnight success.

Seven years later, however, MTV had become the victim of its own success. Now it had to compete with a new crop of upstart rivals that tailored content to language, culture, and current events in specific countries. One successful competitor is Germany's VIVA, launched in 1993 and featuring German veejays and more German artists (like Fantascishen 4 and

Scooter) than MTV Europe. Managers at MTV Networks were not overly concerned because MTV was still extremely popular. But they did realize they were losing their edge (and some customers) to the new national networks. What should the company do? Split up MTV Europe into MTV Germany and MTV Spain?

Because they had spent almost two decades building a global brand identity, MTV executives initially rejected that idea. Little by little, however, they changed their collective mind. They decided to move forward because a certain technological innovation made it possible for MTV to think globally and act locally at very little cost. The breakthrough was digital compression technology, which allows suppliers to multiply the number of services offered on a single satellite feed. "Where there were three or four services," explained one MTV official, "now we can broadcast six or eight."

Today, not only teens in Europe but teens all over the world have their MTV cake and eat it, too. German teens, for instance, see shows created and produced in Germany—in German—along with the usual generous helpings of U.S., British, and international music and the ever-popular duo Beavis and Butthead. And there's an added side benefit for MTV: National advertisers who had shunned the channel during its pan-European days are now coming onboard to beam ads targeted specifically to their consumers.

thinking globally

1. The last decade has witnessed a growing similarity in the attitudes and spending habits of youthful consumers around the world. As one journalist puts it, "It may still be conventional wisdom to 'think globally and act locally,' but in the youth market, it is increasingly a case of one size fits all." Do you agree or disagree? Why or why not?

2. Some people are concerned that teens exposed to large doses of U.S. youth culture via 24-hour MTV networks will begin to identify less and less with their own cultures and societies. Others worry that teenage consumers in developing countries want more and more Western goods that they can't afford. MTV's response to such criticism: "It's just fun," says one network executive. "It's only TV."

   What do you think? Are there dangers in broadcasting U.S. programs and ads to both developed and developing countries?

3. Digital compression technology made it possible for MTV to program over a global network. Can you think of any other technological innovations that have helped companies to think globally and act locally?

a question of ethics

1. We often characterize ethical dilemmas as "right-versus-wrong" situations. But consider the opinion of Rushworth Kidder, president of the Institute for Global Ethics: "The very toughest choices people face are not questions of right versus wrong, but questions of right versus right," such as a choice between the values of truth and loyalty. For instance, should you tell the truth about a superior's wrongdoing, or should you remain loyal to your boss? Describe an ethical dilemma in which an international executive might face a tough choice between "right" and "right." Have you ever faced such a choice? How do *you* define ethical behavior? Do you think that people can be made to act ethically?[31]

2. Nike called upon civil rights leader Andrew Young to look into its labor practices at Asian plants in order to determine if the company was adhering to its own code of ethical conduct.

After a monthlong investigation, Young reported no evidence of widespread or systematic mistreatment of Nike workers abroad. Critics charged that the report was shallow because Young admitted to spending only three hours in any factory, always accompanied by Nike officials. They were also skeptical because Young presented his findings to Nike's board and senior management a week before making them public. If you were the CEO of Nike, how would you respond to these criticisms? Do you think that there are more effective or objective means of monitoring a company's overseas activities? If so, what are they?[32]

3. The North American Free Trade Agreement (NAFTA) requires the United States to spend over $1 billion for environmental cleanup. By the end of 1996, however, the United States had spent nothing in this area. According to Guillermo Perez Diaz, general manager of the water department of San Luis Rio Colorado, a Mexican border city, "The mutual promises made by our two governments have not yet been kept. Our city . . . has serious environmental problems. Our drainage system serves only 38 percent of the population, and our sewage, for which we have no treatment plant, is seriously contaminating the dry bed of the Colorado River. After more than a year of presenting projects to the Border Environment Cooperation Commission and the North American Development Bank, we have yet to receive any help." Do the businesses who have set up in San Luis Rio Colorado bear any responsibility for the environmental problems there? What can business leaders do when governments ignore environmental promises?[33]

integrative video case
PART ONE: OVERVIEW OF INTERNATIONAL BUSINESS
lands' end and yahoo!

background

This video case shows how two very different companies, Lands' End and Yahoo!, approached the same goal: expansion into international markets. Lands' End is a retail business that sells its products through its print and on-line catalogs. Yahoo! is an Internet search engine that supplies its service to Web surfers worldwide.

A firm may decide to go international for any number of reasons, including the drive to increase sales volume and to access resources in other national markets. Lands' End wanted to increase its sales volume in markets such as Japan, Germany, and the United Kingdom. Yahoo! wanted to dominate the global Internet industry by penetrating markets such as China, Japan, Sweden, Norway, France, and others. This video illustrates how the two companies entered a particular country and localized their products and services to meet the needs and preferences of consumers in new markets.

lands' end

In 1963, Gary C. Comer, a former advertising copywriter and an avid sailor, founded Lands' End, Inc., in Chicago, Illinois. The company began by selling sailboat hardware equipment by catalog. In 1978, Lands' End warehouse and phone operations moved to Dodgeville, Wisconsin, a rural community located 40 miles southwest of Madison, Wisconsin. In 1980, the company established a toll-free phone operation that ran 24 hours a day, and in 1985, the Lands' End catalog started coming out monthly. The company went public in 1986. In 1990, three new specialty catalogs were launched: Coming Home (bed and bath supplies), Lands' End Kids, and Beyond Buttonwoods (men's tailored

clothing). In 1991, Lands' End sent its catalog to customers in the United Kingdom for the first time, and in 1993 the company opened a warehouse and phone center there. In 1994, Lands' End opened operations in Japan. That same year Lands' End purchased the trademark of Willis & Geiger, an U.S.-based adventure outfitters company. In 1995, Lands' End launched its Web site on the Internet. Still building its overseas presence, Lands' End opened a phone center in Germany in 1996. By 1997 Lands' End sales had reached $1.2 billion, making the company one of the largest apparel brands in the United States.

yahoo! inc.

Yahoo! is an Internet search engine headquartered in Santa Clara, California, that helps people navigate the World Wide Web. The company's principal product is an ad-supported Internet directory that links users to millions of Web pages. The site leads the field in traffic (95 million pages viewed each day) and is second only to Netscape in on-line advertising revenues. Yahoo! has targeted guides for geographic audiences (Yahoo! Finance and Yahoo! News), demographic audiences (see Yahooligans!, a Web guide for children), special-interest audiences (for example, Yahoo! Finance and Yahoo! News), and community services (Yahoo! Chat). The company is moving into the Internet access market through an alliance with AT&T and has agreed to acquire fellow Internet player GeoCities. Japan's SOFTBANK, which owns 28 percent of Yahoo!, has 15 international Web properties outside the United States. Yahoo! now has offices in Europe, the Asian Pacific, and Canada. Net income for 1998 was $25.6 million. In 1997, the company employed 386 people, and in 1998 its staff climbed to 803.

discussion questions

While you watch the video, keep the following discussion questions in mind. You might want to take notes.

1. Why did the two companies go international?

2. What is the difference between international and global? Answer this question from the perspectives of Lands' End and Yahoo!.

3. How did Lands' End succeed in establishing itself in Germany, the United Kingdom, and Japan?

4. How did Yahoo! succeed in Japan, France, Sweden, China, and Latin America?

5. What international issues have challenged the two companies?

6. How did Yahoo! localize its global products and services?

student exercises

1. Break into groups of two or three people. Discuss the national and international environments for Lands' End and Yahoo!. Present your analysis to the rest of the class with a 10- to 15-minute talk.

2. Choose any company from any country in the world and write up the reasons why this company should or should not go international.

3. Compare and contrast the differences between a global and an international business.

APPENDIX
world atlas

This atlas presents the global landscape in a series of maps designed to assist your understanding of global business. By knowing the locations of countries and the distances between them, managers in the global marketplace are able to make more informed decisions. Knowing the geography of a place also gives managers insight into the culture of the people living there. Because international managers must know where borders meet, this atlas captures the most recent changes in national political boundaries.

As the global marketplace continues to absorb previously isolated business environments, each one of us needs a thorough grasp of the global landscape. Familiarize yourself with each of the maps in this appendix and then try to answer the following 20 questions. We urge you to return to this atlas frequently in order to refresh your memory of the global landscape and especially when you encounter the name of an unfamiliar city or country.

MAP EXERCISES

1. Which of the following countries border the Atlantic Ocean?
   a. Bolivia
   b. Australia
   c. South Africa
   d. Japan
   e. United States

2. Which of the following countries are found in Africa?
   a. Guyana
   b. Morocco
   c. Egypt
   d. Pakistan
   e. Niger

3. Which one of the following countries does *not* border the Pacific Ocean?
   a. Australia
   b. Venezuela
   c. Japan
   d. Mexico
   e. Peru

4. Prague is the capital city of:
   a. Uruguay
   b. Czech Republic
   c. Portugal
   d. Tunisia
   e. Hungary

5. If transportation costs for getting your product from your market to Japan are high, which of the following countries might be good places to locate a manufacturing facility?
   a. Thailand
   b. Philippines
   c. South Africa
   d. Indonesia
   e. Portugal

6. Seoul is the capital city of:
   a. Vietnam
   b. Cambodia
   c. Malaysia
   d. China
   e. South Korea

7. Turkey, Romania, Ukraine, and Russia border the body of water called the _____ Sea.

8. Thailand shares borders with:
   a. Cambodia
   b. Pakistan
   c. Singapore
   d. Malaysia
   e. Indonesia

9. Which of the following countries border no major ocean or sea?
   a. Austria
   b. Paraguay
   c. Switzerland
   d. Niger
   e. all of the above

10. Oslo is the capital city of:
    a. Germany
    b. Canada
    c. Brazil
    d. Australia
    e. Norway
11. Chile is located in:
    a. Africa
    b. Asia
    c. the Northern Hemisphere
    d. South America
    e. Central Europe
12. Saudi Arabia shares borders with:
    a. Jordan
    b. Kuwait
    c. Iraq
    d. United Arab Emirates
    e. all of the above
13. The body of water located between Sweden and Estonia is the _____ Sea.
14. Which of the following countries are located on the Mediterranean Sea?
    a. Italy
    b. Croatia
    c. Turkey
    d. France
    e. Portugal
15. The distance between Sydney (Australia) and Tokyo (Japan) is shorter than that between:
    a. Tokyo and Cape Town (South Africa)
    b. Sydney and Hong Kong (China)
    c. Tokyo and London (England)
    d. Sydney and Jakarta (Indonesia)
    e. all of the above
16. Madrid is the capital city of (capitals are designated with red dots.):
    a. Madagascar
    b. Italy
    c. Mexico
    d. Spain
    e. United States
17. Which of the following countries is *not* located in central Asia?
    a. Afghanistan
    b. Uzbekistan
    c. Turkmenistan
    d. Kazakhstan
    e. Suriname
18. If you were shipping your products from your production facility in Pakistan to market in Australia, they would likely cross the _____ Ocean.
19. Papua New Guinea, Guinea-Bissau, and Guinea are alternative names for the same country.
    a. true
    b. false
20. Which of the following countries are island nations?
    a. New Zealand
    b. Madagascar
    c. Japan
    d. Australia
    e. all of the above

Answers

1. c. South Africa, e. United States; 2. b. Morocco, c. Egypt, e. Niger; 3. b. Venezuela; 4. b. Czech Republic; 5. a. Thailand, b. Philippines, d. Indonesia; 6. e. South Korea; 7. Black; 8. a. Cambodia, d. Malaysia; 9. e. all of the above; 10. e. Norway; 11. d. South America; 12. e. all of the above; 13. Baltic; 14. a. Italy, c. Turkey, d. France; 15. a. Tokyo and Cape Town (South Africa), c. Tokyo and London (England); 16. d. Spain; 17. e. Suriname; 18. Indian; 19. b. false; 20. e. all of the above.

Self-Assessment

If you scored 15 correct answers or more, well done: You are well prepared for your international business journey. If you scored fewer than 8 correct answers, you may wish to review this atlas before moving on to Chapter 2.

THE WORLD IN 1999 This global view identifies each continent and acts as reference for the six maps that follow.

MAP A.2

NORTH AMERICA

MAP A.3

SOUTH AMERICA

MAP A.4

EUROPE

Pacific
Ocean

CAROLINE I.

PALAU I.

Arafura Sea

MOLUCCA I.

Banda Sea

Bering
Sea

KURIL IS.

Sea of
Okhotsk

JAPAN

Tokyo

I N D O N E S I A

Davao

PHILIPPINES

Baguio

Manila

Arctic Ocean

Vladivostok

Sea of
Japan

Kyoto
Csaka

Kitakyushu
Nagasaki
Kagoshima

RYUKYU IS.

East
China
Sea

Taipei

TAIWAN
(FORMOSA)

Hong Kong

Macau

South
China
Sea

HAINAN I.

BRUNEI

SINGAPORE

MALAYSIA

Jakarta

Harbin

Qiqihar

Changchun

Shenyang

N. KOREA

Pyongyang

S. KOREA

Seoul

Beijing

Tianjin

Nanjing

Shanghai

Wuhan

Fuzhou

Changsha

Guangzhou

Hanoi

George Town

Kuala Lumpur

Lake
Baikal

Ulaanbaatar

MONGOLIA

Taiyuan

C H I N A

Chengdu

Chongqing

Kunming

Mandalay

VIETNAM

LAOS

Vientiane

THAILAND

Bangkok

CAMBODIA

Phnom Penh

Ho Chi Minh City
(Saigon)

R U S S I A

Novosibirsk

BHUTAN

MYANMAR

Yangon

BANGLADESH

Dhaka

NEPAL

Calcutta

Bay of
Bengal

SRI
LANKA

Moscow

(European
Russia)

Yekaterinburg

Chelyabinsk

Omsk

Aqmola

Lake
Balkhash

Aral
Sea

KAZAKHSTAN

Almaty

Bishkek

KYRGYZSTAN

Tashkent

TAJIKISTAN

Samarkand

Dushanbe

UZBEKISTAN

TURKMENISTAN

Ashgabat

AFGHANISTAN

Herat

Mashhad

Kabul

Peshawar

Islamabad

Lahore

Multan

PAKISTAN

Delhi

New Delhi

Hyderabad

Karachi

Kanpur

I N D I A

Nagpur

Hyderabad

Chennai
(Madras)

Colombo

Bangalore

Mumbai
(Bombay)

Arabian
Sea

Indian
Ocean

Atlantic
Ocean

Black Sea

Istanbul

Izmir

TURKEY

Ankara

GEORGIA

Tbilisi

ARMENIA

Yerevan

AZERBAIJAN

Baku

Caspian
Sea

Tehran

IRAN

Hamadan

Shiraz

LEBANON

Beirut

SYRIA

Damascus

ISRAEL

Jerusalem

JORDAN

Amman

IRAQ

Baghdad

Basra

KUWAIT

Kuwait

BAHRAIN

Manama

QATAR

Doha

U.A.E.

Abu Dhabi

Muscat

OMAN

Medina

Riyadh

SAUDI
ARABIA

YEMEN

San'a

Jeddah

Mecca

Red
Sea

Mediterranean Sea

MAP A.5

ASIA

MAP A.6

AFRICA

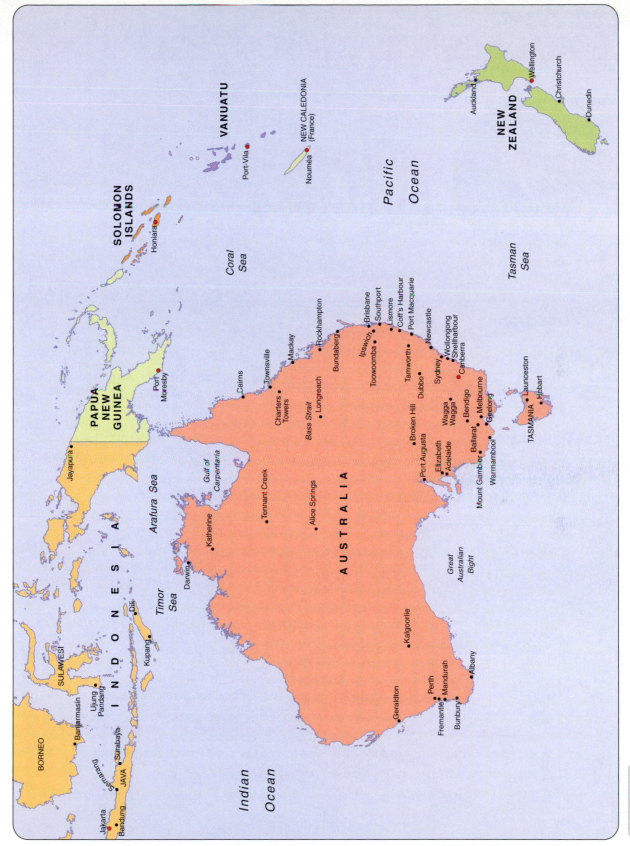

INDONESIA

BORNEO

Jakarta
Bandung
JAVA
Semarang
Surabaya
SULAWESI
Ujung
Pandang
Banjarmasin
Kupang
Dili

Indian
Ocean

Timor
Sea

Arafura Sea

Darwin
Katherine
Tennant Creek

Jayapura

PAPUA
NEW
GUINEA

Port
Moresby

Gulf of
Carpentaria

Alice Springs

AUSTRALIA

Geraldton
Perth
Mandurah
Fremantle
Bunbury
Albany
Kalgoorlie

Great
Australian
Bight

Cairns
Townsville
Charters
Towers
Longreach
Bass Strait

Mackay
Rockhampton
Bundaberg
Toowoomba
Ipswich
Brisbane
Southport
Lismore
Coff's Harbour
Port Macquarie
Newcastle
Tamworth
Sydney
Dubbo
Wollongong
Shellharbour
Canberra
Broken Hill
Wagga
Wagga
Bendigo
Port Augusta
Ballarat
Melbourne
Elizabeth
Geelong
Adelaide
Warrnambool
Mount Gambier

Launceston
Hobart
TASMANIA

Coral
Sea

SOLOMON
ISLANDS

Honiara

VANUATU

Port-Vila

NEW CALEDONIA
(France)

Nouméa

Pacific
Ocean

Tasman
Sea

NEW
ZEALAND

Auckland
Wellington
Christchurch
Dunedin

culture in business

Beacons

A Look Back

CHAPTER 1 presented a global perspective on business. We learned why companies "go international" and about the many external and internal forces with which companies must deal when managing an international business.

A Look at This Chapter

This chapter introduces the important role of culture in international business. We explore the main elements of culture and show how they affect business policies and practices. We learn different methods of classifying cultures and how these methods can be applied to business.

A Look Ahead

CHAPTER 3 describes the political and legal systems of nations. We learn how these systems differ from one country to another and how they influence international business operations. We also show how managers reduce the effects of political risk.

Learning Objectives

After studying this chapter, you should be able to

1. Describe *culture* and explain the influence of both national culture and subcultures.

2. Identify the *components of culture* and describe their impact on business activities around the world.

3. Describe *cultural change* and explain how companies and culture affect one another.

4. Explain how the *physical environment* and *technology* influence culture.

5. Describe the *frameworks* and *dimensions* used to classify cultures and explain how they are applied.

Consumers around the world purchase personal computers, clothing, perfume, and soft drinks. Broad popular appeal, however, doesn't mean that a product can be made and marketed the same way in every country.

Lands' End, for example, modifies shirts, trousers, coats, sweaters, and almost every other article of clothing to accommodate differences in human physique, climate, and shopping habits worldwide. Commodore once used a photo of a naked young man to sell computers in Germany, but the same approach in Saudi Arabia would be highly offensive to Islamic values, not to mention illegal.

Even products that seem "universal" may need to be adapted for international markets. Arab-Malaysian Bank developed a credit card for Malaysians that doesn't allow purchases at "unholy" businesses such as gambling casinos, massage parlors, and nightclubs. But it does offer discounts on pilgrimages to Islam's holy city of Mecca, Saudi Arabia. Even the Walt Disney Company modified long-standing staffing policies at Disneyland Paris when French employees, complaining that Disney was disregarding local values, objected to bans on mustaches, beards, and short skirts.

Thus companies often adapt their marketing and management processes to suit local conditions. Careful evaluation of the local culture helps managers decide whether they will follow the maxim "When in Rome, do as the Romans do."[1]

This chapter is the first of three that discuss aspects of a nation's business environment (culture, politics, laws, and economics) that affect international business activities. One might ask, Why study topics that seem to be only indirectly related to international business? The short answer is they have *everything* to do with international business. Many failures by international businesses are directly related to their neglect of these crucial environmental factors.

The first step in the process of analyzing a nation's potential as a host for international business activity is to assess its overall business climate. This process means addressing some important questions. Are the local people open to new ideas and new ways of doing business? Is the political situation stable enough so that assets and employees are not placed at unacceptable levels of risk? Do government officials and the people want our business? By what ground rules do local businesses play? Answers to these kinds of questions—plus statistical data on such items as income level and labor costs—allow businesses to evaluate the attractiveness of a particular location as a place for doing business.

Understanding culture is crucial when a company does business in *its own* country. It is even more crucial when operating *across* cultures. From individual consumers to entrepreneurs to huge global firms, people inhabit the core of all business activity. When buyers and sellers from around the world come together to conduct business, they bring with them different backgrounds, expectations, and methods of communication. It is very important for businesspeople to understand how to communicate with their counterparts in other cultures.

This chapter defines *culture* in the context of international business. We explore the ways in which social institutions, religion, language, and other elements of culture affect international business activities. We learn how each nation's culture affects such things as its business practices and international competitiveness.

WHAT IS CULTURE?

culture
Set of values, beliefs, rules, and institutions held by a specific group of people.

When traveling in other countries, we often perceive differences in the way people live and work. In the United States dinner is commonly eaten around six; in Spain it's not served until eight or nine. In the United States people shop in large supermarkets once a week; Italians shop in small local grocery stores every day. These are differences in **culture**—the set of values, beliefs, rules, and institutions held by a specific group of people.[2] Culture is a highly complex portrait of a people. It includes everything from high tea in England, to the tropical climate of Barbados, to Mardi Gras in Brazil, to segregation of the sexes in Saudi Arabian schools. As we shall see later in this chapter, the main components of any culture include its *aesthetics, values* and *attitudes, manners* and *customs, social structure, religion, personal communication, education,* and *physical* and *material environments.*

ethnocentricity
Belief that one's own ethnic group or culture is superior to that of others.

Accommodating Culture: Overcoming Ethnocentricity Ethnocentricity is the belief that one's own ethnic group or culture is superior to that of others. It causes people to *view other cultures in terms of their own*—causing them to overlook important human and environmental differences among cultures.

International business projects are often undermined by ethnocentricity, primarily because firms' employees fail to be sensitive to cultural nuances. The annals of business are full of projects that failed because of resistance put up by government, labor, or the general public when companies tried to change something culturally fundamental at a factory or office in someone else's homeland.

Today globalization demands that businesspeople approach other cultures far differently than they did in the past. In particular, new technologies and their applications allow suppliers and buyers to treat the world as a single interconnected global

e·biz

marketplace. Because globalization is bringing companies face-to-face with each other and their global customers, companies need employees who are not blinded by ethnocentricity.

Understanding Culture: Developing Cultural Literacy   Globalization demands that everyone involved in business exhibit a certain degree of **cultural literacy**—detailed knowledge about a culture that enables people to live and work within it. Cultural literacy improves the ability to manage employees, market products, and conduct negotiations in other countries. Global brand names like MTV and Gucci provide a competitive advantage, but cultural differences continue to force modifications to suit local markets. Because culture still dictates that many products incorporate local tastes and preferences, cultural literacy brings us closer to customer needs and desires and improves our competitiveness. We discuss different types of cultural training used for developing cultural literacy in Chapter 14.

<aside>
cultural literacy
Detailed knowledge about a culture that enables people to live and work within it.
</aside>

NATIONAL CULTURE AND SUBCULTURES

Whether rightly or wrongly, we tend to invoke the concept of the *nation-state* when speaking of culture. In other words, we usually refer to British and Indonesian cultures as if all Britons and all Indonesians were culturally identical. Why? Because we have been conditioned to think in terms of *national culture*. But this is at best a generalization. For example, campaigns for Scottish and Welsh independence in Great Britain continue to gain momentum. In remote parts of Indonesia, people build homes in the treetops even as other parts of the nation pursue ambitious economic development programs.

Let's take a closer look at national cultures and the diversity that lies within them.

National Culture   Nation-states support and promote the concept of a national culture by building museums and monuments to preserve the legacies of important events and people. In so doing, they affirm the importance of national culture to their citizens and organizations.

Many companies take advantage of the public relations value of supporting national culture. In Russia, for example, where the national budget cannot afford adequate support for the arts, financially sound Russian firms are leading the way in buying Russian art and returning it to Russian museums. Consumers respond to such goodwill activities by purchasing these companies' products.

Nation-states also intervene in business to help preserve their national cultures. Most nations, for example, regulate culturally sensitive sectors of the economy such as filmmaking and broadcasting. In particular, France continues to voice fears that its language is being tainted with English and its media with U.S. programming.[3] To stem the English invasion, new French laws limit the use of English in product packaging and storefront signs. At peak listening times, at least 40 percent of all radio station programming must be reserved for French artists. Similar laws apply to television broadcasting. Recently, the French government even fined the local branch of a U.S. university for failing to provide a French translation on its English-language site on the World Wide Web.

e·biz

Subcultures   A group of people who share a unique way of life within a larger, dominant culture is called a **subculture**. Unfortunately, our impressions of the cultures of many nations often do not incorporate the influence of important subcultures. Subcultures can differ from the dominant culture in language, race, lifestyle, values, attitudes, or other characteristics. They often play important roles in forming the national image and in the determination of the business strategies that companies employ.

<aside>
subculture
Group of people who share a unique way of life within a larger, dominant culture.
</aside>

Subcultures exist in all nations. For example, the official portrait of Chinese culture often ignores the fact that the total population of China is comprised of more than 50 distinct ethnic groups. Decisions regarding product design, packaging, and advertising must consider each group's distinct culture. Marketing directed at Tibetans must respect their unique history and ethnic pride. Tibetans would resent any campaign referring to them as Chinese. Marketing campaigns in China must also acknowledge that Chinese dialects in the Shanghai and Canton regions differ from those of smaller areas in the country's interior. Not everyone is fluent in the official Mandarin dialect.

Firms must take special care when marketing medicines, dangerous chemicals, and other products requiring detailed instructions. If a product's labels and warnings cannot be read and understood by all subcultures, it might be more likely to inflict physical harm than to satisfy a need.

Although nation-states play a role in the development of national culture, political boundaries do not always correspond to cultural boundaries. This means that subcultures sometimes cross national borders. People who live in different nations but share the same subculture can have more in common with one another than with fellow nationals. Arab culture, for instance, extends from northwest Africa to the Middle East. Arabs—who include any of the Semitic peoples who were once native to Saudi Arabia but who now inhabit every surrounding land—also live in Turkey, in many European countries, and in the United States. Because Arabs tend to share attitudes and purchasing behaviors related to Islamic religious beliefs, marketing to Arab subcultures can sometimes be accomplished with a single marketing campaign. A common language (Arabic) also eliminates translation costs and increases the likelihood of correct message interpretation. To see how small businesses can exploit the knowledge of subcultures and cultural literacy, see the Entrepreneurial Focus "Entrepreneurs Respect Culture."

Entrepreneurial Focus

Entrepreneurs Respect Culture

What do Clifford Lichaytoo in the Philippines, Jiri Bradle in the Czech Republic, and Sterry Chong in China possibly have in common? They are small-business owners who have taken risks because they live in cultures that value and reward risk taking. A close look at the businesses founded by these three entrepreneurs shows how cultural forces affect small businesses.

➡ Clifford Lichaytoo learned the cruel reality of the global economy when he lost textile contracts to competitors in countries like Nicaragua, which have 75 percent lower labor costs. So he started a company in a higher-value-added business—importing premium wines. As Filipinos have prospered, their consumer behavior has begun to resemble that of consumers in other industrialized countries—for example, drinking fine wines, as the French and Italians do.

➡ Jiri Bradle discovered the value that his new advertising agency could provide Western companies doing business in Prague, capital of the Czech Republic. Having learned some lessons in cultural literacy, Colgate Palmolive hired Bradle to integrate Czech culture into its marketing campaign for Colgate toothpaste.

➡ Sterry Chong and his brother hope to strike it rich in a U.S.-China joint venture with TCBY (The Country's Best Yogurt). As their spending power has grown, Chinese consumers, like Filipinos, have begun to behave like consumers in any industrialized nation. Because they are in the market for healthier diets, the selection of available goods has widened. The Chongs are exploiting this trend and their thorough understanding of Chinese culture. "Each city," explains Sterry Chong, "is very different; each province has its own culture. You can't just make one single television commercial and broadcast it across the country. You have to find out what the interest is in each city or province." Accordingly, the Chongs are designing yogurt products and flavors to suit the needs of each individual market in the country.

Both the actions of nation-states and the presence of subcultures help define the culture of a group of people. But a people's culture also includes what they consider beautiful and tasteful, their underlying beliefs, their traditional habits, and the ways in which they relate to one another and their surroundings. This section covers the main components of culture: *aesthetics, values* and *attitudes, manners* and *customs, social structure, religion, personal communication, education,* and *physical* and *material environments.*

AESTHETICS

What a culture considers to be in "good taste" in the arts (including music, painting, dance, drama, and architecture), the imagery evoked by certain expressions, and even the symbolism of certain colors is called **aesthetics**.

Aesthetics are important when a firm considers doing business in another culture. Major blunders can result from selecting inappropriate colors for advertising, product packaging, and even work uniforms. For instance, green is a favorable color in Islam and adorns the national flags of most Islamic nations, including Jordan, Pakistan, and Saudi Arabia. This results in product packaging that is often green to take advantage of this emotional attachment. Across much of Asia, on the other hand, green is associated with sickness. In Europe, Mexico, and the United States, black is the color of death and mourning; in Japan and most of Asia, it's white.

Consider this actual example of the importance of both color imagery and symbolism in marketing. In 1997, Britain transferred administrative control of Hong Kong to the Chinese after its 99-year lease expired. Understandably, the residents of Hong Kong were fearful about what Communist Chinese control would mean for their civil liberties. American Craft Brewing International wished to mark the occasion by brewing a special red-colored lager at its Hong Kong brewery. Because red is a favorite color in China and dawn is the symbol for change, the brewer called its product Red Dawn. For Hong Kong's residents, however, *red* is also seen as the official color of the Chinese Communist Party. Moreover, *dawn* stirs memories of the popular communist song "Dong Fang Hong." These are hardly the images with which Hong Kong residents wanted to relax while pondering the transfer of control to China. As a rule, companies must carefully research product colors and names to be sure they do not evoke any unintended response.[4]

Likewise, music is deeply embedded in culture and should be considered when developing promotions. It can be used in clever and creative ways or in ways that are offensive to the local population. The architecture of buildings and other structures should also be researched to avoid making cultural blunders due to the symbolism of certain shapes and forms.

VALUES AND ATTITUDES

Ideas, beliefs, and customs to which people are emotionally attached are **values**. Values include things like honesty, marital faithfulness, freedom, and responsibility.

Values are important to business because they affect a people's work ethic and desire for material possessions. Whereas certain cultures (say, Singapore) value hard work and material success, others (Greece, for instance) value leisure and a modest lifestyle. The United Kingdom and United States value individual freedom, whereas Japan and South Korea value group consensus. Because values are so important to both individuals and groups, the influx of values from other cultures can be fiercely resisted. Muslims believe drugs, alcohol, and certain kinds of music and literature will undermine

aesthetics
What a culture considers to be in "good taste" in the arts, the imagery evoked by certain expressions, and the symbolism of certain colors.

values
Ideas, beliefs, and customs to which people are emotionally attached.

important values. Nations under Islamic law (such as Iran and Saudi Arabia) exact severe penalties for the possession of such items as drugs and alcohol.

attitudes
Positive or negative evaluations, feelings, and tendencies that individuals harbor toward objects or concepts.

Attitudes are positive or negative evaluations, feelings, and tendencies that individuals harbor toward objects or concepts. For instance, a Westerner expresses an attitude if he or she were to say, "I do not like the Japanese purification ritual because it involves being naked in a communal bath." Attitudes reflect underlying values. The Westerner quoted above, for instance, might hold conservative beliefs regarding exposure of the body.

Like values, attitudes are learned from role models, including parents, teachers, and religious leaders. Like values, they also differ from one country to another because they are formed within a cultural context. Generally, although values concern only important matters, people hold attitudes toward both important and unimportant aspects of life. And whereas values are quite rigid over time, attitudes are more flexible.

Cultural knowledge can tell a businessperson when products or promotions must be adapted to local preferences that reflect values and attitudes. In most countries, for instance, Virginia Slims fosters an image of its cigarette as a cigarette especially for women. Hence, a recent U.S. ad campaign bearing the slogan "It's a Woman Thing." But because South Korean men find its mild taste appealing and similar to the country's traditional brand, Virginia Slims adapted its advertising plans to exploit this attitude toward its cigarette, using such advertisement tag lines in South Korea as "The Cigarette for the Successful Man."[5] Among the important aspects of life that directly affect business activities, people tend to have different cultural attitudes toward time, work and achievement, and cultural change.

Attitudes toward Time   People in many Latin American and Mediterranean cultures are casual about time. They maintain flexible schedules and would rather enjoy their time than sacrifice it to unbending efficiency. Businesspeople, for example, often arrive after scheduled meeting times and prefer to spend time building personal trust before discussing business. Not surprisingly, it usually takes longer to conduct business in these parts of the world than in the United States or northern Europe.

In contrast, people in Japan and the United States typically arrive promptly for meetings, keep tight schedules, and work long hours.[6] The emphasis on using time efficiently reflects the underlying value of hard work in both these countries. However, Japanese and Americans sometimes differ in how they use their work time. Americans, for example, strive toward workplace efficiency and sometimes leave early if the day's tasks are done. This attitude reflects the value that Americans place on producing individual results. In Japan, it is important to look busy in the eyes of others even when business is slow. Japanese workers want to demonstrate their dedication to superiors and co-workers—an attitude grounded in values such as the concern for group cohesion, loyalty, and harmony.

Attitudes toward Work   Whereas some cultures display a strong work ethic, others stress a more balanced pace in juggling work and leisure. People in southern France like to say "We work to live, while people in the United States live to work." Work, they say, is for them a means to an end. In the United States, they charge, it is an end in itself. Not surprisingly, the lifestyle in southern France is slower paced. People tend to concentrate on earning enough money to enjoy food, wine, and good times. Businesses practically close down during August, when many workers take month-long paid holidays (usually outside the country). This attitude is unheard of in many Asian countries, including Japan.

The perceived opportunity for success and reward is a strong element in a culture's attitude toward work. People tend to work hard when risk taking is rewarded with low

In the new China, the state-owned sector has been radically downsized. China is in the midst of converting about 300,000 state-owned businesses into shareholder-owned corporations managed to compete on a global scale. Beijing Enterprises, a conglomerate that franchises tourist concessions, is one of thousands of companies trying to survive in a market economy. Such firms support a rapidly growing middle class of independent businesspeople, professionals, and corporate employees whose attitudes toward work and success has changed significantly. You can find out more about Beijing Enterprises, which handles Chinese McDonald's franchises, at ⟨**www.irasia.com/listco/hk/behl/index.htm**⟩.

taxes on profits and when capital is available for new business start-ups. In both the United Kingdom and France, start-ups are considered quite risky, and capital for entrepreneurial ventures is scarce. If at some point an entrepreneur's venture in those countries goes bust, he or she can find it very hard to obtain financing for future projects. The opposite attitude tends to prevail in the United States. Reference to prior bankruptcy in a business plan is sometimes considered valuable learning experience (assuming, of course, that some lessons were learned). As long as U.S. bankers see promising business plans, they are generally willing to loan money.

Today, many European nations are trying to foster an entrepreneurial spirit like that in the United States. If we look at the record on job creation, the reason is simple. For every 100 jobs in the United States 25 years ago, there are now 160; for every 100 jobs in the European Union 25 years ago, there are now 96.[7]

The need to compete globally is another strong cultural influence on attitudes toward work. Europeans, for example, have not adopted computer technology in the way companies have in the United States, nor is there any equivalent to the support from the public sector that fostered the Internet in the United States. Over a recent 10-year period, for example, 35 percent of all U.S. investment dollars went into technology; in Britain, the total was 16 percent. U.S. venture capitalists—companies that invest in firms with high growth potential—pumped $2.3 billion into new technology in 1996 alone; in Britain, the total was $1.1 billion. But British and other European firms are beginning to realize that global markets require them to connect to the Internet and forge alliances in Asia and the United States. Venture capitalist firms are sprouting up across Europe with large amounts of capital at their disposal.[8]

Finally, people's attitudes toward work are being affected in countries undergoing transition to free market economies. Employees in many of these nations are no longer satisfied with the old dictatorial ways of doing things and want fulfillment from their jobs. A recent poll of soon-to-be business and engineering graduates in eastern Europe found that 65 percent want their ideal manager to be receptive to their ideas. The students also desire their managers to be highly skilled at their jobs. Thirty-seven percent want managers with solid industry experience and 34 percent want managers

e·biz

World Business Survey

Listen Up, Employers

A poll was recently conducted of final-year business and engineering students in the Czech Republic, Hungary, and Poland to learn what they wanted in their first jobs. The results show that these soon-to-be graduates expect their jobs to be fulfilling experiences. The fact that competitive pay ranks highly does not diminish this expectation because these students are jumping into the workplace in well-performing emerging economies.

- A working environment with people I also enjoy socializing with — 52%
- Competitive salaries — 43%
- Being able to specialize in my particular field of interest — 26%
- A good reference for my future career — 22%
- Provision of corporate trainee programs — 21%
- Opportunities to work with a variety of tasks — 20%

that display rational decision making. For more on what these students desire in their first jobs, see the World Business Survey "Listen Up, Employers."

Attitudes toward Cultural Change   A **cultural trait** is anything that represents a culture's way of life, including gestures, material objects, traditions, and concepts. Such traits include bowing to show respect in Japan *(gesture)*, a Buddhist temple in Thailand *(material object)*, relaxing in a *dwaniyah* (tearoom) in Kuwait *(tradition)*, and practicing democracy in the United States *(concept)*. Let's look more closely at how cultures change over time and the roles that international companies play in cultural change.

Cultural Diffusion   The process whereby cultural traits spread from one culture to another is called **cultural diffusion**. *Cultural change* occurs as new traits are accepted and absorbed into a culture. It occurs naturally and, as a rule, gradually. Globalization and technological advances are increasing the pace of both cultural change and diffusion. Satellite television, videoconferencing, and the Internet are increasing the frequency of international contact and exposing people of different nations to new ideas and practices.

When Companies Change Culture: Cultural Imperialism   International companies are often agents of cultural change. As trade and investment barriers fall, for example, consumer-goods and entertainment companies—Coca-Cola, Walt Disney, and MTV among them—are moving into untapped markets. Critics in some target markets charge that in exporting the products of such firms, the United States is practicing **cultural imperialism**—that is, the replacement of one culture's traditions, folk heroes, and artifacts with substitutes from another. Thus products from the Walt Disney

cultural trait
Anything that represents a culture's way of life, including gestures, material objects, traditions, and concepts.

cultural diffusion
Process whereby cultural traits spread from one culture to another.

e·biz

cultural imperialism
Replacement of one culture's traditions, folk heroes, and artifacts with substitutes from another.

Company and its Disneyland Paris theme park met opposition from the French, who saw them as harmful to local culture. Some central and eastern Europeans resent Ronald McDonald and Mickey Mouse because they so quickly dominate domestic markets. Politicians in Russia have decried the so-called Snickerization of their culture—a snide term that refers to the popularity of Snickers candy bars.

Conservative groups in India criticized the Miss World Pageant when it was recently held in the southern city of Bangalore. Farmers criticized Western corporate sponsors for spreading messages of consumerism. More than 500 women protested the portrayal of women as sex objects and threatened to set themselves on fire if the contest took place. One man reportedly burned himself to death in protest.

Companies must be sensitive to the needs and desires of people in every culture in which they do business. They must not only focus on meeting people's product needs, but on how their activities and products affect people's traditional ways and habits. When resistance to cultural change peaks, it often leads to laws designed to preserve culture. In such cases, rather than view their effects on culture as the inevitable consequence of doing business, companies can take several steps to soften those effects.

Policies and practices that are at odds with deeply held beliefs must be introduced gradually. Managers should consult highly respected individuals in the local culture about such activities (in many developing countries elders play a leading role). There are, of course, volatile times in every society, and trying to inject new values or attitudes into an already unstable environment could be disastrous. Launching new investment projects or implementing unfamiliar management methods are best reserved for times when a culture is experiencing relative stability. In any case, managers should always make clear to workers the benefits of any proposed changes.

When Cultures Change Companies Firms often need to adapt policies and practices to local cultures. Managers from the United States, for instance, often encounter cultural differences that force changes in how they motivate Mexican employees. Although it's a time-consuming practice, they might try *situational management*, a system in which a supervisor walks an employee through every step of an

Among the "have" countries of Eastern Europe, Poland enjoys a booming consumer economy (fueled largely by an annual 24 percent growth in exports). Poles once considered interest payments a capitalist evil, but retail credit has grown by 50 percent in each of the past two years. The credit binge hardly rivals that of the United States in the 1960s, but the changes in lifestyles and values are similar: "I see a lot of people around me going into debt," says one young professional, "so it's less embarrassing now to buy on credit."

assignment or task and monitors the results at each stage. This technique helps employees fully understand the scope of their jobs and clarifies the boundaries of their responsibilities.

Exposure to new cultural practices can have subtle effects on a company's local operations. Many U.S. and European companies are rushing to build factories and encourage an emerging consumer culture in Vietnam. But because Vietnam has a traditionally agriculture-based economy, people's concept of time revolves around the seasons. The local "timepiece" is the monsoon, not the clock. Managers must consequently modify their approach and take a more patient, long-term view of business.

Companies also must often modify employee evaluation and reward systems. In Vietnam, individual criticism must be delivered privately to save employees from losing "face" among co-workers. Individual praise for good performance can be delivered either in private or publicly. But because the Vietnamese place great value on group harmony, an individual can be embarrassed if singled out publicly as superior to the rest of the work unit.[9]

Is a Global Culture Emerging? What does the world's high level of cultural change mean for international business? Are we witnessing the emergence of a new, truly global culture in which people around the world share similar lifestyles, values, and attitudes? The rapid pace of cultural diffusion and high degree of human interaction across national borders are causing cultures to converge to some extent. Perhaps it is even true that people in different cultures are developing similar perspectives on the world and beginning to think along similar lines.[10]

But it seems that just as often as we see signs of an emerging global culture, we discover some new habit unique to one culture. When that happens, we are reminded of the roles of history and tradition in defining culture. Whereas cultural convergence is certainly taking place in some market segments for some products (say the teenage market for pop music), it seems likely that a broader global culture will take a very long time to develop, if ever. Values and attitudes are under continually greater pressure as globalization continues. But because they are so deeply ingrained in culture, their transformation will continue to be gradual rather than abrupt.

MANNERS AND CUSTOMS

When doing business in another culture, it is important to understand a people's manners and customs. At a minimum, understanding manners and customs helps managers to avoid making embarrassing mistakes or offending people. In-depth knowledge, meanwhile, improves the ability to negotiate in other cultures, market products to them effectively, and manage international operations. Let's explore some of the important differences in manners and customs around the world.

Manners   Appropriate ways of behaving, speaking, and dressing in a culture are called **manners**. In Arab cultures from the Middle East to northwest Africa, one does not extend a hand to greet an older person unless the elder first offers the greeting. In going first, a younger person would be displaying bad manners. Moreover, because Arab culture considers the left hand the "toilet hand," using it to pour tea or serve a meal is considered very bad manners.

Conducting business during meals is common practice in the United States. In Mexico, however, it is poor manners to bring up business at mealtime unless the host does so first. Business discussions typically resume when coffee and brandy arrive. Likewise, toasts in the United States tend to be casual and sprinkled with lighthearted humor. A similar toast in Mexico, where it should be philosophical and full of passion, would be offensive.[11]

manners
Appropriate ways of behaving, speaking, and dressing in a culture.

Customs   When habits or ways of behaving in specific circumstances are passed down through generations, they become **customs**. They differ from manners in that they define appropriate habits or behaviors in *specific* situations. Sharing food gifts during the Islamic holy month of Ramadan is a custom, as is the Japanese tradition of throwing special parties for young women and men who turn age 20. We now define two types of customs and see how instances of each vary around the world.

Folk and Popular Customs   A **folk custom** is behavior, often dating back several generations, that is practiced within a homogeneous group of people. The wearing of turbans by Muslims in southern Asia and the art of belly dancing in Turkey are folk customs.

A **popular custom** is behavior shared by a heterogeneous group or by several groups. Popular customs can exist either in just one culture or in two or more cultures at the same time. Wearing blue jeans and playing golf are both popular customs. Many folk customs that have spread by cultural diffusion to other regions have developed into popular customs.

We can distinguish between folk and popular food. Popular Western-style fast food, for instance, is rapidly replacing folk food around the world. In many Asian countries, widespread acceptance of "burgers 'n' fries" (born in the United States), and "fish 'n' chips" (born in Britain) is actually altering deep-seated dietary traditions, especially among young people. They are even becoming part of home-cooked meals in Japan and South Korea.

One custom that is similar across cultures is children's play patterns. Companies like Mattel take advantage of children's interest in similar types of toys. Although it relies on managers in each country to adapt promotions to local culture and languages, Mattel often markets standardized products globally.

The Business of Gift Giving   Although giving token gifts to business and government associates is customary in many countries, the proper type of gift varies. A knife, for example, should not be offered to associates in Russia, France, or Germany, where it signals the severing of a relationship. In Japan, gifts must be wrapped in such a delicate way that it is wise to ask someone trained in the practice to do the honors. It is also Japanese custom not to open a gift in front of the gift giver. Tradition dictates that the giver protest that the gift is something small and unworthy of the recipient. In turn, the recipient waits until later to open the gift so that the giver is not embarrassed by the gift's insignificance. Remember, however, that this tradition does not endorse trivial gifts; it is simply a custom.

On the other hand, large gifts to business associates sometimes raise suspicion. Cultures differ in their legal and ethical rules against giving or accepting bribes. The U.S. Foreign Corrupt Practices Act, which prohibits companies from giving large gifts to win business favors, applies to U.S. firms operating at home *and* abroad. In many cultures, however, bribery is woven into a social fabric that has worn well for centuries. In Germany, bribe payments may even qualify for tax deductions.[12] However, the issue remains controversial. Although governments around the world are adopting stricter measures to control bribery, in some cultures large gifts continue to be an effective means of obtaining contracts, entering markets, and securing protection from global competition.

SOCIAL STRUCTURE

Social structure embodies a culture's fundamental organization, including its groups and institutions, its system of social positions and their relationships, and the process by which its resources are distributed. Naturally, social structure affects business decisions ranging from production-site selection to advertising methods and the costs of

customs
Habits or ways of behaving in specific circumstances that are passed down through generations in a culture.

folk custom
Behavior, often dating back several generations, that is practiced within a homogeneous group of people.

popular custom
Behavior shared by a heterogeneous group or by several groups.

social structure
A culture's fundamental organization, including its groups and institutions, its system of social positions and their relationships, and the process by which its resoursces are distributed.

doing business in a country. Three important elements of social structure differ across cultures: *social group associations, social status,* and *social mobility.*

Social Group Associations

People in all cultures associate themselves with a variety of **social groups**—collections of two or more people who identify and interact with one another. Social groups contribute to each individual's identity and self-image. Two groups that play especially important roles in affecting business activity everywhere are *family* and *gender.**

social group
Collection of two or more people who identify and interact with one another.

Family   There are two different types of family groups:

➡ The *nuclear family* consists of a person's immediate relatives, including parents, brothers, and sisters. This concept of family prevails in Australia, Canada, the United States, and much of Europe.

➡ The concept of the *extended family* broadens the nuclear family to include grandparents, aunts and uncles, cousins, and relatives through marriage. It is more important as a social group in much of Asia, the Middle East, North Africa, and Latin America.

Extended families can present some interesting situations for businesspeople unfamiliar with the concept. In some cultures, owners and managers in extended families obtain supplies and materials from another company in which someone in the family works before looking elsewhere. Gaining entry into such family arrangements can be difficult because quality and price are not sufficient motives to ignore family ties.

In extended-family cultures, managers and other employees often try to find jobs for relatives inside their own companies. This practice can present a challenge to the human resource operations of a Western company, which typically must establish explicit policies on nepotism (the practice of hiring relatives).

Gender   Let's first define *gender.* Gender refers to socially learned traits associated with, and expected of, men or women. Gender refers to such socially learned behaviors and attitudes as styles of dress and activity preferences. It is not the same thing as sex, which refers to the biological fact that a person is either male or female.

Although many countries have made great strides toward gender equality in the workplace, others have not. For instance, countries operating under Islamic law sometimes segregate women and men in schools, universities, and social activities, and restrict women to certain professions. Sometimes they are allowed teaching careers but only in all-female classrooms. At other times they can be physicians but for female patients only.

In Japan, women have traditionally been denied equal opportunity in the workplace. While men held nearly all positions of responsibility, women generally served as office clerks and administrative assistants until their mid to late twenties when they were expected to marry and stay at home tending to family needs. Although this is still largely true today, progress is being made in expanding the role of women in Japan's business community. Figure 2.1 shows that women own 23 percent of all businesses in Japan. But many of these businesses are very small and do not carry a great deal of economic clout. The figure shows that greater gender equality prevails in Australia, Canada, Germany, and the United States. However, women in these countries still tend to earn less money than men in similar positions and are sometimes subjected to sexual harassment.

---

*We put these two "groups" together for the sake of convenience. Strictly speaking, a gender is not a group. Sociologists regard it as a category—people who share some status. A key to group membership is mutual *interaction.* Individuals in categories know that they are not alone in holding a particular status, but the vast majority remain strangers to one another.

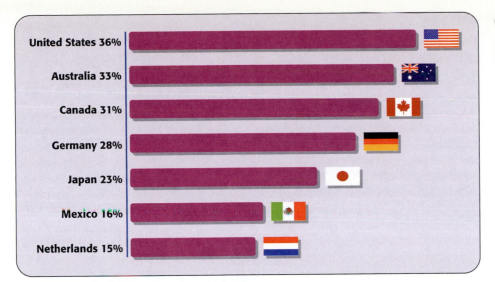

FIGURE 2.1
PERCENTAGE OF WOMEN-OWNED BUSINESSES

United States 36%
Australia 33%
Canada 31%
Germany 28%
Japan 23%
Mexico 16%
Netherlands 15%

Social Status   Another important aspect of social structure is the way a culture divides its population according to *status*—that is, according to positions within the structure. Although some cultures have only a few categories, others have many. The process of ranking people into social layers or classes is called **social stratification**. Class membership places individuals on a sort of "social ladder" that tends to persist across cultures.

social stratification
Process of ranking people into social layers or classes.

Social status is normally determined by one or more of the following three factors: family heritage, income, and occupation. In most societies, the highest social layers are occupied by royalty, government officials, and top business leaders. Scientists, medical doctors, and others with a university education occupy the middle rung. Below are those with vocational training or a secondary-school education that dominate the manual and clerical occupations. Although rankings are fairly stable, they can and do change over time. For example, because Confucianism (a major Chinese religion) stresses a life of learning, Chinese culture frowned on businesspeople for centuries. In modern China, however, those who have obtained wealth and power through business are now counted among those who are important role models for young people.

Social Mobility   Moving to a higher social class is easy in some cultures and difficult or impossible in others. **Social mobility** is the ease with which individuals can move up or down a culture's social ladder. For much of the world's population today, one of two systems regulates social mobility: a *caste system* or a *class system*.

social mobility
Ease with which individuals can move up or down a culture's social ladder.

Caste Systems   A **caste system** is a system of social stratification in which people are born into a social ranking, or *caste*, with no opportunity for social mobility. India is the classic example of a caste culture. Little social interaction occurs between castes, and marrying out of caste is taboo. Opportunities for work and advancement are defined within the system and certain occupations are reserved for members of each caste. Because personal clashes would be inevitable, a member of one caste cannot supervise someone of a higher caste. The caste system forces Western companies to make some hard ethical decisions when entering the Indian marketplace. For example, should they adjust to local human resource policies or import their own because they think of them as so-called "more developed?"

caste system
System of social stratification in which people are born into a social ranking, or caste, with no opportunity for social mobility.

Although the Indian constitution *officially* bans discrimination by caste, its influence persists. Change, however, is taking place at a breakneck pace in India, and as globalization introduces new values, the social system will undoubtedly adapt.

Class Systems A system of social stratification in which personal ability and actions decide social status and mobility is a **class system**. It is the most common form of social stratification in the world today. But class systems vary in the amount of mobility they allow. Highly class-conscious cultures offer less mobility and, not surprisingly, experience greater class conflict. In Western Europe, for instance, wealthy families have retained power for generations by restricting social mobility. As a result, they must deal with class conflict that often translates into labor-management conflict and so increases the cost of doing business. Strikes and property damage are common today when European companies announce plant closings or layoffs.

Conversely, lower levels of class consciousness encourage mobility and lessen conflict. Most U.S. citizens, for instance, share the belief that hard work can improve living standards and social status. They attribute higher status to greater income or wealth, but

class system
System of social stratification in which personal ability and actions decide social status and mobility.

MAP 2.1

MAJOR RELIGIONS OF THE WORLD

Religion is not confined to national political boundaries but can exist in different regions of the world simultaneously. Different religions can also dominate different regions in a single nation. This map shows where the world's major religions are prominent. The map shows several religions in addition to those discussed in this chapter including: **Taoism**, which began in the 100s B.C. in China. Taoists pray to a mixture of deceased humans who displayed extraordinary powers during their lives, and nonhuman spirits embodying various elements of Tao; **Sikhism**, dating back to 1469, teaches breaking the continuous cycle of reincarnation by waking early, cleansing, meditating, and devoting all activities to God; **Animism**, describes all religions involving honoring the souls of deceased humans and worshiping spirits in nature; **Lamaist Buddhism** is a Buddhist sect that emphasizes meditation and has as its spiritual leader, the Dalai Lama; and **Southern Buddhism**, the Buddhist sect that is older than Lamaism and stresses following the teachings of the Buddha.

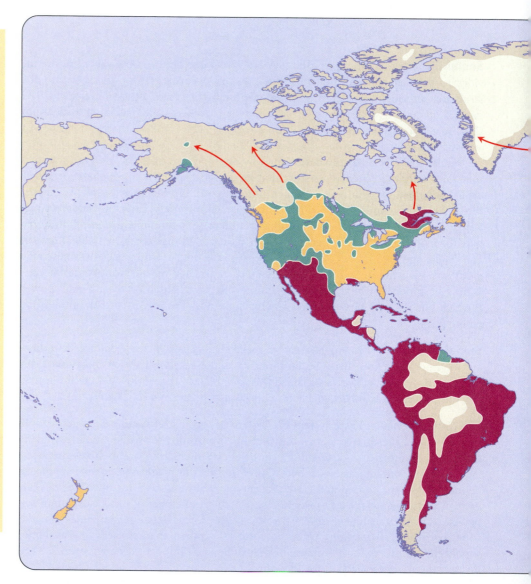

often with little regard for family background. Material well-being is important primarily because it affirms or improves status. A more cooperative atmosphere in the workplace tends to prevail when people feel that a higher social standing is within their reach.

RELIGION

Human values often derive from religious beliefs. Different religions take different views of work, savings, and material goods. Understanding why they do so helps us to understand why companies from certain cultures are more competitive than companies from other cultures. It also helps us understand why some countries develop more slowly than others do. Knowing how religion affects business practices is especially important in countries with religious governments.

Map 2.1 shows where the world's major religions are practiced. In the following sections, we explore several of these religions—Christianity, Islam, Hinduism, Buddhism, Confucianism, Judaism, and Shinto—to examine their effects, both positive and negative, on international business activity.

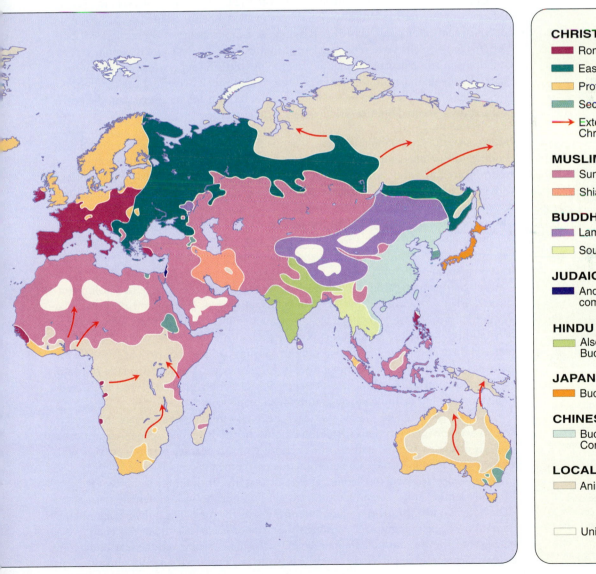

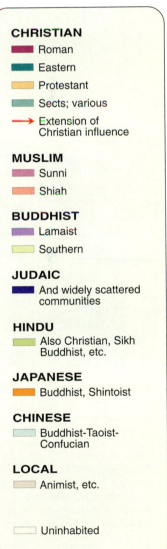

CHRISTIAN
- Roman
- Eastern
- Protestant
- Sects; various
- → Extension of Christian influence

MUSLIM
- Sunni
- Shiah

BUDDHIST
- Lamaist
- Southern

JUDAIC
- And widely scattered communities

HINDU
- Also Christian, Sikh Buddhist, etc.

JAPANESE
- Buddhist, Shintoist

CHINESE
- Buddhist-Taoist-Confucian

LOCAL
- Animist, etc.

- Uninhabited

Christianity   Christianity was born in Palestine nearly 2,000 years ago among Jews who believed that God sent Jesus of Nazareth to be their savior. Christianity now boasts more than 300 denominations, but most Christians belong to the Roman Catholic, Protestant, or Eastern Orthodox churches. With over 1.7 billion followers, Christianity is the world's single largest religion.

The Roman Catholic faith asks its followers to refrain from placing material possessions above God and others. Protestants believe that salvation comes from faith in God and that hard work gives glory to God—a tenet known widely as the Protestant work ethic. Many historians believe this conviction to be a main factor in the development of capitalism and free enterprise in nineteenth-century Europe.

Christian organizations sometimes get involved in social causes that affect business policy. For example, the political wings of some Christian groups have recently called for boycotts against the Walt Disney Company. Among other things, some conservative Christians have charged that in portraying young people as rejecting parental guidance, Disney films impede the moral development of young viewers worldwide.

Christian activism is by no means limited to the United States. In 1998, the French Bishops' Conference sued Volkswagen-France over a billboard ad that, according to the conference, insulted Christians by parodying the famous image of Leonardo Da Vinci's *The Last Supper*. The conference explained that it was reacting to increasing use of sacred things in advertising throughout Europe. "Advertising experts," said a spokesman, "have told us that ads aim for the sacred in order to shock because using sex does not work anymore." Volkswagen halted the $16 million campaign in response to the power of the church to mold opinion and marshal legal resources.[13]

Islam   With 925 million adherents, Islam is the world's second-largest religion. The prophet Muhammad founded Islam around the year 600 in Mecca, the holy city of Islam located in Saudi Arabia. Islam developed from Judaism and Christianity and thrives in northwestern Africa, the Middle East, Central Asia, Pakistan, and some Southeast Asian nations, including Indonesia. Muslim concentrations are also found in most U.S. and European cities. The word *Islam* means "submission to Allah," and *Muslim* means "one who submits to Allah." Two important religious rites include observance of the holy season of Ramadan and making the pilgrimage (the *Hajj*) to Mecca at least once in one's lifetime.

Religion strongly affects the kinds of goods and services acceptable to Muslim consumers. Islam, for example, prohibits the consumption of alcohol and pork. Popular alcohol substitutes are soda pop, coffee, and tea. Substitutes for pork include lamb, beef, and poultry (all of which must be slaughtered in a prescribed way). Because hot coffee and tea often play ceremonial roles in Muslim nations, the markets for them are quite large. Because usury (charging interest for money lent) violates the laws of Islam, credit card companies collect management fees rather than interest, and each cardholder's credit line is limited to an amount held on deposit.[14]

Nations governed by Islamic law (see Chapter 3) sometimes segregate the sexes at certain activities and locations such as in schools. In Saudi Arabia, women cannot drive cars. In orthodox Islamic nations, men cannot conduct market research surveys with women at home unless they are family members. Women visiting Islamic cultures need to be especially sensitive to Islamic beliefs and customs. In Iran, for instance, the Ministry of Islamic Guidance and Culture posts a reminder to visiting female journalists: "The body is a tool for the spirit and the spirit is a divine song. The holy tool should not be used for sexual intentions." Although the issue of *hejab* (Islamic dress) is hotly debated, both Iranian and non-Iranian women are officially expected to wear body-concealing garments and scarves over their hair (which is considered sexually alluring).[15]

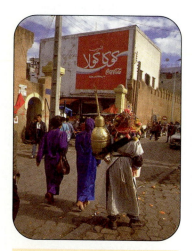

In Islamic countries, where alcohol is forbidden, soft drinks are a popular substitute. And among soft drinks Coke is the preferred brand, hands down. Coke now sells a billion drinks per day—2 percent of the whole world's daily beverage consumption. Eighty percent of the company's profits come from outside the United States. The Arabic sign in this photo is read from right to left.

Hinduism Formed around 4,000 years ago in present-day India, where over 90 percent of its nearly 690 million adherents live, Hinduism is the world's oldest religion. It is also the majority religion of Nepal and a secondary religion in Bangladesh, Bhutan, and Sri Lanka. Considered by some to be a way of life rather than a religion, Hinduism recalls no founder and recognizes no central authority or spiritual leader. Integral to the Hindu faith is the caste system described earlier.

Hindus believe in reincarnation—the rebirth of the human soul at the time of death. For many Hindus the highest goal of life is *moksha*—escaping from the cycle of reincarnation and entering a state of eternal happiness called *nirvana*. Hindus do not eat or willfully harm any living creature because it may be a reincarnated human soul. Because Hindus consider cows sacred animals they do not eat beef. However, consuming milk is considered a means of religious purification. Firms like McDonald's must work closely with government and religious officials to respect Hindu beliefs. In many Hindu regions, McDonald's has removed all beef products from its menu and prepares vegetable and fish products in separate kitchen areas.

In India, there have been attacks on Western consumer-goods companies in the name of preserving Indian culture and Hindu beliefs. Pepsi bottles have been smashed and posters burned, and local officials shut down a KFC restaurant for a time. Although it currently operates in India, Coca-Cola once left the market completely rather than succumb to demands that it must reveal its secret formula to authorities. India's investment environment has improved greatly in recent years. Yet labor-management relations have deteriorated to such a degree that regular strikes cut deeply into productivity. India, for example, makes just five cars per worker per year, compared to a global standard of forty.[16]

Buddhism Buddhism was founded about 2,600 years ago in India by a Hindu prince named Siddhartha Gautama. Today, Buddhism has approximately 311 million followers, mostly in such Asian nations as China, Tibet, Korea, Japan, Vietnam, and Thailand. There also are small numbers of Buddhists in Europe and North and South America. Although founded in India, Buddhism has relatively few adherents there, and unlike Hinduism, it rejects the sort of caste system that dominates Indian society. But like Hinduism, Buddhism promotes a life centered on spiritual rather than worldly matters. Buddhists seek *nirvana* (escape from reincarnation) through charity, modesty, compassion for others, restraint from violence, and general self-control.

Although monks at many rural temples are devoted to lives of meditation and discipline, many Buddhist priests are dedicated to lessening the burden of human suffering. They have financed schools and hospitals across Asia and have been active in worldwide peace movements. In Tibet, where most people still acknowledge the exiled Dalai Lama as the spiritual and political head of the Buddhist culture, the Chinese Communist government suppresses allegiance to any outside authority. Similarly, the official Catholic Church of China must reject the principle of the pope as supreme leader. In the United States, a coalition of religious groups, human rights advocates, and supporters of the Dalai Lama have pressed the U.S. Congress to apply economic sanctions against countries that, like China, are judged to practice religious persecution.[17]

Confucianism An exiled politician and philosopher named Kung-fu-dz (pronounced *Confucius* in English) began teaching his ideas in China nearly 2,500 years ago. Today, China is home to most of Confucianism's 150 million followers. Confucian thought is also ingrained in the cultures of Japan, South Korea, and nations with large numbers of ethnic Chinese, including Singapore.

South Korean business practice reflects Confucian thought in its rigid organizational structure and unswerving reverence for authority. Whereas Korean employees do not question strict chains of command, non-Korean managers and workers often feel differently. Efforts to apply Korean-style management in overseas subsidiaries have caused some high-profile disputes with U.S. executives and even physical confrontations with factory workers in Vietnam.[18]

Some observers contend that the Confucian work ethic and educational commitment helped spur east Asia's phenomenal economic growth. But others respond that the link between culture and economic growth is weak. They argue that economic, historical, and international factors are at least as important as culture.[19]

Chinese leaders distrusted Confucianism for centuries because they believed that it stunted economic growth. Likewise, many Chinese despised merchants and traders because their main objective (earning money) violated Confucian beliefs. As a result, many Chinese businesspeople moved to Indonesia, Malaysia, Singapore, and Thailand, where they launched successful businesses. Today, these countries (along with Taiwan) are continuing to develop and are financing much of China's economic growth.[20]

Judaism   More than 3,000 years old, Judaism was the first religion to preach belief in a single God. Nowadays, Judaism has roughly 18 million followers worldwide. In Israel, Orthodox (or "fully observant") Jews make up 12 percent of the population and constitute an increasingly important economic segment. In Jerusalem, there is even a modeling agency that specializes in casting Orthodox Jews in ads aimed both inside and outside the Orthodox community. Models include scholars and even one rabbi. In keeping with Orthodox principles, women model only modest clothing and never appear in ads alongside men.[21]

Employers and human resource managers must be aware of important days in the Jewish faith. Because the Sabbath lasts from sundown on Friday to sundown on Saturday, work schedules might need adjustment. Devout Jews want to be home before sundown on Fridays. On the Sabbath itself, they do not work, travel, or carry money. Several other important observances are Rosh Ha-Shanah (the two-day Jewish New Year, in September or October), Yom Kippur (the Day of Atonement, ten days after New Year), Passover (which celebrates the Exodus from Egypt, in March or April each year), and Hanukkah (which celebrates an ancient victory over the Syrians, usually in December).

Marketers must take into account foods that are banned among strict Jews. Pork and shellfish (such as lobster and crab) are prohibited. Meat and milk are stored and served separately. Other meats must be slaughtered according to a practice called *shehitah*. Meals prepared according to Jewish dietary traditions are called *kosher*. Most airlines, for example, offer kosher meals.

Shinto   Shinto (meaning "way of the gods") arose as the native religion of the Japanese. But today Shinto can claim only about 3.5 million strict adherents in Japan. Because modern Shinto preaches patriotism, it is sometimes said that Japan's real religion is nationalism. Shinto teaches sincere and ethical behavior, loyalty and respect toward others, and enjoyment of life.

Shinto beliefs are reflected in the workplace through the traditional practice of lifetime employment and through the traditional trust extended between firms and customers. Japanese competitiveness in world markets has benefited from loyal work forces, lower employee turnover, and greater labor-management cooperation. The success of Japanese companies since World War II gave rise to the concept of a Shinto work ethic, certain aspects of which have been emulated by Western managers.

PERSONAL COMMUNICATION

communication
System of conveying thoughts, feelings, knowledge, and information to others through speech, actions, and writing.

People in every culture have a **communication** system to convey thoughts, feelings, knowledge, and information through speech, actions, and writing. Understanding a culture's *spoken* language gives us great insight into why people think and act the way that they do. Understanding a culture's *unspoken* language helps us avoid sending unintended or embarrassing messages. Let's take a closer look at each of these.

Spoken Language   Spoken language is the part of a culture's communication system that is embodied in its spoken and written vocabulary. It is the most obvious difference we notice when traveling in another country. We overhear and engage in a multitude of conversations, and must read many signs and documents to find our way. Because we can never truly understand a culture until we learn its language, language is critical to all international business activities.

Linguistically different segments of a population are often culturally, socially, and politically distinct. For instance, Malaysia's population is comprised of Malay (60 percent), Chinese (30 percent), and Indian (10 percent). Malay is the official national language, but each ethnic group speaks its own language and continues its traditions. The result has sometimes been physical confrontation. The United Kingdom includes England, Northern Ireland, Scotland, and Wales—each of which has its own language and traditions. Recently Scotland has vigorously renewed its drive for independence, and Ireland's native language, Gaelic, is staging a comeback on Irish television and in Gaelic-language schools.[22]

Lingua Franca   A *lingua franca* is a third or "link" language that is understood by two parties who speak different native languages. Although only 5 percent of the world population speaks English as a first language, it is the most common *lingua franca* in international business, followed by French and Spanish.[23] Even the Cantonese dialect of Chinese spoken in Hong Kong and the Mandarin dialect spoken in Taiwan and on the Chinese mainland are so different that a *lingua franca* is often preferred. Although India's official language is Hindi, its *lingua franca* is English because it was once a British colony. MTV is considering Indian programs in Hindi or Tamil, another widely spoken Indian language. "But for now," reports the president of MTV Networks in Asia, "Hinglish works. It's what young people are speaking." *Hinglish* is a combination of Hindi, Tamil, and English words alternated within a single sentence.[24]

Because they operate in many nations, each with its own language, multinationals sometimes choose a *lingua franca* for official internal communications. Philips NV (a Netherlands-based electronics firm) and Asea Brown Boveri AG (a Swiss-based industrial giant) use English for all internal correspondence. Japan-based Sony and Matsushita also use English abroad, even in some non-English-speaking countries.

Properly translating all communications is critical in international business. For instance, Microsoft Corporation recently purchased a thesaurus (a categorized index of terms) for the Spanish-language version of its word processing program. Unfortunately, the index offered some extremely offensive synonyms, equating *man-eater, cannibal,* and *barbarian* with a black person and *man-eating savage* with American Indian; *bastard* meant someone of mixed race, and *vicious* and *perverse* were associated with lesbian. Meanwhile, *Occidental* (referring to the Western Hemisphere) was equated with white, civilized, and cultured. Microsoft issued an apology but still suffered negative publicity in Spain, Mexico, and the United States.[25] (For some more linguistic mistakes made by well-known international companies, see Figure 2.2.)

Language proficiency is critical in production facilities where nonnative managers are supervising local employees. In the wake of the North American Free Trade Agreement, for example, U.S. corporations continue to expand operations in Mexico. Because Mexican factory workers generally appear relaxed and untroubled at work, one U.S. manager was confused when his workers went on strike at his seemingly happy plant. The problem lay in different cultural perspectives. Mexican workers do not take the initiative in matters of problem solving and workplace complaints. In this case, they concluded that the plant manager knew but did not care about their complaints because he did not trouble to question employees about work conditions.[26]

lingua franca
Third or "link" language that is understood by two parties who speak different languages.

FIGURE 2.2

WHAT DID YOU SAY?

Advertising slogans and company documents must be translated carefully so that messages are received precisely as intended. Some humorous (but sometimes expensive) translation blunders include the following:

Braniff Airlines' English-language slogan "Fly in Leather" was translated into "Fly Naked" in Spanish.

A sign for non-Japanese-speaking guests in a Tokyo hotel read, "You are respectfully requested to take advantage of the chambermaids."

An English sign in Moscow hotel read, "If this is your first visit to the USSR, you are welcome to it."

A Japanese knife manufacturer labeled its exports to the United States with "Caution: Blade extremely sharp! Keep out of children."

Japan-based Kinki Nippon Tourist Company changed its name in English-speaking markets after people called looking for "kinky" sex tours.

unspoken language
Language communicated through unspoken cues, including hand gestures, facial expressions, physical greetings, eye contact, and the manipulation of personal space.

Unspoken Language   Unspoken language communicates through unspoken cues, including hand gestures, facial expressions, physical greetings, eye contact, and the manipulation of personal space. Like spoken language, unspoken language communicates both information and feelings and differs greatly from one culture to another. Italians, French, Arabs, and Venezuelans, for example, animate conversations with lively hand gestures and other body motions. Japanese and Koreans, although more reserved, communicate just as much information through their own unspoken languages; a look of the eye can carry as much or more meaning as two flailing arms.

Bows of respect in many Asian cultures may carry different meanings, usually depending upon the recipient. Associates of equal standing bow about 15 degrees toward one another. But proper respect for an elder requires a bow of about 30 degrees. Bows of remorse or apology should be about 45 degrees.

Most unspoken language is subtle and takes time to recognize and interpret. Physical gestures, for example, often convey different meanings in different cultures: the thumbs-up sign is vulgar in Italy and Greece but means "all right" or even "great" in the United States. Former U.S. President George Bush once gave a backward peace sign with his fore- and middle fingers (meaning "peace" or "victory" in the United States) to a crowd in Australia. He was unaware that he was sending a message similar to that given in the United States with the middle finger. Figure 2.3 demonstrates how the meaning of certain gestures varies in different countries.

EDUCATION

Education is crucial for passing on traditions, customs, and values. Each culture educates its young people through schooling, parenting, religious teachings, and group memberships. Families and other groups provide informal instruction about customs and how to socialize with others. In most cultures, intellectual skills, including reading and mathematics, are taught in formal educational settings.

FIGURE 2.3
SOME REGIONAL DIFFERENCES
IN THE MEANING OF GESTURES

Although Western Europe may be moving toward economic unity, its tapestry of cultures remains diverse. Gestures, for example, continue to reflect centuries of cultural differences. As in the United States, the thumb-and-index circle means "okay" in most of Europe; in Germany, it's an indelicate reference to the receiver's anatomy. In most of Great Britain—England and Scotland—the finger tapping the nose means, "You and I are in on the secret"; in nearby Wales, however, it means, "You're very nosy." If you tap your temple just about anywhere in Western Europe, you're suggesting that someone is "crazy"; in Holland, however, you'll be congratulating someone for being clever.

Education Level   Data provided by governments on the education level of their people must be taken with a grain of salt. Because many nations rely on literacy tests of their own design, they often provide little basis for comparison across countries. Some administer standardized tests; others require only a signature as proof of literacy. Unfortunately, because few other options exist, searching for an untapped market and searching for a new factory site forces managers to rely on such undependable benchmarks. Moreover, as you can see from Table 2.1, some countries have further to go in increasing national literacy rates.

TABLE 2.1   *Illiteracy Rates of Selected Countries*

Country	Adult Illiteracy Rate (Percent of People 15 and Above)	Country	Adult Illiteracy Rate (Percent of People 15 and Above)
Niger	86	South Africa	18
Pakistan	62	Turkey	18
Morocco	56	Brazil	17
Haiti	55	Indonesia	16
Egypt	49	Zimbabwe	15
India	48	Jordan	13
Guatemala	44	Mexico	10
Nigeria	43	Singapore	9
Rwanda	40	Venezuela	9
Saudi Arabia	37	Thailand	6
Cambodia	35	Vietnam	6
Nicaragua	34	Chile	5
Kenya	22	Philippines	5
China	19	Argentina	4

High-wage industries are often attracted to nations with excellent programs for basic education. Nations that invest in worker training are usually repaid in productivity increases and rising incomes. It is an undisputed fact that whereas nations with skilled, well-educated workforces attract all sorts of high-paying jobs, poorly educated countries attract the lowest-paying manufacturing jobs. By investing in education, a country can attract (and even create) the kind of high-wage industries that are often called "brainpower" industries.[27]

Newly industrialized economies in Asia owe much of their rapid economic development to solid education systems. Hong Kong, South Korea, Singapore, and Taiwan focus on rigorous mathematical training in primary and secondary schooling. University education concentrates on the hard sciences and aims to train engineers, scientists, and managers.

The "Brain Drain" Phenomenon

Just as a country's quality of education affects its economic development, the level and pace of economic development affects its education system. **Brain drain** is the departure of highly educated people from one profession, geographic region, or nation to another. It transfers know-how from one profession to another because people can apply education and skills to alternate occupations. China is traditionally strong in teaching and research in the basic sciences and mathematics. But economic reform is stranding many university professors with much less income than they could earn by working for private companies or even starting their own businesses. A recent report states that more than 50 percent of those leaving teaching positions at Beijing Normal University have advanced degrees. It's easy to understand brain drain from education when we learn that while university professors in China earn as little as 400 renminbi ($50) per month, multinationals in the private sector are paying secretarial assistants 3,000 renminbi ($375) and bilingual administrative assistants 16,000 ($2,000).[28]

Although the United States controls two thirds of the $300 billion global market for software products and services, there are still nearly 200,000 unfilled high-tech jobs in the United States, mostly for computer programmers. Moreover, because the number of

brain drain
Departure of highly educated people from one profession, geographic region, or nation to another.

e·biz

In high-tech industries, the United States is suffering a severe shortage of brain power. Because they still have about 200,000 jobs to fill, companies like Microsoft have begun draining the brain power of such places as Europe, where 18 million workers are unemployed. These recruits in Ireland are among 3,000 Europeans who have received free training from Microsoft. Ninety-eight percent have found jobs. For the view of the National Science foundation on the mobility of highly skilled personnel, visit its Web site at ⟨**www.nsf.gov**⟩, and search for the phrase "brain drain."

computer-science graduates at U.S. universities plummeted from 48,000 in 1984 to 26,000 in 1997, demand for brainpower in this field will continue to outstrip supply for another decade. More and more U.S. software firms are thus recruiting in markets like Europe, where 18 million people are unemployed. In one year alone, Microsoft put 3,000 Europeans through a free training program and proceeded to place 98 percent in U.S.-paid jobs.[29]

Meanwhile, many developing countries—India, Pakistan, Russia, South Africa, and Taiwan among them—are experiencing high levels of brain drain among scientists, engineers, and researchers in all fields, many of them to the United States. But as the economies of these and other nations continue to develop, they are luring professionals back to their homelands—a process known as *reverse brain drain*.

PHYSICAL AND MATERIAL ENVIRONMENTS

The physical environment and material surroundings of a culture heavily influence its development and pace of change. In this section, we learn how physical environment and culture are related. We then explore the important effect on business of material culture.

Physical Environment   Although culture is *affected* by the physical environment, it is not directly *determined* by it. Two aspects of the physical environment—topography and climate—heavily influence a people's culture.

Topography   All the physical features that characterize the surface of a geographic region constitute its **topography**. Some surface features such as navigable rivers and flat plains facilitate travel and contact with others. In contrast, treacherous mountain ranges and large bodies of water can discourage contact and cultural change. Cultures isolated by impassable mountains or large bodies of water will be less exposed to the cultural traits of other peoples. Cultural change tends to occur more slowly in isolated cultures than in cultures not isolated in such a manner.

Topography can have an impact on consumers' product needs. There is little market for Honda scooters in most mountainous regions because their engines are too small. These are better markets for rugged, maneuverable, fuel-efficient motorcycles with larger engines. Thinner air at higher elevations might also entail modifications in carburetor design for gasoline-powered vehicles.

Topography and Communication   Topography can have a profound impact on personal communication in a culture. For instance, two thirds of China is consumed by mountain ranges (including the Himalayas in southern Tibet) and the formidable Gobi Desert. Groups living in mountain valleys have in fact held to their own ways of life and developed their own languages. Although the Mandarin dialect was decreed the national language many years ago, the mountains, desert, and great land area of China still impair personal communication and the proliferation of Mandarin.

Climate   The weather conditions of a geographic region are called its **climate**. Climate affects where people settle and helps direct systems of distribution. In Australia, for example, intensely hot and dry conditions in two large deserts, combined with jungle conditions in the northeast, have pushed settlement to coastal areas. As a result—and because water transport is less costly than land transport—coastal waters are still used to distribute products between distant cities.

Climate, Lifestyle, and Work   Climate plays a large role in lifestyle and work habits. In the countries of southern Europe, northern Africa, and the Middle East, because the heat of the summer sun grows intense in the early afternoon hours, people often take afternoon work breaks of one or two hours during July and August. During

topography
All the physical features that characterize the surface of a geographic region.

climate
Weather conditions of a geographic region.

This cartoon suggests that climate is a strong determinant of a culture's food preferences. Here, people in a cold-climate culture are shown enjoying a fire-cicle to warm up as opposed to having a pop-cicle to cool down in warm weather.

this time, people perform errands, such as shopping, or even take short naps before returning to work until about 7 or 8 P.M. Companies doing business in these regions must adapt. Production schedules, for instance, must be adjusted for periods during which machines stand idle. Shipping and receiving schedules must reflect afternoon downtime while accommodating shipments made during later working hours.

Climate and Customs Climate also impacts customs such as clothing and food. For instance, people in many tropical areas wear little clothing and wear it loosely because of the warm, humid climate. In the desert areas of the Middle East and North Africa, people also wear loose clothing, but they wear long robes to protect themselves from intense sunshine and blowing sand.

A culture's food customs are perhaps more influenced by the physical environment than by any other aspect of culture. But here, too, beliefs can have a major impact on diet. Pigs, for example, are a good source of protein in China, Europe, and the Pacific Islands. In the Middle East, however, they are regarded as unclean and prohibited by both Judaism and Islam. The taboo probably originated in environmental factors: They were expensive to feed and produced no materials for clothing. However, because some people were still tempted to squander resources by raising pigs, the prohibition became cultural and was incorporated into both Judaic and Islamic religious texts.[30]

Material Culture   All the technology employed in a culture to manufacture goods and provide services is called its **material culture**. Material culture is often used to measure the technological advancement of a nation's markets or industries. Generally, firms enter new markets under one of two conditions: (1) Demand for their products has developed, or (2) the market is capable of supporting its production operations. For example, companies are not flocking to the Southeast Asian nation of Myanmar

material culture
All the technology employed in a culture to manufacture goods and provide services.

(Burma) because economic development under a repressive military government has been stalled by a wide range of political and social problems.

Changes in material culture often cause change in other aspects of a people's culture. Nigeria is the most populous African nation with more than 105 million people. However, the country has only four phone lines per 1,000 people and the typical wait for a phone is 3.5 years. DSC Communications Corporation of the United States recently announced its plans to provide fixed wireless phone service throughout most of Nigeria including the cities of Lagos, Abuja, Kano, Wam, and Port Harcourt.[31] As the African continent continues to upgrade its material culture through economic development programs, a consumer culture will begin to take root.

Uneven Material Culture Material culture often displays uneven development across a nation's geography, markets, and industries. For example, much of China's recent economic progress is occurring in coastal cities such as Shanghai. Shanghai has long played an important role in China's international trade because of its strategic location and superb harbor on the East China Sea. Although it is home to only 1 percent of the total population, Shanghai accounts for 4.3 percent of China's total output—including 12 percent of its industrial production and 11 percent of its financial-services output.[32]

Likewise, Bangkok, the capital city of Thailand, houses only 10 percent of the nation's population but accounts for about 40 percent of its economic output. Meanwhile, the northern parts of the country remain rural, containing farms, forests, and mountains.[33]

CLASSIFYING CULTURES

There are two widely accepted ways to study cultural differences: the *Kluckhohn-Strodtbeck* and *Hofstede frameworks.* Let's look at each of these tools in more detail.

KLUCKHOHN-STRODTBECK FRAMEWORK

The **Kluckhohn-Strodtbeck framework** compares cultures along six cultural dimensions. It studies a given culture by asking the following questions:[34]

1. Do people believe that their environment controls them, that they control the environment, or that they are part of nature?

2. Do people focus on past events, on the present, or on the future implications of their actions?

3. Are people easily controlled and not to be trusted, or can they be trusted to act freely and responsibly?

4. Do people desire accomplishments in life, carefree lives, or spiritual and contemplative lives?

5. Do people believe that individuals or groups are responsible for each person's welfare?

6. Do people prefer to conduct most activities in private or in public?

Case: Dimensions of Japanese Culture By providing answers to each of these six questions, we can briefly apply the Kluckhohn-Strodtbeck framework to Japanese culture:

1. *Japanese believe in a delicate balance between people and environment that must be maintained.* Suppose an undetected flaw in a company's product harms customers

Kluckhohn-Strodtbeck framework
Framework for studying cultural differences along six dimensions, such as focus on past or future events and belief in individual or group responsibility for personal well-being.

using it. In many countries, a high-stakes class-action lawsuit would be filed against the manufacturer on behalf of the victims' families. This scenario is rarely played out in Japan. Japanese culture does not feel that individuals can possibly control every situation—accidents happen. Japanese victims would receive heartfelt apologies, a promise it won't happen again, and a relatively small damage award.

2. *Japanese culture emphasizes the future.* Negotiators from the United States often divulge information about their position to their Japanese counterparts without even realizing it. They also tend to sweeten the deal when negotiations aren't progressing rapidly enough. Japanese negotiators, on the other hand, take a long-term orientation, taking advantage of their U.S. counterparts' desire to wrap things up.

3. *Japanese culture treats people as quite trustworthy.* Crime rates are quite low, and the streets of big cities are safe at night.

4. *Japanese are accomplishment oriented—not necessarily for themselves, but for their employers and work units.*

5. *Japanese culture emphasizes individual responsibility to the group and group responsibility to the individual.*

6. *The culture of Japan tends to be public.* You will often find top managers located in the center of a large, open office surrounded by the desks of many employees. By comparison, many Western executives are often ensconced in offices along outside walls in their home countries.

HOFSTEDE FRAMEWORK

Hofstede framework
Framework for studying cultural differences along four dimensions, such as individualism versus collectivism and power distance.

The **Hofstede framework** grew from a study of one company's worldwide personnel.[35] More than 110,000 people working in IBM subsidiaries in 40 countries responded to a 32-item questionnaire. Based on these responses, Danish psychologist Geert Hofstede developed four dimensions for examining cultures:[36]

1. *Individualism versus collectivism.* Identifies whether a culture holds individuals or the group responsible for each member's welfare. Businesses in individualist cultures place responsibility for poor decisions on the individual in charge; in collectivist cultures, blame for making bad decisions is shared among group members.

2. *Power distance.* Describes the degree of inequality between people in different occupations. In cultures with large power distance, leaders and supervisors enjoy special recognition and privileges. In cultures with small power distance, prestige and rewards are more equally shared between superiors and the company's rank-and-file employees.

3. *Uncertainty avoidance.* Identifies a culture's willingness to accept uncertainty about the future. Cultures that avoid uncertainty normally have lower employee turnover, more formal rules for regulating employee behavior, and more difficulty in implementing change. Organizations in risk-accepting cultures welcome practices from other cultures but suffer from greater employee turnover.

4. *Quantity versus quality of life.* Cultures focused on *quantity of life* emphasize accomplishments like power, wealth, and status. Cultures that stress *quality of life* generally have more relaxed lifestyles; people are more concerned with cultivating relationships and the general welfare of others.

Figure 2.4(a) shows how the Hofstede study ranked selected countries according to the power distance and individualism dimensions. Countries in Quadrant 1 feature little individualism and fairly inequitable reward systems. In contrast, countries in Quadrant 3 display individualistic tendencies and have more equitable cultures.

FIGURE 2.4

HOFSTEDE'S DIMENSIONS

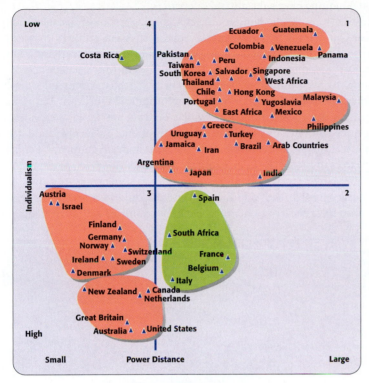

(a)
POWER DISTANCE ×
INDIVIDUALISM-COLLECTIVISM

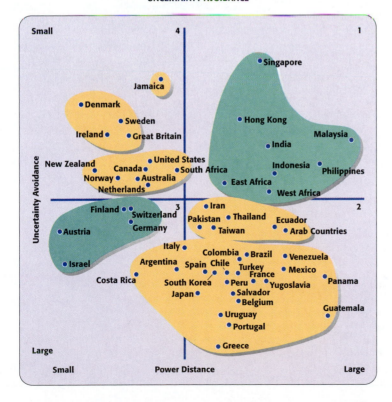

(b)
POWER DISTANCE ×
UNCERTAINTY AVOIDANCE

Quadrant 3 also features economies relying mostly on a free-market economic system. In other words, in terms of welfare and other government social programs, people in Quadrant 3 nations have substantial "safety nets."

Figure 2.4(b) ranks the same countries according to power distance and uncertainty avoidance. Quadrant 1 contains mostly Southeast Asian cultures that extend special privileges to those in power and whose people tend to avoid uncertainty. In Quadrant 2 lie Japan, Korea, and many South American cultures in which people accept greater risk and uncertainty even though the perks of power still exist. Companies are hierarchical and maintain formal, even rigid lines of communication. Quadrant 3 contains Israel and some Western European cultures in which benefits are fairly evenly rewarded even though people still rely largely on formal organizational rules. Quadrant 4 contains the United States, Canada, Great Britain, and the Scandinavian countries. People here share varying degrees of prosperity in an equitable fashion.

Some researchers classify cultures according to similarities in values, religion, language, and geography (see Map 2.2). *Most cross-cultural mistakes made by businesses occur between these clusters*, rather than between countries within any single cluster.

MAP 2.2

A SYNTHESIS OF COUNTRY CLUSTERS

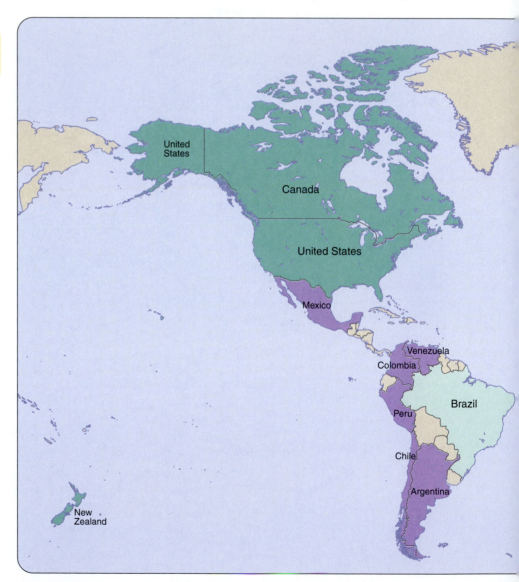

APPLYING THE TWO FRAMEWORKS

If we combine the Kluckhohn-Strodtbeck and Hofstede frameworks, we can recognize ten cultural dimensions that influence managerial decisions, including the design of employee-training programs and reward systems, and approaches to corporate change.[37] These ten dimensions also tell us a great deal about the ways in which people relate to one another and in which cultures organize their business-related institutions. Let's now apply these frameworks to see how cultures *differ* along one very important dimension—the emphasis placed on individual versus group responsibility.

Individual-Oriented Cultures   A culture in which each individual tends to be responsible for his or her own well-being is called an **individual-oriented culture**. This type of culture is found in Europe and North America, including Australia, Canada, Spain, Britain, and the United States. People are given freedom to focus on personal goals but are held responsible for their actions. Children are taught to

> **individual-oriented culture**
> *Culture in which each individual tends to be responsible for his or her own well-being.*

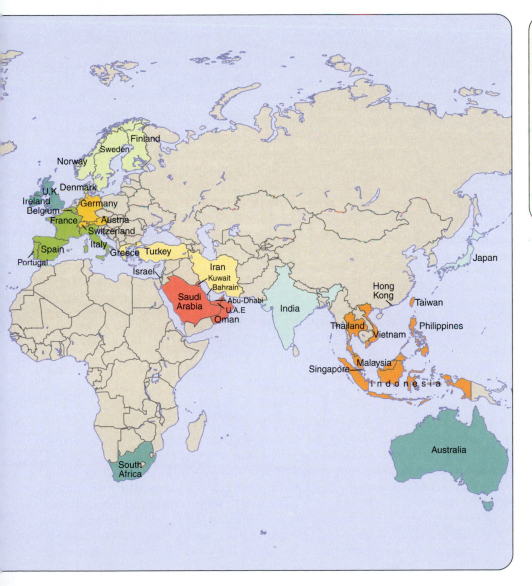

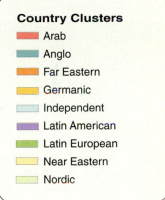

Country Clusters
- Arab
- Anglo
- Far Eastern
- Germanic
- Independent
- Latin American
- Latin European
- Near Eastern
- Nordic

be self-reliant and self-confident at a young age. Such cultures value hard work and entrepreneurial efforts, and the emphasis on individualism promotes risk taking, which in turn fosters invention and innovation. At the same time, the individualist emphasis is also blamed for high turnover among managers and other employees. It's an important consideration: If a key manager who possesses valuable information goes to work for a competitor, the former employer can lose its competitive edge virtually overnight.

It is sometimes hard to develop a cooperative work environment or "team spirit" among employees in individual-oriented cultures. People who are accustomed to receiving personal recognition tend to be more concerned with personal responsibilities than with company-wide performance. Because companies in individual-oriented cultures might find it more difficult to trust one another, cooperative ventures can run into trouble. Partners are more likely to pull out of the venture once their objectives are met.

Group-Oriented Cultures   A culture in which the group shares responsibility for the well-being of each member is called a **group-oriented culture**. People work toward collective rather than personal goals and are responsible to the group for their actions. All social, political, economic, and legal institutions reflect the group's critical role. The goal of maintaining group harmony is most evident in the family structure.

Japan is a classic group-oriented culture. Japanese children learn the importance of groups early by contributing to the upkeep of their schools. They share such duties as mopping floors, washing windows, cleaning chalkboards, and arranging desks and chairs. They carry habits learned in school into the adult workplace, where management and labor work together toward company goals. Japanese managers make decisions only after considering input from subordinates. Materials buyers, engineers, designers, factory floor supervisors, and marketers cooperate at every stage in product development.

Employee-manager trust has long been a hallmark of Japanese organizations. Traditionally, while subordinates promise hard work and loyalty, top managers promise job security. Today's slow-growth Japanese economy makes job security a more difficult promise to keep. From World War II until 1973, for instance, annual economic growth was 9 percent; from 1973 to 1990, it declined to 4 percent and remained at only 2 percent from 1990 to 1996. To remain internationally competitive, Japanese firms have been cutting payroll expenses by eliminating jobs and moving production to low-wage nations like China and Vietnam.[38] As such traditions as job security and the belief that non-Japanese employers provide less job stability fall by the wayside, more and more Japanese workers now consider employment with non-Japanese companies. They are finding that many non-Japanese firms offer better pay and quicker advancement.[39]

> **group-oriented culture**
> *Culture in which the group shares responsibility for the well-being of each member.*

A FINAL WORD

This chapter discussed many of the cultural differences that impact international business. We saw how problems can erupt from cultural misunderstandings and learned how companies can improve their performance with cultural literacy. Being culturally literate can mean the difference between returning home with a contract in hand or returning empty-handed. As globalization propels more and more companies into the international business arena, "Thinking global, and acting local" can help managers succeed. Knowing a people's values, beliefs, rules, and institutions makes managers more effective marketers, negotiators, and production managers. In the next two chapters we explore differences between nations' political, legal, and economic systems.

There is a variety of additional material available on the companion Web site that accompanies this text. You can access this information by visiting the Web site at ⟨**www.prenhall.com/wild**⟩.

summary

❶ Describe *culture* and explain the influence of both national culture and subcultures. *Culture* is the set of values, beliefs, rules, and institutions supported by a specific group of people. Successfully dealing with members of other cultures means overcoming *ethnocentricity* (the tendency to view one's own culture as superior to others) and developing *cultural literacy* (gaining the detailed knowledge necessary to work and live in another culture).

We are conditioned to think in terms of *national culture*—that is, to equate a nation-state and its people with a single culture. In reality, most nation-states are home to numerous *subcultures*—groups of people who share a unique way of life within a larger, dominant culture. But nations affirm the importance of "national culture" by building museums and monuments to preserve national legacies that cut across subcultures. Nation-states often intervene in business to help protect the national culture from the unwanted influence of other cultures. Even so, subcultures contribute greatly to national culture and must be considered in marketing and production decisions.

❷ Identify the *components of culture* and describe their impact on business activities around the world. Culture includes a people's beliefs and traditional habits and the ways in which they relate to one another. These factors fall into one or more of the eight major components of culture: (1) *aesthetics*; (2) *values* and *attitudes*; (3) *manners* and *customs*; (4) *social structure*; (5) *religion*; (6) *personal communication*; (7) *education*; and (8) *physical* and *material environments*.

All of these components affect business activity. Aesthetics, for instance, determines which colors and symbols will be effective (or offensive) in advertising. Values influence a people's attitudes toward time, work and achievement, and cultural change. Knowledge of manners and customs is necessary for negotiating with people of other cultures, marketing products to them, and managing operations in their country. Social structure affects business decisions ranging from production-site selection to advertising methods to the costs of doing business in a country. Different religions take different views of work, savings, and material goods. Understanding a people's system of personal communication provides insight into their values and behavior. A culture's education level affects the quality of the workforce and standard of living. The physical and material environments influence work habits and preferences regarding such products as clothing and food.

❸ Describe *cultural change* and explain how companies and culture affect one another. *Cultural change* occurs when a people integrate into their culture the gestures, material objects, traditions, or concepts of another culture. Globalization and technology are increasing the pace of cultural change around the world. Companies can influence culture when they import business practices or products into the host country. In order to avoid charges of *cultural imperialism*, they should import new products, policies, and practices during times of stability. Cultures also affect management styles, work scheduling, and reward systems. Adapting to local cultures around the world means heeding the maxim "Think global, act local."

❹ Explain how the *physical environment* and *technology* influence culture. A people's *physical environment* includes topography and climate and the ways (good and bad) in which they relate to their surroundings. Cultures isolated by topographical barriers, such as mountains or seas, normally change very slowly, and their languages are often distinct. *Climate* affects the hours of the day that people work. For example, people in hot climates normally take siestas when afternoon temperatures soar. Climate also influences customs, such as the type of clothing a people wear and the types of foods they eat.

Material culture refers to all the technology that people employ to manufacture goods and provide services. It is often used to measure the technological advancement of a nation and often used by businesspeople to determine whether a market has developed adequate demand for a company's products and whether it can support production activities. Material culture tends to be uneven across most nations.

⑤ Describe the *frameworks* and *dimensions* used to classify cultures and explain how they are applied. There are two widely accepted frameworks for studying cultural differences: (1) The *Kluckhohn-Strodtbeck framework* compares cultures along six dimensions by seeking answers to certain questions including: Do people believe that their environment controls them or vice versa? Do people focus on past events or the future? Do they prefer to conduct activities in public or private? (2) The *Hofstede framework* develops four dimensions, such as individualism versus collectivism and quantity versus quality of life. In using one or both of these frameworks, we can analyze cultural differences to find out whether a culture is individual- or group-oriented. This orientation affects attitudes toward such business-related cultural values as risk taking, innovation, job mobility, team cooperation, pay levels, and hiring practices.

questions for review

1. What is *culture*? Explain how *ethnocentricity* distorts one's view of other cultures.

2. What is *cultural literacy*? What factors are forcing businesspeople to understand more about other *cultures*?

3. How do *nation-states* and *subcultures* affect a nation's cultural image?

4. What is meant by a culture's *aesthetics*? Give several examples from several different cultures.

5. How do *values* and *attitudes* differ? Explain how cultures differ in their attitudes toward time, work, and cultural change.

6. How do one culture's practices spread to other cultures? Why are practices from one culture not always welcome in another? Explain why international businesses should be sensitive to accusations of *cultural imperialism*.

7. How do *manners* and *customs* differ? Give some examples of each from several different cultures.

8. What are *folk* and *popular customs*? Describe how a folk custom can become a popular custom.

9. To what does *social structure* refer? How do social rank and mobility affect business activities?

10. Identify the dominant religion in each of the following countries.
    a. India   e. China
    b. Ireland   f. Brazil
    c. Mexico   g. Thailand
    d. Russia

11. What specific advantages do companies gain when they learn how to communicate in another culture?

12. Why is the *education* of a country's people important to both native and nonnative companies operating there? What is meant by *brain drain* and *reverse brain drain*?

13. How are a people's culture and *physical environment* related? How does technology affect culture?

14. Describe the dimensions of the *Kluckhohn-Strodtbeck* and *Hofstede frameworks*. Contrast two cultures by applying each of these frameworks to them.

15. What are the primary characteristics of *individual-oriented cultures*? Of *group-oriented cultures*? How might business practices and competitiveness differ between these two types of cultures?

questions for discussion

1. Two students are discussing the various reasons why they are *not* studying international business. "International business doesn't affect me," declares the first. "I'm going to stay here, not work in some *foreign* country." "Yeah," agrees the second. "Besides, some cultures are real *strange*. The sooner other countries start doing business our way, the better." What counterarguments can you present to these students' perceptions?

2. A recent survey of European business executives obtained some interesting results. They were asked which nation's executives had the strongest work ethic and demonstrated the best leadership abilities. Germany ranked high on both di-

mensions. What parts of German culture do you think explain its high ratings? On the other hand, Greece received low ratings. What is it about Greek culture that, in your opinion, may explain its low rankings on each dimension? Give specific examples if you can.

3. In this exercise, two groups of four students each will debate the benefits and drawbacks of individual- versus group-oriented cultures. After the first student from each side has spoken, the second student questions the opponent's arguments, looking for holes and inconsistencies. A third student attempts to reply to these counterarguments. Then a fourth student summarizes each side's arguments. Finally, the class votes on which team has presented the more compelling case.

in practice

Read the short newspaper article below and answer the questions that follow.

Nike Building Playground at Virginia Mosque

FALLS CHURCH, Va. (AP) - Shoe manufacturer Nike Corp. has begun building a playground at a northern Virginia mosque, one of several projects to make amends for a marketing gaffe.

About two years ago, Nike emblazoned a new shoe model with the word "Air" written in what looked like flames. However, the squiggly lines made the word look like Arabic script for the word Allah.

Under threat of a worldwide boycott by hundreds of millions of Muslims, who considered it a sacrilege, Nike recalled more than 38,000 pairs of the shoes and agreed to build several playgrounds for Muslim communities.

Groundbreaking for the Falls Church playground took place Saturday at the Dar Al-Hijrah Islamic Center, and some 80 children told Nike representatives what the playground should include.

1. What components of culture did Nike disregard in its development of this new shoe? Briefly explain how they disregarded each one.

2. List the countries around the world in which a large percentage of their people would be offended by this marketing mistake.

3. Do you think Nike could have prevented such a gaffe from occurring? If so, what preventative steps could it have taken?

4. Write a short paragraph describing another company that offended a group of people by ignoring relevant cultural components.

projects

1. Select a recent business periodical in print or online—say, *Fortune* ⟨**www.fortune.com**⟩, the *Far Eastern Economic Review* ⟨**www.feer.com**⟩, or *CNN Interactive* ⟨**www.cnn.com**⟩—and find an article discussing the role of culture in international business. Then write a short summary detailing the cultural elements identified by the author, being sure to explain how they pertain to actual business activities in the country under discussion.

2. Select a company in your city or town that interests you and make an appointment to interview the owner or a manager. Your goal is to learn how international opportunities and competition affect the decisions of this owner/manager and his or her company. Be sure to ask for specific examples.

Write a short report of your interview and present a brief talk on your findings to the class.

3. Go to your library or link to a business information service on the Internet. Locate annual reports or similar information issued by companies like Nike, Guess, Lands' End, or Coca-Cola—most libraries have annual reports in both paper and computer-readable form. Review this information and report on the (1) main products or services the company offers, (2) extent to which the company pursues international business operations (often expressed as percentage of sales or assets), and (3) ways that the company has adapted to local cultures around the world.

Many cultures in Asia are in the midst of an identity crisis. In effect, they are being torn between two worlds. Pulling in one direction is a traditional value system derived from agriculture-based communities and extended families—that is, elements of a culture in which relatives take care of one another and state-run welfare systems are unnecessary. Pulling from the opposite direction is a new set of values emerging from manufacturing- and finance-based economies—elements of a culture in which workers must often move to faraway cities to find work, sometimes leaving family members to fend for themselves.

For years, spectacular rates of economic growth elevated living standards in many Asian countries far beyond what was thought possible in a few short decades. Young people in countries like Malaysia and Thailand felt the lure of Western brands. Gucci handbags, Harley-Davidson motorcycles, and other global brand names became common symbols of success. Some parents even encouraged brand-consciousness among their teenage children because it signaled familywide success. Meanwhile, polls of young people showed them holding steadfast to traditional values such as respect for family and group harmony. Youth in Hong Kong, for example, overwhelmingly continued to believe that parents should have much to say about how hard they study, about how they treat family members and elders, and about their choice of friends.

But events took an unpleasant turn in the middle of 1997. The currencies of Thailand, Indonesia, Malaysia, South Korea, and other nations crumbled. Within weeks, currencies were worth about half as much as before and spending power was sharply reduced. Financial investments throughout Southeast Asia fled to safe havens in highly industrialized countries, and future investment plans were either scaled back or put on hold. Some Asians blame the West for the crippling economic crisis. Even more blame economic development and "westernization" for a decaying value system and declining morality. Many Asians, it seems, want modernization but also want to hold on to traditional beliefs and values. They do not want Western companies and governments imposing their ways of doing business on cultures that they might not fully comprehend. Nevertheless, following the crisis, Western companies are scooping up failing enterprises from Thailand to Japan and implementing Western business practices.

Prior to the financial crisis, Asians thought they had discovered an "Asian" way of doing business that was uniquely their own. Many respected analysts in Asia, Europe, and the United States discussed the virtues of the so-called "Asian model." But the crisis put an abrupt end to that discussion. Some observers say that talk of an "Asian" way of doing business was overstated and misplaced. They argue that belief in the importance of family became the practice of nepotism, belief in the importance of relationships became cronyism, belief in the building of consensus became corrupt politics, and belief in conservatism and respect for authority became rigidity and an inability to innovate. If Asian culture esteems family loyalty so highly, why was it necessary for Singapore to enact legislation *requiring* that children take care of elderly parents?

thinking globally

1. If your international firm were doing business in Asia, would you feel partly responsible for these social trends? Is there anything that your company could do to ease the tensions being experienced by these cultures? Be specific.

2. In your opinion, is globalization among the causes of the increasing incidence of divorce, crime, and drug abuse in Asia? Why or why not?

3. Broadly defined, Asia comprises over 60 percent of the world's population—a population that practices Buddhism, Confucianism, Islam, and numerous other religions. Given the fact that there are considerable cultural differences between countries such as China, India, Indonesia, Japan, and Malaysia, is it possible to carry on a valid discussion of "Asian" values? Why or why not?

4. Consider the following statement: "Economic development and capitalism require a certain style of doing business for the twenty-first century. The sooner Asian cultures adapt, the better." Do you agree or disagree? Explain.

a question of ethics

1. Some businesspeople and other experts argue that bribery helps cut through mounds of red tape. Do you agree? By calling for reforms in nations that condone bribery, are international agencies (strongly backed by U.S. interests) promoting a certain set of values and morals? Are they practicing cultural imperialism?

2. When international firms enter the Indian market, they soon learn about the various ways in which a rigid caste system can

affect business activities. Should these companies adjust to local management styles and human resource practices? Or should they import their own styles and practices because they are so-called "more developed" and equitable?

3. Companies often relocate factories from industrialized nations with high labor costs to such low-wage countries as China, India, Mexico, and the nations of Central America. Is there any reasonable response to charges that, in so doing, they frequently exploit child labor, force women to work 75-hour weeks, and destroy family units?

3 politics and law in business

Beacons

A Look Back

CHAPTER 2 introduced the important role of culture in international business. We explored the main elements of culture and showed how they affect business practices. We also saw how different methods of classifying cultures can be applied to business.

A Look at This Chapter

This chapter explores the roles of politics and law in international business. We explain how companies adapt to different political and legal environments and how managers cope with the risks presented by these environments.

A Look Ahead

CHAPTER 4 discusses the world's different economic systems. We learn about economic development and explore the challenges faced by countries transforming their national economies into free-market systems.

Learning Objectives

After studying this chapter, you should be able to

1. Distinguish among the main types of *political systems*.
2. Identify the origins of *political risk* and how managers can reduce its effects.
3. List the main types of *legal systems* and explain how they differ.
4. Describe the major *legal issues* facing international companies.
5. Explain how *international relations* affect international business activities.

The criminals encircled them like lions on a hunt. Javier Hernández had to think fast. His own life and those of his wife and two children were on the line. As a company spokesperson later emphasized, "[The criminals] were there to rob or kidnap him, and he did exactly what he learned he should do: He ran them over and got out of there. If the training is good, a reaction like that should be instinctive. You should do it without thinking."

International business operations often take companies and their employees to exotic and enchanting places. Yet, unfamiliar risks often lurk in the shadows. Such risks pose unique and real threats to a company's employees and its assets. In response, companies often reward their employees with "combat pay" in the most risky business environments.

Criminals can even threaten the competitiveness of nations. For instance, the minister of the French Interior once called the U.S. Ambassador to France into her office and gave him the bad news. Three U.S. citizens had just been arrested by the French Directorate of Territorial Surveillance. What was their crime? They offered cash to French government employees in return for information about France's position on trade negotiations and telecommunications policies. Such are the risks of international business.

What can a company do to lessen its exposure in risky environments? For one, it can lower its profile to become a less attractive target. It's like the old joke about two campers threatened by a grizzly bear in the dark of night. When one crouched to put on a pair of running shoes, the other asked, "Are you crazy? You'll never outrun that bear!" His friend looked up and said, "I don't have to. I only have to outrun you."[1]

Reports like these remind one of scenes from a James Bond film. But unfortunately, they are all too real. The potential for higher returns from international business operations often yield greater risk. Chapter 2 described how an understanding of culture is essential in successfully working in the international marketplace. Yet, it is only one element of that success. Another crucial element is political and legal savvy. This includes awareness of the risks involved and of the reasons why they exist.

The global nature of business obliges people to secure contracts, set up manufacturing facilities, and select distributors in unfamiliar countries. Many times it requires working in developing and emerging economies. Not all these countries observe the same political and legal rules or business practices as the traveling businessperson's home nation. In some countries such as the United States, bribing a public official is a serious crime. For example, the Lockheed Corporation (now Lockheed Martin), a U.S. defense contractor, recently had to pay a $24.8 million penalty for bribing an Egyptian legislator. But in some other nations bribery is more common and may even be expected because of weak legal enforcement. It was not until 1997 that the 29 industrialized nations of the Organization for Economic Cooperation and Development formally banned the practice of bribing officials of other nations.[2] But reality does not always adhere to legal codes.

Our understanding of the nature of politics and laws in other nations lessens the risks of conducting international business. In this chapter, we describe the basic differences among political and legal systems around the world. We show how disputes grounded in political and legal matters affect business activities as well as how companies can manage the associated risks.

POLITICAL SYSTEMS

political system
Structures, processes, and activities by which a nation governs itself.

A **political system** includes the structures, processes, and activities by which a nation governs itself. The Japanese system, for instance, features a prime minister who is chosen by the Japanese Diet (Parliament) and carries out the operations of the government with the help of the Cabinet ministers. The Diet consists of two houses of elected representatives that enact the nation's laws. These laws affect not only the personal lives of people living in or visiting Japan but also the activities of companies doing business there.

POLITICS AND CULTURE

Politics and *culture* are closely related. A country's political system derives from the history and culture of its people. Factors such as current population, age and race composition, and per capita income influence a country's political system.

Consider the case of Switzerland, where the system actively encourages all eligible members of society to vote. By means of *public referendums*, Swiss citizens vote *directly* on many national issues. Contrast this practice with that of most other democracies, in which *representatives of the people, not the people themselves*, vote on such issues. The Swiss system works because Switzerland consists of a relatively small population in a small geographic area.

POLITICAL PARTICIPATION

Political systems can be characterized by *who* participates in them and *to what extent* they participate. *Participation* occurs when people voice their opinions, vote, and show general approval or disapproval of the system.

Participation can be wide or narrow. *Wide participation* occurs when people who are capable of influencing the political system make an effort to do so. For example, most adults in the United States have the right to participate in the political process. Everyone has the right to approve or disapprove of elected representatives and the government in general. *Narrow participation* occurs when few people participate. For instance, in Kuwait participation is restricted to those citizens who can prove Kuwaiti ancestry at some time in the past.

POLITICAL IDEOLOGIES

We can think of the world's political systems as falling on a continuum anchored by two extremes. Let's now identify three political ideologies and learn where different systems lie on the political continuum:

➡ At one extreme is *anarchism*—the belief that only individuals and private groups should control a nation's political activities. It views public government as unnecessary and unwanted because it tramples personal liberties.

➡ At the other extreme is *totalitarianism*—the belief that every aspect of people's lives must be controlled in order for a nation's political system to be effective. Totalitarianism has no concern for individual liberties; in fact, people are often considered slaves of the political system. Institutions such as family, religion, business, and labor are considered subordinate to the state. Totalitarian political systems include such authoritarian regimes as communism and fascism.

➡ Between anarchism and totalitarianism lies *pluralism*—the belief that both private and public groups play important roles in a nation's political activities. Each of these groups (consisting of people with different ethnic, racial, class, and lifestyle backgrounds) serves to balance the power that can be gained by the other. Pluralistic political systems include democracies, constitutional monarchies, and some aristocracies.

Let's take a look at two prevalent types of political systems—democracy and totalitarianism—to gain a fuller understanding of the kinds of political elements that can cause differences in business practices in different countries.

Democracy A **democracy** is a political system in which government leaders are elected directly by the wide participation of the people or by their representatives. The foundations of modern democracy go back at least as far as the ancient Greeks. The Greeks tried to practice a *pure democracy* in which all citizens participated freely and actively in the political process.

Because some people have neither the time nor the desire to get involved in the process, "pure" democracy is more an ideal than a workable system. As population and the barriers of distance and time increase, each citizen's ability to participate completely and actively is reduced. Also, because direct voting usually results in conflicting popular opinion, it is usually impossible for leaders in pure democracies to form cohesive policies.

> **democracy**
> *Political system in which government leaders are elected directly by the wide participation of the people or by their representatives.*

Representative Democracies For practical reasons, most nations have resorted to **representative democracies** in which citizens nominate individuals from their groups to represent their political needs and views. These representatives then help govern the people and pass laws. If the people are satisfied with them, they can vote them back in to office. Those who fail to retain popular support are voted out of office.

To varying degrees, all representative democracies guarantee five freedoms:

➡ *Freedom of expression.* A constitutional right in most democracies, freedom of expression grants the right to voice opinions freely and without fear of punishment.

> **representative democracy**
> *Democracy in which citizens nominate individuals from their groups to represent their political needs and views.*

- ➡ *Periodic elections.* Each elected representative serves for a specific period of time, after which the people (or *electorate*) decide whether or not to retain these representatives. Thus U.S. presidential elections are held every four years, whereas those in France are held every seven years.

- ➡ *Full civil and property rights.* Civil rights include freedom of speech, freedom to organize political parties, and the right to a fair trial. Property rights are the privileges and responsibilities of owners of property (homes, cars, businesses, and so forth).

- ➡ *Minority rights.* In theory, democracies try to preserve peaceful coexistence among groups of people with diverse cultural, ethnic, and racial backgrounds. The same rights and privileges are by law extended to each group, no matter how few its members.

- ➡ *Nonpolitical bureaucracies.* The *bureaucracy* is the part of government that implements the rules and laws passed by elected representatives. In *politicized bureaucracies*, bureaucrats tend to implement decisions according to their own political views rather than those of the people's representatives. This clearly contradicts the purpose of the democratic process.

Despite such shared principles, countries vary greatly in the practice of representative democracy. Britain, for example, practices *parliamentary democracy*. The nation is divided into geographical districts, and people in each district vote for competing *parties* rather than individual candidates. The party winning the greatest number of legislative seats in an election does not automatically win the right to run the country. Rather, a party must gain an *absolute majority*: The number of representatives that it gets elected must be *greater than the number of representatives elected of all other parties*.

Julie Quinonez is a labor activist in Mexico. She runs the Border Committee of Women Workers, a group that educates both female and male workers in Mexico's border assembly plants (called *maquiladoras*) about their rights. Quinonez fights for much needed labor-reform laws in a country where the average salary of maquiladora workers is $50 per week, where plant working conditions are often unbearable, and where many plant managers recognize only those unions that are backed by the government. Workers charge that their right to form independent unions, as reaffirmed in the North American Free Trade Agreement, is not being upheld and that while Mexico's economy is booming, laborers are paid wages far below the cost of living.

If the party with the largest number of representatives lacks an absolute majority, it can join with one or more other parties to form a so-called *coalition government*. In a coalition government, the strongest political parties share power by dividing government responsibilities among themselves. Coalition governments are often formed in Italy, Israel, and the Netherlands. The large number of political parties in these countries makes it difficult for single parties to gain absolute majorities.

Nations also differ in the relative power possessed by each of its political parties. In some democratic countries, a single political party has effectively controlled the system for extended periods. In Mexico, for example, the Institutional Revolutionary Party (PRI) has run the country almost continuously since 1929.[3] In Japan, the Liberal Democratic Party (which is actually conservative) has enjoyed nearly uninterrupted control of the government since the 1950s.

Doing Business in Democracies Democracies maintain stable business environments primarily through laws protecting individual property rights. In theory, commerce prospers when the **private sector** includes independently owned firms that exist to make profits. Bear in mind, that although participative democracy, property rights, and free markets tend to encourage economic growth, they do not always do so. India, for example, is the world's largest democracy but experienced slow economic growth for decades. Meanwhile, some countries achieved rapid economic growth under undemocratic political systems. The so-called "four tigers" of Asia—Hong Kong, Singapore, South Korea, and Taiwan—for example, built strong market economies in the absence of truly democratic practices.

> **private sector**
> *Segment of the economic environment comprised of independently owned firms that exist to make a profit.*

Totalitarianism In a **totalitarian system**, individuals govern without the support of the people, government maintains control over many aspects of people's lives, and leaders do not tolerate opposing viewpoints. In this sense, totalitarianism and democracy are opposites. Nazi Germany under Adolf Hitler and the former Soviet Union under Joseph Stalin are historical examples of totalitarian governments. Today, Cambodia, Myanmar (formerly Burma), China, Cuba, the Democratic Republic of Congo (formerly Zaire), and Iraq are prominent examples of totalitarian governments.

Another important distinction between democratic and totalitarian governments is the concentration of power. Totalitarian leaders attempt to silence those with opposing political views. Unlike democracies, therefore, totalitarian regimes require the near-total centralization of political power. Much like the ideal of "pure democracy," a "pure" form of totalitarianism is not possible either. No totalitarian government is capable of entirely silencing all its critics.

Totalitarian governments tend to share three features:

> **totalitarian system**
> *Political system in which individuals govern without the support of the people, government maintains control over many aspects of people's lives, and leaders do not tolerate opposing viewpoints.*

➡ *Imposed authority.* An individual or group forms the political system without explicit or implicit approval of the people it governs. Thus a totalitarian system is marked by narrow participation. Leaders often acquire and retain power by military force or fraudulent elections. In some cases, they come to power through legitimate means but then remain in office after their terms expires.

➡ *Lack of constitutional guarantees.* Totalitarian systems deny citizens the constitutional guarantees woven into the fabric of democratic practice. They limit, abuse, or reject outright such institutions as freedom of expression, periodically held elections, guaranteed civil and property rights, and minority rights. Also, the bureaucracy is politicized rather than nonpolitical.

➡ *Restricted participation.* Political representation is limited either to parties that are sympathetic to the government or to those that pose no credible threat. In most cases, political opposition is completely banned, and resisters are severely punished.

Do democratic governments provide more "stable" national business environments than totalitarianism? This is a question not easily answered. Democracies, for example, pass laws to protect individual civil liberties and property rights. But totalitarian governments could also grant such rights. What would be the difference? Whereas democracies *guarantee* such rights, totalitarian governments retain the power to repeal them whenever they wish.

Map 3.1 illustrates the extent to which people of 191 nations around the world have political rights and civil liberties. As defined by Freedom House, political rights refer to people's ability to vote and run for public office and, as elected officials, to vote on public policies. Civil liberties include people's freedom to develop views, institutions, and personal autonomy apart from the state. The 16 countries rated worst include Afghanistan, Bhutan, Burma, Burundi, China, Equatorial Guinea, Libya, Saudi Arabia, Somalia, Syria, Turkmenistan, and Vietnam. The worst of these are Cuba, Iraq, North Korea, and Sudan.[4]

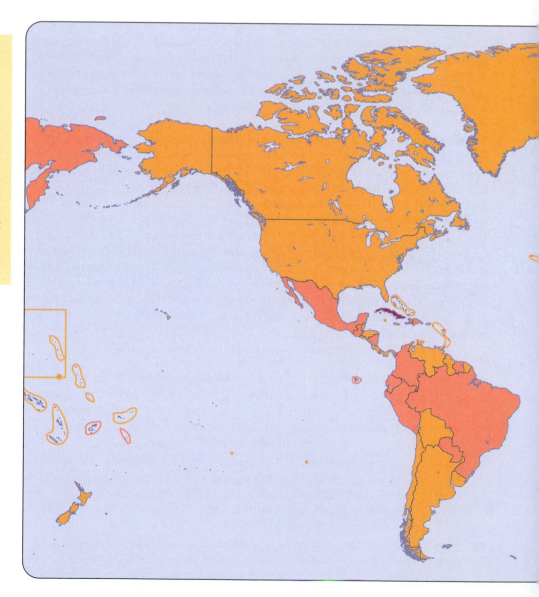

MAP 3.1

POLITICAL AND CIVIL LIBERTIES AROUND THE WORLD

This map illustrates the level of political rights and civil liberties of the people of each nation and territory. It does not rate national governments but represents the rights and liberties of individuals. In all, 81 countries (22 percent of the world population) are listed as being *free*, 57 countries (39 percent of world population) as *partly free*, and 53 countries (39 percent of world population) as *not free*.

We can say with certainty only that a democracy does not guarantee high rates of economic growth and that totalitarianism does not doom a nation to slow economic growth. Rate of *growth*—the increase in the amount of goods and services produced by a nation—is influenced by many variables other than political and civil liberty. These include a country's tax system, its encouragement or discouragement of investment, the availability of its capital, and the trade and investment barriers that it erects or guards against.

Beginning in mid-1997, economic turmoil gripped Asia, and the region is still feeling its effects today. Among other things, the crisis sparked debate over the extent to which Western-style democratic freedoms would have fostered greater economic stability in the region. This chapter's World Business Survey reflects the views of business executives across Asia on this matter.

Let's take a closer look at the two most common types of totalitarianism: *theocratic* and *secular*.

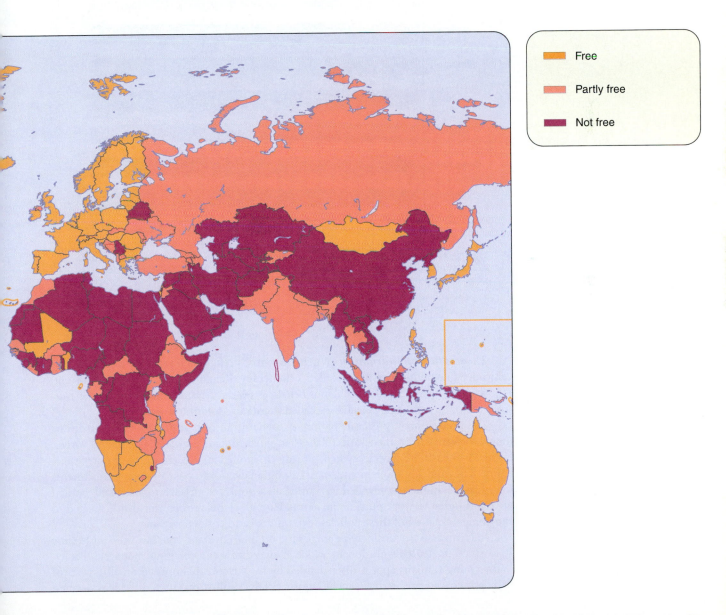

Free

Partly free

Not free

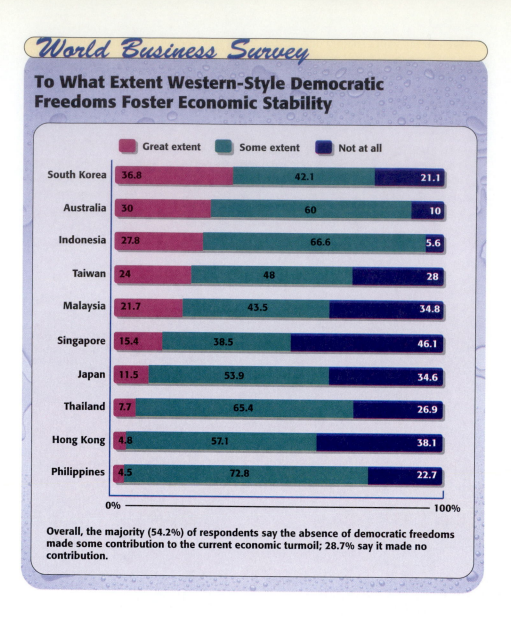

World Business Survey

To What Extent Western-Style Democratic Freedoms Foster Economic Stability

	Great extent	Some extent	Not at all
South Korea	36.8	42.1	21.1
Australia	30	60	10
Indonesia	27.8	66.6	5.6
Taiwan	24	48	28
Malaysia	21.7	43.5	34.8
Singapore	15.4	38.5	46.1
Japan	11.5	53.9	34.6
Thailand	7.7	65.4	26.9
Hong Kong	4.8	57.1	38.1
Philippines	4.5	72.8	22.7

0% ————————————————— 100%

Overall, the majority (54.2%) of respondents say the absence of democratic freedoms made some contribution to the current economic turmoil; 28.7% say it made no contribution.

---

theocracy
Political system in which a country's political leaders are religious leaders who enforce laws and regulations based on religious beliefs.

theocratic totalitarianism
Political system in which religious leaders govern without the support of the people and do not tolerate opposing viewpoints.

Theocratic Totalitarianism When a country's religious leaders are also its political leaders, its political system is called a **theocracy**. Religious leaders enforce laws and regulations that are based on religious beliefs. A political system that is under the control of totalitarian religious leaders is called **theocratic totalitarianism**.

The predominantly Islamic nation of Afghanistan is expected to emerge from its long civil war with a theocratic totalitarian government. As of 1999, military forces, backed by pro-theocracy clergymen, already controlled 90 percent of the country's territory. They quickly implemented strict Islamic law and imposed severe punishments for violators. In these controlled territories, all schools for girls were closed and women were forbidden to work outside the home. Human rights groups worldwide reacted to the implementation of these policies with outrage and condemnation.

Iran can also be considered a theocratic totalitarian state. Iran has been an Islamic state since its 1979 revolution in which it overthrew the reigning monarch. Today, many young Iranians appear disenchanted by the strict code imposed on all aspects of their public and private lives, including strict laws against products and ideas deemed too "Western." They do not question their religious beliefs but yearn for a more open society. The recently elected Iranian president, Muhammad Khatami, was able to make some changes in government policies in recent years despite opposition from conservative religious leaders.[5] Although Afghanistan and Iran are both characterized by theocratic totalitarianism, they are very distrustful of one another. Whereas Afghan Muslims are of the Sunni branch, Iranian Muslims are predominantly Shiite.

Secular Totalitarianism   A political system in which political leaders rely on military and bureaucratic power is called **secular totalitarianism**. It takes three forms: *communist*, *tribal*, and *right-wing*.

Communist Totalitarianism   Under *communist totalitarianism* (referred to here as simply *communism*), the government has sweeping political and economic powers. The Communist Party controls all aspects of the political system, and opposition parties are given little or no voice. In general, each Party member holding office is required to support all government policies, and dissension is rarely permitted. **Communism** is the belief that social and economic equality can be obtained only by establishing an all-powerful Communist Party and by instituting a **socialist** economic system—that is, by granting the government ownership and control over all types of economic activity. This includes ownership of the means of production (such as capital, land, and factories) and the power to decide what the economy will produce and the prices at which goods are sold.

Important distinctions, however, separate communism from socialism. Communists follow the teachings of Marx and Lenin, believe that a violent revolution is needed to seize control over resources, and wish to eliminate political opposition. Socialists believe in none of these. Thus communists are socialists, but socialists are not necessarily communist.

Communist and socialist beliefs differ markedly from those of **capitalism**—the conviction that ownership of the means of production belongs in the hands of individuals and private businesses. Capitalism is also frequently referred to as the *free market*. (The economics of communism and capitalism are covered in detail in Chapter 4.)

Communist totalitarianism and economic socialism seem to have lost the battle against capitalism. In the late 1980s, shortly after the former Soviet Union implemented its twin policies of *glasnost* (political openness) and *perestroika* (economic reform), its government began to crumble as people complained openly about their government. Communist governments in central and eastern Europe soon followed suit, and today such countries as the Czech Republic, Hungary, Poland, Romania, and Ukraine have elected republican governments. As a result, there are far fewer communist nations than there were two decades ago. Map 3.2 shows that only Cuba and North Korea remain avowedly committed to communist ideals.

Tribal Totalitarianism   Under *tribal totalitarianism*, one tribe (or ethnic group) imposes its will on others with whom it shares a national identity. The least understood form of totalitarianism, it characterizes the governments of many African nations, including Kenya, Nigeria, Burundi, and Rwanda. With the departure of European colonial powers, many national boundaries in Africa were created with little regard to ethnic differences among the inhabitants. Thus people of different ethnicities live within the same nation, whereas members of the same ethnicity live in different nations. Over time, certain ethnic groups gained political and military power, and historical enmity among different groups often erupted in bloody conflict.

Right-Wing Totalitarianism   Under *right-wing totalitarianism*, the government endorses private ownership of property and a market-based economy but grants few (if any) political freedoms. Leaders generally strive for economic growth while opposing

secular totalitarianism
Political system in which leaders rely on military and bureaucratic power.

communism
The belief that social and economic equality can be obtained only by establishing an all-powerful Communist Party and by granting the government ownership and control over all types of economic activity.

socialism
The belief that social and economic equality is obtained through government ownership and regulation of the means of production.

capitalism
The belief that ownership of the means of production belongs in the hands of individuals and private businesses.

MAP 3.2

communism, or *left-wing* totalitarianism, which espouses government ownership of property and a centrally planned economy. Argentina, Brazil, Chile, and Paraguay all had right-wing totalitarian governments in the 1980s. Singapore and Indonesia stand out as prominent examples today.

Despite the theoretical differences between the two ideologies, the Chinese political system is currently a mix of communist and right-wing totalitarianism. China is currently engineering high economic growth by implementing certain characteristics of a capitalist economy while still retaining a hard line in the political sphere. For example, China is privatizing many of its decrepit state-run factories and changing laws to further encourage the international investment needed to modernize the country's production technologies. However, the government still has little patience for dissidents demanding greater political freedom.

Doing Business in Totalitarian Countries What are the costs and benefits of doing business in a totalitarian nation? On the plus side, international companies need not be concerned with political opposition to their activities by those outside the gov-

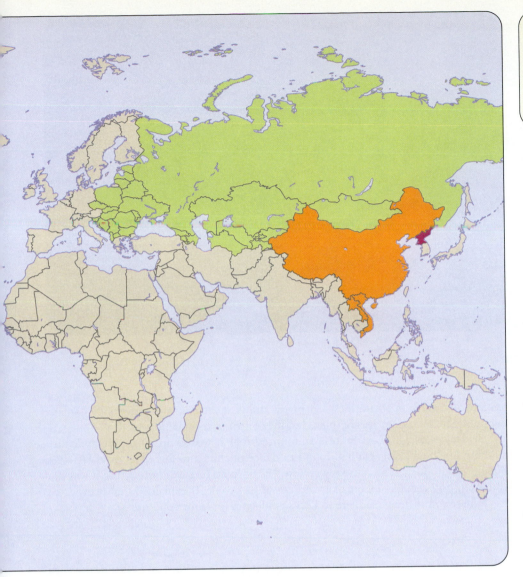

	Postcommunist
	Communist in transition
	Communist not in transition

ernment. On the negative side, they might need to pay bribes and kickbacks to government officials. Refusal to pay could result in loss of market access or even forfeiture of investments in the country.

In any case, doing business in a totalitarian country can be a risky proposition. Many facets of business law pertain to contractual disputes. In a country such as the United States, laws regarding the resolution of such disputes are quite specific. In most totalitarian nations, the law is either vague or nonexistent, and people in powerful government positions can interpret laws largely as they please. "It doesn't matter what the law says," reports the merchandising director of a U.S.-based megastore doing business in China. "What matters is what the guy behind the desk interprets the law to say."[6] The arbitrary nature of totalitarian governments makes it hard for companies to know how laws will be interpreted and applied to their particular business dealings.

Companies operating in totalitarian nations are sometimes criticized for lacking compassion for the people hurt by the oppressive political policies of their hosts. They must decide whether to refrain from investing in totalitarian countries—and miss po-

Many people argue that the United States' embargo against Cuba is no longer effective. They say that a policy which is supposed to drive a wedge between Cuban leader Fidel Castro's regime and its deprived populace is now counterproductive and that the Castro government is scarcely a threat to American influence. The effects of the embargo are yet to be seen, but many American goods—or close substitutes—reach Cuba anyway. These entrepreneurs could have bought these American munchies from an intermediary company—a company in another country that buys goods from the United States and then resells them in Cuba at a minimal price increase that still allows Cubans to buy them without much financial strain.

tentially profitable opportunities—or invest and bear the brunt of potentially damaging publicity. The issues are complex, and the controversy remains heated.

Several years ago, Levi Strauss announced that it would no longer manufacture clothing in China because it had found evidence of child and forced labor at factories making its products. The company reversed its position in 1998, stating that it was not endorsing any change in China's treatment of its people. It explained that it expected its Chinese contractors to adhere to Levi's guidelines for labor conditions.[7]

POLITICAL SYSTEMS IN TIMES OF CHANGE

Globalization is causing fundamental changes in people's values and attitudes toward political systems. People all around the world are demanding greater participation in the political process, and many nations are abandoning totalitarian for democratic systems. Most notably, almost all of the formerly communist countries of central and eastern Europe now have some form of democratic government. Although the transition from a sluggish state-owned white elephant to a vibrant privately operated enterprise has been difficult, there are some remarkable success stories coming out of central and eastern Europe:

➡ Behind the shabby gray walls of Poland's Stomil Sanok, workers use high-tech molding machines to churn out rubber parts for Fiat and Daewoo Corporation. Sales now top $51.5 million; profits grew 86 percent in one recent year, and the company is expanding throughout eastern Europe.

➡ Martin Kratochvil—who used to earn $10,000 a year writing television jingles in Boston—has capitalized on the expanding consumer culture of the Czech Republic to build a $38 million entertainment conglomerate called Bonton. The company already operates multiplex cinemas and is currently building a network of music megastores.

➡ One small company that has cashed in on Hungary's high literacy rates and mathematics skills is Semilab, which makes machines to test silicon for semiconductors. The company now supplies machines to Sharp, Philips Electronics, and Texas Instruments. Annual profits recently soared 182 percent.[8]

When a nation is in the midst of economic and political change, its business environment can range from unstable to chaotic. Even then, small companies prosper by finding opportunity in adversity. In postapartheid South Africa, for instance, one local entrepreneur started a tourism business. He trucks tourists out to the black townships to see first-hand the place where South African democracy took root. In 1998, Donald H. Barden, one of the United States' most successful black entrepreneurs, joined singer Michael Jackson in an investment venture headquartered in the tiny, impoverished African nation of Namibia. Barden and Jackson intend to use Namibia as a tax-free base from which to market various goods—starting with canned foods and drinks, mattresses, and General Motors cars—to the larger war-torn nations of Angola and the Democratic Republic of Congo.[9] Meanwhile, Coca-Cola is building a $30 million bottling plant in Angola despite threats to its distribution channels that include land mines and bandit ambushes.[10]

POLITICAL RISK

All companies doing business internationally confront **political risk**—the likelihood that a government or society will undergo political changes that negatively affect local business activity. Political risk affects different companies in different ways. It can threaten the market of an exporter, the production facilities of a manufacturer, or the ability of a company to remove profits from the country in which they were earned. Map 3.3 shows that the level of political risk varies greatly from nation to nation.

political risk
Likelihood that a government or society will undergo political changes that negatively affect local business activity.

On August 31, 1997, Malaysians crowded Merdeka Square to celebrate their independence from Great Britain—and from the West. With this independence came a need to create a national identity from a mix of Malays, Chinese, and Indians. And so the new government looked to—and needed—a strong economy as a uniting force. Recognizing this need, foreign companies have continued to invest in Malaysia despite Prime Minister Mahathir Mohamad's public criticism of Western culture. The risk, with all its political overtones, didn't boil over until late 1997, when Mohamad blamed foreigners for domestic currency and stock market woes, restricted trade with the West, and gave preferential treatment to Malaysians hurt by it all. Foreign investors fled, taking their money with them. For more on Malaysia, go to ⟨**www.mymalaysia.net.my**⟩.

MAP 3.3

LEVELS OF POLITICAL RISK

A nation's political risk is an important factor in a company's decision to do business with or in that country. This map shows how much political risk can vary from one country to another. Some of the factors included in this assessment of political risk levels include government stability, internal and external conflict, military and religion in politics, corruption, law and order, and bureaucracy quality.

Political risk arises from a variety of sources, including the following:

➡ Corrupt or poor political leadership

➡ Frequent changes in the form of government

➡ Political involvement of religious or military leaders

➡ An unstable political system

➡ Conflict among races, religions, or ethnic groups

➡ Poor relations with other countries

International businesses can unwittingly *increase* their own political risk by stirring up local emotions and sentiments. For example, they can add to their political risk if they harm the local society in some way or damage the natural environment without

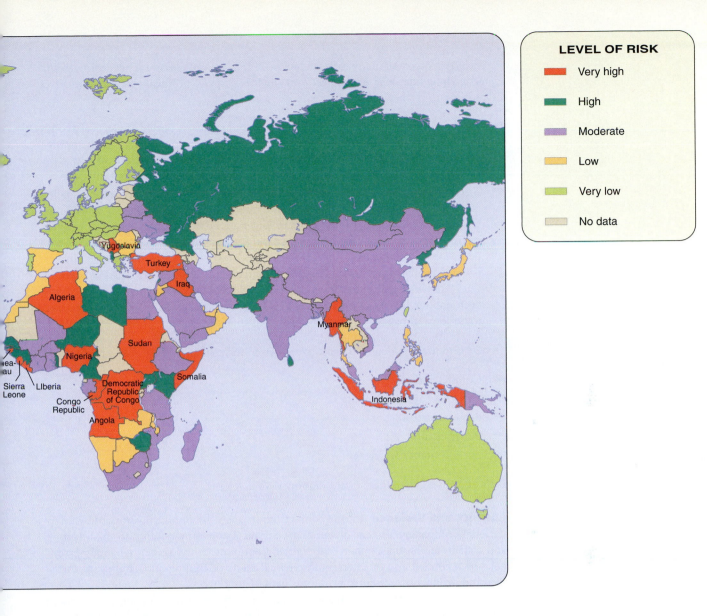

LEVEL OF RISK

- Very high
- High
- Moderate
- Low
- Very low
- No data

fair compensation. They can also increase political risk if they fail to respect local cultural values, customs, and traditions and may even spur lawmakers to change local business laws. In Malaysia, for instance, one of the strongest emerging markets in Asia, people strongly defend varied religious traditions that include Islam and Buddhism. But Westerners, charges Malaysian Prime Minister Mahathir Mohamad,

> *generally cannot rid themselves of their sense of superiority. They still consider their values and political and economic systems better than any others. It would not be so bad if it stopped at that; it seems, however, that they will not be satisfied until they have forced other countries to adopt their ways as well.*

Managers of international subsidiaries there would do well to look at the world through Malaysian eyes. Political leaders and lawmakers often make political capital out of the offensive behavior of multinational companies doing business within their borders.[11]

CLASSIFYING POLITICAL RISK

Political risk can take many different forms. First, we can classify it according to *the range of companies who are subject to it*. In this respect, political risk falls into two categories:

➡ *Macro risk* threatens all companies regardless of industry. For example, every company now doing business in Myanmar fears violence against its assets and employees and shares an abiding concern about government corruption. Macro risks equally affect all companies in a country—both domestic and international.

➡ *Micro risk* threatens companies within a particular industry or even smaller groups. One example is the risk recently confronting oil companies in Nigeria. Groups opposed to the ruling *junta* in Nigeria accused oil companies from developed nations of siphoning off huge quantities of oil and leaving little to the local people except severe environmental damage. The risk for oil companies in Nigeria is that a civilian government could form and change business laws back in favor of the Nigerian people. Changes could include higher corporate tax rates or perhaps even nationalization of the country's oil-drilling industry. In 1999, there appeared to be some movement toward free elections in Nigeria.

Second, we can identify at least five different forms that political risk can take:

➡ Conflict and violence
➡ Terrorism and kidnapping
➡ Property seizure
➡ Policy changes
➡ Local content requirements

Let's examine each of these forms in more detail.

Conflict and Violence   Local conflict can strongly discourage investment by international companies. Violent disturbances impair a company's ability to manufacture and distribute products, obtain materials and equipment, and recruit talented personnel. Open conflict also threatens both physical assets (including office buildings, factories, and production equipment) and the lives of employees.

Conflict arises from several sources. First, it may result from people's resentment toward their own government. When peaceful resolution of disputes between people (or factions) and the government fails, violent attempts to change political leadership often ensue. This was the case in the Democratic Republic of Congo when forces under the command of President Laurent Kabila overthrew the 32-year dictatorship of Mobutu Sesse Seko in 1997.

Second, conflict may arise over territorial disputes between countries. India and Pakistan, for example, continue their dispute over the Kashmir territory (officially called Jammu and Kashmir). The two nations have already clashed three times over the intensely disputed region. Another border dispute is that between Ecuador and Peru. These South American nations have gone to war three times over disputed territory—most recently in 1995.

Finally, disputes between ethnic, racial, and religious groups may erupt in violent conflict. In addition to its dispute with Pakistan, conflict frequently erupts between Hindus and Muslims within India itself. Companies doing business in India constantly face the risk that religious violence will disrupt business operations.

Terrorism and Kidnapping   Kidnapping and other terrorist activities are means of making political statements. *Terrorism*, which aims to create fear and force change through the sudden and unpredictable destruction of life or property, is often employed by small groups dissatisfied with current political or social situations. Such groups sometimes have silent approval from a substantial portion of the local population, but just as often do not. In just one recent year, there were 304 separate acts of worldwide terrorism, resulting in 222 deaths and more than 693 injuries.[12]

Kidnapping and the taking of hostages may be used to fund a terrorist group's activities. Executives of large international companies are prime targets because their employers have the "deep pockets" from which to pay large ransoms. Latin American countries have some of the world's highest kidnapping rates. Several years ago, a Japanese executive working in the United States for Sanyo Electric was kidnapped while watching a baseball game in Mexico. He was freed nine days later, after Sanyo paid a $2 million ransom.[13] When high-ranking executives are required to enter countries with high kidnapping rates (for example, to make decisions that cannot be relegated to subordinates), they should enter unannounced, meet with only a few key people in secure locations, and leave just as quickly and quietly.

The New York-based international security firm Kroll Associates estimates that 8,000 people worldwide were held for ransom in one recent year. "It's a growing problem abroad," admits one Kroll official, "especially in regions where poverty is profound and law enforcement is lax." Some companies even purchase kidnap, ransom, and extortion insurance, but most security experts agree that training managers and executives to avoid trouble in the first place is a far better investment.[14] For a checklist of ways to avoid risk during overseas assignments, see the Global Manager "Your Global Security Checklist."

Property Seizure   Governments sometimes seize the assets of companies doing business within their borders. Seizure of assets falls into one of three categories: *confiscation*, *expropriation*, or *nationalization*.

Confiscation   **Confiscation** is the forced transfer of assets from a company to the government *without compensation*. The former owners normally have no legal basis for requesting compensation or the return of assets. The U.S. 1996 Helms-Burton Law is designed to punish international companies using property seized from U.S. companies following Cuba's communist revolution in 1959.

> **confiscation**
> *Forced transfer of assets from a company to the government without compensation.*

Expropriation   **Expropriation** is the forced transfer of assets from a company to the government *with compensation*. The government doing the expropriating normally determines compensation. There is no framework for legal appeal, and compensation is typically far below market value. In the early 1990s, for example, the government of Lebanon created a company with sweeping authority to expropriate property in Beirut's central business district. The move was the core of the government's effort to rebuild and attract international investors after a civil war ravaged the capital city from 1975 to 1990.

> **expropriation**
> *Forced transfer of assets from a company to the government with compensation.*

Today, governments rarely resort to confiscation or expropriation. Why? By doing so, they jeopardize future investment in their countries. Companies already doing business there may leave for fear of losing valuable assets. This same fear prevents new companies from starting up local operations.

Nationalization   Nationalization is more common than confiscation and expropriation. Whereas expropriation involves one or a small number of companies in an industry, **nationalization** means government takeover of an entire industry. Likely

> **nationalization**
> *Government takeover of an entire industry.*

Global Manager

Your Global Security Checklist

➡ **Know the Territory** Discover all you can about the host country. This includes its culture, politics, laws, economic system, and its rates and patterns of crime. When possible, talk to employees who in the past were stationed in the country. They can provide crucial advice on what to do and what locations to avoid.

➡ **Avoid the Spotlight** Don't call attention to personal position or wealth, and don't attract attention by ostentatious spending or self-promoting media exposure. Leave fancy jewelry and electronic equipment at home. Dress down, but always in tune with local culture. Don't carry luggage—or any item—bearing the company logo, not even business documents.

➡ **Keep Quiet** Don't release any personal information that can be used to track you down. You should have an unlisted phone number, checks containing no home address details, and tight-lipped employees at both home and office. If someone asks for your phone number, always give a work number. Instruct family members to do the same.

➡ **Be Aware** If you're on the road, be on the lookout for a car that keeps showing up in the rear-view mirror. When you're walking, check out who's behind or alongside you. Children, especially those at international schools, are high-visibility targets, and they should be gently told what to look for. Older children

can also be enlisted in security efforts. Kids who live in the neighborhood know who should be there and who shouldn't.

➡ **Vary Routines** You wouldn't think that being predictable would have life-threatening consequences, but in terms of corporate kidnappings, it does. Kidnappers typically watch victims for weeks before making their move. Leave your house, office, or hotel by alternate exits and at different times every day. Swap cars with your spouse occasionally, or one day take a cab and ride the train the next. The key is to avoid establishing a pattern.

➡ **Be Prudent—Not Paranoid** Personal protection is a big business, and you can buy a wide array of personal-protection devices, such as pepper spray, stun guns, and electrical Tasers that can shock an assailant at 15 feet. But most security experts agree that gadgetry—including firearms—isn't a good idea because of the potential for things to go wrong in a high-stress situation.

➡ **Know S.O.S. Procedures** Suppose you're working abroad and your apartment is broken into while you're at home. You can't dial 911 or follow the emergency protocol recommended in your home country. Rather, you should follow the host country's emergency procedures, and you should be familiar with them before trouble strikes.

candidates include industries important to a nation's security and those generating large revenues. In the 1970s, Chile nationalized its vast copper industry and paid international companies a price substantially below market value. Nationalization appeals to governments for four main reasons:

1. Governments may nationalize industries when they believe that international companies are transferring profits to operations in other countries with lower tax rates. Nationalization gives the government control over the cash flow generated by the industry.

2. Governments may nationalize an industry for ideological reasons. The leading political party, for instance, might believe that the government can protect an industry with subsidies. Such was the ideology of the Labor Party that governed Britain for many years following World War II.

3. Nationalization is sometimes used as a political tool. Candidates may promise to save local jobs by nationalizing ailing industries.

4. Government ownership may support industries in which private companies are unwilling or unable to invest. For instance, the investment required to build public utilities and train employees is more than most private companies can afford. Governments often approach this problem by controlling utilities industries and financing them through subsidies obtained from tax revenues.

The extent of nationalization varies widely from country to country. Whereas the governments of Cuba, North Korea, and Vietnam control practically every industry, those of the United States and Canada own very few. Many countries, including France, Brazil, Mexico, Poland, and India, try to strike a balance between government and private ownership.

Policy Changes   In April 1998, the Chinese government unexpectedly banned all direct selling to consumers, claiming that direct-selling operations were really pyramid schemes that fostered social unrest. Amway Corp., with 70,000 sales agents doing $180 million in annual sales, appeared to have been summarily evicted from an extremely lucrative market. In China, however, such regulations are typically open to negotiation *after* they have been passed. Amway was able to convince officials to make it an exception to their rules.[15]

Government policy changes can also result from civil or social unrest or might represent the views of newly empowered political parties. One common policy tool restricts ownership to only domestic companies. When PepsiCo first entered India, for example, its ownership of local companies was restricted to 49 percent. Similarly, governments may restrict participation in certain industries to national companies only.

Local Content Requirements   Laws stipulating that a specified amount of a good or service be supplied by producers in the domestic market are called **local content requirements**. These requirements can force companies to use locally available raw materials, to procure parts from local suppliers, or to employ a certain number of local workers. They allow governments to ensure that international companies foster local business activity and to ease regional or national unemployment. They also help governments maintain some degree of control over international companies without resorting to such extreme measures as confiscation and expropriation.

local content requirements Laws stipulating that a specified amount of a good or service be supplied by producers in the domestic market.

Local content requirements may jeopardize a firm's long-term survival. Specifically, they pose two potential disadvantages to internationally active firms:

1. Requiring an employer to hire local personnel might oblige it to take on an inadequately trained workforce.
2. Requiring companies to obtain raw materials or parts locally might increase production costs, reduce quality, or both.

MANAGING POLITICAL RISK

Aside from monitoring and predicting potential political changes, international companies must try to manage political risks that threaten current operations and future earnings. There are five main methods of managing political risk: *avoidance, adaptation, dependency maintenance, information gathering,* and *influencing local politics.*

Avoidance   *Avoidance* simply means restraining from investing in a country: a poor choice when opportunity knocks. When risk is manageable and the local market is appealing, managers find another way to deal with political risk.

Adaptation   *Adaptation* means incorporating risk into business strategies, often with the help of local officials. Companies can incorporate risk by means of five strategies: *local equity and debt, localization, development assistance, partnerships,* and *insurance.*

Local Equity and Debt   *Local equity and debt* involves financing local business activities with the help of local firms, trade unions, financial institutions, and government. As partners in local business activities, these groups ensure that political forces do not interrupt operations. If they own shares in local operations (*equity*), the partners get cuts of the profits. If they loan cash (*debt*), they receive interest. Risk exposure is reduced because local partners take an interest in the operation's success.

Localization   *Localization* entails modifying operations, the product mix, or some other business element—even the company name—to suit local tastes and culture. When McDonald's opened franchise operations in India, for example, it replaced Big Macs with a similar sandwich containing no beef. In so doing, the company displayed its sensitivity to the religious beliefs of a large portion of the Indian population.

Development Assistance   Offering *development assistance* allows an international business to assist the host country or region in developing its distribution and communications networks and improving the quality of local life. Because the company and the nation become partners, they both benefit.

The scope of development assistance varies widely. For small-scale projects, firms sometimes build employee housing. For larger projects, firms might contribute millions of dollars to build schools and hospitals and upgrade local infrastructure. In the Southeast Asian country of Myanmar, for instance, the U.S. oil company Unocal and France's Total have not only invested billions of dollars to develop natural gas fields, but have also spent another $6 million on local education, medical care, and other improvements.[16] Canon, the Japanese copier and printer company, espouses a policy designed to go beyond mere assistance. Its practice of *kyosei* is best translated as "spirit of cooperation." By practicing *kyosei*, international firms actively use their economic influence in pressing local governments to make social and political reforms.[17]

Partnerships   An increasingly popular way of managing risk, *partnerships* can be excellent for leveraging a company's development plans. "The issue," explains one executive at equipment manufacturer FMC, "is finding ways of sharing risk in these [developing] countries, because you can lose your shirt. So more and more it is a matter of partnering or working with several companies so you can spread your knowledge—or your ignorance—and the risk."[18]

Insurance   Companies entering risky national business environments routinely purchase *insurance* against the potential effects of political risk. The *Overseas Private Investment Corporation (OPIC)*, for example, insures internationally active U.S. companies. Some policies protect companies when local governments restrict the convertibility of local money into home-country currency. Others insure against losses created by violent events, including war and terrorism. The *Foreign Credit Insurance Association (FCIA)* insures companies against damages from war, revolution, and the cancellation of licenses.

Dependency Maintenance

Occasionally, a firm tries to keep the host country dependent on its local activities. Companies have developed three approaches to implementing this strategy:

1. They impress upon local officials and citizens the importance of their activities to local economic development and quality of life. In other words, they try to convince local interests that they really *need* the activities of international companies.

2. They may try to control raw materials, technology, or parts essential to other local businesses. They try to convince local officials that seizure of any local assets would make it extremely difficult for many local operations to continue.

3. If a company is sufficiently large and powerful, it can obtain near-total control of local distribution channels. If it is subsequently threatened, it can refuse to supply local consumers or corporate buyers with the products they need.

Azerbaijan is on the cusp of an economic boom, fueled by, well, fuel. It is estimated that by 2005, this Caspian Sea nation, which has oil reserves of 38 billion barrels, will receive $5 billion annually from oil production—five times more than the country's 1997 budget. This worker for British Petroleum-Amoco (BP Amoco), which has been drilling in Azerbaijan since 1994, is helping build a pipeline in the capital city of Baku. Azerbaijan looks to companies such as BP Amoco to help revive its ineffective refinery equipment and help the country achieve economic independence. To find out more about BP Amoco's work in global markets go to its Web site at ⟨**www.bpamoco.com**⟩.

There are ethical implications of dependency maintenance. First, the deception promoted by companies that locals need their expertise can thwart the development of local talent. Entrepreneurs and small-business owners might be discouraged from trying to compete because of the apparent power of international competitors. Second, international companies can disrupt many sectors of an economy by restricting production of components that they require. Third, international companies can hold an economy hostage to their products by refusing to release their output into distribution channels. This practice can adversely affect the local population's well-being and safety, particularly when a product is important to health or security.

Information Gathering   International firms must monitor and even try to predict political events that threaten local operations and future earnings. There are two sources of data needed to conduct accurate political risk forecasting:

1. A company can ask employees for information bearing on political-risk levels. Employees who have worked in a country long enough to gain insight into local culture and politics are often good sources of information. Likewise, individuals who formerly had decision-making authority while on international assignment probably had contact with local politicians and other officials. Because political power can shift rapidly and dramatically, it is important that the employee's international experience is recent.

2. A firm can obtain information from agencies specializing in political-risk services. These include banks, political consultants, news publications, and risk-assessment services—all of which estimate risk using a variety of criteria and methods. Many of these agencies offer political-risk reports that detail the levels and sources of such risks for each nation. Because such services can be expensive, small companies and enterpreneurs might consider the many free sources of information that are available, notably from their federal governments. Government intelligence agencies are excellent, inexpensive sources to consult.

Influencing Local Politics   Managers must be able to deal with the rules and regulations that apply in each national business environment. Moreover, laws in many nations are susceptible to frequent change, with new laws continually being enacted and existing ones modified. To influence local politics in their favor, managers can propose changes that positively affect their local activities.

Lobbying   Influencing local politics always involves dealing with local lawmakers and politicians, either directly or through lobbyists. **Lobbying** is the policy of hiring people to represent a company's views on political matters. Lobbyists meet with local public officials and try to influence their position on issues relevant to the company. They describe the benefits that a company brings to the local economy, natural environment, infrastructure, and workforce. Their ultimate goal is getting favorable legislation passed and unfavorable legislation rejected.

lobbying
Policy of hiring people to represent a company's views on political matters.

Corruption   As we saw in Chapter 2, bribes are one method of gaining political influence. They are routinely used in some countries to get distributors and retailers to push a firm's products through distribution channels. Sometimes they mean the difference between obtaining important contracts and being completely shut out of certain markets.

In the early 1970s, for example, the president of Lockheed Corp. (now Lockheed Martin) bribed Japanese officials in order to obtain large sales contracts. Public disclosure of the incident in the United States resulted in passage of the 1977 U.S. **Foreign Corrupt Practices Act (FCPA)**, which forbids U.S. companies from bribing gov-

Foreign Corrupt Practices Act (FCPA)
1977 statute forbidding U.S. companies from bribing government officials or political candidates in other nations.

ernment officials or political candidates in other nations (except when a person's life is otherwise in danger). A bribe can constitute "anything of value"—money, gifts, and so forth—and cannot be given to any "foreign government official" empowered to make a "discretionary decision" that may be to the payer's benefit. The FCPA also requires firms to keep accounting records that reflect their international activities and assets.

Like many cultural and political elements, the prevalence of corruption varies from one country to another. Corruption is detrimental to society and business for many reasons. Among them, corruption leads to the misallocation of resources (not always to their most efficient uses), can hurt economic development, distorts public policy, and can damage the integrity of "the system." Table 3.1 shows the countries perceived by businesspeople as being the least and most corrupt as recorded by Transparency International—a nongovernmental organization in Germany dedicated to reducing corruption.

Table 3.1 shows those countries ranked the ten least and most corrupt by businesspeople. In addition to those listed, the United Kingdom ranked 11 (along with Australia and Luxembourg), Germany ranked 15, and the United States ranked 17 (along with Austria).

Because they often place domestic companies at a globally competitive disadvantage, bribery and other forms of corruption can throw whole industries—even economies—into turmoil. For example, because of a corrupt financial system, Japanese banks until 1998 were sheltered from having to compete against international banks in their home market. But because of new laws passed, Japanese banks must now contend with such international competitors as Citibank, Merrill Lynch, Morgan Stanley, Dean Witter, and Britain's Mercury Asset Group.[19] They are likely to have a hard time of it. In July 1998, Japanese officials announced that the country's banking practices had led to an accumulation of $1 trillion in bad debts. Such news has a ripple effect in national economies and is bad for other countries as well. Countries that export to Japan will see their exports fall. Other Asian nations are being especially hard-hit because they are heavily dependent on trade, investment, and borrowing from Japan.[20]

In our discussion of political systems and how companies deal with political uncertainty, we touched on several important legal issues. Although there is a good deal of overlap between a nation's political and legal systems, they are distinct. In the next section we take a closer look at several types of legal systems and their influence on the activities of international companies.

TABLE 3.1 Corruption Perceptions Index

The Least Corrupt . . .	. . . and the Most Corrupt
1. Denmark	76. Russia
2. Finland	77. (*tie*) Ecuador
3. Sweden	77. (*tie*) Venezuela
4. New Zealand	79. Colombia
5. Iceland	80. Indonesia
6. Canada	81. (*tie*) Nigeria
7. Singapore	81. (*tie*) Tanzania
8. (*tie*) Netherlands	83. Honduras
8. (*tie*) Norway	84. Paraguay
10. Switzerland	85. Cameroon

A country's **legal system** consists of its laws and regulations, including the processes by which its laws are enacted and enforced, and the ways in which its courts hold parties accountable for their actions. A legal system is influenced by many cultural variables. These include class barriers, religious beliefs, and whether independent behavior or group conformity is emphasized. Many laws, rules, and regulations are used to safeguard cultural values and beliefs. A country's legal system is also influenced by its political system. Totalitarian governments tend to favor public ownership of economic resources and enact laws limiting entrepreneurial behavior. In contrast, democracies tend to encourage entrepreneurial activity and to protect small businesses with strong property-rights laws.

The rights and responsibilities of parties to business transactions differ from one nation to another. Business strategies, therefore, must be flexible enough to adapt to different legal systems. Laws protecting intellectual property, for example, are quite important for international companies, particularly those in industries that stake considerable investments in R&D.

Also important are political "moods," including upsurges of **nationalism**—the devotion of a people to their nation's interests and advancement. It typically involves intense national loyalty and cultural pride and is often associated with drives toward national independence. In India, for instance, because most business laws originated when the country was struggling for "self-sufficiency," the legal system tended to protect local businesses from international competition. In the 1960s and 1970s, India nationalized many industries and intensely scrutinized applicants wanting licenses to start new businesses. Today, however, although nationalism still runs strong in India, the government is responding to globalization by passing laws that are more pro-business.

legal system
Set of laws and regulations, including the processes by which a country's laws are enacted and enforced and the ways in which its courts hold parties accountable for their actions.

nationalism
Devotion of a people to their nation's interests and advancement.

Used car lots in Korea are filling up with imported brands because Koreans don't want them. Even though Korea's domestic car market is suffering, partly because of sluggish output (Korean-owned Hyundai recently laid off 1,569 workers, whose response invoked a visit from the riot police), Koreans bitterly reject the huge influence of non-Korean companies. To pull itself out of economic crisis, Korea is courting international investors—a risky move considering the country's strong nationalism and distrust of the West. Angry Korean laborers are striking. Wages are dropping. Unemployment is rising. Korea's economic problems are partly attributed to the reckless borrowing and investing of its *chaebol*, or traditional, family-run conglomerates.

TYPES OF LEGAL SYSTEMS

There are three main types of legal systems (called legal traditions) in use around the world: *common law, civil law,* and *theocratic law.* This section examines each of these legal traditions and shows how it affects international business activities.

Common Law   The practice of common law originated in England in the eleventh century and was adopted in its territories around the world. Thus the U.S. legal system, for example, though integrating elements of civil law, is based largely on the common law tradition. A **common law** legal system reflects three factors:

➡ *Tradition:* a country's legal history
➡ *Precedent:* past cases that have come before the courts
➡ *Usage:* the ways in which laws are applied in specific situations

Under common law, the justice system decides cases by interpreting the law on the basis of tradition, precedent, and usage. Each law, however, may be interpreted somewhat differently in each case to which it is applied. In turn, each new interpretation sets a *precedent* that may be followed in future cases. As new precedents arise, laws are altered to clarify vague wording or to accommodate new situations not previously considered.

Business *contracts*—legally enforceable agreements between two parties—tend to be lengthy because they must consider the many possible interpretations of the law that may apply in case of a dispute. Companies must commit a good deal of time to devising clear contracts and large sums of money to acquiring legal advice. On the positive side, common law systems are flexible. Instead of applying uniformly to all situations, laws take into account particular situations and circumstances. The common law tradition is practiced in Australia, Britain, Canada, Ireland, New Zealand, the United States, and parts of Asia and Africa.

Civil Law   The civil law tradition can be traced back to Rome in the fifth century B.C. It is the world's oldest and most common legal tradition. A **civil law** system is based on a detailed set of written rules and statutes that constitute a legal *code.* Civil law is less adversarial than common law because there is no need to interpret laws according to tradition, precedent, and usage. Because all laws are codified and concise, parties to contracts need be concerned only with the explicit wording of the code. All obligations, responsibilities, and privileges directly follow from the relevant code. Less time and money, therefore, are typically spent on legal matters. But civil law systems tend to ignore the unique circumstances of particular cases. The civil law tradition is practiced in Cuba, Puerto Rico, Quebec, all of Central and South America, most of Western Europe, and many parts of Asia and Africa.

Theocratic Law   A legal tradition based on religious teachings is called **theocratic law**. Three prominent theocratic legal systems are Islamic, Hindu, and Jewish law. Although Hindu law was restricted by India's 1950 constitution whereby the state appropriated most legal functions, it does persist as a cultural and spiritual force. Likewise, after most Jewish communities were stripped of judicial autonomy in the eighteenth century, Jewish law lost much of its influence and today serves few legal functions—although it remains a strong religious force.

Islamic law is the most widely practiced theocratic legal system today. Islamic law was initially a code governing moral and ethical behavior and was later extended to commercial transactions.[21] It restricts the types of investments that companies can make and sets guidelines for the conduct of business. Following Islamic law, for exam-

commonn law
Legal system based on a country's legal history (tradition), past cases that have come before its courts (precedent), and the ways in which laws are applied in specific situations (usage).

civil law
Legal system based on a detailed set of written rules and statutes that constitute a legal code.

theocratic law
Legal system based on religious teachings.

ple, banks cannot charge interest on loans or pay interest on deposits. Instead, borrowers give banks portions of the profits earned on their investments, and depositors receive returns based on the profitability of the banks' investments. Likewise, because such products violate Islamic belief, firms abiding by Islamic law cannot invest in alcohol- and tobacco-related businesses.

Firms operating in countries under theocratic legal systems must be extremely sensitive to local values and beliefs. They should evaluate all business activities including hiring practices and investment policies, to ensure compliance not only with the law but also with those cultures' values and beliefs.

GLOBAL LEGAL ISSUES

In general, laws related to product quality, product liability, environmental pollution, and the treatment of employees are far tougher in European countries and the United States than they are in many countries in Africa, Asia, and Latin America. Some international companies take advantage of these differences in standards. For example, they might sell products abroad that are banned in their home countries. Thus *legal* differences often develop into *ethical* issues for many international businesspeople.

STANDARDIZATION

Because of differences among legal systems, companies often hire legal experts in each country in which they operate. This can be a very costly practice. Fortunately, standardization of laws across countries is occurring in some areas. *Standardization*, however, refers to *uniformity in interpreting and applying laws in more than one country*, not to the standardizing of entire legal systems.

Although there is no well-defined body of international law, several existing treaties and agreements constitute a first step toward a universal legal system. International treaties already govern several areas, including intellectual property rights, antitrust regulation, taxation, contract arbitration, and general matters of trade. In addition, several international organizations promote the standardization process. Among others, the *United Nations (U.N.)*, the *Organization for Economic Cooperation and Development (OECD)*, and the *International Institute for the Unification of Private Law in Rome* work to standardize rules of conduct in international business. In order to remove legal barriers for companies operating in the Western European market, the European Union is also standardizing some areas of its nations' legal systems.

In addition to standardization, several other legal issues are important to both international companies and the governments under which they conduct business. Let's briefly explore some of these issues.

INTELLECTUAL PROPERTY

Property that results from people's intellectual talent and abilities is **intellectual property**. It includes graphic designs, novels, computer software, machine-tool designs, and secret formulas such as that for making Coca-Cola. Technically, it results in *industrial property* (in the form of either a *patent* or a *trademark*) or *copyright* and confers a limited monopoly on its holder.

Many legal systems protect **property rights**—the legal rights to resources and any income they generate. Like other types of property, intellectual property can be traded, sold, and licensed in return for fees and/or royalty payments. Intellectual property laws are designed to compensate people whose rights are infringed.

Nations vary widely in their intellectual property laws. For instance, whereas illegal copies of software recently made up 27 percent of the U.S. domestic market, pirated soft-

intellectual property
Property that results from people's intellectual talent and abilities.

property rights
Legal rights to resources and any income they generate.

ware made up a whopping 96 percent of the Chinese market. Running a close second was Russia (95 percent). Illegal copies of CDs and cassettes recently made up 90 percent of both Bulgaria's and Paraguay's domestic markets. However, the value of the pirated CD and cassette market was greatest in Russia, standing at $165 million. Russia also had the largest market value for pirated movie videos ($312 million), although piracy level was greatest in Ukraine (99 percent). Tables 3.2, 3.3, and 3.4 list the worst national offenders against copyright holders in the software and electronic-media industries.[22]

As such figures suggest, laws in some countries are soft in comparison to those in places such as Canada, Western Europe, and the United States. Thus companies going into China with sophisticated production technology must weigh the benefits of market access against the potential costs of intellectual-property theft or piracy. Most of the world's most powerful electronics firms—including IBM, Siemens, and Texas Instruments—declined an offer to build a $1 billion computer chip factory in Shanghai. They concluded that such a deal posed far too great a risk to their investment in intellectual property. But NEC Corporation of Japan finally stepped in when it was guaranteed complete management control.[23]

Currently, European and U.S. companies are lobbying their governments to pressure other nations into adopting stronger laws. So far, their efforts have had mixed results. One promising development is the power recently given the World Trade Organization (WTO) to enforce intellectual-property laws. The Agreement on Trade-Related Aspects of Intellectual Property Rights (TRIPS) Enforcement of the WTO sets detailed minimum standards of protection that each member nation must provide.

Intellectual property can be broadly classified as either *industrial property* or *copyrights*. Let's examine the main issues associated with each category.

Industrial Property   Industrial property includes patents and trademarks—often a firm's most valuable assets. Laws protecting industrial property are designed to reward inventive and creative activity. The purpose of the U.S. Federal Patent Statute is to provide an incentive for inventors to pursue inventions and make them available to consumers. Likewise, trademark law creates incentives for manufacturers to invest in new-product development and also allows consumers to be sure that they are always getting the same product from the same producer. Industrial property is protected internationally under the Paris Convention for the Protection of Industrial Property, to which nearly 100 countries are signatories.

Patents   A **patent** is a right granted to the inventor of a product or process that excludes others from making, using, or selling the invention. Current U.S. patent law went into effect on June 8, 1995, and is in line with the systems of most developed nations. Its provisions are those of the **World Trade Organization (WTO)**, the international organization regulating trade between nations. The WTO typically grants patents for a period of 20 years. The 20-year term begins when a patent application is *filed* with a country's patent office, not when it is finally *granted*. Patents can be sought for any invention that is new, useful, and not obvious to any individual of ordinary skill in the relevant technical field.

Consider the case of tiny Fonar Corp. of Melville, New York. Two decades ago, Fonar founder Raymond V. Damadian obtained patents to the technology underlying modern magnetic resonance imaging (MRI) machines. This technology has revolutionized medicine by yielding far more accurate images than X-ray machines, without the radiation risk. Most MRI machines, however, carry the brand names of such international goliaths as Hitachi, Johnson & Johnson, Siemens, Philips Electronics, and, especially, General Electric. These firms claimed that they developed their technology independently, but Dr. Damadian insisted that "No sooner did we invent than the big guys took it away." Fonar went to court around the world, eventually settling for undis-

industrial property
Patents and trademarks.

patent
Property right granted to the inventor of a product or process that excludes others from making, using, or selling the invention.

World Trade Organization (WTO)
International organization regulating trade between nations.

TABLE 3.2   *Illegal Copies of Entertainment Software**

	Value ($ Millions)	Share of Domestic Market (%)
United States	$2,780	27%
China	1,409	96
Russia	226	95
Mexico	163	82
South Korea	146	62
Hong Kong	111	70
Turkey	97	84
Indonesia	87	89
Thailand	86	85
Germany	85	45

*data is for 1997

TABLE 3.3   *Illegal Copies of CDs and Cassettes**

	Value ($ Millions)	Share of Domestic Market (%)
Russia	$165	65%
China	150	56
Paraguay	130	90
Bulgaria	125	90
Mexico	70	50
Israel	67	30
Czech Republic	63	6
Italy	60	20
Colombia	54	60
Peru	40	80

*data is for 1997

TABLE 3.4   *Illegal Copies of Videos**

	Value ($ Millions)	Share of Domestic Market (%)
Russia	$312	85%
Italy	220	30
China	120	75
Germany	72	22
India	66	80
Turkey	59	95
Mexico	55	55
Greece	50	25
Ukraine	40	99
Venezuela	40	70

*data is for 1997

closed sums from all major defendants except GE, which controls 38 percent of the world market for MRI machines. Not until June 1997 did a U.S. Federal Court of Appeals order GE to pay Fonar $128.7 million.[24]

Trademarks **Trademarks** are words or symbols distinguishing a product and its manufacturer. The Nike "swoosh" is a trademark, as is the name "SONY" as it appears on the firm's products. Consumers benefit from trademarks because they know what to expect when they buy a well-known brand. A bottle of beer with "Fosters" on the label is not expected to taste like one labeled "Heineken" or "Sapporo."

trademark
Property right in the form of words or symbols distinguishing a product and its manufacturer.

Trademark protection typically lasts indefinitely, provided the word or symbol continues to be distinctive. Ironically, this stipulation presents a problem for companies like Coca-Cola and Xerox, whose trademarks "Coke" and "Xerox" have evolved into generic terms for all products in their respective categories.

Designers who own trademarks such as Chanel, Christian Dior, and Gucci, have long been plagued by shoddily made counterfeit handbags, shoes, shirts, and other products. But recently, pirated products *of equal quality* are turning up, especially in Italy. Most Italian makers of luxury goods—notably leather and jewelry—outsource production to small manufacturers across the country. It's not hard, therefore, for these same artisans to counterfeit extra copies of a high-quality product for sale on the black market. Bootleg copies of a Prada backpack costing $500 in New York can be bought for $70 in Rome. Jewelry shops in Milan can buy Bulgari and Rolex watches for $300 and retail them for $2,500. Illegal commerce in Italy is now worth $6 billion annually and growing.[25]

Like trademark laws, enforcement policies differ by country. The maximum penalty in Italy is three years in prison and a $4,000 fine; in Germany, it's five years and an unlimited fine. But some progress toward standardization has been made. The European Union, for example, has opened a new trademark-protection office to police trademark infringement against firms operating in any EU country.

Copyrights **Copyrights** give creators of original works the freedom to publish or dispose of them as they choose. The existence of a copyright is typically denoted by inclusion of the well-known symbol ©, a date, and the copyright holder's name. A copyright holder has such rights as the following:

copyright
Property right giving creators of original works the freedom to publish or dispose of them as they choose.

➡ To reproduce the copyrighted work
➡ To derive new works from the copyrighted work
➡ To sell or distribute copies of the copyrighted work
➡ To perform the copyrighted work
➡ To display the copyrighted work publicly

Copyright holders include authors and publishers of literary works; composers of musical scores; developers of computer-software programs; and artists, photographers, and painters. Works created after January 1, 1978, are automatically copyrighted for the creator's lifetime plus 50 years. Publishing houses receive copyrights for either 75 years from the date of publication or 100 years after creation, whichever comes first. A copyright is granted for the *tangible expression* of an idea, not for the idea itself. For example, no one can copyright the idea of a movie about the sinking of the *Titanic*. However, once the film itself is made to express its creator's treatment of the subject, that film can be copyrighted. A major problem for software companies like Microsoft is that counterfeiters easily skirt weak copyright laws in many countries.

Copyrights are protected under the **Berne Convention**, an international copyright treaty to which the United States is a member, and the 1954 Universal Copyright Convention. More than 50 countries abide by one or both of these treaties.

Berne Convention
International treaty protecting copyrights.

PRODUCT SAFETY AND LIABILITY

Most countries have product safety laws that lay down standards to be met by manufactured products. **Product liability** holds manufacturers, sellers, and others, including individual company officers, responsible for damage, injury, or death caused by defective products. Injured parties can sue for both monetary compensation through *civil* lawsuits and fines, or imprisonment through *criminal* lawsuits. Civil suits are frequently settled before cases go to court.

product liability
Responsibility of manufacturers, sellers, and others for damage, injury, or death caused by defective products.

The United States has the toughest product liability laws in the world, with Europe a close second. Less developed and emerging countries have the weakest laws. By the same token, insurance premiums and legal expenses are greater in those nations with strong product liability laws. Awarded damages tend to be several times larger in the United States than in other developed countries.

Conforming to different international laws can be a complex process. Consider a product as seemingly straightforward as "Made in China" teddy bears. Bears that were assembled in China with parts made all over the world must meet manufacturing and safety specifications for customers in Brazil, Canada, the European Union, Japan, Mexico, and the United States. Before a teddy bear can be shipped to the United States, four different certificates from four different labs must be obtained. Each one certifies that the toy complies with various U.S. federal regulations, including ASTM F-963, the U.S. voluntary toy-safety standard. Teddy bears headed for Brazil need certification from a recognized U.S. or Brazilian laboratory. Shipments headed toward Japan must comply with Japanese toy-safety regulations, and those destined for sale in the European Union must comply with ENZI, the European safety standard.[26]

Enforcement of product liability laws differs from nation to nation. In the United States, for instance, tobacco companies are under attack for failing to warn consumers about the health effects of tobacco and nicotine. In countries like India and Sri Lanka, however, they are free from scrutiny by public-welfare organizations. Because of far less stringent regulation, the biggest market for U.S. cigarette makers is Asia, followed closely by eastern Europe. Philip Morris, the world's biggest tobacco company, increased international sales by 80 percent (to 660 billion cigarettes) between 1990 and 1997. In Poland market potential is still quite large despite the curbing of cigarette advertising, the raising of taxes, and the banning of smoking on the job. About 50 percent of all Polish adults smoke, compared to 25 percent in the United States.[27]

TAXATION

National governments use income and sales taxes for many purposes. They use tax revenue to pay government salaries, to build military capacity, and to shift earnings from people with high incomes to the poor. They also pass indirect taxes called *consumption taxes*, which serve two main purposes:

1. To help pay for the consequences of using a particular product
2. To make imports more expensive

Consumption taxes on such products as alcohol and tobacco help pay the health-care costs of treating resulting illnesses. Similarly, gasoline taxes help pay for road and bridge repairs needed to counteract the effects of vehicle use and weathering. Taxes on imports give locally made products an advantage among price-sensitive consumers.

As with other aspects of government regulation, countries differ in the portion of their citizens' incomes taken in taxes. Figure 3.1 shows the percentage of income the world's richest nations take from their citizens through various means of taxation. We

FIGURE 3.1

TOTAL TAX REVENUES

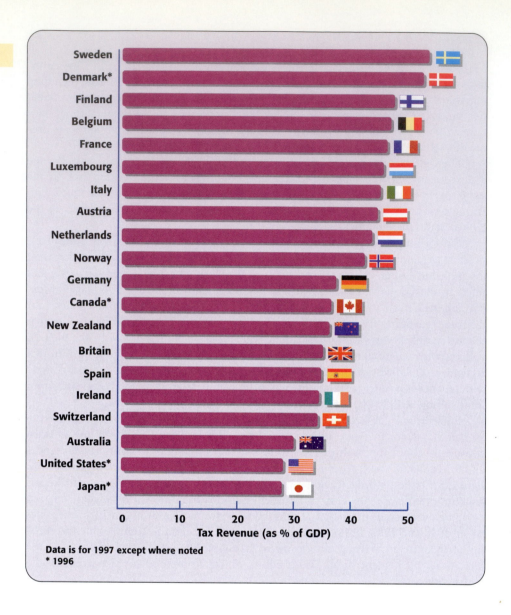

value added tax (VAT)

Tax levied on each party that adds value to a product throughout its production and distribution.

see that both Sweden and Denmark take more than 50 percent of national output, although citizens in the United States and Japan pay-in less than 30 percent.

Unlike the United States, many countries employ a so-called **value added tax (VAT)**—a tax levied on each party that adds value to a product throughout its production and distribution. Supporters of the VAT system contend that it distributes taxes on retail sales more evenly between producers and consumers. Suppose, for instance, that a shrimper sells the day's catch of shrimp for $1/kilogram and that the country's VAT is 10 percent (see Table 3.5). The shrimper, processor, wholesaler, and retailer pay taxes of $0.10, $0.07, $0.11, and $0.10, respectively, for the value that each adds to the product as it makes its way to consumers. Because the government collects taxes from each player on this team, consumers pay no tax at the point of sale. If, however, producers and distributors simply increase prices to compensate for their tax burdens, consumers end up paying the total amount taxed. So that the poor are not overly burdened, many countries exclude the VAT on certain items such as children's clothing.

TABLE 3.5	Effect of Value-Added Taxes (VAT)			
Production Stage	**Selling Price**	**Value Added**	**10% VAT**	**Total VAT**
Shrimper	$1.00	$1.00	$0.10	$0.10
Processor	1.70	0.70	0.07	0.17
Wholesaler	2.80	1.10	0.11	0.28
Retailer	3.80	1.00	0.10	0.38

ANTITRUST REGULATIONS

Laws designed to prevent companies from fixing prices, sharing markets, and gaining unfair monopoly advantages are called **antitrust laws**. Such laws try to provide consumers with a wide variety of products at fair prices. The United States has the strictest antitrust regulation in the world and is the strictest enforcer. Germany also has rather strict antitrust regulation. In Japan, the Fair Trade Commission enforces antitrust laws but is often ineffective because *absolute proof* of wrongdoing is needed to bring charges.

Companies based in strict antitrust countries often argue that they are at a disadvantage against competitors whose home countries condone *market sharing,* whereby competitors agree to serve only designated segments of a certain market. Thus firms in strict antitrust countries often lobby for exemptions in certain international transactions. Small businesses also argue that they could better compete against large international companies if they could join forces without fear of violating antitrust laws.

In the absence of a global antitrust enforcement agency, antitrust complaints are often stirred by an urge to protect local markets rather than by any real threat of unfair competition. For instance, the European Commission challenged the merger of U.S. airplane makers Boeing and McDonnell Douglas in 1997. The commission argued that the merger would increase Boeing-McDonnell's market share in Europe to a level that would impede competition. In the United States, meanwhile, many industry observers viewed the EU complaint as a ploy to protect the large European aerospace company, Airbus Industrie. To win commission approval, Boeing made certain concessions, such as adjusting contracts so that it could not become the exclusive supplier to several U.S. air carriers.

In 1998, pressure from Australia, Canada, and Europe forced the U.S. accounting firms Ernst & Young and KPMG Peat Marwick to abandon merger plans. The official response of those nations' regulatory bodies indicated that they would refuse to approve the merger, principally because of its projected impact in their home markets.[28] Experts admit that until a neutral governing body is established it will be hard to distinguish nationalist self-interest from genuine concern about competitive fairness.[29]

> **antitrust laws**
> Laws designed to prevent companies from fixing prices, sharing markets, and gaining unfair monopoly advantages.

BUSINESS AND INTERNATIONAL RELATIONS

Political relationships between a company's home country and those in which it does business will affect its international activities. Favorable political relationships foster stable business environments and increase international cooperation in many areas, including the development of communications and distribution infrastructures. In turn, a stable environment requires a strong legal system through which disputes can be resolved quickly and fairly. In general, favorable political relations lead to increased business opportunities and lower risk.

To generate stable business environments, some countries have turned to *multilateral agreements*—treaties concluded among several nations, each of whom agrees to abide by treaty terms even if tensions develop. According to the European Union's founding treaty, goods, services, and citizens of member nations are free to move across members' borders. Every nation must continue to abide by such terms even if it has a conflict with another member. Thus although Britain and France disagree on many issues, neither can treat goods, services, and citizens moving from one country to the other any differently than it treats those of any other EU nation.

THE UNITED NATIONS

United Nations (*U.N.*)
International organization formed after World War II to provide leadership in fostering peace and stability around the world.

Although individual nations sometimes have the power to influence the course of events in certain parts of the world, they cannot monitor political activities everywhere at once. Similarly, no single country has the resources or support to act as an undisputed global leader. The **United Nations (UN)** was formed after World War II to provide leadership in fostering peace and stability around the world. The U.N. and its many agencies provide food and medical supplies, educational supplies and training, and financial resources to poorer member nations. The U.N. receives its funding from member contributions based primarily on gross national product (GNP). Practically all nations in the world are U.N. members—except for Switzerland and several other small countries and territories that have only observer status.

The U.N. strives to maintain a neutral position, free of political bias. By mid-1997, for instance, years of bad grain harvests and poor economic policy had made it quite difficult for the government of North Korea to feed its people. North Korean leaders asked for assistance from Japan, South Korea, and the United States. But because hostilities remain between these three nations and North Korea, the three nations demanded political concessions before beginning grain shipments. Under the cover of the United Nations, however, all three made unconditional shipments of grain and other foodstuffs to help ease North Korea's food shortage.

Figure 3.2 gives an overview of the U.N. system. It is headed by a Secretary General, who is elected by all members for a five-year term, and consists of six main organs:

➡ All members have an equal vote in the *General Assembly*, which discusses and recommends action on any matter that falls within the U.N. Charter. It approves the U.N. budget and the makeup of the other bodies.

➡ The *Security Council* consists of 15 members. Five (China, France, the United Kingdom, Russia, and the United States) are permanent. Ten others are elected by the General Assembly for two-year terms. The Council is responsible for ensuring international peace and security, and all U.N. members are bound by its decisions.

➡ As you can see from Figure 3.2, the *Economic and Social Council*, which is responsible for economics, human rights, and social matters, administers a host of smaller organizations and specialized agencies.

➡ The five permanent members of the Security Council make up the *Trusteeship Council*, which administrates all trustee territories under U.N. custody.

➡ The *International Court of Justice* consists of 15 judges elected by the General Assembly and Security Council. It can hear disputes only between nations, not cases brought against individuals or corporations. It has no compulsory jurisdiction, and its decisions can be, and have been, disregarded by specific nations.

➡ Headed by the Secretary General, the *Secretariat* administers the operations of the U.N.

A FINAL WORD

Differences in political and legal systems create both costs and risks for international companies. Because of the inherent connections among politics, laws, and culture, gaining satisfactory control over costs and risks is extremely difficult in any national

FIGURE 3.2   **THE UNITED NATIONS SYSTEM**

Figure 3.2 — The United Nations System

INTERNATIONAL COURT OF JUSTICE

GENERAL ASSEMBLY

ECONOMIC AND SOCIAL COUNCIL

SECURITY COUNCIL

TRUSTEESHIP COUNCIL

SECRETARIAT

- Main and other sessional committees
- Standing committees and ad hoc bodies
- Other subsidiary organs and related bodies

UNRWA
United Nations Relief and Works Agency for Palestine Refugees in the Near East

IAEA
International Atomic Energy Agency

INSTRAW
International Research and Training Institute for the Advancement of Women

ODCCP
United Nations Office for Drug Control and Crime Prevention

OHCHR
Office of the United Nations High Commissioner for Human Rights

UNCHS
United Nations Centre for Human Settlements (Habitat)

UNCTAD
United Nations Conference on Trade and Development

UNDP
United Nations Development Program

UNIFEM
United Nations Development Fund for Women

UNV
United Nations Volunteers

UNEP
United Nations Environment Program

UNFPA
United Nations Population Fund

UNHCR
Office of the United Nations High Commissioner for Refugees

UNICEF
United Nations Children's Fund

UNICRI
United Nations Interregional Crime and Justice Research Institute

UNIDIR
United Nations Institute for Disarmament Research

UNITAR
United Nations Institute for Training and Research

UNOPS
United Nations Office for Project Services

UNU
United Nations University

WFP (UN/FAO)
World Food Program

ITC
International Trade Centre UNCTAD/WTO

FUNCTIONAL COMMISSIONS
Commission for Social Development
→ United Nations Research Institute for Social Development (UNRISD)
Commission on Human Rights
Commission on Narcotic Drugs
Commission on Science and Technology for Development
Commission on Sustainable Development
Commission on the Status of Women
Commission on Population and Development
Statistical Commission

REGIONAL COMMISSIONS
Economic Commission for Africa (ECA)
Economic Commission for Europe (ECE)
Economic Commission for Latin America and the Caribbean (ECLAC)
Economic and Social Commission for Asia and the Pacific (ESCAP)
Economic and Social Commission for Western Asia (ESCWA)

SESSIONAL AND STANDING COMMITTEES

EXPERT, AD HOC AND RELATED BODIES

- Military Staff Committee
- Standing committees and ad hoc bodies
- International Tribunal for the former Yugoslavia
- International Criminal Tribunal for Rwanda

UNSCOM
United Nations Special Commission (Iraq)

ILO
International Labour Organization

FAO
Food and Agriculture Organization of the United Nations

UNESCO
United Nations Educational, Scientific and Cultural Organization

WHO
World Health Organization

WORLD BANK GROUP

IBRD
International Bank for Reconstruction and Development

IDA
International Development Association

IFC
International Finance Corporation

MIGA
Multilateral Investment Guarantee Agency

IMF
International Monetary Fund

ICAO
International Civil Aviation Organization

UPU
Universal Postal Union

ITU
International Telecommunication Union

WMO
World Meteorological Organization

IMO
International Maritime Organization

WIPO
World Intellectual Property Organization

IFAD
International Fund for Agricultural Development

UNIDO
United Nations Industrial Development Organization

WTO*
World Trade Organization

OSG
Office of the Secretary-General

OIOS
Office of Internal Oversight Services

OLA
Office of Legal Affairs

DPA
Department of Political Affairs

DDA
Department of Disarmament Affairs

DPKO
Department of Peacekeeping Operations

OCHA
Office for the Coordination of Humanitarian Affairs

DESA
Department of Economic and Social Affairs

DGAACS
Department of General Assembly Affairs and Conference Services

DPI
Department of Public Information

DM
Department of Management

UNSECOORD
Office of the United Nations Security Coordinator

UNOG
UN Office at Geneva

UNOV
UN Office at Vienna

PEACEKEEPING OPERATIONS

UNTSO
United Nations Truce Supervision Organization (HQ: Jerusalem), June 1948 to date

UNMOGIP
United Nations Military Observer Group in India and Pakistan, January 1949 to date

UNFICYP
United Nations Peacekeeping Force in Cyprus, March 1964 to date

UNDOF
United Nations Disengagement Observer Force (Golan Heights), June 1974 to date

UNIFIL
United Nations Interim Force in Lebanon, March 1978 to date

UNIKOM
United Nations Iraq-Kuwait Observation Mission, April 1991 to date

MINURSO
United Nations Mission for the Referendum in Western Sahara, April 1991 to date

UNOMIG
United Nations Observer Mission in Georgia, August 1993 to date

UNMOT
United Nations Mission of Observers in Tajikistan, December 1994 to date

UNPREDEP
United Nations Preventive Deployment Force (The former Yugoslav Republic of Macedonia), March 1995 to date

UNMIBH
United Nations Mission in Bosnia and Herzegovina, December 1995 to date

UNMOP
United Nations Mission of Observers in Prevlaka, January 1996 to date

MONUA
United Nations Observer Mission in Angola, July 1997 to date

MINPONUH
United Nations Civilian Police Mission in Haiti, December 1997 to date

United Nations Civilian Police Support Group
(Croatia) January 1998 to date

MINURCA
United Nations Mission in the Central African Republic, April 1998 to date

▶ United Nations programs and organs
■ Specialized agencies and other autonomous organizations within the system
● Other commissions, committees and ad hoc and related bodies

* Although not a specialized agency it cooperates with the United Nations

business environment, even the most stable. Even so, understanding differences in culture, politics, and law is the first step for any company that hopes to manage the risks of doing business in unfamiliar environments.

In the next chapter, we will continue our discussion of national business environments by examining the different ways in which *economic systems* function. Our study of national business environments will then be complete.

 There is a variety of additional material available on the companion Web site that accompanies this text. You can access this information by visiting the Web site at ⟨**www.prenhall.com/wild**⟩.

summary

① Distinguish among the main types of *political systems.* A *political system* consists of the structures, processes, and activities by which a nation governs itself. It derives from the history and *culture* of the nation's people, and it is generally characterized by either *wide participation*, whereby large numbers of people can and do influence the system, or *narrow participation*, whereby only a few people may act to influence it.

Today, two main types of political systems are most common. In a *democratic system*, leaders are elected directly by the wide participation of the people or the people's representatives. Very few pure democracies exist. Most take the form of the *representative democracy*, in which citizens nominate individuals from their groups to represent their political needs and views. Typically, democracies guarantee five rights: (1) freedom of expression, (2) periodic elections, (3) full civil and property rights, (4) minority rights, and (5) nonpolitical bureaucracies.

In a *totalitarian system*, individuals govern without the support of the people, maintain control over nearly all aspects of people's lives, and do not tolerate opposing viewpoints. Under *theocratic totalitarianism*, a country's religious leaders are also its political leaders who enforce laws and regulations based on religious and totalitarian beliefs. Under *secular totalitarianism*, political leaders rely on military and bureaucratic power. There are three forms of secular totalitarianism. Under *communist totalitarianism*, the government aims for social equality by planning all types of economic activity. Under *tribal totalitarianism*, one tribe imposes its will on other populations in the country. *Right-wing totalitarianism* is characterized by capitalist economics but denies most political freedoms.

② Identify the origins of *political risk* and how managers can reduce its effects. *Political risk* is the likelihood that a government or society will undergo political changes that negatively affect local business activity. It arises from a variety of sources, including (1) corrupt or poor political leadership; (2) frequent changes in the form of government; (3) political involvement of religious or military leaders; (4) an unstable political system; (5) conflict among races, religions, or ethnic groups; and (6) poor relations with other countries. *Macro risk* threatens all companies in a nation regardless of industry. *Micro risk* threatens firms within a particular industry or even smaller groups.

There are at least five different forms of political risk: (1) conflict and violence, (2) terrorism and kidnapping, (3) property seizure, (4) policy changes, and (5) local content requirements. *Property seizure*—the taking of a company's assets by a local government—may take one of three forms: *confiscation* (forced transfer of assets without compensation); *expropriation* (forced transfer with compensation); or *nationalization* (forced takeover of an entire industry). *Local content requirements* are regulations requiring manufacturers to use local resources.

In managing political risk, companies can adopt one or more of five strategies: (1) *avoidance* (not investing in a country); (2) *adaptation* (incorporating risk into business strategy); (3) *dependency maintenance* (keeping the host nation dependent on the firm's local activities); (4) *information gathering* (monitoring local political events); and (5) *political influence* (such as by *lobbying*—hiring people to represent the firm's views on local political matters).

③ List the main types of *legal systems* and explain how they differ. A *legal system* is a country's set of laws and regulations, including the processes by which its laws are enacted and enforced and the ways in which its courts hold parties accountable for their actions. There are three categories of legal systems. Under *common law*, the justice system decides cases by interpreting the law on the basis of *tradition* (legal history), *precedent* (past cases), and *usage* (application of laws in specific situations). *Civil law* is based on a detailed set of written rules and statutes that constitute a legal *code*. All obligations, responsibilities, and privileges follow directly from the written code. *Theocratic law* is based on religious teachings.

4 **Describe the major *legal issues* facing international companies.** Laws around the world adhere to widely varying standards, and there is no well-defined body of international law. There are, however, some efforts being made to achieve *standardization*—uniformity in interpreting and applying laws in more than one country.

Chief among the legal issues affecting international business are the following: (1) protection of *property rights* (legal rights to resources and any income they generate); (2) protection of *intellectual property*, including *patents, trademarks*, and *copyrights* that result from intellectual talent and ability; (3) *product liability* standards applying to companies responsible for damage, injury, or death caused by

defective products; (4) *taxation* policies (which may discourage the use of a product or increase the prices of imports); and (5) *antitrust regulations* designed to prevent companies from fixing prices, sharing markets, and gaining unfair monopoly advantages.

5 **Explain how *international relations* affect international business activities.** Political relations between a company's home country and those with which it does business strongly affect its international activities. In general, favorable political relations lead to increased opportunity and stable business environments. Because no single country has the resources or the support to act as an undisputed global leader, the mission of the *United Nations* (*U.N.*) is to provide leadership in fostering peace and stability around the world. The U.N. strives to achieve a neutral position, free of political bias. Although its global peacekeeping efforts have had mixed results, its many agencies continue to aid poorer nations by providing food and medical supplies, educational supplies and training, and financial resources.

questions **for review**

1. What is a *political system*? Explain the relation between a "political system" and a "culture."

2. Distinguish between *wide* and *narrow political participation*.

3. What is *democracy*? Describe the effects of a democratic environment on business activities.

4. What is the difference between a *pure democracy* and a *representative democracy*?

5. What is a *coalition government*?

6. What is *totalitarianism*? Explain the different forms of totalitarianism and describe how each affects business.

7. Define *political risk*. Identify the five main types of political risk and explain how each affects international business activities.

8. Distinguish among *confiscation, expropriation*, and *nationalization*.

9. List five different methods that businesses use to manage political risk.

10. Describe the three main types of *legal systems*. Identify the differences among them and give examples of countries employing each type.

11. How does *standardization* of laws benefit international companies?

12. Identify the different categories and sub-categories of *intellectual property*.

13. What are *property rights*?

14. What are *product liability* laws? Explain how product liability laws differ from country to country.

15. Why do countries collect *taxes*? What are the ramifications for international business?

16. How does the enforcement of *antitrust laws* benefit consumers?

17. How do positive *international relations* benefit the activities of international companies?

questions **for discussion**

1. The Internet is forcing politicians to change their governing methods. How might the Internet affect change in totalitarian political systems like Cuba and North Korea? What might the Net's future expansion mean for nations with theocratic systems (for example, Iran)? What changes might technology bring to the way that democracies function?

2. Under a totalitarian political system, the Indonesian economy has grown quite strong over the last 30 years. In India, meanwhile, the economic system of the world's largest functioning democracy has been relatively poor over the past 40 years. Relying on what you learned in this chapter, do you think the Indonesian economy grew despite, or because of, a totalitarian regime? What might explain India's relatively poor performance under a democratic political system?

3. The United Nations seems to be experiencing an identity crisis. What do you think should be its role and responsibilities? Do you believe the U.N. should continue in its present form? What opportunities and challenges will likely confront the U.N. in the near future?

4. Consider the following statement: "Democratic political systems, as opposed to totalitarian ones, provide international companies with more stable environments in which to do business." Do you agree? Why or why not? Support your argument with specific country examples.

in practice

This chapter discussed the nuances of different political and legal systems that make international business activities dynamic, yet fraught with potential pitfalls. Read the following excerpt from the *Wall Street Journal* and answer the questions at the end.

India Clears Insurance Reform

In news that could alter the game plans of some of the world's biggest insurance companies, India decided to open the nation's insurance business to the private sector and allow foreign investor's to acquire stakes of up to 26 percent in Indian insurers.

The decision, which still needs the approval of Parliament, is expected to give foreign investors a bit more confidence in the economy of the world's biggest democracy—especially since the proposal managed to stay on track and intact in recent weeks.

There had been fears that when the matter moved from a committee to the full cabinet, left-leaning coalition members might force the government to lower that foreign-investment ceiling to 20 percent.

1. Give a brief sketch of India's political and legal systems (3 to 4 paragraphs). Why is it typical for one coalition government or another to be in power in India? What is meant by the phrase "left-leaning coalition members?" Why would they want to lower the investment ceiling?

2. Briefly describe the current relations between India and your home country (2 to 3 paragraphs). Next, identify several instances of how the status of these relations has benefited or damaged the operations of businesses from either your country or India. Be specific.

3. Update this article by searching the business press or the World Wide Web for relevant information. Was the foreign investment law eventually passed? If so, what final ceiling was agreed upon? If so, did companies enter the Indian insurance market as was hoped? If the law was not passed, what caused its failure in Parliament?

projects

1. Two groups of four students each will debate the ethics of doing business in countries with totalitarian governments. After the first student from each side has spoken, the second student will question the opposing side's arguments, looking for holes and inconsistencies. The third student will attempt to answer these arguments. A fourth student will present a summary of each side's arguments. Finally, the class will vote to determine which team has offered the more compelling argument.

2. Select two recent articles from business magazines (in print or on their Web sites). One article should discuss the political element of a country's business environment, the other a legal element of the same environment. Potential topics include corruption, and pending legislation relevant to interna-

tional companies. Summarize both articles and explain what businesses can do to prepare for, or respond to, any special problems the articles discuss. Here are some good starting points for your research:

- *The Economist* ⟨**www.economist.com**⟩
- *Far Eastern Economic Review* ⟨**www.feer.com**⟩
- *Financial Times* ⟨**www.ft.com**⟩

3. Select a country that interests you. What type of political and legal systems does the country have? Do free elections take place? Is the government heavily involved in the economy? Is the legal system effective and impartial? Do political and legal conditions suggest that it should be further considered as a potential market? Present your findings to the class.

business case 3
INTELLECTUAL PROPERTY RIGHTS IN ASIA

As we saw in this chapter, the piracy of intellectual property—computer software, films, books, music CDs, and pharmaceutical drugs—is a common problem. Due to piracy, companies doing business in Asian countries (including China, India, Indonesia, Japan, the Philippines, South Korea, Taiwan, and Thailand) lose more than $3 billion in sales every year. Often, criminals are connected to political leaders and receive legal protection from prosecution.

The following two examples are illustrative:

➡ Indian law gives international pharmaceutical firms five- to seven-year patents on *processes used to manufacture drugs*—but *not on the drugs themselves*. Local companies pirate this property of the international pharmaceutical companies by slightly modifying production processes in order to arrive at the finished drugs.

➡ In China, political protection for pirates of intellectual property is common. In fact, many factories churning out pirated products are operated by government officials, people working for the government, and even the People's Liberation Army (China's national army). Many operate on government-owned land.

Despite high piracy rates, because of expanding markets and rapid economic growth, Asian countries remain attractive to international companies. Although the U.S. government complains about China's piracy practices, it tends to renew normal trading relations status (formerly known as most favored nation (MFN) trading status) to China annually.

thinking globally

1. What actions can companies and governments take to ensure that products cannot be easily pirated? Be specific.

2. Do you think that the international business community is being too lax about the abuse of intellectual property rights in China and other Asian countries? Are international companies simply afraid to speak out for fear of jeopardizing access to the markets of these countries?

3. The Internet is making it easier to transmit digital information around the world. This increased trade in digital communication poses a threat to intellectual property because digital technology allows the manufacture of perfect clones of original works. How might the Internet affect intellectual-property laws?

4. How might the Internet potentially *reduce* a company's ability to sell its products internationally?

a question of ethics

1. Pharmaceutical marker Glaxo Wellcome holds patents on the powerful anti-AIDS drug AZT. Those patents protect its monopoly on the drug until the year 2005 and prevent other companies from manufacturing cheaper generic versions. For an average patient, the annual cost of the drug is about $3,000. However, makers of generic drugs claim that this price could be cut in half. Is it ethical for the patent holder to keep lower-cost versions off the market? Why or why not?

   Think, too, about the possibilities for AZT in developing countries, where AIDS has reached epidemic proportions. In 1994, it was discovered that AZT lowered by nearly 70 percent the risk of a mother transmitting the HIV virus to her baby. This finding, however, meant little to women who can afford neither AZT nor the modern clinics needed to administer it. Should pharmaceutical companies donate AZT to those in need, as Merck did with Metzican, a treatment for river blindness in tropical Africa and Latin America?[30]

2. At a shopping arcade in Shanghai, China, several hundred small shops sell all sorts of computer paraphernalia. Although a few shops sell original packaged software, neighboring stores outsell them with illegal copies of the same software at one-tenth the price. Sophisticated business application software that sells in the United States for hundreds of dollars can be had here for just a few bucks. Government officials in Asia sometimes have different attitudes toward software piracy than their counterparts in the United States. Why such a casual attitude toward theft on a billion-dollar scale? "A certain amount of piracy is welcomed," suspects one official at Lotus 1-2-3, "because very few people can afford software at market prices."[31]

   Imagine that you're the owner of a fledgling graphics company in Shanghai. With an income of only a few thousand dollars a year, you cannot afford to buy the original packaged graphics software that you need to get your business off the ground. Do you think that piracy is always unethical, or do you think that despite its illegality, it can help facilitate small-business development in your country?

3. To pressure the government of Myanmar (formerly Burma) to end its repressive policies, the Clinton administration in 1997 imposed sanctions on U.S. companies investing in Myanmar. Companies with existing business in the country at that time were exempt from the sanctions. One such U.S. company is oil giant Unocal, which is part of an international consortium investing $1.2 billion to develop Myanmar's Yadana natural gas fields.

   Using the Internet and more traditional forums, grassroots protesters have accused Unocal and its partners of collaborating with the Myanmar government. They have accused Unocal of everything from using slave labor to ignoring human rights abuses by the military regime. Top Unocal executives respond that another large company would gladly take its place if it withdrew. Unocal believes that its presence is helping the 35,000 people who live near the project area, where Unocal and Total of France are spending $6 million on education, medical care, and other improvements. What do you think is the ethical stance to take here?[32]

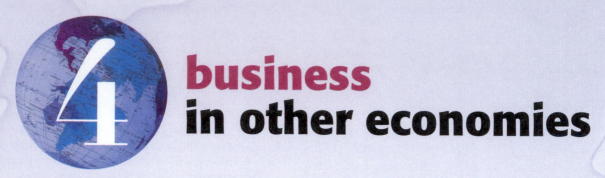

business
in other economies

Beacons

A Look Back

CHAPTER 3 discussed ways in which different political and legal systems affect international business activities. We also explored some of the ways managers can cope with the risks presented by political and legal uncertainties.

A Look at This Chapter

This chapter introduces and explains different economic systems. We examine the relation between culture and economics and describe their combined effects on international business. We also discuss economic development and the difficulties faced by countries undergoing transition to market economies.

A Look Ahead

CHAPTER 5 introduces us to a major form of international business activity—international trade. We examine the patterns of international trade and outline several theories that attempt to explain why nations conduct trade.

Learning Objectives

After studying this chapter, you should be able to

1 Identify the three main categories of *economic systems*.

2 Define *economic development* and explain how it can be measured.

3 Describe the process of *economic transition*.

4 Identify obstacles to business in *transitional economies*.

5 Describe the experiences of *nations and regions* undergoing economic transition.

"Individualism," declared the last North Vietnamese President Ho Chi Minh, "is the cruel enemy of socialism." For years, countries under communist and socialist systems criticized industrialized nations for emphasizing individualism and free markets over collective economic welfare. But today it seems that communism and extreme socialism are being swept into the dustbin of history as economies based on free-market principles thrive.

By making their economies as efficient as possible, reform-minded governments everywhere are trying to keep pace with neighbors by instituting free-market reforms. But economic reform is hardly an easy task. Corruption, unemployment, income inequality, and pollution are just some of the common side effects of massive economic change. The corruption and underground economies that so often spring up during reform reduce governments' revenues and thereby hamper further needed reforms. In fact, the confusion surrounding reform often makes corruption attractive and inevitable.

Chu Shijan is manager of Red Pagoda, a tobacco company. He is a local hero for bringing jobs and prosperity (but mostly cash) to his city, Yuxi, China. For years, the Chinese government required Chu to report his company's income at the state-mandated selling price for cigarettes. But that price was only about one-half the black-market price. Thus Chu was selling his cigarettes at twice the price as he was reporting for tax purposes. Taking advantage of the system, Chu tucked away $145 million in company bank accounts. As one Chinese businessman put it, under conditions such as these, "Only a fool reports his company's income accurately."[1]

Like culture and systems of politics and law, economic systems differ from one country to another. In Chapter 2, we saw that one defining element of a culture is its tendency toward *individualism* or *collectivism*. Economic systems in individual-oriented cultures tend to provide incentives and rewards for individual business initiative. Group-oriented cultures tend to offer fewer such incentives and rewards. In the United States, for example, *entrepreneurs*—businesspeople who accept the risks and opportunities involved in creating and operating new business ventures—are rewarded with a top corporate tax rate of about 40 percent. Meanwhile, the less individual-oriented cultures of Germany, Italy, and Japan have corporate tax rates in excess of 50 percent.[2]

Furthermore, national culture affects a nation's level of economic development. In turn, the development of a country's economy can dramatically affect many aspects of its culture. In this chapter, we introduce the world's different economic systems and examine the link between culture and economics. We begin by explaining the three main types of economic systems. Then we explore economic development and ways of classifying nations using several development indicators. We conclude by looking at ways in which different countries are dealing with economic challenges and the implementation of market-based economic reform.

ECONOMIC SYSTEMS

economic system
Structure and processes that a country uses to allocate its resources and conduct its commercial activities.

A country's **economic system** consists of the structure and processes that it uses to allocate its resources and conduct its commercial activities. No nation is either completely "individualist" or completely "collectivist" in its cultural orientation. Likewise, no economic system reflects a completely individual or group orientation. The economies of all nations express a blend of individual and group values (the latter of which are often reflected in government involvement in business activities). In other words, no economy is entirely focused on individual reward at the expense of social well-being. Nor is any economy so completely focused on social well-being that it places no value on individual incentive and enterprise.

Because every system displays a tendency toward individual- or group-oriented economic values, we can, as in Figure 4.1, organize systems along a continuum that characterizes them as *centrally planned, mixed,* or *market economies.* Let's take a look at each of these three types of economic systems.

CENTRALLY PLANNED ECONOMY

centrally planned economy
Economic system in which a nation's land, factories, and other economic resources are owned by the government which plans nearly all economic activity.

A **centrally planned economy** is a system in which a nation's land, factories, and other economic resources are owned by the government. Government makes nearly all economy-related decisions—including who produces what and the prices of products, labor, and capital. Central planning agencies specify production goals for factories and other production units and even decide prices. In the former Soviet Union, for in-

FIGURE 4.1

CONTINUUM OF ECONOMIC SYSTEMS

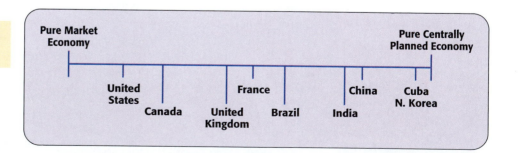

stance, communist officials set prices for such staples as milk, bread, eggs, and other essential goods. The ultimate goal is to achieve a wide range of political, social, and economic objectives by taking complete control over production and distribution of the nation's resources.

Origins of the Centrally Planned Economy   Central planning is rooted in the ideology that the welfare of the group is more important than individual well-being. Just as group-oriented cultures emphasize group over individual goals, a centrally planned economy strives to achieve economic and social equality.

The German philosopher Karl Marx popularized the idea of central economic planning in the nineteenth century. Marx's ideas were a reaction to the hardship he witnessed working people endure in Europe during and following the Industrial Revolution. Marx argued that the economy could not be reformed, but that it must be overthrown and replaced with a more equitable "communist" system.

Different versions of Marx's ideas were implemented in the twentieth century by means of violent upheaval. Revolutions installed totalitarian (see Chapter 3) economic and political systems in Russia in 1917, China and North Korea in the late 1940s, and Cuba in 1959. By the 1970s, central planning was the economic law in lands stretching across central and eastern Europe (Czechoslovakia, Hungary, Poland, Yugoslavia, Romania, Bulgaria, Albania, East Germany), Asia (China, Vietnam, North Korea, and Cambodia), Africa (Angola and Mozambique), and Latin America (Cuba and Nicaragua).

Decline of Central Planning   In the late 1980s, however, nation after nation began to dismantle communist central planning in favor of market-based economies (see Map 3.2 in Chapter 3, pp. 86–87). Economists, historians, and political scientists attribute the collapse of centrally planned economies to a combination of four factors.

Failure to Create Economic Value   Central planners paid little attention to the task of producing quality goods and services at the lowest possible cost. In other words, they failed to see that commercial activities succeed when they create economic value for customers. Along the way, scarce resources were wasted in the pursuit of commercial activities that were not self-sustaining.

Failure to Provide Incentives   Government ownership of economic resources drastically reduced incentives for people and organizations to maximize the benefits obtained from those resources. There were few incentives to create new technologies, new products, and new production methods (except in the areas of aerospace, nuclear power, and other sciences, in which government scientists excelled). The result was little or no economic growth and consistently low standards of living.

Even today, for example, North Korea remains perhaps the most closed economy in the world. For the most part, the policy of *juche* (self-reliance) is causing extreme hardship for its people. After floods in 1995 and 1996 wiped out or badly damaged 20 percent of the nation's crops, the government was forced to cut rice rations to about half a bowl per day.[3] Shortages were so severe because government policy had systematically eliminated incentives to create wealth and develop effective production techniques.

Failure to Measure Up   The world took note of high rates of economic growth in countries like Hong Kong, Singapore, South Korea, and Taiwan—the so-called "four tigers." The realization that a once-poor region of the world had achieved such growth awakened central planners. They realized that an economic system based on private ownership fosters growth much better than one hampered by central planning. This belief persists despite economic difficulties in Asia since mid-1997.

Failure to Satisfy Consumer Needs Would-be consumers in many centrally planned economies were tired of standards of living that had slipped far below those of their counterparts in predominantly market economies. Ironically, although central planning was conceived as a means for creating a more equitable system for distributing wealth, too many central planners failed even to provide such basic necessities as adequate food, housing, and medical care. Underground economies (black markets) for all kinds of goods and services flourished and in some cases even outgrew "official" economies. Prices on black markets were much higher than official prices set by governments.

MIXED ECONOMY

mixed economy
Economic system in which land, factories, and other economic resources are more equally split between private and government ownership.

A **mixed economy** is a system in which land, factories, and other economic resources are more equally split between private and government ownership. In a mixed economy, the government owns fewer economic resources than the government in a centrally planned economy. In a mixed economy, the government tends to control those economic sectors that it considers important to national security and long-term stability. Such sectors usually include iron and steel manufacturing (for building military equipment), oil and gas production (to guarantee continued manufacturing and availability), and automobiles (to guarantee employment for a large portion of the workforce). Many mixed economies also maintain generous welfare systems to support the unemployed and provide health care for the general population.

Mixed economies are found all around the world: France, Germany, Spain, Norway, Denmark, and Sweden in Western Europe; Brazil in Latin America; South Africa; and India, Indonesia, Malaysia, Pakistan, and Sri Lanka in Asia. Although all the governments of these nations do not centrally plan their economies, they all influence economic activity by means of special incentives, including hefty subsidies to key industries.

Origins of the Mixed Economy Proponents of mixed economies contend that a successful economic system not only must be efficient and innovative but also should protect society from the excesses of unchecked individualism and organizational greed. The goal is to achieve low unemployment, low poverty, steady economic growth, and an equitable distribution of wealth by means of the most effective policies.

Proponents point out that throughout the 1990s, European and U.S. rates of productivity and growth were almost identical. Although the United States has created more jobs, it has done so at the cost of widening social inequality. Proponents argue that nations with mixed economies should not dismantle their social-welfare institutions but modernize them so that they contribute to national competitiveness. Austria, the Netherlands, and Sweden are taking this route. In the Netherlands, for example, labor unions and the government agreed to an epic deal involving wage restraint, shorter working hours, budget discipline, new tolerance for part-time and temporary work, and the trimming of social benefits. As a result, Dutch unemployment is just 6.6 percent, and the country has recently created 200,000 jobs in just two years.[4] Jobless rates elsewhere in Europe are typically at least twice as high.

Decline of Mixed Economies Many mixed economies are converting to market-based systems. Reasons for the decline of mixed economies are similar to those for centrally planned economies. When assets are owned by the government, there seems to be less incentive to eliminate waste and practice innovation. Extensive government ownership tends to result in a lack of responsibility and accountability, rising costs, defective products, and slow economic growth. Many government-owned businesses in mixed economies needed large infusions of taxpayers' money to survive as world-class competitors. In turn, taxes and prices were higher and standards of living lower. Underpinning the move toward more market-based systems is large-scale *privatization*.

Move Toward Privatization The selling of government-owned economic resources to private operators is called **privatization**. The main goal of privatization is to increase economic efficiency. It also removes subsidies formerly paid to government-owned companies and curtails the practice of appointing managers for political reasons rather than reasons of managerial expertise. Because privatized companies compete in open markets for material, labor, and capital, they can go out of business if they do not produce competitive products at fair prices. This is extremely rare for government-owned companies.

To improve its competitiveness, France has recently sold off more than $30 billion worth of government assets.[5] But even as France is privatizing its government-owned businesses, the French electorate continues to hold fast to a deeply embedded tradition of social welfare. Indeed, in one recent poll, 66 percent of respondents preferred France's combination of rich benefits and high unemployment to the low jobless rates and smaller social safety net of the United States. This attitude was certainly borne out by the 1997 election of a left-of-center government. "Here," reports Ernest Antoine-Seilliere, president of the French conglomerate CGIP, "social security and social solidarity weigh more than efficiency."[6]

MARKET ECONOMY

In a **market economy**, the majority of a nation's land, factories, and other economic resources are privately owned, whether by individuals or businesses. Nearly all economy-related decisions—including who produces what and the prices of products, labor, and capital—are determined by the interplay of two forces:

➡ **Supply**—the quantity of a good or service that producers are willing to provide at a specific selling price.

➡ **Demand**—the quantity of a good or service that buyers are willing to purchase at a specific selling price.

As supply and demand change for a good or service, so does its selling price. The lower the price, the more people will demand the product; the higher the price, the less people will demand it. Likewise, the lower the price, the smaller the quantity that producers will supply; the higher the price, the more they will supply. In this respect, supply and demand are dictated by what is called the "price mechanism."

Chocolate lovers, for example, should consider the story told by the three graphs in Figure 4.2. Figure 4.2(a) shows that, despite some ups and downs, worldwide consumption of cocoa, the principal ingredient in chocolate, has begun to outstrip production. Figure 4.2(b) shows that total worldwide reserves have consequently begun to fall. The pressure is being felt from both the demand side (consumption in such countries as Germany, Britain, France, Japan, and especially the United States has risen consistently over the past decade) and the supply side (disease and pests have plagued crops in such producer countries as the Ivory Coast, Ghana, Indonesia, Brazil, Nigeria, and Malaysia). Figure 4.2(c) shows that the price of cocoa futures—agreements to buy cocoa at a future date—on the New York Coffee, Sugar and Cocoa Exchange have risen during the same period.[7]

Origins of the Market Economy Market economics is rooted in the belief that individual concerns should be placed above group concerns. In this view, the group benefits when individuals receive incentives and rewards to act in certain ways. If people are allowed to own their homes, for example, they are more likely to take care of the property. Conversely, under a system of publicly owned property, individuals have little incentive to care for property.

privatization
Policy of selling government-owned economic resources to private companies and individuals.

market economy
Economic system in which the majority of a nation's land, factories, and other economic resources are privately owned, whether by individuals or businesses.

supply
Quantity of a good or service that producers are willing to provide at a specific selling price.

demand
Quantity of a good or service that buyers are willing to purchase at a specific selling price.

FIGURE 4.2   COCOA SUPPLY AND DEMAND

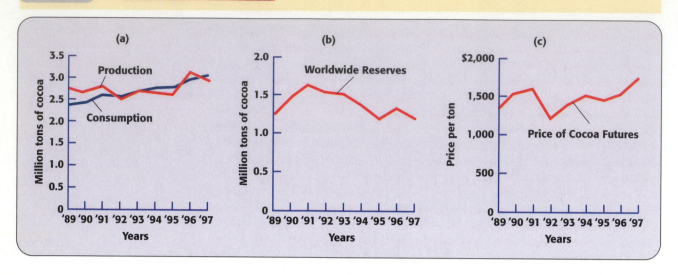

Laissez-Faire Economics For many centuries the world's dominant economic philosophy supported government control of most of a society's assets and direct government involvement in its international trade. In the mid-1700s, a new approach to national economics called for less government interference in commerce and greater individual economic freedom. This approach became known as a *laissez-faire* system, loosely translated from French as "allow them to do [without interference]."

Canada and the United States are examples of contemporary market economies. It is no accident that both these countries have individual-oriented cultures. As much as an emphasis on individualism fosters a democratic form of government, it also supports a market economy.

Features of a Market Economy

To function smoothly and properly, a market economy requires three things: *free choice*, *free enterprise*, and *price flexibility*.

➡ *Free choice* gives individuals access to alternative purchase options. In a market economy, few restrictions are placed on consumers' ability to make their own decisions and exercise free choice. For example, a consumer shopping for a new car is guaranteed a variety from which to choose. The consumer can choose among dealers, models, sizes, styles, colors, and mechanical specifications, such as engine size and transmission type.

➡ *Free enterprise* gives companies the ability to decide which goods and services to produce and the markets in which to compete. They are free to enter new and different lines of business, select geographic markets and customer segments to pursue, hire workers, and advertise their products. They are, therefore, guaranteed the right to pursue interests profitable to them.

➡ *Price flexibility* allows most prices to rise and fall to reflect the forces of supply and demand. In contrast, nonmarket economies often set and maintain prices at stipulated levels (as the Chinese government did for state-produced tobacco products in this chapter's opening example). Interfering with the price mechanism violates a fundamental principle of the market economy.

Government's Role in a Market Economy In a market economy, government has little direct involvement in business activities. Even so, it usually plays an important role in four areas: *enforcing antitrust laws, preserving property rights, providing a stable fiscal and monetary environment,* and *preserving political stability.* Let's look briefly at each of these areas.

Enforcing Antitrust Laws When one company is able to control a product's supply—and, therefore, its price—it is considered a *monopoly.* The goal of antitrust laws is to encourage the development of industries with as many competing businesses as the market will sustain. In such industries, prices are kept low by the forces of competition. By enforcing antitrust laws, governments prevent monopoly businesses from exploiting consumers and constraining the growth of commerce through competition.

Consider the case of Microsoft Corporation. In 1997, rival companies complained about Microsoft's plan to release a free version of its Windows software that included its Internet Explorer Web browser. Competitors argued that Microsoft's plan would stifle competition. In a preliminary ruling, a federal appeals court affirmed certain principles of free-enterprise decision making. It ruled that Microsoft was free to determine the features and functions of its products as long as it offered advantages to consumers that could not be obtained by combining separately purchased products.[8] But in 1999 Microsoft's problems were continuing as it was battling an antitrust suit brought by the U.S. government.

e·biz

Traders shouted in frustration when the Hong Kong stock market plunged 10.4 percent in October 1997, putting a spotlight on the Asian economic crisis. In the more than thirty years leading up to this plunge, Asian countries had experienced rapid and consistent growth and earned the confidence of international investors. Although it's hard to pinpoint the exact reason for the abrupt tumble, many economists attribute it to excessive debt. During the boom, companies in Asia borrowed huge sums of money, mostly in U.S. dollars at low interest rates. In 1995, the dollar's value rose, making Asian exports higher-priced and less competitive. Many Asian countries had to devalue their currency to compete overseas. Companies who had borrowed the huge sums in dollars then needed to earn much more in local currency to repay their loans, and the long slide began.

Preserving Property Rights A smoothly functioning market economy rests on a legal system that safeguards individual property rights. By preserving and protecting individual property rights, governments encourage individuals and companies to take risks such as investing in technology, inventing new products, and starting new businesses. Strong protection of property rights ensures entrepreneurs that their claims to assets and future earnings are legally safeguarded. This protection also supports a healthy business climate in which a market economy can flourish.

Providing a Stable Fiscal and Monetary Environment Unstable economies are often characterized by high inflation and unemployment. These forces create general uncertainty about the nation's suitability as a place to do business. Governments can help control inflation through effective *fiscal policies* (policies regarding taxation and government spending) and *monetary policies* (policies controlling money supply and interest rates). A stable economic environment helps companies to better forecast costs, revenues, and the future of the business in general. Such conditions reduce the risks associated with future investments such as product development and business expansion.

MAP 4.1

ECONOMIC FREEDOM AROUND THE WORLD

This map classifies countries according to their levels of economic freedom. Only 9 countries and territories are considered completely "free" whereas 64 nations are "mostly free." But the scale tips in favor of a lack of economic freedom: There are 58 nations labeled "mostly not free" and 25 nations labeled "repressed." Those countries ranking highest on economic freedom also tend to have the highest economic growth rates and living standards.

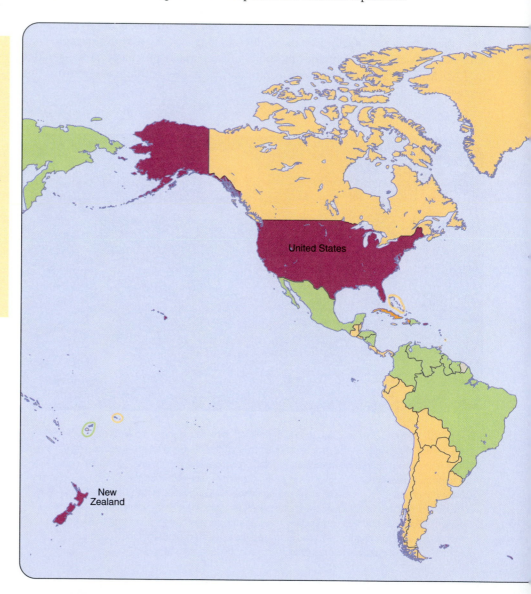

Preserving Political Stability A market economy depends on a stable government for its smooth operation and, indeed, for its future existence. Political stability helps businesses engage in activities without worrying about terrorism, kidnappings, and other political threats to their operations. (See Chapter 3 for extensive coverage of political risk and stability.)

Economic Freedom So far, we have discussed the essence of market economies as being grounded in freedom: free choice, free enterprise, free prices, and freedom from direct intervention by government. Map 4.1 shows how 156 countries rank according to their levels of economic freedom. Some of the factors involved in the rankings include trade policy, government intervention in the economy, property rights, black markets, and wage and price controls.

Recall that in Chapter 3, we said that the connection between political freedom and economic growth is not at all certain. Likewise, we can say only that countries with the greatest economic freedom *tend to have* the highest standards of living, whereas those with the lowest freedom tend to have the lowest standards of living. Moreover,

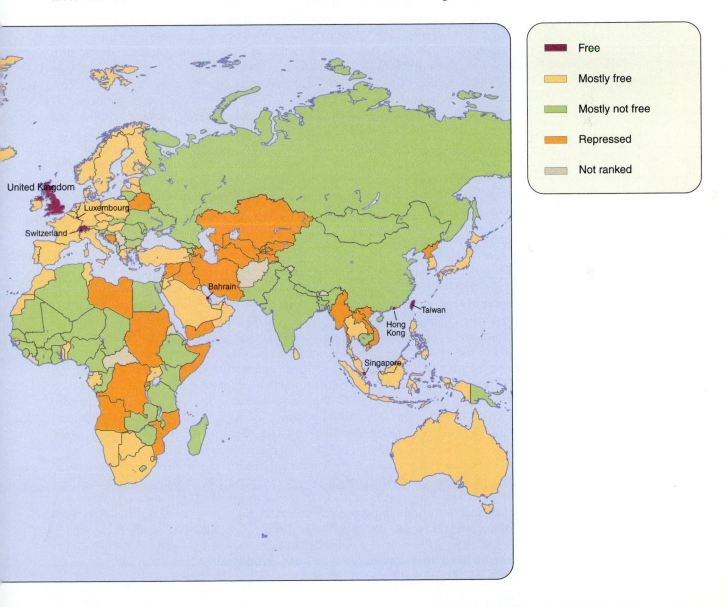

comparing Map 3.1 (pp. 82–83) and Map 4.1, we see that countries with the greatest political freedom also tend to have the greatest economic freedom. Three of the worst-rated countries on political freedom appear on the list of the worst-rated countries on economic freedom: North Korea, Cuba, and Iraq. The four highest-rated countries on economic freedom are Hong Kong, Singapore, Bahrain, and New Zealand. The United States comes in sixth, after Switzerland.

DEVELOPMENT OF NATIONS

economic development
Measure for gauging the economic well-being of one nation's people, as compared to that of another nation's people.

The economic well-being of one nation's people compared to that of another nation's people is reflected in the country's level of **economic development**. Level of economic development reflects several economic and human indicators, including a nation's economic output (agricultural and industrial), infrastructure (power and transport facilities), and people's physical health and level of education. Cultural, political, legal, and economic differences between nations can cause great differences in economic development from one country to another.

Economic development is an increasingly important topic for international businesspeople. Today international businesses commonly expand into countries that are low-cost production bases. These countries tend to be poor, yet can have ambitious development programs. A fuller understanding of economic development should help managers to more effectively accomplish their objectives.

Businesspeople use many different measures to estimate a country's level of economic development. In fact, one Hong Kong-based investment research company, Jardine Fleming Securities, monitors Nike's production patterns to gauge industrial and economic development in Asian nations. The company takes its theory seriously, arguing that as companies follow Nike into a country, workers' paychecks and skills increase and the country's currency grows stronger—encouraging yet more investment and development.[9] For those who are uneasy with such informal indicators, there are other more formal methods of gauging a country's level of development. Let's take a look at several of these.

NATIONAL PRODUCTION

gross national product (GNP)
Value of all goods and services produced by a country during a one-year period, including income generated by both domestic and international activities.

gross domestic product (GDP)
Value of all goods and services produced by a country's domestic economy over a one-year period.

GNP or GDP per capita
Nation's GNP or GDP divided by its population.

The broadest measure of economic development is **gross national product (GNP)**—the value of all goods and services produced by a country during a one-year period. This figure includes income generated both by domestic production and by the country's international activities. **Gross domestic product (GDP)** is the value of all goods and services produced by the domestic economy over a one-year period. In other words, when we add to GDP the income generated from exports, imports, and the international operations of a nation's companies, we get GNP. A country's **GNP per capita** is simply its GNP divided by its population. GDP per capita is calculated similarly.

Both GNP per capita and GDP per capita measure a nation's income per person. Map 4.2 on pages 126–127 classifies countries according to GNP per capita. Those nations with the highest GNP per capita are Switzerland, Japan, and Norway; those nations with the lowest are Mozambique, Ethiopia, and Tanzania.

Marketers often use GNP or GDP per capita figures to determine whether a country's population is wealthy enough to begin purchasing its products. For instance, the Asian nation of Myanmar, with a GDP per capita of only $120 per year, is very poor. Here, you won't find computer companies marketing laptops or designer-apparel firms selling expensive jeans. Yet several large makers of personal-care products are staking out territory in Myanmar. Companies like Colgate-Palmolive and the Anglo-Dutch firm Unilever are traditional explorers of uncertain but promising markets in which they can offer relatively cheap items such as soap and shampoo.[10]

Although GNP and GDP are the most popular indicators of economic development, they have several important drawbacks. In the following sections, we discuss each of these in some detail.

Proliferation of Uncounted Transactions   Many of a nation's transactions are not counted in either GNP or GDP. Some of the activities not included are:

➡ Volunteer work
➡ Unpaid household work
➡ Illegal activities such as gambling and black market (underground) transactions
➡ Unreported transactions conducted in cash

In many cases, the underground economy is so large and prosperous that official statistics like GDP per capita are almost meaningless. In the case of Myanmar, for instance, economists report that official numbers mask a thriving underground economy spurred by differences between official and black-market currency exchange rates.[11]

Figure 4.3 shows the percentage of overall GDP that is accounted for by the unofficial economy in several central and eastern European countries. In Ukraine, according to official statistics, GDP has *shrunk* by 52 percent since the break from Moscow in 1991. Why, then, do kids in Reeboks dash through Kiev streets snarled with Jeeps and shiny Mercedes-Benzes? The answer is that $30 billion a year—a whopping 49 percent of GDP—flows through the country in unreported cash. Who generates this cash? There's little incentive for a small Kiev manufacturer to go the official route when faced with a gauntlet of 14 regulatory and permit steps just to export a batch of socks to neighboring Poland. It is much simpler for the company to do business in the underground economy.[12]

In addition, *barter* (the exchange of goods and services for other goods and services instead of money) regularly occurs in many developing countries. Barter is a popular alternative for buyers lacking the hard currency needed to pay for imports. In one well-known case, Pepsi-Cola traded soft drinks in the former Soviet Union for 17 submarines, a cruiser, a frigate, and a destroyer. Pepsi then converted its payment into cash by selling the military goods as scrap metal.[13] Because of their lack of currency, Russians still make extensive use of barter. In one incident, the Russian government paid

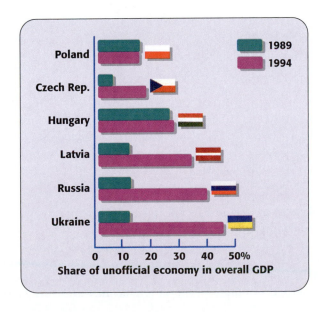

FIGURE 4.3

UNOFFICIAL ECONOMIES

MAP 4.2

COUNTRY CLASSIFICATION BY GROSS NATIONAL PRODUCT PER CAPITA

SEE INSET

8,000 teachers in the Altai republic (1,850 miles east of Moscow) their monthly salaries with 15 bottles of vodka each. Teachers had previously refused an offer to receive part of their salaries in toilet paper and funeral accessories.[14]

Question of Growth   Because gross product figures are a snapshot of *one year's economic output*, they do not tell us whether a nation's economy is growing or shrinking. In predicting a country's future output, its expected economic growth rate should be examined. Thus even a nation with moderate GNP or GDP figures will inspire greater investor confidence and international investment if growth rates are high.

Problem of Averages   Remember that per capita numbers give an average figure for an entire country. Although these numbers can be broadly helpful in estimating quality of life and level of economic development, averages do not tell the story in much detail. In most countries, urban areas are more developed than rural areas and have higher per capita income. In less advanced countries, regions surrounding good harbors or other transportation facilities are usually more developed

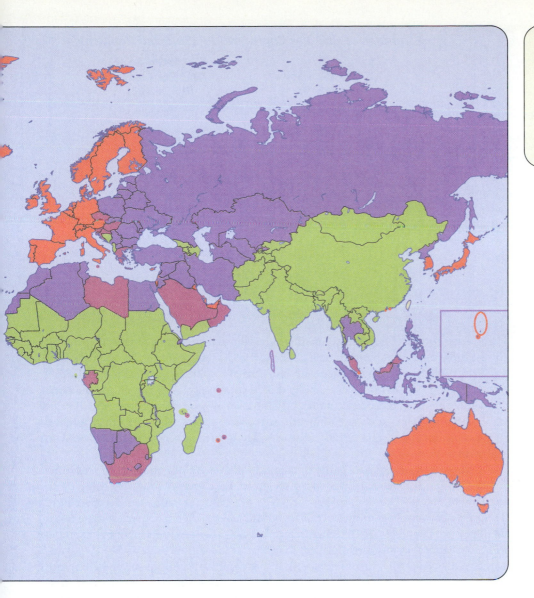

	High-income ($9,386 or more)
	Upper-income ($3,036–$9,385)
	Lower-income ($766–$3,035)
	Low-income ($765 or less)

than interior regions. Sometimes industrial parks boasting companies with advanced technology in production or design can generate a disproportionate share of a country's earnings.

Because Shanghai, Hong Kong, and other coastal regions of China are far more developed than the country's interior, GNP or GDP per capita figures for the country as a whole are quite misleading. Mercedes-Benz does a fair amount of business in Shanghai, whereas many agricultural regions deep inside China still rely on bicycles and animals for a good deal of their transport.

Pitfalls of Comparison   Country comparisons using gross product figures can be misleading. In order to compare gross product per capita, each currency involved must be translated into a single currency unit (usually the dollar) at official exchange rates. But official exchange rates provide only limited data. Although they tell us *how many units of one currency it takes to buy one unit of another*, they do not tell us *what that unit of local currency can buy in its home country*. Thus to understand the value of a currency in its home country, we must apply the concept of *purchasing power parity*.

TABLE 4.1	Estimates of GNP Per Capita at PPP (Selected Countries)	
Country	GNP Per Capita (U.S. $)	PPP Estimate of GNP Per Capita (U.S. = 100)
United States	$26,980	$26,980
Switzerland	40,630	25,860
Japan	39,640	22,110
Canada	19,380	21,130
Russia	2,240	4,480
Mexico	3,320	6,400
Nigeria	260	1,220
India	340	1,400

PURCHASING POWER PARITY

purchasing power
Value of goods and services that can be purchased with one unit of a country's currency.

purchasing power parity (PPP)
Relative ability of two countries' currencies to buy the same "basket" of goods in those two countries.

Using gross product figures to compare production across countries does not account for the different cost of living in each country. **Purchasing power** is the value of goods and services that can be purchased with one unit of a country's currency. **Purchasing power parity (PPP)** is the relative ability of two countries' currencies to buy the same "basket" of goods in those two countries. This basket of goods is representative of ordinary, daily-use items such as toothpaste, soap, rice, apples, and so forth. Estimates of gross product per capita *at PPP* allow us to see what a currency can actually buy in real terms.

Using purchasing power parity to compare the wealth of nations produces some interesting results. Table 4.1, for instance, shows how several countries compare to the United States when their respective GNPs per capita are adjusted to reflect PPP. Thus if we convert Swiss francs to dollars at official exchange rates, we estimate Swiss GNP per capita at $40,630. If, however, we estimate Switzerland's GNP per capita at PPP, we realize that it is actually lower than that of the United States—$25,860, compared to $26,980. Why the difference? GNP per capita at PPP is lower in Switzerland because of its higher cost of living. This means that it costs more to buy the same basket of goods in Switzerland than it does in the United States. The opposite phenomenon occurs in the case of Nigeria. Because the cost of living is lower in Nigeria than in the United States, Nigeria's GNP per capita rises from $260 to $1,220 when PPP is considered. We discuss PPP in far greater detail in Chapter 10.

HUMAN DEVELOPMENT

human development index (HDI)
Measure of the extent to which a government satisfies its people's needs and the extent to which these needs are addressed equally across a nation's entire population.

The purchasing power parity concept does a fairly good job in revealing differences between nations' levels of economic development. Unfortunately, it leaves much to be desired *as an indicator of a people's total well-being*. Table 4.2 shows how selected countries rank according to the United Nations' **human development index (HDI)**—the measure of the extent to which a government satisfies its people's needs and the extent to which these needs are addressed equally across a nation's entire population. As such, the HDI goes beyond calculations of a country's *financial* wealth. It measures the extent to which a government satisfies its people's needs along three dimensions: (1) a long and healthy life, (2) an education, and (3) a decent standard of living.

TABLE 4.2 Rankings of National Wealth Versus Human Development Index (HDI)

Country	HDI Value	HDI Rank	Real GDP Per Capita Rank (at PPP)	Population Not Expected to Live to Age 40 (%)
Industrial Countries				
Canada	0.960	1	8	3.1
France	0.946	2	15	4.0
Norway	0.943	3	9	2.7
United States	0.942	4	3	4.0
Iceland	0.942	5	14	2.6
the Netherlands	0.940	6	19	2.5
Japan	0.940	7	7	2.2
Finland	0.940	8	23	3.1
New Zealand	0.937	9	24	4.3
Sweden	0.936	10	21	2.7
Spain	0.934	11	30	3.0
Austria	0.932	12	13	3.7
Belgium	0.932	13	12	3.5
Australia	0.931	14	18	3.5
United Kingdom	0.931	15	20	2.6
Greece	0.923	20	35	3.8
Luxembourg	0.899	27	1	3.8
Nonindustrial Countries				
Hong Kong	0.914	22	5	2.4
Cyprus	0.907	24	32	3.1
Barbados	0.907	25	36	4.2
Singapore	0.900	26	11	3.2
Bahamas	0.894	28	28	5.5
Chile	0.891	30	43	4.6
Uruguay	0.883	37	52	5.4
Panama	0.864	45	59	6.2
Mexico	.853	50	50	8.3
Malaysia	0.832	60	47	7.2
Mauritius	0.831	61	31	6.2
Brazil	0.783	68	68	14.0
Saudi Arabia	0.774	73	41	8.8
Algeria	0.737	82	65	10.6
Oman	0.718	88	39	8.8
Botswana	0.673	97	67	15.9
Philippines	0.672	98	86	12.8
China	0.626	108	105	9.1
Honduras	0.575	116	109	10.8
Namibia	0.570	118	83	21.1
Vietnam	0.557	121	147	12.1
Kenya	0.463	134	139	22.3
India	0.446	138	143	19.4
Bangladesh	0.368	144	144	26.4
Cambodia	0.348	153	154	31.9
Angola	0.335	157	133	38.9
Guinea	0.271	167	153	41.3
Ethiopia	0.244	170	174	35.7
Sierra Leone	0.176	175	171	52.1

The HDI uses three factors to evaluate a government's success in these three areas:

1. Life expectancy
2. Educational attainment
3. Income

Table 4.2 also illustrates the disparity between wealth and HDI for selected countries. We see that France ranks only fifteenth according to GDP per capita but second in providing health care, education, and a decent standard of living. On the other hand, although Luxembourg ranks first on the basis of GDP per capita, it ranks only twenty-seventh on the HDI. Perhaps most striking in Table 4.2 is the column showing each nation's population that is not expected to reach age 40. Figures for countries near the bottom of the table reveal a close link between income and living standards. People in countries that rank low on wealth and HDI have dramatically shorter life spans.

Unlike the other measures we discussed, the HDI looks beyond financial wealth. By stressing the human aspects of economic development, the HDI demon-

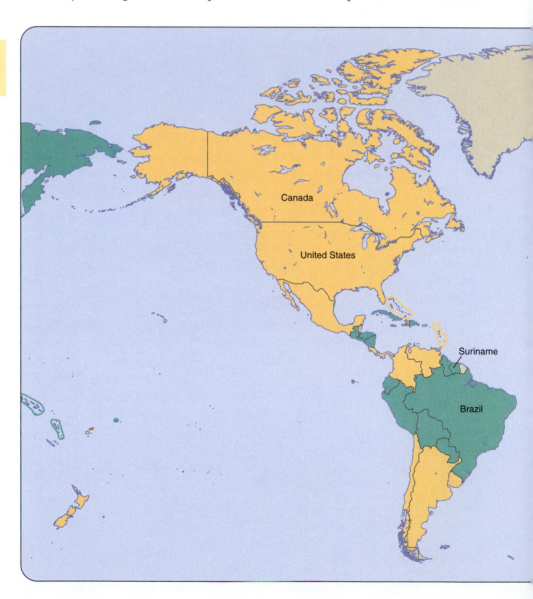

MAP 4.3

COUNTRY CLASSIFICATION BY HUMAN DEVELOPMENT INDEX

strates that high national income alone does not guarantee human progress. The importance of national income, however, should not be underestimated. Countries need money to build good schools, provide quality health care, support environmentally friendly industries, and underwrite other programs designed to improve quality of life. As you can see from Map 4.3, the HDI divides countries into three categories: those with high, medium, and low *quality of life*.

CLASSIFYING COUNTRIES

Nations are commonly classified as being *developed*, *newly industrialized*, or *developing*. These classifications are based on national indicators such as GNP per capita, portion of the economy devoted to agriculture, amount of exports in the form of industrial goods, and overall economic structure. There are, however, no consensus lists of countries in any category, and borderline countries are often classified differently in different listings. Let's take a closer look at each of these classifications.

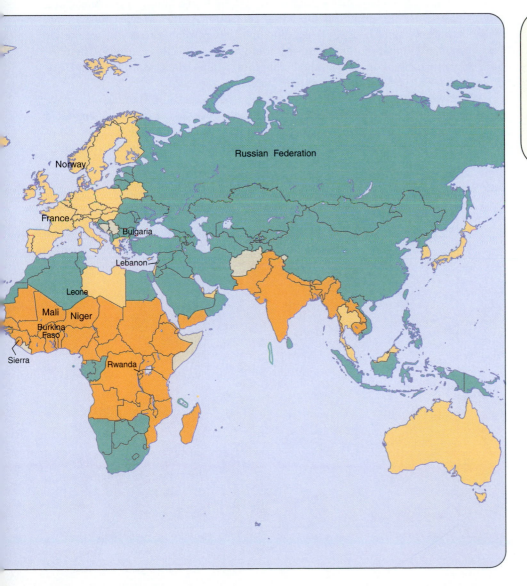

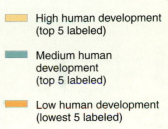

High human development (top 5 labeled)

Medium human development (top 5 labeled)

Low human development (lowest 5 labeled)

developed country
Country that is highly industrialized, highly efficient, and whose people enjoy a high quality of life.

Developed Countries   Those countries that are highly industrialized, highly efficient, and whose people enjoy a high quality of life are **developed countries**. People in developed countries usually receive the finest health care and benefit from the best educational systems in the world. Most developed nations also support aid programs for helping poorer nations improve their economies and standards of living. Countries in this category include Australia, Canada, Japan, New Zealand, the United States, all Western European nations, and Greece.

Newly Industrialized Countries   Those countries that recently increased the portion of their national production and exports derived from industrial operations are **newly industrialized countries (NICs)**. The NICs are located primarily in Asia and Latin America. Over the past two to three decades, they have attracted an increasing share of total world investment. Figure 4.4 shows just how much this type of investment has grown. Since 1990, according to the World Bank, investment flowing into these nations has totaled $210 billion.[15]

newly industrialized country (NIC)
Country that has recently increased the portion of its national production and exports derived from industrial operations.

Although economic problems in Asia have slowed their progress since 1997, most listings of NICs still include Asia's "four tigers" (Hong Kong, South Korea, Singapore, and Taiwan). Also appearing on most lists are South Africa, Brazil, China, India, Malaysia, Mexico, and Thailand. Depending upon the pivotal criteria that we use for classification, a number of other countries could be placed in this category. These include Argentina, Chile, Indonesia, the Philippines, Brunei, the Czech Republic, Hungary, Poland, Russia, Slovakia, Turkey, and Vietnam.

emerging markets
Newly industrialized countries plus those with the potential to become newly industrialized.

When we combine newly industrialized countries with those countries that have the potential to become newly industrialized, we arrive at a category often called **emerging markets**. Generally, emerging markets have developed some (but not all) of the operations and export capabilities associated with NICs.[16] However, debate contin-

FIGURE 4.4

INVESTMENT IN NEWLY INDUSTRIALIZED COUNTRY STOCKS

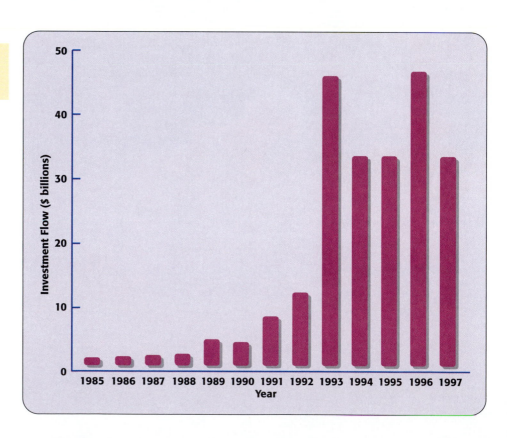

ues over the defining characteristics of such classifications as *newly industrialized country* and *emerging market.*

Developing Countries   Nations having the poorest infrastructures and lowest personal incomes are called **developing countries** (also called *less developed countries*). These countries often rely heavily on one or a few sectors of production, such as agriculture, mineral mining, or oil drilling. They might show potential for becoming newly industrialized countries, but typically lack the necessary resources and skills to do so. Most lists of developing countries include many nations in Africa, the Middle East, and the poorest formerly communist nations in Europe and Asia.

Developed countries employ the latest technological advances in their manufacturing sectors. However, developing countries (and NICs as well) are sometimes characterized by a high degree of **technological dualism**—use of the latest technologies in some sectors of the economy coupled with the use of outdated technologies in others.

developing country
(*also called* less developed country) *Nation that has a poor infrastructure and extremely low personal incomes.*

technological dualism
Use of the latest technologies in some sectors of the economy coupled with the use of outdated technologies in other sectors.

Over the last two decades, countries with centrally planned economies have been remaking themselves in the image of stronger market economies. This process, called **economic transition**, involves changing a nation's fundamental economic organization and creating entirely new free-market institutions. Some nations take transition further than others do, but the process typically involves five reform measures:[17]

ECONOMIC TRANSITION AND ITS OBSTACLES

economic transition
Process by which a nation changes its fundamental economic organization and creates new free-market institutions.

1. Macroeconomic stabilization to reduce budget deficits and expand credit availability
2. Liberalization of economic activity that is decided by prices reflecting supply and demand
3. Legalization of private enterprises and privatization of state-owned enterprises in accord with an effective system of individual property rights
4. Removal of trade and investment barriers in goods and services, and removal of controls on convertibility of the nation's currency
5. Development of a social-welfare system designed to ease the transition process.

There is little doubt that transition from central planning to free-market economics is generating tremendous international business opportunities. But difficulties arising from years of socialist economic principles have hampered progress from the start. Let's now take a look at the key remaining obstacles that are hindering former socialist and communist countries in their transition to free-market economies; *lack of managerial expertise*, *shortage of capital*, *cultural differences*, and *environmental degradation*.

LACK OF MANAGERIAL EXPERTISE

One of the biggest challenges facing companies in transitional economies is a lack of managers qualified to conduct operations in a highly competitive global economy. Because central planners formerly decided nearly every aspect of the nation's commercial activities, there was little need for production, distribution, and marketing plans or strategies—or for the trained individuals to devise them.

Likewise, because the types of goods and services to be offered were decided by central planning committees, there was little need to investigate consumer wants and needs—or for the specialists capable of conducting such research. Because central planners set prices, very little thought was given to strategies for delivering competitively priced products—or to the need for experts in operations, inventory, distribution, or logistics. Because all products were basically the same, there was no need for marketers with advertising skills.

Factory managers at government-owned firms had only to meet production requirements already set by central planners. In fact, some products rolled off assembly lines merely to be stacked outside the doors of the factory. After all, knowing where they went after that—and who took them there—was not the factory manager's job.

Managers in transitional countries tend to lack training in all areas of business management. But the situation is improving in countries where organizations and consultants are helping to develop local managerial talent. For instance, the World Bank's Economic Development Institute has launched a training program to support enterprise restructuring and privatization in transition economies. One Russian success story is that of a Mrs. Smirnova, deputy director of the textile conglomerate, Mayak, in Nizhniy Novgorod. Fresh out of the program, Smirnova instituted international accounting standards before they were required by Russian law and personally retrained the firm's accountants. She then initiated the company's breakup into 13 independent businesses. Today 70 percent of Mayak's production is exported to Britain.[18]

SHORTAGE OF CAPITAL

Not surprisingly, transition is very expensive. To facilitate the process and ease the pain, governments must usually spend a great deal of money in three areas:

1. Developing a telecommunications and infrastructure system, including highways, bridges, rail networks, and sometimes subways
2. Setting up financial institutions, including stock markets and a banking system
3. Educating people in the ways of market economics

Unfortunately, governments of transition economies can often afford only a portion of the required investment. Usually they lack capital because of the same financial management practices that they are trying to replace. However, outside sources of capital are available. These include national and international companies, other governments, and international financial institutions, such as the World Bank, the International Monetary Fund (IMF), and the Asian Development Bank.[19] But another problem facing many transition countries is that they already owe substantial amounts of money to international lenders.

Thailand was one of the first countries to lead the Asian market into turmoil and many investors believe it'll be the first country to lead them out. Thailand's economy came to a grinding halt—just like this highway construction in Bangkok—when, in July 1997, its currency crashed. Economists cite many possible reasons for the crash. One reason is that Thailand's companies borrowed heavily from banks—almost 80 percent of their total financing. In contrast, most U.S. companies raise money from the stock market, borrowing only 22 percent on average from banks.

CULTURAL DIFFERENCES

Economic transition and reform make deep cultural impressions on a nation's people. As we saw in Chapter 2, cultures differ greatly, with some more open to change than others. Likewise, certain cultures welcome economic change more easily than others. Transition often replaces dependence on government with greater emphasis on individual responsibility, incentives, and rights. Such changes can be traumatic in some cultures. Deep cuts in welfare payments, unemployment benefits, and guaranteed government jobs can present a major shock to a nation's people.

Importing modern management practices without tailoring them to the local culture can also have serious consequences. For instance, South Korea's Daewoo Motors is currently facing a potentially disabling culture clash in central Europe. Korea's management system is based on a rigid hierarchical structure and an obsessive work ethic. Managers at Daewoo's domestic car plant in Pupyong-Gu are expected to arrive an hour early for work to stand at the company gates and greet workers—who arrive singing the company anthem. The Korean work ethic is tricky to implement at the factory of Avia, Daewoo's Czech carmaker. Korean managers have trouble understanding why employees want holidays that coincide with their children's school breaks or why European managers so frequently switch companies. However, Daewoo is working to help bridge the cultural and workplace gaps. At any one time, 500 Romanians, Poles, and Uzbeks study their Korean colleagues' work habits and methods by staffing assembly lines at Daewoo Motors' plant in Korea for six-month stretches. Traveling in the other direction are Korean managers and technicians who specialize in assembly line efficiency.[20]

ENVIRONMENTAL DEGRADATION

The economic and social policies of former communist governments in central and eastern Europe were disastrous for the natural environment. Similarly, the headlong rush in Asia to catch up to developed countries is leaving serious environmental damage in its wake. The direct effects of environmental destruction are evident in increased levels of sickness and disease, including asthma, blood deficiencies, and cancer—the result of which is lower productivity in the workplace.

Sometimes a country's transition to a new, stronger economy comes at the expense of the environment. Oddly enough, one indicator of a country's wealth is the heat its landfills emit; vegetable peels don't burn as hot as paper and plastic. Ironically, this "hot" landfill in Taiwan is indicative of both Taiwan's miraculous productivity and its serious pollution problem. Activists in Taiwan have started grass-roots organizations such as the Green Party and Homemaker's Union, which they model somewhat after the U.S. Environmental Protection Agency.

Countries in transition often suffer periods in which the negative effects of a market economy seem to outweigh its benefits. It's hard to enjoy a larger paycheck when the streets are choked with smog and the parks and rivers are polluted with garbage. In Bangkok, Thailand, commuters suffer carbon monoxide poisoning, and according to one study, children attending a school near a highway lost 10 IQ points from lead poisoning. Meanwhile, Taiwan's ability to produce garbage is rising at least as fast as its capacity to produce electronics equipment. "Living here is like living in hell by American standards," says mechanical engineering professor Jeff Chiang as he looks out over a smoky landscape studded with refinery smokestacks and rivulets of oil. In Kaohsiung, Taiwan's second-biggest city and home to steel, oil, plastics, and petrochemicals, people claim that you can almost "chew" the air, and some recall times when they could light the ground water with matches.[21]

FOCUS ON SELECTED MARKETS

Now that we have examined the process and challenges of economic development and transition, let's focus on the transition experiences of several countries and regions. In the following sections, we describe cultural, political, and economic events in nations that are undergoing transition from centrally planned or mixed economies to market economies. As such, we draw upon concepts from Chapters 2, 3, and 4.

CHINA

China began its experiment with central planning in 1949, when communists defeated the nationalists in a long and bloody civil war. Today, the country's leaders describe its economic philosophy as "socialism with Chinese characteristics." There is possibly no country on earth that has done more for its people economically in the last 20 years than China. Glistening skyscrapers dominate the Shanghai and Beijing cityscapes. Although rural China continues to look and function much as it has for centuries, people in large cities have good job prospects, the likes of which were never before known in China. The country's immense population, rising incomes, and expanding opportunities are attracting new business ventures like never before.

Transition Moves Forward   China is the location of some of the most fascinating economic, political, and social changes currently taking place in Asia. From 1949 until reforms were initiated in the late 1970s, the nation had a unique economic system. Agricultural production was organized into groups of people who formed production "brigades" and production "units." *Communes* were larger entities responsible for planning agricultural production quotas and industrial production schedules.

But even in the early days of communism, private ownership found a place in the Chinese economy. Families in rural areas owned their own homes and parcels of land on which to produce particular crops. Production surpluses could be consumed by the family or sold at a profit on the open market. In 1979, the government initiated important economic reforms in the agricultural sector. These reforms strengthened work incentives in this sector, which is the main source of income for nearly 75 percent of all Chinese. Family units could then grow whatever crops they chose and sell the produce at prices set by the forces of supply and demand. Rural income doubled within just six years.

At about the same time, *township and village enterprises*, or *TVEs*, began to appear. The government initially regarded TVEs as illegal operations unrelated to the officially sanctioned communes. Each TVE relied on the open market for materials, labor, and capital and used a nongovernmental distribution system. Each TVE employed managers who were directly responsible for profits and losses. Between 1979 and 1991, TVE output grew at an average annual rate of more than 27 percent, compared to total gross product growth in the nation as a whole of less than 11 percent. TVEs were legalized in 1984, and by 1993 they accounted for more than 32 percent of China's total GDP.[22] Clearly, the TVEs were laying the groundwork for a market economy.

Initially, and in line with communist ideology, outside companies were restricted from participating in the Chinese economy. But over time investment policies aimed at non-Chinese companies were softened. In the mid-1980s, outside companies were allowed much greater freedom to enter joint ventures with Chinese partners. The government identified 14 cities in which tax breaks were extended to firms establishing international trading and manufacturing operations. It also established five special economic zones characterized by an even greater market orientation.

Patience and Guanxi Success, however, is often won only after a hard struggle. IBM invested heavily in China in the 1980s, trying to push its unpopular PS/2 computer systems on Chinese consumers. When the PC market finally did take off in China, competitors with better products zoomed ahead. Still, IBM persisted. It moved its Chinese headquarters from Hong Kong to Beijing, launched cheaper PCs onto the market, and developed world-class manufacturing lines and research labs inside China. It also got to know its Chinese customer through creation of a national network of service centers. Its persistence paid off. IBM's China sales rose 50 percent annually from 1994 to 1997.

Consumer-goods companies and retailers must also be willing to wait until China's purchasing power catches up to levels in the West. Wal-Mart has two stores in China, and company leaders say that the best is yet to come. CFO John Menzer is counting on strong gains in Chinese purchasing power to boost sales of such items as washing machines and TV sets.[23]

But are patience and dogged persistence enough? In short, no. One of the most important factors in forming a successful venture in China is *guanxi*—personal relationships. Consider the tale of two companies, one from the United States, the other France. Each badly wanted a $20 million contract to supply papermaking equipment in

In August 1996, Wal-Mart Stores, Inc. opened two Wal-Marts and one Sam's Club store in China, acting on forecasts that China's total purchasing power will equal current U.S. levels in five to seven years. The giant retailer adapted its goods to local tastes but imported its information systems to China—a strategy that has also worked for Wal-Mart in Mexico, Puerto Rico, Argentina, Brazil, Germany, and Canada. For more information on Wal-Mart's international business go to (**www.wal-mart.com/ stores/interdiv.shtml**).

China. Although the U.S. managers showed that their company's equipment was state-of-the-art and competitively priced, the contract went to their French competitors. It seems the French won the contract not because they offered a better deal, but because they spent more time listening than talking and took special care to make the Chinese feel comfortable during their visit to France. As you can see from the Global Manager "Guidelines for Good *Guanxi*," learning the secrets of *guanxi* is extremely important for success in China.

Global Manager

Guidelines for Good *Guanxi*

Research, Research, Research   China is not a single market, but many different regional markets with different cultures and even different languages. Chinese hosts are particularly impressed when someone goes the extra mile to acquire in-depth knowledge of their business, their region, and their country. No one knows this more than Bob Wilner, director of international human resources for McDonald's Corporation. Wilner was part of the market-opening team for China. He initially went to China to learn as much as possible about the market, how people were managed, and the country's employment systems. "Unlike the way we cook our hamburgers exactly the same in all 101 countries," says Wilner, "the way we manage, motivate, reward and discipline is more sensitive to the culture." Wilner and other McDonald's managers were able to develop that sensitivity only through repeated visits. As a result, McDonald's has been very successful in China.

The Importance of Contacts, Not Contracts   In China, face-to-face communication and personal relationships take priority over written contracts. Mu Dan Ping, a partner in the Chinese Business Group at Ernst & Young's Los Angeles office, offers the following diagram to show the different priorities:

> United States: Reason → Law → Relationship
> China: Relationship → Reason → Law

Managers from the United States look for the rationale or *reason* first, says Mu. Is there a market with profit potential? If so, they want a *legal contract* before they spend time on a business *relationship*. Conversely, explains Mu, the Chinese need to establish a trust *relationship* first. Then they look for common goals as a *reason* for doing business. In a way, the *legal contract* is just a formality, serving to ensure mutual understanding.

Pleasure Before Business   It seems impossible *not* to talk business when you've come to China for the express purpose of conducting business. But experts advise that you leave your sales pitches on the back burner and follow the lead of your Chinese hosts. Jay Rothstein, a business consultant on China, says that many companies seeking partnerships in China overlook the importance of personal relationships. They send their top performers to wow Chinese businesspeople with savvy sales pitches. "Companies that send their salesperson of the year will come back empty-handed," warns Rothstein. "In China, you must become friends before you do business."

Guanxi Hides in the Details   Managers from other countries often feel constrained by the socially oriented schedules arranged by their Chinese hosts. Busy executives sometimes resent all of the sightseeing and banquets as a waste of time. The Chinese, however, see such activities as opportunities to get to know each other before committing to a business deal.

Business Partners Are Family Members, Too   In China, family is extremely important. Visiting businesspeople should never turn down invitations to partake in a Chinese executive's family life. When Lauren Hsu was market analyst for Kohler Company, a manufacturer of plumbing fixtures, she was responsible for researching the Chinese market and identifying potential joint venture partners. Once, in the midst of negotiations, Hsu was invited to go bowling with the partner's daughter and then to a piano concert with the entire family. Such activities had little to do with promoting Kohler plumbing fixtures, but it helped push the deal to the next stage.

Good Things Take Time   Researching and visiting China, finding trustworthy partners, paying attention to details, and attending family events all take time. The joint venture deal that Lauren Hsu eventually oversaw involved two years of meetings and visits just getting acquainted. The Chinese negotiation process is rather slow because of the number of people involved. The Chinese are highly interdependent and tend to operate on a collaborative basis.

Challenges Ahead for China   Economic reforms are moving along very well in China, and the country continues to experience strong growth. Political and social problems, however, pose threats to China's future economic performance. Unrest continues in China, though not on the highly publicized scale of the Tiananmen Square incident in 1989. Skirmishes occasionally erupt between secular and Muslim Chinese in western provinces, and terrorist attacks sometimes occur in Beijing. Meanwhile, political leaders continue to restrict democratic reforms. Some observers believed that the death of Deng Xiaoping in 1997 would allow a new generation of leaders to speed up democratic reforms. However, as of 1999 political liberties had not increased.

Hong Kong and Macao, Yes, but Taiwan?   In July 1997, China regained control of Hong Kong after 99 years under British rule. Speeches by President Jiang Zemin to mark the ceremonies squelched the possibility of political reform in China, at least in the near future. Jiang credited the success of communist ideals for the return of Hong Kong, even while strongly supporting the preservation of human rights, personal freedoms, and property rights in Hong Kong. Mainland China's promise of "one country, two systems" would be kept. In other words, while the economic and political freedoms of people in Hong Kong would remain largely intact, the rest of China would continue along the lines drawn by the communist leadership.

The southern coastal territory of Macao is also under Chinese control as of December 1999. Only one hour's ferry ride from Hong Kong, Macao has been under Portugese administration since its founding in 1557. Although Macao's main function used to be that of trading post, today it serves mainly as a gambling outpost. In fact, it is commonly referred to as "Asia's Vegas."

It is important that China manage its one country, two systems policy well to preserve order in China, Hong Kong, and Macao. The island of Taiwan is watching very closely: Any chance of its eventual reunification with the Chinese mainland depends on the successful integration of Hong Kong and Macao. For now at least, things appear to be going smoothly. People in Hong Kong and Macao go about their business of creating wealth, whereas mainland Chinese have curtailed demands for political reform.

When it comes to Hong Kong, China has good reason to keep its "one country, two systems" policy. Prior to leaving British rule, Hong Kong had the world's third most competitive economy, with a gross domestic product per capita of $25,300—higher than Australia and the United Kingdom. It also boasted a low unemployment rate of 2.5 percent and had very low tax rates (15 percent salary rate and 16.5 percent corporate rate). To see how Hong Kong fares today, go to the English-language portion of its government's Web site at 〈**www.info.gov.hk/eindex.htm**〉.

Unemployment Although the economy rumbles forward and transition continues steadily, one potential problem is unemployment. Intensified competition and the entry of international companies into China is placing greater emphasis on efficiency and the cutting of payrolls in some industries. But the biggest contributor to the unemployed sector seems to be migrant workers, hundreds of thousands of whom left their farms and go from city to city searching for better-paying factory work or construction jobs. Unhappiness with economic progress in the countryside and the misery of migrant workers are serious potential sources of social unrest for the Chinese government.

People's Liberation Army Finally, one concern of Western governments is China's expanding defense industry. For one thing, China's military police (the People's Liberation Army—PLA) is deeply involved in international business activities. It is estimated that the PLA owns 15,000 businesses and 50,000 factories and employs 1 million troops in commercial activities. Some observers believe that China is using the revenue generated by economic reform to modernize its military. Although China officially reports annual military spending of $7 billion, the cash generated by PLA-run businesses could increase that figure to more than $25 billion. Moreover, companies like Baskin-Robbins, Intel, Visa, Motorola, Citibank, and Dunkin' Donuts now do business with PLA-connected firms.[24] Despite calls as recently as 1998 by China's leaders that the PLA reduce its commercial interests, many China watchers doubt significant change anytime soon.

VIETNAM

Communist Vietnam, like China, is one of the new investment darlings of Asia, and multinational companies are rushing to penetrate this promising market. Vietnam has vast natural resources such as gas, gold, and timber. It boasts a pristine coastline longer than the distance between San Diego and Seattle, which is sure to become a popular tourist locale. It has a large population of 72 million, 80 percent of whom are under the age of 40. Add to these factors the dynamism of the Vietnamese people and years of pent-up consumer demand, and you have a marketer's or investor's dream.

Vietnam has attracted international interest since the late 1980s, when the government announced its policy of *doi moi* (economic reform), similar to *perestroika* in the former Soviet Union. However, because the United States did not lift its 18-year-long trade embargo until 1994, U.S. firms have been late in joining the party. Now they are making up for lost time. Within hours after the embargo was lifted, a giant Pepsi can appeared on a main Ho Chi Minh City square. Not to be outdone, Coca-Cola flew in a 30-foot inflatable Coke bottle for a celebration at the city's concert hall.

Granted, other large companies are not as enthusiastic about Vietnam as PepsiCo and Coca-Cola. Many potential investors are turned off by reports of crime and corruption, a poor infrastructure, and shifting ground rules. Indeed, many businesspeople call Vietnam the "land of the moving goalposts." It's easy to get into the game, they say, but scoring is difficult once you're in because conditions always seem to be changing, usually due to government policy. Thus, of the $23 billion pledged to Vietnam by Western investors, only one third has actually been spent. The main reason is the country's tangled bureaucracy and archaic legal system.

Those who are perhaps least affected by the stranglehold of government in Vietnam are its entrepreneurs. A newly arrived visitor will notice a constant buzz of entrepreneurial activity. Upon arriving at the airport of Ho Chi Minh City (still called Saigon by most who live there), incoming passengers are greeted by crowds of drivers offering their services in or on vehicles ranging from antique Mercedes limousines to modern motorcycles. Once downtown, the teams of peddlers are over-

Vietnam, Inc.: Youth Seek Their Fortunes

In a crowded Saigon nightspot called Apocalypse Now, young U.S. "expats" in their twenties and thirties mingle with the international crowd and swap stories of their lives in the new Vietnam. Some see Vietnam as the place to make their fortunes whereas others see it as a smart career move. Still others are just hanging out because it's a cool place to go after college.

What unites them is a total lack of emotional baggage; memories of the Vietnam War belong to their parents or to the parents of Vietnam's own twentysomethings. Indeed, the war has been reduced to a decor theme: At Apocalypse Now, sandbags are piled in the corner to conjure up foxholes, dollops of blood-red paint drip on white globe lights, and painted helicopters buzz from the ceiling. Says 31-year-old David Case, a self-styled entrepreneur and jack-of-all-investment-trades: "A lot of people in the States say, 'Wow, don't the Vietnamese hate you?' Or they tell me they spent the better part of their youth staying out of Vietnam. But Vietnam is not a war anymore. It's a country." For people like David Case, you might even say, "Vietnam is not a country anymore. It's a business opportunity." Here are three brief "snapshots" of some of the brave new entrepreneurs:

➡ Luu Hue-Chan, 29, a Vietnamese American who emigrated to the United States when she was 9, launched VietLink two years ago with six partners. The privately funded start-up specializes in cross-cultural training and human resource projects to help bridge the gap between the U.S. and Vietnamese business communities.

So far, VietLink has served as an intermediary for a variety of U.S. concerns. In one recent year, the company expected to turn a profit on revenues of $250,000.

➡ James Wolf, 26, hardly looks like your typical CEO (he claims he got a *D* in business class), and his partner Doug Lewis, also 26, is a college dropout. Yet, the two manage some 100 Vietnamese workers at their own Bamboo Hardwoods factory outside Saigon. Founded by Lewis, the company makes bamboo panels for furniture and flooring to be assembled and sold around the world. Lewis became a fan of bamboo as an ecologically sound alternative to hardwood when he helped run a bamboo nursery in Seattle. Private investors enabled him to open his factory, and then he hired Wolf, a graduate of the Rhode Island School of Design, at a bamboo trade show in Bali. The company made a profit in 1996, less than two years after Lewis started it.

➡ Then there's David Case, probably more a mix of artist and entrepreneur. By his own admission, his life in Vietnam is "pretty schizoid." On some days, he might be working with young girls from the countryside to make and sell blankets (partly in an effort to keep them from prostitution). Other days might find him working on a deadline as a freelance writer for Reuters, covering Vietnam's volatile economic scene. He's also a studio musician in the midst of cutting 10 jazz-influenced pop tracks for the first Western CD ever recorded in Vietnam.

whelming. At the marketplace, entrepreneurs sell oranges, bananas, papayas, and *jeruk*, a green fruit larger and sweeter than a grapefruit. In addition, young entrepreneurs from the United States are getting in on the action, although they are more likely to be peddling $500,000 multimedia proposals than papayas.[25] For more on this phenomenon, see the Entrepreneurial Focus "Vietnam, Inc.: Youth Seek Their Fortunes."

RUSSIA

Russia's experience with communism dates back to 1917. For the next 75 years, factories, distribution, and all other facets of operations, as well as the prices of labor, capital, and products, were controlled by the government. While China was experimenting with private farm ownership and a limited market-price system, the Soviet Union remained staunchly communist under a system of complete government ownership. This total absence of market institutions has badly impaired transition in Russia today. Unlike China, Russia is enduring massive political and economic reforms at the same time.

Slow Transition   Mikhail Gorbachev's rise to the presidency of the Soviet political system signaled the beginning of the end for central economic planning in what is now the former Soviet Union. Gorbachev ushered in a new era of freedom of thought, freedom of expression, and economic restructuring. For the first time since the communist takeover, people were allowed to speak freely about their lives under economic socialism. And speak freely they did—venting their frustrations over a general lack of consumer goods, poor-quality products, and long lines at banks and grocery stores.

However, the transition from government ownership and central planning has been challenging for ordinary Russians. Except for criminals and wealthy businesspeople, who the Russians call the "oligarchs," people are having difficulty maintaining their standard of living and affording many basic items such as food and clothing. In fact, in the winter of 1998–1999, the Russian government requested food from Western Europe and the United States to help its people avoid starvation. These hard times are causing increased alcohol abuse and depression among Russians. See the World Business Survey "The Pain of Being Set Free" for one effect of these hard times on ordinary people.

The main force hampering Russians' ability to improve living standards is inflation. Once released from artificial government control, prices soared, destroying the ordinary Russian's ability to buy almost anything, including food. For example, in 1992 inflation in Russia was running around 2,500 percent per year! Although inflation is now under better control today, industrial output appears to be stagnant. Some Russians are surviving because they were factory managers under the old system and retained their jobs in the new. Others have turned to the black market, creating organized-crime syndicates and relying on extortion payments to create personal wealth. Still others are working hard to build legitimate companies but find themselves being forced into making "protection" payments to organized crime.

Challenges Ahead for Russia   Several challenges lie ahead for Russia. As in so many other transitional economies, managerial talent needs to be fostered. Years of central planning hampered development of the managerial skills needed to operate companies in a market-based economy. Russian managers must improve their skills in financial control, research and development, employee hiring and training, marketing, and pricing—in short, in every facet of management practice.

Most importantly, the country's economy for the most part collapsed in autumn 1998. The reason was that the Asian currency crisis in 1997–1998 rippled through the world economy, causing a "credit crunch" (a shortage of investment capital) in the world's emerging markets. Russia needs this money to establish the institutions that are essential to the functioning of a market economy, such as well-functioning stock markets, a strong central bank, and an effective tax system.

The absence of an operational tax code is one of the major problems facing the nation today. Without being able to collect taxes from individuals and corporations, the government's coffers are continuously empty—they cannot afford to pay coal miners, teachers, the pensions of the elderly, or to invest in education and infrastructure. Payment for goods and services through barter, not cash, is now the norm in Russia. International lending institutions (such as the International Monetary Fund) and governments of developed nations (such as Britain, Canada, France, Germany, Italy, Japan, and the United States) sent financial aid packages to help Russia's transition. But much of that aid was siphoned off to swell personal offshore bank accounts and those of organized crime. The nation is in the same (or perhaps worse) situation that it was in the earliest days of transition. The Russian government (with help from other world powers) is working to develop the basics of a sound market economy before further badly needed reform and transition can take place.

The Pain of Being Set Free

Since the fall of communism, people in Russia and central and eastern Europe are having a difficult time making ends meet. The mental anguish of rapid social change, crumbling welfare systems, and rocketing unemployment are creating a gloomy atmosphere in some nations. Suicides in Russia have jumped about 48 percent in postcommunist times. Statistics for the Baltic States are similar, with Latvia's suicide rate increasing about 44 percent, Estonia's 46 percent, and Lithuania's 70 percent! Officials point to alcoholism and depression, and a slow response in recognizing and treating these afflictions.

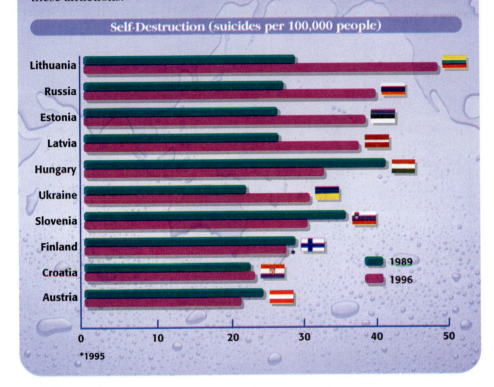

Self-Destruction (suicides per 100,000 people)

Lithuania, Russia, Estonia, Latvia, Hungary, Ukraine, Slovenia, Finland*, Croatia, Austria

■ 1989 ■ 1996

*1995

In addition, political instability, especially in the form of intensified nationalist sentiment, could threaten progress toward transition. Also, some experts worry about the future disposition of Russia's nuclear weapons stockpiles. Almost everyone in Russia is badly in need of currency and sales of such stockpiles can earn large sums of hard currency. Although the temptation to sell weapons to other nations is particularly great, in the wrong hands they can threaten global security, and that of Russia itself.

CENTRAL AND EASTERN EUROPE

Many countries undergoing transition in the broad region of central and eastern Europe were once mixed economy nations. Shortly after World War II, however, nearly all turned to communist practice under political and military pressure from the former Soviet Union. They deposed their communist regimes only after change gripped the former Soviet Union itself. Most have introduced democratic political reforms and market-oriented economic reforms, but they still feel the residual effects of central planning and communist ideology.

Countries are experiencing different degrees of success, with those nations that remained more autonomous from the Soviet Union faring better than those previously integrated into the Soviet Union itself. Poland, for example, is outpacing Russia in the race toward a free market. While Russia's economy contracted by 50 percent between 1991 and 1997, the Polish economy posted better than 5 percent annual growth through 1997 and is expected to continue along this path into the twenty-first century.[25] To explain this discrepancy, economists point to the different roles played by the Russian and Polish governments. In Russia, for instance, regulatory burdens add more than three months to the process of registering a business; in Poland, it only takes a few weeks. In Poland, leading multinationals like Nestlé, Proctor & Gamble, and Unilever are already major investors, and their success there has encouraged more and more medium-size companies to look at Poland as an investment base.[26]

Why are conditions in non-Soviet nations so much better than in the nations of the former Soviet Union? First, in many non-Soviet countries, political reform preceded economic reform. Policy makers, therefore, had popular mandates to implement economic reforms that were sometimes quite painful. Second, market reform in former Soviet nations often took place before government-owned companies were ready to compete in the national or international marketplace. As transition brought world competition into previously centrally planned economies, inefficient producers were forced into layoffs or even bankruptcies. Poorly trained employees, outdated production techniques, and a lack of capital for start-ups created stumbling blocks on the road to transition.

Despite the attractiveness of a market of roughly 150 million people, why do many international companies remain reluctant to commit to large-scale investments in the region? First, progress toward a fully free-market economy has been slow. The cultures of these nations have never been as individual-oriented as those of Canada, the United Kingdom, or the United States. People tend to place faith in strong central governments and to distrust completely free markets. Thus government bureaucrats are often able to retain power over many political and economic decisions. Therefore, international companies find it very hard to surmount administrative delays and bureaucratic red tape.

Second, certain political disadvantages obstruct the transition process. Some countries lack strong central governments capable of dealing effectively with important national matters. In early 1997, for instance, Albania was badly crippled by a collapsed "pyramid" investment scandal that cost many people their entire life savings. As chaos ensued, the government sat by helplessly as looters and rioters took control of the streets with weapons seized from government storage.

Finally, many central and eastern Europeans are faced with the high levels—and the resulting expense—of pollution bequeathed them by the communist era. The former regimes disregarded the environment for two main reasons: (1) They had access only to poor-quality coal as a source of energy, and (2) they could not afford basic pollution-control equipment. Their successors must now find the money to pay for environmental cleanup programs and pollution-control equipment.

Despite these problems, there are positive signs. In about one third of these countries, the private sector is already responsible for roughly half the total gross national product. Some nations were also sustaining tolerable inflation rates into 1999—around 8 percent in the Czech Republic, 11 percent in Hungary, and 9 percent in Poland. Sound fiscal and monetary policies are largely responsible for eliminating the outrageously high rates of earlier years, but current rates are still rather high. During the same period, inflation was only 1 percent in France, 2.2 percent in Japan, and 1.4 percent in the United States. Because inflation rates this high in central and eastern Europe continue to erode consumer spending power, living standards, and further development, they must be brought lower.

AFRICA

When most African nations gained independence from European colonial powers between the late 1940s and mid-1960s, many adopted socialist or communist economic policies. During the Cold War, unfortunately, the former Soviet Union and the United States struggled against one another for political influence across much of the continent. The situation was most extreme and blatant in Angola, where each nation provided weapons and other supplies to different sides in a bloody civil war.

Most African governments have a tradition of exercising strong central control over the economy while withholding incentives for private business activity. Tanzania and Zambia were among the staunchly socialist countries that "exported" the socialist ideology to other African countries, and today evidence of poor central planning is apparent across the continent in low gross national product, high unemployment, runaway inflation, low quality of life, and overall economic stagnation.

In addition, the profits generated from business conducted with international companies are often siphoned off by corrupt leaders and used to bloat personal bank accounts. In the West African nation of Equatorial Guinea, for example, an oil boom has increased economic growth by 67 percent in just one year. Unfortunately, the family of the president controls almost all of the country's oil income. A separatist group from one region that receives virtually no benefits whatsoever has emerged to challenge central government control. Equatorial Guinea, reports one diplomat, "is a patrimonial state with a complete absence of rule of law."[28]

During the last 10 years, however, many African nations have initiated transition toward free-market economics, and governments appear to be loosening their control over commercial affairs. Uganda, for instance, has introduced several measures to privatize its agricultural sector, which was under government control for a long time. In all, about 30 African countries are currently experimenting with some form of market economic system. Malawi, Mozambique, and South Africa have already held their first democratic elections, and Mali, Tanzania, and Zambia are currently peaceful democracies.

In other parts of Africa, however, political and economic stability remain elusive goals. In Algeria, Nigeria, and Sierra Leone for instance, antidemocratic forces have forced legitimately elected politicians from office. In the Central African Republic and the Democratic Republic of Congo (formerly Zaire), corrupt leaders have enriched themselves and allowed the living standards to slide to unimaginably low levels. In Rwanda and Burundi, ongoing warfare among ethnic groups destroys property and destabilizes social organization. In Kenya, where relatively peaceful elections returned the president for a fifth term, conflict between his ethnic group and that of the runner-up resulted in political violence that scared off both international investors and tourists. Citing rampant corruption among top officials, the IMF also suspended a $205 million low-interest loan.[29] Until market-based economic reform and democratic legal reform take place, Africa remains a gamble for international companies in many industries.

LATIN AMERICA

For much of the 1970s, Argentina, Brazil, Chile, and Peru had economies under repressive government control; all four suffered from rapid inflation, rising unemployment, and declining qualities of life. Chile was the first to loosen government control and implement sweeping changes in economic policy, and other countries slowly followed suit. Most of Latin America is now characterized by growing market economies. Latin America's enormous population is attracting large investments from international companies in many industries.

The largest challenge facing companies entering Latin America is political and economic uncertainty. Economic reform in Mexico, for instance, was jeopardized when the Mexican peso tumbled steeply at the end of 1994. Mexican politics faced another crisis in 1994 when President Carlos Salinas de Gortari not only lost his reelection bid but was later forced into exile amid accusations of corruption and politically sanctioned murder. In the long term, however, the outlook for Mexico and all of Latin America is promising. Financial aid and other assistance from developed countries has helped to revive the Mexican economy and kept the nation—and, indeed, the entire region—on the track of economic reform. Continued political and economic reforms are increasing Latin America's appeal to international companies.

WESTERN EUROPE

Although Western Europe is not undergoing transition from central planning, many countries are experiencing the pain associated with the reform of mixed economies. Since World War II, the region has experienced relative prosperity and political stability under democratic governments. For decades, governments controlled certain economic sectors, including rail networks, power companies, telecommunications, and banking. One of the lingering results of this policy has been a high payroll tax. In Germany, for instance, workers pay about 40 percent of their salaries in taxes and social security contributions, and employers match many of those payments. In addition, strong labor unions have secured liberal fringe benefits. As you can see from Figure 4.5, labor costs in much of Europe are higher than that in the United States. The Organization for Economic Cooperation and Development reports correspondingly lower returns on business investment in Europe.[30]

FIGURE 4.5

INTERNATIONAL COMPARISON OF LABOR COSTS

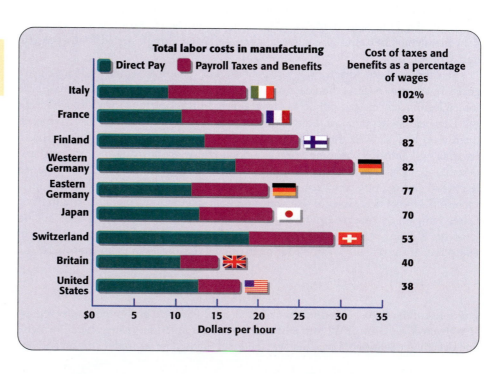

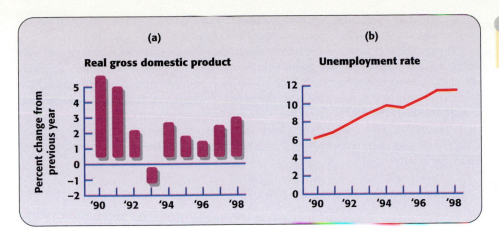

FIGURE 4.6

GERMAN ECONOMIC GROWTH

(a)

Real gross domestic product

(b)

Unemployment rate

Such high wage rates are creating correspondingly high unemployment rates. The French government passed legislation that requires all companies to go from 39- to 35-hour workweeks by 2002, arguing that the policy will create rather than jeopardize jobs. Many French businesspeople contend, however, that the program will succeed on a broad basis only if employers can reach agreement with labor unions, which are reluctant to grant concessions. Nevertheless, some companies are responding. Toyota Motor Company of Japan is building a $670 million assembly plant in northern France that will create 2,000 jobs.[31]

In Germany, where unemployment stands at around 10 percent, many companies, citing rigidly unionized work rules, high payroll taxes, and a weak domestic economy, are contracting work out to other countries rather than hiring German workers. Porsche, for example, now builds some of its popular two-seat Boxsters in Finland. Currently, German firms are investing about 10 times as much abroad as others are investing in Germany. Thus, as you can see from the two charts in Figure 4.6, although the German economy is growing (largely through exports), so is the unemployment rate.[32]

Most member countries of the European Union have established monetary union through a single currency, called the *euro*. To achieve this goal, several countries needed to strengthen their economies by further cutting government spending. France, for example, is trying to reduce the power of its labor unions and make changes that will likely add to already high unemployment rates. Both France and Italy had jobless rates of about 12 percent in 1999, while Spain's stood at a crippling 18 percent. In contrast, the jobless rate in the United States was around 4.2 percent.

Divisions between the countries of Western Europe will continue to surface as they debate the merits of giving up some measure of national control to a European-wide parliament. These are normal growing pains for a continent trying to pool resources after centuries of conflict. However, it looks increasingly likely that the European Union, which was modeled after the United States, might not become a "United States of Europe," but rather a "united Europe of states."[33]

A FINAL WORD

Ongoing market reforms in formerly centrally planned and mixed economies are having a profound effect on international business. Freer markets are spurring major shifts in manufacturing activity. Lured by such incentives as low wages and growing markets, international companies are forging ties in newly industrialized countries and exploring opportunities in developing nations. Global capital markets are making it easier for these companies to set up factories abroad, and some newly industrialized countries are even producing world-class competitors of their own.

International companies are keenly aware that many countries experiencing difficulties have immense potential for growth. Some experts, for instance, estimate the middle class in India will soon climb over 300 million people—more than the entire U.S. population. As long as one-time centrally planned economies continue down the path toward free markets, they will spur domestic entrepreneurial activity and attract international investors. This chapter completes our coverage of national business environments. The next chapter introduces Part 3 of the text—the international trade and investment environment.

There is a variety of additional material available on the companion Web site that accompanies this text. You can access this information by visiting the Web site at ⟨**www.prenhall.com/wild**⟩.

summary

① Identify the three main categories of *economic systems*. An *economic system* consists of the structure and processes that a country uses to allocate its resources and conduct its commercial activities. Economic systems can be organized along a continuum embracing three types.

In a *centrally planned economy*, the government owns land, factories, and other economic resources, and plans nearly all economic-related activities. The philosophy of central planning stresses the group over individual well-being and strives for economic and social equality.

In a *mixed economy*, land, factories, and other economic resources are split between private and government ownership, with governments tending to control economic sectors crucial to national security and long-term stability.

In a *market economy*, private individuals or businesses own the majority of land, factories, and other economic resources. Economic decisions are influenced by the interplay of *supply* (the quantity of a product that producers are willing to provide at a specific selling price) and *demand* (the quantity of a product that buyers are willing to purchase at a specific selling price). To function smoothly, the market economy requires *free choice* (in buyers' purchase options), *free enterprise* (in producers' competitive decisions), and *price flexibility* (reflecting supply and demand).

② Define *economic development* and explain how it can be measured. *Economic development* refers to the economic well-being of one nation's people com-

pared to that of another nation's people. Formal methods for gauging economic development include the following: (a) *National production* includes such measures as *gross national product* (*GNP*) (the value of all goods and services produced in one year by a country) and *gross domestic product* (*GDP*) (the value of all goods and services produced in one year by the domestic economy). (b) *Purchasing power parity* (*PPP*) refers to the relative ability of two countries' currencies to buy the same "basket" of goods in those two countries. This index is used to correct comparisons that are made at official exchange rates and, therefore, ignore different costs of living in different nations. (c) The United Nations' *human development index* (*HDI*) goes beyond estimates of financial wealth in order to measure the extent to which a people's needs are satisfied and addressed equally across the population. HDI tries to determine if a government is successful in three areas: life expectancy, educational attainment, and income.

③ Describe the process of *economic transition*. The process whereby a nation changes its fundamental economic organization in order to create free-market institutions is called *economic transition*. Typically, five reform measures are involved: (a) macroeconomic stabilization to reduce budget deficits and expand credit availability; (b) liberalization of economic activity that is decided by prices reflecting supply and demand; (c) legalization of private enterprises and privatization of state-owned enterprises in keeping with an effective system of individual property rights; (d) removal of barriers to trade and investment in goods and services and to the free flow of currency; and (e) development of a social welfare system to ease the transition process.

4 **Identify obstacles to business in** *transitional economies.* The major obstacles to successful economic transition fall into four categories: (a) *Lack of managerial expertise.* Because central planners made virtually all operations and pricing decisions, and because the satisfaction of consumer needs was rarely a consideration, very few people developed the kinds of managerial skills needed in a highly competitive global economy. (b) *Shortage of capital.* Transition requires heavy expenditures in three areas: (1) developing a communications and infrastructure system, (2) setting up financial institutions, and (3) educating people about the working of a market economy. Most governments of transition nations lack the capital needed to make these investments. (c) *Cultural differences.* Some cultures are more open to change than others. Shocks to the economic system may include cuts in welfare payments, unemployment benefits, and guaranteed jobs. Importing modern management practices means tailoring them to the local culture. (d) *Environmental degradation.* Rapid industrialization and unsustainable economic growth rates in newly industrialized and developing nations are contributing to high levels of pollution. The costs of environmental destruction include lower workforce productivity due to substandard health conditions.

5 **Describe the experiences of** *nations and regions* **undergoing economic transition.** The experiences of seven countries or areas are particularly instructive.

China. China has been a centrally planned economy since 1949. Beginning in 1979, the government initiated economic reform. Chinese purchasing power, however, has not yet come close to standards in the West and growing unemployment is a problem. There also are significant cultural obstacles to doing business in China.

Vietnam. The Vietnamese government began liberalizing in the late 1980s, and the United States lifted an 18-year trade embargo in 1994. With vast natural resources and a population of 72 million, Vietnam is now a promising market and investment opportunity. Unfortunately, crime, corruption, and constantly changing ground rules are discouraging investors.

Russia. Because the former Soviet Union remained a staunchly communist system from 1917 until the late 1980s, the transition there has been slower than in China. The main impediment to transition has long been inflation. Although the erosion of purchasing power seems to have slowed, industrial production remains stagnant.

Central and Eastern Europe. These nations are experiencing differing degrees of success in transition. Countries like Poland are making headway, but progress in the nations that once belonged to the former Soviet Union itself has been slower. The private sector is making itself felt in many of these countries, controlling about half of gross domestic product.

Africa. Political and economic instability and corrupt leadership remain the biggest stumbling blocks. Some countries, such as Uganda, are making progress in establishing a free market. Broad market-based economic and legal reforms are needed for Africa to attract significant international investment.

Latin America. Under repressive right-wing government control for much of the 1970s, many countries suffered high inflation, unemployment, and poor living standards. Today, Latin America is characterized by growing market economies, and its huge population is attracting significant international investment.

Western Europe. The transition in much of Western Europe is from socialist to more pure free-market economies. European governments are aggressively privatizing and forcing companies to be globally competitive. Transition to a single currency has sparked efforts to strengthen economies by cutting government spending.

questions **for review**

1. What is an *economic system*? How are culture and economics related?

2. What is a *centrally planned economy*? Describe the link between central planning and communism. Name two countries that have or had centrally planned economies.

3. What is a *mixed economy*? Explain the origin of mixed economies, and name three countries with mixed economies.

4. Define *market economy*. What are the three requirements of a market economy?

5. Define *economic development*. Which three broad categories are used to classify countries according to level of economic development? Name three countries in each category.

6. Describe three *measures of economic development*. What are the advantages and disadvantages of each?

7. How does *GNP* differ from *GDP*?

8. Which three countries have the highest GNP per capita at *purchasing power parity*?

9. Explain the value of the *Human Development Index* (*HDI*).

10. What are the main characteristics of *developed countries*? *Newly industrialized countries*? *Developing countries*?

11. What types of countries tend to be characterized by *technological dualism*?

12. List the five reform measures involved in making the *transition* from a centrally planned or mixed economy to a market economy.

13. What is *privatization*? Explain its importance to economic transition.

14. What are the four main *obstacles* to businesses in transitional economies? Briefly describe each.

15. How did *China* get an early start on the transition process? Describe *guanxi*.

16. Describe how transition is proceeding in *Vietnam*.

17. Why is transition proceeding so slowly in *Russia*?

18. What is the main force holding back the transition to freer markets in *Africa*? Support your answer with three examples.

19. How is economic transition faring in *Latin America*?

20. Why are countries in *Western Europe* having an easier time in their transition efforts than those in *central and eastern Europe*?

questions for discussion

1. The Internet is quickly penetrating many aspects of business and culture in developed countries, but it is barely available in many poor countries. Do you think that this technology is going to widen the economic development gap between rich and poor countries? Why or why not? Is there a way that developing countries can use such technology as a tool for economic development?

2. Imagine that you are the director of a major international lending institution supported by funds from member countries. What one area in newly industrialized and developing economies would be your priority for receiving development aid? Do you suspect that any member countries will be politically opposed to aid in this area? Why or why not?

3. Two students are discussing the pros and cons of different measures of economic development. "GNP per capita," declares the first, "is the only true measure of how developed a country's economy is." The second student counters: "I disagree. The only true measure of a country's economic development is its people's quality of life, regardless of its GNP." Why is each of these students incorrect? Respond to each with a one-paragraph comment.

in practice

Countries in eastern and central Europe cast off the chains of communism in the late 1980s. This caused most nations to experience severe economic recessions caused by the "shock therapy" of implementing economic reforms. By the middle to late 1990s, many nations had turned their economies around and were growing steadily (see the "Winners and Losers" charts below). In 1998,

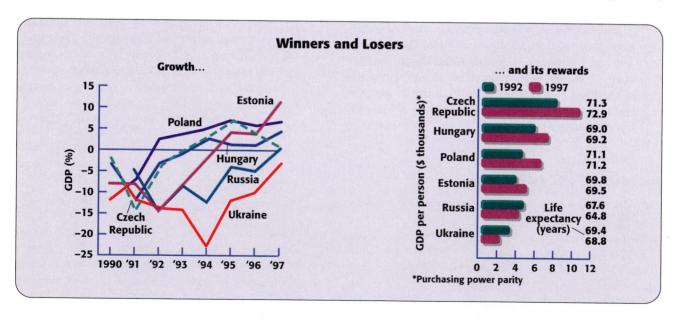

the economics of the Baltic States (Estonia, Latvia, and Lithuania) were expected to post GDP gains of more than 5 percent.

1. Why do you think Poland, Hungary, the Baltic States, and other countries outperformed Russia and the Ukraine throughout their postcommunist transitions? Identify several possible economic factors and social/cultural factors, and briefly describe why you think each was important.

2. How do you reconcile the high growth rates being experienced by the Baltic States and their large increases in suicide rates as shown in the World Business Survey on page 143? Why do you think a nation's people can be so depressed when the economy is performing so well?

3. Companies explicitly or implicitly supplement their analysis of a nation's attractiveness as a new market or production base with human development indicators. Do you think this is appropriate? List several human development issues that can affect company operations in a nation and, therefore, the decision to enter the market.

projects

1. In this project, two groups of four students debate the benefits and drawbacks of both market and mixed economies. After the first student from each side has spoken, the second student questions the opponent's arguments, looking for holes and inconsistencies. The third student attempts to answer these arguments. The fourth student presents a summary of each side's arguments. Finally, the class votes on which team has offered the more compelling argument.

2. Select a recent article from a business magazine or Web site discussing some economic issue within a particular country. Potential topics include privatization of state-owned companies, the influence of a capital shortage on transition, and investment in advancing human development such as public health programs. Summarize the article and explain how local and international companies will be affected by the decision

and how they can respond to it. Some good starting points include the following:

- CNN ⟨www.cnn.com⟩
- *The Economist* ⟨**www.economist.com**⟩
- *Far Eastern Economic Review* ⟨**www.feer.com**⟩
- *The Financial Times* ⟨**www.ft.com**⟩

3. Select a country that interests you. What type of economic system does it have? Has it always had this type of economic system? Is it developed, newly industrializing, or developing? How does it rank on the various measures of economic development? Has it undergone any form of economic transition within the last 10 years? If so, what have been the effects of that transition on the culture and the country's political, legal, and economic systems? Present a brief report to the class.

business case 4
BUSINESS ADMINISTRATION, HAVANA STYLE

Like M.B.A. students all over the world, students in Havana University's first M.B.A. program take courses ranging from accounting to international trade. Yet for the 50 members of HU's first graduating class in 1997, applying the principles of capitalist business in communist Cuba is another matter entirely. As one HU student complains: "I am studying about investing capital when Cubans cannot invest in Cuba. If you are a foreigner abroad, you can invest. But if you are a Cuban, no." Still, the mere existence of an M.B.A. program in Cuba, plus the recent influx of investment, are signs that the aging dictator, Fidel Castro, is loosening his iron grip on the island's planned economy.

When the Soviet Union collapsed in 1989, Cuba had to kiss Soviet subsidies goodbye. With state-owned industrial dinosaurs wheezing away and the economy under immense strain, Castro opened up key state industries to non-Cuban investment. As a result, joint ventures have become a key plank in the effort to prop up Cuba through limited economic reforms. Thus in 1994, $1.5 billion in investment flowed into Cuba. The money comes chiefly from Canada, Mexico, and Europe—all of whom benefit from the absence of Cuba's neighbor and nemesis, the United States, which has maintained a trade embargo against Cuba since

1960. The biggest player in Cuba today is Canada's Sherritt International Corporation. Sherritt's flag flutters outside the island's biggest nickel mine, and Sherritt rigs are reviving output from old oil fields. After turning around the ailing nickel mine at Moa, Sherritt received Castro's go-ahead to develop beach resorts and beef up communications and transport networks.

Yet, although international concerns like Sherritt are free to invest in Cuba, they face some harsh realities and a number of restrictions. For instance, Ricardo Elizondo came to Cuba from Mexico to help manage his company's stake in Etecsa, the firm that provides all of Cuba's phone service. Elizondo reports that anyone who wants to do business in Cuba must accept the reality of partnership with a socialist state. Cuba lacks a legal system to enforce commercial contracts; it lacks a banking system to offer credit, and there are no private-property rights. One thing the government doesn't lack is plenty of labor laws—and these are onerous. Non-Cuban partners cannot hire, fire, or even pay workers directly. They must pay the government to provide laborers who, in turn, are paid only a fraction of these payments.

Why do companies investing in Cuba put up with such restrictions? For one thing, they are getting a great return on their investment. "Cuba's assets are incredibly cheap, and the potential return is huge," says Frank Mersch, VP at Toronto's Altamira Management Ltd., which holds 11 percent of Sherritt. Castro, say analysts, is offering outsiders deals with rates of return up to 80 percent a year. Moreover, international investors tend to agree with the widespread belief that the Castro regime won't last very long. Once Castro loses his hold on Cuba, whether through capitulation, exile, or death, the United States will likely end its embargo. In that case, property prices will soar. Companies like Sherritt and Etecsa, who stepped in first, will have gained a valuable toehold in what could be a vibrant market economy.

thinking globally

1. Sherritt pays the Cuban government $9,500 per year per worker. According to Frank Calzon of Freedom House, a New York–based human rights group, the government then pays workers only $120 to $144 per year. Why do you think the Cuban government requires non-Cuban businesses to hire and pay workers only through the government? Do you think it is ethical for non-Cuban businesses to enter into partnerships with the Cuban government? Why or why not?

2. Do some brief research on Cuba, and describe a scenario for economic transition in the event that the Castro regime collapses. How do you think that the transition to a market economy in Cuba would be the same as or different than the transitions now taking place in Russia and China?

3. The United States not only has maintained a trade embargo against Cuba since 1960 but also has enacted a law permitting U.S. companies to sue companies from other nations that traffic in the property of U.S. firms nationalized by Castro when he took over. It also empowers the U.S. government to deny entry visas to the executives of such firms as well as their families. Given the fact that the Cold War is over, why do you think the United States maintains such a hard line against doing business with Cuba? Do you think this embargo is in the United State's best interests? Why or why not?

a question of ethics

1. At the same time that deregulation and free-market forces have reduced health care inflation in the United States, 12 states have passed laws to safeguard the rights of patients and to limit the secret financial incentives that insurance plans offer to doctors. Furthermore, the federal government has just issued regulations limiting what health-maintenance organizations can do to pare costs and has barred insurers from denying coverage to people with preexisting medical conditions. Free-market theorists, such as Peter Huber of the Manhattan Institute for Policy Research, argue that this kind of lingering regulatory involvement is just a way station on the road to complete deregulation. Eventually, they say, there will be a giant free-for-all to provide health care, information service, electric power, entertainment, and financial services to both business and individual consumers. Do you think that it would be profitable to provide health insurance for a cancer patient in a market economy? What about providing electricity and phone service for people in rural areas and inner-city neighborhoods? What are the ethical ramifications of eliminating all government regulations?[34]

2. As you discovered in this chapter, China's People's Liberation Army (PLA) has built a sprawling network of businesses—enterprises that do everything from raise pigs to run airlines and hospitals, mine coal, manage hotels, and operate paging and cellular networks. As a business conglomerate, of course, the PLA partners with international investors. According to *New York Times* columnist Abraham Rosenthal, "The great part of U.S. business in China is with companies and cartels controlled by the Chinese military." Other observers, however, argue that it's easy to read too much into the PLA's foray into business. They point out that there is little centralized coordination among the thousands of businesses with military affiliations and that whereas many of the larger military-affiliated companies are run by individual or retired officers, others are managed by civilians. If you were looking for a joint venture partner in China, would you have any ethical concerns about partnering with the PLA? If so, what would those be? Suppose you were managing a Canadian-Chinese joint venture involving the PLA, when a clash between pro-democracy demonstrators and the PLA turns bloody. How would this turn of events affect business relations with your PLA partner? Given the country's record on human rights, are the ethical issues of partnering with the Chinese military any different than those that arise from investing in or exporting to China? Why or why not?[35]

3. The social-welfare states of western Europe were founded after the Second World War with specific ethical considerations in mind: reduce social and economic inequality, improve living standards for the poor, and provide health care for everyone. Now many of these countries have begun to trim social-welfare provisions and increase their reliance on market forces. Do you think that the ethical concerns of half a century ago are a thing of the past, or do you feel that market reforms will simply re-create the conditions that motivated the development of the welfare state in the first place? Argue the merits of each case.

integrative video case
PART TWO: NATIONAL BUSINESS ENVIRONMENTS
mtv europe and yahoo!

background

This video case shows how MTV Europe and Yahoo! have taken into consideration sociocultural and political factors in penetrating markets abroad. In essence, the message from both companies is, "When in Rome, do as the Romans do." Both companies have been very sensitive to the various countries' culture, social structure, and political climate, and accordingly they have customized their products and services to satisfy local demands. These companies also looked at the long traditions and histories of the countries they wanted to do business in, such as China, France, Denmark, Sweden, and Mexico.

mtv europe

Since it was launched in 1981, MTV has become an international player, especially in Europe, by "thinking globally and acting locally." Peter Einstein, president of MTV Europe, led the charge when he said, "Be there,

giving them what they want, in whatever form." MTV Europe, currently reaching 77 million homes, has adopted a European strategy; it offers local versions of its satellite/cable TV network programming to compete in individual European countries. These more-focused offerings have gradually been replacing MTV Europe's wider regional programming, and versions for the Netherlands, Spain, and Eastern European countries are now being considered. The network only recently launched MTV Central Germany, which added 11.2 million homes to its customer base. Wider regional advertisers still make up the largest share of the network's ad revenues, but the number of advertisers has increased to 600 (local and regional) from 235 advertisers (most of which were regional) in 1995.

yahoo! inc.

For information on this company, please refer to the Part I video case on pages 30–31.

discussion questions

While you watch the video, keep the following discussion questions in mind. You might want to take notes.

1. How did MTV Europe and Yahoo! deal with the cultures of the countries they penetrated?

2. How did the companies express their sensitivity to concerns such as politics, religion, and social issues?

3. How would the cultures of the countries the two companies had dealings with be classified in Hofstede's framework?

4. How would you use Kluckhohn-Strodtbeck's framework to analyze the cultures of Japan, France, Mexico, Sweden, China, and Denmark?

5. How did MTV Europe approach penetrating the cultures of the various countries they have dealings with? Give details. What approach did Yahoo! take? Give details.

6. Give your own interpretation of the phrase "When in Rome, do as the Romans do."

student exercises

1. Break into groups of two or three people. Draw up a strategy focusing on culture and politics for how an international company might penetrate markets in China and France.

2. Assume that Yahoo! is about to attempt to penetrate Africa. What would be the challenges facing the company in selected

African countries? How should it proceed in its efforts in Nigeria? In Liberia? In Egypt? In South Africa?

3. Assume that MTV Europe is about to try to expand into the same countries listed in question 2. Where might it succeed? Where might it fail? Why?

international trade

Beacons

A Look Back

CHAPTERS **2, 3,** and **4** examined the important ways in which cultural, political, and legal elements influence business activities in other countries. We also learned that business is often conducted differently in different economies around the world.

A Look at This Chapter

This chapter begins our study of the international trade and investment environment. We explore the oldest form of international business activity—international trade. We discuss the benefits and volume of international trade and explore the major theories that attempt to explain why trade occurs.

A Look Ahead

CHAPTER **6** explains government involvement in international trade. We explore the motives and methods of government intervention and how the global trading system works to promote free trade.

Learning Objectives

After studying this chapter, you should be able to

1. Describe the *volume* of international trade, how trade volume and *world output* are related, and *international trade patterns*.

2. Describe *mercantilism* and explain its historical impact on the world powers and their colonies.

3. Identify the differences between *absolute advantage* and *comparative advantage*.

4. Explain the *factor proportions* and *international product life cycle* theories.

5. Explain the *new trade* and *national competitive advantage* theories.

S'bu Mngadi, chief spokesperson for Coca-Cola Southern Africa, mentions with pride the entrepreneurial spirit of the people of many African nations. He tells the story of two brothers from Mpumalanga, South Africa, who started selling Coke years ago out of a "spaza shop"—a small store run out of the back of a tin and cinderblock house. Now they own a multimillion-dollar Coca-Cola bottling business.

Throughout the twentieth century, many African nations were devastated by bloody wars, both internally and with their neighbors. Although all of Africa accounts for less than 1 percent of world commerce, a new age seems to be dawning in some African nations. Besides South Africa, countries showing promise include Botswana, Ghana, Nigeria, Mozambique, and Uganda. The United States now leads the world in trade with Africa—annual trade figures top $10 billion and are expected to rise. Economic growth rates for countries south of the Sahara Desert are expected to be 5 percent per year through the year 2006.

Coca-Cola is doing what it can to ride the wave of growing trade and investment activity in Africa. Apart from humanitarian contributions, Coke offers budding micro-entrepreneurs free business management courses. "What we've seen in South Africa," says Charles Frenette, Coke's chief marketing officer, "is somebody who starts by standing on a street corner, then moving up to a kiosk." It sounds like a slow process, but engaging in such basic forms of business is how the most successful Southeast Asian economies began their climb out of abject poverty. Maybe, just maybe, it can work for Africa too.[1]

Today, people around the world are accustomed to purchasing goods and services from companies in other countries. In fact, many consumers get their first taste of another country's culture through merchandise purchased from that country. Chanel No. 5 perfume evokes the romanticism of France. The fine artwork on Imari porcelain conveys the Japanese attention to detail and quality. MTV, The Gap, and Levi's jeans portray the casual lifestyle of people in the United States.

In this chapter, we explore international trade in goods and services. We begin by examining the benefits, volume, and patterns of international trade. We then explore a number of important theories that attempt to explain why nations trade with one another.

OVERVIEW OF INTERNATIONAL TRADE

The purchase, sale, or exchange of goods and services across national borders is called **international trade**. This is in contrast to domestic trade, which occurs between different states, regions, or cities within a country. Another important form of international busi-

MAP 5.1

THE IMPORTANCE OF TRADE

This map shows each nation's trade volume as a share of its GDP, adjusted for purchasing power parity.

Trade as a share of GDP at purchasing power parity is defined as the sum of merchandise exports and imports measured in current U.S. dollars divided by the value of GDP converted to international dollars using purchasing power parity conversion factors.

This is a conservative measure: Because the GDP of many developing countries is larger in PPP terms than when converted at official exchange rates, the resulting ratios tend to be lower.

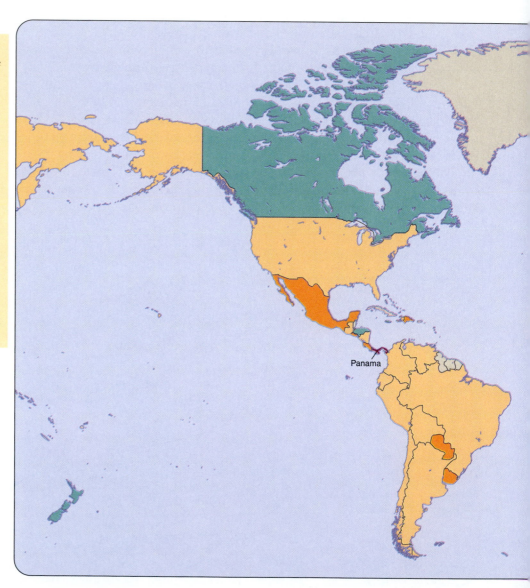

Panama

ness activity is **foreign direct investment (FDI)**—the purchase of physical assets or a significant amount of the ownership of a company in another country to gain a measure of management control. We discuss foreign direct investment in detail in Chapter 7.

A majority of the world's economies have seen an increase in the importance of trade over the past decade. One way to measure the importance of trade to a nation is to examine the volume of an economy's trade relative to its total output. Map 5.1 shows the sum of each country's exports and imports divided by its GDP at purchasing power parity. As the map demonstrates, the value of trade passing through some nations' borders actually exceeds the amount of goods and services that they produce (the 100.1% and up category).

BENEFITS OF INTERNATIONAL TRADE

As we saw in our opening example, international trade is opening doors to new entrepreneurial opportunity across Africa. It also provides a country's people with a greater choice of goods and services. For example, because Finland has a cool climate, it cannot

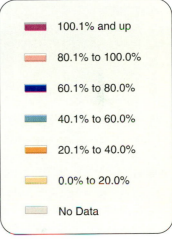

international trade
Purchase, sale, or exchange of goods and services across national borders.

foreign direct investment (FDI)
Purchase of physical assets or a significant amount of the ownership of a company in another country to gain a measure of management control.

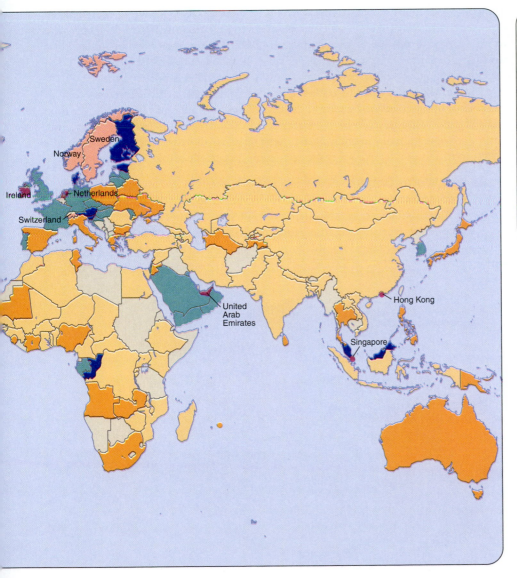

	100.1% and up
	80.1% to 100.0%
	60.1% to 80.0%
	40.1% to 60.0%
	20.1% to 40.0%
	0.0% to 20.0%
	No Data

be expected to grow cotton. But it can sell paper and other products made from lumber (which it has in abundance) to the United States. It can then use the proceeds from the sale to buy Pima cotton from the United States. Thus people in Finland get cotton they would otherwise not have. Although the United States has vast forests, the wood-based products from Finland might be of a certain quality or price that fills a gap in the U.S. marketplace. Importing these products from Finland might also allow workers in the United States to work in other industries that pay higher wages.

International trade is an important engine for job creation in many countries. For example, the Department of Commerce of the United States estimates that for every $1 billion increase in exports, 22,800 jobs are created in the country. Thus growing exports between 1993 and 1997 created more than 6.5 million jobs in the United States. Moreover, the U.S. Trade Representative's office reports that trade-related jobs pay 13 percent to 17 percent more than jobs not related to international trade.[2] Expanded trade has similar benefits for other countries.

VOLUME OF INTERNATIONAL TRADE

The volume of international trade continues to increase. In 1997, world merchandise exports stood at $5.4 trillion and service exports $1.4 trillion. Figure 5.1 shows the world's largest exporters of merchandise in 1997 according to the portion of total world exports for which each is responsible. Perhaps not surprisingly, the United States, Germany, and Japan dominate the rest of the world in export volume.

Most of world merchandise trade is comprised of trade in manufactured goods. The dominance of manufactured goods in the trade of merchandise has persisted over time and will likely continue to do so (see Figure 5.2). Although the importance of service exports is growing for many nations, it tends to be relatively more important for the world's richest countries. Service exports make up roughly 20 percent of total world trade.

Trade and World Output   The level of world output in any given year influences the level of international trade in that year. Slower world economic output slows the volume of international trade, and higher output spurs greater trade. Trade slows in times of economic recession because people are less certain about their own financial futures and thus buy fewer domestic and imported products. Another reason output

FIGURE 5.1

WORLD'S TOP MERCHANDISE EXPORTERS

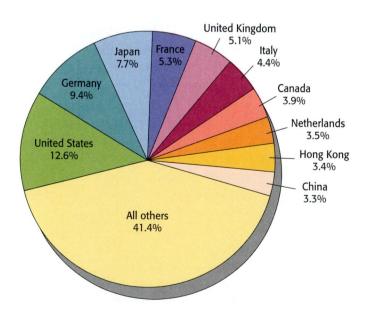

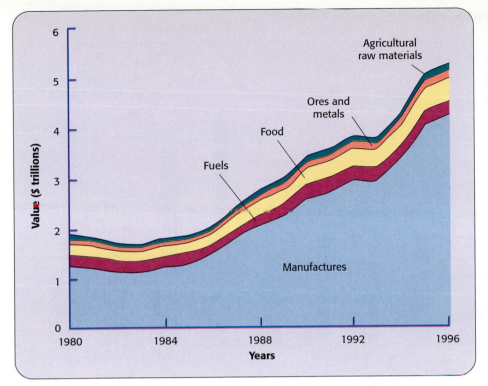

FIGURE 5.2

BREAKDOWN OF WORLD MERCHANDISE EXPORTS

The value of merchandise exports has more than doubled since 1980, while manufactured exports have more than tripled. Traditional exports of primary commodities remain important for many developing countries, but world trade is increasingly dominated by manufactured goods.

and trade move together is that a country in recession also often has a weak currency relative to other nations. This makes imports more expensive relative to domestic products. We discuss the relation between currency values and trade fully in chapter 10. In addition to trade and world output moving in lockstep fashion, trade has consistently grown faster than output (see Figure 5.3).

INTERNATIONAL TRADE PATTERNS

Exploring the volume of international trade and world output provides useful insights into the international trade environment. However, it does not tell us who trades with whom. For instance, we do not know whether trade occurs primarily between the world's richest nations or whether there is significant trade activity involving poorer nations.

Customs agencies in most countries record the destination of exports, the source of imports, and the physical quantities and values of goods crossing their borders. This type of data is very revealing, although it is sometimes misleading. For example, governments sometimes deliberately distort the reporting of trade in military equipment or other sensitive goods. In other cases, extensive trade in underground economies (black markets) can distort the real picture of trade between nations. Nevertheless, customs data tend to reflect general trade patterns among nations rather well.[4]

Who Trades with Whom?   Figure 5.4 shows the broad pattern of merchandise trade between the world's richest and poorest nations (data on trade in services is unavailable). As we see, trade among the world's high-income economies accounts for nearly 60 percent of total world merchandise trade. Two-way trade between high-income countries and low- and middle-income nations accounts for about 34 percent of world merchandise trade. But we also notice the lack of significant merchandise trade among low- and middle-income nations—only about 6 percent of total world

FIGURE 5.3   GROWTH OF WORLD MERCHANDISE EXPORTS AND GDP, 1987–1997

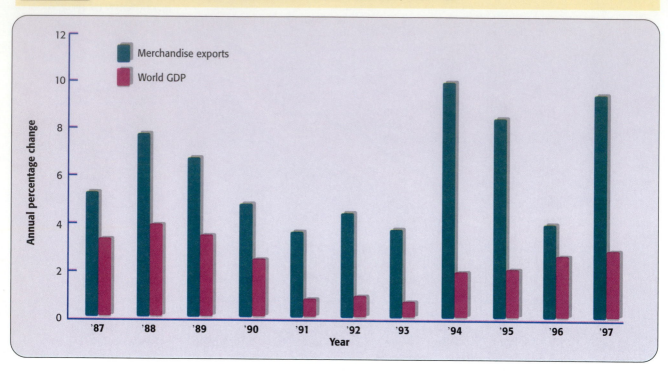

trade. These figures reveal the low purchasing power of the world's poorest nations and indicate their general lack of economic development.

Table 5.1 shows data on trade among high-income economies that account for a large portion of total worldwide trade—the European Union, Japan, and the United States. The table demonstrates that whereas U.S. imports from Japan account for 2.2 percent of total world merchandise trade, Japan's imports from the United States account for just 1.3 percent—slightly more than half the value of trade flowing in the op-

FIGURE 5.4

DIRECTION OF INTERNATIONAL TRADE (% OF WORLD TRADE)

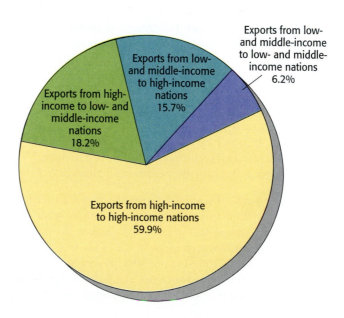

TABLE 5.1

Trade Among Several High-Income Nations (% of World Trade)

	Importer		
Exporter	United States	European Union	Japan
United States	—	2.5	1.3
European Union	2.8	23.5	0.9
Japan	2.2	1.2	—

posite direction. These statistics reveal why headlines in the United States often complain that Japan's markets are not open to U.S. goods. The value of goods traded between the European Union and the United States is much more balanced. Finally, the table reveals the very large portion of world merchandise trade occurring solely among European Union nations—nearly a quarter of the worldwide total.

Asian Crisis and World Trade   Economic crises in several Asian countries has curtailed their output and influenced trade. But so far it has had less of an impact than some predicted.[3] The five most affected Asian countries are Indonesia, Malaysia, the Philippines, South Korea, and Thailand. However, as the crises continue to play themselves out, Hong Kong and China could be hit still harder and thus jeopardize recovery for the entire region. We discuss the reasons behind the Asian financial crisis in Chapter 10.

Why has the Asian crisis so far not strongly affected world trade volume? Because the five most affected countries just listed account for just 3.6 percent of world GDP, about 7 percent of world trade, and under 4 percent of international bank lending. In addition, no country outside Asia relied on these five nations for as much as 10 percent of its total merchandise exports or imports in the year before the crisis struck. For example, these nations accounted for only 8.6 percent of the United States' total merchandise imports and just 8.4 percent of its merchandise exports. They comprised only 2.5 percent of Western Europe's imports and exports.

The Asian crisis will mostly affect trade among those countries in crisis and among other economies in the region. For example, in contrast to the United States and Europe, the five most affected economies accounted for 16.5 percent of Japan's total imports and 19.6 percent of its exports prior to the crisis. If Japan can revitalize its own economy, it will pull the rest of Asia along with it to increased economic activity and output. In any case, as the Asian economies recover, they will emerge from the crisis stronger than ever. Wasteful business practices will have been drastically curtailed. Companies now joining forces with European or North American firms will have the financial capital with which to research and develop new products and penetrate markets at home and abroad. Thus managers outside Asia would do well to take the opportunity to both learn more about the Asian marketplace and prepare for the renewed competitiveness of Asian companies. See the Global Manager "Five Rules for Building Good Relations in the 'Rim' and Beyond" for some quick pointers on doing business in Pacific Rim nations.

TRADE DEPENDENCE AND INDEPENDENCE

All countries fall on a continuum of trade interdependencies, with total dependence on another country at one end and total independence from other countries at the other end. Complete independence was considered desirable from the sixteenth through

A South Korean bank employee prepares for a run on the country's cash supply. Rapid depreciation, high interest rates and unemployment, and the flow of private funds out of Korea and other Asian countries have precipitated a major economic crisis in which Asian economies are expected to shrink by more than 5 percent, a striking contrast to the much-heralded growth they sustained in the 1980s.

Global Manager

Five Rules for Building Good Relations in the "Rim" and Beyond

To do business in Asia–Pacific Rim countries (those that rim the Pacific Ocean in Asia), start by recognizing two facts: (1) Asian customers can be as diverse as their individual cultures, and (2) aggressive salesmanship doesn't work in the land of the "four tigers." Cultural nuances and business etiquette demand a little homework before you visit these countries. Some general rules apply, however. Here are five:

1. **Count on third-party contacts.** Asians prefer to do business with people they know. Cold calls—in which you call a company with no prior contact—and other direct-contact methods seldom work. Meeting the right people in an Asian company almost always depends on having the right introduction. Use a proper intermediary. If the person with whom you hope to do business respects your intermediary, chances are he or she will respect you.

2. **Carry a bilingual business card.** To make a good first impression, have bilingual cards printed even though many Asians speak English—the international language of business. It shows both respect for the language and commitment to doing business in a particular country. It also translates your title into the local language. Asians generally are not comfortable until they know your position and whom you represent.

3. **Leave the hard sell at home.** Asian businesspeople are tough negotiators, but they dislike argumentative exchanges. Harmony and consensus are the bywords. Be prepared to be patient but firm.

4. **Go easy with legalese.** Legal documents are not as important as personal relationships. Most Asians do not like detailed contracts and will often insist that agreements be left flexible so that adjustments can easily be made to fit changing circumstances. It's very important to foster good relations based on mutual trust and benefit. The importance of a contract in many Asian societies is not what it stipulates, but rather who signed it.

5. **Build personal rapport.** Social ease and friendship are prerequisites to doing business. Accept invitations and be sure to reciprocate. As much business is transacted in informal dinner settings as in corporate settings.

much of the eighteenth centuries. On the other hand, some remote island nations were completely independent simply because they lacked methods of transportation to engage in trade. Today, however, this is far less common and isolationism is generally considered undesirable.

Effect on Developing and Transition Nations   Developing and transition nations that share borders with developed countries are often dependent upon their wealthier neighbors. This is now the case in Europe, as Germany leapfrogs Austria and the United States to become central Europe's biggest investor. A large number of joint ventures now bridge the borders between Germany and its neighbors—Germany has more than 6,000 in Hungary alone. Germany also is central Europe's most generous aid donor and mightiest trading partner, accounting for more than half of the European Union's total trade with the 12 central and east European countries that have applied to join the union. The benefit for central European nations is a chance to increase their prosperity. By combining German technology with lower central European production costs, German companies are already gaining an edge over the competition. Central European workers, for instance, are highly skilled but don't enjoy the expensive benefits that their German counterparts do. That's why Opel, the German arm of General Motors Corporation, built a $440 million plant in Szentgotthard, Hungary, using local talent to make parts for and assemble its Astra hatchbacks for export. J. P. Morgan estimated that in 1997 alone the region bought 10 percent of Germany's exports and accounted for a quarter of its roughly 6 percent export growth. Nearly every central European country gets at least 30 percent of its imports from Germany.[5]

Dangers of Trade Dependency   Trade dependency can be dangerous. Economic recession or political turmoil in the nation depended upon can cause serious economic or political problems for the dependent nation. Perhaps as central European countries prosper, they will try to diversify away from trade dependence on Germany. Recently, some poorer countries have tried to become less dependent upon trade with the United States. However many of these nations have adopted a more pragmatic stance, hoping that trade with the United States will bolster their own economies, allowing them to diversify gradually.

Countries today lie somewhere along the continuum between total dependence and complete independence. Thus it is generally acknowledged that trade between most nations is characterized by a degree of interdependency. The level of interdependency between certain pairs of countries often reflects the amount of trade that occurs between a company's subsidiaries in the two nations. For example, transactions between subsidiaries of international companies account for about one-third of U.S. exports and about two-fifths of U.S. imports. The Mercedes-Benz plant in Tuscaloosa, Alabama, imports most of its components for production of its Mercedes-Benz sport utility vehicle from Germany. The completed vehicle is then sent back to Germany or to affiliates in other countries.[6]

THEORIES OF INTERNATIONAL TRADE

Trade between different groups of people has occurred for many thousands of years. But it was not until the fifteenth century that people tried to explain why trade occurs and why trade can benefit both parties to an exchange. Figure 5.5 shows a timeline of when the main theories of international trade were proposed. Today, efforts to refine existing trade theories and develop new ones continue. Let's now discuss the first theory that attempts to explain why nations should engage in international trade—*mercantilism*.

FIGURE 5.5   **TRADE THEORY TIMELINE**

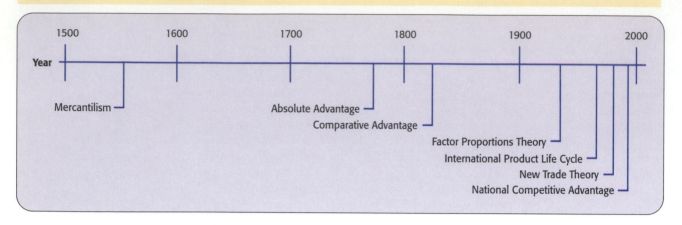

MERCANTILISM

mercantilism

Trade theory holding that nations should accumulate financial wealth, usually in the form of gold, by encouraging exports and discouraging imports.

The trade theory that nations should accumulate financial wealth, usually in the form of gold, by encouraging exports and discouraging imports is called **mercantilism**. It states that other measures of a nation's well-being, such as living standards or human development, are irrelevant. Nation-states in Europe followed this economic philosophy from about 1500 to the late 1700s. The most prominent mercantilist nations included Britain, France, the Netherlands, Portugal, and Spain.

How Mercantilism Worked   When navigation was a fairly new science, Europeans explored the world by sea, claiming the lands they encountered in the name of the European monarchy who was financing their voyage. Early exploration led them to Africa, Asia, and North, South, and Latin America. Subsequent colonization meant subduing native populations and imposing upon them alien ways of life. Colonial trade was conducted for the benefit of mother countries, and colonial nations were generally treated as exploitable resources.

In recent times, former colonies have struggled to diminish their reliance on the former colonial powers. For example, in an effort to decrease their dependence on the former colonial masters, African nations are welcoming trade relationships with partners from Asia and North America. But because their geographic isolation is a factor in the cost of their trading relationships, many former colonies have joined the Lome Convention, which gives them duty-free access to the European Union for a range of exports.[7]

trade surplus

Condition that results when the value of a nation's exports is greater than the value of its imports.

Trade Surpluses   Just how did countries implement mercantilism? First, nations increased their wealth by maintaining a **trade surplus**—the condition that results when the value of a nation's exports is greater than the value of its imports. In mercantilism, a trade surplus meant that a country was taking in more gold on the sale of its exports than it was paying out for its imports. A **trade deficit** is the opposite condition—one that results when the value of a country's imports is greater than the value of its exports. In mercantilism, trade deficits were to be avoided at all costs. We discuss the importance of national trade balance more fully in Chapter 7.

trade deficit

Condition that results when the value of a country's imports is greater than the value of its exports.

Intervention   Second, national governments actively intervened in international trade to maintain a trade surplus. According to mercantilism, accumulation of wealth depended on increasing a nation's trade surplus, not necessarily expanding its total value or volume of trade. The governments of mercantilist nations did this by either banning certain imports or imposing various restrictions on them such as tariffs or quotas. At the same time, they subsidized home-based industries to expand exports. Governments also typically outlawed the removal of their gold and silver to other nations.

Colonialization   Third, mercantilist nations acquired less developed territories (colonies) around the world to serve as sources of inexpensive raw materials and as markets for higher priced finished goods. Colonies were the source of many essential raw materials including tea, sugar, tobacco, rubber, and cotton. These resources would be shipped to the mercantilist nation where they were incorporated into finished goods such as clothing, cigars, and other products. These finished goods would then be sold to the colonies. Trade between mercantilist countries and their colonies were a huge source of profits for the mercantilist powers. The colonies received low prices for basic raw materials but paid high prices for finished goods.

The mercantilist and colonial policies greatly expanded the wealth of nations employing them. This wealth allowed nations to build armies and navies to control their far-flung colonial empires and to protect their shipping lanes from attack by other nations. It was a source of a nation's economic power that in turn increased its political power relative to other countries. Today, countries seen by others as trying to maintain a trade surplus and expanding their national treasuries at the expense of other nations are accused of practicing *neo-mercantilism* or *economic nationalism*. Fairly or not, Japan has often been accused of practicing neo-mercantilism because of its consistently high trade surplus with several industrial nations—particularly the United States. France has also been labeled neo-mercantilist by its trading partners when it has tried to export its way out of difficult economic times in the past.

Flaws of Mercantilism   Despite its seemingly positive benefits for any nation implementing it, mercantilism is inherently flawed. Mercantilist nations believed that the world's wealth was limited and that a nation could increase its share of the pie only at the expense of its neighbors—called a *zero-sum game*. The main problem with mercantilism is that if all nations were to barricade their markets from imports and push their exports onto others, international trade would be severely restricted. In fact, trade in all nonessential goods would likely cease altogether.

In addition, paying colonies little for their exports but charging them high prices for their imports impaired their economic development. Thus their appeal as markets for goods was less than it would have been if they were allowed to accumulate greater wealth. These negative aspects of mercantilism were made apparent by a new trade theory developed in the late 1700s—*absolute advantage*.

ABSOLUTE ADVANTAGE

Scottish economist Adam Smith first put forth the trade theory of absolute advantage in 1776.[8] The ability of a nation to produce a good more efficiently than any other nation is called an **absolute advantage**. In other words, a nation with an absolute advantage can produce greater output of a good or service than other nations using the same amount of, or fewer, resources.

absolute advantage
Ability of a nation to produce a good more efficiently than any other nation.

Among other things, Smith reasoned that international trade should not be banned or restricted by tariffs and quotas, but allowed to flow according to market forces. If people in different countries were able to trade as they saw fit, no country would need to produce all the goods it consumed. Instead, a country could concentrate on producing the goods in which it holds an absolute advantage. It could then trade with other nations to obtain the goods it needed but did not produce.

Suppose Mark McGwire (baseball's single-season home run king) needs to install a jacuzzi in his family's home during the baseball season. Should he do the job himself or hire a professional installer to do it for him? Suppose McGwire (who has never installed a jacuzzi before) would have to take one month off from baseball and forgo roughly $800,000 in salary to complete the job. On the other hand, the professional installer (who does not play professional baseball) can complete the job for $10,000 and do it in two weeks. Although McGwire has an absolute advantage in playing major league baseball, the installer has an absolute advantage in installing jacuzzis. Whereas it takes McGuire one month to do the job, the installer can do it in two weeks. Thus McGwire should hire the professional to install the jacuzzi to save himself both time and money resources.

Let's now apply the absolute advantage concept to an example of two trading countries to see how trade can increase production and consumption in both nations.

Case: Riceland and Tealand

Suppose that we live in a world of just two countries (Riceland and Tealand), two products (rice and tea), and transporting goods between these two countries costs nothing. Riceland and Tealand currently produce and consume their own rice and tea. The table below shows the number of units of resources (labor) each country expends in creating rice and tea. In Riceland, just 1 resource unit is needed to produce a ton of rice, but 5 units of resources are needed to produce a ton of tea. In Tealand, 6 units of resources are needed to produce a ton of rice whereas 3 units are needed to produce a ton of tea.

	Rice	Tea
Riceland	1	5
Tealand	6	3

Another way of stating each nation's efficiency in the production of rice and tea is the following:

➡ In Riceland, 1 unit of resources = 1 ton of rice *or* $\frac{1}{5}$ ton of tea
➡ In Tealand, 1 unit of resources = $\frac{1}{6}$ ton of rice *or* $\frac{1}{3}$ ton of tea

These numbers also tell us one other thing about rice and tea production in these two countries. Because one unit of resources produces 1 ton of rice in Riceland compared to Tealand's output of only $\frac{1}{6}$ ton of rice, Riceland has an absolute advantage in rice production—it is the more efficient rice producer. However, because one resource unit produces $\frac{1}{3}$ ton of tea in Tealand compared to Riceland's output of just $\frac{1}{5}$ ton, Tealand has an absolute advantage in tea production.

Gains from Specialization and Trade Suppose now that Riceland specializes in rice production to maximize the output of rice in our two-country world. Likewise, Tealand specializes in tea production to maximize world output of tea. Although each country now specializes and world output increases, both countries face a problem. Riceland can consume only its rice production and Tealand can consume only its tea production. The problem can be solved if the two countries trade with each other to obtain the good that it needs, but does not produce.

Suppose that Riceland and Tealand agree to trade rice and tea on a one-to-one basis—a ton of rice costs a ton of tea and *vice versa.* Thus Riceland can produce 1 ton extra of rice with an additional resource unit and trade with Tealand to get 1 ton of tea.

This is a lot better than the $\frac{1}{5}$ ton of tea that Riceland would have gotten by investing that additional resource unit in making tea for itself. Thus Riceland definitely benefits from the trade. Likewise, Tealand can produce $\frac{1}{3}$ ton extra of tea with an additional resource unit and trade with Riceland to get $\frac{1}{3}$ ton of rice. This is twice as much as the $\frac{1}{6}$ ton of rice it could have produced using that additional resource unit to make its own rice. Thus Tealand also benefits from the trade. The gains resulting from this simple trade are shown in Figure 5.6.

Although Tealand does not gain as much as Riceland from the trade, it does get more rice than it would without trade. The gains from trade for actual countries would depend on the total number of resources each country had at its disposal. Another important determinant of the actual benefits from trade is the demand for each good in each country.

As this example shows, the theory of absolute advantage destroys the mercantilist idea that international trade is a zero-sum game. Instead, because there are gains to be had by both countries party to an exchange, international trade is a *positive-sum game*. The theory also calls into question the objective of national governments to acquire wealth through restrictive trade policies. It argues that nations should instead open their doors to trade so their people can obtain a greater quantity of goods more cheaply. Thus the theory does not measure a nation's wealth by how much gold and silver it has on reserve, but by the living standards of its people.

Despite the power of the theory of absolute advantage in showing the gains from trade, there is one potential problem. What happens if one country does not hold an absolute advantage in the production of any product? Are there still benefits to trade, and will trade even occur? To answer these questions, let's take a look at an extension of absolute advantage, the theory of *comparative advantage*.

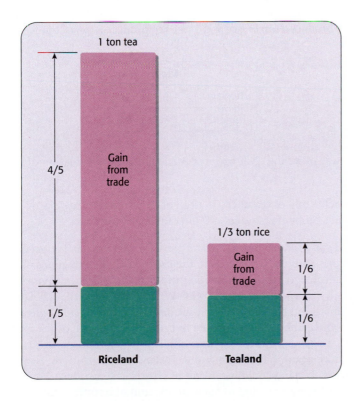

FIGURE 5.6

GAINS FROM SPECIALIZATION AND TRADE: ABSOLUTE ADVANTAGE

COMPARATIVE ADVANTAGE

An English economist named David Ricardo developed the theory of comparative advantage in 1817.[9] He proposed that if one country (in our example of a two-country world) held absolute advantages in the production of both products, specialization and trade could still benefit both countries. A country has a **comparative advantage** when it is unable to produce a good more efficiently than other nations, but produces the good more efficiently than it does any other good. In other words, *trade is still beneficial even if one country is less efficient in the production of two goods, so long as it is less inefficient in the production of one of the goods.*

comparative advantage
Inability of a nation to produce a good more efficiently than other nations, but an ability to produce that good more efficiently than it does any other good.

Let's return to our jacuzzi example. Now suppose that Mark McGwire has previously installed many jacuzzis and can do the job in one week—twice as fast as the jacuzzi installer. Thus Mark McGwire now holds absolute advantages in both baseball and jacuzzi installation. Although the professional installer is at an absolute disadvantage in both jacuzzi installation and baseball, he is *less inefficient* in jacuzzi installation. However, despite his absolute advantage in both areas, McGwire would still have to give up $200,000 to take time off baseball to complete the work. Is this a wise decision? No. McGwire should hire the professional installer. The installer earns money he would not earn if McGwire did the job himself. McGwire earns more money continuing to play baseball than he would save if he installed the jacuzzi himself.

Gains from Specialization and Trade To see how the theory of comparative advantage works with international trade, let's return to our example of Riceland and Tealand. In our earlier discussion, Riceland had an absolute advantage in rice production and Tealand had an absolute advantage in tea production. Suppose that Riceland now holds absolute advantages in the production of both rice *and* tea. The table below shows the number of units of resources each country now expends in creating rice and tea. Riceland still needs to expend just 1 resource unit to produce a ton of rice but now needs to invest only 2 units of resources (instead of 5) to produce a ton of tea. Tealand still needs 6 units of resources to produce a ton of rice and 3 units to produce a ton of tea.

	Rice	Tea
Riceland	1	2
Tealand	6	3

Another way of stating each nation's efficiency in the production of rice and tea is the following:

➡ In Riceland, 1 unit of resources = 1 ton of rice *or* $\frac{1}{2}$ ton of tea
➡ In Tealand, 1 unit of resources = $\frac{1}{6}$ ton of rice *or* $\frac{1}{3}$ ton of tea

Thus Riceland can produce more rice and tea than Tealand for every unit of resource employed—it has absolute advantages in the production of both goods. But if Riceland has absolute advantages in the production of both goods, it can't possibly gain from trading with a less efficient producer, right? Wrong, because although Tealand has absolute disadvantages in both rice and tea production, it has a *comparative* advantage in tea. In other words, although it is unable to produce either rice or tea more efficiently than Riceland, Tealand produces tea more efficiently than it produces rice.

Assume once again that Riceland and Tealand decide to trade rice and tea on a one-to-one basis. Tealand could use 1 unit of resources to produce $\frac{1}{6}$ ton of rice. But it would do better to produce $\frac{1}{3}$ ton of tea with this unit of resources and trade with Riceland to get $\frac{1}{3}$ ton of rice. Thus by specializing and trading, Tealand gets twice as much rice than it could if it were to produce the rice itself. There are also gains from trade for Riceland despite its dual absolute advantages. Riceland could invest 1 unit of resources in the production of $\frac{1}{2}$ ton of tea. However, it would do better to produce 1 ton of rice with the 1 unit of resources and trade that rice for 1 ton of tea. Thus Riceland gets twice as much tea through trade than if it were to produce tea itself. This is in spite of the fact that it is a more efficient producer of tea than Tealand.

The benefits for each country from this simple trade are shown in Figure 5.7. Again, the benefits from trade for actual countries depends on the amount of resources at their disposal and each market's desired level of consumption of each product.

Assumptions and Limitations   Throughout the discussion of absolute and comparative advantage, we made several important assumptions that limit the real-world application of the theories. First, we assumed that countries are driven only by the maximization of production and consumption. This is often not the case. In fact, governments of most nations involve themselves in international trade issues out of a concern for workers or consumers. The role of government in international trade is discussed in detail in Chapter 6.

Second, the theories assume that there are only two countries engaged in the production and consumption of just two goods. This obviously does not reflect the situation existing in the real world. There currently are more than 180 countries and literally a countless number of products being produced, traded, and consumed worldwide.

Third, it is assumed that there are no costs of transporting traded goods from one country to another. In reality, transportation costs are a major expense of international trade for some products. If transportation costs for a good are higher than the savings generated through specialization, trade will not occur.

Fourth, the theories consider labor the only kind of resource for the production process. The reason is that labor accounted for a very large portion of the total pro-

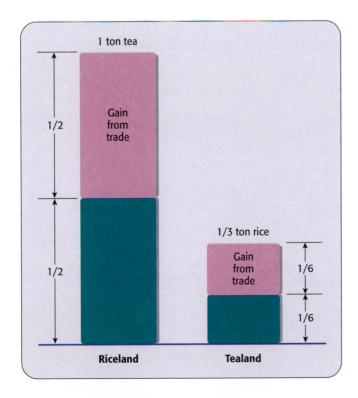

FIGURE 5.7

GAINS FROM SPECIALIZATION AND TRADE: COMPARATIVE ADVANTAGE

duction cost of most goods at the time the theories were developed. Moreover, it is assumed that resources are mobile within each nation but cannot be transferred between them. Labor, and especially natural resources, can be difficult and costly to transfer between nations. However, this is definitely changing. For example, people from a nation belonging to the European Union are allowed to live and work in any other member nation.

Finally, it is assumed that specialization in the production of one particular good does not result in gains in efficiency. But we know that specialization causes increased knowledge of a task and perhaps even future improvements in how that task is performed. Thus the amount of resources needed to produce a specific amount of a good should decrease over time.

Despite the assumptions made in the theory of comparative advantage, research reveals that it appears to be supported by a substantial body of evidence.[10] Nevertheless, economic researchers continue to develop and test new theories to explain the international purchase and sale of products. Let's now examine one of these, the theory of *factor proportions*.

FACTOR PROPORTIONS THEORY

In the early 1900s, an international trade theory emerged that focused attention on the proportion (supply) of resources in a nation. The cost of any resource is simply the result of supply and demand: Factors in great supply relative to demand will be less costly than factors in short supply relative to demand. **Factor proportions theory** states that countries produce and export goods that require resources (factors) that are abundant and import goods that require resources in short supply.[11] The theory resulted from the research of two economists, Eli Heckscher and Bertil Ohlin, and is therefore sometimes called the Heckscher-Ohlin theory.

Thus factor proportions theory differs considerably from the theory of comparative advantage. Recall that the theory of comparative advantage states that countries specialize in producing the good that it can produce more efficiently than any other good. Thus the focus of the theory (and absolute advantage as well) is on the *productivity* of the production process for a particular good. In contrast, factor proportions theory says that a country specializes in producing and exporting goods using the factors of production that are most *abundant*, and thus *cheapest*—not the goods in which it is most productive.

Labor versus Land and Capital Equipment   Factor proportions theory breaks a nation's resources into two categories: labor on the one hand, land and capital equipment on the other. It predicts that a country will specialize in products that require labor if the cost of labor is low relative to the cost of land and capital. Alternatively, a country will specialize in products that require land and capital equipment if their cost is low relative to the cost of labor.

Factor proportions theory is conceptually appealing. For example, Australia has a great deal of land (nearly 60 percent of which is in meadows and pastures) and a small population relative to its size. Australia's exports consist largely of mined minerals, grain, beef, lamb, and dairy products—products requiring a great deal of land and natural resources. Australia's imports, on the other hand, consist mostly of manufactured raw materials, capital equipment, and consumer goods—things needed in capital-intensive mining and modern agriculture. But instead of looking at simply this type of anecdotal evidence, let's see how well factor proportions theory stands up to scientific testing.

factor proportions theory
Trade theory holding that countries produce and export goods that require resources (factors) that are abundant and import goods that require resources in short supply.

Evidence on Factor Proportions Theory: The Leontief Paradox Despite its conceptual appeal, factor proportions theory is not supported by studies examining the trade flows of nations. The first large-scale study to document such evidence was performed by a researcher named Wassily Leontief in the early 1950s.[12] Leontief tested whether the United States, which uses an abundance of capital equipment, exports goods requiring capital-intensive production and imports goods requiring labor-intensive production. Contrary to the predictions of the factor proportions theory, his research found that U.S. exports require more labor-intensive production than its imports. This apparent paradox between predictions of the theory and actual trade flows is called the *Leontief paradox*. Leontief's findings are supported by more recent research on the trade data of a large number of countries.

What might account for the paradox? One possible explanation is that factor proportions theory considers a country's production factors to be homogeneous—particularly labor. But we know that labor skills vary greatly within a country—more highly skilled workers emerge from training and development programs. When expenditures on improving the skills of labor are taken into account, the theory seems to be supported by actual trade data. Further studies on international trade data will help us better understand what reasons actually account for the Leontief paradox.

Because of the drawbacks of each of the international trade theories mentioned so far, researchers continue to propose new ones. Let's now examine a theory that attempts to explain international trade on the basis of the life cycle of products.

INTERNATIONAL PRODUCT LIFE CYCLE

Raymond Vernon put forth an international trade theory for manufactured goods in the mid-1960s. His **international product life cycle theory** says that a company will begin by exporting its product and later undertake foreign direct investment as the product moves through its life cycle. The theory also says that for a number of reasons a country's export eventually becomes its import.[13]

Although Vernon developed his model around the United States, we can generalize the model today to apply to any of the developed and innovative markets of the world such as Australia, the European Union, Japan, and North America. Let's now examine how his theory attempts to explain international trade flows.

> **international product life cycle theory**
> *Trade theory holding that a company will begin by exporting its product and later undertake foreign direct investment as the product moves through its life cycle.*

Stages of the Product Life Cycle International product life cycle theory follows the path of a good through its life cycle (from new to maturing to standardized product) to determine where it will be produced (see Figure 5.8). In the *new product stage*, stage 1, the high purchasing power and demand of buyers in an industrialized country spur a company to design and introduce a new product concept. Because the exact level of demand in the domestic market is highly uncertain at this point, the company keeps production volume low and based in the home country. Keeping production where initial research and development occurred and staying in contact with customers allows managers to monitor buyer preferences and modify the product as needed. Although initially there is virtually no export market, exports do begin to pick up late in the new product stage.

In the *maturing product stage*, stage 2, the domestic market and markets abroad become fully aware of the existence of the product and its benefits. Demand rises and is sustained over a fairly lengthy period of time. As exports begin to account for an increasingly greater share of total product sales, the innovating company introduces production facilities in those countries with the highest demand. Near the end of the maturity stage, the product begins generating sales in developing nations and perhaps some manufacturing presence is established there.

FIGURE 5.8   **INTERNATIONAL PRODUCT LIFE CYCLE**

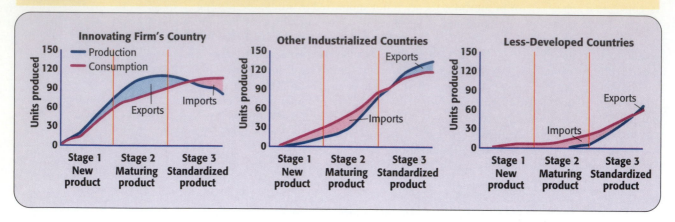

In the *standardized product stage*, stage 3, competition from other companies selling similar products pressures companies to lower prices in order to maintain sales levels. As the market becomes more price sensitive, the company begins searching aggressively for low-cost production bases in developing nations to supply a growing worldwide market. Furthermore, as most production now takes place outside the innovating country, demand in the innovating country is supplied with imports from production in developing and other industrialized nations. Late in this stage, domestic production might even cease altogether.

Limitations of the Theory   Vernon developed his theory at a time when most of the new products being developed in the world were originating and being sold first in the United States. One reason U.S. companies were strong globally in the 1960s was that their domestic production bases were not destroyed as was the case in Europe (and to some extent Japan) during the Second World War. In addition, production of many durable goods including automobiles was shifted to production of military transportation and weaponry in the United States during the war. This laid the foundation for an enormous demand for new capital-intensive consumer goods following the war such as autos and home appliances including stoves and refrigerators. Furthermore, advances in technology originally developed with military purposes in mind were integrated into consumer goods. A wide range of new and innovative products including televisions, photocopiers, and computers, met the seemingly insatiable appetite of consumers in the United States.

Thus the theory seemed to explain world trade patterns quite well when the United States dominated world trade. But today its ability to depict the trade flows of nations accurately is weak. The United States is no longer the sole innovator of products in the world. New products seem to be springing up everywhere as research and development activities of companies continue to globalize.

Furthermore, companies today design new products and make product modifications at a very quick pace. The result is quicker product obsolescence and a situation in which companies "cannibalize" their existing products with new product introductions. This is forcing companies to introduce products in many markets simultaneously to recoup a product's research and development costs before its sales decline and it is dropped from the product line. The theory has a difficult time explaining the resulting trade patterns.

In fact, older theories might better explain today's global trade patterns. Much production in the world today more closely resembles what is predicted by the theory of comparative advantage. For example, Tata Unisys Ltd. (a partnership between Tata of India and Unisys of the United States) oversees software programming in India for Chase Manhattan Bank of New York. The software is destined for the bank's operations in Hong Kong and the United States. "You consider all of the available resources," explains Gene Friedman, vice president of applied technology at Chase Manhattan. Labor in India costs half as much as in the United States yet is highly skilled in software programming.[14] This pattern resembles the theory of comparative advantage in that a product's components are made in the country that can produce them at a high level of productivity. Components are later assembled in another location where productivity in assembly is high.

Finally, the theory is challenged by the fact that more companies are operating in international markets from their inception.[15] Many small companies are teaming up with companies in other markets to develop new products or production technologies. This strategy is particularly effective for small companies that would otherwise be unable to participate in international production or sales. See the Entrepreneurial Focus "Teaming Up: Prospering from Alliances with Other Entrepreneurs" for a profile of one small French company that is profiting from its global connections.

The international product life cycle theory does retain some explanatory power when applied to technology-based products that are eventually mass-produced. However, other more powerful international trade theories continue to emerge. Let's now look at a theory that says countries export products that they were among the first to produce—*new trade theory*.

Entrepreneurial Focus

Teaming Up: Prospering from Alliances with Other Entrepreneurs

Gerard Compain spends his day in Paris talking on the phone to his "global network," a group of entrepreneurs scattered around the world. They are his agents and their mission is to give him a local face and help him conquer markets abroad.

Compain is managing director of Ingenico, one of the world's leading vendors of smart-card readers—a smart card looks like a credit or debit card but is embedded with a computer chip that can store a great deal of financial and personal information. Ingenico is currently focused on opening subsidiaries abroad with the help of local companies. He targets businesses with an entrepreneurial spirit similar to that of Ingenico's. "Entrepreneurs," he explains, "do things in a way that's smarter, quicker and simpler. These people know their countries better than we do. And they know how to design and sell products for those markets."

Compain starts his global assault by targeting advance customers. "We look for the most innovative customers, sell them a new product idea, make it, and then go to other customers. We tell them, 'Look, we have an incredible new concept. Are you interested?'" Ingenico recently developed a portable smart-card reader for the police in Shanghai,

China, who use smart cards to gather information on traffic violators. Ingenico has made and sold other products based on the same model including a portable card reader for kiosk and newsstand owners, and terminals for Australian taxicabs.

When it came time to expand into such countries as Australia, China, Germany, Russia, Singapore, and the United States (in all of which Ingenico now has subsidiaries), Compain looked for local entrepreneurs who would treat Ingenico like their own businesses. "I wasn't interested in hiring managers," he says. "Since we're a relatively small company, I can't bring these people to Paris every month to take their orders." Compain's strategy helped Ingenico double its sales recently to $60 million.

The only country that has resisted smart-card technology is the United States. But Compain thinks that things will soon change. "Americans don't like to adopt foreign technology," he says, amused. "So we formed an alliance with a North American company [International Verifact Inc. of Toronto]. Now we'll be viewed not as a French company but as a North American one. We will train Americans, and they will eventually adopt our technology. It's just a matter of time."

NEW TRADE THEORY

new trade theory
Trade theory holding that (1) there are gains to be had from specialization and increasing economies of scale, (2) those companies first to market can create barriers to entry, and (3) government may have a role to play in assisting its home companies.

During the 1970s and 1980s, a new theory emerged to explain trade patterns.[16] The **new trade theory** states that (1) there are gains to be had from specialization and increasing economies of scale, (2) those companies first to enter a market can create barriers to entry, and (3) government may have a role to play in assisting its home-based companies. Because the theory emphasizes productivity rather than a nation's resources, it is in line with the theory of comparative advantage but at odds with factor proportions theory.

First-Mover Advantage   According to the new trade theory, as a company increases the extent to which it specializes in the production of a particular good, output rises because of gains in efficiency. Regardless of the amount of a company's output, it has fixed production costs such as the cost of research and development, and the plant and equipment needed to produce the product. As output increases, the company can spread the fixed costs of production over a greater number of units, thereby reducing the total cost of each unit of output. Thus as the company expands, it can lower prices to buyers and force potential new companies to produce at a similar level of output if they want to be price competitive. This results in the first market entrant gaining what is called a **first-mover advantage**—the economic and strategic advantage gained by being the first company to enter an industry. This first-mover advantage can create a formidable barrier to entry for potential rivals.[17]

first-mover advantage
Economic and strategic advantage gained by being the first company to enter an industry.

Because of the potential benefits of being the first company to enter an industry, some businesspeople and researchers make a case for government assistance. They say that by working together to target potential new industries, a government and its home-based companies can take advantage of the benefits of being the first mover in an industry. Government involvement has always been widely accepted in undertakings such as space exploration for national security reasons, but less so in purely commercial ventures. But the fear that governments of other countries might participate with industry to gain first-mover advantages spurs many governments into action.

The theory is still too fresh and not enough evidence is yet available to judge its accuracy or value. Let's now look at the last major theory of international trade—*national competitive advantage.*

Honda unveiled its new gas-electric powered hybrid car in Tokyo at the end of 1998. The unique engine may offer Honda a first-mover advantage, a strong barrier to entry for rival carmakers in a growing segment of the auto industry. To read more about Honda's electric car, go to ⟨**www.honda1999.com/cars/ev**⟩.

NATIONAL COMPETITIVE ADVANTAGE

Michael Porter put forth a new theory in 1990 to explain why certain countries are leaders in the production of certain products.[18] His **national competitive advantage theory** states that a nation's competitiveness in an industry depends on the capacity of the industry to innovate and upgrade. Porter's work incorporates certain elements of previous international trade theories but also makes some important new discoveries.

Porter is not preoccupied with explaining the export and import patterns of nations, but with explaining why some nations are more competitive in certain industries. He identifies four elements present in every nation to varying degrees that form the basis of national competitiveness. Figure 5.9 shows the *Porter diamond*, which consists of the following four elements: (1) factor conditions; (2) demand conditions; (3) related and supporting industries; and (4) firm strategy, structure, and rivalry. Let's take a look at each of these elements and see how they all interact to support national competitiveness.

national competitive advantage theory
Trade theory holding that a nation's competitiveness in an industry depends on the capacity of the industry to innovate and upgrade.

Factor Conditions Factor proportions theory considered a nation's resources, such as a large labor force, natural resources, climate, or surface features, as paramount factors in what products a country will produce and export. Porter acknowledges the value of such resources, which he terms *basic* factors, but also discusses the significance of what he calls *advanced* factors.

Advanced Factors Advanced factors include such things as the skill levels of different segments of the workforce and the quality of the technological infrastructure in a nation. Advanced factors are the result of investments in education and innovation

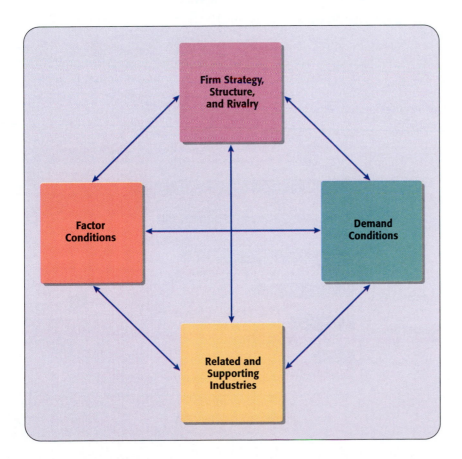

FIGURE 5.9

DETERMINANTS OF NATIONAL COMPETITIVE ADVANTAGE

such as worker training and technological research and development. Whereas the basic factors can be the initial spark for why an economy begins producing a certain product, advanced factors account for the sustained competitive advantage a country enjoys in that product.

Today for example, Japan has an advantage in auto production and the United States in the manufacture of airplanes. In the manufacture of computer components, Taiwan reigns supreme (see the World Business Survey "On Top of the World"). These countries did not attain their status in their respective areas because of basic factors. For example, Japan did not acquire its advantage in autos because of its natural resources of iron ore—it has virtually none and must import most of the iron it needs. These countries developed their productivity and advantages in producing these products through deliberate efforts including worker training and development, and improvements in technology and work processes.

Demand Conditions   Sophisticated buyers in the home market are also important to national competitive advantage in a product area. A sophisticated domestic market drives companies to modify existing products to include new design features and develop entirely new products and technologies. Companies in markets with sophisticated buyers should see the competitiveness of the entire group improve. For example, the sophisticated market in the United States for computer software has helped give companies based in the United States an edge in developing new software products.

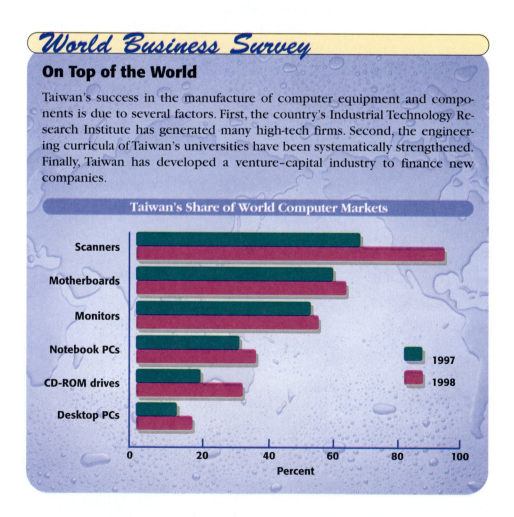

World Business Survey

On Top of the World

Taiwan's success in the manufacture of computer equipment and components is due to several factors. First, the country's Industrial Technology Research Institute has generated many high-tech firms. Second, the engineering curricula of Taiwan's universities have been systematically strengthened. Finally, Taiwan has developed a venture–capital industry to finance new companies.

Taiwan's Share of World Computer Markets

Related and Supporting Industries   Companies belonging to a nation's internationally competitive industries do not exist in isolation. Rather, supporting industries spring up to provide the inputs required by the industry. How does this happen? Companies that can benefit from the product or process technologies of an internationally competitive industry begin to form clusters of related economic activities in the same geographic area. The presence of these clusters serves to reinforce the productivity and therefore competitiveness of each industry within the cluster.[19] For example, Italy is home to a successful cluster in the footwear industry that greatly benefits from the country's closely related leather-tanning and fashion-design industries. Map 5.2 shows the locations of some important clusters in the United States. Looking at the cluster in Colorado, for instance, we see that mining and the exploration of oil and gas depend heavily on the provision of engineering services that in turn require advanced computer hardware and software.

Firm Strategy, Structure, and Rivalry   The last determinant of the Porter diamond to discuss is the strategy, structure, and rivalry of firms. The strategic decisions of firms have lasting effects on their future competitiveness. Managers committed to producing quality products that are valued by buyers while maximizing the firm's market share and/or financial returns are essential. But highly skilled managers are not all that are needed. Equally as important is the industry structure and rivalry between a nation's companies. The more intense the competition to survive between a nation's domestic companies, the greater will be their competitiveness. This heightened competitiveness helps them compete against imports and against companies that might develop a production presence in the home market.

Government and Chance   Apart from these four factors identified as part of the diamond, Porter identifies the roles of government and chance in fostering national competitiveness of industries. For example, the import-substitution policies of many countries in Latin America in past decades had a severe distorting effect on its home demand conditions. Although the policies designed to protect young industries within these nations were well intentioned, their effect was mostly negative. Labor unions and industry leaders were able to secure protection from higher quality imports, but at the expense of consumers. As the quality of locally produced goods continued to decline, consumers demanded less from local producers and the local producers became more dependent on continued protection.[20]

Another example that illustrates how the various determinants of national competitive advantage are related is high-definition television (HDTV). Japanese companies were first to develop the technology on which HDTV is based. To thwart any advantage Japanese companies might possess, network broadcasters in the United States sought government support for the creation of an industry standard for HDTV. In the early 1990s it was agreed that the standard in the United States would be digital. This decision put Japanese producers at a disadvantage because their system was based on analog technology. But U.S. broadcasters and television makers were at battle over who would commit first to the new technology. Meanwhile, Matsushita focused on television programming as the key driver of the future of HDTV and did an end-around on the bickering parties. Matsushita allied itself with Hollywood studios to coproduce shows in the new format and stepped ahead of its competition.[21]

Porter's theory holds promise but has just begun to be subjected to research using actual data on each of the factors involved and national competitiveness. There are important implications for companies and governments if the theory accurately identifies the important drivers of national competitiveness. For instance, government policies should not be designed to protect national industries that are not internationally com-

MAP 5.2   **MAPPING SELECTED U.S. CLUSTERS**

Here are just some of the clusters in the United States. A few—Hollywood's entertainment cluster and North Carolina's Carolina's household-furniture cluster—are well known. Others are less familiar, such as golf equipment in Carlsbad, California, and optics in Phoenix, Arizona. A relatively small number of clusters usually account for a major share of the economy within a geographic area as well as for an overwhelming share of its economic activity that is "exported" to other locations. *Exporting clusters*—those that export products or make investments to compete outside the local area—are the primary source of an area's economic growth and prosperity over the long run. The demand for local industries is inherently limited by the size of the local market, but exporting clusters can grow far beyond that limit.

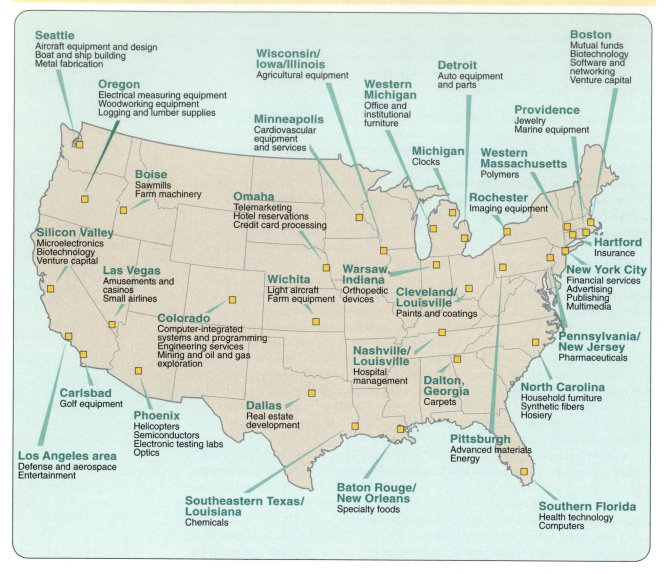

Seattle
Aircraft equipment and design
Boat and ship building
Metal fabrication

Oregon
Electrical measuring equipment
Woodworking equipment
Logging and lumber supplies

Boise
Sawmills
Farm machinery

Silicon Valley
Microelectronics
Biotechnology
Venture capital

Las Vegas
Amusements and casinos
Small airlines

Colorado
Computer-integrated systems and programming
Engineering services
Mining and oil and gas exploration

Carlsbad
Golf equipment

Phoenix
Helicopters
Semiconductors
Electronic testing labs
Optics

Los Angeles area
Defense and aerospace
Entertainment

Wisconsin/ Iowa/Illinois
Agricultural equipment

Minneapolis
Cardiovascular equipment and services

Omaha
Telemarketing
Hotel reservations
Credit card processing

Wichita
Light aircraft
Farm equipment

Warsaw, Indiana
Orthopedic devices

Dallas
Real estate development

Southeastern Texas/ Louisiana
Chemicals

Western Michigan
Office and institutional furniture

Michigan
Clocks

Cleveland/ Louisville
Paints and coatings

Nashville/ Louisville
Hospital management

Dalton, Georgia
Carpets

Baton Rouge/ New Orleans
Specialty foods

Detroit
Auto equipment and parts

Western Massachusetts
Polymers

Rochester
Imaging equipment

Pittsburgh
Advanced materials
Energy

Boston
Mutual funds
Biotechnology
Software and networking
Venture capital

Providence
Jewelry
Marine equipment

Hartford
Insurance

New York City
Financial services
Advertising
Publishing
Multimedia

Pennsylvania/ New Jersey
Pharmaceuticals

North Carolina
Household furniture
Synthetic fibers
Hosiery

Southern Florida
Health technology
Computers

petitive, but develop the components of the diamond that contribute to increased competitiveness. Support for or against this latest and influential theory will accumulate over time as research into its value continues.

A FINAL WORD

This chapter introduced and explained a number of concepts regarding international trade. We explored the benefits of international trade and its volume and pattern in the world today. As we saw in this chapter's opening example, trade can feed a nation's entrepreneurial spirit and bring economic development. As the volume of trade continues to expand worldwide, new theories will likely emerge to explain why countries trade and why they have advantages in producing certain products. In the next chapter we discuss the important role of governments in influencing the volume and pattern of international trade.

There is a variety of additional material available on the companion Web site that accompanies this text. You can access this information by visiting the Web site at ⟨**www.prenhall.com/wild**⟩.

summary

❶ Describe the *volume* of international trade, how trade volume and *world output* are related, and *international trade patterns*. *International trade* is the purchase, sale, or exchange of goods and services across national borders. International trade provides a country's people with a greater choice of goods and services and is an important engine for job creation in many countries. One way to measure the importance of trade to a nation is to examine the volume of an economy's trade relative to its total output. In this respect, a majority of the world's economies have seen an increase in the importance of trade over the past decade. Most of world merchandise trade is comprised of trade in manufactured goods. Service exports make up roughly 20 percent of total world trade.

Slower world economic output slows the volume of international trade, and higher output spurs greater trade. Trade slows in times of economic recession because an uncertain financial future causes reduced purchases of imports. Also, a weak currency relative to other nations makes imports more expensive relative to domestic products, thus reducing trade. Although levels of trade and world output tend to move in lockstep fashion, trade has consistently grown faster than output.

The pattern of international trade in merchandise is dominated by flows among the high-income economies of the world (60 percent), followed by trade among high-income countries and low- and middle-income nations (34 percent). Trade among the low- and middle-income nations is just 6 percent of the total. Furthermore, the value of U.S. merchandise imports from Japan is almost twice Japan's imports from the United States. The value of goods traded between the European Union and the United States is much more balanced. Finally, nearly a quarter of total world merchandise trade occurs solely among European Union nations.

❷ Describe *mercantilism* and explain its historical impact on the world powers and their colonies. The trade theory that nations should accumulate financial wealth, usually in the form of gold, by encouraging exports and discouraging imports is called *mercantilism*. Under this theory, other measures of a nation's well-being, such as living standards or human development, are irrelevant. Nation-states in Europe followed this economic philosophy from about 1500 to the late 1700s. The most prominent mercantilist nations included Britain, France, the Netherlands, Portugal, and Spain.

Countries implemented mercantilism by doing three things. First, they increased their wealth by maintaining a *trade surplus*—the condition that results when the value of a nation's exports is greater than the value of its imports. Second, national governments actively intervened in international trade to maintain a trade surplus. Finally, mercantilist nations acquired less developed territories (colonies) around the world to serve as sources of inexpensive raw materials and as markets for higher priced finished goods.

Despite its seemingly positive benefits for any nation implementing it, mercantilism is inherently flawed. Mercantilism states that a nation increases its wealth only at the expense of other nations—called a *zero-sum game*. But if all nations were to barricade their markets from imports and push their exports onto others, international trade in all nonessential goods would likely cease altogether. In addition, paying colonies little for their exports but charging them high prices for their imports reduced their wealth and lessened their appeal as markets for goods.

❸ Identify the differences between *absolute advantage* and *comparative advantage*. The ability of a nation to produce a good more efficiently than any other nation is called an *absolute advantage*. According to this theory, international trade should not be banned or restricted by tariffs and quotas, but allowed to flow according to market forces. If people in different countries were able to trade as they saw fit, a country could concentrate on producing the goods in which it holds an absolute advantage. It could then trade with other nations to obtain the goods it needed but did not produce.

The theory of absolute advantage destroys the mercantilist idea that international trade is a zero-sum game. Instead, because there are gains to be had by both countries party to an exchange, international trade is a *positive-sum game*. The theory does not measure a nation's wealth by how much gold and silver it has on reserve, but by the living standards of its people.

But what happens if one country does not hold an absolute advantage in the production of any product? Efforts to solve this problem inspired the theory of *comparative advantage*. A nation holds a comparative advantage in production of a good when it is unable to produce the good more efficiently than other nations, but can produce that good more efficiently than it does any other good. As a result, *trade is still beneficial even if one country is less efficient in the production of two goods, so long as it is less inefficient in the production of one of the goods.*

4 **Explain the *factor proportions* and *international product life cycle* theories.** *Factor proportions theory* states that countries produce and export goods that require resources (factors) that are abundant and import goods that require resources in short supply. Factor proportions theory breaks a nation's resources into two categories: labor on the one hand, land and capital equipment on the other. It predicts that a country will specialize in products that require labor if its cost is low relative to the cost of land and capital. Alternatively, a country will specialize in products that require land and capital equipment if their cost is low relative to the cost of labor.

Unfortunately, factor proportions theory is not supported by studies examining the trade flows of nations. Research found, for example, that U.S. exports require more labor-intensive production than its imports. This apparent paradox between predictions of the theory and actual trade flows is called the *Leontief paradox*.

International product life cycle theory says that a company will begin exporting its product and later undertake foreign direct investment as the product moves through its life cycle. This theory follows the path of a good through its life cycle (from new to maturing to standardized product) to determine where it will be produced. In the *new product stage*, stage 1, uncertain domestic demand and the importance of staying close to customers keeps production volume low and based in the home country. In the *maturing product stage*, stage 2, as exports begin to account for an increasingly greater share of total product sales, the innovating company introduces production facilities in those countries with the highest demand. In the *standardized product stage*, stage 3, competition from other companies selling similar products pressures companies to lower prices in order to maintain sales levels. As the market becomes more price sensitive, the company begins searching aggressively for low-cost production bases in developing nations to supply a growing worldwide market.

5 **Explain the *new trade* and *national competitive advantage* theories.** The *new trade theory* argues that (a) there are gains to be had from specialization and increasing economies of scale, (b) those companies first to market can create barriers to entry, and (c) government may have a role to play in assisting its home companies.

New trade theory holds that as its output increases, a company can spread the fixed costs of production over a greater number of units, thereby reducing the total cost of each unit of output. As the company expands, it can lower prices to buyers and force potential new companies to produce at a similar level of output if they want to be price competitive. This results in the first market entrant gaining what is called a *first-mover advantage*—the economic and strategic advantage gained by being the first company to enter an industry. The theory says that by working together, governments and home-based companies can target potential new industries in which to become first-movers.

National competitive advantage theory states that a nation's competitiveness in an industry (and, therefore, trade flows) depends on the capacity of the industry to innovate and upgrade. The *Porter diamond* identifies four elements present in every nation to varying degrees that form the basis of national competitiveness.

(a) *Factor conditions.* The theory acknowledges the value of such *basic* factors as labor force and natural resources, but greater emphasis is placed on *advanced* factors, which include such things as the skill levels of different segments of the workforce and the quality of the technological infrastructure in a nation.

(b) *Demand conditions.* A sophisticated domestic market drives companies to improve existing products and develop entirely new products and technologies—thus improving competitiveness.

(c) *Related and supporting industries.* Companies belonging to a nation's internationally competitive industries do not exist in isolation. Rather, supporting industries spring up to provide the inputs required by the industry and form clusters of related economic activities in the same geographic area—once again, reinforcing productivity and competitiveness.

(d) *Firm strategy, structure, and rivalry.* The strategic decisions of managers in producing their companies' goods and services have lasting effects on their firms' competitiveness. In addition, the more intense the competition to survive between a nation's domestic companies, the greater will be their competitiveness. This heightened competitiveness helps them compete against imports and against companies that might develop a production presence in the home market. Finally, the actions of *governments* and the occurrence of *chance events* can also affect the competitiveness of a nation's companies, thus influencing trade flows.

questions for review

1. What is *international trade*? Explain how it differs from *foreign direct investment*.

2. Identify how important trade is to the economies of five nations.

3. What are some of the *benefits* of international trade?

4. Of the 10 countries responsible for much of the world's merchandise trade, how many are from Africa? Asia? Europe? North America? South America?

5. What portion of total world trade occurs in merchandise? In services?

6. Explain the relation between trade and *world output*.

7. Describe the *patterns* that international trade follows.

8. Why is a nation's level of *dependence* or *independence* important?

9. What is *mercantilism*? Explain how mercantilism worked and its flaws.

10. How does a *trade surplus* differ from a *trade deficit*?

11. What types of policies might a country be doing to be called *neomercantilist*?

12. What is an *absolute advantage*? Describe how it works using a numerical example.

13. Explain what is meant by a *comparative advantage*. Why can countries gain from trade despite not having an absolute advantage?

14. What is the *factor proportions theory*? Identify the two categories of national resources.

15. Describe *international product life cycle theory* including its three stages.

16. What is the *new trade theory*? Explain what is meant by the term *first-mover advantage*.

17. Describe *national competitive advantage theory*. What are the four elements of the *Porter diamond* and the two other factors influencing competitiveness?

questions for discussion

1. If the nations of the world were to suddenly cut off all trade with one another, what products might you no longer be able to obtain in your country? Choose one other country and identify the products it would need to do without.

2. Despite economic problems in Asia recently, the twenty-first century is being dubbed the "Pacific Century" by many economists. Why do you think this enthusiasm is present? What will this mean for trade between Asia, Europe, and North America?

3. Because of its abundance of natural resources, Brazil was once considered a nation certain to attain advanced economic status quickly. Yet over the past two decades Brazil has sometimes been referred to as an economic "basket case." What forces do you think are preventing Brazil's economic progress?

4. National competitive advantage theory emphasizes advanced factor conditions, such as a skilled and productive workforce, as having a significant effect on a nation's competitiveness. Do you think that governments, companies, communities, or individuals are responsible? Or are none of these parties responsible? Explain your answer.

in practice

Among other things, the theory of national competitive advantage states that a country gains a competitive advantage in an industry when its home-based companies form a cluster of activities that support one another. Read the following article taken from a business publication and answer the questions that follow.

France Opens "Genetic Valley"

In late October, France unveiled "Genopole," a designated area for genetic research and development, biotech companies, and public and private research and diagnostic laboratories. The site, located in Evry, a city 20 miles south of Paris, is also being called "Genetic Valley."

Genopole's tenants already include Genethon (a gene research facility), Genoscope (the national gene sequencing center), the National Genotyping center, and the research arm of the French Muscular Dystrophy Association. Private companies include Genset, Rhone-Poulenc-Rorer, and Euro Sequence Gene Services.

Nearby the Genopole area is the Université d'Evry/Val d'Essone which is well known in France for its biology and molecular biology departments. The French government is working with the University to offer high-level courses in gene sequencing and genomes. Pierre Tambourin, Genopole's director, said one of his tasks is "to create a research campus" consisting of a "core of researchers in key disciplines."

1. Identify the various participants (public and private) mentioned in the article. What do you think each party has to offer the cluster to encourage the cross-fertilization of ideas and innovations?

2. Why is it that today governments often try to create clusters around groundbreaking research in high technology products and processes?

3. Two recent, influential theories (new trade theory and the theory of national competitive advantage) emphasize a role for governments in helping domestic companies become strong internationally. Do you think governments should undertake such efforts or let markets, on their own, decide who should succeed and fail?

4. Can you identify a cluster that exists in your hometown or city, or that of your college or university? If so, identify the members of the cluster and what each one has to offer.

projects

1. Select a recent business periodical, such as the *Far Eastern Economic Review, Wall Street Journal,* or *World Trade.* Find an article discussing the advantages and/or disadvantages of international trade. Write a summary of the points made in the article and express why you agree or disagree with them.

2. Go to your library, or link to a company's site on the Internet. Locate the annual report (or other information) of a large international firm such as British Airways, Daimler-Chrysler, Harley-Davidson, Sony, or Wal-Mart. To what extent does the company rely on imports to supply its production facilities in various countries? How much of the company's total sales are outside the home country? Does the company import from and export to mostly high-income countries only or low- and middle-income countries as well? Is the company's export revenue increasing or decreasing and at what rate? Supply other information you think is relevant and write a one or two page report of your findings.

3. Select a recent business periodical, such as the *Far Eastern Economic Review, Wall Street Journal,* or *World Trade.* Find an article that discusses the international trade situation of one or more of the Asian economies affected by economic crisis in recent years. Have the countries tried to export their way out of slow economic growth? If so, what forces led them to resort to increasing exports to stimulate their economies? If not, why not? What is the projection for recovery of these economies in the near term? Write a short report of your findings.

business case 5
DHL EXPRESS WORLDWIDE: FIRST IN ASIA AND THE WORLD

Question: What company is the leading international express carrier? If you answered Federal Express, UPS, or Airborne Express you're wrong. Try DHL Worldwide Express. The Redwood City, California-based company actually carved out the niche for international express service in 1969 when it began shipping bills of lading and other documents from San Francisco to Honolulu. Soon the company got requests to deliver and pick up in Japan and other Asian countries, and the whole business of international express delivery was born.

Today the company delivers and picks up from 80,000 destinations in 224 countries and employs over 35,000 employees worldwide, 11,000 of them based in Asia, the company's first and most important international market. Customer service and reliability are what DHL prides itself on most. For instance, the company hires DHL personnel in the countries in which it operates and sees this practice as key to forging relationships with customers in its overseas markets. "Unlike many of our competitors," says one DHL executive, "we don't take a package and hand it off to an agent. We ensure that our deliveries and pick-ups are made by DHL personnel and that we can manage business locally by using local people who know local customs." Because relationships are the name of the game in service businesses, DHL is currently cultivating relationships with customs agents. The byzantine customs clearance procedures in many countries are the biggest obstacle to speedy international deliveries.

Express air delivery is now a huge business in Asia, but DHL has several formidable competitors snapping at its heels.

These include Federal Express, which offers competitive rates, and local players like Hong Kong Delivery, whose small size makes it highly flexible. DHL cannot simply rest on its number-one position or boast of its long years of experience to stay ahead. The dangers of complacency were brought home to the company in the mid-1980s, when its DHL Japan office faced customer resistance to a price hike. DHL employees had simply assumed that the firm would always be number one and had grown lax on service. In fact, an objective "shipment test" revealed that DHL Japan provided the worst service at what were already the highest prices. Japanese customers simply continued to use DHL because it was the first in the business and because loyalty was important. Yet, the proposed price hike might have been the decisive factor in convincing formerly compliant cus-tomers to defect. Fortunately, DHL Japan's then-president, Shinichi Momose, was able to get the affiliate back on track through initiatives generated by a series of intensive meetings with his staff.

Today DHL's customer service record is winning repeated kudos in Asia. In 1997, for the eleventh year running, DHL International was voted the "Best Express Service" of the year at the Asian Freight Industry Awards. "We operate in an increasingly competitive business," explains DHL Far East Regional Managing Director John A. Kerr, "and our customers are demanding both increased levels of services and sophisticated logistics solutions. . . . We cannot afford to be so complacent in the years ahead. We will continue to listen to our customers, understand their needs, and work to meet their requirements."

thinking globally

1. As the first to set up an international air express business in 1969, DHL had the first-mover advantage over other companies. Is being a first mover as advantageous for a service company, such as DHL Worldwide Express, as it is for a manufacturing company like Boeing? Explain.

2. When it comes to global expansion and setting up overseas affiliates, how is a service company's focus different from that of a manufacturing company? What are the elements that you think are necessary for a service company to achieve global success? What are the obstacles to global expansion?

3. DHL prides itself on having its own staff of 35,000 spread out across the globe instead of relying on foreign agents. Discuss the merits and drawbacks of this international staffing approach.

4. After reading the above case, what do you think are the dangers, if any, of being a first mover?

5. Whereas Federal Express uses only its own aircraft and ground fleets, DHL has long-standing relationships with airlines all over the world. Owning its own aircraft is a key part of Federal Express' global expansion philosophy, yet, interestingly, DHL's Quarterly Export Indicator Survey found that ownership of its own airline network was the least important criterion for selecting a freight partner. In contrast, customer service was listed as the most important criterion. Which do you think would be most important to the success of an international express courier and why?

a question of ethics

1. In actual international trade practice, both physical resources and capital cross international borders freely whereas labor is heavily restricted. In fact, it is very difficult in many nations to get a permit allowing you to be gainfully employed within that country. Thus while companies are free to set up production in markets where labor is cheap, labor cannot move to markets where wages are higher. Why do you think this situation prevails? Is it ethical that of all the components of production, labor is the one most subject to restrictions on its international mobility? Discuss.

2. Banana producers in the island nations of the West Indies sell all of their exports to the European Union, accounting for about 3 percent of the world trade in bananas. Nations belonging to the European Union prefer to buy bananas from these nations who happen to be their former colonies. They also want to support the struggling economies of Africa, the Caribbean, and the Pacific, where bananas make up a large percentage of gross national product. Several years ago, the European Union cut a deal that restricts imports of bananas from dollar-based producers and provides incentives to buy from African, Caribbean, and Pacific producers. Recently, with the interests of the large U.S. fruit companies such as Dole, Chiquita, and Del Monte in mind, the United States challenged the European Union deal in an international court and won. Those U.S. companies alone already account for nearly two-thirds of the fruit traded worldwide. Discuss the ethics of attempting to manage trade in the interest of countries occupying a highly vulnerable position in the global economy. Given the scenario above, would you argue on behalf of the United States or the European Union? Why?[22]

3. Recent international trade theories propose that a nation's standard of living is harmed by protectionist actions that restrict imports—an argument for free trade. Yet, think about what happens when free trade and global competition spur companies to move production to cheaper locations abroad, thereby eliminating jobs in their home countries. The gains and losses of free trade are not always distributed evenly across the population. Argue either for or against the necessity of measures that protect products and jobs at home.

government impact on international trade

Beacons

A Look Back

CHAPTER 5 explored theories that, over the years, have tried to explain the pattern that international trade should take. We examined the important concept of comparative advantage and the conceptual basis for how international trade benefits nations.

A Look at This Chapter

This chapter discusses the active role of national governments in international trade. We examine the motives for government intervention and the tools that nations use to accomplish their goals. We then explore the global trading system and show how it promotes free trade.

A Look Ahead

CHAPTER 7 continues our discussion of the international business environment. We explore recent patterns of foreign direct investment, theories that try to explain why it occurs, and the role of governments in influencing investment flows.

Learning Objectives

After studying this chapter, you should be able to

1. Describe the *cultural*, *political*, and *economic motives* behind governmental intervention in trade.
2. List and explain the *methods governments use to promote international trade*.
3. List and explain the *methods governments use to restrict international trade*.
4. Discuss the importance of both the *GATT* and *WTO* in promoting free trade.

The French try to keep their language free of such alien English words as *jeans* and *hamburger*. French law bans foreign-language words from virtually all business and government communications, radio and TV broadcasts, public announcements, and advertising messages—at least whenever a suitable French alternative is available. You can't advertise a *best-seller*; it has to be a *succès de librairie*. You can't sell *popcorn* at *le cinéma*; French moviegoers must snack on *mais soufflé*. A select group of individuals comprising the Higher Council on French Language works against the inclusion of such so-called "Franglais" phrases as *le marketing*, *le cash flow*, and *le brainstorming* into commerce and other areas of French culture.

Although many people consider music the universal language, not all cultures are equally open to the world's diverse musical influences. To prevent Anglo-Saxon music from "corrupting" French music, French law requires radio programs to include at least 40 percent French content. Such *local content requirements* are intended to protect both French cultural identity and jobs of French artists from other nations' pop culture that regularly washes up on French shores.

How does the English language so easily infiltrate the cultures of other nations? Despite the grand conspiracy theories put forth by some individuals and groups, it is the natural result of international trade. International trade in all sorts of goods and services is exposing people around the world to new words, ideas, products, and ways of life. But as international trade continues to expand, many governments try to limit potential adverse effects on their cultures and economies. This is where the theory of international trade meets the reality of international business today.[1]

The previous chapter discussed theories that describe what the patterns of international trade *should* look like. The theory of comparative advantage states that the country having a comparative advantage in the production of a certain good will produce that good when barriers to trade do not exist. However, this ideal does not accurately characterize trade in today's global marketplace. Despite efforts by supranational organizations (such as the World Trade Organization) and smaller groups of countries, nations still retain many barriers to trade.

In this chapter we look in detail at government involvement in international trade. We first explain why nations erect barriers to trade, exploring the cultural, political, and economic motives for such barriers. We then examine the instruments countries use to restrict both imports and exports. We then discuss efforts of the global trading system to promote trade by reducing trade barriers. We cover how smaller groups of countries are eliminating barriers to trade and investment in Chapter 8.

WHY DO GOVERNMENTS INTERVENE IN TRADE?

free trade
Pattern of imports and exports that would result in the absence of trade barriers.

The pattern of imports and exports that would result in the absence of trade barriers is called **free trade**. Despite the advantages of free trade that we discussed in chapter 5, national governments have long intervened in the trade of goods and services. Why do governments impose restrictions on free trade? In general, they do so for reasons that are cultural, political, or economic—or some combination of the three. Countries often intervene in trade by strongly supporting their domestic companies' exporting activities. But the more emotionally charged aspect of trade intervention revolves around troubled economies. Businesses and workers in tough economic times will often lobby their governments to protect them from imports that are reducing work and eliminating jobs in the domestic market. Figure 6.1 shows the population for and against free trade in various countries around the world. How does your country rank? Let's now take a closer look at government involvement in trade by examining the cultural, political, and economic motives for intervention.

CULTURAL MOTIVES

Nations often restrict trade in goods and services to achieve cultural objectives, the most common being protection of national identity. In Chapter 2 we saw how culture and trade are intertwined and significantly affect one another. The cultures of countries are slowly altered by exposure to the people and products of other cultures. Unwanted cultural influence in a nation can cause great distress and cause governments to block imports that it believes are harmful—recall our discussion of *cultural imperialism* in Chapter 2. As we saw in this chapter's opening example, the French government tries to block the cultural influence of other nations. In fact, France has laws that guarantee French artists a minimum amount of airtime on French radio programs. The law's purpose is to encourage the growth of France's own national music industry and curtail the imports of music by artists from other nations, particularly the United States.

Canada is another country making headlines for its attempts to mitigate the cultural influence of entertainment products imported from the United States. Since 1999 Canada requires at least 35 percent of music played over Canadian radio to be by Canadian artists. It is also proposing new restrictions including a hefty tax on imported magazines and subsidies for Canadian magazines, or a ban on Canadian advertising in magazines that do not have at least 60 percent Canadian content.[2] In fact, many countries are considering laws to protect their media programming for cultural reasons. The problem with such restrictions is that they reduce the selection of products available to consumers.

FIGURE 6.1

PROTECTIONISM OVERSEES
FREE TRADE

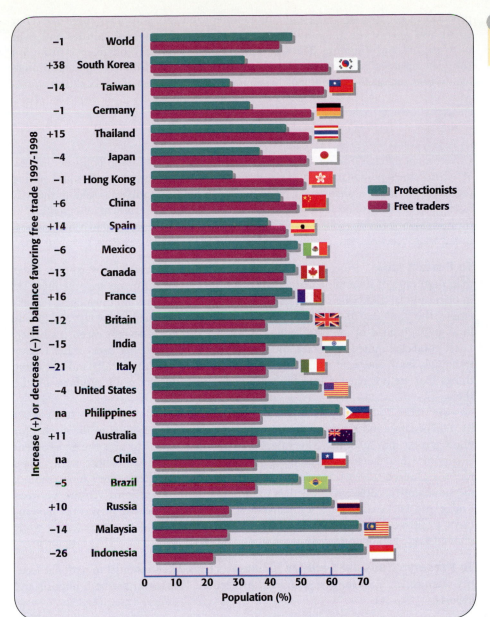

Increase (+) or decrease (−) in balance favoring free trade 1997-1998		
−1	World	
+38	South Korea	
−14	Taiwan	
−1	Germany	
+15	Thailand	
−4	Japan	
−1	Hong Kong	
+6	China	
+14	Spain	
−6	Mexico	
−13	Canada	
+16	France	
−12	Britain	
−15	India	
−21	Italy	
−4	United States	
na	Philippines	
+11	Australia	
na	Chile	
−5	Brazil	
+10	Russia	
−14	Malaysia	
−26	Indonesia	

Protectionists
Free traders

Population (%)

Cultural Influence of the United States

Certainly, the United States, more than any other nation, is seen as a threat to national cultures around the world. Why is this? The reason is the global strength of the United States in entertainment and media (such as movies, magazines, and music) and consumer goods. Such products are highly visible to all consumers and cause groups of various kinds to lobby government officials for protection from their cultural influence. Because the rhetoric of protectionism tends to receive widespread public support, domestic producers of competing products find it easy to join in the calls for protection. Cultural concerns even caused talks on a global investment agreement to fall apart in early 1998.

How can the United States reduce the perception that it is trying to dominate the cultures of nations? Companies based in the United States can support efforts of entrepreneurs in all types of media and entertainment industries in other countries. They could also finance teaching and production of films on regional cultures and their histories, art, and literature. The U.S. government could back off from insisting on complete openness in sensitive cultural industries. It could also offer funding through institutions such as the World Bank to support the preservation of local cultures worldwide.[3]

POLITICAL MOTIVES

Government officials often make trade-related decisions based upon political motives. Why? Because a politician's very survival might depend on pleasing voters and getting reelected. However, a trade policy based purely on political motives is seldom the wisest long-run policy. The main political motives behind government intervention in trade include protecting jobs, preserving national security, responding to other nations' unfair trade practices, and gaining influence over other nations.

To Protect Jobs Short of an unpopular war, nothing will oust a government faster than high rates of unemployment. Thus practically all governments become involved in international trade when jobs created by domestic businesses are threatened. For example, the president of Guyana, in South America, urged her fellow citizens to buy local goods instead of imports saying, "A foreign product does not mean it's better. Local goods are quite good. I use them all the time." Making her case on her weekly radio talk show, she went as far as to ask importers to act "as patriots and not bring things that are not needed into the country to crowd locally made products off the shelves."[4]

But efforts to curb domestic jobs are typically more subtle and receive less publicity. Fuji of Japan and Kodak of the United States control large shares of the market for photographic film in China. This caused Chinese nationalists to urge the government to support China Lucky Film, the struggling state-owned company whose market share recently plunged to 7 percent. Fearing the death of yet another major Chinese brand, the government considered whether to prohibit a proposed joint venture between Kodak and Lucky. China's National Association of Light Industry urged the government to provide $240 million in cash and low-interest loans to rescue Lucky while maintaining a ban on joint ventures in film manufacturing.[5]

To Preserve National Security Industries considered essential to national security often receive government-sponsored protection. This is true for both imports and exports.

National Security and Imports Preserving national security by restricting certain imports is supported by the argument that a government must have access to a domestic supply of certain items—such as weapons, fuel, and air, land, and sea transportation—in the event that war could restrict their availability. For example, many nations (particularly the United States) continue to search for oil within their borders in case war would disrupt the flow of oil from outside sources. National security reasons for intervention are very difficult to argue against, and they tend to have the support of most of a country's people.

Agriculture is also typically protected for national security reasons because a nation importing its food supplies could face starvation in times of war. France has come under attack by other European nations as well as countries outside Europe for protecting its agricultural sector. French agricultural subsidies are intended to provide a fair financial return for French farmers who traditionally operate on a small scale and therefore have high production costs and low profit margins. But many developed nations are exposing agribusiness to market forces, thus causing farms to increase their efficiency. As a result, farmers are discovering new ways to manage risk and improve efficiency. "What I've tried to do with our farm," says Jerry Schillinger, a third-generation Montana wheat farmer, "is get more involved in diversification, such as machine rental." Other farmers are experimenting with alternating crops, more intensive land management, high-tech "precision farming," and greater use of biotechnology.[6]

However, protection from import competition does have its drawbacks. Perhaps the main one is the added cost of continuing to produce a good or provide a service that could be supplied more efficiently by an international supplier. Also, once a policy of protection is adopted it may remain in place much longer than necessary. Thus policy makers should consider whether the trade policy decision is truly a matter of national security before intervening.

National Security and Exports Governments also have national security motives for banning certain defense-related goods from export to other nations. Most industrialized nations have agencies that review requests to export technologies or products that are said to have *dual uses*—meaning they have both industrial and military applications. Products designated as being dual use are classified as such and require special governmental approval before export can take place. Bans on the export of dual use products were strictly enforced in the years of the Cold War between the Western powers and the former Soviet Union. Some countries have relaxed enforcement of these controls since the early 1990s. However, due to the continued presence of terrorist threats and rogue nations that badly want weapons of mass destruction, such bans are receiving renewed support.

For example, in mid-1999 a special committee of the U.S. House of Representatives revealed that recent technology transfers to China fell into the dual use category. The committee charged that Hughes Electronics Corporation and Loral Space and Communications (both of the United States) helped China improve its long-range ballistic missile capabilities. The companies used Chinese rockets to launch satellites and helped Chinese scientists improve their rocket technology following the failure of some launches. Both companies denied wrongdoing and acted only after receiving approval for the technology transfers from the Bush and Clinton administrations. Loral responded to the charges in a written statement, saying "We believe we demonstrated that any material exchanged with the Chinese was from open sources, readily available in standard engineering textbooks."[7] The situation worries officials who fear that China (as it has in the past) might sell the missile technology to India's longtime foe Pakistan, thus disrupting the balance of power in the region.

To Respond to "Unfair" Trade   Many observers argue that it makes no sense for one nation to allow free trade if other nations actively protect their own industries. Governments often threaten to close their ports to another nation's ships or impose extremely high tariffs on its goods if it does not concede on some trade issue seen as being unfair. In other words, if one government thinks another nation is not playing fair, it will also often threaten to play unfair unless certain concessions are agreed.

To Gain Influence   Governments of the world's largest nations may become involved in trade to gain influence over smaller nations. For example, Japan has a certain amount of influence in Asia. Many countries throughout Asia and Southeast Asia rely on Japan for a large amount of their imports and exports. Japan lent the region a large amount of money to help countries recover from financial crises in recent years. No doubt the Japanese government expects to generate goodwill among its neighbors through of such deals.

The United States maintains a trade embargo on communist Cuba in the hope of exerting political influence against Fidel Castro's 20-year-old regime. Some observers believe the embargo is punishing ordinary people in Cuba, while the Cuban government claims it is having minimal effects on daily life.

Similarly, the United States goes to great lengths to gain and maintain control over events in all of Central, North, and South America as well as the Caribbean basin. This is one reason behind the free trade initiatives in the Americas that are strongly supported by the United States. The potential to exert influence on internal politics is also a primary reason why the United States is keeping its embargo on communist Cuba.

ECONOMIC MOTIVES

Although governments intervene in trade because of highly charged cultural and political reasons, they also have economic motives for intervention. The most common economic reasons given for nations' attempts to influence international trade are protection of young industries from competition and promotion of a strategic trade policy.

To Protect Infant Industries   According to the *infant industry argument*, a country's emerging industries need protection from international competition during their development phase until they become sufficiently internationally competitive. The argument is based on the idea that infant industries need protection because of a steep learning curve. In other words, as an industry grows and matures, it gains the knowledge it needs to become more innovative, efficient, and competitive.

Although this argument is conceptually appealing, it does have several problems. First, the argument requires governments to distinguish between industries that are worth protecting and those that are not. This is very difficult to do, if not impossible. For years, Japan (through the Ministry of International Trade and Industry, or MITI) has targeted infant industries for protection, low-interest loans, and other benefits. Its performance on assisting these industries was very good from the 1950s to the early 1980s but has been less successful since then. However, some observers note the Ministry of Finance (MOF) was more influential in the Japanese government during the years of lackluster performance. It is thought that the MOF, not MITI, was responsible for poor decision making and losing focus. Recently, there are signs that MITI is regaining its stature in the government.[8] Until MITI achieves future success in identifying and targeting industries, supporting this type of policy remains questionable.

Second, protection from international competition can cause domestic companies to become complacent toward innovation. This can limit a company's incentives to obtain the knowledge it needs to become more competitive. The most extreme examples of complacency are industries within formerly communist nations. When their communist protections collapsed in the late 1980s and early 1990s, practically all the state-run companies were decades behind their international competitors. Indeed many required financial assistance in the form of infusions of capital or outright purchase to survive.

Third, once protection of an industry is given, it can be politically difficult to eliminate that protection. At stake if protection is removed may be industry profits, the existence of companies that supply the domestic industry, and the welfare of perhaps thousands of families whose jobs might be lost in the face of fierce competition.

Fourth, protection can do more economic harm than good. Consumers often end up paying more for products because a lack of competition typically creates fewer incentives to cut production costs or improve quality. Meanwhile, companies become more reliant on protection. For example, protection of domestic industries in Japan has caused a two-tier economy to emerge. In one tier are protected and noncompetitive domestic industries; in the other are highly competitive multinationals. In the flagging domestic industries of banking, property, construction retailing, and local manufacturing, higher costs are the result of protected markets, high wages, overregulation, and barriers to imports. In contrast, multinationals such as NEC, Sony, Toyota, and Toshiba enjoy low-cost advantages because of their efficient production facilities in East Asia, Europe, Latin America, and the United States. Because these multinationals regularly face rivals in overseas markets, they must be strong competitors if they are to survive.[9]

Fifth, the infant industry argument also holds that it is not always possible for small, promising companies to obtain funding in capital markets, and thus they need financial support from their government. However, international capital markets today are far more sophisticated than in the past, and promising business ventures can normally obtain funding from private sources.

To Pursue Strategic Trade Policy   Recall from our discussion in Chapter 5 that new trade theorists believe government intervention can help companies take advantage of economies of scale and be first movers in their industries. First-mover advantages result because economies of scale in production limit the number of companies that an industry can sustain.

Benefits of Strategic Trade Policy   Supporters of strategic trade policy argue that it results in increased national income. Companies should earn a good profit if they obtain first-mover advantages and solidified positions in their markets around the world. It is assumed that these home-based companies will bring profits earned abroad back home. However, this is not necessarily the case. Many large international companies reinvest profits abroad, for example, to develop new products or construct new production capacity.

They also claim that strategic trade policies helped South Korea build global conglomerates (called *chaebol*) that dwarf the competition. For example, Korean shipbuilders over many years received a variety of government subsidies, including low-cost financing from the Korean Development Bank. The *chaebol* made it possible for companies to survive poor economic times because of the wide range of industries in which they competed. Such policies also had spinoff effects on related industries such as transport. By the mid-1990s one of the country's largest shipping firms, Hanjing Shipping, had become the largest cargo transporter between Asia and the United States.[10]

Drawbacks of Strategic Trade Policy Although it sounds as if strategic trade policy has only benefits, there can be drawbacks as well. Government assistance to domestic companies caused inefficiency and high costs for both South Korean and Japanese companies in the late 1990s. For example, because of high wages at home due to large government concessions to local labor unions, Korea's *chaebol* were operating under very low profit margins. When the Asian currency crisis hit in the summer of 1997, the *chaebol* were not prepared for the consequences. The government realized it had given away too much in the good times and pulled back some of its support by, for one thing, passing a law to make it easier for companies to fire employees.[11]

In addition, when governments decide to support specific industries, their choice is often subject to political lobbying by the groups seeking government assistance. It is possible that special-interest groups could capture all the gains from assistance with no benefit for consumers. If this were to occur, consumers will end up paying more for lower-quality goods than they could otherwise obtain.

Finally, strategic trade policies have the potential to spark destructive competition or even a trade war between nations. In fact, some actions can provoke retaliation against companies in another nation that are not even directly related to a conflict. For instance, when the U.S. government pressured China to control the counterfeit production of videos, compact disks, and computer software, unrelated companies felt the repercussions. Soon afterward, Aetna Insurance of the United States saw its negotiations to enter the Chinese market collapse.

FREE TRADE AND THE UNITED STATES

The United States government and its various agencies often are front and center on the world stage promoting free trade. They often criticize nations for policies designed to restrict trade and praise those that open their borders to freer trade. It is fair, then, to examine how people in the United States feel about the fairness of trade and whether they think freer trade is a good idea.

U.S. Attitudes toward Trade The office of the U.S. Trade Representative and recent administrations of U.S. presidents have worked hard to convince the people of the United States that trade is good for the economy and, in turn, for them individually. But despite their best efforts and a booming economy for much of the 1990s, success in convincing people of trade's benefits has been elusive.

As recently as late 1998, Commerce Secretary William Daley was given the task of promoting the benefits of international trade to the U.S. citizenry through a new "trade-education initiative." "There's a basic sense among the public that it's not a level playing field," says Daley. David Iannelli, a pollster who recently surveyed people's opinions on the issue of trade, says a continued "us-vs.-them outlook would help explain why in these good economic times, Americans see the international economy as a threat rather than an opportunity." But another pollster, Ed Sarpolus, says that "Americans do not want to build trade walls. The more information you give people—even when it includes negative information—support for free trade goes up. They understand we have to trade."[12] For some actual figures on people's attitudes in the United States toward international trade, see the World Business Survey "To Trade Freely, or Not to Trade Freely."

World Business Survey

To Trade Freely, or Not to Trade Freely

A recent poll by the *Wall Street Journal* and NBC News revealed some interesting figures on how ordinary citizens in the United States feel about international trade and the role that their government should play in U.S. competitiveness in the world. As evidence that the U.S. population is aware of world economic events, 24 percent of those surveyed said that the Asian financial crisis (which began in 1997) posed the single greatest threat to the health of the U.S. economy. But as the following charts show, a lopsided majority (58 percent) believes that international trade is predominantly bad for the nation. The population is more split on the role of government involvement in ensuring U.S. competitiveness around the world. Forty-nine percent of those surveyed felt that the government should play a direct, active role in ensuring U.S. global competitiveness.

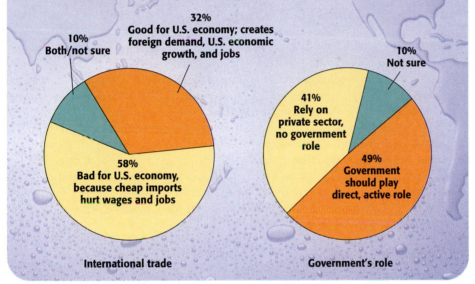

10% Both/not sure

32% Good for U.S. economy; creates foreign demand, U.S. economic growth, and jobs

58% Bad for U.S. economy, because cheap imports hurt wages and jobs

International trade

10% Not sure

41% Rely on private sector, no government role

49% Government should play direct, active role

Government's role

In the previous discussion we alluded to the types of instruments available to governments in their efforts at promoting or restricting trade with other nations. The four most common instruments that governments use to promote trade are *subsidies*, *export financing*, *foreign trade zones*, and *special government agencies*.

METHODS OF PROMOTING TRADE

SUBSIDIES

Financial assistance to domestic producers in the form of cash payments, low-interest loans, tax breaks, product price supports, or some other form is called a **subsidy**. Regardless of the form a subsidy takes, it is intended to assist domestic companies in fending off international competitors. This can mean becoming more competitive in the home market or increasing competitiveness in international markets through exports. Because of the many forms a subsidy can take, it is virtually impossible to calculate the amount of subsidies any country offers its producers. In fact, most arguments over whether one nation is giving unfair subsidies to its companies are often settled by the World Trade Organization only after a long and arduous inves-

subsidy
Financial assistance to domestic producers in the form of cash payments, low-interest loans, tax breaks, product price supports, or some other form.

tigation. Even then, the losing party generally disagrees with the verdict but is bound to accept the organization's ruling (the World Trade Organization is discussed in detail shortly).

Subsidies in Media and Entertainment   As mentioned earlier, media and entertainment are commonly subsidized in many nations. However, France does stand out as being very generous with its subsidies to entertainment. The French film authority, Le Centre National de la Cinématographie, subsidizes many films each year. In one recent year, some French films received "automatic" subsidies to the tune of about $54 million while others benefited from about $20 million a year in advances against box-office receipts. The French government argues that such subsidies are necessary to counteract the influence of Hollywood films and TV programs. Whereas Hollywood films are privately financed and driven by market demand, critics contend that France's films are less competitive because they have to satisfy bureaucratic agendas for funding.[13] However, the fact that many French films are critically acclaimed worldwide might present one argument against removing subsidies that apparently stoke artistic inspiration.

Drawbacks of Subsidies   Critics charge that subsidies cover costs that truly competitive industries should be able to absorb on their own. In this sense, it is argued, subsidies simply encourage inefficiency and complacency. Because governments generally pay for subsidies with funds obtained from income and sales taxes, it is widely believed that subsidies benefit companies and industries that receive them but harm consumers. Thus although subsidies provide short-term relief, the idea that government subsidies help the nation's citizens in the long term is highly questionable.

One fact recently catching the attention of policy makers concerned with the environmental consequences of government policies is that subsidies lead to an overuse of resources. For example, subsidies in developing nations to cover the high cost of energy total more than $230 billion a year—more than four times the total amount of financial assistance to developing countries. Such wasteful spending deprives developing countries of resources that could be invested in other more productive ways, including the transition to more sustainable forms of energy.[14]

EXPORT FINANCING

Governments often promote exports by helping companies finance their export activities. They can offer loans that a company could otherwise not obtain or charge them an interest rate that is lower than the market rate. Another option is for a government to guarantee that it will repay the loan of a company if the company should default on repayment—called a *loan guarantee*.

Many nations have special agencies dedicated to helping their domestic companies gain export financing. For example, a very well-known institution is called the *Export-Import Bank of the United States*—or *Ex-Im Bank* for short. The Ex-Im Bank finances the export activities of companies in the United States and offers them reasonably priced cargo insurance. Another U.S. government agency, the *Overseas Private Insurance Corporation* (*OPIC*), also provides insurance services. Through OPIC, both exporters and those companies investing abroad can insure against loss of assets due to social unrest in a nation, expropriation by a host-nation government, and unfavorable changes in currency values.

Receiving financing from government agencies is often crucial to the success of small businesses just beginning to export. In fact, taken together the "little guys" account for over 80 percent of all transactions handled by the Ex-Im Bank. According to Lalitha Swart, senior vice president at Silicon Valley Bank in Santa Clara, California, most of the customers that her bank links up with Ex-Im Bank are small to medium-size exporters. "I would describe them as emerging high-growth companies," says

Swart. "They tend to be in industries such as telecommunications, life sciences, software, computer peripherals, [and] managed healthcare."[15]

In recent years, the Ex-Im Bank has launched several programs to fuel growth in small business exporting. For instance, a revolving loan to Lynch Machinery of Bainbridge, Georgia, allowed the firm to hire 60 new employees and fill orders for $50 million in glass presses for computers and high-definition TVs for export to China and other Asian markets.[16] Changes for 1999 and beyond include creating a new system that makes it easier for the Ex-Im Bank to approve small loan requests. Another new program is designed to reach small businesses that are owned by minorities and women, are in depressed urban and rural areas, and that produce environmentally beneficial products. For a survey of ways in which the Ex-Im Bank helps businesses gain export financing, see the Entrepreneurial Focus "Ex-Im Bank: Experts in Export Financing."

Export financing programs, however, are not immune to controversy. In general, few criticize government support of small business exporting activities. But support for large multinational corporations is often controversial. The Ex-Im Bank's financing of

Entrepreneurial Focus

Ex-Im Bank: Experts in Export Financing

What follows are some of the ways that businesses can obtain expertise and financing from Ex-Im Bank. You can also click on ⟨www.exim.gov⟩ for more information.

Telephone Hotline   Through a special toll-free number (1-800-565-3946), Ex-Im Bank provides information on export credit insurance, pre-export financing through working-capital guaranteed loans, and medium- and long-term loans as well as guarantees to overseas buyers. The bank also offers briefings and seminars on export financing. In Alaska, Hawaii, and the District of Columbia, the number to call is 202-565-3946.

City-State Program   The bank works with state and local governments to offer export counseling and financial assistance to businesses within their respective jurisdictions. Cooperative programs currently operate in Puerto Rico and in more than 30 states and regions.

Working Capital Guarantee Program   This program helps small and midsize businesses obtain pre-export financing from commercial lenders. The bank will guarantee 100 percent of the principal and interest or extend revolving lines of credit to eligible exporters. These funds may be used for such pre-export activities as buying raw materials or international marketing.

Credit Information Services   The Ex-Im Bank uses its repayment records to provide credit information to U.S. exporting firms and the commercial banking community. The bank can provide information useful in financing export sales to a specific country or an individual company abroad. However, the bank will not divulge confidential financial data on non-U.S. buyers to whom it has extended credit, nor will it disclose classified or confidential information regarding particular credits or conditions in other countries.

Export Credit Insurance   The New-to-Export Policy is available to firms just beginning to export or with average annual export-credit sales of less than $2 million over the preceding two years. Firms must also be classified as small businesses, as defined by the U.S. Small Business Administration. Typically, insurance policies cover 100 percent of political risk and 95 percent of commercial risk. Insurance premiums vary across transactions, depending on the repayment term and the type of buyer. However, these premiums are usually lower than those charged by commercial insurers.

Guarantee Program   This program provides repayment protection for private-sector loans made to creditworthy buyers of U.S. capital equipment and services exports. Coverage is available for loans up to 85 percent of the U.S. export value, with repayment terms of one year or more. Most guarantees provide comprehensive coverage against political and commercial risks, but narrower coverage is also available for political risk only. Ex-Im Bank's guarantee is available for fixed- or floating-rate export loans denominated in U.S. dollars or convertible currencies of other countries.

Loan Program   This program provides fixed-interest-rate financing for export sales of U.S. capital equipment and related services. Ex-Im Bank extends direct loans to non-U.S. buyers of U.S. exports and intermediary loans to creditworthy parties that provide loans to non-U.S. buyers.

large companies has angered critics who contend that subsidizing large private companies at taxpayer expense amounts to corporate welfare. Furthermore, the Ex-Im Bank's original mandate was to support domestic employment and thus offered low-cost financing only for exports whose content was 100 percent domestic. But companies pressured the Ex-Im Bank to relax this restriction, and now it will finance exports with at least 50 percent domestic content.[17]

FOREIGN TRADE ZONES

foreign trade zone (FTZ)
Designated geographic region in which merchandise is allowed to pass through with lower customs duties (taxes) and/or fewer customs procedures.

Most countries promote trade with other nations by creating what is called a **foreign trade zone (FTZ)**—a designated geographic region in which merchandise is allowed to pass through with lower customs duties (taxes) and/or fewer customs procedures. The intended purpose of foreign trade zones is often times increased employment, with increased trade a by-product. Figure 6.2 is an ad for Turkey's "Aegean Free Zone," in which the Turkish government allows companies to conduct manufacturing operations free of taxes.

Customs duties increase the total amount of a good's production cost and increase the time it takes to get it to market. Companies can reduce such costs and time by establishing a facility inside a foreign trade zone. A common purpose of many companies' facilities in such zones is final product assembly. For example, Japanese car plants in Indiana, Kentucky, Ohio, and Tennessee are designated as foreign trade zones that are administered by the U.S. Department of Commerce. The car companies are allowed to import parts from other production facilities around the world at 50 percent of the normal duty charged on such parts. After assembly the vehicles are sold within the United States market with no further duties being charged. Thus instead of assembly taking place elsewhere, state governments offer lower customs duties in return for the creation of jobs.

China has established a number of large foreign trade zones to reap the employment advantages they offer. Goods imported into these zones do not require import licenses or other documents, nor are they subject to import duties. International companies can also store goods in these zones before shipping them on to other countries without incurring taxes in China. Moreover, five of these zones are located within specially designated economic zones in which local governments can offer additional opportunities and tax breaks to international investors.[18]

Another country that has enjoyed the beneficial effects of foreign trade zones is Mexico. As early as the 1960s, Mexico established such a zone along its northern border with the United Sates. Creation of the zone caused development of companies called *maquiladoras* along the border inside Mexico. The *maquiladoras* import materials or parts from the United States without duties, perform some processing on them, and export them back to the United States, which charges duties only on the value added to the product in Mexico. The program has expanded rapidly over the three decades since its inception. In one recent year, *maquiladoras* employed more than 860,000 people and exported more than $40 billion worth of goods.[19]

SPECIAL GOVERNMENT AGENCIES

The governments of most nations have special agencies responsible for promoting exports. Such agencies can be particularly helpful in obtaining contracts for small and midsize businesses that have limited financial resources. Government trade-promotion agencies also often organize trips for trade officials and businesspeople to visit other countries to meet potential business partners and generate contracts for new business. They also typically open trade offices in other countries. These offices are designed to promote the home country's exports and introduce businesses to potential business partners in the host nation. Government trade-promotion agencies typically do a great

FIGURE 6.2

THE AEGEAN FREE ZONE

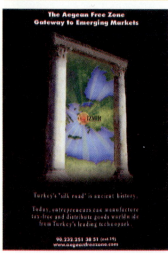

deal of advertising in other countries to promote the nation's exports. Figure 6.3 is an ad for ProChile—the government of Chile's Trade Commission, which has 35 commercial offices worldwide (and a Web site at ⟨www.chileinfo.com⟩).

Governments not only promote trade by encouraging exports but also can encourage imports that the nation does not or cannot produce. For example, in Japan the Japan External Trade Organization (JETRO) is a trade-promotion agency of the government. The agency coaches small and midsize overseas businesses on the protocols of Japanese deal making, arranges meetings with suitable Japanese distributors and partners, and even assists in finding temporary office space for first-time visitors.

Town & Country (T&C) Cedar Homes, based in Petoskey, Michigan, manufactures prefabricated homes. The company credits JETRO for making Japan indispensable to its livelihood. Says T&C president Stephan Biggs: "JETRO's office in Michigan received requests from Japan, searched their database, and put our hand in theirs. And that was it. It has to do with relationships, and we couldn't have done it without JETRO." By linking with the Intercontinental Trading Corporation, a Japanese distributor, T&C has introduced a new style of home to affluent Japanese. Now sales to Japan comprise 20 percent of T&C's total sales.[20]

For all companies, and particularly small ones with fewer resources, just finding out about the wealth of government regulations in other countries is a daunting task. What are the tariffs charged on a product? Are quotas placed on certain products? Fortunately, it is now possible to get answers to questions like these through the Internet. For a list of some very informative Web sites, see the Global Manager "Surfing the Regulatory Seas."

FIGURE 6.3
PROMOTING CHILE TO THE WORLD

e·biz

Global Manager

Surfing the Regulatory Seas

U.S. DEPARTMENT OF COMMERCE

→ The International Trade Administration (ITA) has a Web site at ⟨www.ita.doc.gov⟩ that offers trade data by country, region, and industry sector. It also has information on export assistance centers around the United States, a national export directory, and detailed background information on each trading partner of the United States.

→ The FedWorld Web site at ⟨www.fedworld.gov⟩ is a comprehensive central access point for locating and acquiring information on U.S. government activities and trade regulations.

→ The Stat-USA Web site ⟨www.stat-usa.gov⟩ lists databases on trade regulations and documentation requirements on a country-by-country basis.

U.S. CHAMBER OF COMMERCE

Dun & Bradstreet's 2,000 page Exporter's Encyclopedia has been called the "bible of exporting," and it's now available online on the U.S. Chamber of Commerce's International Business Exchange Web site at ⟨www.uschamber.org/International⟩. Access to the encyclopedia is offered as part of a $250 chamber membership package, which also includes information on a variety of international trade topics.

TRADE COMPASS INC.

By paying $49 a month to this private organization, you can search full-text articles from the Federal Register, Congressional Bills dataset, and the U.S. Code of Federal Regulations, as well as information on tariff actions, rules of origin, free trade issues, and more.

U.S. NATIONAL TRADE ESTIMATES

This Web site at ⟨www.ustr.gov/reports/nte/1996/contents.html⟩ lists the most important barriers affecting U.S. exports to other countries. It shows foreign direct investment by U.S. persons and discusses protection of intellectual property rights.

U.S. TRADE POLICY AGENDA AND ANNUAL REPORT

This Web site at ⟨www.ustr.gov/reports/tpa/1996/contents/html⟩ provides one-stop information on trade negotiations, including a wide range of documents on all subjects relating to trade talk agendas, as well as a helpful section on acronyms to help you get through the entries.

METHODS OF RESTRICTING TRADE

We saw earlier in this chapter some of the cultural, political, and economic reasons why governments intervene in trade. In this section we discuss the methods governments can employ to restrict unwanted trade. There are two general categories of trade barrier available to governments: *tariffs* and *nontariff barriers*. Tariffs add to the cost of imported products because they levy an additional tax upon them. In turn, the higher price tends to lower the quantity sold of the products levied with a tariff. Nontariff barriers limit the quantity of an imported product. In turn, the lower quantity of product available in the market tends to increase its price and thus decrease sales. Let's now take a closer look at tariffs and the various types of non-tariff barriers.

TARIFFS

tariff
Government tax levied on a product as it enters or leaves a country.

A **tariff** is a government tax levied on a product as it enters or leaves a country. We can classify tariffs into three categories according to the country that levies the tariff. First, a tariff levied by the government of a country that is exporting a product is called an *export tariff*. Countries can use export tariffs when they think that the price of an export is lower than it should be. Developing nations whose exports consist mostly of low-priced natural resources often levy export tariffs. Second, a tariff levied by the government of a country that a product is passing through on its way to its final destination is called a *transit tariff*. Transit tariffs have been almost entirely eliminated worldwide through international trade agreements. Third, a tariff levied by the government in a country that is importing a product is called an *import tariff*. The import tariff is by far the most common tariff used by governments today.

We can further break down the import tariff into three subcategories based on the manner in which it is calculated. First, an **ad valorem tariff** is levied as a percentage of the stated price of an imported product. Second, a **specific tariff** is levied as a specific fee for each unit (measured by number, weight, etc.) of an imported product. Third, a **compound tariff** is levied on an imported product and calculated partly as a percentage of its stated price, and partly as a specific fee for each unit. There are two main reasons why countries levy tariffs.

ad valorem tariff
Tariff levied as a percentage of the stated price of an imported product.

specific tariff
Tariff levied as a specific fee for each unit (measured by number, weight, etc.) of an imported product.

compound tariff
Tariff levied on an imported product and calculated partly as a percentage of its stated price, and partly as a specific fee for each unit.

To Protect Domestic Producers   First, tariffs are a way of protecting domestic producers of a product. Because import tariffs raise the effective cost of an imported good, domestically produced goods can appear more attractive to buyers. In this way, domestic producers gain a protective barrier against imports. Although producers receiving tariff protection can gain a price advantage, protection can keep them from increasing efficiency in the long run. A protected industry can be devastated if protection encourages complacency and inefficiency if it is later thrown into the lion's den of international competition. Mexico, for example, began reducing tariff protection in the mid-1980s as a prelude to NAFTA negotiations. Although Mexican producers struggled to become more efficient, many were forced into bankruptcy.

To Generate Revenue   Second, tariffs are a source of government revenue. Using tariffs to generate government revenue is most common among relatively less developed nations. The main reason is that less developed nations tend to have less formal domestic economies that presently lack the capability to record domestic transactions accurately. The lack of accurate record keeping makes collection of sales taxes within the country extremely difficult. Nations solve the problem by simply raising their needed revenue through import and export tariffs. Map 6.1 shows that those nations obtaining a greater portion of their total revenue from taxes on international trade are indeed the poorer nations.

The Argentine province of Entre Rios has benefited greatly from the expanded international commerce made possible by the trade union Mercosur. However, the lack of trade restrictions that has brought new prosperity has also made it possible for Brazilian chicken farmers to sell cheaper poultry products across their borders in Buenos Aires, Argentina. The Argentine government is now feeling the pressure from poultry farmers in Entre Rios, like the one pictured here, to install trade barriers and recoup their advantage in the poultry market.

The discussion so far leads us to question who, then, benefits from tariffs? We've already mentioned the two principle reasons for tariff barriers—protecting domestic producers and raising government revenue. Thus on the surface it appears that governments and domestic producers benefit. We also discussed that tariffs raise the effective price of a product because importers typically must charge buyers a higher price to recover the cost of this additional tax. Thus it appears on the surface that consumers do not benefit. As we also mentioned earlier, there is the danger that tariffs will create inefficient domestic producers that may go out of business once protective import tariffs are removed. Analysis of the total cost to a country is far more complicated and goes beyond the needs of our discussion here. Suffice to say that tariffs tend to exact a cost on countries as a whole because they lessen the gains from trade to a nation's people.

QUOTAS

A restriction on the amount (measured in units or weight) of a good that can enter or leave a country during a certain period of time is called a **quota**. After tariffs, a quota is the second most common type of trade barrier. Governments typically administer their quota systems by granting quota licenses to the companies or governments of other nations (in the case of import quotas), and domestic producers (in the case of export quotas). Governments normally grant such licenses on a year-by-year basis.

quota
Restriction on the amount (measured in units or weight) of a good that can enter or leave a country during a certain period of time.

Reasons for Import Quotas   There are two reasons why a government imposes *import quotas*. First, it may wish to protect its domestic producers by placing a limit on the amount of goods allowed to enter the country. This helps domestic producers maintain their market shares and prices because competitive forces are restrained. In this case, domestic producers win because of the protection of their markets. Consumers lose because of higher prices and less selection due to lower competition. Other losers include domestic producers whose own production requires the import slapped with a quota. Companies relying on the importation of so-called "intermediate" goods will find the final cost of their own products increase.

Second, a government may impose import quotas to force the companies of other nations to compete against one another for the limited amount of imports allowed.

MAP 6.1

Governments of low-income economies typically raise relatively larger shares of their revenues from taxes on international trade. As they develop, however, they tend to generate a greater portion of their revenues from taxes on income, capital gains, and other economic activity.

Note: Taxes on international trade include import duties, export duties, profits of import or export monopolies, exchange profits, and exchange taxes.

Thus those wishing to get a piece of the action will likely lower the price that they are asking for their goods. In this case, consumers win from the resulting lower prices. Domestic producers of competing goods win if external producers do not undercut their prices, but lose if they do.

In the mid-1990s China had in place an import quota system in its filmmaking industry. One year, state-run China Film Corporation imported just 10 blockbuster movies—all through revenue-sharing agreements with international distributors. The agreement resulted in Buena Vista International earning a mere $500,000 in China on its immensely popular Disney film *The Lion King*, although the film grossed more than $1.3 million in Shanghai alone. "[Chinese] taxes are unlike [those] anywhere else in the world," reports Buena Vista executive Larry Kaplan. "A hit there brings in less than in a small central European country." Under international pressure China later abolished its quota system.[21]

Countries historically have placed import quotas on the textiles and apparel products of other countries under what is called the Multi-Fiber Arrangement which is part of the GATT agreement (discussed shortly). Countries affected by this arrangement ac-

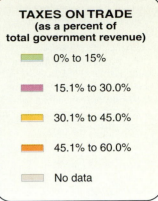

TAXES ON TRADE
(as a percent of
total government revenue)

- 0% to 15%
- 15.1% to 30.0%
- 30.1% to 45.0%
- 45.1% to 60.0%
- No data

count for over 80 percent of world trade in textiles and clothing each year. Although the 1974 arrangement was originally planned to last just four years, it has since been continually revised and extended. However, all quotas in this industry are expected to phase out completely by 2005.

Reasons for Export Quotas   There are at least two reasons why a country imposes *export quotas* on its domestic producers. First, it may wish to maintain adequate supplies of a product in the home market. This motive is most common among countries exporting natural resources that are essential to domestic business or the long-term survival of a nation.

Second, a country may restrict exports to restrict supply on world markets, thereby increasing the international price of the good. This is the motive behind the formation and activities of the Organization of Petroleum Exporting Countries (OPEC). This group of nations from the Middle East and Latin America attempts to restrict the world's supply of crude oil to earn greater profits. Although OPEC was quite successful

International pressure forced China to abandon its import quota system. In the mid 1990s, when the system was still in effect, Buena Vista International earned a mere $500,000 showing the popular Disney film, *The Lion King*, although the film grossed more than $1.3 million in Shanghai alone.

in its early years, the 1970s, it is finding it difficult to get a consensus among its members to restrict oil production in recent years—the end result being near-record lows in world crude oil prices.

Voluntary Export Restraints A unique version of the export quota is called a **voluntary export restraint (VER)**—a quota that a nation imposes on its exports usually at the request of another nation. Countries normally self-impose a voluntary export restraint in response to the threat of an import quota or total ban on the product by an importing nation. The classic example of the use of a voluntary export restraint is the automobile industry in the 1980s. Japanese carmakers were making significant market share gains in the U.S. market. The closing of U.S. carmakers' production facilities in the United States was creating a volatile anti-Japan sentiment among the population and the U.S. Congress. Fearing punitive legislation in Congress if Japan did not limit its auto exports to the United States, the Japanese government and its carmakers self-imposed a voluntary export restraint on cars headed for the United States.

Consumers in the country that imposes an export quota benefit from greater supply and the resulting lower prices if domestic producers do not curtail production. Producers in an importing country benefit because the goods of producers from the exporting country are restrained, which may allow them to increase prices. Export quotas hurt consumers in the importing nation because of reduced selection and perhaps higher prices. However, export quotas might allow these same consumers to retain their jobs if imports were threatening to put domestic producers out of business. Again, detailed economic studies are needed to determine the winners and losers in any particular export quota case.

Tariff-Quotas A hybrid form of trade restriction is called a **tariff-quota**—a lower tariff rate for a certain quantity of imports and a higher rate for quantities that exceed the quota. Figure 6.4 shows how a tariff-quota actually works. Imports entering a nation under a quota limit of, say, 1,000 tons are charged a 10 percent tariff. But subsequent imports that do not make it under the quota limit of 1,000 tons are charged a tariff of 80 percent. Tariff-quotas are used extensively in the trade of agricultural products. Many countries implemented tariff-quotas in 1995 following permission of their use by the international trade agency, the GATT (we discuss the GATT later in this chapter).

voluntary export restraint (VER)
Unique version of export quota that a nation imposes on its exports usually at the request of an importing nation.

tariff-quota
Lower tariff rate for a certain quantity of imports and a higher rate for quantities that exceed the quota.

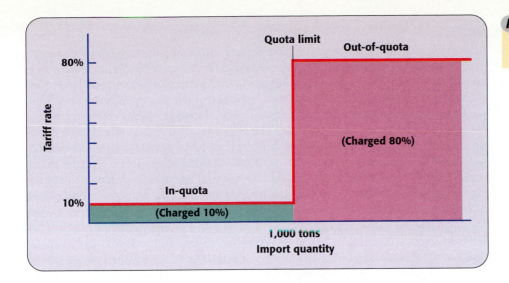

FIGURE 6.4

HOW A TARIFF-QUOTA WORKS

EMBARGOES

A complete ban on trade (imports and exports) in one or more products with a particular country is called an **embargo**. An embargo may be placed on one or a few goods or completely ban trade in all goods. It is the most restrictive nontariff trade barrier available and is typically applied to accomplish political goals. Embargoes can be decreed by individual nations or by supranational organizations such as the United Nations. Because they can be very difficult to enforce, embargoes are used less today than in the past. One example of a total ban on trade with another country is the United States' embargo on trade with Cuba. In fact, not even U.S. tourists are allowed to vacation in Cuba.

After a military coup ousted elected President Aristide of Haiti in the early 1990s, restraints were applied to force the military junta either to reinstate Aristide or to hold new elections. One restraint was an embargo by the Organization of American States. Because of difficulties in actually enforcing the embargo and after two years of fruitless United Nations diplomacy, the embargo failed. Then the United Nations stepped in with a ban on trade in oil and weapons. Despite some smuggling through the Dominican Republic, which shares the island of Hispaniola with Haiti, the embargo was generally effective and Aristide was eventually reinstated.

embargo
Complete ban on trade (imports and exports) in one or more products with a particular country.

LOCAL CONTENT REQUIREMENTS

Laws stipulating that a specified amount of a good or service be supplied by producers in the domestic market are called **local content requirements**. These requirements can state that a certain portion of the end product consist of domestically produced goods, or that a certain portion of the final cost of a product have domestic sources.

The purpose of local content requirements is to force companies from other nations to employ local resources in their production processes—particularly labor. Similar to other restraints on imports, such requirements help protect domestic producers from the price advantage of companies based in other, low-wage countries. Today, companies can circumvent local content requirements by locating production facilities inside the nation stipulating such restrictions.

local content requirements
Laws stipulating that a specified amount of a good or service be supplied by producers in the domestic market.

ADMINISTRATIVE DELAYS

administrative delays
Regulatory controls or bureaucratic rules designed to impair the rapid flow of imports into a country.

Regulatory controls or bureaucratic rules designed to impair the rapid flow of imports into a country are called **administrative delays**. This nontariff barrier includes a wide range of government actions such as requiring international air carriers to land at inconvenient airports; requiring product inspections that damage the product itself; purposely understaffing customs offices to cause unusual time delays; and requiring special licenses that take a long time to obtain. The objective of all such administrative delays for a country is to discriminate against imported products—in a word, protectionism.

Although Japan has removed some of its trade barriers, many subtle obstacles to imports remain. Products ranging from cold pills and vitamins to farm products and building materials find it hard to penetrate the Japanese market. One journalist visiting Japan reports that because her Drixoral cold tablets contained more pseudoephedrine sulfate than Japanese law allows, she had to hand them over to customs agents—they were considered narcotics! Planning to take some extra strength Excedrin to Japan? The journalist says don't bother because it will likely be a major headache. Explains one employee of Bristol-Myers Lion, "The dosage of aspirin, caffeine, and acetaminophen in Excedrin Extra-Strength is too high. Japanese maximum dosages must be lower [for the Japanese people]." Instead of risking their health on U.S.-made Excedrin (priced in New York at 24 for $3.29), Japanese consumers would rather pay $5.40 for a package of 10 made in Japan.[22]

Recently, Saudi Arabia opened its markets to imports by simplifying its customs clearance process. Government agencies eliminated the annual review of product registration and lowered registration fees that it charges importers. They also will begin allowing 60 product-testing facilities and more than 180 laboratories located outside Saudi Arabia to provide certification testing services for conformity to Saudi laws. Some of the products covered by the recent changes include children's toys and playground equipment.[23]

CURRENCY CONTROLS

currency controls
Restrictions on the convertibility of a currency into other currencies.

Restrictions on the convertibility of a currency into other currencies are called **currency controls**. A company that wishes to import goods generally must pay for those goods in a common, internationally acceptable currency such as the U.S. dollar, European Union euro, or Japanese yen. Generally, it must also obtain the currency from its nation's domestic banking system. Governments can require that companies desiring such a currency apply for a license to obtain it. Thus a country's government can discourage imports by restricting who is allowed to convert the nation's currency into the internationally acceptable currency.

Another way governments apply currency controls to reduce imports is by stipulating an exchange rate that is unfavorable to potential importers. Because the unfavorable exchange rate can force the cost of the imported good to an impractical level, many potential importers simply give up on the idea. Meanwhile, the country will often allow exporters to exchange the home currency for an international currency at favorable rates to encourage exports.

GLOBAL TRADING SYSTEM

The global trading system certainly has seen its ups and downs. World trade volume reached a peak in the late 1800s, only to be devastated when the United States passed the Smoot-Hawley Act in 1930. The act represented a major shift in U.S. trade policy from one of free trade to one of protectionism. The act set off round after round of competitive tariff increases among the major trading nations. Other nations felt that if the United States was going to restrict its imports, they were not going to give exports from the United States free access to their domestic markets. The Smoot-Hawley Act and the global trade wars that it helped to usher in crippled the economies of the industrialized nations and helped spark the Great Depression. Living standards around the world were devastated throughout most of the 1930s.

GENERAL AGREEMENT ON TARIFFS AND TRADE (GATT)

Attitudes toward free trade changed markedly in the late 1940s. In the previous 50 years, extreme economic competition among nations and national quests to increase their resources of production helped create two world wars and the worst global economic recession ever. As a result, economists and policy makers proposed that the world band together and agree on a trading system that would help to avoid similar calamities in the future. A system of multilateral agreements was developed that became known as the **General Agreement on Tariffs and Trade (GATT)**—a treaty that was designed to promote free trade by reducing both tariff and nontariff barriers to international trade. The GATT was formed in 1947 by 23 nations—12 developed and 11 developing economies—and came into force in January 1948.[24]

The GATT was highly successful throughout its early years. Between 1947 and 1988, the treaty helped to reduce average tariffs from 40 percent to 5 percent and multiply the volume of international trade by 20 times. But by the middle to late 1980s, rising nationalism worldwide and trade conflicts led to a nearly 50 percent increase in nontariff barriers to trade. Also, services (not covered by the original GATT) had become increasingly important—accounting for between 25 to 30 percent of total world trade. It was clear that a revision of the treaty was necessary, and in 1986 a new round of trade talks began—called the *Uruguay Round*.

Uruguay Round of Negotiations   The ground rules set by the GATT result from periodic "rounds" of negotiations between its members. Though relatively short and straightforward in the early years, negotiations became more prolonged as issues grew more complex. Table 6.1 shows the eight negotiating rounds that have occurred since the GATT's formation. Note that whereas tariffs were the only topic of the first five rounds of negotiations, other topics were added in subsequent rounds.

The *Uruguay Round* of GATT negotiations began in 1986 in Punta del Este, Uruguay (hence its name), and was the largest trade negotiation in history. It was the eighth round of GATT talks within a span of 40 years and took more than 7 years to complete. Although it had its good and bad moments, the Uruguay Round made significant progress in reducing trade barriers by revising and updating the 1947 GATT. In addition to developing plans to further reduce barriers to merchandise trade, the negotiations modified the original GATT treaty in several important ways:

➡ *International trade in services* was included in the GATT for the first time.

➡ *Intellectual property rights* were clearly defined—giving protection to copyrights (including computer programs, databases, sound records, and films), trademarks and service marks, and patents (including trade secrets and know-how).

➡ *Tariff and nontariff barriers in agricultural trade* were to be reduced significantly.

➡ The *World Trade Organization* (*WTO*) was established with power to enforce the new GATT—an agency that the 1947 GATT lacked.

Agreement on Services   Because of the ever-increasing importance of services to the total volume of world trade, nations wanted to include GATT provisions for trade in services. Trade in goods is a straightforward concept—goods are exported from one country and imported to another. But negotiating trade agreements in services presents

General Agreement on Tariffs and Trade (*GATT*) *Treaty that was designed to promote free trade by reducing both tariff and nontariff barriers to international trade.*

TABLE 6.1 The Rounds of GATT

Year	Site	Number of Countries Involved	Topics Covered
1947	Geneva, Switzerland	23	Tariffs
1949	Annecy, France	13	Tariffs
1951	Torquay, England	38	Tariffs
1956	Geneva	26	Tariffs
1960–1961	Geneva (Dillon Round)	26	Tariffs
1964–1967	Geneva (Kennedy Round)	62	Tariffs, antidumping measures
1973–1979	Geneva (Tokyo Round)	102	Tariffs, nontariff measures, "framework agreements"
1986–1994	Geneva (Uruguay Round)	123	Tariffs, nontariff measures, rules, services, intellectual property, dispute settlement, investment measures, agriculture, textiles and clothing, natural resources, creation of the WTO

problems because of the difficulty in defining exactly what a service is. The General Agreement on Trade in Services (GATS) created during the Uruguay Round identifies four different forms that international trade in services can take:

1. *Cross-border supply*: Services supplied from one country to another (for example, international telephone calls).
2. *Consumption abroad*: Consumers or companies using a service while in another country (for example, tourism).
3. *Commercial presence*: A company establishing a subsidiary in another country to provide a service (for example, banking operations).
4. *Presence of natural persons*: Individuals traveling to another country to supply a service (for example, business strategy consultants).

The GATS extended the principle of nondiscrimination to cover international trade in all services, although talks regarding some sectors were more successful than were others. One area not making much headway was trade in telecommunications. The main reason for little progress in this area during the Uruguay Round was that many governments were still trying to privatize their state-owned telecommunications providers. To remove protection at such a delicate point in time, it was argued, would not give the newly independent telecommunication companies a fighting chance to be competitive. Other areas achieving limited progress were maritime transport services, international movement of people, and provision of financial services. Talks in these areas are ongoing.

Agreement on Intellectual Property Like services, products consisting entirely or largely of intellectual property are accounting for an increasingly large portion of international trade. Recall from Chapter 3 that intellectual property refers to property that results from people's intellectual talent and abilities.

Products classified as intellectual property are supposed to be legally protected by copyrights, patents, and trademarks. High-tech industries (such as pharmaceutical drugs and computer software) have long been victimized by the ease with which patents and copyrights are bypassed or completely ignored in many nations. Other low-tech industries (such as apparel, films, and music) have long been cheated out of revenue by counterfeit versions of global brands. For instance, purveyors of fake Dooney & Bourke handbags in Mexico along the border with the United States pride themselves on how well the leather details of the genuine product have been copied.

Although international piracy continues, the Uruguay Round has taken an important step in getting it under control. It created the Agreement on Trade-Related Aspects of Intellectual Property (TRIPS) to help standardize intellectual-property rules around the world. The TRIPS Agreement concurs that protection of intellectual-property rights benefits society because it encourages the development of new technologies and other creations. It supports the articles of both the Paris Convention and the Berne Convention (see Chapter 3) and in certain instances takes a stronger stand on intellectual-property protection.

Agreement on Agricultural Subsidies Trade in agricultural products has long been a bone of contention for most of the world's trading partners at one time or another. Countries protect their domestic agricultural sector to ensure that adequate food is produced, to protect farmers from price swings on world markets due to weather conditions, and to preserve rural communities. Some of the more popular barriers countries use to protect their agricultural sectors include import quotas and subsidies paid directly to farmers. In general, trade barriers promote domestic inefficiency in agricultural production that results in higher domestic prices for consumers.

The Uruguay Round addressed the main issues of agricultural tariffs and nontariff barriers in its Agreement on Agriculture. The agreement aims to increase the exposure of national agricultural sectors to market forces and increase predictability in international agricultural trade. The agreement forces countries to convert all nontariff barriers to tariffs—a process called "tariffication." It then stipulates that developed nations cut their agricultural tariffs 36 percent by the year 2000. Developing nations must reduce their tariffs 24 percent by the year 2004. No requirements are placed on the least developed economies.

WORLD TRADE ORGANIZATION (WTO)

Perhaps the greatest achievement of the Uruguay Round was creation on January 1, 1995, of the **World Trade Organization (WTO)**—the only international organization regulating trade between nations. The three main goals of the WTO are to help the free flow of trade, to help negotiate further opening of markets, and to settle trade disputes between its members. One key component of the WTO that was carried over from GATT is the principle of nondiscrimination called **normal trade relations** (formerly called **most-favored nation status**)—a requirement that WTO members extend the same favorable terms of trade to all members that they extend to any single member. For example, if Japan were to reduce its import tariff on German automobiles to 5 percent, it must reduce the tariff it charges imports from all other WTO nations to 5 percent.

The newly formed WTO replaced the *institution* of GATT but absorbed the various GATT *agreements* (such as on services, intellectual property, and agriculture) into its own agreements. Thus the GATT institution no longer officially exists. In 1999, the WTO recognized 133 members, and of 35 observer members, 31 had applied for membership but 4 had not (see Map 6.2).

World Trade Organization (WTO)
Only international organization regulating trade between nations.

normal trade relations
(*formerly **most-favored nation status***)
Requirement that GATT (and WTO) members extend the same favorable terms of trade to all members that they extend to any single member.

MAP 6.2

MEMBERSHIP OF GATT AND WTO

In 1947, there were just 23 original members to the General Agreement on Tariffs and Trade (GATT). In 1999, the World Trade Organization (WTO) recognized 133 members, 31 observer members who had applied for full membership, and 4 observer members who had not.

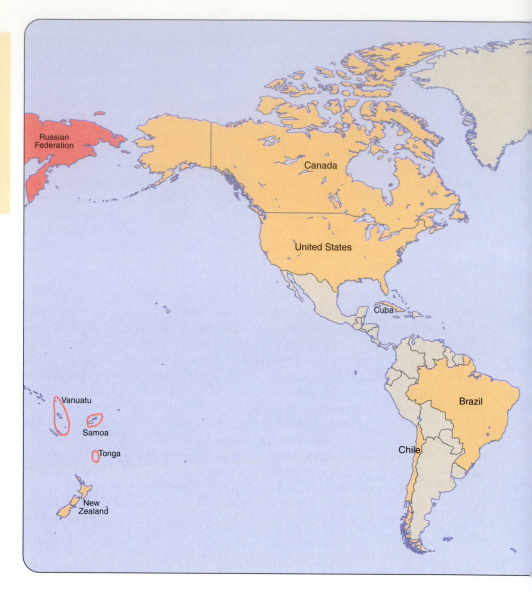

Dispute Settlement in the WTO

The power of the WTO to settle trade disputes is what really sets it apart from the GATT. Under the GATT, nations could file a complaint against another member and a committee would investigate the matter. If appropriate, the GATT would identify the unfair trade practices and member countries would pressure the offender to change its ways. But in reality, GATT rulings (usually given only after very long investigative phases that sometimes lasted years) were more likely to be ignored than heeded.

In contrast, the various WTO agreements are essentially contracts between member nations that commit them to maintaining fair and open trade policies. When one WTO member files a complaint against another, the Dispute Settlement Body of the WTO moves into action swiftly. Decisions are to be rendered in less than one year—nine months if the case is urgent, fifteen months if the case is appealed. The WTO dispute settlement system is not only faster and automatic, but its rulings cannot be ignored or blocked by members. Offenders must realign their trade policies according to WTO guidelines or suffer financial penalties and perhaps trade sanctions. Because of its

	Original GATT members (1947)
	WTO observer members who have applied for full membership
	Other WTO observer members

ability to penalize offending member nations, the WTO's dispute settlement system is the spine of the global trading system.

Dumping and the WTO   The WTO also gets involved in settling disputes that involve "dumping" and the granting of subsidies. When a company exports a product at a price lower than the price normally charged in its domestic market, it is said to be **dumping**. Charges of dumping are made (fairly or otherwise) against almost every nation at one time or another and can occur in any type of industry. For example, Western European plastic producers considered retaliating against Asian competitors whose prices were substantially lower in European markets than at home.[25] In a more recent incident, U.S. steel producers and their powerful union charged that steelmakers in Brazil, Japan, and Russia were dumping steel on the U.S. market at low prices. The problem arose as nations tried to improve their economies (through exporting) in the wake of continued reverberations from the Asian financial crisis, which first struck in 1997 but spread to other emerging markets.[26] In fact, one report

dumping
Practice of exporting a product at a price lower than the price that the product normally commands in the domestic market.

noted U.S. imports of Japanese hot rolled steel rose 500 percent in the first eight months of 1998.[27]

Because dumping is an act by a company, not a country, the WTO cannot punish the country in which the company accused of dumping is based. Rather, it can only respond to the steps taken by the country that retaliates against the company. The WTO allows a nation to retaliate against dumping if it can show that dumping is actually occurring, can calculate the damage to its own companies, and can show that the damage is significant. The normal way a country retaliates is to charge an **antidumping duty**—an additional tariff placed on an imported product that a nation believes is being dumped on its market. But such measures must expire within five years of the time they are initiated unless a country can show that circumstances warrant their continued existence. Table 6.2 shows the number of antidumping cases recorded by the World Trade Organization over a recent one-year period. Gary Horlick, an antidumping lawyer in Washington, DC, says that the rise in antidumping cases looks like "Smoot-Hawley in slow motion."[28]

However, by imposing antidumping duties a government can protect one industry or segment of an industry while harming another. For instance, it was reported in early 1999 that the U.S. International Trade Commission (ITC) slapped a 149 percent antidumping duty on imports of preserved mushrooms from Chile and was investigating petitions against China, India, and Indonesia. The whole affair started when the U.S. *fresh* mushroom industry complained to the ITC that imports of *preserved* mushrooms were harming its industry. Nature's Farm Products of Hayward, California, owns facilities in Chile that import preserved mushrooms into the United States. Its vice president, Pete Pizzo, does not understand the logic of the antidumping duty. "They [domestic U.S. growers and processors] have never accused us of undercutting them or dumping. They just don't like the competition," laments Pizzo. Referring to other effects of the punitive duty, Pizzo says, "Not only will prices jump, but our business and the customers we serve will be harmed."[29]

Subsidies and the WTO   Governments also often retaliate when the competitiveness of their companies is threatened by a subsidy that another country pays its own domestic producers. Like antidumping measures, nations can retaliate against product(s) receiving an unfair subsidy by charging a **countervailing duty**—an additional tariff placed on an imported product that a nation believes is receiving an unfair subsidy. Unlike dumping, because payment of a subsidy is an action by a country, the WTO regulates the actions of both the government that pays the subsidy and the government that reacts to the subsidy.

antidumping duty
Additional tariff placed on an imported product that a nation believes is being dumped on its market.

countervailing duty
Additional tariff placed on an imported product that a nation believes is receiving an unfair subsidy.

TABLE 6.2   *Dumpers or Dumped-Upon?*

Anti-dumping cases* Main Users		Main Targets	
Australia	42	China	31
European Union	41	South Korea	16
South Africa	23	Taiwan	16
United States	16	United States	15
Argentina	15	Germany	14
South Korea	15	Japan	12
Canada	14	Indonesia	9
India	13	India	7
Brazil	11	Britain	6

*Data is for 1997.

New Round of "Millenium" Negotiations A new round of negotiations is slated to begin with a December 1999 meeting of the World Trade Organization in Washington, DC. The European Union is tentatively calling this next series of negotiations as the "Millenium Round." But some, referring to the more than 7 years it took to complete the Uruguay Round, jokingly say that the name implies that it may take 1,000 years to complete.

In any case, the European Union wants the negotiations to have a broad scope and include barrier reduction in all areas of international trade. It says that in this way, countries can make tariff concessions in one area and balance these against gains in other areas. The United States, however, prefers a narrowly focused, sector-by-sector approach. Moreover, it wants the talks to concentrate on making further gains in agriculture, intellectual property, high technology, the boom in cybertrade, and environmental technology. If previous rounds of negotiations can be used as a guide, the new talks should produce meaningful reductions in a range of tariff and nontariff barriers to trade.[30]

e-biz

GLOBAL TRADE AND THE ENVIRONMENT

Steady gains in global trade and rapid industrialization in many developing and emerging economies have generated environmental concerns among both governments and special-interest groups. Of concern to many people are levels of carbon dioxide emissions—the principal greenhouse gas and believed to contribute to global warming. Most carbon dioxide emissions are created from the burning of fossil fuels and the manufacture of cement. Map 6.3 shows national per capita levels of carbon dioxide emissions. Recent responses to these concerns within the global trading system have occurred within the context of the WTO and the United Nations.

WTO Policies The World Trade Organization has no separate agreement dealing with environmental issues. It explicitly states that the WTO is not to become a global environmental agency responsible for setting environmental standards. It leaves such tasks to national governments and the many intergovernmental organizations that already exist for such purposes. The WTO works alongside the roughly 200 international agreements on the environment. Some of these include the Montreal Protocol for protection of the ozone layer, the Basel Convention on international trade or transport of hazardous waste, and the Convention on International Trade in Endangered Species.

Nevertheless, the preamble to the agreement that established the WTO does mention the objectives of environmental protection and sustainable development. The WTO also has an internal committee called the Committee on Trade and Environment. The committee's responsibility is to study the trade/environment relationship and recommend possible changes in the WTO trade agreements.

In addition, the WTO does take explicit positions on some environmental issues related to trade. First, although the WTO supports national efforts at labeling "environmentally friendly" products as such, it states that labeling requirements or policies cannot discriminate against the products of other WTO members. Second, the WTO supports policies of the least developed countries that require full disclosure of potentially hazardous products entering their markets for reasons of public health and environmental damage.

United Nations Earth Summits Rio de Janeiro, Brazil, hosted a United Nations Conference on the Environment and Development (the "Earth Summit") in 1992. The

MAP 6.3

CHARTING CARBON DIOXIDE EMISSIONS

Carbon dioxide emissions are believed to contribute to global warming. The United Nations sponsors meetings among national government leaders to reduce the significant contributor to greenhouse gases. High-income economies emit 32 times as much carbon dioxide per capita as low-income countries, excluding China and India. Protecting the environment from the dangerous by-products will require greater cooperation among the leaders of all nations.

Note: Carbon dioxide emissions are those released by the burning of fossil fuels and the manufacture of cement. They include carbon dioxide produced during the consumption of solid, liquid, and gas fuels and gas flaring.

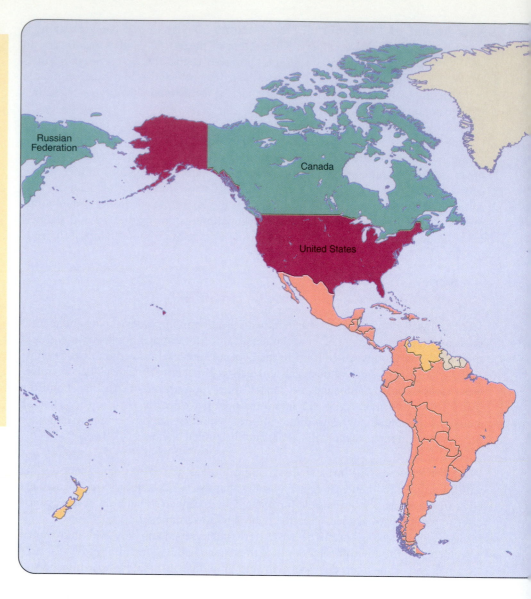

summit resulted in several conventions—including one on climate and one on biodiversity—and a statement of intent on forests. A document called *Agenda 21* was intended to set the framework for environmental and developmental policies into the twenty-first century. As such, the document was not a call to action because it created no timetables, financial targets, or assignment of accountability.

A more recent conference in Kyoto, Japan, in 1997 addressed concerns over global climate change. For the most part, it was an attempt to get those governments that had accepted the Rio Summit's Climate Convention to initiate modest reductions in greenhouse gas emissions. It was agreed that by the years 2008 to 2012, emission levels would be below 1990 levels by 7 percent for the United States, 8 percent for the European Union, and 6 percent for Japan. But each nation's government needed to ratify the agreement, and there was little optimism for its success. For example, the

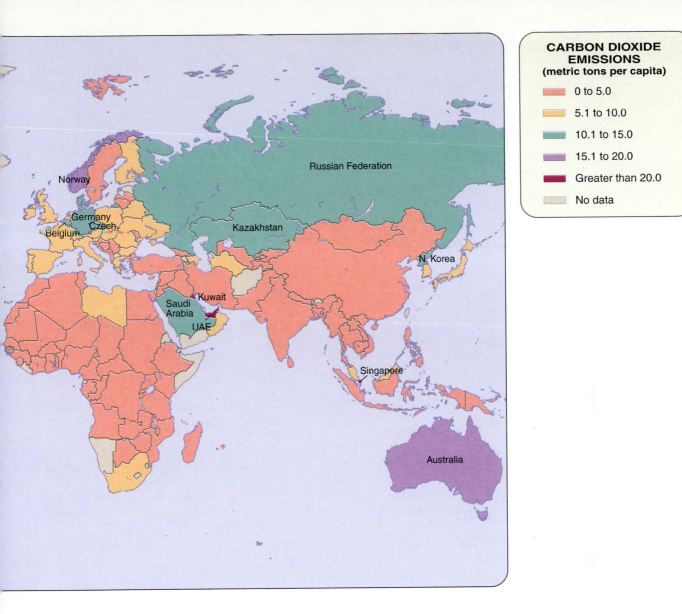

CARBON DIOXIDE EMISSIONS
(metric tons per capita)

- 0 to 5.0
- 5.1 to 10.0
- 10.1 to 15.0
- 15.1 to 20.0
- Greater than 20.0
- No data

U.S. Congress was not expected to pass the agreement at least until follow-up summits were held.[31]

The current lack of progress can be traced to a decision made at Rio de Janeiro to divide the world into rich and poor nations. Although rich nations were supposed to take steps to cut gas emissions, poor ones were not required to do so. That single decision created an "us-versus-them" mentality that prevails today and poisons current discussions on environmental issues. There is no question, however, that industrial and industrializing nations account for the majority of the world's carbon dioxide emissions (see Figure 6.5). In fact, the European Union, Japan, and the United States comprise 13 percent of the world's population, but 42 percent of its carbon dioxide emissions. Whether the global trading system will find a way to cooperate more fully on environmental issues remains to be seen.

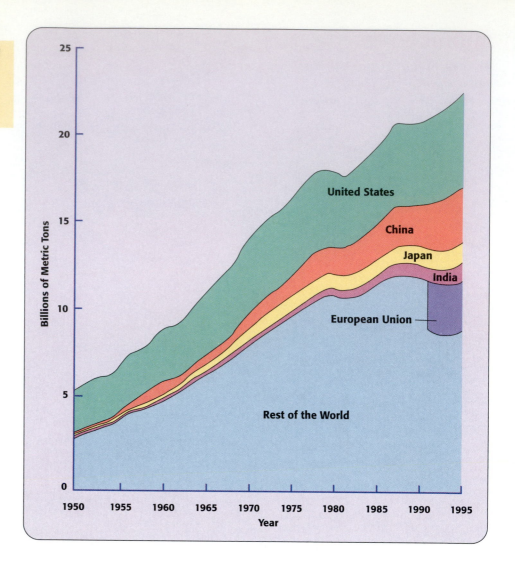

FIGURE 6.5

THE RISING TIDE OF CARBON DIOXIDE EMISSIONS

Note: Pre-1991 data for the European Union are included in the total for the rest of the world.

A FINAL WORD

Despite the theoretical benefits of trade that we discussed in chapter 5, nations do not simply throw open their doors to free trade and force all their domestic businesses to sink or swim. This chapter has discussed reasons why national governments continue to protect all or some of their national industries and how they go about it. The global trading system through the various GATT agreements and the World Trade Organization tries to strike a balance between national desires for protection and international desires for free trade. But as we've seen, even the world's greatest free trade supporter, the United States, has difficulty convincing its citizens of the benefits of free trade.

In the next chapter we continue our discussion of the international trade and investment environment by discussing foreign direct investment. We look at recent patterns in foreign direct investment flows, examine theories that try to explain why it occurs, and discuss how governments intervene in foreign direct investment flows.

There is a variety of additional material available on the companion Web site that accompanies this text. You can access this information by visiting the Web site at ⟨**www.prenhall.com/wild**⟩.

summary

① Describe the *cultural, political,* and *economic motives* behind governmental intervention in trade. The pattern of imports and exports that would result in the absence of trade barriers is called *free trade.* Despite the advantages of free trade, governments intervene in free trade. Perhaps the most common cultural motive for trade intervention is protection of national identity. The cultures of countries are slowly altered by exposure to the people and products of other cultures. Unwanted cultural influence in a nation can cause great distress and cause governments to block imports that it believes are harmful.

The main political motives behind government intervention in trade include (a) protecting jobs, (b) preserving national security, (c) responding to other nations' unfair trade practices, and (d) gaining influence over other nations.

The most common economic reasons given for nations' attempts to influence international trade are (a) protection of young industries from competition and (b) promotion of a strategic trade policy. According to the *infant industry argument,* a country's emerging industries need protection from international competition during their development phase until they become sufficiently internationally competitive.

Although this argument is conceptually appealing, it does have several problems. First, governments are likely to be unable to distinguish between industries that are worth protecting and those that are not. Second, protection from international competition can cause domestic companies to become uncompetitive. Third, once protection of an industry is given, it can be politically difficult to eliminate that protection. Fourth, protection can cause consumers to pay more for products because of a lack of competition.

Believers in *strategic trade policy* argue that government intervention can help companies take advantage of economies of scale and be first movers in their industries. Companies should earn a good profit if they obtain first-mover advantages and solidified positions in their markets around the world.

Although it sounds as if strategic trade policy has only benefits, government assistance to domestic companies can result in both inefficiency and high costs. In addition, groups seeking government assistance could capture all the gains from assistance and leave consumers paying more for lower-quality goods. Finally, strategic trade policies have the potential to spark destructive competition or even trade wars between nations.

② List and explain the *methods governments use to promote international trade*. A *subsidy* is financial assistance to domestic producers in the form of cash payments, low-interest loans, tax breaks, product price supports, or some other form. It is intended to assist domestic companies in fending off international competitors.

Critics charge that subsidies cover costs that truly competitive industries should be able to absorb on their own. It is widely believed that subsidies benefit companies and industries that receive them but not consumers.

Governments also promote exports by providing *export financing.* They can offer loans that a company could otherwise not obtain or charge them an interest rate that is lower than the market rate. Another option is to guarantee that the government will repay a company's loan if the company should default on repayment—called a *loan guarantee.* Many nations also have special agencies dedicated to helping their domestic companies gain export financing.

Most countries promote trade with other nations by creating what is called a *foreign trade zone* (FTZ)—a designated geographic region in which merchandise is allowed to pass through with lower customs duties (taxes) and/or fewer customs procedures. Finally, most nations have *special government agencies* responsible for promoting exports. These agencies often organize trips for trade officials and businesspeople to visit other countries to meet potential business partners and generate contracts for new business. They also typically open trade offices in other countries to promote the home country's exports and introduce businesses to potential business partners in the host nation.

③ List and explain the *methods governments use to restrict international trade*. There are two general categories of trade barrier available to governments: *tariffs* and *nontariff* barriers. A *tariff* is a government tax levied on a product as it enters or leaves a country. We can classify tariffs into three categories according to the country that levies the tariff. (a) A tariff levied by the government of a country that is exporting a product is called an *export tariff.* (b) A tariff levied by the government of a country that a product is passing through on its way to its final destination is called a *transit tariff.* (c) A tariff levied by the government in a country that is importing a product is called an *import tariff.* The import tariff is by far the most common tariff used by governments today.

We can further break down the import tariff into three subcategories based on the manner in which it is calculated. (a) An *ad valorem tariff* is levied as a percentage of the stated price of an imported product. (b) A *specific tariff* is levied as a specific fee for each unit (measured by number, weight, etc.) of an imported product. (c) A *compound tariff* is levied on an imported product and calculated partly as a percentage of its stated price, and partly as a specific fee for each unit. Countries levy tariffs to protect domestic producers, or to earn revenue.

A restriction on the amount (measured in units or weight) of a good that can enter or leave a country during a certain period of time is called a *quota*. A government may impose an *import quota* to protect its domestic producers by placing a limit on the amount of goods allowed to enter the country or to force companies from other nations to compete for a limited amount of imports allowed. A country may impose an *export quota* on its domestic producers to maintain adequate supplies in the home market or to restrict supply on world markets to increase its price on world markets.

A complete ban on trade (imports and exports) in one or more products with a particular country is called an *embargo*. An embargo may be placed on one or a few goods or completely ban trade in all goods. Laws stipulating that a specified amount of a good or service be supplied by producers in the domestic market are called *local content requirements*. These requirements can state that a certain portion of the end product consist of domestically produced goods, or that a certain portion of the final cost of a product have domestic sources. Regulatory controls or bureaucratic rules designed to impair the rapid flow of imports into a country are called *administrative delays*. Restrictions on the convertibility of a currency into other currencies are called *currency controls*. A country's government can discourage imports by restricting who is allowed to convert the nation's currency into the internationally acceptable currency.

4 **Discuss the importance of both the *GATT* and *WTO* in promoting free trade.** The *General Agreement on Tariffs and Trade* (*GATT*) is a treaty that was designed to promote free trade by reducing both tariff and nontariff barriers to international trade. The GATT was formed in 1947 and came into force in January 1948. The ground rules set by the GATT result from periodic "rounds" of negotiations between its members. The 1986 *Uruguay Round* of GATT negotiations made significant progress in reducing trade barriers by revising and updating the 1947 GATT. In addition to developing plans to further reduce barriers to merchandise trade, the negotiations modified the original GATT treaty in several important ways: (1) International trade in services was included for the first time; (2) intellectual property rights were clearly defined; (3) tariff and nontariff barriers in agricultural trade were reduced significantly; (4) the *World Trade Organization* (*WTO*) was established with power to enforce the new GATT—an agency that the 1947 GATT lacked.

The newly formed WTO replaced the *institution* of GATT and absorbed the various GATT *agreements* (such as on services, intellectual property, and agriculture) into its own agreements. The three main goals of the WTO are to help the free flow of trade, to help negotiate further opening of markets, and to settle trade disputes between its members. One key component of the WTO that was carried over from GATT is the principle of nondiscrimination called *normal trade relations* (formerly called *most-favored nation status*)—a requirement that WTO members extend the same favorable terms of trade to all members that they extend to any single member.

When a company exports a product at a price lower than the price it normally charges in its domestic market, it is said to be *dumping*. Because dumping is an act by a company, not a country, the WTO cannot punish the country in which the company accused of dumping is based but can only respond to the steps taken by the country that retaliates against the company. The WTO allows a nation to retaliate against dumping if it can show that dumping is actually occurring, can calculate the damage to its own companies, and can show that the damage is significant. Finally, although the World Trade Organization has no separate agreement dealing with environmental issues, the WTO works alongside the roughly 200 international agreements on the environment.

questions for review

1. Identify the *cultural motives* for nations to intervene in free trade.

2. Identify four *political motives* for government intervention in trade. Explain how national security concerns affect *exports and imports*.

3. What are the two main *economic motives* for government trade intervention? Explain the drawbacks of each approach.

4. List *four methods* governments can use *to promote international trade*.

5. What is a *subsidy*? Identify the drawbacks of using subsidies.

6. Explain how *export financing* helps promote trade. Why is it especially important to small and midsize businesses?

7. What is a *foreign trade zone*? Explain how it promotes trade and illustrate with an example.

8. How can *special government agencies* help promote trade?

9. Identify *six methods* governments can use *to restrict international trade*.

10. Explain the difference between a *tariff* and a *quota*.

11. What is a *voluntary export restraint*? Explain how it is used and how it differs from a quota.

12. Explain what an *embargo* is and why it is seldom used today.

13. What is the purpose of a *local content requirement*?

14. Explain how *administrative delays* and *currency controls* are used to restrict trade.

15. What is the *General Agreement on Tariffs and Trade (GATT)*?

16. What was the *Uruguay Round*? What were its four main accomplishments?

17. What is the *World Trade Organization (WTO)*? Describe how the WTO settles trade disputes.

18. Explain what it means for a nation to have *normal trade relations* (or *most-favored nation status*).

19. Explain the difference between an *antidumping duty* and a *countervailing duty*.

20. Identify efforts at *protecting the environment* from international trade and rapid industrialization.

questions for discussion

1. Imagine that the people in your nation are convinced that international trade is harmful to their wages and jobs and that your task is to change their minds. What kinds of programs would you implement to educate your people about trade's benefits? Describe how each would help change people's attitudes.

2. Most countries create a list of "hostile" countries and require potential exporters to those nations to apply for special permission before they are allowed to proceed. Which countries would you place on just such a list for your nation, and why? Which products are you most concerned about, and why?

3. Two students are discussing efforts within the global trading system to reduce trade's negative effects on the environment. One student says, "Sure, there may be pollution effects, but they're a small price to pay for a higher standard of living." The other student agrees saying, "Yeah, those 'tree-huggers' are always exaggerating those effects anyway. Who cares if some little toad in the Amazon goes extinct? I sure don't." What counterarguments can you offer to these students?

in practice

Please read the short article below and answer the questions that follow.

Japan Slammed on Agricultural Import Testing

The World Trade Organization (WTO) has ruled that Japan's complicated testing requirements for imports of cherries, apples, nectarines, and walnuts are not backed by scientific or health necessities.

The ruling comes in response to a charge by the United States that the testing requirements were a nontariff trade barrier raised by Japanese officials wanting to block U.S. exports of the food products into the country. "We fully expect Japan to comply with the WTO ruling and fully open its market to U.S. apples and other produce," said U.S. trade representative Charlene Barshefsky.

The WTO ruling is the third successful outcome for U.S. trade disputes with Japan. The two prior cases involved differential tax policies for distilled spirit imports and intellectual property regarding sound recordings.

1. Do you think Japan is being singled out unfairly by the United States? Explain your answer.

2. What cultural, political, or economic objectives do you think motivated Japan to maintain barriers to the importation of these products?

3. Do you think that the WTO should have the power to dictate the trade policies of individual nations and punish them if they do not comply? Why or why not?

4. Japan was in the midst of a serious economic recession at the time the WTO made this ruling. Do you think countries experiencing economic difficulties should be allowed to erect temporary tariff and nontariff barriers? Why or why not? What effect do you think such an allowance would have on the future of the global trading system?

projects

1. Select a recent business periodical in print or online—say, the *Far Eastern Economic Review* ⟨**www.feer.com**⟩, the *Wall Street Journal* ⟨**www.wsj.com**⟩, *CNN Interactive* ⟨**www.cnn.com**⟩— and find an article discussing government intervention in promoting or restricting trade. Write a short summary (about 800 words) of what motivated the action, which industries or individual companies are affected, and the reaction of other nations or the World Trade Organization.

2. Select a company involved in importing or exporting in your city or town. Make an appointment to interview the owner or a manager. Your goal is to understand how government involvement in international trade has helped or harmed the company's business activities. Be sure to inquire about specific past examples and future potential impacts of government intervention. Write a short report of your interview and present a brief talk in which you present your findings to the class.

3. In this project, two groups of four students each will debate the case for/against protectionism due to a recent dramatic rise in the import of coffee into your country. One team represents businesspeople in your country who welcome the imports because they benefit their livelihood. The other group represents businesspeople who oppose the imports because it hurts their livelihood. The goal is to try to convince your government to introduce or not introduce protection for domestic coffee growers. After the first student from each side has spoken, the second student questions the opponent's arguments, looking for holes and inconsistencies. The third student attempts to answer these arguments. The fourth student presents a summary of each side's arguments. Finally, the class votes on which team has offered the more compelling argument.

business case 6
"UNFAIR PROTECTION OR VALID DEFENSE?"

"**M**exico Widens Anti-dumping Measure . . . Steel at the Core of U.S.–Japan Trade Tensions . . . Competitors in Other Countries Are Destroying an American Success Story . . . It Must Be Stopped," scream headlines around the world.

International trade theories argue that nations should open their doors to trade. Conventional free-trade wisdom says that by trading with others, a country can offer its citizens a greater quantity and selection of goods at cheaper prices than it could in the absence of trade. Nevertheless, truly free trade still does not exist because national governments intervene. Despite the efforts of the World Trade Organization (WTO) and smaller groups of nations, governments seem to be crying foul in the trade game now more than ever.

We see more efforts at protection in the increase of governments charging foreign producers with "dumping" their goods on world markets. Table 6.2 "Dumpers or Dumped Upon?" (page 210) shows the countries most often charging others with dumping, and their most common targets. Worldwide, the number of antidumping cases that were initiated stood at about 150 in 1995, 225 in 1996, 230 in 1997, and were estimated at around 300 in 1998.

There is no shortage of examples. The United States charges Brazil, Japan, and Russia with dumping their products in the U.S. market as a means to export their way out of tough economic times. The U.S. steel industry wants the government to slap a 200 percent tariff on certain types of steel. But carmakers within the United States are not complaining, and General Motors even spoke out against the antidumping charge—it is enjoying the benefits of low-cost steel for use in its auto production. Canadian steel makers followed the lead of the United States and are pushing for antidumping actions against four nations.

Emerging markets, too, are jumping into the fray. Mexico recently expanded coverage of its Automatic Import Advice System. The system requires importers (from a select list of countries) to notify Mexican officials of the amount and price of a shipment 10 days prior to its expected arrival in Mexico. The 10-day notice gives domestic producers advanced warning of low-priced products so they can complain of dumping before the products clear customs and enter the marketplace. India is also getting onboard by setting up a new government agency to handle antidumping cases. Even Argentina, China, Indonesia, South Africa, South Korea, and Thailand are using this recently popular tool of protectionism.

Why is dumping on the rise in the first place? Oddly enough, the WTO allows it. The WTO has made major inroads on the use of tariffs, slashing them across almost every product category in recent years. But the WTO does not have authority to punish companies, only governments. Thus, the WTO cannot make judgments against individual companies that are dumping products in other markets. It can only pass rulings against the government of the country that imposes an antidumping duty. But the WTO allows countries to retaliate against nations whose producers are suspected of dumping when it can be shown that (1) the alleged offenders are significantly hurting domestic producers, and (2) the export price is lower than the cost of production or lower than the home-market price.

Supporters of antidumping tariffs claim that they prevent dumpers from undercutting the prices charged by producers in a target market and driving them out of business. Another claim in support of antidumping is that it is an excellent way of retaining some protection against potential dangers of totally free trade. Detractors of antidumping tariffs charge that once such tariffs are imposed they are rarely removed. They also claim that it costs companies and governments a great deal of time and money to file and argue their cases. It is also argued that the fear of being charged with dumping causes international competitors to keep their prices higher in a target market than would otherwise be the case. This would allow domestic companies to charge higher prices and not lose market share—forcing consumers to pay more for their goods.

thinking globally

1. "You can't tell consumers that the low price they are paying for that fax machine or automobile is somehow unfair. They're not concerned with the profits of some company. To them, it's just a great bargain and they want it to continue." Do you agree with this statement? Do you think that people from different cultures would respond differently to this statement? Explain your answers.

2. As we've seen, the WTO cannot currently get involved in punishing individual companies—its actions can only be directed toward governments of countries. Do you think this is a wise policy? Why or why not? Why do you think the WTO was not given authority to charge individual companies with dumping? Explain.

3. Identify a recent antidumping case that was brought before the WTO. Locate as many articles in the press as you can that discuss the case. Identify the nations, product(s), and potential punitive measures involved. Supposing you were part of the WTO's Dispute Settlement Body, would you vote in favor of the measures taken by the retaliating nation? Why or why not?

a question of ethics

1. Ever since the early 1980s, the United States has drawn fire from the business community for imposing economic sanctions (similar to an embargo) against Iran for mainly political reasons. Those sanctions disallow international trade and investment between U.S. and Iranian businesspeople. Business leaders in the United States would like the sanctions removed so they could be included in lucrative Iranian oil and gas deals. Other sanction opponents wonder if a policy of offering "all stick and no carrot" is undermining social and political change in Iran. In 1997, a moderate cleric won Iran's presidential election by a landslide. The new president, Seyyid Mohammed Khatami, waged a vigorous campaign for human rights and press freedom as well as improved relations with the West.[33]

    Opponents of unilateral sanctions say that too often, they result in competitors from other countries being handed contracts on silver platters while the offending regime goes unpunished. They also claim that ordinary people suffer the brunt of sanctions while privileged members of ruling classes and political groups remain unscathed. Do you think sanctions can be effective at changing the behavior of governments? Why or why not? Do you think that one country acting alone can bring about reforms through the use of economic sanctions or embargoes?

2. A nonprofit trade and industry group, the National Foreign Trade Council (NFTC), based in Washington, DC, recently criticized a Massachusetts law that it says harms U.S. companies. The NFTC requested the U.S. District Court in Boston to strike down a Massachusetts law that imposes a 10 percent penalty on any company that submits a bid for state contracts that also does business with Myanmar (Burma). The NFTC argues that the law is an attempt to shape foreign policy, although the U.S. Constitution states that "foreign policy is exclusively reserved for the federal government." The NFTC says it does not support the human rights abuses occurring in Myanmar, but instead supports the companies that are being financially penalized.[34]

    Do you think that companies should be penalized in their domestic business dealings because of where they do business abroad? Do you think that the World Trade Organization should get into domestic/international political matters? Why or why not?

3. Trade in services constitutes a continually greater portion of international trade. One such service, hosting international tourists, is becoming especially important for many developing and emerging economies. Under the cover of darkness on November 22, 1998, workers and police officers raided and destroyed an ancient wooden mosque in Chengdu, the capital city of Sichuan Province. Local Muslims transformed the mosque, built in 1666, into a symbol of China's dying cultural heritage and adamantly opposed its destruction. But the mosque was located on a valuable piece of property adjacent to a new city square that might help turn Chengdu into an international destination for tourists.[35]

    Do you think it would have been important to save the mosque? If so, how could it have been saved? Would it have been proper for international development agencies to step in and preserve the mosque where it stood, or perhaps move it to a new location? Was there a role to play for private businesses around the world, such as international tour operators?

7 foreign direct investment

Beacons

A Look Back

CHAPTER 6 explained government involvement in the free trade of goods and services. We explored the motives and methods of government intervention. We also examined the global trading system and how it promotes free trade.

A Look at This Chapter

This chapter examines another significant form of international business, foreign direct investment (FDI). Again, we are concerned with the patterns of FDI and the theories on which it is based. We also explore why and how governments intervene in FDI activity.

A Look Ahead

CHAPTER 8 explores the trend toward greater regional integration of national economies. We explore the benefits of closer economic cooperation and examine prominent regional trading blocs that exist around the world.

Learning Objectives

After studying this chapter, you should be able to

1. Describe the worldwide patterns of *foreign direct investment (FDI)* and the reasons for these patterns.

2. Describe each of the *theories* that attempt to explain why foreign direct investment occurs.

3. Discuss the important *management issues* in the foreign direct investment decision.

4. Explain why governments intervene in the free flow of foreign direct investment.

5. Discuss the *policy instruments* that governments use to restrict and promote foreign direct investment.

It's one of the wonders of the industrial world. The Boeing assembly plant in Everett, Washington, contains 98 acres of manufacturing activity under one roof and is thought to be the largest building on earth. In the cavernous plant as many as 40 cranes work their delicate way through a network of 10-story steel girders. An air-traffic control center is needed just to coordinate construction of the wide-body aircraft known as the 747, 767, and 777, the "babies" of the world's preeminent manufacturer of large-body commercial aircraft.

Visitors to the Everett plant—and some 100,000 tourists come every year might consider the vista before them as uniquely American: bigger than anything else and clear evidence of can-do spirit and industrial might. Yet, one look at the shop floor shows the truly international nature of Boeing's operations. Wooden crates marked "Belfast, Ireland" contain nose landing-gear doors. On a metal rack, there is a stack of outboard wing flaps from Alenia of Italy. The entire fuselage of the 777 has traveled in quarter sections from Japan. Its wing tip assembly comes from Korea, its rudders from Australia, and so on.

At one time, entire Boeing aircraft were made in the United States, but now they are constructed from parts manufactured all over the world. At one time, too, Boeing's sales were 75 percent domestic; today, however, 60 percent of the company's sales are to markets worldwide. To maintain control over such a global operation, Boeing buys a large portion of either their international suppliers' physical assets or publicly traded stock. This part ownership gives Boeing some decision making power in their supplier organizations.

Not surprisingly, the increase of international production and sales are intimately intertwined. To gain access to international markets, Boeing contracts to produce parts abroad, giving other countries much-needed jobs and technology transfer. "You've got to maintain tit for tat if you expect to keep selling airplanes," says one Boeing middle manager.[1]

Many early trade theories were created at a time when most production factors (such as labor, financial capital, capital equipment, and land or natural resources) either could not be moved or could not be moved easily across national borders. But today, all these factors except land are internationally mobile. In fact, inequities in the distribution of factors among countries often propel resources toward those countries where scarcity exists. Companies can easily finance expansion from international financial institutions and whole factories can be picked up and moved to another country. Even labor is more mobile than in years past, although many barriers restrict the complete mobility of labor.

Due to technological advancements in telecommunications and international transportation, companies can do more than simply export their products. Today even entrepreneurs and small companies, not just huge global firms, can engage in **foreign direct investment (FDI)**—the purchase of physical assets or a significant amount of the ownership (stock) of a company in another country to gain a measure of management control. Thus at the core of foreign direct investment are international flows of capital. But there is wide disagreement on what exactly constitutes foreign direct investment. Nations set different thresholds at which they classify an international capital flow as FDI. Most governments set the threshold at anywhere from 10 to 25 percent of stock ownership in a company abroad—the U.S. Commerce Department sets it at 10 percent. In contrast, an investment that does not involve obtaining a degree of control in a company is called a **portfolio investment**.

In this chapter, we examine the importance of foreign direct investment to the operations of international companies. We begin by exploring the pattern FDI has taken in recent years—investigating its sources and destinations. We then take a look at several theories that attempt to explain foreign direct investment flows. Next, we turn our attention to several important management issues that arise in most decisions of whether a company should undertake FDI. We then focus on the reasons why governments try to encourage or restrict foreign direct investment and the methods they employ to accomplish these goals.

foreign direct investment (FDI)
Purchase of physical assets or a significant amount of the ownership (stock) of a company in another country to gain a measure of management control.

portfolio investment
Investment that does not involve obtaining a degree of control in a company.

PATTERNS OF FOREIGN DIRECT INVESTMENT

Just as international trade displays distinct patterns, so too does foreign direct investment. In this section we first take a look at the factors that have led to robust growth in FDI over the past decade. We then turn our attention to the destinations and sources of foreign direct investment.

GROWTH OF FOREIGN DIRECT INVESTMENT

Growth rates in worldwide flows of FDI throughout the early 1990s were approximately 40 percent per year for both inflows and outflows.[2] Although FDI growth rates did slow in 1997, they seemed to be picking up steam again in the late 1990s. There are two main reasons that account for the rising tide of FDI flows over the past decade or so—*globalization* and *mergers and acquisitions*.

Globalization   The forces that are causing the globalization of industries are part of the reason for growth in foreign direct investment. Recall from Chapter 6 that in the 1980s old barriers to trade were not being reduced and new, creative barriers seemed to be popping up in many nations. This presented a problem for companies that were trying to export their products to markets around the world. In response, many companies got around such barriers and undertook foreign direct investment in those markets that promised adequate sales volumes. The Uruguay Round of GATT negotiations (see Chapter 6) created renewed determination to further reduce barriers to trade. As countries lowered their trade barriers, companies realized that they could now produce in the most efficient and productive locations in the world, and simply export to their markets worldwide. This set off another round of foreign direct investment flows into low-cost newly industrialized and emerging nations worldwide. The wave continues as we march into a new century.

Increasing globalization is also causing a growing number of international companies from emerging markets to undertake FDI. For example, companies from Taiwan began investing heavily in other nations in the mid-1980s. Acer, headquartered in Singapore but founded in Taiwan, manufactures personal computers and computer components. Just 20 years after it opened for business, Acer had spawned 10 subsidiaries worldwide and even became the dominant industry player in many emerging markets.[3]

Mergers and Acquisitions   The number of *mergers and acquisitions* (M&A) and their exploding values also underlie the growth in foreign direct investment flows. A great deal of M&A activity has been occurring in domestic markets. In fact, the number of mergers and acquisitions throughout the world (domestic and international) has risen from around 16,000 per year in the early 1990s to more than 26,000 per year in the last years of the decade. In 1998, the M&A deal between Travelers Group and Citicorp merged their financial services powerhouses. The deal was valued at $70 billion. At one point in the merger talks, a director apparently asked the question: "Can anyone stop us?" After a brief silence, someone replied, "NATO" (the military alliance between the United States, Canada, and nations across Europe). Such confidence is fueling "merger mania." Exxon and Mobil announced a proposed $80 billion deal later that year—causing M&A experts to wonder who will do the first-ever $100 billion deal.[4]

Such confidence at home is causing companies to venture abroad for new M&A targets. The number of deals that involve companies from different countries has more than doubled since the mid-1990s. Many cross-border M&A deals are driven by the desires of companies to do any or all of the following:

➡ Get a foothold in a new geographic market
➡ Increase a firm's global competitiveness
➡ Fill gaps in companies' product lines in a global industry
➡ Reduce costs in such areas as R&D, production, or distribution

Consider the merger between Daimler Benz of Germany and Chrysler of the United States. Though valued at around $39 billion, the new mammoth car company (called DaimlerChrysler) does $130 billion in worldwide sales each year. The deal was done for several very good reasons. First, the deal is designed to trim $3 billion in purchasing and research and development costs from the budget of the new carmaker. Second, it will reduce excess production capacity in an industry with high and expanding rates of capacity underutilization. The new company will concentrate pro-

Critical M&A Considerations

A recent survey of major employers across Asia with experience in mergers and acquisitions found that M&A is pursued (a) to gain market share, (b) to gain access to new markets, and (c) to achieve competitive size.

The survey also asked managers about the major internal concerns for companies involved in an M&A deal. The reason internal matters are important is that as soon as a deal is announced, employees wonder: Will I lose my job? Will my pay go up or down? What will working for "them" be like? If such issues are not addressed, they can undo an otherwise done deal. As you can see in the figure below, maintaining open lines of communication, retaining key talented employees, and retaining key managers rank at the top of the list.

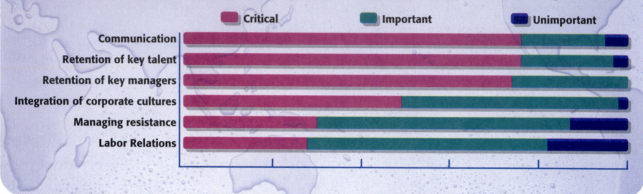

duction at the most efficient plants and close inefficient ones. Finally, the deal combines the prestigious product line of Mercedes-Benz with the economy and middle-of-the-road product line of Chrysler. Thus the combined company can offer its customers a full line of cars from which to choose.[5] For a look at the internal company issues that concern managers during the M&A process, see the World Business Survey "Critical M&A Considerations."

But large global companies and the mergers and buyouts occurring among them do not comprise all foreign direct investment. Entrepreneurs and small businesses also play important roles in the expansion of FDI flows. Let's now take a look at how entrepreneurs and small businesses contribute to FDI and the kinds of investments that they undertake.

Role of Entrepreneurs and Small Businesses   Statistics do not exist that specifically state the portion of worldwide FDI that is contributed by entrepreneurs and small businesses. Nevertheless, we know from anecdotal evidence that these companies are engaged in FDI. Casa Rustica is a small company based in the United States that distributes rustic furniture from Mexico to large and small U.S. retailers. But a frequent problem arises when its Mexican suppliers do not have the productive capacity needed to meet demand. In such cases, Casa Rustica takes matters into its own hands and helps them expand capacity by not only offering loans, but by taking part ownership in their operations in Mexico.

Unhindered by many of the constraints of a large company, entrepreneurs investing in other markets often demonstrate an inspiring can-do spirit mixed with ingenuity and bravado. For a day-in-the-life look at a young entrepreneur who is realiz-

Entrepreneurial Focus

Cowboy Candy Rides into Manchuria

Tom Kirkwood, though just 28 years old, has turned his dream of introducing his grandfather's taffy to China into a fast-growing, if still unprofitable, business. Kirkwood's story—his hassles and hustling—provides some lessons on the purest form of global investing. The basics that small investors in China can follow are as basic as they get. Find a product that's easy to make, widely popular, and cheap to sell and then choose the least expensive, investor-friendliest place to make it.

Kirkwood, whose family runs the Shawnee Inn, a ski and golf resort in Shawnee-on-Delaware, Pennsylvania, decided to make candy in Manchuria—China's gritty, heavily populated, industrial northeast. Chinese often give individually wrapped candies as a gift, and Kirkwood reckoned that China's rising, increasingly prosperous urbanites would have a lucrative sweet tooth. "You can't be M&Ms, but you don't have to be penny candy, either," Kirkwood says. "You find your niche. Because a niche in China is an awful lot of people."

Kirkwood decided early on that he wanted to do business in China. In the mid-1980s after prep school, he spent a year in Taiwan and China learning Chinese and working in a Shanghai engineering company. The experience gave him a taste for adventure capitalism on the frontier of China's economic development. In 1991, while in China advising other firms on how to set up business, Kirkwood set up a partnership with Bulgarian student Peter S. Moustakerski. The two eventually came up with what they considered a sure-fire idea—candy. Using $400,000 of Kirkwood's family money, they bought equipment and rented a factory in Shenyang, a city of 6 million people in the heart of Manchuria. Roads and rail transport were convenient, and wages were low. The local government seemed amenable to a 100 percent foreign-owned factory, and the Shenyang Shawnee Cowboy Food Company was born.

It's a small operation with only 51 employees, but running your own business in China is a rigorous life. On a Sunday evening, Kirwood and his wife, Kate, leave their apartment in Shanghai to take a plane to Shenyang, about 750 miles away. The two are met two hours later by the company's general manager, Michael Fu, and an assistant general manager. They immediately brief Kirkwood on the latest business issues: adding new flavors to the line; collecting debts; a broken production machine; and a fire at Shenyang's largest department store, which is also Cowboy Candy's largest customer. After lunch the next day, Kirkwood and his wife view the burned-out remains of the department store. Then they tour a wholesale market, one of seven in Shenyang. Each market sells 100 to 600 boxes of candy a day. If he can get 5 percent of the local market, figures Kirkwood, he could roll out an additional half ton of candy a day. That would help push his factory close to its capacity of 4 tons a day.

At 3 A.M. the next morning, it's time for Kirkwood to be on the road for a three-hour predawn ride across Manchuria to the port of Dalian. There Kirkwood meets with a local distributor who is behind on payments and then has a chat with one of China's new singing talents, Quidi Aixinjueluo, who has agreed to appear in a Cowboy Candy commercial. Over breakfast at a hotel overlooking the ocean, Kirkwood agrees to sponsor a music video if Quidi will promote Cowboy Candy. The deal done, Kirkwood heads for the airport and his afternoon flight to Beijing for a meeting with a distributor interested in Cowboy Candy. As he's boarding the plane, he realizes he has a bag full of candy. He offers one to a flight attendant. When lunch is over, he vows, "Everybody on this plane will know Cowboy Candy."

ing his dreams in China, see the Entrepreneurial Focus "Cowboy Candy Rides into Manchuria."

Some entrepreneurs are motivated to seek out true adventure in some of the poorest nations of the world—seeing opportunity where others see only risk. Consider the case of Brian Bowen and a few adventurous buddies from Perry, Georgia. When Uzbekistan (a former Soviet Union republic) opened its borders to investment in the 1990s, Bowen and five fellow entrepreneurial friends took their savings and went in to set up cellular phone service in Tashkent, Uzbekistan. Tashkent was almost entirely leveled by an earthquake in 1966 and the surviving landline telephone service dated from the 1920s. But today, the country would shut down without the cellular service provided by Bowen's company, International Communication Group (ICG). Bowen and his friends share ownership of the company with the Uzbekistan government. Bowen admits that the arrangement did present some difficulties: "I don't have any experience dealing with the KGB, the mafia, or the family connections in the bureaucracy here." In addition to learning the ins and outs of the government bureaucracy, Bowen has learned to eat horsemeat, drink vodka toasts, and enjoy *plov*—a dish of pilaf rice and mutton. The company has 7,000 subscribers, 240 employees, and could be worth as much as $100 million by some industry estimates.[6]

WORLDWIDE FLOWS OF FDI

As we said earlier, FDI flows grew rapidly throughout the early 1990s though it slowed some in 1997 (see Figure 7.1). There is little doubt that the financial turmoil and economic problems in a handful of Asian nations and the dark clouds that it cast over many other emerging markets had a role in this. But as we close out one century and begin a fresh one, preliminary figures suggest that FDI flows are once again rising at a fast pace.

Although the *destination* of most FDI inflows are industrialized countries, they are attracting a declining share of worldwide total FDI. However, as Map 7.1 (pages 228–229) and its accompanying table shows, the United States is the top destination of FDI among all countries. Two other industrialized nations making it into the top five are France and the United Kingdom. So industrialized nations are attracting less FDI, while newly industrialized nations and emerging markets are attracting more. Map 7.1 also shows that China and Brazil appear in the "top five" list. These are two of the biggest emerging markets that have become magnets for investment from around the world.

Industrialized countries are also the *source* for about 85 percent of worldwide FDI. In fact, the five largest sources of FDI (France, Germany, Japan, the United Kingdom, and the United States) account for roughly two-thirds of investment outflows. Just as the portion

FIGURE 7.1

WORLDWIDE FLOWS OF FOREIGN DIRECT INVESTMENT

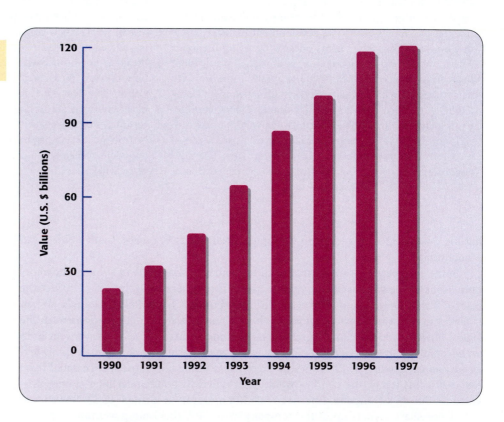

of FDI being sent *to* industrialized nations is declining, the portion of FDI being sent *from* industrialized nations is also declining. In fact, a recent "Multinationals Top 50" list of the largest international companies showed that many are headquartered in Asia, particularly China, Hong Kong, South Korea, Taiwan, and Singapore. Latin America also had many companies represented, with Mexico home to eight and Brazil home to six of the world's largest multinationals.[7]

Let's now take a closer look at some examples of the kinds of investments companies are undertaking in two regions attracting much FDI—*East Asia and the Pacific* and *Latin America and the Caribbean.*

East Asia and the Pacific　　The East Asia and Pacific region is luring a great deal of capital in the form of foreign direct investment. India's success at market liberalization in the mid-1990s was rewarded with a tripling of FDI inflows in a single one-year period.[8] Multinationals find it important to have a presence in the developing world of Asia to tap into low-cost resources and to service local markets. The late 1990s saw a revival of interest in Asia among European Union nations. This was demonstrated by the launch of an Asia-Europe Investment Promotion Action Plan. Privatization of telecommunications, as well as other large-scale infrastructure projects, should sustain FDI flows to Asia well into the twenty-first century.

The dream of reaching India's 100 million middle-class consumers has lured such companies as Coca-Cola, General Electric, Rank Xerox, Revlon, and Kellogg. Although these companies see vast potential in India (a "big emerging market"), they realize that pitfalls also abound such as a poor infrastructure, inefficient bureaucracy, and a rather unexpected sophisticated demand of consumers. Mercedes-Benz opened a plant in India in the mid-1990s to manufacture its E-class sedan and win over India's rich new business class. But two years later the plant was operating at just 10 percent of its capacity of 20,000 cars per year. It turns out that the wealthy in India were not at all interested in buying an outdated European design, but demanded the latest models available in the most advanced markets.

Latin America and the Caribbean　　The Latin America and Caribbean region is also a magnet for FDI inflows, although the volume varies widely from one year to the next. Much of this FDI is directed at ongoing projects with exceptionally large investment requirements such as privatization within the infrastructure, mining, and petrochemical industries.

There also are large auto assembly projects by Volkswagen, Fiat, General Motors, and Ford. Awed by double-digit sales growth in auto markets throughout Latin America, European, Japanese, and U.S. carmakers are pouring a total of $18 billion into new factories in South America. Mark Hogan, president of General Motors-Brazil, predicts that as a single market, Brazil and Argentina "will surpass Germany and become one of the top three markets in the world, behind the United States and Japan." Driving the optimism are economic conditions the likes of which have not been seen for decades. Brazilian Jose Filho and his wife, Theresinha, watched in amazement as their three married children bought a total of 10 new cars among them. Filho and his wife have one car, a Chevy Chevette. Because the South American continent was seen as a dumping ground for obsolete technology and outdated models in the 1990s, GM's plant there turned out Chevy Chevettes—out of production in the United States for years. Now GM wants to turn these markets into a showcase for the latest in technology and lean manufacturing. By offering a new model every two months, GM-Brazil increased production from 170,000 to 500,000 units a year over the past 5 years. One auto-industry analyst estimates that the plant con-

MAP 7.1

**VOLUME OF INWARD
FOREIGN DIRECT INVESTMENT**

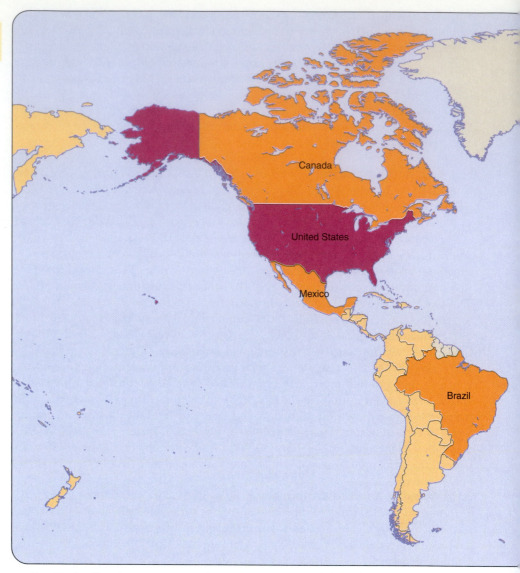

Canada

United States

Mexico

Brazil

Note: **Foreign direct investment** is net inflows of investment to acquire a lasting management interest (10 percent or more of voting stock) in an enterprise operating in an economy other than that of the investor. It is the sum of equity capital, reinvestment of earnings, other long-term capital, and short-term capital as shown in the balance of payments.

tributed 25 percent to the parent company's operating profit during that period. Brazilian demand for GM cars is so high that the plant at San Jose dos Campos operates 23 hours a day.[9]

EXPLANATIONS FOR FOREIGN DIRECT INVESTMENT

So far we have seen how the flows of foreign direct investment increased dramatically over recent decades only to rise more slowly in the late 1990s. But what we have not investigated are explanations for why FDI occurs. There are four main theories that attempt to explain why companies engage in foreign direct investment: *international product life cycle, market imperfections (internalization), eclectic theory,* and *market power*. Let's now look at each of these in detail.

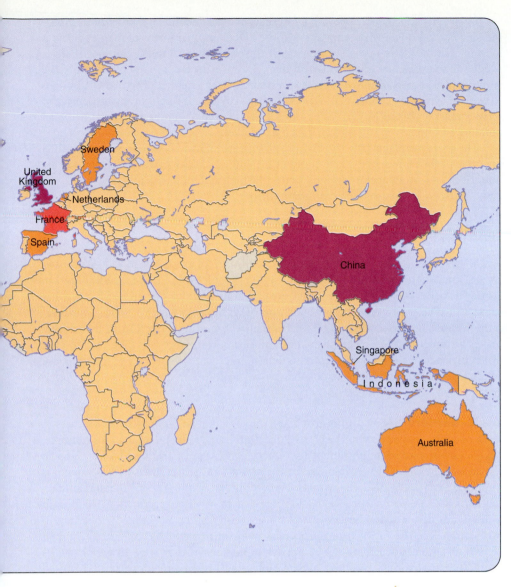

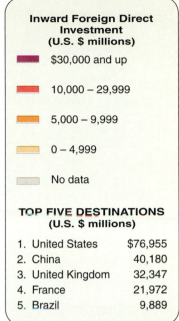

**Inward Foreign Direct
Investment
(U.S. $ millions)**

- $30,000 and up
- 10,000 – 29,999
- 5,000 – 9,999
- 0 – 4,999
- No data

**TOP FIVE DESTINATIONS
(U.S. $ millions)**

1. United States $76,955
2. China   40,180
3. United Kingdom   32,347
4. France   21,972
5. Brazil   9,889

INTERNATIONAL PRODUCT LIFE CYCLE

Although we introduced the international product life cycle in Chapter 5 in the context of international trade, it can also explain foreign direct investment.[10] The **international product life cycle** states that a company will begin by exporting its product and later undertake foreign direct investment as a product moves through its life cycle. In the *new product stage*, a good is produced in the home country because of uncertain domestic demand and to keep production close to the research department that developed the product. In the *maturing product stage*, the company directly invests in production facilities in those countries where demand is great enough to warrant its own production facilities. In the final *standardized product stage*, increased competition creates pressures to reduce production costs. In response, a company builds production capacity in low-cost developing nations to serve its markets around the world.

> **international product
> life cycle**
> *Theory stating that a
> company will begin by
> exporting its product and
> later undertake foreign direct
> investment as a product
> moves through its life cycle.*

Despite its conceptual appeal, the international product life cycle theory is limited in its power to explain why companies choose FDI over other forms of market entry. A local firm in the target market could pay for the right (license) to use the special assets needed to manufacture a particular product. In this way, a company could avoid the additional risks associated with direct investments in the market. The theory also fails to explain why firms choose FDI over exporting activities. It might be less expensive to serve a market abroad by increasing output at the home-country factory rather than building additional capacity within the target market.

The theory explains why the FDI of some firms follows the international product life cycle of their products. But it does not explain why other market entry modes are inferior or less advantageous options. Let's now look at a more recently developed theory—*market imperfections (internalization)* theory.

MARKET IMPERFECTIONS (INTERNALIZATION)

A market that is said to operate at peak efficiency (prices are as low as they can possibly be) and where goods are readily and easily available is said to be a *perfect market*. However, perfect markets are rarely, if ever, seen in business because of factors that cause a breakdown in the efficient operation of an industry—called *market imperfections*. **Market imperfections** theory states that when an imperfection in the market makes a transaction less efficient than it could be, a company will undertake foreign direct investment to internalize the transaction and thereby remove the imperfection. There are two market imperfections that are relevant to this discussion—trade barriers and specialized knowledge.

market imperfections
Theory stating that when an imperfection in the market makes a transaction less efficient than it could be, a company will undertake foreign direct investment to internalize the transaction and thereby remove the imperfection.

Trade Barriers   One common market imperfection in international business is trade barriers, such as tariffs. The North American Free Trade Agreement, for example, stipulates that a sufficient portion of a product's content must originate within Canada, Mexico, or the United States in order for the product to escape tariff charges when it is imported to any of these three markets. Therefore, a large number of Korean manufacturers of videocassette recorders (VCRs) invested in Mexican production facilities in Tijuana, Mexico, just south of Mexico's border with California. Thus by investing in production facilities in Mexico, the Korean companies were able to skirt the North American tariffs and thereby earn a greater profit than if they were to export VCRs from Korean factories. Thus the presence of a market imperfection (tariffs) caused companies to undertake foreign direct investment.

Specialized Knowledge   The unique competitive advantage of a company sometimes consists of specialized knowledge. This knowledge could be the technical expertise of engineers or the special marketing abilities of managers. When the knowledge is technical expertise, companies can charge a fee to companies in other countries for use of the knowledge in producing the same or a similar product. But when a company's specialized knowledge is embodied in its employees, the only alternative to exploit a market opportunity in another nation may be to undertake FDI.

However, the possibility that a company will create a future competitor by charging another company for access to its knowledge is a market imperfection that can encourage FDI. Rather than trade a short-term gain (the fee charged another company) for a long-term loss (lost competitiveness), a company will prefer to undertake investment. For example, as Japan rebuilt its industries in the 1950s following the Second World War, many Japanese companies paid Western firms for access to special technical knowledge embodied in their products. These Japanese companies became adept at revising and improving many of these technologies and became leaders in their industries such as electronics and autos. The Western companies would have been better off not licensing their technologies, but undertaking foreign direct investment.

ECLECTIC THEORY

The **eclectic theory** states that firms undertake foreign direct investment when the features of a particular location combine with ownership and internalization advantages to make a location appealing for investment.[11] A *location advantage* is the advantage of locating a particular economic activity in a specific location because of the characteristics (natural or acquired) of that location.[12] These advantages have historically been natural resources such as oil in the Middle East, timber in Canada, and copper in Chile. However, they can also be acquired advantages such as a productive workforce. An *ownership advantage* is the advantage that a company has due to its ownership of some special asset, such as brand recognition, technical knowledge, or management ability. An *internalization advantage* is the advantage that arises from internalizing a business activity rather than leaving it to a relatively inefficient market. The theory states that when all these advantages are present, a company will undertake FDI.

eclectic theory
Theory stating that firms undertake foreign direct investment when the features of a particular location combine with ownership and internalization advantages to make a location appealing for investment.

MARKET POWER

Firms often seek the greatest amount of power possible in their industries relative to rivals. The **market power** theory states that a firm tries to establish a dominant market presence in an industry by undertaking foreign direct investment. The benefit of market power is greater profit because the firm is far better able to dictate the cost of its inputs and/or the price of its output.

One way a company can achieve market power (or dominance) is through **vertical integration**—the extension of company activities into stages of production that provide a firm's inputs (*backward integration*) or absorb its output (*forward integration*). Sometimes a company can effectively control the world supply of an input needed by its industry if it has the resources or ability to integrate backward into supplying that input. Companies may also be able to achieve a great deal of market power if they can integrate forward to increase control over output. For example, they could perhaps make investments in distribution to leapfrog channels of distribution that are tightly controlled by competitors.

market power
Theory stating that a firm tries to establish a dominant market presence in an industry by undertaking foreign direct investment.

vertical integration
Extension of company activities into stages of production that provide a firm's inputs (backward integration) or absorb its output (forward integration).

MANAGEMENT ISSUES IN THE FDI DECISION

Decisions of whether or not to engage in foreign direct investment involve several important issues regarding management of the company and the firm's market. Some of these issues are grounded in the inner workings of firms undertaking FDI such as the control desired over operations abroad or the firm's cost of production. Others are related to the market and industry in which a firm competes such as the preferences of customers or the actions of rivals. Let's begin our examination of each of these important issues by exploring how the desire for control plays a role in the FDI decision.

CONTROL

When many companies invest abroad they are greatly concerned with controlling the activities occurring in the local market for a variety of reasons. Perhaps the company wants to be certain that its product is being marketed the same in the local market as it is at home. Or maybe it wants to ensure that the selling price remains the same in both markets. Some companies try to maintain ownership of a large portion of the local operations, say even up to 100 percent, in the belief that greater ownership gives them greater control.

However, for a variety of reasons even complete ownership does not *guarantee* control. For example, the local government might intervene and require a company to hire some local managers rather than bringing them all in from the home office. Companies may need to prove a scarcity of skilled local managerial talent before the government will let them bring managers in from the home country. Governments might also require that all goods produced in the local facility be exported so they do not compete with products of the country's native firms.

Partnership Requirements   Because of the importance of control, many companies have strict policies regarding how much ownership they will take in firms in other nations. In fact, prior to the 1990s IBM had the strict policy that international subsidiaries needed to be 100 percent owned by the home office. However, companies must sometimes abandon such policies when a country demands shared ownership in return for access to its market.

Partnership requirements were more common in the past than they are today. Governments saw such requirements as a way to shield their workers and industries from what they perceived as exploitation or domination by large international firms. But these policies are being phased out worldwide. Companies would sometimes sacrifice control to pursue a market opportunity but frequently did not. By the 1980s, most countries retreated from such a hard-line stance and began to open their doors to investment by multinationals. For example, Mexico in the 1980s was making its decisions on investment by multinationals on a case-by-case basis. IBM was trying to negotiate for 100 percent ownership of a facility in Guadalajara and got the go-ahead after the company made numerous concessions in other areas.

Benefits of Cooperation   Recent years have seen greater harmony between governments and international companies, though the business press still tends to highlight the controversies. The reason is that governments of many developing and newly industrialized countries have come to realize the benefits of investment by multinationals: decreased unemployment, increased tax revenues, training to create a more highly skilled workforce, and the transfer of technology. In addition, countries with reputations for overly restricting the operations of multinational enterprises see their inward investment flows dry up—diminishing such potential gains. Indeed, this was the case in India prior to its market reforms of the early 1990s. As a result, the nation was unable to garner the benefits of the foreign direct investment in the proportions that flowed into neighboring Southeast Asian nations.[13]

Cooperation also frequently opens important communication channels that help firms to maintain positive relationships in the host country. Both parties tend to walk a fine line—cooperating most of the time, but holding fast on those occasions where the stakes are especially high.

Cooperation with a local partner and respect for national pride in central Europe contributed to the successful acquisition of Hungary's Borsodi brewery (formerly a state-owned enterprise) by Belgium's Interbrew. From the start, Interbrew wisely insisted it would move ahead provided (a) the local brand would receive total backing, (b) local management would be in charge, and (c) Interbrew would assist local management with technical, marketing, sales, distribution, and general management training. After four years of operation within the Interbrew group, Borsodi recently became one of the parent company's key subsidiaries. It is now run entirely by Hungarian managers following modern management methods and focusing on quality and profitability. The positive experience in Hungary encouraged Interbrew to recently acquire breweries in Croatia, Romania, and Bulgaria.[14]

PURCHASE-OR-BUILD DECISION

Another important matter for managers is whether to purchase an existing business or build a subsidiary abroad from the ground up—called a *greenfield investment.* An acquisition generally provides the investor with an existing plant and equipment as well as personnel. The acquiring firm may also benefit from the goodwill the existing company has built up over the years and, perhaps, brand recognition of the existing firm. In addition, purchase of an existing business can perhaps allow for alternate methods of financing the purchase, such as an exchange of stock ownership between the companies. Factors that reduce the appeal of purchasing existing facilities include obsolete equipment, poor relations with workers, and an unsuitable location.

But adequate facilities are sometimes simply unavailable and a company must go ahead with a greenfield investment. Poland is a source of skilled and inexpensive labor—appealing to car manufacturers. But the country had little in the way of advanced car production facilities when General Motors was considering investing there. GM wound up investing $323 million in a new facility built in Poland's Silesian region. The factory went on-line in 1998 and has the potential to produce 200,000 units annually (some of which are designated for export). GM expects the plant to function as a back door to the profitable markets of Western Europe.[15] However, greenfield investments can have there share of headaches—obtaining the necessary permits and financing and hiring local personnel can be a real problem in some markets.

Mexico's Cemex, S.A. is a multinational company that made a fortune by buying struggling, inefficient plants around the world and reengineering them. Chairman Lorenzo Zambrano has long figured that it was "Buy big globally, or be bought." The success of Cemex in using FDI has confounded, even rankled, its competitors in developed nations. In the early 1990s, for example, escaping recession at home in Mexico, Cemex borrowed money and carried out a $1.8 billion purchase of Spain's two largest cement companies, Valenciana and Sanson. "For Spaniards," recalls Zambrano, "the idea of [Mexicans] coming to Spain and changing top management, 500 years after the conquest of Mexico, was unthinkable. . . . They said a Mexican company couldn't manage in Europe. But we increased our operating margin in Spain by more than three times in three years. We made that company much better than before, but also made it much better than our competitors in Europe." The international assets of Cemex were nearly half of its total assets of $8 billion at the time.[16]

We have only addressed some of the issues important to managers when considering purchasing or building in a market abroad. We will have more to say on this topic in Chapter 14 when we see how companies actually take on such an ambitious goal. In the meantime, for additional insight into the concerns of managers in this situation see the Global Manager "Investing Abroad? Be Prepared for Surprises."

PRODUCTION COSTS

There are many factors that affect the cost of production in any national market. For example, labor regulations can increase the hourly cost of production several times. Companies may be required to provide benefits packages for their employees that are over and above hourly wages. More time than was planned for might be required to adequately train workers to bring productivity up to an acceptable standard. Although

Investing Abroad? Be Prepared for Surprises

The decision of whether to build facilities in a market abroad or purchase the existing operations of a company already in the local market can be a difficult task. Managers can minimize their risk by preparing themselves and their company for any number of surprises that their firms might face, including the following:

➡ **Human Resource Policies.** This aspect of FDI often holds the biggest surprise. Many managers erroneously assume the policies they use at home can simply be imported into the local culture with minimal revision. Unfortunately, these policies seldom address local customs and abide by local regulations. For example, many European countries require government approval for a plant to run a continuous operation in several shifts and have regulations governing shift work for women in certain manufacturing operations.

➡ **Labor Costs.** This factor of production is often higher than expected. Denmark, for instance, has a minimum wage of about $13 an hour—more than twice as high as that of the United States. Mexico has a minimum daily rate of only $3. But the effective rate is nearly double because of government-mandated benefits and employment practices.

➡ **Mandated Benefits.** These often cover elements totally alien to managers and can include such things as company-supplied clothing and meals, required profit sharing, guaranteed employment contracts, and generous dismissal policies. Costs of these programs can top 100 percent of an employee's wage. Such programs are typically nonnegotiable and strictly enforced. Violations can result in government seizure of company property,

assessment of large fines, and even prison terms for executives.

➡ **Unions.** These differ a great deal from country to country. In some countries organized labor is present at almost every company, although relations can be more or less hostile than in the home market and strikes at individual plants can be frequent or seldom. In Scandinavia, rather than dealing with a single union at its plant, an employer may have to negotiate with five or six unions—each representing a different skill or profession.

➡ **Economic-Development Incentives.** Existing in most countries these can be substantial and can change constantly. The European Union, for example, is trying to standardize incentives based upon unemployment levels. But some member countries continually stretch the rules and several have been penalized for exceeding guidelines.

➡ **Information.** Comprehensive and comparable data on such vital factors as the availability of labor, utility services, and plant sites simply don't exist in some countries. Such information, although varying in quality and availability, is generally good in developed countries; in undeveloped countries it is suspect at best. Therefore, any firm considering international expansion must perform careful research early in the decision process.

➡ **Personal and Political Contacts.** These types of contacts can be extremely important—especially in developing and emerging nations—and are sometimes the only way to get operations established. But using them can be difficult. Moreover, complying with practices that are common in the local market can create ethical dilemmas for managers.

---

the cost of land and the tax rate on profits can be lower in the local market (or purposely lowered to attract multinationals), it cannot be assumed that they will remain constant. Companies from around the world using Taiwan as a production base in the past decade or so have witnessed rising wages and land prices that erode profits as the economy continues to industrialize.

rationalized production
System of production in which each of a product's components are produced where the cost of producing that component is lowest.

Rationalized Production   One approach companies use to contain production costs is **rationalized production**—a system of production in which each of a product's components are produced where the cost of producing that component is lowest. All the components are then brought together at one central location for assembly into the final product. Consider the typical stuffed animal made in China whose components are all imported to China (with the exception of the polycore thread with which it's sewn). The stuffed animal's eyes are molded in Japan. Its outfit is imported from France. The polyester-fiber stuffing comes from either Germany or the United States, and the pile-fabric "fur" is produced in Korea. Only final assembly of these components occurs in China.

Although highly efficient, a potential problem with this production model is that a work stoppage in one country can bring the entire production process to a standstill. Production of autos is highly rationalized with parts coming in from a multitude of countries for assembly. When the United Auto Workers (UAW) union held a strike for many weeks against General Motors in 1998, many of GM's international assembly plants were threatened. The plant that the UAW chose to launch their strike supplied brake pads to virtually all of GM's plants throughout North America.

Case: The Mexican *Maquiladora* Stretching 2,000 miles long from the Pacific Ocean to the Gulf of Mexico, this 130-mile-wide strip along the U.S.-Mexico border may well be North America's fastest-growing region. With 11 million people and $150 billion in output, the region's economy is larger than that of Poland's and close to the size of Thailand's. The combination of a low-wage regional economy nestled inside a prosperous giant is now becoming a model for other regions that are split by wage or technology gaps. Some analysts compare the U.S.-Mexico border region to that between Hong Kong and its manufacturing realm, China's Guangdong Province. Officials from cities along the border between Germany and Poland are also studying the U.S.-Mexico experience.

But no matter how popular this model becomes, businesses must also consider the dark side of the border economy's allure—when goods and capital flow freely, so does contraband. Unfortunately, a great deal of the construction, retailing, and other business along the border is spurred by an estimated $22 billion in cross-border drug trafficking. Another profitable business is the smuggling of illegal immigrants from Mexico to the United States. Moreover, ethical dilemmas have arisen over the wide gap between Mexican and U.S. wages and over the loss of U.S. union jobs to *maquiladora* nonunion jobs. *Maquiladoras* also do not operate under the same stringent environmental regulations to which companies across the border must adhere.[17] Furthermore, human rights groups and consumer organizations frequently criticize U.S. companies for taking advantage of low-wage labor in this region.

Cost of R&D As the role of technology as a powerful competitive factor continues to grow, the soaring cost of developing subsequent stages of technology has led multinationals to engage in cross-border alliances and acquisitions. For instance, huge multinational pharmaceutical companies are intensely interested in the pioneering biotechnology work done by smaller, entrepreneurial start-ups. Cadus Pharmaceutical Corporation of Tarrytown, New York, is using yeast to determine the function of 400 genes that are related to so-called receptor molecules. Many disorders are associated with the improper functioning of these receptors—making them good targets for drug development. In 1997, Cadus invested up to $68 million with the United Kingdom's SmithKline Beecham to allow it access to its yeast work. Glaxo, another British pharmaceutical giant, cut a deal with Sequana Therapeutics Inc., a genomics firm in La Jolla, California, for access to its work on nematodes.[18]

One indicator of the significance of technology in foreign direct investment is the amount of R&D being conducted by affiliates of parent companies in other countries. The globalization of innovation and the phenomenon of foreign direct investment in R&D are not necessarily motivated by demand factors such as the size of local markets. Instead, foreign direct investment in R&D appears more likely to be spurred by supply factors such as gaining access to high-quality scientific and technical human capital.[19]

Israel attracts foreign direct investors with its growing high-tech industries. Here a researcher tests a sample of DNA-containing material at the Weismann Institute in Israel. To see more of Israel's technological industries, go to Virtual Jerusalem's *Israel Technological Letter* site at ⟨**www.virtualjerusalem.com/ business/i_tech**⟩.

CUSTOMER KNOWLEDGE

The behavior of buyers is frequently an important issue in the decision of whether to undertake foreign direct investment. A local presence might help companies gain valuable knowledge about its customers that it could not obtain from the home market. For example, when customer preferences for a product differ a great deal from country to country, a local presence might help companies to better understand such preferences and tailor their products accordingly.

Some countries have quality reputations in certain product categories. German engineering, Italian shoes, French perfume, and Swiss chocolate impress customers as being of superior quality. Because of these perceptions, it can be profitable for a firm to produce its product in the country with the quality reputation although it is based in another country. For example, a cologne or perfume producer might want to bottle its fragrance in France and give it a name in French. Such image appeal can be strong enough to encourage foreign direct investment.

FOLLOWING CLIENTS

Firms commonly engage in foreign direct investment when doing so puts them close to firms for which they act as supplier. This practice of "following clients" can be expected in industries where many component parts are obtained from suppliers with whom a manufacturer has a close working relationship. It also tends to result in clusters whereby companies that supply one another's inputs congregate in a certain geographic region (see Chapter 5). For example, when Mercedes opened its first international plant just outside Tuscaloosa, Alabama, as many as nine auto-parts suppliers also moved to the area from Germany. Together, they brought with them $225 million in additional investment.[20]

FOLLOWING RIVALS

In industries with a limited number of large firms, FDI decisions frequently resemble a "follow the leader" scenario. In other words, many of these firms believe that choosing not to make a move parallel to that of the "first mover" might result in being shut out of a potentially lucrative market. For example, when firms based in industrial countries moved back into South Africa following the end of apartheid, their competitors followed. Of course, each market can sustain only a certain number of rivals. Firms that cannot compete will choose the "least damaging option." This seems to have been the case for Pepsi, which went back into South Africa in 1994, but withdrew in 1997 after being crushed by Coke.[21]

GOVERNMENT INTERVENTION IN FDI

Nations often intervene in the flow of foreign direct investment to protect their cultural heritages, domestic companies, and, of course, jobs. Thus nations frequently enact laws, create regulations, or construct administrative hurdles to which companies from other nations must adhere if they wish to invest in the nation.

In a general sense, a bias toward protectionism or openness is rooted in a nation's culture, history, and politics. Values, attitudes, and beliefs form the basis for much of a government's position regarding foreign direct investment. For example, South American nations with strong cultural ties to a European heritage (such as Argentina) are generally enthusiastic about investment received from European nations. South American nations with stronger indigenous influences (such as Ecuador) are generally less enthusiastic.

Opinions vary widely on the appropriate amount of foreign direct investment a country should allow. At one extreme are those who favor complete economic self-sufficiency and oppose any form of FDI. At the other extreme are those who favor free markets with no government intervention at all. However, most countries believe that a certain amount of FDI is desirable in raising national output and enhancing the standard of living for their people. Thus in between the two extremes are those who believe that the decision of whether or not to allow investment depends on the particular situation. Besides philosophical ideals, countries intervene in FDI for a host of far more practical reasons. But before we take a look at these we must understand what is meant by a country's *balance of payments*.

The French government, wanting to preserve its country's culture, hopes that films like *Astérix and Obélix Against Caesar*, starring Gérard Depardieu and made with French, Italian, and German backing, will provide an "image of resistance to American cinematographic imperialism," as the newspaper *Le Monde* proclaimed it.

BALANCE OF PAYMENTS

balance of payments
A national accounting system that records all payments to entities in other countries and all receipts coming into the nation.

A country's **balance of payments** is a national accounting system that records all payments to entities in other countries and all receipts coming into the nation. International transactions that result in payments (outflows) to entities in other nations are reductions in the balance of payments accounts and therefore recorded with a (−) minus sign. International transactions that result in receipts (inflows) from other nations are additions to the balance of payments accounts and thus recorded with a (+) plus sign. For example, when a U.S. company buys 40 percent of the publicly traded stock of a Mexican company on Mexico's stock market, the U.S. balance of payments records the transaction as an outflow of capital and it is recorded with a minus sign (−). Table 7.1 shows the balance of payments accounts for the United States. As shown in the table, any nation's balance of payments consists of two major components—the *current account* and *capital account*. Let's now describe each of these accounts and discuss how to read Table 7.1.

current account
A national account that records transactions involving the import and export of goods and services, income receipts on assets abroad, and income payments on foreign assets inside the country.

Current Account   The **current account** is a national account that records transactions involving the import and export of goods and services, income receipts on assets abroad, and income payments on foreign assets inside the country. The *merchandise* account in Table 7.1 includes exports and imports of tangible goods such as computer software, electronic components, and apparel. The *services* account includes exports and imports of services such as tourism, business consulting, and banking services. For example, suppose a company in the United States receives payment for consulting services provided to a company in another country. The receipt is recorded as an "export of services" and assigned a (+) plus sign in the services account in the balance of payments.

The *income receipts* account includes income earned on U.S. assets held abroad. When a U.S. company's subsidiary in another country remits profits back to the parent in the United States, the receipt is recorded in the income receipts account and given a

TABLE 7.1	**United States Balance of Payments Accounts, 1997 (U.S. $ millions)**	
Current Account		
Exports of goods, services, and income	1,179,380	
Merchandise	679,325	
Services	258,268	
Income receipts on U.S. assets abroad	241,787	
Imports of goods, services, and income		−1,294,904
Merchandise		−877,279
Services		−170,520
Income payments on foreign assets in U.S.		−247,105
Current account balance		−155,215
Capital Account		
Increase in U.S. assets abroad (capital outflow)		−478,502
U.S. official reserve assets		−1,010
Other U.S. government assets	174	
U.S. private assets		−477,666
Foreign assets in the U.S. (capital inflow)	733,441	
Foreign official assets	15,817	
Other foreign assets	717,624	
Capital account balance	254,939	
Statistical discrepancy	−99,724	

(+) plus sign. The *income payments* account includes income paid to entities in other nations that is earned on assets they hold in the United States. For instance, when a French company's U.S. subsidiary sends profits earned in the U.S. back the parent company in France, the transaction is recorded in the income payments account as an outflow and given a (−) minus sign .

A **current account surplus** occurs when a country exports more goods, services, and income than it imports. Thus the nation is running a *trade surplus.* Conversely, a **current account deficit** occurs when a country imports more goods, services, and income than it exports—called a *trade deficit.* Table 7.1 shows that the United States had a current account deficit in 1997. Figure 7.2 shows the U.S. current

current account surplus
When a country exports more goods, services, and income than it imports (also called a trade surplus).

current account deficit
When a country imports more goods, services, and income than it exports (also called a trade deficit).

FIGURE 7.2

CURRENT ACCOUNT BALANCES FOR THE THREE BIGGEST TRADERS

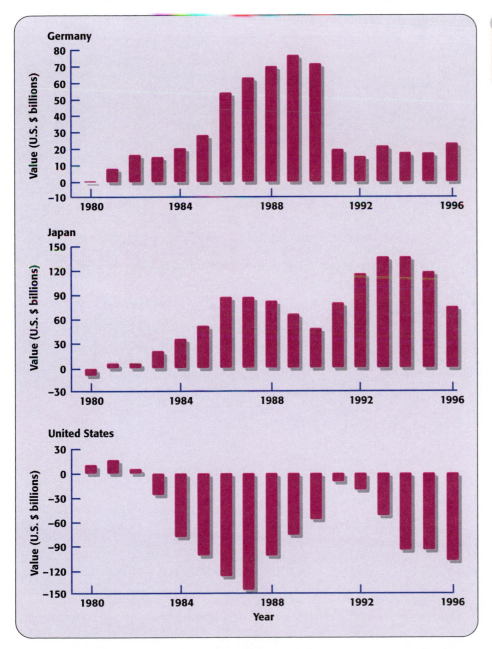

account balance alongside that of Germany and Japan—together, the world's three biggest traders. We will address this matter shortly.

Capital Account   The **capital account** is a national account that records transactions involving the purchase or sale of *assets*. Favorable political events in Mexico in the late 1990s caused some financial experts to recommend investing in Mexico's stock market.[22] If a U.S. citizen followed that advice and invested in Mexican stocks, the transaction would show up on the capital accounts of both the United States and Mexico—as an outflow of assets from the United States and an inflow of assets to Mexico. Conversely, in earlier years Mexican investors bought real estate in the United States as a hedge against a currency whose value was declining. Those transactions also showed up on the capital accounts of both nations—as an inflow of assets to the United States and as an outflow of assets from Mexico. Although the balances

capital account
A national account that records transactions involving the purchase or sale of assets.

MAP 7.2

CURRENT ACCOUNT BALANCE

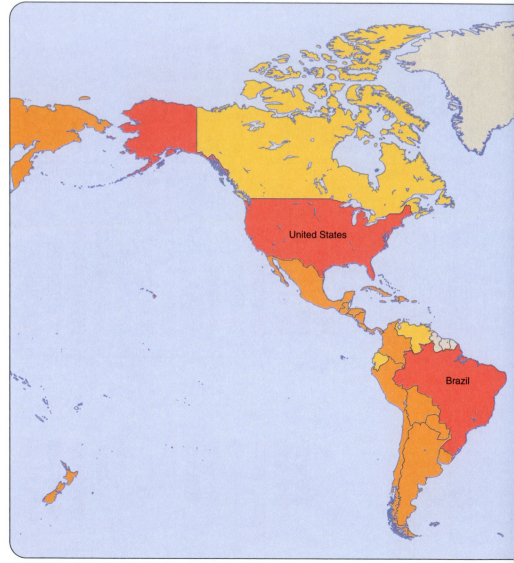

Notes: Data is for 1996.
Current account balance is the sum of net exports of goods and services, income, and current transfers.

of the current and capital accounts should be the same, there commonly is error due to recording methods. This figure is recorded in Table 7.1 as a *statistical discrepancy*.

Persistent U.S. Trade Deficit   Much is made in the business press about the persistent deficit in the current account (trade deficit) of the United States. Map 7.2 shows the current account balances for nations around the world. Notice that the United States has the most negative current account balance of any nation and seems out of place in the group of countries listed as the "Five Most Negative." Let's take a moment to analyze what a deficit may mean for nations in general and the United States in particular.

A trade deficit simply means a country is importing more than it is exporting. This is often pointed to as evidence of declining U.S. competitiveness abroad and/or unfair trading practices by other nations. But the deficit can also be viewed as the ex-

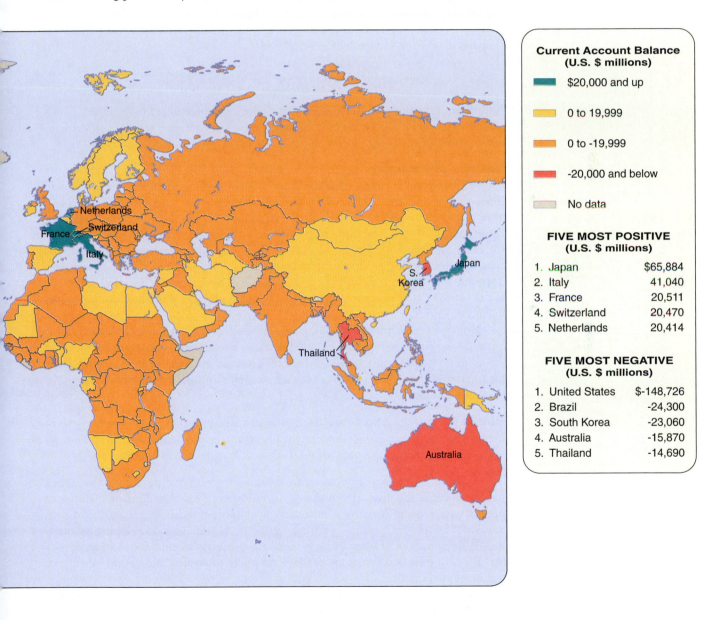

Current Account Balance
(U.S. $ millions)

- ■ $20,000 and up
- ☐ 0 to 19,999
- ☐ 0 to -19,999
- ☐ -20,000 and below
- ☐ No data

FIVE MOST POSITIVE
(U.S. $ millions)

1.	Japan	$65,884
2.	Italy	41,040
3.	France	20,511
4.	Switzerland	20,470
5.	Netherlands	20,414

FIVE MOST NEGATIVE
(U.S. $ millions)

1.	United States	$-148,726
2.	Brazil	-24,300
3.	South Korea	-23,060
4.	Australia	-15,870
5.	Thailand	-14,690

cess of domestic spending over production. Thus it can be thought of as U.S. borrowing from other nations to finance the purchase of goods and services. The key question then is: Does the deficit imply borrowing to finance a consumption binge or does it reflect borrowing to purchase productive equipment that will have long-term payoffs? Although this question is difficult to answer, it appears that a large portion of the deficit is related to investment in productivity-enhancing goods and services. But it is too early to determine the long-term effect of the persistent U.S. trade deficit. All we can say at this point is that it appears that a fair amount of investment (as opposed to consumption) may allow for less apprehension over the persistent deficit.[23]

However, trade deficits can create a vicious circle if gone unchecked. As a nation's borrowing increases it must pay higher interest rates and dividends for international borrowing. The nation must then send more and more resources out of the country to pay off debt—money that could otherwise be invested in productivity-enhancing projects. As a result, long-term economic growth is further impaired by current consumption and the need to service debt.

REASONS FOR HOST COUNTRY INTERVENTION

A number of reasons underlie a government's decisions regarding foreign direct investment by international companies. Let's now look at the two main reasons countries intervene in FDI flows—the *balance-of-payments* and *to obtain resources and benefits*.

Balance of Payments   Many governments see intervention as the only way to keep their balance of payments under control. First, because foreign direct investment inflows are recorded as additions to the balance of payments, a nation also gets a balance-of-payments boost from an initial FDI inflow. Second, as we saw in Chapter 6, countries can impose local content requirements on investors from other nations coming in for the purpose of local production. This gives local companies the chance to become suppliers to the production operation. This can help to reduce the nation's imports and thereby improve its balance of payments. Third, exports (if any) generated by the new production operation can have a favorable impact on the host country's balance of payments.

However, many international companies wish to send at least part of its profits back to the home country. These capital outflows decrease the balance of payments of the country where the investment is located. To shore up its balance of payments, the host nation may prohibit or restrict the nondomestic company from removing profits to its home country.

Obtain Resources and Benefits   Beyond balance-of-payments reasons, governments might intervene in FDI flows to acquire resources and benefits such as *technology* and *management skills and employment*. Let's look at each of these in turn.

Access to Technology   Investment in technology, whether in products or processes, tends to increase the productivity and competitiveness of individual nations. Thus host nations have a strong incentive to encourage the import of technology. Consider the situation for many Asian nations. Throughout the 1970s and 1980s, developing countries in Asia were introduced to expertise in industrial processes as multinationals set up factories within their borders. Some of them are trying to acquire and develop their own technological expertise.

Singapore, for instance, has been particularly successful in gaining access to high technology. In the mid-1990s, the German industrial giant Siemens chose Singapore as

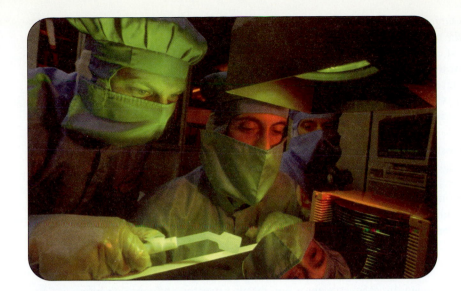

Siemens (**www.siemens.com**), a German industrial firm, is a partner with Singapore in producing high-tech components like the silicon chips being manufactured here. The relationship benefits Siemens in providing low-cost manufacturing, and Singapore gains by developing its own technological expertise.

the site for an Asia-Pacific microelectronics design center employing 60 people. Siemens sets high targets for technology transfer because it knows that the higher the targets, the more help it will get from Singapore's government. To ensure that it's getting technological value for its money, Singapore's National Science and Technology board regularly audits the design center. Singapore has also gained valuable semiconductor technology by joining with U.S.-based Texas Instruments and other investors to set up the country's first wafer-fabrication plant.[24]

Management Skills and Employment As we saw in Chapter 4, many onetime communist nations suffer from a serious lack of the management skills needed to succeed in the global economy. By encouraging FDI, these nations can allow in talented managers who can train locals so that, over time, the international competitiveness of domestic companies will improve. Furthermore, locals who are trained in modern management techniques may eventually leave the firm to start their own local businesses—thereby expanding employment opportunities even more.

However, detractors argue that although FDI may create jobs, it may also destroy jobs because less competitive local firms may be forced out of business.

REASONS FOR HOME COUNTRY INTERVENTION

Home nations (those from which international companies launch their investments) may also seek to encourage or discourage *outflows* of FDI for a variety of reasons. However, there generally tends to be fewer concerns among home nations because they tend to be prosperous, industrialized nations. For these countries, an outward investment seldom has a national impact—unlike the impact on developing or emerging nations that receive the FDI. Nevertheless, among the most common reasons for discouraging outward FDI are the following:

➡ *Investing in other nations sends resources out of the home country.* Thus fewer resources are used for development and economic growth at home. On the other hand, profits on assets abroad that are returned home increase both a home country's balance of payments and its available resources.

➡ *Outgoing FDI may ultimately damage a nation's balance of payments by taking the place of its exports.* This can occur when a new production facility in a market abroad servicing that market replaces exports that used to be sent there from the home country. For example, if the Mercedes-Benz plant in the United States fills a demand that U.S. buyers would otherwise satisfy with purchases of German-made autos, Germany's balance of payments is correspondingly decreased.

➡ *Jobs resulting from outgoing investments may replace jobs at home.* This is often the most contentious issue for home countries. The relocation of production to a low-wage nation can have a strong impact on a locale or region. However, the impact is rarely national and its effects are often muted by other job opportunities in the economy. In addition, there may be an offsetting improvement in home-country employment if additional exports are needed to support the activity that was represented by the outgoing FDI. For example, if Hyundai of South Korea builds an auto plant in Brazil, Korean employment may increase in order to supply the Brazilian plant with parts.

But foreign direct investment is not always a negative influence on home nations. In fact, under certain circumstances they actually might encourage it. Specifically, countries promote outgoing FDI for the following reasons:

➡ *Outward FDI can increase long-run competitiveness.* Today, businesses frequently compete on a global scale. The most competitive firms tend to be those that conduct business in the most favorable location anywhere in the world, continuously improve their performance relative to competitors, and derive technological advantages from alliances formed with other companies. Japanese companies have become masterful at benefiting from FDI and cooperative arrangements with companies from other nations. The key to their success is that Japanese companies see every cooperative venture as a learning opportunity.

➡ *Nations may encourage FDI in industries that they have determined to be "sunset" industries.* Sunset industries are those that use outdated and obsolete technologies or employ low-wage workers with few skills. These jobs are not greatly appealing to countries having industries that pay skilled workers high wages. By allowing some of these jobs to go abroad and retraining workers in higher-paying skilled work, they can upgrade their economies toward "sunrise" industries. This represents a tradeoff for governments between a short-term loss of jobs and the long-term benefit of developing workers skills.

GOVERNMENT POLICY INSTRUMENTS AND FDI

Over time, both host and home nations have developed a range of methods to either promote or discourage FDI (see Table 7.2). Governments use these tools for many reasons including improving balance-of-payments positions, acquiring resources, and, in the case of outward investment, keeping jobs at home. Let's now take a look at these methods.

HOST COUNTRIES: RESTRICTION

Host countries have a variety of methods to restrict incoming FDI. These take two general forms—*ownership restrictions* and *performance demands.*

TABLE 7.2 — *Methods of Restricting and Promoting FDI*

	Methods of Restricting FDI	Methods of Promoting FDI
Host Countries	Ownership restrictions Performance demands	Tax incentives Low-interest loans Infrastructure improvements
Home Countries	Differential tax rates Sanctions	Insurance Loans Tax breaks Political pressure

Ownership Restrictions   Governments can impose *ownership restrictions* that prohibit nondomestic companies from investing in certain industries or owning certain types of businesses. Most often, such prohibitions apply to businesses in cultural industries and companies vital to national security. For instance, as India and some Islamic countries in the Middle East try to protect traditional values, accepting investment by Western companies is a controversial issue between purists and moderates. Also, most nations do not allow FDI in their domestic weapons or national defense firms. See Chapter 6 for complete coverage of the security issues surrounding national defense.

Another ownership restriction is a requirement that nondomestic investors hold less that a 50 percent stake in local firms when they undertake foreign direct investment. This requirement was popular in earlier times when host countries thought that 51 percent local ownership gave them control over a local subsidiary. We saw earlier in this chapter how this is not necessarily the case.

New methods increase the ability of local firms to profit from knowledge transfers regardless of the portion of local ownership. For example, when GM was deciding in the mid-1990s whether to invest $110 million in an aging auto plant in Jakarta, Indonesia, to get the deal the Indonesian government scrapped many of its ownership restrictions—including eventual forced divestment to Indonesians. Indonesia's action was no doubt prompted by the fact that China and Vietnam were also courting GM for its financial investment. In another instance, even though Siemens owns 100 percent of the plant in Singapore that we mentioned earlier, Singapore's government still feels that it is gaining valuable know-how and technology.[25]

Performance Demands   More common than ownership requirements are *performance demands* that influence how international companies operate in the host nation. Although typically viewed as intrusive, most international companies allow for them in the same way they allow for home-country regulations. As a Hewlett-Packard executive once remarked, "Yes, I jump through hoops for the Mexican government, but I learned long ago to do that for the U.S. government."[26] As we saw in Chapter 6, performance demands can take many forms. Some of these include ensuring that a portion of the product's content originates locally, stipulations regarding the portion of output that must be exported, or requirements that certain technologies be transferred to local businesses.

HOST COUNTRIES: PROMOTION

Host countries also offer a variety of incentives to encourage inflows of FDI. Again, these take two general forms—*financial incentives* and *infrastructure improvements*.

Financial Incentives   Host governments of all nations grant companies financial incentives if they will invest within their borders. One method includes *tax incentives* such as lower tax rates or offers to waive taxes on local profits for a period of time—extending as far out as five or more years. A country may also offer *low-interest loans* to investors.

However, the downside of incentives such as these is that it can allow multinationals to create bidding wars between locations that are vying for the investment. In such cases, the company eventually invests in the most appealing location after the locations endure rounds of escalating incentives. Companies have even been accused of engaging other governments in negotiations so as to force concessions from locations already selected for investment. The cost to taxpayers of snaring FDI can be up to $250,000 per job—especially in the case of a bidding war. This can be many times the average worker's wage in most cases of FDI.[27]

e·biz

Infrastructure Improvements   Because of the problems associated with financial incentives, some governments are taking an alternative route to luring investment. Lasting benefits for communities surrounding the investment location can result from making local *infrastructure improvements*—better seaports suitable for containerized shipping, improved roads, and increased telecommunications systems. For instance, Malaysia is carving a $40 billion Multimedia Super Corridor (MSC) into a region's forested surroundings. The region has planned a paperless government, an intelligent city called Cyberjaya, two telesuburbs, a technology park, a multimedia university, and an intellectual-property-protection park. The MSC is dedicated to creating the most advanced technologies in telecommunications, medicine, distance learning, and remote manufacturing.[28]

HOME COUNTRIES: RESTRICTION

To limit the effects of outbound FDI on the national economy, home governments may exercise any of the following options:

➡ Impose *differential tax rates* that charge income from earnings abroad at a higher rate than domestic earnings.

➡ Impose outright *sanctions* that prohibit domestic firms from making investments in certain nations.

HOME COUNTRIES: PROMOTION

On the other hand, to encourage outbound FDI home-country governments can do any of the following:

➡ Offer *insurance* to cover the risks of investments abroad. We discussed these risks in detail in Chapter 3. They include, among others, insurance against expropriation of assets, losses from armed conflict, kidnappings, and terrorist attacks.

➡ Grant *loans* to firms wishing to increase their investments abroad. A home-country government may also guarantee the loans that a company takes from financial institutions.

- Offer *tax breaks* on profits earned abroad or negotiate special tax treaties. For example, several multinational agreements reduce or eliminate the practice of double taxation—profits earned abroad being taxed both in the home and host countries.

- Apply *political pressure* on other nations to get them to relax their restrictions on inbound investments. Non-Japanese companies often find it very difficult to invest inside Japan. The United States, for one, repeatedly pressures the Japanese government to open its market further to FDI. But because such pressure has achieved little success, many U.S. companies cooperate with local Japanese businesses. For example, California-based Silicon Graphics is cooperating with Nippon Telephone and Telegraph to provide video servers and other multimedia technology for use in interactive video.[29]

A FINAL WORD

In this chapter, we learned about the second major way of conducting international business—foreign direct investment (FDI). We saw that, like trade decisions, many factors influence a company's decision of whether to invest in markets abroad. Companies can be thwarted in their efforts or encouraged to invest in a nation depending on the philosophy of its government. The balance of payments positions of both home and host nations are also important because FDI flows affect the economic health of both nations. We learned that companies ranging from massive global corporations to adventurous entrepreneurs all contribute to FDI flows.

The next chapter will conclude our study of the trade and investment aspects of the international business environment. Specifically, we see how groups of nations, anywhere from several to several dozen, are joining forces to integrate their economies and thereby facilitate international trade and investment.

There is a variety of additional material available on the companion Web site that accompanies this text. You can access this information by visiting the Web site at ⟨www.prenhall.com/wild⟩.

summary

① Describe the worldwide patterns of *foreign direct investment* (*FDI*) and the reasons for these patterns. Foreign direct investment grew very rapidly throughout the early 1990s, slowed somewhat in 1997, but seemed to be picking up steam again in the late 1990s.

The forces causing the *globalization* of industries are encouraging growth in foreign direct investment. Lower trade barriers encouraged FDI in those markets that promised adequate sales volumes. Companies could produce in the most efficient and productive locations in the world, and simply export to their markets worldwide. Increasing globalization is also causing a growing number of international companies from emerging markets to undertake FDI.

The number of *mergers and acquisitions* (M&A) and their exploding values also underlie the growth in foreign direct investment flows. A great deal of M&A activity in domestic markets is causing companies to venture abroad for new M&A targets. The number of deals that involve companies from different countries has more than doubled since the mid-1990s. *Entrepreneurs* and *small businesses* also contribute to the expansion of FDI flows. Unhindered by many of the constraints of a large company, entrepreneurs investing in other markets often demonstrate an inspiring can-do spirit and ingenuity.

Although the destination of most FDI inflows are industrialized countries, they are attracting a declining share of worldwide total FDI. Also, the industrialized nations are contributing less to the flow of FDI while the newly industrialized nations and emerging markets are contributing more. The East Asia and Pacific region is luring a great deal of capital in the form of foreign direct investment. Multinationals find it important to have a presence in the developing world of Asia to tap into low-cost resources and to service local markets. The Latin America and Caribbean region is also a magnet for FDI inflows, although the volume varies widely from one year to the next.

2 **Describe each of the *theories* that attempt to explain why foreign direct investment occurs.** Four main theories attempt to explain why companies engage in foreign direct investment: *international product life cycle, eclectic theory, market power,* and *market imperfections* (*internalization*).

The *international product life cycle* states that a company will begin by exporting its product and later undertake foreign direct investment as a product moves through its life cycle. In the *new product stage,* a good is produced in the home country. But in the *maturing product stage,* the company directly invests in production facilities in those countries where demand is high. In the final *standardized product stage,* a company builds production capacity in low-cost nations to serve its markets around the world. Despite its conceptual appeal, the international product life cycle theory is limited in its power to explain why companies choose FDI over other forms of market entry, such as exporting or licensing.

Market imperfections theory states that when an imperfection in the market makes a transaction less efficient than it could be, a company will undertake foreign direct investment to internalize the transaction and thereby remove the imperfection. One common market imperfection that causes FDI is trade barriers such as tariffs. Also, when a company's specialized knowledge is embodied in its employees, the only alternative to exploit a market opportunity in another nation may be to undertake FDI.

The *eclectic theory* states that firms undertake foreign direct investment when the features of a particular location combine with ownership and internalization advantages to make a location appealing for investment. A *location advantage* is the advantage of locating a particular economic activity in a specific location. An *ownership advantage* is the advantage that a company has due to its ownership of some special asset. An *internalization advantage* is the advantage that arises from internalizing a business activity rather than leaving it to a relatively inefficient market. When all these advantages are present, a company will undertake FDI.

The *market power* theory states that a firm tries to establish a dominant market presence in an industry by undertaking foreign direct investment. The benefit of market power is greater profit because the firm is far better able to dictate the cost of its inputs and/or the price of its output. One way a company achieves market power is through backward or forward *vertical integration.*

3 **Discuss the important *management issues* in the foreign direct investment decision.** Decisions of whether or not to engage in foreign direct investment involve several important issues regarding management of the company and the firm's market.

When many companies invest abroad they are greatly concerned with *controlling* the activities occurring in the local market for a variety of reasons. But a greater ownership percentage does not guarantee greater control. Also, local governments might require a company to hire local managers or require that all goods produced in a local facility be exported so they do not compete with products of native firms.

Another matter of concern is whether to *purchase an existing business or build an international subsidiary from the ground up.* An acquisition generally provides the investor with an existing plant and equipment as well as personnel. On the other hand, factors that reduce the appeal of purchasing existing facilities include obsolete equipment, poor relations with workers, and an unsuitable location. But adequate facilities are sometimes simply unavailable and a company must go ahead with a greenfield investment.

The *cost of production* in a market is also important. Labor regulations can increase the hourly cost of production several times. One approach companies use to contain production costs is *rationalized production*—a system of production in which each of a product's components are produced in that location in which the cost of producing that component is lowest. All the components are then brought together at one central location for assembly into the final product.

A local market presence might help companies gain valuable knowledge about the *behavior of buyers* that it could not obtain from the home market. Also, a company might want to produce in a nation that has a quality image in a certain product. Firms commonly engage in foreign direct investment when doing so puts them close to firms for which they act as supplier—called *following clients*. The practice tends to result in clusters whereby companies that supply one another's inputs congregate in a certain geographic region. Sometimes companies engage in FDI simply because a rival does and they do not want to be shut out of a potentially lucrative market—called *following rivals*.

④ **Explain why governments intervene in the free flow of foreign direct investment.** Both host and home countries interfere in the free flow of FDI for a variety of reasons—many of them related to their balance of payments position.

A country's *balance of payments* is a national accounting system that records all payments to entities in other countries and all receipts coming into the nation. International transactions that result in payments (outflows) to entities in other nations are reductions in the balance of payments accounts. International transactions that result in receipts (inflows) from other nations are additions to the balance of payments accounts. The *current account* is a national account that records transactions involving the import and export of goods and services, income receipts on assets abroad, and income payments on foreign assets inside the country. A *current account surplus* (trade surplus) occurs when a country exports more goods, services, and income than it imports. A *current account deficit* (trade deficit) occurs when a country imports more goods, services, and income than it exports. The *capital account* is a national account that records transactions that involve the purchase or sale of *assets*.

One reason why governments of *host* countries intervene in foreign direct investment flows is to protect their *balance-of-payments*. Allowing FDI to come in gives a nation a balance-of-payments boost. Countries also improve their balance-of-payments position from the exports of local production operations

created by FDI. However, when direct investors send profits made locally back to the parent company in the home country, the balance of payments decreases. Local investment in *technology* also tends to increase the productivity and competitiveness of the nation. By encouraging FDI, nations can also bring in people with *management skills* who can train locals and thus improve the competitiveness of local companies. Furthermore, many local *jobs* are also created as a result of incoming FDI.

Home countries also intervene in FDI flows. For one thing, investing in other nations sends resources out of the home country—lowering the balance of payments. On the other hand, profits on assets abroad that are returned home increase a home country's balance of payments. Also, outgoing FDI may ultimately damage a nation's balance of payments by taking the place of its exports. In addition, jobs resulting from outgoing investments may replace jobs at home that were based on exports to the host country.

⑤ **Discuss the *policy instruments* that governments use to restrict and promote foreign direct investment.** Both host and home nations have a range of methods to either promote or discourage FDI.

Host countries have a variety of methods to restrict incoming FDI. Governments can impose *ownership restrictions* that prohibit nondomestic companies from investing in businesses in cultural industries and those vital to national security. They can also create *performance demands* that influence how international companies operate in the host nation. Performance demands can take the form of stipulations regarding the portion of the product's content originating locally, the portion of output that must be exported, or requirements that certain technologies be transferred to local businesses.

Host governments can also grant companies *tax incentives* such as lower tax rates or offer to waive taxes on local profits for a period of time. A country may also offer *low-interest loans* to investors. However, the downside of incentives such as these is that it can allow multinationals to create bidding wars between locations that are vying for the investment. Because of the problems associated with financial incentives, some governments prefer to lure investment by making local *infrastructure improvements*—better seaports suitable for containerized shipping, improved roads, and increased telecommunications systems.

To limit the effects of outbound FDI on the national economy, home governments may impose *differential tax rates* that charge income from earnings abroad at a higher rate than domestic earnings. Or they can impose outright *sanctions* that prohibit domestic firms from making investments in certain nations. On the other hand, to encourage outbound FDI home-country governments can offer *insurance* to cover the risks of investments abroad. They can also grant *loans* to firms wishing to increase their investments abroad. A home-country government may also guarantee the loans that a company takes from financial institutions. They might also offer *tax breaks* on profits earned abroad or negotiate special tax treaties. Finally, they may apply *political pressure* on other nations to get them to relax their restrictions on inbound investments.

questions for review

1. What is *foreign direct investment* (*FDI*)? Explain how FDI differs from *portfolio investment*.

2. What are three factors contributing to the growth in FDI.

3. Identify at least three motivations behind companies' decisions to engage in FDI.

4. What are the main destinations and sources of FDI? Describe how each is changing.

5. Describe how the *international product life cycle* explains FDI. What are the three product stages?

6. How does the theory of *market imperfections* (*internalization*) explain FDI?

7. Explain the *eclectic theory*. Identify the three advantages that must be present for FDI to occur, according to the theory.

8. How does the theory of *market power* explain the occurrence of FDI? Describe the importance of *vertical integration* to the theory.

9. Why is control important to the FDI decision?

10. Describe the role of production costs in the FDI decision. What is *rationalized production*?

11. How does the need for each of customer knowledge, following clients, and following rivals impact the FDI decision?

12. What is a country's *balance of payments*? Explain its usefulness briefly.

13. Identify the difference between the *current account* and the *capital account*.

14. For what reasons do *host* countries intervene in FDI?

15. For what reasons do *home* countries intervene in FDI?

16. Identify the main methods *host* countries use to restrict and promote FDI.

17. What methods do *home* countries use to intervene in FDI?

questions for discussion

1. You overhear your superior tell another manager in the company, "I'm fed up with this nation's companies always leaving the country to hire low-wage workers elsewhere. Don't any of them have any national pride?" The other manager responds, "I disagree. It is every company's duty to make as much profit as possible for its owners. If that means going abroad to reduce costs, so be it." Do you agree with either of these managers? Why or why not? Now step into the conversation and give a description of where you stand on the issue.

2. The global carmaker you work for is investing in an auto assembly facility in Costa Rica with a local partner. Explain the potential reasons for this investment. Will your company want to exercise a great deal of control over this operation? Why or why not? What areas might your company want to exercise control over and what areas might it cede control to the partner?

3. This chapter presented several theories that have been proposed to explain the flow of foreign direct investment. Which of these theories seems most appealing to you? Why is it appealing? Can you think of one or more companies that seem to fit the pattern described by the theory? In your opinion, what faults do the alternative theories have?

in practice

Please read the following brief article and answer the questions that follow.

Lebanon to Encourage Foreign Investment

Attendees from more than a dozen countries at the recent Forum on Industrial Development in Beirut heard Lebanese Prime Minister Salim Hoss outline a range of measures designed to open the country to increased foreign investment.

Among Hoss's measures are plans to pass by June a law protecting intellectual and industrial property rights; establish free economic trade zones; create regulations to prevent double taxation; and simplify and modernize the country's tax and investment structure. Hoss emphasized that Lebanon's role is "to complement, not rival, its Arab neighbors" and maximize "its ability to adapt to both change and market needs."

The Lebanese State Institute for developing Investment has said it is actively looking for foreign investment in the country's food production and construction sectors, either in joint ventures or alone.

1. We live in an era of intense national competition to attract investment from abroad to create jobs and raise living standards. Why, then, do you think prime minister Hoss explicitly stated that Lebanon wishes "to complement, not rival, its Arab neighbors?" Is this standard diplomacy or might there be something cultural or historical involved?

2. Find a recent article in the business press or on the World Wide Web that updates this article that appeared in early 1999. Did Lebanon actually get these measures passed by June? If so, what has been the reaction by international companies? How have domestic companies reacted?

3. Investigate the economies of Lebanon and its neighbors. In what economic sectors is each country strong? Do the strengths of each country really complement one another or do they compete directly with one another? If you were considering investing in Lebanon, what management issues would concern you? Be specific.

projects

1. In the business press, locate at least two articles that discuss a cross-border merger or acquisition that has taken place within the past year. What reasons did each company give for the merger or acquisition? Was it a marriage of equals or did a larger partner absorb a far smaller one? Do the articles identify any internal issues that managers had to deal with following the merger or acquisition? What is the performance of the new company? Write a one- to two-page report of your findings.

2. With several of your classmates, select a country that interests you. For the most recent data you can find, what is its balance-of-payments position? What is its current account balance? What is its capital account balance? What are some possible causes for the surplus or deficit you see? What are some of the effects on the nation of this surplus or deficit? Prepare a brief report and present it to the class.

3. With one or two of your classmates, visit your city's chamber of commerce office and/or its economic development office. Does the city have a practice of offering incentives to lure companies into the area? Does it try to attract international companies and, if so, how? Does it try to persuade companies in certain industries to invest in the region? Ask other questions you feel are pertinent. Present your findings to the class.

business case 7

MERCEDES-BENZ: FOOT-LOOSE IN TUSCALOOSA

"Aloof." "Serious." "Not youthful." Definitely "not fun." These were the unfortunate epithets applied to Mercedes-Benz by a market research firm that assesses product personalities. Research among American dealers also revealed that consumers felt so intimidated by Mercedes that they wouldn't sit in the cars at the showroom. In order to increase sales and broaden the market to a more youthful and value-conscious consumer, Mercedes-Benz of North America came up with a series of inventive, free-spirited ads featuring stampeding rhinos and bobbing aliens. Although the new ads boosted sales, the company needed more than a new marketing message to ensure its future growth. What it needed was an all-new Mercedes. Enter the Mercedes M-Class, a sports utility vehicle (SUV). With a base price of $35,000 and a luxury lineage, Mercedes is hoping to pit its M-Class against the Ford Explorer and Jeep Grand Cherokee.

Not only is the M-Class Mercedes' first SUV, but it's also the first car that Mercedes has manufactured outside of Germany—in the heart of Dixie, no less. The rough-hewn town of Vance, Alabama (population 400), where people hang out at the local barbecue joint, is the last place you'd expect to find button-down engineers from Stuttgart, Germany. But this small town outside of Tuscaloosa appealed to Mercedes for several reasons. Labor costs in the U.S. Deep South are 50 percent lower than in Germany. Also, Alabama offered an attractive $250 million in tax refunds and other incentives to win the much-needed Mercedes jobs. Mercedes also wanted to be closer to the crucial U.S. market and to create a plant from the ground up, one that would be a model for its future international operations.

The gleaming, E-shaped Mercedes plant is the brainchild of engineer-turned-CEO, Andreas Renschler. When Japanese carmakers entered the U.S. market in the 1980s, they reproduced their car-building philosophies, cultures, production practices, and management styles in the United States. But Mercedes started with the proverbial blank sheet of paper. In order to appeal to U.S. workers, Mercedes knew it had to abandon the rigid hierarchy of the typical Mercedes production line and create a more egalitarian shop floor. Thus administrative offices in the Vance plant run through the middle of the manufacturing area, and while it's all glassed in, team members still have easy access to administrators. The plant is also designed so workers can unilaterally stop the assembly line to correct manufacturing problems. So far, the system has been a catalyst to communication among the Alabama plant's 1,500 U.S. workers, German trainers, and diverse management team that includes executives from both Detroit and Japan. Even so, Mercedes has spent an enormous amount of time and effort to train its U.S. workforce. Explains Sven Schoolman, a 31-year-old trainer from Sindelfingen, "In Germany, we don't say we build a car. We say we build a Mercedes. We had to teach that."

So far the Mercedes' M-class is competing very well against the entrenched competition. The company is also gaining valuable experience in how to set up and operate a plant in another country. "It was once sacrosanct to talk about our cars being 'Made in Germany,'" says Jurgen E. Schrempp, CEO of Mercedes' parent, Daimler Benz. "We have to change that to 'Made by Mercedes,' and never mind where they are assembled."

thinking globally

1. What were the chief factors involved in Mercedes' decision to undertake FDI in the United States?

2. Why do you think Mercedes decided to build the plant from the ground up in Alabama rather than buying an existing plant in, say Detroit?

3. Do you think Mercedes risks diluting its "Made in Germany" reputation for engineering quality by building its M-class in Alabama? Why or why not?

4. What do you see as the pros and cons of Mercedes' approach to managing FDI—abandoning the culture and some of the practices of its home country? What are the pros and cons of the approach of the Japanese carmakers—trying to duplicate the culture and production practices of the home country?

a question of ethics

1. In the opening of this chapter, we talked about Boeing's overseas production of parts. It's becoming more and more common for companies like Boeing to promise manufacturing contracts to overseas suppliers in exchange for entry into that country's market. Labor union representatives argue that these kinds of deals are made at the expense of jobs at home. After all, if a company can have parts made in China at lower wages, why keep factories going at home? They also are concerned that the transfer of technology will breed strong competitors in other nations and thereby threaten even more domestic jobs. Others argue, however, that the increase in sales abroad actually helps create more jobs at home. Discuss the ethics of companies contracting out production to factories abroad in exchange for sales contracts.

2. Although foreign direct investment continues to run up against national barriers, worldwide talks on international business and globalization have tended to focus on trade barriers. But now the United States and nations in the Organization for Economic Cooperation and Development (OECD) are pushing for a Multilateral Agreement on Investment (MAI) that would create a comprehensive set of rules to liberalize and safeguard FDI. Such an agreement would outlaw all restrictions and controls that national governments might wish to impose on FDI. Opponents are concerned that an agreement on investment would make multinationals exempt from minimum wage legislation or requirements to draw workforces from the host nation. Others fear that decisions affecting the fair treatment of labor

and consumer and environmental protection might be wrested from national governments and placed in the hands of powerful multinationals.

What ethical issues should be considered in the formation of an MAI? What are the risks to labor and to the environment if an MAI gives multinationals free reign on foreign direct investment and limits the role of national governments?[30]

3. In order to become a major export platform for the semiconductor industry, Malaysia's government not only offered tax breaks but also guaranteed that electronics workers would be prohibited from organizing independent labor unions. The government decreed that the goal of national development required a "union-free" environment for the "pioneers" of semiconductors. Under pressure from U.S. labor unions, the Malaysian government offered a weak alternative to industry unions—company-by-company "in-house" unions. Yet as soon as workers organized one at a Harris Electronics plant, the 21 union leaders were fired and the new union disbanded. In another instance, when French-owned Thomson Electronics inherited a Malaysian factory with a union of 3,000, it closed the plant and moved the work to Vietnam.

Newly industrialized nations such as Malaysia feel that their future depends upon investment by multinationals. Their governments are acutely aware that in the absence of incentives such as a "union-free" workforce, international companies can easily take their investment elsewhere. Discuss the problems that these governments face in balancing the needs of their citizens with the long-term quest for economic development.[31]

8 regional economic integration

Beacons

A Look Back

CHAPTER 7 examined recent patterns of foreign direct investment. We explored the theories that try to explain why it occurs and how governments influence investment flows.

A Look at This Chapter

This chapter explores the global trend of increased integration of national economies. We examine the reasons why nations are making significant efforts at regional integration and study the most prominent regional trading blocs in place today.

A Look Ahead

CHAPTER 9 begins our inquiry into the international financial system. We describe the structure of the international capital market and explain how the foreign exchange market operates.

Learning Objectives

After studying this chapter, you should be able to

1 Define *regional economic integration* and identify the five levels of integration.

2 Discuss the *benefits* and *drawbacks* associated with regional economic integration.

3 Describe regional integration in *Europe* and explain how companies are adapting.

4 Discuss regional integration in *the Americas* and analyze its future prospects.

5 Characterize regional integration in *Asia* and discuss how it differs from integration elsewhere.

6 Explain regional integration in the *Middle East* and *Africa* and explain why progress there has been slow.

Formation of the North American Free Trade Agreement (or NAFTA) is changing attitudes among Mexican manufacturers. "Each day," observes Alberto Romo Chavez, president of the successful Mexican trading house Alro Exportaciones, "I'm finding more people focused on exporting professionally." Alro relies on more than 80 manufacturers in 7 Mexican states to manufacture such decorative household and garden accessories as vases and candleholders for international customers. The post-NAFTA climate helped Alro's billings grow from $680,000 in 1992 to $7 million in 1996. Since then, Romo has witnessed firsthand the extent to which exporting fever has gripped his country. Ninety days after he conducted an exporting seminar to 300 businesspeople in one Mexican state, his company added to its exporting clientele 13 new manufacturers from that state alone.

Meanwhile, the European Union (EU) is changing the attitudes and expectations of young people in Europe. Vincent Wauters is a 26-year-old Belgian with a degree in history who speaks three languages. His willingness to pick up and move made him a good catch for French catalog retailer La Redoute. "I have a vision that is clearly European," says Wauters. "I have a sense of our common history, our cultural diversity, and I'm used to the kind of flexibility that's needed for people to adapt to one another." Anne-Marie Ronayne, a consultant with the international recruiting firm EMDS, agrees: "Companies," she says, "are looking for their future leaders. That means finding people with good attitudes, who can think across borders."[1]

Trade agreements such as NAFTA and the EU (which we will learn more about shortly) are changing the landscape of the global marketplace. Companies are finding that these agreements are lowering trade barriers and opening up new markets for goods and services. Markets otherwise off-limits because tariffs made imported products too expensive can become quite attractive once tariffs are lifted. But trade agreements can be double-edged swords for many companies. Not only do they allow domestic companies to seek new markets abroad, but they let competitors from other nations enter the domestic market. Such mobility increases competition in every market taking part in an agreement.

Trade agreements can thus force a company to alter strategies, sometimes radically. Korea-based Samsung, for example, manufactured 1.5 million color TVs at its complex outside Tijuana, Mexico, in 1997. Indeed, Korean and Japanese investment in Mexico have made it the largest TV-producing country in the world. Why are some of the largest Asian electronics firms producing TVs in Mexico? They not only want to make TVs where labor is inexpensive, but, in order to avoid tariffs and other trade barriers, they want to make them where they are sold. Locating production in Mexico ensures that Samsung TVs have at least the 62.5 percent regional content required by NAFTA to qualify them as "North American" products. In fact, Samsung recently opened a plant for making TV picture tubes, raising the North American content of its Mexican-made TVs to 85 percent.[2] As we will see throughout this chapter, such agreements profoundly affect marketing as well as production strategies.

We began part III of this book by discussing the gains of specialization and trade. We now close this part by showing how groups of countries are cooperating to dismantle barriers that threaten these potential gains. In this chapter, we focus on regional efforts to encourage freer trade and investment. We begin by defining *regional economic integration* and describing its five different levels. Then we examine the benefits and drawbacks of regional trade agreements. Finally, we explore in detail several long-established trading agreements and several agreements that are in the earliest stages of development.

WHAT IS REGIONAL ECONOMIC INTEGRATION?

regional economic integration
Process whereby countries in a geographic region cooperate with one another to reduce or eliminate barriers to the international flow of products, people, or capital.

regional trading bloc
Group of nations in a geographic region undergoing economic integration.

The process whereby countries in a geographic region cooperate with one another to reduce or eliminate barriers to the international flow of products, people, or capital is called **regional economic integration**. A group of nations in a geographic region undergoing economic integration is called a **regional trading bloc**.

The goal of nations undergoing economic integration is not only to increase cross-border trade and investment but also to raise living standards for their people. We saw in Chapter 5, for instance, how specialization and trade create real gains in terms of greater choice, lower prices, and increased productivity. Regional trade agreements are designed to help nations accomplish these objectives. As we saw in our opening discussion, regional integration can also enable people like Vincent Wauters to move from one country to another simply to find work or earn a higher wage. Thus regional integration can help improve quality of life and living standards for a nation's people. Regional economic integration sometimes has additional goals such as protection of intellectual property rights or the environment, or even eventual political union.

LEVELS OF REGIONAL INTEGRATION

Since the development of theories demonstrating the potential gains available through international trade, nations have tried to reap benefits in a variety of ways (see Chapter 5). Figure 8.1 shows five potential levels (or degrees) of economic and political integra-

FIGURE 8.1

LEVELS OF REGIONAL INTEGRATION

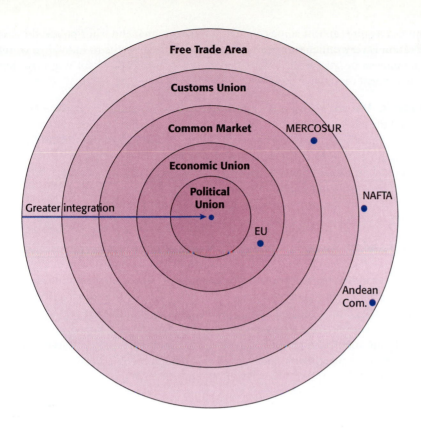

Free Trade Area

Customs Union

Common Market

MERCOSUR

Economic Union

NAFTA

Political Union

Greater integration

EU

Andean Com.

tion for regional trading blocs. A *free trade area* is the lowest extent of national integration, *political union* the greatest. Each level of integration incorporates the properties of those levels that precede it.

Free Trade Area   Economic integration whereby countries remove all barriers to trade between themselves but each country determines its own barriers against nonmembers is called a **free trade area**. A free trade area is the lowest level of economic integration that is possible between two or more countries. Countries belonging to the free trade area remove all tariffs and nontariff barriers such as quotas and subsidies on international trade in goods and services. However, each country is able to maintain whatever policy it sees fit against nonmember countries. These policies can differ widely from country to country. Countries belonging to a free trade area also typically establish a process by which trade disputes, if they arise, can be resolved.

Customs Union   Economic integration whereby countries remove all barriers to trade between themselves but erect a common trade policy against nonmembers is called a **customs union**. Thus the main difference between a free trade area and a customs union is that the members of a customs union agree to treat trade with all nonmember nations in a similar manner. Countries belonging to a customs union might also negotiate as a single entity with other supranational organizations such as the World Trade Organization.

Common Market   Economic integration whereby countries remove all barriers to trade *and* the movement of labor and capital between themselves but erect a common trade policy against nonmembers is called a **common market**. Thus a common market integrates the elements of free trade areas and customs unions while adding the free movement of important factors of production—people and cross-border investment.

free trade area
Economic integration whereby countries remove all barriers to trade between themselves but each country determines its own barriers against nonmembers.

customs union
Economic integration whereby countries remove all barriers to trade between themselves but erect a common trade policy against nonmembers.

common market
Economic integration whereby countries remove all barriers to trade and the movement of labor and capital between themselves but erect a common trade policy against nonmembers.

Because it requires at least some cooperation in economic and labor policy, this level of integration is very difficult to attain. Furthermore, the benefits to individual countries can be uneven because skilled labor may move to countries where wages are higher, and investment capital may flow where returns are greater.

economic union
Economic integration whereby countries remove barriers to trade and the movement of labor and capital, erect a common trade policy against nonmembers, and coordinate their economic policies.

Economic Union   Economic integration whereby countries remove barriers to trade and the movement of labor and capital, erect a common trade policy against non-members, *and* coordinate their economic policies is called an **economic union**. An economic union goes beyond the demands of a common market by requiring that member nations harmonize their tax, monetary, and fiscal policies, and create a common currency. Economic union requires that member countries concede a certain amount of their national autonomy (or sovereignty) to the supranational union of which they are a part.

political union
Economic and political integration whereby countries coordinate aspects of their economic and political systems.

Political Union   Economic and political integration whereby countries coordinate aspects of their economic *and* political systems is called a **political union**. A political union requires member nations to accept a common stance on economic and political policies regarding nonmember nations. However, nations are allowed a degree of freedom in setting certain political and economic policies within their territories. Canada and the United States are examples of early formations of political unions. In both these nations smaller states and provinces are combined to form larger entities. A group of nations currently taking steps in this direction is the European Union—discussed later in this chapter.

EFFECTS OF REGIONAL ECONOMIC INTEGRATION

Few topics in international business are as hotly contested and involve as many groups as the effects of regional trade agreements on people, jobs, companies, culture, and living standards. The result is that the topic often spurs debate over the merits and demerits of such agreements. On one side of the debate are people who see the bad that regional trade agreements have done—on the other, those who see the good. Each party to the debate cites data on trade and jobs that bolster their position. They point to companies that have picked up and moved to another country where wages are lower after a new agreement was signed, or companies that have stayed at home and kept jobs there. Then there is the cultural aspect of such agreements: Some people argue that they will lose their unique cultural identity if their nation cooperates too much with other nations. The only thing made clear as a result of such debates is that both sides are right some of the time. Let's now take a closer look at the benefits and drawbacks of regional integration.

BENEFITS OF REGIONAL INTEGRATION

Recall from Chapter 5 that nations engage in specialization and trade because of the gains in output and consumption. Greater specialization, increased efficiency, greater consumption, and higher standards of living all should result from higher levels of trade between nations.

trade creation
Increase in level of trade between nations that results from regional economic integration.

Trade Creation   As we have seen, economic integration removes barriers to trade and/or investment for nations belonging to a trading bloc. The increase in the level of trade between nations that results from regional economic integration is called **trade creation**. One result of trade creation is that consumers and industrial buyers in member nations are faced with a wider selection of goods and services not available before-hand. Thus although Mexico is home to several internationally popular beers (includ-

One factor motivating European nations to seek economic integration in the second half of the twentieth century was the widespread destruction of two world wars. This scene in Dresden, Germany, where bombing completely destroyed the city and killed more people than died at Hiroshima, Japan, was typical of the European landscape after World War II.

ing Tecate, Corona, and Dos Equis), stores inside Mexico stock popular beers imported from Canada and the United States. This is a result of the free trade agreement between Canada, Mexico, and the United States (this agreement will be discussed shortly).

Another result of trade creation is that buyers can acquire goods and services at less cost following the lowering of trade barriers such as tariffs. Furthermore, lower costs tend to lead to higher demand for goods because people have more money left over after a purchase to buy other products.

Greater Consensus   We saw how the General Agreement on Tariffs and Trade (GATT) and the World Trade Organization (WTO) work to lower barriers on a global scale in Chapter 6. Efforts at regional economic integration differ in that they comprise smaller groups of nations—ranging anywhere from several countries to as many as 30 or more nations. The benefit of trying to eliminate trade barriers in smaller groups of countries is that it can be easier to gain consensus from fewer members as opposed to, say, the 133 countries that comprise the WTO.

Political Cooperation   There can also be political benefits from efforts at regional integration. A group of nations can have significantly greater political weight in the world than the nations have individually. Thus nations can have more say when negotiating with other countries in forums such as the World Trade Organization or perhaps even the United Nations. Moreover, integration involving political cooperation can reduce the potential for military conflict between member nations. In fact, peace was at the center of early efforts at integration in Europe in the 1950s. The devastation of two world wars in the first half of the twentieth century caused Europe to see integration as one way of preventing further armed conflicts.

DRAWBACKS OF REGIONAL INTEGRATION

Although trade tends to benefit countries, it can also have substantial negative effects. Let's now examine the more important of these.

Trade Diversion   The flip side of trade creation is **trade diversion**—the diversion of trade away from nations not belonging to a trading bloc and toward member nations. Trade diversion can occur after formation of a trading bloc because of the lower

trade diversion
Diversion of trade away from nations not belonging to a trading bloc and toward member nations.

tariffs charged between member nations. It can actually result in reduced trade with a more efficient nonmember producer and increased trade with a less efficient producer within the trading bloc. In this sense, economic integration can unintentionally reward a less efficient producer within the trading bloc. Unless there is other internal competition for the producer's good or service, buyers will be paying more after trade diversion due to the inefficient production methods of the producer.

A World Bank report recently caused a stir over the results of the free trade bloc between Latin America's largest countries, MERCOSUR (discussed later in this chapter). The report suggested that formation of the bloc only encouraged free trade in the lowest-value products of local origin, while deterring competition for more sophisticated goods manufactured outside of the market. Closer analysis shows that although the member nations have benefited since formation of the common market, outside countries also sharply increased their exports to MERCOSUR. Hence, while imports from one member state to another tripled between 1991 and 1996, imports from the rest of the world also tripled, increasing in value from $25 billion to $75 billion. Thus the net effect of the agreement has been trade creation, not trade diversion as critics had charged.[3]

Shifts in Employment   Perhaps the most controversial aspect of regional economic integration is how people's jobs are affected. Because the formation of trading blocs significantly reduces or eliminates barriers to trade among members, the producer of a particular good or service is more likely to be the most productive producer. Industries requiring mostly unskilled labor, for example, will tend to shift production to low-wage nations within a trading bloc. It is estimated that by the end of 1997 somewhere between 32,000 and 100,000 manufacturing jobs were lost in the United States as a direct result of the free trade agreement between Canada, Mexico, and the United States. However, there is also evidence that between 90,000 and 160,000 jobs of various sorts were created in the United States because of greater exports to Mexico. One engine for this job growth is the formation or expansion of companies in the transportation and warehousing industries on the U.S. side of the border.[4] Thus trade agreements do cause dislocations in labor markets—some jobs are lost while others are gained.

It is highly likely that countries protecting low-wage domestic industries from competition will see these jobs move to the country where wages are lower once trade and investment barriers are removed. But this is also an opportunity for workers to upgrade their skills and gain more advanced job training. This can help nations increase their competitiveness because a better educated and more skilled workforce attracts higher paying jobs than does a less skilled workforce. However, an opportunity for a nation to improve some abstract "factors of production" is little consolation to people finding themselves suddenly without work.

Loss of National Sovereignty   Successive levels of integration require that nations surrender more of their national sovereignty. The least amount of sovereignty that must be surrendered to the trading bloc occurs in a free trade area. Countries are allowed to set their own barriers to trade against all nonmember nations as they see fit. However, political union requires nations to give up a high degree of sovereignty in foreign policy. This is why political union is so hard to achieve. Long histories of cooperation or animosity between nations do not disappear when a group of countries forms a union. Because some members have very delicate ties with nonmember nations whereas others have very strong ties, the setting of a common foreign policy can be extremely tricky.

Because of the benefits and despite the drawbacks of regional trade agreements, economic integration is taking place throughout the world. Europe, the Americas, Asia, the Middle East, and Africa are all undergoing integration to some degree. In the remaining sections of this chapter we examine the most prominent efforts at integration in each of these regions. We begin by looking at the region with the longest history and highest level of integration—Europe.

The most sophisticated and advanced example of regional integration that we can point to today is occurring in Europe. European efforts at integration began shortly after the Second World War as a cooperative effort between a small group of countries and involved a few, select industries. Regional integration now encompasses practically all of Western Europe and all industries. Let's now explore integration in Europe beginning with its earliest attempts at cooperation.

EUROPEAN COAL AND STEEL COMMUNITY

In the middle of the twentieth century, many would have scoffed at the idea that the European countries, which had spent so many years at war with one another, could present a relatively unified whole by the close of the century. How has Europe come so far in such a relatively short time? A war-torn Europe emerged in 1945 facing two challenges. First, it needed to rebuild itself and avoid further armed conflict. Second, it needed to increase its industrial strength to stay competitive with an increasingly powerful United States.

Cooperation seemed to be the only way of facing these challenges. In 1951, Belgium, France, West Germany, Italy, Luxembourg, and the Netherlands took the first step toward cooperation. Together, these six nations created what was called the *European Coal and Steel Community*. This community of nations was designed to remove barriers to trade in coal, iron, steel, and scrap metal among the member nations. The European Coal and Steel Community continued to evolve and would one day be known as the forerunner of today's European Union.

EUROPEAN ECONOMIC COMMUNITY

The members of the European Coal and Steel Community signed the Treaty of Rome in 1957 and created the *European Economic Community* (*EEC*) (see Map 8.1). The Treaty of Rome took the bold step of outlining a future common market for these nations. Thus the treaty called for not only the elimination of tariffs between member nations and the creation of a common external tariff, but also the free internal movement of goods, services, labor, and capital. In 1967 the EEC broadened its scope to include additional industries, notably atomic energy, and changed its name to the *European Community* (*EC*).

The community once again changed its name in 1994 to the *European Union* (*EU*) and we refer to it by this name throughout the remainder of the discussion. As the goals of integration for the EU continued to expand, so too did its membership. The population of the trading bloc is today estimated at about 370 million people with a GDP of over $6 trillion.

The Treaty of Rome also aimed at establishing common policies among member nations for transportation and agriculture. The common agricultural policy became a highly contentious issue between the EU and other nations because EU price supports and direct subsidies to farmers were very large. To be sure, price supports and subsidies for agriculture are not unusual in any of the industrialized countries. But the EU policy consumed an enormous amount of financial resources and caused difficulties at world-

MAP 8.1 REGIONAL INTEGRATION IN EUROPE

European Union members by date of entry:

- ■ 1957
- ■ 1973
- ■ 1981
- ■ 1986
- ■ 1995

- ■ Candidates for future EU membership

- ■ Members of the European Free Trade Association (EFTA)

wide trade talks under the auspices of the GATT, especially during the Uruguay Round of negotiations. Generous subsidies to farmers were at last seriously questioned in 1995 when it appeared that their continuance might severely strain the EU budget. At that point, total EU subsidies accounted for approximately one half of the Union's overall expenditures.

SINGLE EUROPEAN ACT

By the mid-1980s, member nations of the European Union were feeling increasingly frustrated by a lack of harmony on several important matters including taxation, law, and regulations. A plethora of bureaucratic rules and regulations in each country served to protect national companies and industries just as they did before the EU was created. Distribution of goods across national borders between member nations required a gargantuan amount of paperwork. The important objective of harmonizing laws and policies was beginning to appear unachievable.

In response to mounting disappointment, a special commission was formed to study what could be done to get the EU moving forward once again. This commission (called the Delors Commission after the French finance minister at the time, Jacques Delors) produced a proposal for eliminating all remaining obstacles to a common market by the end of 1992. The proposal became known as the *Single European Act* (*SEA*). The goal of the SEA was to increase the ability of European companies to compete against companies from Japan and North America. The SEA, which was ratified by member nations and became law in 1987, had the following stated objectives:

- Harmonizing product standards throughout the Union
- Allowing suppliers to compete for government contracts in all nations of the Union
- Removing barriers to trade between member nations
- Removing restrictions on the international sale of currencies
- Lifting barriers to competition in financial services
- Abolishing restrictions on the right of logistics companies to pick up and deliver goods inside other member countries.

Impact on European Businesses   During the 1980s, European firms treated the emerging "pan-European" market as a self-fulfilling prophecy. Companies were changing tactics and market strategies and positioning themselves to take advantage of the opportunities that the SEA offered. For firms within the EU, this resulted in a wave of mergers and acquisitions.

The SEA is generally considered to have benefited large EU firms most. The reason is that these firms were able to combine their special understanding of European needs, capabilities, and cultures with the ability to produce in large quantities for all national markets in the EU and thereby cut costs. However, some of the restructuring observed certainly would have taken place without passage of the SEA.[6] But not only large firms benefited from the SEA. Small and medium-size companies were encouraged through EU institutions to engage in networking with one another to offset any negative consequences resulting from, for example, changing product standards. Although much standardization has occurred, the seemingly simple matter of deciding on the shape of a common electrical plug remains a particularly troublesome matter.

On the other hand, efforts to increase transportation efficiency have had little success. The cost of air travel within Europe remains high relative to other markets. Regarding the transport of goods, intermodal transport (containerized shipments that can be easily loaded onto trucks, trains, or ships) has been promoted for several years to increase the use of rails. However, most freight still travels by road.[7]

Impact on Non-European Businesses   Although much standardization did occur following passage of the act, problems remain for some companies outside the European Union. For instance, the rule that individual countries can prohibit imports that threaten public security has made breaking into the European market difficult. The problem arises because countries have a great deal of latitude when deciding what is a public security threat.

For example, Evan Segal is president of Dormont Manufacturing Company based, strangely enough, in Export, Pennsylvania. Dormont manufactures hoses that hook deep fat fryers up to gas outlets. Although Dormont once sold its product freely throughout Europe, it began to be denied entry into several countries that exploited the public security loophole. Dormont's top customer is Frymaster Corporation—a supplier of deep fat fryers to McDonald's. Frymaster told Dormont that British restaurants no longer allow McDonald's to use Dormont hoses. Also, shortly before Disneyland

Paris opened its theme park, French inspectors demanded that Dormont hoses be replaced with French-approved equipment. Evan Segal and other small exporters around the world still must cope with disparate standards in what is supposedly a unified Europe. Trade officials in the United States estimate that at least $300 million of the $112 billion that the U.S. exports to Europe are goods that once needed no separate national approval, but now require it from each country.[8]

One other consequence for non-EU firms was the need to gain a place within the market before the close of 1992. A Pfizer representative was quoted as saying, "Pfizer does not have a choice about whether to manufacture in the European Union or not. If we are going to sell in Europe, we have to manufacture there."[9]

MAASTRICHT TREATY

Well before the SEA deadline even arrived, some members of the EU wanted to take European integration even further. Members of the European Union met in 1991 for a summit meeting in Maastricht, Netherlands, to plan for more advanced stages of integration. The result was the *Maastricht Treaty* that was signed by the EU members in late 1993.

The Maastricht Treaty took the European trading bloc beyond what many had believed possible. First, it called for banking in a single, common currency after January 1, 1999, and circulation of coins and paper currency on January 1, 2002. A common currency clearly benefits firms doing business in the EU. The costs (commissions) inherent in converting from the currency of one member nation to another can be avoided. Business owners also need not worry about the potential loss of money due to shifting exchange rates between national currencies on cross-border deals in the EU (exchange rates are discussed in Chapter 9). Not having to cover such costs and risks frees up capital for greater investment. However, investments must be made to adjust company and banking methods to keep track of transactions in two currencies until eventual full conversion in 2002.

Second, the treaty set up monetary and fiscal targets for countries wishing to take part in monetary union. These targets call for government deficits less than 3 percent of GDP, government debt less than 60 percent of GDP, and inflation and interest rates within 1.5 percent and 2 percent, respectively, of those of the three best-performing member nations.[10] Of the current 15 EU members only Britain, Denmark, Greece, and Sweden have chosen not to take part in monetary union for now. Monetary union is discussed in much greater detail in Chapter 10 under the topic of the European monetary system.

Third, the treaty called for political union of the member nations—including development of a common foreign and defense policy and common citizenship. However, progress on political integration will wait until the countries see how smoothly the final stages of economic and monetary union go.

Impact of Maastricht   The economic pressure generated by the drive to a single currency is so great that it has created mild social unrest in many countries. In one incident in Belgium, home to the European Commission, nurses jammed Brussels' streets to register their anger over proposed cuts in house-call reimbursements. They were not alone in blaming Belgium's public spending cuts on the strict Maastricht criteria for taking part in monetary union. "For my parents, Europe went together with peace and prosperity," recalls Tony Vandeputte, chief executive officer of the Federation of Belgian Industries. "Today, it is associated with spending cuts."[11] But despite such unrest, many observers warned that amending Maastricht would open up a whole new round of negotiations that could threaten future progress and therefore counseled against any such moves.[12]

Monetary union has also caused political upheaval in some nations, especially those choosing not to take part initially. The election of new governments in Britain, France, and Germany in the late 1990s made a murky picture murkier. Britain's Prime Minister Tony Blair helped keep that country out of the monetary union in January 1999, but not to the delight of all parties. The Confederation of British Industry came out in favor of Britain participation in the single currency. The stance of British industry was prompted by views held by investors from other countries such as Toyota's president, Hiroshi Okuda. Okuda said that Toyota would undertake a "rethinking" of its investment in Britain should Britain remain outside monetary union.[13]

STRUCTURE OF THE EUROPEAN UNION

The more complex the integration efforts of a group of nations, the larger and more complex the bureaucracy seems to be. This seems logical since full monetary union and even political union must coordinate the policies of all member nations. The additional layer of bureaucracy overlays that which already exists in each member country. In the case of the European Union, five institutions play important roles in monitoring and enforcing economic and political integration.

European Council   The European Council consists of the European Commission (discussed next) and the heads of state of each member nation. Twice each year, the Council holds meetings to discuss and resolve any policy issues including foreign policy.

European Commission   The European Commission is headquartered in Brussels, Belgium, where its job is to draft and implement new legislation and ensure compliance by member nations. The commission comprises twenty commissioners appointed by each member country—larger nations get two commissioners, smaller countries, one. A president and six vice presidents selected from among the group of twenty commissioners govern the commission. Each commissioner is assigned a specific policy area such as competitive policy or agricultural policy. Although commissioners are appointed by their national governments, they are expected to behave in the best interest of the EU as a whole, not in the interest of their own country.

Council of Ministers   The Council of Ministers is also headquartered in Brussels where it votes on the passage of laws after receiving proposed legislation from the European Commission. The Council of Ministers is composed of one representative from each member country. The membership of the council changes depending on what topic is currently under discussion. For instance, when the discussion turns to environmental issues, environmental ministers attend the meetings, for agricultural issues, the ministers of agriculture attend, and so on.

Because no proposed legislation becomes law unless the Council of Ministers votes it into law, the council has a great deal of power within the EU. Although passage into law for all legislation used to require a unanimous vote, some legislation today requires only a simple majority to win approval. Particularly sensitive areas such as immigration and taxation still require a unanimous vote.

European Parliament   In spite of its title, the European Parliament acts as a consultative rather than legislative body. Its main purpose is to debate and amend legislation proposed by the European Commission and its power is therefore limited. But it has the right to vote on the appointment of commissioners, as well as veto power over some laws (including the annual budget of the EU). The more than 600 members of parliament are expected to voice their particular political views on matters and are

British Chancellor of the Exchequer Gordon Brown formally presents to the assembled European Parliament the unanimous recommendation of the fifteen European Union finance ministers that eleven member states join in launching the euro in 1999. For more information on European business and the euro, go to ⟨**www.eubusiness.com/emu/ euroamue.htm**⟩.

elected by popular vote within each member nation. There is a call for increased democratization within the EU, and some believe this could be achieved by strengthening the powers of the parliament.

Court of Justice   The Court of Justice is the court of appeals in the European Union. It is composed of one justice from each member country. One type of case that the Court of Justice hears are those in which a member nation is accused of not meeting its treaty obligations. Another type are those in which the commission or council is charged with failing to live up to their responsibilities under the terms of a treaty. Like the commissioners, justices are required to act in the interest of the EU as a whole, not in the interest of their own countries.

FUTURE EU MEMBERSHIP

As of mid-1999, the European Union had 15 members. For talks on future enlargement of EU membership, potential new member countries have been divided into two tiers. The first-tier countries include Cyprus, Czech Republic, Estonia, Hungary, Poland, and Slovenia. The second tier includes Bulgaria, Latvia, Lithuania, Malta, Romania, and Slovakia (see Map 8.1). One country that is a logical but highly unlikely candidate for future membership is Turkey. One reason for the failure of Turkey to win support in the EU is charges (fair or not) by member nations of human rights abuses. Another reason is intense opposition by Greece, a longtime foe of Turkey. However, Turkey does have a customs union with the EU, and this is increasing trade between Turkey and the EU. One other country that has tried but failed to gain support for membership is Morocco. Despite disappointment for some countries that are EU hopefuls and despite intermittent setbacks for EU members themselves, integration in Europe continues to move forward.

EUROPEAN FREE TRADE ASSOCIATION (EFTA)

Certain European nations were reluctant to join in the ambitious goals of the EU, fearing destructive rivalries and a loss of national sovereignty. Some of these nations did not want to be part of a common market but instead wanted the benefits of a free trade area. In 1960, seven countries—Austria, Denmark, Norway, Portugal, Sweden, Switzerland, and the United Kingdom—formed the *European Free Trade Association* (*EFTA*). The focus of EFTA is trade in industrial, not consumer, goods. But over time many EFTA members recognized the potential for greater integration and joined the European Union. Countries came and went and by 1999, EFTA consisted of only Iceland, Liechtenstein, Norway, and Switzerland (see Map 8.1). Combined, they have a population of slightly less than 12 million people. Nevertheless, EFTA members remain committed to free trade principles and raising standards of living for their people.

Let's now examine the progress of economic integration in the Americas and see how far it has come and where it is headed.

INTEGRATION IN THE AMERICAS

Europe's success at economic integration caused other regions to consider the benefits of forming their own regional trading blocs. Latin American countries began forming regional trading arrangements in the early 1960s but only made substantial progress in the 1980s and 1990s. North America was about three decades behind Europe in taking major steps toward economic integration. Let's now explore the major efforts toward economic integration in North, South, and Central America, beginning with North America.

U.S.-CANADA FREE TRADE AGREEMENT

There has always been a good deal of trade between Canada and the United States. In fact, the two nations are each other's largest trading partner. Canada and the United States had in the past established trade agreements in several industrial sectors of their economies including automotive products. But the idea of a comprehensive free trade agreement between the two countries was proposed in 1987. In January 1989, the *U.S.-Canada Free Trade Agreement* went into effect. The goal was to eliminate all tariffs on bilateral trade between Canada and the United States by 1998. An international tribunal was established to settle any trade disputes that should arise. Due to accelerating progress in Europe in the late 1980s and early 1990s, the task of creating a North American trading bloc that included Mexico took on new urgency and resulted in the North American Free Trade Agreement.

NORTH AMERICAN FREE TRADE AGREEMENT (NAFTA)

While Canada and the United States were negotiating their free trade agreement, Mexico was quietly working toward increasing its global competitiveness. It joined the GATT in 1986 and began taking a more pro-market stance by targeting several state-owned enterprises for privatization in 1988. Mexico and the United States began discussing the potential for integration in early 1991, and talks between Canada, Mexico, and the United States began later that year. The *North American Free Trade Agreement* (*NAFTA*) became effective in January 1994, creating a market of 360 million consumers and a GDP of about $6.5 trillion (see Map 8.2).

As a free trade agreement, NAFTA seeks to eliminate most tariffs and nontariff trade barriers on most goods originating from within North America by 2008. The agreement also calls for liberalized rules regarding government procurement practices, the granting of subsidies, and the imposition of countervailing duties (see Chapter 6). Other provisions deal with such issues as trade in services, intellectual property rights, and standards of health, safety, and the environment.[14]

MAP 8.2  **REGIONAL INTEGRATION IN NORTH AMERICA**

Local Content Requirements and Rules of Origin   Manufacturers and distributors are finding that while NAFTA encourages free trade between Canada, Mexico and the United States, the resulting trade is anything but hassle free. Local content requirements and rules of origin are among the agreement's most complex criteria. These rules create special problems for producers and distributors. Although they rarely know the precise origin of every part or component in a piece of industrial equipment, they are responsible for determining whether a product has sufficient North American content to qualify for tariff-free status. The producer or distributor must also provide a NAFTA "certificate of origin" to an importer to claim an exemption from tariffs. Four criteria determine whether a good meets NAFTA rules of origin:[15]

➡ Goods wholly produced or obtained in the NAFTA region

➡ Goods containing nonoriginating inputs but meeting Annex 401 origin rules (which covers regional input)

➡ Goods produced in the NAFTA region wholly from originating materials

➡ Unassembled goods and goods classified in the same harmonized system category as their parts that do not meet Annex 401 rules but have sufficient North American regional value content

Effects of NAFTA   Between 1993 and 1996, trade among the North American nations increased from about $290 billion to $420 billion in 1996—a 43 percent gain.[16] United States exports to Canada rose 13 percent in 1997 over the previous year while exports to Mexico jumped 26 percent. What is notable about this increase in trade is that Mexico became the second largest export market of the United States for the first time ever in 1997. In fact, bilateral trade between the United States and Mexico reached a record $174 billion in 1998.[17] Canada remains in the number-one position with almost $1 billion of goods crossing the U.S.-Canada border each day. Meanwhile, Japan was bumped to number three behind Mexico. This is despite the fact that Mexico's economy is one-twelfth the size of Japan's.[18]

Canada traded very little with Mexico before NAFTA went into effect. However, between 1991 and 1997, Canada's exports to Latin America and the Caribbean more than doubled from under $3 billion to almost $6.5 billion. In fact, Canada now exports more to this region than Germany and France combined.[19] There is little doubt that NAFTA either directly or indirectly spurred this sharp rise in trade.

The agreement's effect on employment and wages is not as easy to determine. The United States Trade Representative Office claims that NAFTA has created 311,000 jobs in the United States and displaced only 116,000 workers. However, the AFL-CIO labor union claims that the cost of NAFTA was 420,000 jobs in the United States.[20] Despite these conflicting views, the U.S. government maintains that export-related jobs created by NAFTA pay higher wages than the national average for production workers. But the government report does not specify whether the new jobs pay more than the jobs that were lost.[21]

Despite the disparity in the different numbers that are referenced by different groups, it is certainly true that some U.S. companies headed for the border after NAFTA came into being. One firm from the United States making a massive manufacturing commitment to Mexico is Delphi Automotive Systems. Delphi recently became Mexico's largest employer with 70,000 employees in 45 facilities—half of them along the border with the United States. Delphi manufactures a variety of lighting, electric, and steering assemblies for 27 of the world's automotive companies. The company cemented its commitment to Mexico by opening a Tech Center in Ciudad Juarez, its first major engineering effort outside the United States. By siting this center closer to manufacturing facilities the company is reducing lead times and start-up costs.[22]

The NAFTA agreement also included provisions for environmental protection. However, Mexico still does not have the facilities to deal with the impact that greater economic activity will have on the environment. For instance, figures released two years after NAFTA took effect reported that Mexico was handling only 12 percent of its 8 million tons of hazardous materials in a legitimate manner.[23] But progress is being made. Mexico's Instituto Nacional de Ecologia (National Ecology Institute) has launched a new industrial waste management program, including an incentive system to encourage waste reduction and recycling.

Expansion of NAFTA   Continued ambivalence about the long-term effects of NAFTA including concerns of union leaders and environmental watchdogs is delaying the expansion of NAFTA. After Chile made significant economic progress in the late 1980s and early 1990s, business leaders argued for its integration into NAFTA. The slender nation of 14 million people is no economic giant but might be a model for economic reform in other South American nations. Chile began its market reforms about

Air pollution from increased industrialization mixes with fog over Mexico City. On the day this photo was taken, visibility was so poor that the city's airport had to close. NAFTA provisions for waste reduction, recycling, and disposal of hazardous materials were inspired in part by such damage to the air and water of member nations. To read more about NAFTA's provisions go to its site at ⟨**www.nafta-sec-alena.org**⟩.

15 years ahead of Brazil (the largest economy in South America), and today is largely open to trade and investment.

However, Chile's entry into NAFTA was dealt a severe blow when the U.S. Congress failed to grant fast track negotiating authority to the Clinton administration. Fast track authority allows an administration to engage in all necessary talks surrounding a trade deal without the official involvement of Congress. After the deal's details are decided, Congress then simply votes up or down on the deal and cannot revise the treaty's provisions. The granting of fast track authority was shot down in the U.S. Congress for two reasons: a renewed affinity for isolationism among some and a desire to include labor and environmental clauses in future trade deals among others.

Integration of Chile into NAFTA could benefit many small companies in Canada, Mexico, and the United States that cannot afford to invest in production facilities in Chile. For example, Amigo Mobility International is a Bridgeport, Michigan, company that manufactures electric scooters for the disabled. The small $17 million company exports to Argentina, Brazil, Chile, and Mexico. Amigo's chief operating officer, Clarence Rivette, estimates that if Chile were to participate in NAFTA, Chilean customers could expect an initial price reduction of up to 5 percent on the company's products priced between $2,000 and $4,000.[24]

ANDEAN COMMUNITY

Early attempts at integration among Latin American countries had a rocky beginning. The first try, the *Latin American Free Trade Association (LAFTA)*, was formed in 1961. The agreement first called for the creation of a free trade area by 1971 but then extended that date to 1980. Yet due to a crippling debt crisis in South America and a reluctance of member nations to do away with protectionism, the agreement was doomed to an early demise. Disappointment with LAFTA led to the creation of two other regional trading blocs—the Andean Community and the Latin American Integration Association.

The *Andean Community* (originally the Andean Pact) was formed in 1969 between five South American countries located in the Andes mountain range—Bolivia, Chile, Colombia, Ecuador, and Peru. Venezuela joined the pact in 1973 but Chile left in 1976 (see Map 8.3). Today the group comprises a market of about 100 million consumers and a combined GDP of over $480 billion. The main objectives of the pact included tariff reduction for trade among member nations, a common external tariff, and common policies in both transportation and certain industries. But once again, cooperation was difficult to achieve. The political ideology of each of the members was somewhat hostile to the concept of free markets and favored a good deal of government involvement in business affairs. Thus inherent distrust made lower tariffs and more open trade with other members hard to achieve.

The Andean Community received a new lease on life in 1990 when its members promised to create a free trade area by 1992, a customs union by 1994, and a common market by 1995. The Andean countries posted nearly 30 percent annual gains in trade from 1990 to 1997. All the countries except Peru have liberalized trade with the other members. Three countries (Colombia, Ecuador, and Venezuela) have established a common external tariff for most products. Thus the free trade area is in place for the most part.

But the customs union, not to mention the common market, is behind schedule. The common market will be difficult to implement within the framework of the Andean Community because each country has been given significant exceptions in the tariff structure they have in place for trade with nonmember nations. One obstacle to further progress is that countries continue to sign agreements with just one or two

MAP 8.3   *REGIONAL INTEGRATION IN LATIN AMERICA*

Note: Chile and Bolivia are associate members of MERCOSUR.

countries outside the Andean Community framework.[25] Such independent action impairs progress internally and hurts the credibility of the Andean Community in the eyes of the rest of the world. Furthermore, Bolivia and Chile have gained associate membership in the trading bloc known as MERCOSUR (discussed shortly), which indicates a lack of confidence in the future success of the Andean Community.

LATIN AMERICAN INTEGRATION ASSOCIATION (ALADI)

The *Latin American Integration Association (ALADI)* was formed in 1980. Map 8.3 shows the countries belonging to the ALADI trading bloc. Because of the failure of the first attempt at integration (LAFTA), the objectives of ALADI were scaled back significantly. The ALADI agreement calls for preferential tariff agreements to be made between pairs of member nations (called *bilateral* agreements) that reflect the economic development of each nation. Although the agreement resulted in roughly 24 bilateral agreements and 5 subregional pacts, the agreements did not accomplish a great deal of cross-border trade. Dissatisfaction with progress once again caused certain nations to form another trading bloc of their own—MERCOSUR.

SOUTHERN COMMON MARKET (MERCOSUR)

The Southern Common Market (MERCOSUR) was established in 1988 between just Argentina and Brazil but expanded to include Paraguay and Uruguay in 1991. In 1996, it underwent another expansion when Bolivia and Chile became associate, but not full, members of the bloc (see Map 8.3). Chile is expected to become a full member by the end of 1999, but Bolivia will likely need to wait some time for full membership. Two other countries showing interest in MERCOSUR are Peru and Venezuela. In fact, Peru's President Alberto Fujimori stated in 1997 that his country would leave the Andean Community, although he gave no date or timetable.

Today MERCOSUR acts as a customs union and boasts a market of more than 220 million consumers (nearly half of Latin America's total population) and 60 percent of its total economic output.[26] Its first years of existence were very successful—trade between members grew nearly four-fold during the 1990s.[27] MERCOSUR continues to make progress on trade and investment liberalization and is emerging as the most powerful trading bloc in all of Latin America. In fact, if all goes well, it has the goal of incorporating all of the countries of South America into a South American Free Trade Agreement by the year 2005, when it would link up with NAFTA to form a Free Trade Area of the Americas (discussed shortly).

Regional economic integration in Latin America has certainly caught the eye of European business. European companies gobbled up lucrative contracts for rebuilding Latin America's infrastructure when those countries instituted free-market reforms and privatization of public utilities. For instance, Telefónica de España of Spain paid $5 billion to buy phone companies in Argentina, Brazil, Chile, and Peru. Seven of the ten largest private companies in Brazil are European owned, compared to two controlled by U.S. companies. Some notable European companies setting up shop in Latin America include Germany's Volkswagen and Italy's Fiat in autos, France's supermarket chain Carrefours, and the British/Dutch personal-care products group Unilever. As European companies continue making inroads into Latin America, U.S. companies are pressuring their government to move more quickly in integrating Chile into NAFTA and accelerating the creation of the Free Trade Area of the Americas. The appeal of Latin America to both the European Union and the United States is not only its large consumer base but its potential as a low-cost production platform for worldwide export.[28]

CENTRAL AMERICA AND THE CARIBBEAN

Attempts at economic integration in Central American countries and throughout the Caribbean basin have been much more modest than efforts elsewhere in the Americas. Nevertheless, let's look at two efforts at integration in these two regions—CARICOM and CACM.

Caribbean Community and Common Market (CARICOM)   The *Caribbean Community and Common Market* (*CARICOM*) trading bloc was formed in 1973. Map 8.4 shows the countries and territory encompassed by CARICOM. As a whole, CARI-

MAP 8.4   **REGIONAL INTEGRATION IN CENTRAL AMERICA AND THE CARIBBEAN**

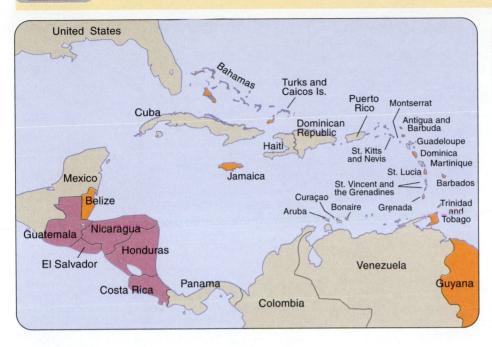

COM has a combined GDP of about $28.6 billion and a consumer market of about 5.8 million. The trading bloc seeks to establish free movement of tourists within the region, and the free movement of factors of production, including skilled workers and professionals. Other than establishment of a common external tariff by most members, CARICOM has not made much progress. The main difficulty CARICOM faces, and what will continue to hamper its progress, is that most of the members trade more with nonmembers than they do with members simply because members do not have the imports each needs.

Central American Common Market (CACM)

The *Central American Common Market (CACM)* was formed in 1961 to create a common market between Costa Rica, El Salvador, Guatemala, Honduras, and Nicaragua (see Map 8.4). Together, the members of CACM comprise a market of 28 million consumers and have a combined GDP of about $85 billion.[29] However, the common market was never realized because of a long and bloody war between El Salvador and Honduras and civil wars in the region. But renewed peace is creating more business confidence and optimism, which is driving growth in trade between members at about 25 percent per year.[30]

After being revived in 1991, the CACM has chosen to focus not on trade but on greater deregulation of industry, harmonization of tax laws, and infrastructure improvement. However, it is doubtful that these measures will do much good in protecting these nations from the onslaught of international competition. Nevertheless, progress is continuing and talk of new trade agreements can once again be heard. See the Global Manager "The Central American Market: Staying Ahead of the Curve" for more on what the future might have in store for this region of the world.

The Central American Market: Staying Ahead of the Curve

Falling tariffs are creating a free market in most of Central America. After declining during the 1980s due to war and a lack of convertibility of local currencies, regional trade between these nations now accounts for a fifth of Central America's total. The region's "northern triangle" of El Salvador, Guatemala, and Honduras is looking to build on that process with negotiations for a free trade zone with Mexico. The zone would supplement a similar deal between Costa Rica and Mexico that has tripled trade between the two countries. It would also be a step toward eventual integration with NAFTA.

FDI TARGETS

➤ *Agriculture* will continue to be one of the major forces behind the region's economies, with the notable exception of Panama.

➤ *Services* continue to offer the major investment opportunity in Panama, where the government is keen to promote development near the Panama Canal. Several banking institutions are already being privatized in Costa Rica.

➤ *Mining* is again attracting international interest, particularly in Panama, Nicaragua, and Costa Rica, led by Canadian companies like Greenstone Resources, Teck, and Tiomin Resources.

➤ *Tourism* will also be a major regional investment focus. Panama, in particular, believes it has the same potential as Costa Rica, the current leader.

➤ *Maquiladora operations* will continue to boom, offering a quick fix to the region's chronic unemployment. Asian investors, particularly the Taiwanese, continue to lead the charge.

CORPORATE STRATEGY

Advances toward open markets have been enough to allow multinational firms to plan their investments regionally. Indeed, some companies believe that only when the market is considered as a whole does it muster the critical mass needed for serious investment in the region. For example, Royal Dutch/Shell (UK/Netherlands) is already treating the market as one. The company is reducing material and marketing costs by offering common services throughout Central America and the Caribbean from its base in the Dominican Republic. "The markets by themselves are too small," says Jorge Ardanaz, general manager of Shell Nicaragua, "but together they are interesting."

Normally, multinational companies run operations from one of the three largest Central American economies, typically Costa Rica, with offices in the other two, Panama and Guatemala. El Salvador's central location and rapid economic recovery is gaining attention. But, like Nicaragua, its lack of an Atlantic port means the bulk of its imports have to be brought in through Guatemala and Honduras.

RISKS

➤ *The competition.* International investors face competition from local companies that are also taking advantage of the regional market. Often, several producers band together. The Pellas group, Nicaragua's largest company, this year pooled its brewery interests with peers from Costa Rica, Guatemala, and El Salvador to form Consorcio Cervecero Centroamerica, Coseca, creating the sector's first regional operator.

➤ *Overvalued currency and high interest rates.* The threat of overvalued local currency has been buoyed by remittances from nationals working in the United States and illegal drug trafficking. This is one reason that Johnson & Johnson (U.S.) chose to base its operations in Panama, which uses the U.S. dollar as its official currency. Interest rates, however, can reach over 20 percent and make local manufacturing difficult.

➤ *Violence and crime.* The end of major conflicts in the region has not necessarily meant peace. All the violence has left a lasting culture of crime. Kidnappings are rife in Guatemala, and the murder rate in El Salvador is now higher than during the country's own 10-year conflict. Dow Centroamerica (U.S.) shifted its head office to Costa Rica from Guatemala in the mid-1980s due to fears for the safety of its executives.

FREE TRADE AREA OF THE AMERICAS (FTAA)

Sure to dominate discussion of regional trading blocs in the Americas at least until the year 2005 is creation of a *Free Trade Area of the Americas* (*FTAA*). The objective of the FTAA is to create a trading bloc that reaches from the northern tip of Alaska to the southern tip of Tierra del Fuego, in South America. The FTAA would create the world's largest market comprising 34 nations, 800 million consumers, and have a collective GDP of about $10 trillion. The only Western Hemisphere nation that will not be part of the FTAA is Cuba. The FTAA would work alongside the different trading blocs such as NAFTA, MERCOSUR, the Andean Community, and CACM. Beginning in 2005, the FTAA would remove tariffs and nontariff barriers between all member countries over an unspecified number of years.

Early talks toward a free trade area in the Western Hemisphere were called the Enterprise for the Americas Initiative (EAI). In addition to the creation of a trading bloc, the EAI had as its goal reform in Latin America. The EAI did establish funds for environmental efforts in Argentina, Bolivia, Chile, Colombia, El Salvador, Jamaica, and Uruguay. It also helped many Latin American countries relieve the pressure of massive debts owed to large international banks.[31]

The first official meeting, the 1994 Summit of the Americas in Miami, created the broad blueprint for the agreement. Government representatives reaffirmed their commitment to FTAA at the Second Summit of the Americas in April 1998 in Santiago, Chile. Actual negotiations began in September 1998 and are scheduled to finish in 2005. Signaling the growing economic power of Brazil, it and the United States will co-chair the final three years of the negotiations—widely expected to be the toughest. It also sends a more general message about the growing importance of Brazil. One Brazilian diplomat spoke of past dependence of Brazil on the United States and past mistrust between them. "But we are not so dependent on the U.S. anymore, things are more balanced. We cannot simply be rolled over, and I think Washington understands that."[32]

Similar to the expansion of NAFTA, success in seeing FTAA become a reality hinges a great deal upon fast track negotiating authority for the U.S. President. However, fast track negotiating authority is not as essential early in the negotiations as it is in later stages. It is at that point that countries will want to see some sign that the United States (the driver behind the initiative) is determined to cement the deal.[33]

In addition to trade, the Santiago Summit accomplished some social policy objectives. First, the countries laid aside over $40 billion to achieve 100 percent primary education for all citizens by the year 2010. Further, they created a special office to focus on threats to the freedom of the press and human rights abuses.[34] Running alongside the summit meeting was what was called the "Santiago People's Summit of the Americas." This summit was organized and attended by trade unions, women's organizations, environmental groups, religious groups, and human rights groups. Their goal was to create a forum in which to publicize the need for education, democracy, workers' rights, drug enforcement, rising incomes for ordinary people, and an end to all forms of discrimination within the FTAA. About 1,500 people from the 34 nations attended.[35]

Corruption is an area of contention for Canada and the United States, who fear closer cooperation could mean more piracy and lost sales to counterfeit goods. Latin America has long been identified as a market for pirated merchandise, particularly music on CD-ROM and computer software. Some music is even produced in Macao, China, and sent for sale to Latin America. Big record companies are reluctant to invest there, and the region's local artists are losing royalties from exports that they would otherwise get from official recordings.[36] In addition, the Argentine Supreme Court recently ruled that piracy is not an illegal act. The Software Publishers Association—which represents the computer software industry in the United States—closed its doors until Argentina implements an antipiracy legal framework.[37] See the World Business Survey "Corruption Perceptions in the FTAA" for more on corruption in some FTAA member countries.

World Business Survey

Corruption Perceptions in the FTAA

Corruption is a problem throughout Latin America for all firms doing business there. If the FTAA is going to be a success, corruption will have to be rooted out. The table below shows the results of a survey on how businesspeople perceive corruption in some countries involved in the FTAA.

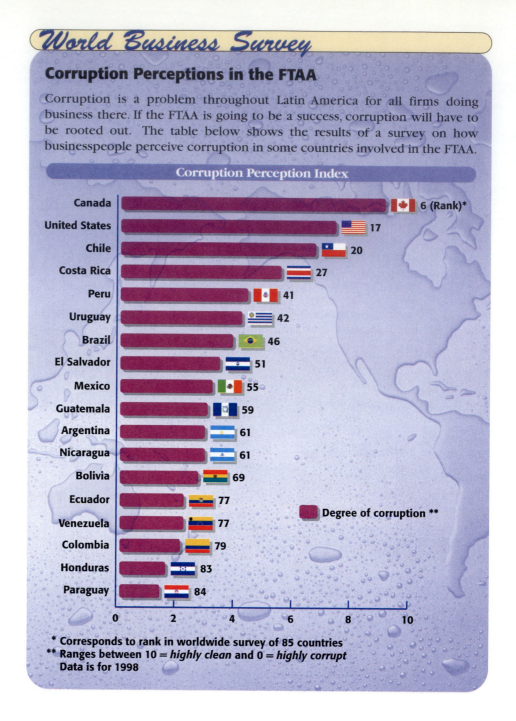

Corruption Perception Index

Country	Index
Canada	6 (Rank)*
United States	17
Chile	20
Costa Rica	27
Peru	41
Uruguay	42
Brazil	46
El Salvador	51
Mexico	55
Guatemala	59
Argentina	61
Nicaragua	61
Bolivia	69
Ecuador	77
Venezuela	77
Colombia	79
Honduras	83
Paraguay	84

Degree of corruption **

* Corresponds to rank in worldwide survey of 85 countries
** Ranges between 10 = *highly clean* and 0 = *highly corrupt*
Data is for 1998

TRANSATLANTIC ECONOMIC PARTNERSHIP (TEP)

The idea for a *Transatlantic Economic Partnership* (*TEP*) between the United States and the European Union first surfaced in May 1998 at the EU-United States summit meeting. The partnership will create a market of nearly 650 million consumers and an annual output of almost $16 trillion. In addition to forging closer economic ties between the EU and the United States, the partnership aims to contribute to stability, democ-

TABLE 8.1 **How the EU and the United States Measure Up**

	EU	U.S.
Area (thousands of square miles)	1,249.0	3,732.0
Population (millions)	373.3	267.6
Population density/square mile	298.9	71.7
Unemployment rate (percent)	10.7	4.9
Gross domestic product (billions of U.S. $)	8,093.4	7,819.3
GDP growth rate (percent)*	2.6	3.8

*All data is for 1997 except for GDP growth rate, which is for years 1995–1996.

racy, and development worldwide. As Table 8.1 shows, although the EU and the United States differ in important ways, the partnership is one of equals in terms of the size of their economies.

There is good reason for the proposed partnership. The United States and the European Union account for 20 percent of one another's merchandise trade and over 38 percent of trade in services. Companies based in the European Union account for nearly 60 percent of all foreign direct investment in the United States while companies from the United States account for 44 percent of investment in the EU. Companies from Europe are the number-one investors in 41 of the 50 states in the United States and number two in the rest.[38] The relation between European countries and the United States is only growing stronger as some big mergers in recent years has shown, notably the 1998 merger between Daimler-Benz and Chrysler.[39]

INTEGRATION IN ASIA

Efforts outside Europe and the Americas at economic and political integration have tended to be looser arrangements. Let's take a look at two important coalitions in Asia and among Pacific Rim nations—the Association of Southeast Asian Nations and the organization for Asia Pacific Economic Cooperation.

ASSOCIATION OF SOUTHEAST ASIAN NATIONS (ASEAN)

Indonesia, Malaysia, the Philippines, Singapore, and Thailand formed the *Association of Southeast Asian Nations (ASEAN)* in 1967. Brunei joined in 1984, Vietnam in 1995, Laos and Myanmar in 1997, and Cambodia in 1998 (see Map 8.5). Together, the ASEAN countries comprise a market of about 500 million consumers and a GDP of more than $800 billion. The three main objectives of the alliance are to (1) promote economic, cultural, and social development in the region; (2) safeguard the region's economic and political stability; and (3) serve as a forum in which differences can be resolved fairly and peacefully.

The intention to admit Cambodia, Laos, and Myanmar (formerly Burma) was met with criticism from some Western nations. The main concern regarding Laos and Cambodia stemmed from their roles in support of the communists during the Vietnam War. The quarrel with Myanmar centers on evidence of its continued violation of human rights. Nevertheless, ASEAN felt that by adding these countries to the coalition, it could counter China's rising strength and its resources of cheap labor and abundant raw materials.[40]

MAP 8.5

REGIONAL INTEGRATION IN ASIA

Doing Business with ASEAN Companies involved in Asia are likely to be doing business with an ASEAN member. Here is how some companies around the world are betting on the growth and future prospects of ASEAN:

➡ General Motors is investing $750 million over 10 years in a car production facility in Thailand. Not only does GM plan to serve that country's domestic market, but it also will produce autos for export.

➡ Mazda Motor Corporation is forming a joint venture for production and assembly of pickup trucks in Thailand's Rayong province. The joint venture's facility will help the company diversify its product line and better respond to buyer preferences in the region.

➡ Matsushita Electric Industrial Company Ltd. already has 38 manufacturing operations in ASEAN, which account for over 50 percent of the Osaka-based firm's total output. "Given the ASEAN region's extremely brisk growth," says Toshiyuki Nakahara, a Matsushita counselor, "we believe that it is not just a large production center for the global market, but also a growing consumer market in and of itself."

Association of Southeast Asian Nations (ASEAN)

Asia Pacific Economic Cooperation (APEC)

But businesses that are unfamiliar with operating in ASEAN do need to exercise caution in their dealings. Some inescapable facts about ASEAN that warrant consideration include:[41]

➡ *Diverse cultures and politics.* The ASEAN nations are culturally and politically diverse. For instance, the Philippines is a representative democracy; Brunei is an oil-rich sultanate; and Vietnam is a state-controlled communist country. Businesses cannot expect to use boilerplate business protocol for all ASEAN countries.

➡ *Corruption and black markets.* Bribery is common in many ASEAN countries and there are active black markets in Indonesia, the Philippines, and Vietnam. In 1990 Triton Energy paid $300,000 to settle a U.S. Securities and Exchange Commission complaint that a Triton consultant in a former subsidiary paid bribes to Indonesian officials.

➡ *Absence of common tariffs and standards.* Executives in ASEAN say companies could cut their transactional costs and enhance production strategies if ASEAN countries harmonized tariffs, quality and safety standards, customs regulations, and investment rules.

Investors in Asia face many challenges. General Motors is investing hundreds of millions of dollars in car production in Thailand, both for sale in that country and for export. While this and other such investment projects will help the government shore up its recovering economy (which has stalled many building projects, such as the one pictured here) and provide work for many unemployed laborers, Thailand is still reluctant to let international investors gain too much control of its domestic banking industry.

ASIA PACIFIC ECONOMIC COOPERATION (APEC)

The organization for *Asia Pacific Economic Cooperation (APEC)* was formed in 1989. Begun as an informal forum among 12 trading partners, APEC now has 21 members (see Map 8.5). Together, the APEC nations account for more than 45 percent of world trade and a combined GDP of more than $16 trillion.

The stated aim of APEC was not to build another trading bloc. Instead, it desired to strengthen the multilateral trading system and expand the global economy by simplifying and liberalizing trade and investment procedures among member nations. More long term, APEC hopes to have free trade and investment throughout the region by 2010 for developed nations and 2020 for developing ones.

Progress is creating some positive benefits for people doing business in APEC nations. It is changing the granting of business visas so businesspeople can travel throughout the region without obtaining multiple visas. It is recommending mutual recognition agreements on professional qualifications so that engineers, for example, could practice in any APEC country, regardless of nationality. It is also ready to simplify and harmonize customs procedures. Eventually businesses could use the same customs forms and manifests for all APEC economies.[42]

Future Prospects for APEC The 1997 APEC summit held in Vancouver was preoccupied with how to respond to a financial crisis that first hit the region that summer and jeopardized economic growth throughout the region. The crisis began in Thailand and created shock waves that were felt throughout the region when currency values plummeted. The summit assured affected Asian nations of $68 billion in bailout money from the International Monetary Fund. In return, the Asian countries committed to freer trade plus doing away with government's close cooperation with banks and big business. For example, South Korea, the last to go into crisis prior to the summit meeting, committed to breaking up many of its powerful conglomerates. See chapter 10 for a complete discussion of the Asian financial crisis.

Matters did not improve much in 1998. Tensions continued and perhaps even grew as certain Asian leaders claimed that Western nations were behind the meltdown of the Asian economies so that they could then buy up banks and companies that had gone broke. One leader in particular, Malaysia's Prime Minister Mahathir Mohamad, is very outspoken on the issue and claims that the West is even plotting to undermine his leadership. The 1998 APEC Summit in Malaysia seemed to push the situation from bad to worse. Virtually nothing was accomplished on economics, and political tensions boiled into the open at times over the desire by the United States for more democratic reform in Asia. All this left many wondering what APEC is all about. It certainly does not have the focus or the record of accomplishments of NAFTA or the EU. Nonetheless, open dialogue and attempts at cooperation should continue to encourage progress toward APEC goals, however slow.[43]

INTEGRATION IN THE MIDDLE EAST AND AFRICA

Economic integration has not left out the Middle East and Africa although progress there is more limited than in any other geographic region. Limited success is due mostly to the small size of the countries involved and their relatively low level of development. The largest of these coalitions are the Gulf Cooperation Council and the Economic Community of West African States.

GULF COOPERATION COUNCIL (GCC)

In response to the hostilities between Iraq and Iran, several Middle Eastern nations formed the *Gulf Cooperation Council* (*GCC*) in 1980. Members of the GCC are Bahrain, Kuwait, Oman, Qatar, Saudi Arabia, and the United Arab Emirates (see Map 8.6).[44] The primary purpose of the GCC at its formation was to cooperate with the increasingly powerful trading blocs in Europe at the time—the EU and EFTA. However,

MAP 8.6   REGIONAL INTEGRATION IN THE MIDDLE EAST AND AFRICA

Legend:
- Gulf Cooperation Council (GCC)
- Economic Community of West African States (ECOWAS)

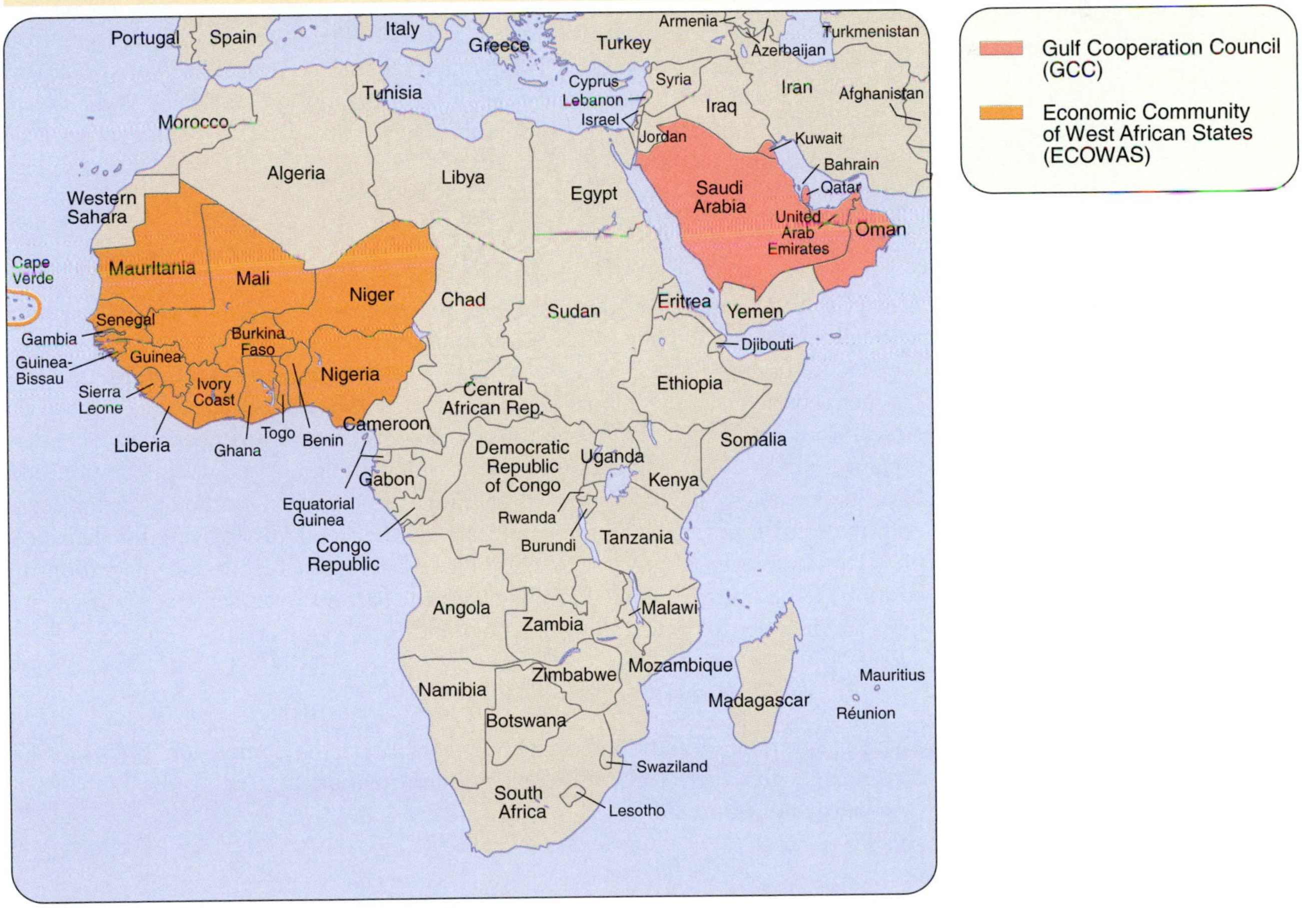

it has become as much a political entity as an economic one as it has evolved. Its cooperative thrust allows citizens of member countries to travel freely without visas in the GCC. It also permits citizens of one member nation to own land, property, and businesses in any other member nation without the need for local sponsors or partners.

ECONOMIC COMMUNITY OF WEST AFRICAN STATES (ECOWAS)

The *Economic Community of West African States (ECOWAS)* was formed in 1975 but relaunched its efforts at economic integration in 1992 because of a lack of early progress (see Map 8.6). One of the most important goals of ECOWAS is the formation of a customs union and eventual common market. Together, the ECOWAS nations comprise most of the economic activity in sub-Saharan Africa.

The group's lack of progress on economic integration largely reflects each nation's lack of economic development. Despite these problems, there are stories of successful dealings with African nations. Companies that have made inroads into Africa include:

e·biz

➡ Digital Equipment snagged a $1.4 million contract to supply the government of the Ivory Coast with personal computers and database management software.

➡ Africa On-line successfully participated in a simulated cyber workshop that depicted a visit to the Ivory Coast via the Internet and is now selling 50 new subscriptions per week in that country.

➡ Penray Companies employs about 85 people and sells its oil and fuel treatment products for car care to Senegal.

However, the most important success stories of these African nations come from the region's own small businesses. For example, the West African Enterprise Network works to help each other and create a better business environment in all West African countries. The ultimate goal of this organization is greater economic integration, and its story is highlighted in the Entrepreneurial Focus "The West African Enterprise Network: Small Businesses with a Large Mission."[45]

A FINAL WORD

This chapter has described the main regional integration efforts that are occurring throughout the world today. Table 8.2 summarizes the members of each regional trading bloc we discussed in this chapter. We saw that there is a great deal of debate about the merits or demerits of regional trade agreements. We also learned about some of the ethical elements of such agreements and the actions of governments and independent organizations to counter the negative effects of integration. Although integration does have its drawbacks, governments will continue to be enticed by the opportunities to reap the gains from increased trade and to raise the standards of living for their peoples. Thus despite its negative aspects, it is likely that regional economic integration will continue to be a growing force in rolling back the barriers to greater trade between nations and between existing trading blocs of nations.

There is a variety of additional material available on the companion Web site that accompanies this text. You can access this information by visiting the Web site at ⟨**www.prenhall.com/wild**⟩.

Entrepreneurial Focus

The West African Enterprise Network: Small Businesses with a Large Mission

Being an entrepreneur is no one's idea of the easy life, and for entrepreneurs in West Africa the going is particularly rough. Government policies restrict entrepreneurs and sometimes even discriminate against the private sector, the supporting infrastructure is weak, and tax and investment incentives for business are skewed and arbitrary. Yet, by banding together, over 300 West African entrepreneurs from 12 countries are pushing for policy reforms, advocating changes in the business environment and promoting cross-border trade and investment.

The creation of the West African Enterprise Network (WAEN) in 1992 was based on the conviction that modern private enterprise provided one of the keys to development in West Africa and that local entrepreneurs are best placed to change a business environment that is hostile to private enterprise. The original idea for WAEN came from the Club du Sahel and the United States Agency for International Development (USAID). Yet after laying the foundation and providing a modest amount of funding, these agencies have stepped aside and largely allowed the businessmen and women of West Africa to build their own networks. Because West Africa is a patchwork of French- and English-speaking communities that do not fully understand one another's requirements, the WAEN members feel it is vital to join forces and pool information if they are to achieve their ultimate goal—a single unified market in the region. Toward that end, the network has set up a Regional Trade Information Centre (RTIC), which not only distributes information about the network but also publishes information on prices, supply availability, new technologies, and business opportunities. The national networks contribute to the RTIC electronically.

Although initially viewed with skepticism by regional and international authorities, the WAEN has now established a reputation for acting as an important catalyst for government and private sector interaction. The Mali network, for instance, now represents the interests of the country's private sector. The national authorities consult the network directly on the design and implementation of economic policy. Thanks to the Ivory Coast's network, five subcontracting firms have been set up, all of them managed and funded nationally. The WAEN is also beginning to gain regional and international recognition. Until now regional integration was always the domain of government. But African firms have a key role to play in developing regional cooperation in West Africa—they know from experience the meaning of trade.

TABLE 8.2	The World's Main Regional Trading Blocs
EU	**European Union**
	Austria, Belgium, Britain, Denmark, Finland, France, Germany, Greece, Ireland, Italy, Luxembourg, Netherlands, Portugal, Spain, Sweden
EFTA	**European Free Trade Association**
	Iceland, Liechtenstein, Norway, Switzerland
NAFTA	**North American Free Trade Agreement**
	Canada, Mexico, United States
Andean	**Andean Community**
	Bolivia, Colombia, Ecuador, Peru, Venezuela
ALADI	**Latin American Integration Association**
	Argentina, Bolivia, Brazil, Chile, Colombia, Ecuador, Mexico, Paraguay, Peru, Uruguay, Venezuela
MERCOSUR	**Southern Common Market**
	Argentina, Brazil, Paraguay, Uruguay (Bolivia and Chile are associate members)
CARICOM	**Caribbean Community and Common Market**
	Antigua and Barbuda, Bahamas, Barbados, Belize, Dominica, Grenada, Guyana, Jamaica, Montserrat, St. Kitts and Nevis, St. Lucia, St. Vincent and the Grenadines, Trinidad and Tobago

(*continued*)

TABLE 8.2	The World's Main Regional Trading Blocs (continued)
CACM	**Central American Common Market**
	Costa Rica, El Salvador, Guatemala, Honduras, Nicaragua
FTAA	**Free Trade Area of the Americas**
	Caribbean, Central America, North America, South America
TEP	**Transatlantic Economic Partnership**
	European Union (15 countries), United States
ASEAN	**Association of Southeast Asian Nations**
	Brunei, Cambodia, Indonesia, Laos, Malaysia, Myanmar, Philippines, Singapore, Thailand, Vietnam
APEC	**Asia Pacific Economic Cooperation**
	Australia, Brunei, Canada, Chile, China, Hong Kong, Indonesia, Japan, South Korea, Malaysia, Mexico, New Zealand, Papua New Guinea, Peru, Philippines, Russia, Singapore, Taiwan, Thailand, United States, Vietnam
GCC	**Gulf Cooperation Council**
	Bahrain, Kuwait, Oman, Qatar, Saudi Arabia, United Arab Emirates
ECOWAS	**Economic Community of West African States**
	Benin, Burkina Faso, Cape Verde, Gambia, Ghana, Guinea, Guinea-Bissau, Ivory Coast, Liberia, Mali, Mauritania, Niger, Nigeria, Senegal, Sierra Leone, Togo

summary

1 **Define *regional economic integration* and identify the five levels of integration.** The process whereby countries in a geographic region cooperate with one another to reduce or eliminate barriers to the international flow of products, people, or capital is called *regional economic integration*. A group of nations in a geographic region undergoing economic integration is called a *regional trading bloc.* There are five potential levels (or degrees) of economic and political integration for regional trading blocs. (A *free trade area* is the lowest extent of national integration, *political union* the greatest.) Each level of integration incorporates the properties of those preceding it. (a) Economic integration whereby countries remove all barriers to trade between themselves but each country determines its own barriers against nonmembers is called a *free trade area.* Countries belonging to the free trade area remove all tariffs and nontariff barriers on the international trade of goods and services but maintain whatever policy they see fit against nonmember countries. (b) Economic integration whereby countries remove all barriers to trade between themselves but erect a common trade policy against nonmembers is called a *customs union.* Thus the main difference between a free trade area and a customs union is that all members of the trading bloc agree to treat trade with all nonmember nations in a similar manner. (c) Economic integration whereby countries remove all barriers to trade *and* the movement of labor and capital between themselves but erect a common trade policy against nonmembers is called a *common market.* Thus a common market extends beyond free trade areas and customs unions by adding the free movement of people and cross-border investment. (d) Economic integration whereby countries remove barriers to trade and the movement of labor and capital, erect a common trade policy against nonmembers, *and* coordinate their economic policies is called an *economic union.* An economic union goes beyond the demands of a common market by requiring that member nations harmonize tax, monetary, and fiscal policies, and create a common currency. (e) Economic and political integration whereby countries coordinate aspects of their economic *and* political systems is called a *political union.* Member nations must accept a common stance on economic and political policies regarding nonmember nations but are allowed a degree of freedom in setting certain internal political and economic policies.

2 Discuss the *benefits* and *drawbacks* associated with regional economic integration. The resulting increase in the level of trade between nations as a result of regional economic integration is called *trade creation.* One result of trade creation is that consumers and industrial buyers in member nations are faced with a wider selection of goods and services not available beforehand. Another result is that buyers can acquire goods and services at less cost following lower trade barriers such as tariffs.

There can also be political benefits from regional integration. A group of nations can have significantly greater political weight in the world than the nations have individually. Thus nations can have more say when negotiating with other countries in forums such as the World Trade Organization or perhaps even the United Nations. Integration involving political cooperation can also reduce the potential for military conflict.

The flip side of trade creation is *trade diversion*—the diversion of trade away from nations not belonging to a trading bloc and toward member nations. Trade diversion can actually result in reduced trade with a more efficient nonmember producer and increased trade with a less efficient producer within the trading bloc. Perhaps the most controversial aspect of regional economic integration is how people's jobs are affected. Countries protecting low-wage domestic industries from competition will likely see these jobs move to the country where wages are lower once barriers are removed. But this is also an opportunity for countries to upgrade the skills of their workers so they can earn higher wages.

Successive levels of integration require that nations surrender more of their national autonomy (or sovereignty). The least amount of sovereignty that must be surrendered to the trading bloc occurs in a free trade area. However, political union requires nations to give up a high degree of sovereignty in foreign policy. This is why political union is so hard to achieve.

3 Describe regional integration in *Europe* and explain how companies are adapting. The *European Coal and Steel Community* was formed in 1951 to remove trade barriers in coal, iron, steel, and scrap metal among the member nations. The members of the European Coal and Steel Community signed the Treaty of Rome in 1957 and created the *European Economic Community (EEC).* The treaty called for not only the elimination of tariffs between member nations and the creation of a common external tariff, but also the free internal movement of goods, services, labor, and capital. In 1967 the EEC broadened its scope and changed its name to the *European Community (EC)* and changed its name once again in 1994 to the *European Union (EU).*

In response to mounting disappointment in the mid-1980s, a proposal was made to eliminate all remaining obstacles to a common market by the end of 1992—it was called the *Single European Act (SEA).* The goal of the SEA was to increase the ability of European companies to compete against companies from Japan and North America. The SEA is generally considered to have benefited large EU firms most. However, small and medium-size companies were encouraged through EU institutions to engage in networking with one another to offset any negative consequences resulting from, for example, changing product standards. Although a great deal of standardization did occur following passage of the Act, problems remain for some companies outside the European Union.

The *Maastricht Treaty* took the European trading bloc beyond what many had believed possible. It called for banking in a single, common currency after January 1, 1999, and circulation of coins and paper currency on January 1, 2002. The treaty also called for political union of the member nations—including development of a common foreign and defense policy and common citizenship.

Today the European Union consists of 15 member nations and encompasses nearly all of Western Europe. Five institutions play important roles in monitoring and enforcing economic and political integration. (a) The European Council meets twice each year to discuss and resolve any policy issues such as foreign policy. (b) The European Commission has the task of drafting and implementing new legislation and ensure compliance by member nations. (c) The Council of Ministers votes on the passage of laws after receiving proposed legislation from the European Commission. (d) The European Parliament's main purpose is to debate and amend legislation proposed by the European Commission. (e) The Court of Justice hears cases in which a member nation is accused of not meeting its treaty obligations, and those in which the commission or council is charged with failing to live up to its responsibilities under the terms of a treaty.

④ Discuss regional integration in *the Americas* and analyze its future prospects. In January 1989, the *U.S.-Canada Free Trade Agreement* went into effect. The goal was to eliminate all tariffs on bilateral trade between Canada and the United States by 1998. The task of creating a North American trading bloc that included Mexico took on new urgency and resulted in the *North American Free Trade Agreement* (*NAFTA*), which became effective in January 1994. As a free trade agreement, NAFTA seeks to eliminate most tariffs and nontariff trade barriers on most goods originating from within North America by 2008.

The *Andean Community* was formed in 1969 and consists of Bolivia, Colombia, Ecuador, Peru, and Venezuela. The main objectives of the pact included tariff reduction for trade among member nations, a common external tariff, and common policies in both transportation and certain industries. However, the Andean Community was not very successful and its future potential is highly questionable. The *Latin American Integration Association* (*ALADI*) was formed in 1980 and consists of Mexico plus 10 South American nations. Although the agreement resulted in roughly 24 bilateral agreements and 5 subregional pacts, the agreements did not accomplish a great deal of cross-border trade.

MERCOSUR, or the *Southern Common Market*, was established in 1988 and includes Argentina, Brazil, Paraguay, and Uruguay. Bolivia and Chile are associate members. Chile is expected to receive full membership by the end of 1999 although Bolivia's full entry is some time off. Today MERCOSUR acts as a customs union and continues to make progress on trade and investment liberalization. It is emerging as the most powerful trading bloc in all of Latin America.

Attempts at economic integration in Central American countries and throughout the Caribbean basin have been much more modest than elsewhere in the Americas. The *Caribbean Community and Common Market* (*CARICOM*) trading bloc was formed in 1973. The main difficulty CARICOM faces is that most members trade more with nonmembers than they do with each other because members do not have the imports each needs. The *Central American Common Market* (*CACM*) was formed in 1961 to create a common market between Costa Rica, El Salvador, Guatemala, Honduras, and Nicaragua. Civil wars and wars among the members hampered progress for much of the existence of the CACM. But peace and renewed hope is driving expanded trade in recent years.

The objective of the *Free Trade Area of the Americas* (*FTAA*) is to create a trading bloc that reaches from the northern tip of Alaska to the southern tip of Tierra del Fuego, Argentina (excluding Cuba). The FTAA would remove tariffs and nontariff barriers between all member countries over an unspecified number of years once agreement is reached in 2005. The goal of a *Transatlantic Economic Partnership* (*TEP*) between the United States and the European Union is to contribute to stability, democracy, and development worldwide, in addition to forging closer economic ties between the two parties.

⑤ Characterize regional integration in *Asia* and discuss how it differs from integration elsewhere. The *Association of Southeast Asian Nations* (*ASEAN*), formed in 1967, has three main objectives: (a) to promote economic, cultural, and social development in the region; (b) to safeguard the region's economic and political stability; and (c) to serve as a forum in which differences can be resolved fairly and peacefully. Some inescapable facts about ASEAN include: (a) The ASEAN nations are culturally and politically diverse. (b) There are active black markets in Indonesia, the Philippines, and Vietnam, and bribery is common in many ASEAN countries. (c) Executives in ASEAN say companies could cut their transactional costs and enhance production strategies if ASEAN countries harmonized tariffs, quality and safety standards, customs regulations, and investment rules. Today ASEAN has 10 members.

The organization for *Asia Pacific Economic Cooperation* (*APEC*) was formed in 1989. Begun as an informal forum among 12 trading partners, APEC now has 21 members. Together, the APEC nations account for more than 45 percent of world trade and a combined GDP of more than $16 trillion. The stated aim of APEC was not to build another trading bloc. Instead, it desired to strengthen the multilateral trading system and expand the global economy by simplifying and liberalizing trade and investment procedures among member nations. More long term, APEC hopes to have free trade and investment throughout the region by 2010 for developed nations and 2020 for developing ones.

⑥ Explain regional integration in the *Middle East* and *Africa* and explain why progress there has been slow. Economic integration has not left out the Middle East and Africa although progress there is more limited than in any other geographic region. The biggest reason for limited success is the small size of the countries involved and their relatively low levels of development. The largest of these coalitions are the Gulf Cooperation Council and the Economic Community of West African States.

In response to the hostilities between Iraq and Iran, several Middle Eastern nations formed the *Gulf Cooperation Council* (*GCC*) in 1980. Members of the GCC are Bahrain, Kuwait, Oman, Qatar, Saudi Arabia, and the United Arab Emirates. The primary purpose of the GCC at its formation was to cooperate with the increasingly powerful trading blocs in Europe at the time—the EU and EFTA. However, it has become as much a political entity as an economic one as it has evolved. Its cooperative thrust allows citizens of member countries to travel freely without visas in the GCC. It also permits citizens of one member nation to own land, property, and businesses in any other member nation without the need for local sponsors or partners.

The *Economic Community of West African States* (*ECOWAS*) was formed in 1975 but relaunched its efforts at economic integration in 1992 because of a lack of early progress. One of the most important goals of ECOWAS is the formation of a customs union and eventual common market. Together, the ECOWAS nations comprise most of the economic activity in sub-Saharan Africa. The group's lack of progress on economic integration largely reflects each nation's lack of economic development.

questions for review

1. What is the ultimate goal of *regional economic integration*?

2. What are the *five levels*, or degrees, of regional integration? Briefly describe each one.

3. Identify three potential benefits of regional economic integration and three potential drawbacks.

4. Explain the difference between *trade creation* and *trade diversion*. Why are these two concepts important?

5. Identify at least two reasons for Europe's initial desires to form a regional trading bloc.

6. What impact is the *European Union* (*EU*) having on European companies? Non-European companies?

7. What is the *Maastricht Treaty*?

8. Identify the five main institutions of the European Union. Briefly describe the function each performs.

9. What is the *European Free Trade Association* (*EFTA*)?

10. What three countries belong to the *North American Free Trade Agreement* (*NAFTA*)?

11. What effect has NAFTA had on trade between these nations?

12. What is the *Andean Community*? Give one reason why it is behind schedule.

13. Who are the members of the *Southern Common Market* (*MERCOSUR*) trading bloc? Briefly describe how it has performed.

14. List the five nations that belong to the *Central American Common Market* (*CACM*). Why is it behind schedule?

15. What is the *Free Trade Area of the Americas* (*FTAA*)?

16. What is the *Transatlantic Economic Partnership* (*TEP*)? Identify its main goals.

17. What are the three main objectives of the *Association of Southeast Asian Nations* (*ASEAN*)?

18. How do the goals of the organization for *Asia Pacific Economic Cooperation* (*APEC*) differ from those of other regional blocs?

19. What is the *Gulf Cooperation Council*? Identify its six members.

20. What is the *Economic Community of West African States* (*ECOWAS*)? Explain why it has had limited success in achieving economic integration.

questions for discussion

1. It is likely that the proliferation and growth of regional trading blocs will continue into the foreseeable future. At what point do you think the integration process will stop (if ever)? Explain your answer.

2. Some people believe that the rise of regional trading blocs threatens free trade progress made by the General Agreement on Tariffs and Trade (GATT) and the World Trade Organization (WTO). Do you agree? Why or why not?

3. Certain groups of countries, particularly in Africa, are far less economically developed than other regions such as Europe and North America. What sort of integration arrangement do you think developed countries could create with less developed nations to improve living standards? Be as specific as you can.

in practice

In this chapter's discussion of regional economic integration, we learned about the proposed Free Trade Area of the Americas (FTAA). Read the following short excerpt from *Latin Trade* and answer the questions that follow.

Building Blocs

If the FTAA is a success, it will be because people in the smaller economies are willing to do the hard work of adapting to free markets. Says Jamaica's ambassador to the United States, "Let's say we all produce sugar, so you will have competition between the smallest, poorest country and the largest, richest country."

Such disparities may strengthen the movement toward the formation of subregional blocs among smaller groups of nations that then harmonize rules with each other. "The FTAA brings together countries and economies of all shapes and sizes," says Jaime Garcia, Peru's former vice minister of industry. "That lends itself toward subregional trade blocs."

1. Small companies in small nations that take part in regional trade agreements typically cannot compete with large multinational companies from industrialized nations. How would you propose that small nations help their small companies adapt to the fierce competition such agreements often create?

2. Do you think by forming subregional trade blocs that small countries can really strengthen their negotiating positions against large nations? Why or why not? Do you think that very small nations should even participate in regional trade agreements with very large nations? Why or why not?

3. Do you think that the FTAA will help lift the living standards for people in the smallest countries (such as Ecuador or Nicaragua) or will it only be a boon for the largest nations such as Brazil, Canada, and the United States?

4. Do you think subregional or regional trade agreements cause instability on a subregional, regional, or global scale, or do you believe they foster cooperation? Explain your answer.

5. After all you've read in this chapter about regional trade agreements, what is your assessment of their value? Should their progress continue or be rolled back?

projects

1. Some analysts believe that NAFTA can extend its current arrangement to more advanced levels of economic integration. In small groups of several students or more, discuss the obstacles that NAFTA nations might face as they seek to bring other nations into their fold. Discuss whether political integration is a possibility.

2. Go to your library or link to a business information service on the Internet. Locate an article or two that describe how a large international company is coping with regional economic integration. Write a one-page report on how the company is responding to the integration. Are the company's strategies paying off or are there problems? Describe the factors behind the company's success or problems.

3. In this project, two groups of four students debate the advantages and disadvantages of regional economic integration. After the first student from each side has spoken, the second student questions the opponent's arguments, looking for holes and inconsistencies. The third student attempts to answer these arguments. The fourth student presents a summary of each side's arguments. Finally, the class votes on which team has offered the more compelling argument.

business case 8
TAINTED TRADE: INCREASING IMPORTS BRINGS INCREASE IN ILLNESS

Today, Americans in the dead of a Minnesota winter can indulge their cravings for summer-fresh raspberries. Europeans who are thousands of miles away from North America can put Mexican mangoes in their breakfast cereal. Japanese shoppers can buy radishes that were grown from seeds cultivated in Oregon. Eating fresh and natural produce is a growing consumer trend, and the globalization of the food industry and the liberalization of markets have now made it possible for people to choose from produce grown all over the world. Unfortunately, these forces have also made it more likely that these same consumers will get debilitating—and even deadly—illnesses from food-borne pathogens.

In the United States several outbreaks linked to the burgeoning global trade in produce have made headlines in recent years. In 1996 and 1997, for instance, 2,300 people were victims of a parasite called cyclospora that had hitched a ride on raspberries grown in Guatemala. Outbreaks of Hepatitis A and salmonella from tainted strawberries and alfalfa sprouts, respectively, have also alarmed consumers. Although health officials say that there is no evidence that imports are inherently more dangerous, they do cite some real reasons for worry. For one thing, imported produce often comes from countries where food hygiene and basic sanitation are less advanced. For another, some microbes that cause no damage in their home country are deadly when introduced on foreign soil. Finally, the longer the journey from farm to table, the more chance of contamination. Just consider the journey taken by the salmonella-ridden alfalfa sprouts: The seeds for the sprouts were bought from Uganda and Pakistan, among other nations, shipped through the Netherlands, flown into New York, and trucked all around the United States.

Food contamination incidences show no signs of abating. Since the passage of NAFTA, U.S. food imports have doubled to 30 billion tons. Over the same time period, federal inspections of those imports by the Food and Drug Administration have dropped to less than half what they were. The increase in imports has clearly strained the U.S. food-safety system, which was built one hundred years ago for a world contained within the country's own borders. Although it isn't feasible for the United States to plant FDA inspectors in every country, the Clinton administration proposed another measure that would make trading partners dance to the FDA's tune. In October 1997, it was announced that the administration would ask Congress to require federal regulators to ban imports of fruit and vegetables from countries that did not meet expanded U.S. food-safety standards. It would also ask for more money for the FDA to enable it to hire investigators to inspect not just produce but also farming methods and government safety systems in other countries. Countries that blocked the new inspections would be forbidden to sell fruit and vegetables in the United States, the administration said. The proposal is likely to irk trading partners of the United States and is certain to be only the beginning of a worldwide debate on food safety and trade.

thinking globally

1. How do you think that countries with a high volume of exports to the United States, such as Mexico, will respond to this proposal? Do you think it is a good way to stem the tide of food-related illnesses? Why or why not?

2. Sue Doneth of Marshall, Michigan, is a mother of one of the schoolchildren who was exposed to the Hepatitis A virus after eating tainted frozen strawberry desserts. She spoke to Congress and said, "We are forcing consumers to trade the health and safety of their families for free trade. That is not fair trade. NAFTA is not a trade issue: it is a safety issue." Do you think food-safety regulations should be built into an extension of NAFTA? Why or why not? What are the benefits and drawbacks of putting food-safety regulations into international trade pacts?

3. The lack of harmonized food-safety practices and standards is just one of the challenges faced by the food industry as it becomes more global. What other challenges face the food industry in an era of economic integration and opening markets?

a question of ethics

1. Jagdish Bhagwati said the term *free trade agreements* in describing NAFTA or the European Union is misleading. Bhagwati says these agreements are really "preferential trade agreements" that offer free trade only to members—ensuring free trade for members and relative protection against non-members. Is this happening to the Caribbean nations who were excluded from NAFTA? A 1997 World Bank study warned that Mexico could gobble up as much as one third of the Caribbean's $12.5 billion in exports to the United States. Some argue that from apparel factories in Jamaica to sugar cane fields in Trinidad, NAFTA has cost jobs, market share, and income for the vulnerable island nations of the region. According to the Caribbean Textile Apparel Institute, more than 150 apparel plants closed in the Caribbean and 123,000 jobs have been lost "as a direct result of trade and investment diversion to Mexico." Given the impact on nonmember nations, do you think such "preferential trade agreements" are ethical? Do you think trade is ever truly "free" between nations? Why do you think islands in the Caribbean basin were not invited to be part of NAFTA? Imagine yourself as a member of the U.S. Congress. Make an argument for including the Caribbean or excluding it from an extension of NAFTA.[46]

2. Pan-European marketing is inhibited not only by different cultural preferences in each EU country but also by various restrictions each country places on advertising. For instance, Greece and Sweden ban all advertising aimed at children, and France outlaws all alcohol and tobacco advertising. The internal market directorate of the European Commission is working on a green paper that would require rewriting all laws that restrict cross-border marketing in the EU—such as Greece's ban on toy advertising. Business leaders supporting the directorate see national advertising restrictions as measures designed to protect countries' domestic industries. How is it possible to know whether such restrictions are the result of ethical concerns or are really protective measures? Do you think that a nation's ethical concerns, such as the impact of advertising on children or the promotion of tobacco and alcohol, should be superseded by regional trade agreements that strive for unified standards and more open trade? Why or why not?[47]

3. Labor unions and environmentalists in the United States aren't the only ones to speak out against NAFTA. There continues to be opposition in Mexico by those who fear a loss of national sovereignty and who feel that the income gap between the two countries will never be narrowed. Average hourly wage on the U.S. side of the border in El Paso, Texas, is $7.71 compared to $1.36 on the Mexican side in Ciudad Juarez. Mexican critics argue that their entire country will be subsumed by companies from the United States that do not contribute to Mexico's economic growth or higher standard of living, but who instead use Mexico as a low-cost assembly site while keeping high-paying, high-skilled jobs at home. Do you think there are ways in which trade agreements can help close the economic gap between poor and wealthy partners? Or will the interests of poorer nations always be subordinate to wealthier countries within regional trading blocs?[48]

integrative video case
PART THREE: INTERNATIONAL TRADE AND INVESTMENT
rollerblade, sebago shoes, and nivea

background

This video looks at Rollerblade and Sebago Shoes, two U.S.-based companies, and NIVEA, a company based in Germany, each of which conducts business throughout the world. Products from all three companies share aspects of the international product life cycle, and all three companies face similar situations. For example, should they undertake foreign direct investment and build manufacturing facilities in other countries? Until now, each company has survived international competition by producing high-quality products. But now each company must decide on the future course of action it will take.

The video discusses the international product life cycle and illustrates what that cycle means in terms of survival and success in the international environment. You will see how Sebago Shoes and Rollerblade have been successful outside the United States and how NIVEA has succeeded in the U.S. market. You will be able to appreciate how certain types of companies have a competitive advantage over other types and how companies from certain countries have a competitive advantage over companies from other countries. Furthermore, you will understand and appreciate how companies conduct business in an era of regional integration.

yahoo!

For information on this company, please refer to the video case for Part I, page 30.

rollerblade, inc.

Rollerblade is a privately held company, based in Minnetonka, Minnesota, whose products are distributed worldwide. In 1980, it developed its skates as an off-season training tool for hockey players, and the skates were quickly taken up by skiers. In 1986, the company redefined and expanded the in-line skate market to include fitness

enthusiasts, recreation seekers, and cross-training athletes from numerous sports. Today, with an estimated 30 million participants, in-line skating has truly come into its own as a sport. Rollerblade, the pioneer of in-line skating, continues to lead the in-line skate industry. It has a majority market share, whereas none of the other 30-plus in-line skate companies have more than a 10% share.

sebago shoes

Shoe manufacturer Sebago Shoes was established in Portland, Maine, in 1946. From the very beginning, Sebago Shoes earned a reputation for its high-quality, hand-made shoes. Although as a small company Sebago Shoes dealt primarily in the U.S. market, it soon started exporting its shoes to the world. Today, the company competes against traditional giants in the shoe industry from countries including Italy, France, Spain, and the Czech Republic. Retailers in 73 countries now carry Sebago Shoes.

nivea

In 1911, Oskar Toplowitz, the owner of Beiersdorf (the German company that manufactures NIVEA), started the development of a skin cream based on new ingredients. He named it NIVEA from the Latin word *nivius*, meaning "snow white." During the 1930s, the company became more visible by introducing products such as shaving cream, facial toner, and shampoo. Following World War II, NIVEA's trademarks were taken over by companies from the countries against which Germany fought. Soon after the war ended, Beiersdorf set about buying back the trademark rights, a process finally completed in 1997. In the 1950s the NIVEA brand became increasingly well-known in many countries, and soon grew into the umbrella brand for a wide range of skin-care products. From the 1960s through the 1980s, NIVEA concentrated on getting its products into markets worldwide, and it succeeded handsomely.

discussion questions

While you watch the video, keep the following questions in mind. You might want to take notes.

1. How could a company such as Rollerblade maintain its international market share through product design and development?

2. How could regional economic integration in Europe help a non-EU company such as Sebago Shoes succeed?

3. Could companies such as Rollerblade, NIVEA, and Yahoo! succeed in regionally integrated economies such as the Middle East and Africa? Why or why not?

4. Describe the international product life cycle for the products of the four companies shown in this video. What are their similarities and differences?

5. How did NIVEA, a German company, become successful in the United States? Use the theory of national competitive advantage to analyze NIVEA, Rollerblade, and Sebago Shoes.

student exercises

1. Break into groups of two or three students. Consider the goods or services of the four companies in the video. Describe their product life cycles, and determine what each company must do to sustain its international success.

2. Compare the different economic regions of the world and determine which ones are most attractive in terms of foreign direct investment. Give reasons for your choices.

6. What role does the government play in terms of Yahoo!'s presence in the French market?

3. Select several countries from various regions of the world, and list the most important goods and services they export and import. How does each country benefit from the others in terms of what they trade? What trade restrictions do they impose on one another?

9 international financial markets

Beacons

A Look Back

CHAPTER 8 introduced the ongoing process of regional economic integration among countries in several areas of the world. We saw how international companies are responding to the challenges and opportunities that regional integration is creating.

A Look at This Chapter

This chapter introduces us to the international financial system by describing the structure of international financial markets. We learn first about the international capital market and its main components. We then turn to the foreign exchange market, explaining how it works and outlining its structure.

A Look Ahead

CHAPTER 10 concludes our study of the international financial system. We discuss the factors that influence exchange rates and explain why and how governments and other institutions try to manage exchange rates. In so doing, we focus on recent currency problems in Asia, Russia, and emerging markets worldwide.

Learning Objectives

After studying this chapter, you should be able to

1. Discuss the purposes, development, and financial centers of the *international capital market*.
2. Describe the *international bond*, *international equity*, and *Eurocurrency markets*.
3. Discuss the four primary functions of the *foreign exchange market*.
4. Explain how currencies are *quoted* and different *rates* given.
5. Identify the main *instruments* and *institutions* of the foreign exchange market.
6. Explain why and how governments restrict *currency convertibility*.

Hamid Mazloomi, still in his twenties, is already a seasoned veteran of the currency markets. "If you want to send money to Frankfurt, we just make a phone call," he says. "We deal in all currencies." He is not speaking from New York, London, or Tokyo, but rather from Peshawar, Pakistan, roughly 30 miles from the Afghanistan border.

Mazloomi and 350 other currency traders belong to Peshawar's Currency Sarafar (money-changing) Association. He can deliver huge payments to Afghanistan, Australia, Germany, Pakistan, Russia, the United Kingdom, and the United States. He does all his business with one phone line and the help of a large extended family that is spread throughout the world.

Peshawar is quickly becoming the linchpin of a regional currency market. Anywhere from $100,000 to $3 million worth of currency is traded there every day. Currency traders in the world's busiest financial centers rely on increasingly complex contracts and the latest technology to do their jobs. But in Peshawar, about the only technology used are mobile phones for relaying the latest currency prices to traders literally out in the street. In Peshawar, there is no need for lawyers and fancy contracts because individual honor is enough—a slap of hands seals a deal.[1]

Well-functioning financial markets are an essential element of the international business environment. They funnel money from organizations and economies with excess funds to those with shortages. International financial markets also allow companies to exchange one currency for another. Such exchanges, as well as the rates at which currencies are exchanged, are critical to international business.

Suppose, for example, you purchase a CD player imported from a company based in the Philippines. Whether or not you realize it, the price you paid for that CD player was affected by the *exchange rate* between your country's currency and the Philippine peso. Ultimately, the Filipino company that sold you the CD player must convert the purchase made in your currency into Philippine pesos. Thus the profit earned by the Filipino company also is influenced by the exchange rate between your currency and the peso. Managers must understand how changes in currency values—and thus in exchange rates—affect the profitability of their international business activities. Among other things, managers at our hypotetical company in the Philippines must know how much to charge you for their CD player.

In this chapter, we launch our study of the international financial system by exploring the structure of the international financial markets. The two interrelated systems that comprise the international financial markets are:

1. The international capital market
2. The foreign exchange market

We start by examining the purposes of the international capital market and tracing its recent development. We then take a detailed look at the international bond, equity, and Eurocurrency markets, each of which helps companies to borrow and lend money internationally. Understanding these issues lays the groundwork for our discussion, in Chapter 14, of the sources from which companies obtain the financial resources they need to fund their investment projects. We then introduce the foreign exchange market (an international market for currencies), which facilitates international business transactions.

INTERNATIONAL CAPITAL MARKET

capital market
System that allocates financial resources in the form of debt and equity according to their most efficient uses.

A **capital market** is a system that allocates financial resources in the form of debt and equity according to their most efficient uses. Its main purpose is to provide a mechanism through which those wishing to borrow or invest money can do so efficiently. Individuals, companies, governments, mutual funds, pension funds, and all types of nonprofit organizations participate in capital markets. An individual, for example, might want to buy her first home; a midsize company might want to add production capacity; and a government may want to develop a new fiber optic telecommunications system. Sometimes these individuals and organizations have excess cash to lend; at other times, they need funds.

PURPOSES OF NATIONAL CAPITAL MARKETS

There are two primary means by which companies obtain external financing: *debt* and *equity*. Capital markets function to help them obtain both types of financing. To understand the international capital market fully, however, we need to review the purposes of capital markets in domestic economies. Quite simply, national capital markets help individuals and institutions borrow the money that other individuals and institutions want to lend. Although in theory borrowers could search individually for various parties willing to lend or invest, this would be a time-consuming process. Consequently, intermediaries of all kinds exist to facilitate financial exchanges. Most of us are familiar with the most common capital-market intermediaries:

➡ *Commercial banks* lend borrowers their investors' deposits at a specific rate of interest. They provide loans for new investment projects and may help to finance a firm's import or export activities.

➡ *Investment banks* help clients to invest excess capital and borrow needed capital. They act as *agents*, introducing clients to organizations that provide either investment or borrowing opportunities.

Role of Debt   **Debt** consists of loans in which the borrower promises to repay the borrowed amount (the *principal*) plus a predetermined rate of *interest*. Company debt normally takes the form of **bonds**—instruments specifying the timing of principal and interest payments. The holder of a bond (the *lender*) can force the borrower into bankruptcy if the borrower fails to pay on a timely basis. Bonds issued for the purpose of funding investments are commonly issued by private sector companies and by municipal, regional, and national governments.

Role of Equity   **Equity** is part ownership of a company in which the equity holder participates with other part owners in the company's financial gains and losses. Equity normally takes the form of **stock**—shares of ownership in a company's assets that give *shareholders* (or *stockholders*) a claim on the company's future cash flows. Shareholders may be rewarded with *dividends*—payments made out of surplus funds—or by increases in the value of their shares. Of course, they may also suffer losses due to poor company performance—and thus decreases in the value of their shares. Dividend payments are not guaranteed but determined by the company's board of directors and based on financial performance. In capital markets, shareholders can either sell one company's stock for that of another or *liquidate* them—exchange them for cash. **Liquidity**, which is a feature of both debt and equity markets, refers to the ease with which bondholders and shareholders may convert their investments into cash.

PURPOSES OF THE INTERNATIONAL CAPITAL MARKET

The **international capital market** is a network of individuals, companies, financial institutions, and governments that invest and borrow across national boundaries. It consists of both formal exchanges (where buyers and sellers meet to trade financial instruments) and electronic networks (where trading occurs anonymously). This market makes use of unique and innovative financial instruments specially designed to fit the needs of investors and borrowers located in different countries who are doing business with one another. Large international banks play a central role in the international capital market. They gather the excess cash of investors and savers around the world, then channel this cash to borrowers across the globe.

Expanding the Money Supply for Borrowers   The international capital market is a conduit for joining borrowers and lenders in different national capital markets. Thus a company unable to obtain funds from investors in its own nation can seek financing from investors elsewhere and thereby undertake an otherwise impossible investment project. The option of going outside the home nation is particularly important to firms in countries with small or developing capital markets of their own—particularly those with emerging stock markets. An expanded supply of money also benefits small but promising companies that might not otherwise get financing if there is an intense competition for capital.

debt
Loans in which the borrower promises to repay the borrowed amount (the principal*) plus a predetermined rate of interest.*

bond
Debt instrument specifying the timing of principal and interest payments.

equity
Part ownership of a company in which the equity holder participates with other part owners in the company's financial gains and losses.

stock
Shares of ownership in a company's assets that give shareholders a claim on the company's future cash flows.

liquidity
Ease with which bondholders and shareholders may convert their investments into cash.

international capital market
Network of individuals, companies, financial institutions, and governments that invest and borrow across national boundaries.

Reducing the Cost of Money to Borrowers   An expanded money supply reduces the cost of borrowing. Like the prices of potatoes, wheat, and other commodities, the "price" of money is determined by supply and demand. If its supply increases, its price—in the form of interest rates—falls. Thus excess supply creates a buyer's (borrower's) market, forcing down interest rates and the cost of borrowing. Projects regarded as infeasible because of low expected returns might be viable at a lower financing cost.

Reducing Risk for Lenders   The international capital market expands the available set of lending opportunities. In turn, an expanded set of opportunities helps reduce risk for lenders (investors) in two ways:

1. *Investors enjoy a greater set of opportunities from which to choose.* They can thus reduce overall portfolio risk by spreading their money over a greater number of debt and equity instruments. In other words, if one investment loses money, the loss can be offset by gains elsewhere.
2. *Investing in international securities benefits investors because some economies are growing while others are in decline.* For example, prices of bonds in Thailand and Kazakhstan do not follow bond-price fluctuations in the United States, which are independent of prices in Hungary.[2] In short, investors reduce risk by holding international securities whose prices move independently.

Unfortunately, small would-be borrowers still face some serious problems in trying to secure loans. In particular, interest rates are often high and many entrepreneurs have nothing to put up as collateral. But as you can see from the Entrepreneurial Focus "Where Microcredit Is Due," some unique methods are available for getting capital into the hands of small businesspeople—particularly in developing nations.

Entrepreneurial Focus

Where Microcredit Is Due

Obtaining capital challenges the entrepreneurial spirit in many developing countries. If a person is lucky enough to obtain a loan, it is typically from a loan shark whose inordinate interest rates devour most of the entrepreneur's profits. However, an alternative money-lending practice is growing in popularity. In obtaining *microcredit*, small groups of low-income entrepreneurs borrow money at competitive rates without having to put up collateral. Besides being collateral-free, microcredit offers the following advantages:

Borrowers Sink or Swim Together   For better or worse, group members are joined at the economic hip: If a member fails to pay off a loan, everyone may lose future credit. Often, however, peer pressure and support help to defend against this contingency. In addition, strong family ties in developing countries tend to furnish important support networks.

Most Loans Go to Women   Although outreach to male borrowers is increasing, most microcredit borrowers are women. Women tend to be better at funneling profits into family nutrition, clothing, and education, as well as business expansion. The successful use of microcredit in Bangladesh has increased wages, community income, and the status of women. One local bank that has already loaned $450 million to 2.1 million borrowers enjoys a 98 percent on-time payback record.

It Might Even Work in Developed Countries   The microcredit concept was pioneered in developed countries as a way for developing countries to create the foundation for a market economy. Nowadays, the use of microcredit within developed nations might be a way to spur economic growth in depressed geographic areas, such as inner cities. But whereas microcredit loans in developing countries typically average less than $100, those in developed nations average a minimum of at least $500.

FORCES EXPANDING THE INTERNATIONAL CAPITAL MARKET

Thirty-five years ago, national capital markets functioned largely as independent markets. But since that time, the amount of debt, equity, and currencies traded internationally has increased dramatically. This rapid growth can be traced to three main factors: (1) *information technology*, (2) *deregulation*, and (3) *innovative financial instruments*.

Information Technology   Information is the lifeblood of every nation's capital market. Investors need information about new investment opportunities and corresponding risk levels.

Large investments in information technology over the past two decades have drastically reduced the costs, in both time and money, of communicating around the globe. Investors and borrowers can now respond in record time to breaking news in the international capital market. The introduction of electronic trading after the daily close of formal exchanges also facilitates faster response times.

e·biz

Ironically, financial institutions in emerging economies sometimes integrate information technology into their financial services even sooner than their counterparts in more developed countries. For example, Thailand's Thai Farmers Bank invested heavily in information technology and sent its vice president of research and development to the United States to find out how its system compared. To his surprise, Ampol Polohakul discovered that Thai Farmers was far ahead of its U.S. counterparts, mainly because it had implemented state-of-the-art technology right from the beginning.[3]

Deregulation   Deregulation of national capital markets has been instrumental in the expansion of the international capital market. Regulation reached its high-water mark in the early 1970s. The need for deregulation became apparent when heavily regulated markets in the largest countries were facing fierce competition from less regulated markets in smaller nations. Subsequent deregulation increased competition, lowered the cost of financial transactions, and opened many national markets to global investing and borrowing.

Continued growth in the international capital market depends on further deregulation. For instance, although Japan talked about deregulation for years, only a devastating

In the decade leading up to the late 1990s, Japanese banks overinvested, racking up $1 trillion in "doubtful" loans. As banks pulled back on new loans, blue-chip companies suffered in turn, and unemployment rose to a post-World War II high of 3.5%. While the government debated whether to merge or close failing banks, many Japanese, like this couple, decided that an at-home safe was preferable to risking their savings for the standard 0.1% interest rate at a shaky Tokyo bank. For updates on how the Japanese economy is performing, see the Bank of Japan's Web site at ⟨**www.boj.or.jp**⟩.

economic slump in the late 1990s finally forced the Japanese government and banking industry to undertake serious reforms. Pension funds, for example, were allowed to invest in riskier assets. Subsequently, $20 billion flowed into the Japanese branch offices of the largest international investment-management companies, such as Morgan Stanley and Goldman Sachs. However, the dismantling of Japan's heavily regulated financial structure will no doubt be painful. The elimination of weak players through competition and consolidation will mean, among other things, loss of jobs.[4]

Financial Instruments   Greater competition in the financial industry is creating the need to develop *innovative financial instruments*. One result of the need for new types of financial instruments is **securitization**—the unbundling and repackaging of hard-to-trade financial assets into more liquid, negotiable, and marketable financial instruments (or *securities*).

> **securitization**
> *Unbundling and repackaging of hard-to-trade financial assets into more liquid, negotiable, and marketable financial instruments (or securities).*

A mortgage loan from a bank, for instance, is not liquid or negotiable because it is a customized contract between the bank and the borrower: Banks cannot sell loans and thus raise capital for further investment because each loan differs from every other loan. Consider, however, the function of U.S. government agencies such as the Federal National Mortgage Association and the General National Mortgage Association. These agencies guarantee mortgages against default and thus accumulate them as pools of assets. In turn, they sell securities in capital markets that are backed by these mortgage pools. When mortgage bankers participate in this process, they are able to raise capital for further investment.[5] The prices of such securities are based on the future expected values of their underlying financial instruments. Securitized bonds then trade on the market in much the same way as do other bonds.[6]

WORLD FINANCIAL CENTERS

The world's three most important financial centers are London, New York, and Tokyo. With the advent of a single European currency (the *euro*) in 1999, Europe's financial markets may eventually merge into three or four electronically linked financial zones. Officials at traditional exchanges worry that information technology may make formal European stock exchanges obsolete. Indeed, unless they continue to modernize, cut costs, and provide new customer services, they might be rendered obsolete by trading on the Internet and other new electronic systems. In Paris, French stock exchange authorities hosted a lavish two-day conference to tout new technological wizardry and remind the global investment community that Paris's financial markets are accommodating the euro.[7]

e·biz

> **offshore financial center**
> *Country or territory whose financial sector features very few regulations and few, if any, taxes.*

e·biz

Offshore Financial Centers   An **offshore financial center** is a country or territory whose financial sector features very few regulations and few, if any, taxes. These centers tend to be characterized by economic and political stability and usually provide access to the international capital market through an excellent telecommunications infrastructure. As we will see in Chapter 10, most governments protect their own currencies by restricting the amount of activity that domestic companies can conduct in foreign currencies. Therefore, companies often find it hard to borrow funds in foreign currencies and so turn to offshore centers, which offer large amounts of funding in currencies other than their own. Moreover, the profits borrowers earn on these funds are then taxed at the lower or nonexistent rates of the offshore centers. In short, offshore centers are sources of funding (and usually cheaper funding) for companies with multinational operations.

Offshore financial centers fall into two categories:

➡ *Operational centers* see a great deal of financial activity. Prominent operational centers include London (which does a good deal of currency trading) and Switzerland (which supplies a great deal of investment capital to other nations).

➡ *Booking centers* are usually located on small island nations or territories with favorable tax and/or secrecy laws. Little financial activity takes place here. Rather, funds simply pass through on their way to large operational centers. In fact, booking centers are typically home to offshore branches of domestic banks that use them merely as bookkeeping facilities to record tax and currency-exchange information.[8] Some important booking centers are the Cayman Islands and the Bahamas in the Caribbean; Gibraltar, Monaco, and the Channel Islands in Europe; Bahrain in the Middle East; and Singapore in Southeast Asia.

Increasingly, offshore centers are attracting attention in the rapidly expanding world of electronic commerce. Anguilla, a small Caribbean island belonging to the United Kingdom, is attempting to become a center for Internet-based companies. How? In Anguilla, such firms are allowed to do all the electronic commerce they want via the Internet and pay no taxes on their profits. To meet one "Webpreneur" who is already working to attract business to Anguilla, see his Web site at ⟨**www.offshore.com.ai**⟩.[9]

e·biz

Now that we have covered the basic features of the international capital market, let's take a closer look at its main components: the *international bond*, *international equity*, and *Eurocurrency markets*. We will explain more fully how companies take advantage of these markets to finance various investment projects in Chapter 14.

MAIN COMPONENTS OF THE INTERNATIONAL CAPITAL MARKET

INTERNATIONAL BOND MARKET

The **international bond market** consists of all bonds sold by issuing companies, governments, or other organizations *outside their own countries*. Issuing bonds internationally is an increasingly popular way to raise needed funding. Typical buyers include medium- to large-size banks, pension funds, mutual funds, and governments with excess financial reserves. Large international investment banks such as Morgan Stanley, Chase Manhattan, and Salomon Brothers typically manage the sales of new international bond issues for corporate and government clients.

international bond market
Market consisting of all bonds sold by issuing companies, governments, or other organizations outside their own countries.

Growth of the International Bond Market   The international bond market is growing very rapidly. From 1992 through 1996, total worldwide volume of international bonds grew over 10 percent per year, to $2.4 trillion at the end of 1996.[10] Issuance of *new* international bonds grew from $454 billion in 1995 to $680 billion in 1996 and to $746 billion in 1997.[11] In 1996 alone, the 20 largest borrowers in the world raised more than $250 billion on the international bond market.[12] Figure 9.1 shows the worldwide issuance of new international bonds by currency and by issuer's location.

Throughout much of the 1990s, the most important factor fueling growth in the international bond market was low interest rates (in other words, the cost of borrowing money). Low interest rates in developed nations resulted from low levels of inflation but also meant that investors were earning little interest on bonds issued by governments and companies in domestic markets.[13] Thus banks, pension funds, and mutual funds sought higher returns in the newly industrialized and developing nations, where

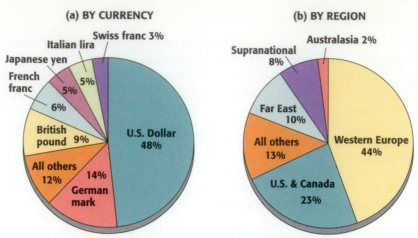

FIGURE 9.1

NEW ISSUANCE OF INTERNATIONAL BONDS

The U.S. dollar continues to dominate the international bond market, with the German mark coming in a distant second. But Western Europe continues to issue a greater volume of international bonds than any other market.

(a) BY CURRENCY

Swiss franc 3%
Italian lira 5%
Japanese yen 5%
French franc 6%
British pound 9%
All others 12%
German mark 14%
U.S. Dollar 48%

(b) BY REGION

Australasia 2%
Supranational 8%
Far East 10%
All others 13%
Western Europe 44%
U.S. & Canada 23%

Supranational includes international and global institutions; *Western Europe* includes Austria, Belgium, Channel Islands, Denmark, Ireland, Finland, France, Germany, Greece, Italy, Luxembourg, Netherlands, Norway, Portugal, Spain, Sweden, Switzerland, and the United Kingdom; the *Far East* includes China, Hong Kong, Indonesia, Japan, South Korea, Malaysia, Philippines, Singapore, Taiwan, and Thailand; *Australasia* includes Australia and New Zealand.

higher interest payments reflected the greater risk of the bonds. At the same time, corporate and government borrowers in developing countries badly needed capital to invest in corporate expansion plans and public works projects. As the demand for money outstripped the supply, interest rates in these markets went even higher.

This situation raises an interesting question: How can investors seeking higher returns and borrowers seeking to pay lower interest rates both come out ahead? The answer, at least in part, lies in the international bond market:

➡ By issuing bonds in the international bond market, borrowers from newly industrialized and developing countries can borrow money from other nations where interest rates are lower.

➡ By the same token, investors in developed countries buy bonds in newly industrialized and developing nations in order to obtain higher returns on their investments (although they also accept greater risk).

In this way, high interest rates outside the developed nations have fueled increased activity in the international bond market. Figure 9.2 shows the growth that has taken place in the flow of private debt capital into emerging markets from commercial banks and other institutions.

One country currently attracting investors to what specialists call "the outer frontier" of bond issuance is Nicaragua. Yielding a whopping 17 percent per year—compared to 6.6 percent on U.S. treasury bonds—Nicaraguan bonds offer the highest returns of any dollar-linked sovereign issue. Moreover, the Nicaraguan government has never missed an interest payment. Not surprisingly, there is a catch: Your broker may have to cold-call Nicaraguan farmers in order to fill your order, and in order to collect your interest checks, you must bring your bond certificates to the Finance Ministry in Managua. Why farmers? The bonds are compensation bonds issued to Nicaraguans whose property was nationalized by the Marxist government that ruled the country in the 1980s. Rather than resettle thousands of people, the pro-market government that took over in 1990 gave affected citizens bonds for everything from office buildings and cotton crops to confiscated chickens. Today, about 40 percent of the estimated $444 million in compensation bonds are believed to be held by U.S. and European

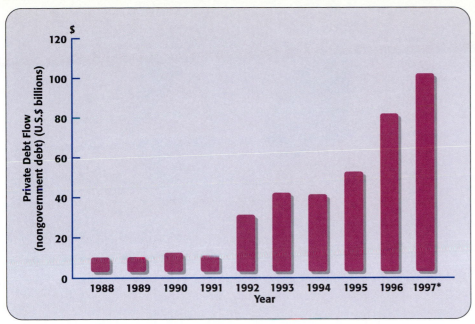

FIGURE 9.2

DEBT FLOWS INTO EMERGING MARKETS

The flow of debt capital into emerging markets has risen dramatically since the late 1980s. Flows in 1997 would certainly have been greater had it not been for the Asian economic crisis in 1997 and its effect on other markets.

*estimate

investors. Traders are salivating at the prospect of another $200 million that may be issued to settle a $1.5 billion backlog in property claims.[14]

Even though the international bond market is thriving, many emerging countries see the need to develop their own national markets. Volatility in the global currency market—such as the drop in value of several major Southeast Asian currencies in 1997 and 1998—can wreak havoc when projects earning funds in Indonesian rupiahs or Philippine pesos must pay off debts in dollars. Why? A drop in a country's currency forces borrowers to shell out more local currency to pay off the interest owed on bonds denominated in an unaffected currency. In the long run, argues Arvind Mathur, head of the Asian Development Bank's capital markets team, "It simply doesn't make sense to borrow abroad for these types of projects."[15]

INTERNATIONAL EQUITY MARKET

The **international equity market** consists of all stocks bought and sold outside the issuer's home country. Both companies and governments frequently sell shares in the international equity market. Buyers include other companies, banks, mutual funds, pension funds, and individual investors. Stock exchanges listing the greatest number of companies from outside their own borders are Frankfurt, London, and New York. Large international companies frequently list their stocks on several national exchanges simultaneously and sometimes offer new stock issues only outside their country's borders.

Growth of the International Equity Market   The volume of *new* international equities issued by companies and governments rose from $49 billion in 1992 to $113 billion in 1996—an average annual increase of over 14 percent.[16] In 1996, private companies alone raised more than $80 billion by selling stocks in the international equity market.[17] Estimates for 1997 ($73 billion for the first three quarters) show that the economic crisis in Asia probably caused a decline in the issues for that year.[18] Figure 9.3 shows the worldwide issuance of new international equity by currency and by issuer's location. As we will see in the following sections, four factors are responsible for most of this growth.

international equity market
Market consisting of all stocks bought and sold outside the issuer's home country.

FIGURE 9.3

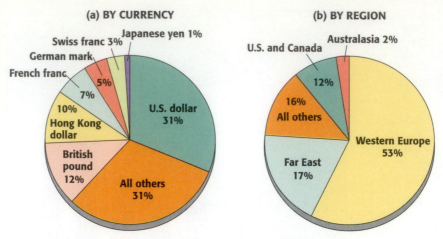

Most new international equity continues to be issued in the U.S. dollar, although the Hong Kong dollar is increasingly popular. Companies in the United States are not likely to issue international equity due to the world dominance of U.S. stock exchanges (Figure 9.3b). On the other hand, Western Europe is aggressively listing shares internationally.

(a) BY CURRENCY

(b) BY REGION

Western Europe includes Austria, Belgium, Channel Islands, Denmark, Ireland, Finland, France, Germany, Greece, Italy, Luxembourg, Netherlands, Norway, Portugal, Spain, Sweden, Switzerland, and the United Kingdom; the *Far East* includes China, Hong Kong, Indonesia, Japan, South Korea, Malaysia, Philippines, Singapore, Taiwan, and Thailand; *Australasia* includes Australia and New Zealand.

Spread of Privatization With many countries continuing to abandon central planning and socialist-style economics, the worldwide pace of *privatization* is accelerating. A single privatization often places billions of dollars of new equity on stock markets. The government of Peru, for instance, recently conducted the largest cross-border stock sale in all of Latin America: By selling its 26 percent share of the national telephone company, Telefonica del Peru, it raised $1.2 billion. Of the total value of the sale, 48 percent was sold in the United States, 26 percent to other international investors, and another 26 percent to domestic retail and institutional investors in Peru.[19]

Increased privatization in Europe is also expanding worldwide equity. Although historically more devoted to debt as a means of financing, Europe has more recently discovered the value of equity, and as investors grow more willing to accept increased risks in anticipation of higher returns, an "equity culture" is beginning to take root. In addition, as the European Union becomes more thoroughly integrated, investors are becoming more willing to invest in the stocks of companies from other European nations. Today, most European investors still base 80 percent of their decision on the national origin of a particular stock and only 20 percent on its economic sector. Experts, however, predict a future about-face, when 80 percent of investors' decisions will hinge on a given stock's economic sector.[20]

Economic Growth in Developing Countries Continued economic growth in newly industrialized and developing countries is also contributing to growth in the international equity market. As companies based in emerging economies succeed and grow, they require greater investment. Because only a limited supply of funds is available in these nations, the international equity market is a major source of funding. Figure 9.4 shows the flows of non-FDI financing into emerging stock markets in recent years. Recall from Chapter 7 that FDI, or foreign direct investment, refers to investment that is accompanied by a degree of managerial control over the investment.

Activity of Investment Banks Investment banks are now contributing more to growth in the international equity market. Investment banks facilitate the sale of a company's stock worldwide by bringing together sellers and large potential buyers.

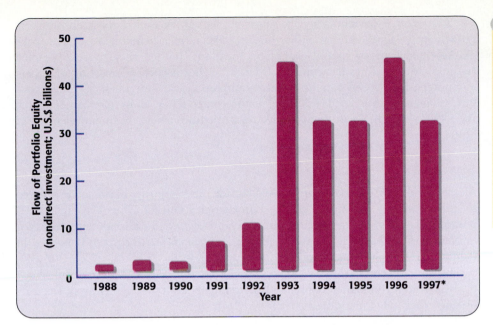

FIGURE 9.4

NON-FDI FLOWS INTO EMERGING MARKETS
As newly industrialized and developing countries continue to develop their economies, companies there require investment financing. The flow of funds into the equities of emerging markets has grown significantly to meet these needs. The drop-off in 1997 was due in part to the Asian economic crisis.

*estimate

Increasingly, investment banks are searching for investors outside the national market in which a company is headquartered. In fact, this method of raising funds is becoming more common than listing a company's shares on another country's stock exchange. The World Business Survey "Ranking the Top Investment Banks" conveys borrowers' satisfaction with the capital-raising abilities of the world's top banks.

World Business Survey

Ranking the Top Investment Banks

Companies rely on investment banks to locate investors who will provide firms with capital to finance their investment projects. Investment banks underwrite new issues of international bonds and equities (among other instruments) on the international capital market. Shown here are the findings of a recent poll asking borrowers what banks provide the best service in the raising of capital.

Rank	Institution
1	JP Morgan (U.S.)
2	Deutsche Bank (Germany)
3	Merrill Lynch (U.S.)
4	Warburg Dillon Read (U.S.)
5	Credit Suisse First Boston (Switzerland)
6	Goldman Sachs (U.S.)
7	Morgan Stanley Dean Witter (U.S.)
8	HSBC Markets (U.K.)
9	Barclays (U.K.)
10	ABN Amro (Netherlands)

e-biz

Advent of Cybermarkets The automation of stock exchanges is encouraging growth in the international equity market. The term *cybermarkets* denotes stock markets that have no central geographic locations. Rather, they consist of global trading activities conducted on the Internet. Cybermarkets (consisting of supercomputers, high-speed data lines, satellite uplinks, and individual personal computers) match buyers and sellers in nanoseconds. They allow companies to list their stocks worldwide through an electronic medium where trading takes place 24 hours a day.[21]

EUROCURRENCY MARKET

Eurocurrency market
Market consisting of all the world's currencies (referred to as Eurocurrency) that are banked outside their countries of origin.

All the world's currencies that are banked outside their countries of origin are referred to as *Eurocurrency* and traded on the **Eurocurrency market**. Thus U.S. dollars deposited in Tokyo's Sumitomo Bank are called *Eurodollars* and British pounds deposited in New York's Chase Manhattan are called *Europounds*. Japanese yen deposited in Frankfurt's Deutsche Bank are called *Euroyen*, and so forth.

Because the Eurocurrency market is characterized by very large transactions, only the very largest companies, banks, and governments are typically involved. Deposits originate primarily from four sources:

➡ Governments with excess funds generated by a prolonged trade surplus
➡ Commercial banks with large deposits of excess currency
➡ International companies with large amounts of excess cash
➡ Extremely wealthy individuals

Growth of the Eurocurrency Market   Eurocurrency originated in Europe during the 1950s—hence the "*Euro*" prefix. Communist governments of eastern European nations feared that they might forfeit dollar deposits made in U.S. banks if claims were filed against them by U.S. citizens. To protect their dollar reserves, they deposited them in banks across Europe. Banks in the United Kingdom began lending these dollars to finance international trade deals, and banks in other countries (including Canada and Japan) followed suit.

Although the Eurocurrency market originated for mainly political reasons, its growth in the last few decades has been due mostly to the financial factors that we will discuss shortly. In the mid-1990s, the Eurocurrency market was valued at around $6 trillion, with London accounting for about 20 percent of all deposits.[22] Other important markets include Canada, the Caribbean, Hong Kong, and Singapore.

Appeal of the Eurocurrency Market   Typically, governments strictly regulate commercial banking activities in their own currencies within their borders. Often, for example, they force banks to pay deposit insurance to a central bank, where they must keep a certain portion of all deposits "on reserve" in non-interest-bearing accounts, and to keep interest rates within a prescribed range. Although such restrictions protect investors, they add costs to banking operations.

The main appeal of the Eurocurrency market, therefore, is the complete absence of regulation. The absence of regulation and its resulting lower costs mean that banks can charge borrowers less, pay investors more, and still earn healthy profits. In addition, extremely large transactions considerably reduce transaction costs. Moreover, **interbank interest rates**—rates that the world's largest banks charge one another for loans—are determined by the free market. The most commonly quoted rate in the Eurocurrency market is the *London Interbank Offer Rate (LIBOR)*—the interest rate that London banks charge other large banks that borrow Eurocurrency. The *London Interbank Bid Rate (LIBID)* is the interest rate offered by London banks to large investors

interbank interest rates
Interest rates that the world's largest banks charge one another for loans.

for Eurocurrency deposits. Different cities quote different interest rates for each Eurocurrency.

An unappealing feature of the Eurocurrency market is greater risk: Government regulations that protect depositors in national markets are nonexistent. Despite the greater risk of default, however, Eurocurrency transactions are fairly safe because of the size of the banks involved.

FOREIGN EXCHANGE MARKET

Unlike domestic transactions, international transactions involve the currencies of two or more nations. Although most nations have their own currency, some nations share a common currency. For example, many African nations share the CFA franc.

In international transactions, companies need a mechanism for exchanging one currency for another. Currencies are bought and sold in, and their prices determined by, the **foreign exchange market**. Financial institutions convert one currency into another at a specific **exchange rate**—the rate at which one currency is exchanged for another. Rates depend on the size of the transaction, the trader conducting it, general economic conditions and, sometimes, government mandate.

In many ways, the foreign exchange market is like the markets for such commodities as cotton, wheat, and copper. The forces of supply and demand determine currency prices, and transactions are conducted through a process of *bid* and *ask quotes*. If someone asks for the current exchange rate of a certain currency, the bank does not know whether it is dealing with a prospective buyer or seller. Thus it quotes two rates: The *bid quote* is the price at which it will buy, the *ask quote* the price that it will pay. Say, for example, that the British pound is quoted in U.S. dollars at $1.6296. The bank may then bid $1.6294 to *buy* British pounds and offer to *sell* them at $1.6298. The difference between the two rates is the *bid-ask spread*. Naturally, banks always buy low and sell high, earning their profits from the bid-ask spread.

> **foreign exchange market**
> *Market in which currencies are bought and sold and in which currency prices are determined.*

> **exchange rate**
> *Rate at which one currency is exchanged for another.*

FUNCTIONS OF THE FOREIGN EXCHANGE MARKET

The foreign exchange market is not really a source of corporate finance. Rather, it facilitates corporate financial activities and international transactions. Investors use the foreign exchange market for four main reasons.

Currency Conversion   Companies use the foreign exchange market to convert one currency into another. Suppose a Malaysian company sells a large number of computers to a customer in France. The French customer wishes to pay for the computers in francs, the French currency, whereas the Malaysian company wants to be paid in its own ringgit. How do the two parties resolve this dilemma? They turn to banks to exchange the currencies for them.

Companies also must convert to local currencies when they undertake foreign direct investment. In addition, when a firm's international subsidiary earns a profit and the company wishes to return some of it to the home country, it must first convert the local money into the home currency.

Currency Hedging   The practice of insuring against potential losses that result from adverse changes in exchange rates is called **currency hedging**. International companies commonly use hedging for one of two purposes:

1. To lessen the risk associated with international transfers of funds
2. To protect themselves in credit transactions in which there is a time lag between billing and receipt of payment

> **currency hedging**
> *Practice of insuring against potential losses that result from adverse changes in exchange rates.*

Suppose our Malaysian computer company has a subsidiary in Germany. The parent company in Malaysia knows that in 30 days—say, on February 1—its German subsidiary will be sending it a payment in German marks. Because the parent is concerned about the value of that payment in ringgit one month in the future, it wants to insure against the possibility that the mark's value will fall over that period—whereby, of course, it will receive less money. On January 2, therefore, the parent company contracts with a financial institution, such as a bank, to exchange the payment in one month at an agreed-upon exchange rate specified on January 2. As of January 2, therefore, the Malaysian company knows exactly how much the payment will be worth on February 1.

currency arbitrage
Instantaneous purchase and sale of a currency in different markets for profit.

Currency Arbitrage **Currency arbitrage** is the instantaneous purchase and sale of a currency in different markets for profit. Assume, for instance, that a currency trader in New York notices that the value of the French franc is lower in Tokyo than in New York. The trader can, therefore, buy francs in Tokyo, sell them in New York, and earn a profit on the difference. Arbitrage, however, is usually more complex. For one thing, our trader will probably need to exchange U.S. dollars for Japanese yen in New York, use those yen to buy French francs in Tokyo, and then sell those francs for U.S. dollars in New York. High-tech communication and trading systems allow the entire transaction to occur within seconds. However, if the difference between the value of the franc in Tokyo and the value of the franc in New York is not greater than the cost of conducting the transaction, it isn't worth making.

Currency arbitrage is a common activity among experienced traders of foreign exchange, very large investors, and companies in the arbitrage business. Firms whose profits are generated primarily by another economic activity, such as retailing or manufacturing, take part in currency arbitrage only if they have very large sums of cash on hand.

interest arbitrage
Profit-motivated purchase and sale of interest-paying securities denominated in different currencies.

Interest Arbitrage **Interest arbitrage** is the profit-motivated purchase and sale of interest-paying securities denominated in different currencies. Companies use interest arbitrage to find better interest rates abroad than those available in their home countries. The securities involved in such transactions include government treasury bills, corporate and government bonds, and even bank deposits. Suppose a trader notices that interest rates paid on bank deposits in Greece are higher than those paid in Sydney, Australia (after adjusting for exchange rates). He can convert Australian dollars to Greek drachmas and deposit the money in a Greek bank account for, say, one year. At the end of the year, he converts the drachmas back into Australian dollars and earns more in interest than the same money would have earned had it remained on deposit in an Australian bank. If, however, the value of the Greek drachma relative to the Australian dollar should fall over that one-year period, our trader's profits could fall, be completely eliminated, or even turn into a loss.

currency speculation
Purchase or sale of a currency with the expectation that its value will change and generate a profit.

Currency Speculation **Currency speculation** is the purchase or sale of a currency with the expectation that its value will change and generate a profit. The shift in value might be expected to occur suddenly or over a longer period. The foreign exchange trader may bet that a currency's price will go either up or down in the future. Suppose a trader in London believes that the value of the Japanese yen will increase over the next three months. She, therefore, buys yen with pounds today at the current price, intending to sell them in 90 days. If the price of yen rises in that time, she earns a profit; if it falls, she takes a loss. Speculation is much riskier than arbitrage because the value, or price, of currencies is quite volatile and is affected by many factors. Like arbitrage, currency spec-

In the wake of the Asian currency crisis that began in 1997, the value of the Thai baht plunged by 63%. To support its suddenly cash-strapped banks, the Thai government increased the money supply, both by lending money to commercial banks and by simply printing more currency. The resultant buildup in the money supply poses the threat of even further devaluations. Consequently, many influential Thais, like the popular actress on the left, urge those holding foreign currencies, especially the U.S. dollar, to convert them into bahts and thereby strengthen the local currency.

ulation is commonly the realm of foreign exchange specialists rather than the managers of firms engaged in other enterprises.

Currency speculation has played a significant role in events that began unfolding in Southeast Asia in 1997. After news emerged in May about Thailand's slowing economy and political instability, currency traders sprang into action. They responded to poor economic growth prospects and an overvalued currency, the Thai baht, by dumping the baht on the foreign exchange market. When the supply glutted the market, the value of the baht plunged. Meanwhile, traders began speculating that other Asian economies were also vulnerable. From the time the crisis first hit until the end of 1997, the value of the Indonesian rupiah fell by 87 percent, the South Korean won by 85 percent, the Thai baht by 63 percent, the Philippine peso by 34 percent, and the Malaysian ringgit by 32 percent.[24] Many currency speculators, of course, made a great deal of money. Certainly, currency speculation of this nature and magnitude is a matter of ethical debate. (We cover the Asian crisis and currency speculation in far more detail in Chapter 10.)

Because of the importance of foreign exchange to trade and investment, businesspeople must understand how currencies are quoted in the foreign exchange market. Managers must understand the financial instruments available to help them protect the profits earned by their international business activities. They must also be aware of government restrictions that may be imposed on the convertibility of currencies and know how to work around these and other obstacles.

HOW THE FOREIGN EXCHANGE MARKET WORKS

QUOTING CURRENCIES

There are two components to every quoted exchange rate: the quoted currency and the base currency. If an exchange rate quotes the number of Japanese yen needed to buy one U.S. dollar (¥/$), the yen is the **quoted currency** and the dollar the **base currency**. When you designate any exchange rate, the quoted currency is always the *numerator* and the base currency the *denominator*. If, for example, you were given a yen/dollar exchange rate quote of 120:1 (meaning that 120 yen are needed to buy 1 dollar), the numerator is 120 and the denominator 1. We can also designate this rate as ¥ 120/$.

quoted currency
In a quoted exchange rate, the currency with which another currency is to be purchased.

base currency
In a quoted exchange rate, the currency that is to be purchased with another currency.

Direct and Indirect Rate Quotes   Table 9.1 lists exchange rates between the U.S. dollar and a number of other currencies as reported in the *Wall Street Journal*. The second column of numbers, under the heading "Currency per U.S. $," tells us *how many units of each listed currency can be purchased with one U.S. dollar*. For example, find the row labeled "Japan (Yen)." The number 117.87 in the second column tells us that 117.87 Japanese yen buys 1 U.S. dollar. We state this exchange rate as ¥ 117.87/$. Because the yen is the quoted currency, we say that this is a *direct quote* on the yen and an *indirect quote* on the dollar. This method of quoting exchange rates is called *European terms* because it is typically used outside the United States.

The first column of numbers in Table 9.1, under the heading "U.S. $ equivalent," tells us how many U.S. dollars it costs to buy one unit of each listed currency. The first column following the words "Japan (Yen)," tells us that it costs $0.008484 to purchase one yen (¥)—less than one U.S. cent. We state this exchange rate as $0.008484/¥. In this case, because the dollar is the quoted currency, we have a *direct quote* on the dollar and an *indirect quote* on the yen. The practice of quoting the U.S. dollar in direct terms is called *U.S. terms* because it is used mainly in the United States.

Whether we use a direct or indirect quote, it is easy to find the other: simply divide the quote into the numeral 1. The following formula is used to derive a direct quote from an indirect quote:

$$Direct\ quote = \frac{1}{Indirect\ quote}$$

And for deriving an indirect quote from a direct quote:

$$Indirect\ quote = \frac{1}{Direct\ quote}$$

For example, suppose we are given an indirect quote on the U.S. dollar of ¥ 117.87/$. To find the direct quote, we simply divide ¥ 117.87 into $1:

$$\$1 \div ¥\ 117.87 = \$0.008484/¥$$

Note that our solution matches the number in the first column of Table 9.1 following the words "Japan (Yen)." Conversely, to find the indirect quote, we divide the direct quote into 1. In our example, we divide $0.008484 into ¥ 1:

$$¥\ 1 \div \$0.008484 = ¥\ 117.87/\$$$

This solution matches the number in the second column of Table 9.1 following the words "Japan (Yen)."

Calculating Percent Change   Why are businesspeople and foreign exchange traders interested in tracking currency values over time as measured by exchange rates? Because changes in currency values can benefit or harm current and future international transactions. **Exchange rate risk** (also known as **foreign exchange risk**) is the risk of adverse changes in exchange rates. Managers develop strategies to minimize this risk by tracking percent changes in exchange rates. For example, take P_N as the exchange rate at the end of a period (the currency's *new* price), and P_O as the exchange rate at the beginning of that period (the currency's *old* price). Now we can calculate percent change in the value of a currency with the following formula:

$$Percent\ change\ (\%) = \frac{P_N - P_O}{P_O} \times 100$$

Note: This equation yields the percent change in the base currency, not in the quoted currency.

exchange rate risk (*or* **foreign exchange risk**)
Risk of adverse changes in exchange rates.

TABLE 9.1   *Exchange Rates, Thursday, October 22, 1998*

The New York foreign exchange selling rates below apply to trading among banks in amounts of $1 million and more, as quoted at 4 P.M. Eastern time by Telerate and other sources. Retail transactions provide fewer units of foreign currency per dollar.

Country	U.S. $ Equivalent	Currency Per U.S. $	Country	U.S. $ Equivalent	Currency Per U.S. $
Argentina (Peso)	1.0001	.9999	3-months forward	.008597	116.32
Australia (Dollar)	.6252	1.5995	6-months forward	.008695	115.01
Austria (Schilling)	.08663	11.544	**Jordan** (Dinar)	1.4094	.7095
Bahrain (Dinar)	2.6525	.3770	**Kuwait** (Dinar)	3.3167	.3015
Belgium (Franc)	.02954	33.850	**Lebanon** (Pound)	.0006629	1508.50
Brazil (Real)	.8404	1.1900	**Malaysia** (Ringgit-b)	.2632	3.8000
Britain (Pound)	1.6950	.5900	**Malta** (Lira)	2.6667	.3750
1-month forward	1.6921	.5910	**Mexico** (Peso)		
3-months forward	1.6872	.5927	Floating rate	.1004	9.9650
6-months forward	1.6801	.5952	**Netherland** (Guilder)	.5409	1.8486
Canada (Dollar)	.6483	1.5425	**New Zealand** (Dollar)	.5261	1.9008
1-month forward	.6483	1.5426	**Norway** (Krone)	.1357	7.3708
3-months forward	.6483	1.5426	**Pakistan** (Rupee)	.02022	49.450
6-months forward	.6482	1.5427	**Peru** (new Sol)	.3301	3.0298
Chile (Peso)	.002162	462.45	**Philippines** (Peso)	.02355	42.470
China (Renminbi)	.1208	8.2782	**Poland** (Zloty)	.2905	3.4425
Colombia (Peso)	.0006259	1597.79	**Portugal** (Escudo)	.005954	167.95
Czech. Rep. (Koruna)			**Russia** (Ruble) (a)	.05967	16.760
Commercial rate	.03461	28.892	**Saudi Arabia** (Riyal)	.2666	3.7503
Denmark (Krone)	.1606	6.2262	**Singapore** (Dollar)	.6176	1.6193
Ecuador (Sucre)			**Slovak Rep.** (Koruna)	.02823	35.420
Floating rate	.0001494	6692.50	**South Africa** (Rand)	.1751	5.7125
Finland (Markka)	.2005	4.9869	**South Korea** (Won)	.0007560	1322.80
France (Franc)	.1820	5.4959	**Spain** (Peseta)	.007186	139.16
1-month forward	.1822	5.4873	**Sweden** (Krona)	.1294	7.7290
3-months forward	.1827	5.4723	**Switzerland** (Franc)	.7461	1.3403
6-months forward	.1832	5.4572	1-month forward	.7488	1.3355
Germany (Mark)	.6103	1.6385	3-months forward	.7535	1.3271
1-month forward	.6112	1.6361	6-months forward	.7596	1.3165
3-months forward	.6129	1.6317	**Taiwan** (Dollar)	.03042	32.878
6-months forward	.6147	1.6269	**Thailand** (Baht)	.02652	37.705
Greece (Drachma)	.003572	279.99	**Turkey** (Lira)	.00000354	282190.00
Hong Kong (Dollar)	.1290	7.7490	**United Arab** (Dirham)	.2723	3.6730
Hungary (Forint)	.004607	217.06	**Uruguay** (New Peso)		
India (Rupee)	.02367	42.255	Financial	.09302	10.750
Indonesia (Rupiah)	.0001288	7763.00	**Venezuela** (Bolivar)	.001755	569.88
Ireland (Punt)	1.5223	.6569	—		
Israel (Shekel)	.2286	4.3744	**SDR**	1.4070	.7107
Italy (Lira)	.0006165	1622.00	**ECU**	1.2011	
Japan (Yen)	.008484	117.87			
1-month forward	.008521	117.36			

Special Drawing Rights (SDR) are based on exchange rates for the U.S., German, British, French, and Japanese currencies. Source: International Monetary Fund.

European Currency Unit (ECU) is based on a basket of community currencies.

a-Russian Central Bank rate. Trading band lowered on 8/17/98. b-Government rate.

The Wall Street Journal daily foreign exchange data for 1996 and 1997 may be purchased through the Readers' Reference Service (413) 592-3600.

Let's illustrate the usefulness of this calculation with a simple example. Suppose that on February 1 of the current year, the exchange rate between the French franc (FF) and the U.S. dollar was FF 5/$. On March 1 of the current year, the exchange rate stood at FF 4/$. What is the change in the value of the base currency—the dollar? If we plug these numbers into our formula, we arrive at the following change in the value of the dollar:

$$\text{Percent change (\%)} = \frac{4 - 5}{5} \times 100 = -20\%$$

Thus the value of the dollar has fallen 20 percent. In other words, one U.S. dollar buys 20 percent fewer French francs on March 1 than it did on February 1.

To calculate the change in the value of the French franc, we must first calculate the indirect exchange rate on the franc; this is necessary because we want to make the franc our base currency. Using the formula presented earlier, we obtain an exchange rate of $.20/FF (1 ÷ FF 5) on February 1 and an exchange rate of $.25/FF (1 ÷ FF 4) on March 1. Plugging these rates into our percent-change formula, we get:

$$\text{Percent change (\%)} = \frac{.25 - .20}{.20} \times 100 = 25\%$$

Thus the value of the French franc has risen 25 percent. One French franc buys 25 percent more U.S. dollars on March 1 than it did on February 1.

How important is this difference to businesspeople and exchange traders? Consider the fact that the typical trading unit in the foreign exchange market (called a *round lot*) is $5 million. Therefore, a $5 million purchase of francs on February 1 would yield FF 25 million. But because the dollar has by March 1 lost 20 percent of its buying power, a $5 million purchase would get us only 20 million French francs—5 million fewer francs than a month earlier.

Cross Rates   International transactions between two currencies other than the U.S. dollar often use the dollar as a vehicle currency. For instance, a retail buyer of merchandise in the Netherlands might convert its Dutch guilders to U.S. dollars and then pay its Japanese supplier in U.S. dollars. The Japanese supplier may then take those U.S. dollars and convert them to Japanese yen. This process was more common years ago, when fewer currencies were freely convertible and when the United States greatly dominated world trade. Today, a Japanese supplier may want payment in guilders. Perhaps it wishes to build a distribution warehouse in the Netherlands and needs guilders to make the investment. In this case, both the Japanese and the Dutch companies need to know the exchange rate between their respective currencies. To find this rate using their respective exchange rates with the U.S. dollar, we calculate what is called their **cross rate**—an exchange rate calculated using two other exchange rates.

Cross rates between two currencies can be calculated using either currency's indirect or direct exchange rates with another currency. If we return to Table 9.1, for instance, we see that the *direct* quote on the Netherlands' guilder (NLG) is NLG 1.8486/$. The *direct* quote on the Japanese yen is ¥ 117.87/$. To find the cross rate between the guilder and the yen, with the yen as the base currency, we simply divide 1.8486 by 117.87:

$$1.8486 \div 117.87 = \text{NLG } 0.01568/¥$$

Thus, it costs 0.01568 guilders to buy one yen.

We can also calculate the cross rate between the guilder and the yen by using the indirect quotes for each currency against the U.S. dollar. Again, we see in Table 9.1 that

cross rate
Exchange rate calculated using two other exchange rates.

the *indirect* quote on the guilder to the dollar is $0.5409/NLG. The *indirect* quote on the yen to the dollar is ¥ 0.008484/$. To find the cross rate between the guilder and the yen, again with the yen as the base currency, we divide 0.5409 by 0.008484:

$$0.5409 \div 0.008484 = 63.7553$$

We must then perform an additional step. Because *indirect* quotes were used in our calculation, we must divide our answer into 1:

$$1 \div 63.7553 = 0.01568$$

Again (as in our earlier solution), we see that it costs 0.01568 guilders to buy one yen.

Table 9.2 shows the cross rates for major world currencies. When finding cross rates using direct (*indirect*) quotes, currencies down the left-hand side represent quoted (*base*) currencies; those across the top represent base (*quoted*) currencies. Look at the intersection of the "Netherlands" row (the quoted currency in our example) and the "Yen" column (our base currency). Note that our solutions for the cross rate between guilder and yen match the listed rate of 0.01568 guilders to the yen.

Naturally, the exchange rate between the guilder and the yen is quite important to both our Japanese supplier and the Dutch retailer. If the guilder's value falls relative to the yen, the Dutch company must pay more in guilders for its Japanese products. This situation will force the Dutch company to take one of two steps: either increase the price at which it resells the Japanese product (perhaps reducing sales) or keep prices at current levels (thus reducing its profit margin). Ironically, the Japanese supplier will suffer if the yen rises too much. Why? Under such circumstances, the Japanese supplier can do one of two things: allow the exchange rate to force its prices higher (thus increasing profits) or counter the exchange rate effect by reducing its prices (and thus reducing its profit margin). Both the Japanese supplier and the Dutch buyer can absorb exchange rate changes by squeezing profits—but only to a point. Once that point is passed, they will no longer be able to trade. The Dutch buyer will be forced to look for a supplier in a country with a more favorable exchange rate or for a supplier in its own country.

SPOT RATES

All the exchange rates we've discussed thus far are called **spot rates**—exchange rates that require delivery of the traded currency within two business days. Exchange of the two currencies is said to occur "on the spot," and the **spot market** is the market for

spot rate
Exchange rate requiring delivery of the traded currency within two business days.

spot market
Market for currency transactions at spot rates.

TABLE 9.2	Key Currency Cross Rates									
	Dollar	**ECU**	**Pound**	**SFranc**	**Guilder**	**Peso**	**Yen**	**Lira**	**D-Mark**	**FFranc**	**CdnDlr**
Canada	1.5425	1.8526	2.6145	1.1509	.83442	.15479	.01309	.00095	.94141	.28066	. . .
France	5.4959	6.6009	9.3156	4.1005	2.9730	.55152	.04663	.00339	3.3542	. . .	3.5630
Germany	1.6385	1.9679	2.7773	1.2225	.88635	.16443	.01390	.00101	. . .	.29813	1.0622
Italy	1622.0	1948.1	2749.3	1210.2	877.42	162.77	13.761	. . .	989.93	295.13	1051.5
Japan	117.87	141.57	199.79	87.943	63.762	11.828	. . .	.07267	71.938	21.447	76.415
Mexico	9.9650	11.969	16.891	7.4349	5.3906	. . .	.08454	.00614	6.0818	1.8132	6.4603
Netherlands	1.8486	2.2203	3.1334	1.3792	. . .	.18551	.01568	.00114	1.1282	.33636	1.1984
Switzerland	1.3403	1.6098	2.2718	. . .	.72504	.13450	.01137	.00083	.81800	.24387	.86891
U.K.	.58997	.70859	. . .	.44018	.31914	.05920	.00501	.00036	.36007	.10735	.38248
ECU	.83260	. . .	1.4113	.62120	.45093	.08355	.00706	.00051	.50815	.15149	.53977
U.S.	. . .	1.2011	1.6950	.74610	.54095	.10035	.00848	.00062	.61031	.18195	.64830

currency transactions at spot rates. The spot market assists companies in performing any one of three functions:

1. Converting income generated from sales in another country into their home-country currency
2. Converting funds into the currency of an international supplier
3. Converting funds into the currency of a country in which they wish to invest

Buy and Sell Rates   The spot rate is available only for trades worth millions of dollars. Thus it is available only to banks and foreign exchange brokers. If you are traveling to another country and want to exchange currencies at your bank before departing, you will not be quoted the spot rate. Rather, banks and other institutions will give you a *buy rate* (the exchange rate at which the bank will buy a currency) and an *ask rate* (the rate at which it will sell a currency). In other words, you will receive what we described when introducing the foreign exchange market as *bid* and *ask quotes*. These rates reflect the amounts that large currency traders are charging, plus a markup.

Suppose, for example, that you are leaving Mexico for a business trip to Germany and need to buy some German marks (DM). The bank will quote you exchange rate terms, such as Peso 4.5373/83 per DM. The bank, in other words, will buy German marks at the rate of Peso 4.5373/DM and sell them at the rate of Peso 4.5383/DM.

FORWARD RATES

forward rate
Exchange rate at which two parties agree to exchange currencies on a specified future date.

forward market
Market for currency transactions at forward rates.

When a company knows that it will need a certain amount of foreign currency on a certain future date, it can exchange currencies using a **forward rate**—an exchange rate at which two parties agree to exchange currencies on a specified future date. Forward rates represent the expectations of currency traders and bankers regarding a currency's future spot rate. Reflected in these expectations are a country's present and future economic conditions (including inflation rate, national debt, taxes, trade balance, and economic growth rate) as well as its social and political situation. The **forward market** is the market for currency transactions at forward rates.

Companies commonly use the forward market to insure themselves against unfavorable exchange-rate changes. It can be used for all types of transactions requiring future payment in other currencies, including credit sales or purchases, interest receipts or payments on investments or loans, and dividend payments to stockholders in other countries. Not all currencies, however, are traded in the forward market. In particular, these include the currencies of countries with high inflation rates or currencies generating little demand on international financial markets.

forward contract
Contract requiring the exchange of an agreed-upon amount of a currency on an agreed-upon date at a specific exchange rate.

Forward Contracts   Suppose a Brazilian bicycle maker imports parts from a German supplier. Under the terms of their contract, the Brazilian importer must pay 1 million German marks in 90 days. The Brazilian firm can wait until one or two days before payment is due, buy marks in the spot market, and pay the German supplier. Unfortunately, in the 90 days between the contract and the due date, the exchange rate will probably change. What if the value of the Brazilian *real* goes down? In that case, the Brazilian importer will have to pay more reals to get the same 1 million German marks. Our importer, therefore, may want to pay off the debt before the 90-day term. But what if it does not have the cash on hand? What if it needs those 90 days to collect accounts receivable from its own customers?

To decrease its exchange-rate risk, our Brazilian importer can enter into a **forward contract**—a contract requiring the exchange of an agreed-upon amount of a currency on an agreed-upon date at a specific exchange rate. Forward contracts are commonly signed for 30, 90, and 180 days into the future, but customized contracts (say, for 76 days) are possible. Note that a forward contract *requires* exchange of an agreed-upon amount of a currency on an agreed-upon date at a specific exchange rate: The bank must deliver the marks, and the Brazilian importer must buy them at the prearranged price. Forward contracts belong to a family of financial instruments called **derivatives**—instruments whose values *derive* from other commodities or financial instruments. These include not only forward contracts but also currency swaps, options, and futures (which we discuss shortly).

In our example, the Brazilian importer can use a forward contract to pay marks to its German supplier in 90 days. It is always possible, of course, that in 90 days, the value of the real will be lower than its current value. But by locking in at the forward rate, the Brazilian firm protects itself against the less favorable spot rate at which it would have to buy marks in 90 days. In this case, the Brazilian company protects itself from paying more to the supplier at the end of 90 days than if it were to pay at the spot rate in 90 days. Thus it protects its profit from further erosion if the spot rate becomes even more unfavorable over the next three months. Remember, too, that such a contract prevents the Brazilian importer from taking advantage of any increase in the value of the real in 90 days that would reduce what the company owed its German supplier.

Premiums and Discounts As we've already seen, a currency's forward exchange rate can be higher or lower than its current spot rate. If its forward rate is higher than its spot rate, the currency is trading at a *premium*. If its forward rate is lower, it is trading at a *discount*. Return once again to Table 9.1 (p. 309). Locate the row labeled "Britain (Pound) 1-month forward." This is the 30-day forward exchange rate for the British pound (GBP). Note that the rate of $1.6921/GBP is *less* than the spot rate of $1.6950/GBP (the spot rate quoted in the previous row of Table 9.1). The pound, therefore, is trading at a *discount* on the 1-month forward contract. We know, then, that a contract to deliver British pounds in 30 days costs $0.0029 less per pound in 30 days than it does today. Likewise, the 3- and 6-month forward rates tell us that pounds cost $0.0078 and $0.0149 less in 90 and 180 days, respectively. Clearly, the pound is also trading at a discount on 3- and 6-month forward contracts.

SWAPS, OPTIONS, AND FUTURES

In addition to forward contracts, three other types of currency instruments are used in the forward market: *currency swaps*, *options*, and *futures*.

Currency Swaps A **currency swap** is the simultaneous purchase and sale of foreign exchange for two different dates. Currency swaps are an increasingly important component of the foreign exchange market. Suppose a Swedish carmaker imports parts from a subsidiary in Turkey. The Swedish company must pay the Turkish subsidiary in Turkish lira for the parts when they are delivered tomorrow. It also expects to receive Turkish liras for cars sold in Turkey in 90 days. Our Swedish company exchanges krona for lira in the spot market today to pay its subsidiary. At the same time, it agrees to a forward contract to sell Turkish lira (and buy Swedish krona) in 90 days at the quoted 90-day forward rate for lira. In this way, the Swedish company uses a swap both to reduce its exchange-rate risk and to lock in the future exchange rate. In this sense, we can think of a currency swap as a more complex forward contract.

Currency Options Recall that a forward contract *requires* exchange of an agreed-upon amount of a currency on an agreed-upon date at a specific exchange rate. In contrast, a **currency option** is a right, or *option*, to exchange a specific amount of a currency

derivative
Financial instrument whose value derives from other commodities or financial instruments.

currency swap
Simultaneous purchase and sale of foreign exchange for two different dates.

currency option
Right, or option, to exchange a specific amount of a currency on a specific date at a specific rate.

on a specific date at a specific rate. In other words, whereas forward contracts require parties to follow through on currency exchanges, currency options do not.

Suppose a company buys an option to purchase, in 30 days, French francs at FF 5.95/$. If, at the end of the 30 days, the exchange rate is FF 6/$, the company would *not* exercise its currency option. Why? It could get 0.05 more francs for every dollar by exchanging at the spot rate in the currency market rather than at the stated rate of the option. Companies often use currency options to hedge against exchange rate risk or to obtain foreign currency.

currency futures contract
Contract requiring the exchange of a specific amount of currency on a specific date at a specific exchange rate, with all conditions fixed and not adjustable.

Currency Futures Contracts   Similar to a currency forward contract is a **currency futures contract**—a contract requiring the exchange of a specific amount of currency on a specific date at a specific exchange rate. All of these conditions are fixed and not adjustable.

FOREIGN EXCHANGE MARKET TODAY

The foreign exchange market is actually an electronic network connecting the world's major financial centers. In turn, each of these centers is a network of foreign exchange traders, currency trading banks, and investment firms. The foreign exchange market is growing rapidly and is dominated by several major trading centers and several currencies.

GROWTH OF THE FOREIGN EXCHANGE MARKET

In a single day, the volume of trading on the foreign exchange market (comprising currency swaps and spot and forward contracts) totals more than $1.2 trillion—roughly the yearly gross national product of Italy.[25] While the total volume of spot transactions is growing, the forward market is growing about twice as fast and is overtaking the spot market.[26]

e·biz

Likewise, although world trade is growing rapidly, it is growing more slowly than the foreign exchange market. Therefore, factors other than world trade must be involved in the growth rate of the foreign exchange market. Two of these factors are *technological innovation* and *financial market deregulation*. First, important advances in electronic communication systems are making it much easier and cheaper to exchange currencies around the world. An electronic system called Real Time Gross Settlements (RTGS) allows banks to settle outstanding currency balances instantaneously with one another. This capability reduces foreign exchange risk by eliminating the time lag between purchases and sales—a time lag during which currency values can change.[27]

Second, less bureaucratic red tape and fewer banking regulations mean an increased international flow of money and a corresponding need for currency conversion. For the same reason, the world's largest international banks recently proposed global standards to speed up the process of worldwide financial deregulation.[28]

TRADING CENTERS

Most of the world's major cities participate in trading on the foreign exchange market. In recent years, however, just three countries have come to account for slightly more than half of all global currency trading: the United Kingdom, the United States, and Japan. Accordingly, most of this trading takes place in the financial capitals of London, New York, and Tokyo.

London dominates the foreign exchange market for historic and geographic reasons. The United Kingdom was once the world's largest trading nation. British merchants needed to exchange currencies of different nations, and London naturally assumed the role of financial trading center. London quickly came to dominate the market and still does so because of its location halfway between North America and Asia. A key factor is its time zone.

Because of differences in time zones, London is opening for business as markets in Asia close trading for the day. When New York opens for trading in the morning, trading continues in London for several hours. As a result, more trading in U.S. dollars takes place in London than in the United States, and more trading in German marks than in Germany.[29]

Map 9.1 shows why it is possible to trade foreign exchange 24 hours a day (except weekends and major holidays). At least one of the three major centers (London, New York, and Tokyo) keeps the market open for 21 hours each day. Moreover, trading does not stop during the three hours they are closed because other trading centers (including San Francisco and Sydney, Australia) remain open. Also, most large banks active in foreign exchange ensure continuous trading by employing overnight traders.

IMPORTANT CURRENCIES

Although the United Kingdom is the major location of foreign exchange trading, the U.S. dollar is the currency that dominates the foreign exchange market. Because the U.S. dollar is so widely used in world trade, it is considered a **vehicle currency**—a currency used as an intermediary to convert funds between two other currencies. Currencies most often involved in currency transactions are (in order of use) the U.S. dollar, the German mark, the Japanese yen, the British pound, and the French franc.[30]

The U.S. dollar is a vehicle currency for two main reasons. First, the United States is the world's largest trading nation. Because the United States is so heavily involved in international trade, many international companies and banks maintain dollar deposits, making it easy to exchange other currencies with dollars. Second, following World War

> **vehicle currency**
> *Currency used as an intermediary to convert funds between two other currencies.*

MAP 9.1

FOREIGN TRADING CENTERS, BY TIME ZONE

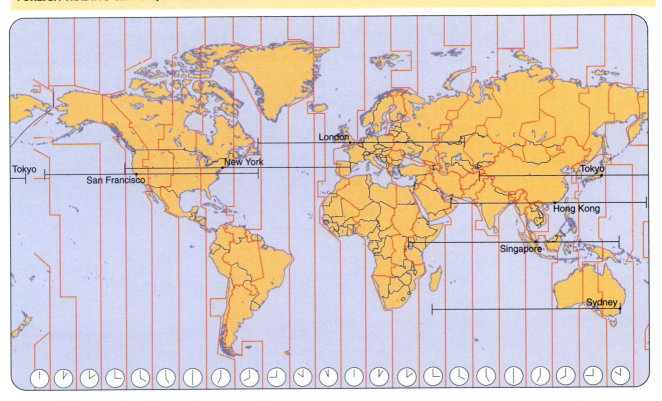

II, all of the world's major currencies were tied indirectly to the dollar because it was the most stable currency. In turn, the dollar's value was tied to a specific value of gold—a policy that held wild currency swings in check. Although world currencies are no longer linked to the value of gold (see Chapter 10), the stability of the dollar, along with its resistance to inflation, helps people and organizations maintain their purchasing power better than their own national currencies. Even today, people in many countries convert extra cash from national currencies into dollars.

INSTITUTIONS OF THE FOREIGN EXCHANGE MARKET

So far, we have discussed the foreign exchange market only in general terms. We now look at the three main components of the foreign exchange market: the *interbank market*, *securities exchanges*, and the *over-the-counter market*.

interbank market
Market in which the world's largest banks exchange currencies at spot and forward rates.

Interbank Market   It is in the **interbank market** that the world's largest banks exchange currencies at spot and forward rates. Many companies receive their foreign exchange services from the banks with which they do most of their business. Each bank satisfies client requests for exchange quotes by obtaining them from other banks in the interbank market. For transactions involving commonly exchanged currencies, the largest banks often have sufficient currency on hand. But rarely exchanged currencies are not typically kept on hand and may in fact be unable to be obtained from another bank. In such cases, banks turn to *foreign exchange brokers* who maintain vast networks through which to obtain seldom traded currencies.

In the interbank market, then, banks act as agents for client companies. In addition to locating and exchanging currencies, banks commonly offer advice on trading strategy, supply a variety of currency instruments, and provide other risk-management services. They also help clients manage exchange-rate risk by providing information on

World Business Survey

Choosing a Foreign Exchange Bank

A survey asked 194 clients what they consider most important when selecting a bank to provide their foreign exchange services.

Ranking	Factor
1	Price alone
2	Relationship with bank
3	Relationship with individual person
4	Quote speed
5	Credit rating
6	Back-office settlement
7	Strategy advice
8	Liquidity
9	Research
10	Innovation
11	Currency breadth
12	Product breadth
13	24-hour service/night desk
14	Technology available
15	Risk management

rules and regulations around the world. The World Business Survey "Choosing a Foreign Exchange Bank" identifies the factors that clients consider most important when selecting a bank to provide foreign exchange services.

Large banks in the interbank market have significant power in currency markets and use their influence to get better rates than smaller players. Clients, of course, benefit when banks pass on savings in the form of lower fees. Small firms, however, often find it difficult to get favorable bank rates because they deal only in small volumes of currencies and do so rather infrequently. For this reason, a small company might choose a discount international payment service to provide it with better quotes.

Clearing Mechanisms Finally, clearing mechanisms are an important element of the interbank market. Banks continuously perform foreign exchange transactions with other banks and foreign exchange brokers. These accounts are not settled after each individual trade in a single currency. Rather, they are settled after a number of transactions have been processed. The process of aggregating the currencies that one bank owes another and then carrying out that transaction is called **clearing**. In the past, clearing was normally done each day or once every two days and involved the actual transportation of currencies from one bank to another. But nowadays clearing is performed more frequently and handled through computerized clearing mechanisms.

Securities Exchanges **Securities exchanges** specialize in currency futures and options transactions. Buying and selling currencies on these exchanges entails the use of securities *brokers*, who facilitate transactions by transmitting and executing clients' orders. Transactions on securities exchanges are much smaller than those in the interbank market and vary with each currency. One important exchange is the Chicago Mercantile Exchange (CME), a nonprofit company with 2,725 members—mostly banks, investment firms, brokers, and independent traders. The CME deals in a variety of financial futures, including futures for most major currencies. It is the second-largest futures exchange, after the Chicago Board of Trade (CBT).

The third-largest exchange is the London International Financial Futures Exchange (LIFFE). In September 1996, it merged with the London Commodities Exchange (LCE) and now offers the most comprehensive collection of futures in the

clearing
Process of aggregating the currencies that one bank owes another and then carrying out the transaction.

securities exchange
Exchange specializing in currency futures and options transactions.

Merrill Lynch and other international investment banks with operations in Tokyo hope to realize huge opportunities in the wake of the Japanese initiative known as *kinyu biggu ban*—the "finance big bang." In theory, an overhaul of the national financial system will open the Japanese market—with a total savings pool of $11 trillion—to competition from international banks and brokers. Merrill Lynch has opened a network of retail-brokerage banks and hired some 2,000 brokers once employed by Japan's fourth-largest brokerage, which went under in recent years. You can check the progress of Merrill Lynch in Japan through the company's Web site at (**www.merrilllynch.com**).

world. On the LIFFE, futures and options are traded for seven currencies. Thanks to a recent deal struck between the two parties, it is now possible to trade LIFFE futures on the CBT.[31] U.S. trading in currency *options* occurs only on the Philadelphia Stock Exchange (PSE), the leading currency options exchange in the world. It deals in both standardized options and customized options, allowing investors flexibility in designing currency option contracts. The PSE deals in 11 currencies and most cross-trades among them, for a total of 110 currency pairs.[32]

over-the-counter (OTC) market
Exchange consisting of a global computer network of foreign exchange traders and other market participants.

Over-the-Counter Market The **over-the-counter (OTC) market** is an exchange with no central trading location: It consists of a global computer network of foreign exchange traders and other market participants. All foreign exchange transactions can be performed in the OTC market. The major players are large financial institutions and investment banks, including Goldman Sachs and Merrill Lynch.

The over-the-counter market is growing rapidly in recent years because it offers several benefits for business. First, it allows businesspeople to search freely for the institution providing the best (lowest) price for conducting a transaction. Second, it offers greater opportunities for designing customized transactions. See the Global Manager "Five Strategies for More Effective Foreign Exchange" for other ways that companies can become more adept in their foreign exchange activities.

e·biz

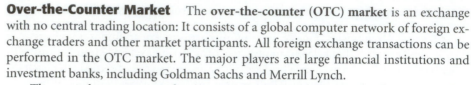

Global Manager

Five Strategies for More Effective Foreign Exchange

1. **Analyze your foreign exchange activities and choose service providers who best fit your needs.** Analyze your needs. What is the nature of your foreign exchange activity? What types of transactions do you undertake and in which currencies? How frequent and how large are your wire transfers? Could repetitive transfers be consolidated? Next, take a close look at the range of service providers available to you. Many businesspeople automatically turn to local bankers when they need to transfer funds overseas, but this may not be the best choice. In some cases, a mix of service providers might offer the best solution.

2. **Trade with major players in the foreign exchange market.** In terms of cost and service, money-center banks—those located in financial centers—who participate directly in the foreign exchange market may have some advantages over local banks. Often, dealing directly with a large trading institution is more cost-effective than dealing with a local bank because it avoids the additional markup that the local bank charges for its services.

3. **Consolidate transactions to boost your buying power and realize economies of scale.** Depending on your circumstances, you may want to time overseas payments in order to consolidate multiple transfers into one large transaction. If you find yourself making multiple smaller payments in the same currency, consider opening an overseas local-currency account against which you can write drafts. Likewise, allowing foreign receiv-

ables to accumulate in an interest-bearing local account until they can be repatriated in a lump sum, may prove more advantageous than exchanging each payment individually.

4. **Encourage competition between providers and be an aggressive negotiator.** If your foreign exchange activity is substantial, work to develop relationships with at least two money-center banks. Then you can play one against the other to get the best rates. You should also monitor the rates you're getting over time. Some institutions raise rates over time, especially if they sense you're not shopping around. To monitor your exchange rates accurately, you'll need access to real-time market rates provided by firms like Reuters, Telerate, and Bloomberg. A word of caution: Beware of less expensive, time-delayed services that delay data by 15 minutes or more—an eternity in the foreign exchange market, where rates can change by the second.

5. **Automate your operations for greater accuracy and efficiency.** Every phone call, fax, or transmittal opens the door to human error and delays in getting funds where and when you need them. That's why it makes sense to harness the power of computers to your international wire transfers and drafts. Widely available from banks and specialized service providers, automated software programs greatly reduce the potential for errors and miscommunication while speeding the execution of transfers.

Our discussion of the foreign exchange market so far assumes that all currencies can be readily converted for another in the foreign exchange market. A **convertible currency** (also called **hard currency**) is traded freely in the foreign exchange market, with its price determined by the forces of supply and demand. Countries that allow full convertibility are those in strong financial positions with adequate reserves of foreign currencies. Such countries have no reason to fear that people will sell their own currency for that of another. However, many newly industrialized and developing countries do not permit the free convertibility of their currencies. Let's now take a look at why governments place restrictions on the convertibility of currencies and how they do it.

CURRENCY CONVERTIBILITY

convertible currency (or hard currency)
Currency that trades freely in the foreign exchange market, with its price determined by the forces of supply and demand.

GOALS OF CURRENCY RESTRICTION

Governments impose currency restrictions to achieve several goals. One goal is to preserve a country's reserve of hard currencies with which to repay debts owed to other nations. Developed nations, emerging markets, and some natural resource exporting countries tend to have the greatest amounts of foreign exchange. Without sufficient reserves (liquidity), a country could default on its loans and thereby discourage future investment flows. This consequence would have occurred during the 1994 Mexican peso crisis. The international bailout of Mexico, however, shored up the nation's financial position by limiting the flight of capital and investment from the country.

A second goal of currency restriction is to preserve hard currencies to pay for imports and to finance trade deficits. Recall from Chapter 7 that a country runs a *trade deficit* when the value of its imports exceeds the vlaue of its exports. Currency restrictions help governments maintain inventories of foreign currencies with which to pay for such trade imbalances. They also make importing more difficult because local companies cannot obtain foreign currency to pay for imports. The resulting reduction in imports directly improves the country's trade balance.

A third goal is to protect a currency from speculators. For instance, in the wake of the 1997–1998 Asian financial crisis, some Southeast Asian nations considered the control of their currencies as an option to limit the damage done by economic downturns.

Back when the Korean won was relatively stable against the U.S. dollar, many Korean companies and banks borrowed money in U.S. dollars. When the value of the won collapsed during the Asian financial crisis, these debts increased by as much as fivefold. Korea was therefore saddled with huge foreign debts, and the weakened won was not convertible into the currencies acceptable to creditors. Many patriotic Koreans thus turned in privately held gold to contribute to the nation's debt payments.

Malaysia, for example, stemmed the outflow of foreign money by preventing local investors from converting their Malaysian holdings into other currencies. The move also curtailed currency speculation but, in the process, effectively cut off Malaysia from investors elsewhere in the world. Critics of this tactic charge that it amounts to abandoning the concept of the free-market economy.[33]

A fourth (less common) goal is to keep resident individuals and businesses from investing in other nations. These policies are designed to generate more rapid economic growth by forcing investment in the home country. Unfortunately, although this might work in the short term, it normally slows long-term economic growth. The reason: There is no guarantee that domestic funds *held* in the home country will be *invested* there. Instead, they might be saved or even spent on consumption. Ironically, increased consumption can mean further increases in imports, making the balance of trade deficit even worse.

POLICIES FOR RESTRICTING CURRENCIES

Certain government policies are frequently used to restrict currency convertibility. Governments can require that all foreign exchange transactions be performed at or approved by the country's central bank. They can also require import licenses for some or all import transactions. These licenses help the government control the amount of foreign currency leaving the country.

Some governments implement systems of *multiple exchange rates*, specifying a higher exchange rate on the imports of certain goods or on the imports from certain countries. The government can thus reduce imports while still ensuring that imports of important goods enter the country. It also can use such a policy to target the goods of countries with which it is running a trade deficit.

Other governments issue *import deposit requirements* that require businesses to deposit certain percentages of their foreign exchange funds in special accounts before being granted import licenses. In addition, *quantity restrictions* limit the amount of foreign currency that residents can take out of the home-country when traveling to other countries as tourists, students, or medical patients.

Countertrade   Finally, one way to get around national restrictions on currency convertibility is **countertrade**—the exchange of goods and services between two parties without the use of money. One simple form of countertrade is a *barter* transaction, in which goods are exchanged for others of equal value. Parties exchange goods and then sell them in world markets for hard currency. Cuba, for instance, once exchanged $60 million worth of sugar for cereals, pasta, and vegetable oils from the Italian firm Italgrani.[34] In the past, Boeing sold aircraft to Saudi Arabia in return for oil.[35] The many different forms of countertrade are covered in detail in Chapter 13.

countertrade
Exchange of goods and services between two parties without the use of money.

A FINAL WORD

This chapter surveyed the most important components of international financial markets. We learned about the international bond, equity, and Eurocurrency markets. Despite the problems in Asia, Russia, and other emerging markets of Latin America, continued growth in the international capital market is expected. We also learned the fundamentals of exchange rates and saw how the foreign exchange market is structured. In the next chapter, we extend our coverage of the international financial system to see how market forces (including interest rates and inflation) impact exchange rates. We then conclude our study of the international financial system by looking at the roles of government and international institutions in managing movements in exchange rates.

There is a variety of additional material available on the companion Web site that accompanies this text. You can access this information by visiting the Web site at ⟨**www.prenhall.com/wild**⟩.

summary

❶ Discuss the purposes, development, and financial centers of the *international capital market.* The international capital market has three main purposes. First, it provides an expanded supply of capital for borrowers because it joins together borrowers and lenders in different nations. Second, it lowers the cost of money for borrowers because a greater supply of money lowers the cost of borrowing (interest rates). Third, it lowers risk for lenders because it makes available a greater number of investments.

Growth in the international capital market is due mainly to three factors. First, advances in *information technology* allow borrowers and lenders to do business more quickly and cheaply. Second, the *deregulation* of capital markets is opening the international capital market to increased competition. Third, *innovation in financial instruments* is increasing the appeal of the international capital market.

The world's most important financial centers are London, New York, and Tokyo. These cities conduct a large number of financial transactions daily. Other locations, called *offshore financial centers*, handle less business but have few regulations and few, if any, taxes.

❷ Describe the *international bond, international equity,* and *Eurocurrency markets.* The *international bond market* consists of all bonds sold by issuers outside their own countries. It is experiencing rapid growth primarily because investors in developed markets are searching for higher rates from borrowers in emerging markets and vice versa. The *international equity market* consists of all stocks bought and sold outside the home country of the issuing company. The four main factors responsible for the recent growth in international equity are *privatization*, greater issuance of stock by *companies in newly industrialized and developing nations*, greater *international reach of investment banks*, and *global electronic trading*—trading that takes place on *cybermarkets*. The *Eurocurrency market* consists of all the world's currencies that are banked outside their countries of origin. The appeal of the Eurocurrency market is its lack of government regulation and, therefore, lower cost of borrowing.

❸ Discuss the four primary functions of the *foreign exchange market.* The foreign exchange market is the market in which currencies are bought and sold and in which currency prices are determined. It has four primary functions. First, individuals, companies, and governments use it, directly or indirectly, to convert one currency into another. Second, it offers tools with which investors can *insure against adverse changes in exchange rates.* Third, it is used to earn a profit from *arbitrage*—the purchase and sale of a currency, or other interest-paying security, in different markets. Finally, it is used to *speculate about a change in the value of a currency.*

❹ Explain how currencies are *quoted* and *different rates* given. Currencies are quoted in a number of different ways. An *exchange-rate quote* between currency A and currency B (A:B) of 10:1 means that it takes 10 units of currency A to buy 1 unit of currency B. This example reflects a *direct quote* of currency A and an *indirect quote* of currency B. The exchange rate in this example is calculated using their actual values. We can also calculate an exchange rate between two currencies by using their respective exchange rates with a common currency; the resulting rate is called a *cross rate.* A *spot rate* is an exchange rate that requires delivery of the traded currency within two business days. This rate is normally obtainable only by large banks and foreign exchange brokers. The *forward rate* is the rate at which two parties agree to exchange currencies on a specified future date. Forward exchange rates represent the market's expectation of what the value of a currency will be at some point in the future.

❺ Identify the main *instruments* and *institutions* of the foreign exchange market. Companies involved in international business make extensive use of certain financial instruments in order to reduce exchange-rate risk. A *forward contract* requires the exchange of an agreed-upon amount of a currency on an agreed-upon date at a specific exchange rate. A *currency swap* is the simultaneous purchase and sale of foreign exchange for two different dates. A *currency option* is the right to exchange a specific amount of a currency on a specific date at a specific rate. It is sometimes used to acquire a needed currency. Finally, a currency *futures contract* requires the exchange of a specific amount of currency on a specific date at a specific exchange rate. It is similar to a forward contract except that none of the terms is negotiable.

The world's largest banks exchange currencies in the *interbank market*. These banks locate and exchange currencies for companies and sometimes provide additional services. *Securities exchanges* are physical locations at which currency futures and options are bought and sold (in smaller amounts than those traded in the interbank market). The *over-the-counter (OTC) market* is an exchange that exists as a global computer network linking traders to one another.

6 **Explain why and how governments restrict *currency convertibility.*** There are four main goals of currency restriction. First, a government may be attempting to preserve the country's hard currency reserves for repaying debts owed to other nations. Second, convertibility might be restricted to preserve hard currency to pay for needed imports or to finance a trade deficit. Third, restrictions might be used to protect a currency from speculators. Finally, such restrictions can be an attempt to *keep* badly needed currency from being invested abroad. Policies used to enforce currency restrictions include government approval for currency exchange, imposed import licenses, a system of multiple exchange rates, and imposed quantity restrictions.

questions for review

1. Distinguish between *debt* and *equity*.
2. What are the three main benefits of the *international capital market*? Explain each briefly.
3. Name three factors responsible for growth in the international capital market.
4. Define and explain *securitization*.
5. Which three cities are considered the most important financial centers in the international capital market?
6. What is an *offshore financial center*? Why are they appealing to business?
7. What is the single most important factor fueling growth in the *international bond market*? Explain the role and influence of this factor.
8. What is the *international equity market*? Explain the factors responsible for its growth.
9. What is the *Eurocurrency market*? Explain how it functions.
10. For what four reasons do investors use the *foreign exchange market*?

11. Distinguish between *currency arbitrage* and *interest arbitrage*.
12. What is a *direct exchange-rate quote*? An *indirect* quote?
13. Explain how to calculate percent changes in currency prices.
14. What are *cross rates*? Why are they important?
15. Distinguish between *spot rate* and *forward rate*. How is each used in the foreign exchange market?
16. Explain the differences among *currency swaps*, *options*, and *futures*.
17. Where are the world's main foreign exchange trading centers located? Which three currencies are used most in the foreign exchange market?
18. What is a *vehicle currency*?
19. Describe the three main institutions in the *foreign exchange market*.
20. Why are restrictions placed on *currency conversion*? What policies can governments use to restrict currency conversion?

questions for discussion

1. What factors do you think are holding back the creation of a truly global capital market? How might a truly global capital market function differently than the current international market? (*Hint:* Some factors to consider are interest rates, currencies, regulations, and types of financial flows between countries.)
2. The use of different national currencies creates a barrier to further growth in international business activity. What are the pros and cons, among companies *and* governments, of replacing national currencies with regional currencies? Do you think a global currency is someday possible? Why or why not?
3. Governments dislike the fact that offshore financial centers facilitate money laundering. Do you think that electronic commerce will make it easier or harder to launder money and camouflage other illegal activities? Do you think offshore financial centers should be allowed to operate as freely as they do now, or do you favor regulation? Explain your answers.

in practice

Read the excerpt below from *Wall Street Journal* and answer the following questions:

> the movie Pocahontas products the fall in the fall, again coinciding with Disney's schedule for global release. This strategy provides ideal balance.
>
> ---
>
> Last week, the dollar ranged from 135.85 to 111.45 yen. While analysts used to see four-yen moves of the dollar as volatile, a repeat of last week's ranges won't come as a surprise this week.
>   Late Friday in New York, the dollar was trading at 116.68 yen, down from 119.45 Thursday. The U.S. currency also traded at 1.6368 marks, up from 1.6350. Sterling was at $1.7065, down from $1.7110.

1. Is the exchange rate quote for the U.S. dollar a direct or indirect quote on the (a) yen? (b) mark? (c) sterling (British pound)?

2. (a) From Thursday to Friday, what percentage change in the value of the dollar occurred against the yen? (b) sterling? (*Remember to mind your quoted and base currencies!*)

3. Using the mark as the base currency, what is Friday's cross rate between the yen and mark?

4. Using sterling as the base currency, what is Friday's cross rate between the mark and sterling?

projects

1. This chapter taught us that information technology, deregulation, and innovative financial instruments are behind much of the growth in the international capital market. Write a short report (about 800 words) on the ways in which recent advances in one of these three areas is helping to grow the international capital market. You might want to focus on a specific technology, nation (other than your own), international organization, or new financial instrument. Report your findings to the class in a brief presentation. Business periodicals such as *Forbes*, the *Economist*, *Euromoney*, and *Business Week*, available either in your library or on the Internet, are a good place to start.

2. With several of your classmates, select a country that interests you. Does the country have a city that is an important financial center? What volume of bonds is traded on the country's bond market? What is the total value of stocks traded on its stock exchange(s)? Does it have an emerging stock market? How has its stock market performed over the last year? What is the exchange rate between its currency and that of your own country? What factors are responsible for the stability or

volatility in that exchange rate? Are there any restrictions on the exchange of the nation's currency? How is the forecast for the country's currency likely to influence business activity in its major industries? Present a brief summary of your findings to the class. (*Hint:* Two good sources to begin your research are the monthly *International Financial Statistics* and the annual *Exchange Arrangements and Exchange Restrictions*, both published by the International Monetary Fund.)

3. Suppose your company has $10 million in excess cash to invest for one month. Your task is to invest this money in the foreign exchange market to earn a profit. (Holding dollars is not an option.) Select the currencies that you wish to buy at today's spot rate, but do not buy less than $2.5 million of any single currency. Track the spot rate for each of your currencies over the next month in the business press. At the end of the month, exchange your currencies at that day's spot rate. Calculate your gain or loss over the one-month period. (Your instructor will determine whether, and how often, you may trade currencies throughout the month.)

business case 9
HONG KONG HANDOVER: "ONE COUNTRY, TWO SYSTEMS"

On the stroke of midnight, July 1, 1997, fireworks showered over Hong Kong as Britain handed over its former colony to China. One minute later, the British flag was taken down and the Chinese flag hoisted all over the island. At the mint, the stern profile of Queen Elizabeth was morphing over and over into a five-petaled bauhinia flower, the new face of Hong Kong's coinage.

But even as the Chinese flag replaced the Union Jack and the bauhinia replaced the queen, much in Hong Kong remained the same—including its currency. The Hong Kong dollar is still pegged to the U.S. dollar, and the remnimbi Yuan, China's currency, cannot be used in Hong Kong. So far, it's clear that China's promise of "one country, two systems" was not a hollow slogan. As a Special Administrative Region, Hong Kong not only retains its own currency and controls its own reserves, but also remains outside Chinese law. It need not send revenues to Beijing, and it will be no easier for Chinese citizens to visit or settle in Hong Kong than anywhere else.

From a Communist viewpoint, such measures may seem extraordinary concessions to the citizens of Hong Kong. But

China desperately needs Hong Kong to facilitate its transformation from state-owned economy to full-fledged free-market powerhouse. Because China's own financial markets are small and crude, its large state-owned companies are scrambling to raise international capital on Hong Kong's stock market. The rise of these so-called "red chip" companies reflects both Beijing's efforts to restructure its economy and Hong Kong's efforts to establish itself as an economic dynamo for the rest of China. Chief executive Gary Coull of Crédit Lyonnais Securities (Asia) Ltd., estimates that for at least a decade, China will pump out as many as 350 public offerings a year on the Hong Kong exchange.

There are, however, dark clouds looming on Hong Kong's glittering financial horizon, not the least of which is the currency crisis that first swept through Southeast Asia in 1997. In addition, although Communist China is reforming its economy at a dizzying pace, political reforms have lagged far behind. In contrast, while Hong Kong itself is not a true democracy, it does enjoy some freedom of the press and the rule of law. Both information and capital flow somewhat unobstructed. Although China has pledged to preserve Hong Kong's freedoms, many people are nervous about the future. With the handover, for instance, the Chinese government abolished Hong Kong's elected legislature and replaced it with a council of hand-picked bureaucrats. In the past, Chinese authorities have arrested journalists who disclosed economic or financial information that the government deemed secret. More recently, an analyst at a Hong Kong–based brokerage firm lost his job after criticizing the management of China Eastern Airlines during a roadshow for the company's public-share offering. Julia Craddock, managing director for equity capital markets at BZW Asia Ltd. in Hong Kong, is uneasy about the handover. "In our business," she says, "you need to be able to rely on a free flow of information."

thinking globally

1. The merging of entrepreneurial Hong Kong with dynamic, developing China poses huge opportunities and huge risks. From a Hong Kong financier's viewpoint, what do you see as the greatest risks and greatest opportunities? From that of a Chinese politician?

2. Why is Hong Kong's currency linked to the U.S. dollar rather than the British pound?

3. At the same time that China is boosting Hong Kong's bottom line with "red chip" listings, the government is trying to restore Shanghai to the financial glory that it enjoyed before the Communist revolution of 1949. Both local civic leaders and Beijing's central planners are spending over $30 billion on the physical infrastructure required by a world-class financial center. However, despite Shanghai's global aspirations and potential, its financial scene is proving a bust for investors. Why do you think it is proving hard to create a flourishing financial exchange in mainland China? Does the problem support Craddock's opinion that the free flow of information is necessary for conducting business in the financial-services sector? Why or why not?

a question of ethics

1. Salomon Brothers Inc. Chairman Deryck C. Maughan once declared, "Markets are not politically correct." Some evidence suggests that the world's capital flows away from developing democracies. Moreover, the developing world's largest recipients of outside capital are single-party dominated states—China, Indonesia, and Vietnam. While the economies of Communist China and Vietnam each grew by about 10 percent in 1996, democratic India's economy expanded only 6.8 percent in the fiscal year ending in March 1997.

   Meanwhile, the World Bank's World Development Report takes the opposite point of view, claiming that in the long run, democratic political systems will have an edge in economic effectiveness. According to the bank, the crucial elements in economic effectiveness are the checks and balances of an open, democratic society. For its own survival if nothing else, says the bank, a democracy will tend to reflect the people's interests. And the people's interests are topped by long-term stable growth. Do you think that capitalism thrives best in more authoritarian countries or that its best prospects are in democratic countries? Explain your answer.

   Say, for example, that you are looking to expand your investment portfolio by investing overseas. Do you think it's ethical to invest in companies in authoritarian countries with questionable human rights records, such as Indonesia and China?[36]

2. In 1968, bank deposits in offshore financial centers (OFCs) were estimated at $11 billion. By 1991, estimates of the total size of the global offshore business had risen to over $1 trillion. "Dirty money" obtained through drug trafficking, gambling, and other illicit activities uses offshore financial centers to escape the same thing as "clean" respectable capital: national taxation and the surveillance of government regulation. According to one expert:

   > The burgeoning international marketplace—destablizing currency flows, using offshore havens to avoid tax—is hostile to expressions of common and public interest. Private interests have too easily slipped the national leash and have used the ungoverned world beyond national frontiers to undermine what they regard as tiresome, inefficient, and bureaucratic efforts to assert the moral and social dimension in human affairs.

Do you agree or disagree with this statement? Explain your answer. Do you think that corporate use of OFCs to avoid home-country bureaucracies and taxes is ethical? Why or why not?[37]

3. The goal of government regulation and supervision of financial-services industries has been to maintain the integrity and stability of financial systems and thereby to protect both depositors and investors. Regulations, for instance, include prohibitions against lending by management to itself or to closely related entities (a practice called "self-dealing"), against insider trading, and against other transactions in which there is a conflict of interest. In less than two decades, however, deregulation has transformed the world's financial markets. Granted, deregulation has spurred competition and growth in financial sectors; it has allowed capital to flow freely across borders and boost the economies of developing countries.

What, however, do you see as the "dark side" of deregulation, in terms of business ethics? What do you think Adam Smith, one of the first philosophers of capitalism, meant when he warned against the dangers of "colluding producers"? How do you think this warning applies to the financial-services sector today?[38]

10 international monetary system

Beacons

A Look Back

CHAPTER 9 examined how the international capital market and foreign exchange market operate. We also explained how exchange rates are calculated and how different rates are used in international business.

A Look at This Chapter

This chapter extends our knowledge of exchange rates and international financial markets. We examine factors that help determine exchange rates and explore rate forecasting techniques. We discuss international attempts to manage exchange rates and review recent currency problems in Asia, Russia, and other emerging markets.

A Look Ahead

CHAPTER 11 introduces the topic of the last part of this book—international business management. We explore how companies screen and research international opportunities and choose among competing investment projects.

Learning Objectives

After studying this chapter, you should be able to

1 Explain how *exchange rates* influence the activities of domestic and international companies.

2 Identify the factors that help determine exchange rates and their impact on business.

3 Describe the primary methods of *forecasting exchange rates*.

4 Discuss the evolution of the current *international monetary system* and explain how it operates.

5 Explain the *European monetary system* and assess its record of performance.

It hit hard for Raul Concepcion and other businesspeople in Manila's Makati business district. Their once bright futures now looked bleak and uncertain. The value of the Philippines' currency, the Philippine peso, unexpectedly plummeted in July 1997. Concepcion's company, Concepcion Industries Inc., which manufactures air conditioners and refrigerators for the domestic market, was hard hit by the weakened currency. Soaring prices for power and oil were the worst. But labor groups were also demanding higher wages to help workers' families offset the hardship caused by the devalued peso. "We'll be back to square one," moaned Concepcion.

Half a world away in Minong, Wisconsin, U.S.A., the future also turned sour for Link Snacks. Link Snacks sells beef and cheese products in Japan, South Korea, Malaysia, the Philippines, and Singapore. Jay Link, vice president of international sales, echoes Concepcion's despair over crumbling Asian economies. "Our orders have slowed by 15 percent to 20 percent over the last six months," reports Link. The crisis came at a particularly bad time for Link Snacks—the company had just launched an aggressive international marketing campaign.

Raul Concepcion and Jay Link are just two of millions of businesspeople worldwide who returned to "square one" in the wake of the Asian financial crisis. Besides throwing global financial markets into turmoil, the Asian crisis caused companies to completely rethink their business expansion strategies in Asia and other emerging markets. Many analysts do not expect the wounded Asian economies to recover fully until perhaps 2001 or 2003. The crisis is a sober reminder to all businesses, whether small exporter or huge global conglomerate, that knowledge and vigilance pay when it comes to the international financial system.[1]

In Chapter 9, we explained the fundamentals of how exchange rates are calculated and how different types of exchange rates are used. But our knowledge in this area is incomplete without a more thorough examination of the factors that influence exchange rates. This chapter extends our understanding of the international financial system by exploring factors that determine exchange rates and various international attempts to manage them. We begin by learning how company activities are affected by exchange-rate movements. We then examine the factors that help determine currency values and in turn exchange rates. Next, we learn about different methods of forecasting exchange rates. We conclude this chapter by exploring international mechanisms designed to manage exchange rates: the international monetary system and the European monetary system.

HOW EXCHANGE RATES INFLUENCE BUSINESS ACTIVITIES

Times of crisis are not the only occasions during which companies are affected by exchange rates. In fact, movement in a currency's exchange rate affects the activities of both domestic and international companies. Let's now examine how exchange-rate changes affect the *production*, *marketing*, and *financial* decisions of companies, and why stable and predictable rates are desirable.

PRODUCTION AND MARKETING DECISIONS

Exchange rates affect demand for a company's products in the global marketplace. When a country's currency is *weak* (valued low relative to other currencies), the price of its exports on world markets declines and the price of imports increases. Lower prices make the country's exports more appealing on world markets. They also give companies the opportunity to take market share away from companies whose products are priced high in comparison.

Furthermore, a company selling in a country with a *strong* currency (one that is valued high relative to other currencies) while paying workers in a country with a weak currency improves its profits. The Asian financial crisis discussed at the beginning of this chapter allowed some companies to follow just such a strategy. For example, Dell Computer makes nearly all its products in Penang, Malaysia, and prices everything it exports in dollars. But at the same time, Dell pays its Malaysian workers and suppliers in the local currency, ringgits. In fact, the Asian financial crisis turned this practice into a winning combination: Revenue was being generated in a strong currency whose value was climbing steadily, while expenses were being paid in a weak currency whose value kept falling. On the downside, companies with such a price advantage might grow complacent about reducing production costs. Long-term competitiveness might be lost if management views the temporary price advantage caused by exchange rates as permanent.[2]

The intentional lowering of the value of a currency by the nation's government is called **devaluation**. The reverse, the intentional raising of its value by the nation's government, is called **revaluation**. These concepts are not to be confused with the terms *weak* and *strong* currencies, although their effects are similar.

Devaluation lowers the price of a country's exports on world markets and increases the price of imports because the country's currency is now worth less on world markets. Thus a government might devalue its currency to give its domestic companies an edge over competition from other countries. It might also devalue to boost exports so that a trade deficit can be eliminated. However, such a policy is not wise because devaluation reduces consumers' buying power. It also allows inefficiencies to persist in domestic companies because there is now less pressure to be concerned with production costs. Revaluation has the opposite effects: It increases the price of exports and reduces the price of imports.

devaluation
Intentional lowering of the value of a nation's currency.

revaluation
Intentional raising of the value of a nation's currency.

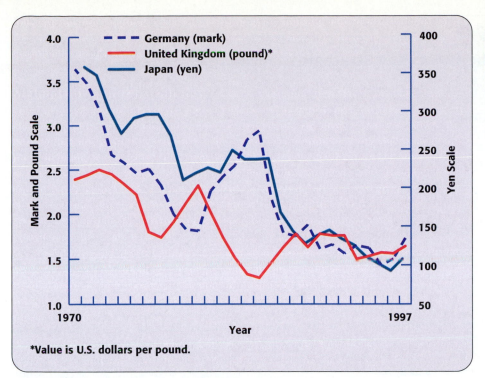

Figure 10.1 shows exchange rates between the U.S. dollar and several major world currencies. We can see that the Japanese yen fell steadily throughout the late 1980s. But in the early 1990s, a strong yen began to hurt Japan's automobile exports by adding about $3,300 to the cost of every Honda, Toyota, and Nissan sold in the United States. But the situation reversed in the middle to late 1990s, when the dollar rose against the yen. Japan's carmakers were once again able to price their exports attractively in the United States. U.S. carmakers were forced to reduce their own prices in order to stay competitive, thus hurting profit margins. Even so, Japan's carmakers increased their U.S. market share by nearly 10 percent in 1997 alone. Meanwhile, Detroit's Big Three carmakers (Chrysler, Ford, and General Motors) were trying to persuade U.S. policy makers that a weaker dollar was important for their short-term survival because it increased the price of imported autos.[3]

There are steps companies can take to counter the negative effects that too strong a currency can have on exports. For example, a strong dollar in 1997 caused some U.S. companies to become more aggressive in boosting exports.[4] For a look at some of these approaches, see the Global Manager "Exporting against the Odds: Key Strategies for Success."

FINANCIAL DECISIONS

Managers' financial decisions are also influenced by exchange rate changes. Exchange rates affect how and when a company pays its dividends. Suppose a company must pay dividends to shareholders (or to its parent company) in another country. If possible, the company will want to pay dividends when the home currency is strong. In this way, it takes less of the company's home currency to obtain the needed amount of the other country's currency to pay the dividends. Exchange rates also affect the amount of profit a company earns from its international subsidiaries. The earnings of international subsidiaries are typically integrated into the parent company's financial statements *in the*

Exporting Against the Odds: Key Strategies for Success

True or false: A nation's exports begin to fall after its currency has risen in value for 18 months.

The answer: Mostly true, but not necessarily so. Companies in the United States exported against the odds in 1997, when the U.S. dollar had climbed 54 percent against the yen and 23 percent against the German mark. Here's how:

➡ **Getting Leaner and Meaner** Companies cut costs by downsizing staff and reengineering factories for greater efficiency. According to the National Association of Manufacturers, thousands of small manufacturers doubled or tripled sales within a few years by finding ways to shave production costs.

➡ **Catering to the Customer** European customers of Chicago-based Bison Gear & Engineering stuck with the company despite it raising prices in French francs and German marks. The reason: Bison was willing to custom-design the transmission gears for every factory machine in which its product was installed. Thus despite the sticker shock, Bison's exports have actually risen.

➡ **Diversifying into Safer Sectors** An increasing number of U.S.-based exporters are in industries such as software, services, and entertainment—industries less affected by currency fluctuations. Demand in these hot-growth categories is growing around the world. Software giant Microsoft draws some 55 percent of its sales from outside the United States.

➡ **Going Where Demand Is Highest** Many U.S. companies today export to developing nations where demand is high. For instance, the share of total exports going to Latin America was more than 18 percent in 1997. This compares to a figure of just 11 percent a decade earlier.

➡ **Cutting or Freezing Prices** A strong dollar means U.S. exports headed for Europe and Japan are more expensive than European- and Japanese-made goods. Some U.S. exporters have frozen prices of their goods in francs, marks, or yen even though it means lower dollar revenues and lower profits. California-based Varian Associates froze prices on its chromatographs—industrial instruments that sell for upward of $40,000. To the company's surprise, it sold nearly 20 percent more units.

home currency. Translating subsidiary earnings into a *strong* home currency *reduces* the amount of these earnings when stated in the home currency. Likewise, translating earnings into a weak home currency increases stated earnings in the home currency.

Ferro Corporation is a $1.4 billion producer of ceramic glaze and porcelain tile. During the 1980s, Latin American countries experienced super-high inflation and a

In October 1998, the world's diplomats, bankers, and finance ministers met at the annual International Monetary Fund (IMF) Conference. The central issue was how to help the world's emerging markets and distressed economies. Brazil, in particular, was troubled with high inflation, interest rates nearing 45 percent, and a growing number of impoverished citizens—like the children shown here. The IMF, along with the World Bank and the United States, put together a $41.5 billion rescue package for Brazil, hoping that an improved Brazilian economy would also strengthen other South American economies.

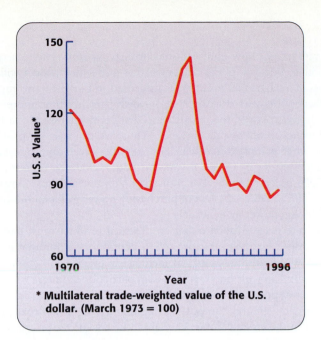

FIGURE 10.2

VALUE OF THE U.S. DOLLAR OVER TIME*

U.S. $ Value*

150

120

90

60

1970   1996

Year

* **Multilateral trade-weighted value of the U.S. dollar. (March 1973 = 100)**

precipitous decline in the values of their currencies. Ferro's sales and earnings in Brazil were growing exponentially—at least as measured in Brazilian *reals*. But in terms of its home currency, U.S. dollars, profits were far less rosy.[5]

DESIRE FOR STABILITY AND PREDICTABILITY

As we have seen, unfavorable movements in exchange rates can be costly for both domestic and international companies. Therefore, managers prefer that exchange rates be *stable*. Stable exchange rates improve the accuracy of financial planning, including cash flow forecasts. Although methods do exist for insuring against potentially adverse exchange-rate movements, most of these are too expensive for small and medium-size businesses. Moreover, as the unpredictability of exchange rates increases, so too does the cost of insuring against the accompanying risk. Figure 10.2 shows how the value of the U.S. dollar has changed over time. The figure reveals the instability of the dollar during the decade of the 1980s.

Managers also prefer that exchange-rate movements be *predictable*. Predictable exchange rates reduce the likelihood that companies will be caught off-guard by sudden and unexpected rate changes. Predictable rates reduce the need for costly insurance (usually by currency hedging) against possible adverse movements in exchange rates. Rather than purchasing insurance, companies would be better off spending their money on more productive activities such as developing new products or designing more efficient production methods.

WHAT FACTORS DETERMINE EXCHANGE RATES?

To improve our knowledge of the factors that help determine exchange rates, we must first understand two important concepts: the law of one price and purchasing power parity. Each of these concepts tells us the level at which an exchange rate *should* be. While discussing these concepts, we will examine some of the many factors affecting *actual* exchange-rate levels.

LAW OF ONE PRICE

An exchange rate tells us how much of one currency we must pay to receive a certain amount of another. But it does not tell us whether a specific product will actually cost us more or less in a particular country (as measured in our own currency). When we travel to another country, we discover that our own currency buys more or less than it does at home. In other words, we quickly learn that exchange rates do not guarantee or stabilize the buying power of our currency. Thus, we can lose purchasing power in some countries while gaining it in others. For example, a restaurant meal for you and a friend costing 420 francs in France might cost you 11,000 yen (about 510 francs) in Japan and 17,500 bolivar (about 170 francs) in Venezuela. Thus compared to your meal in France, you've suffered a loss of purchasing power in Japan but benefited from increased purchasing power in Venezuela.

law of one price
Principle that an identical item must have an identical price in all countries when price is expressed in the same currency.

The **law of one price** stipulates that an identical product must have an identical price in all countries when price is expressed in a common-denominator currency. For this principle to apply, products must be identical in quality and content in all countries, and must be entirely produced within each particular country.

For example, suppose coal mined within both the United States and Germany is of similar quality in each country. Suppose further that a kilogram of coal costs DM 1.5 in Germany and $1 in the United States. Therefore, the law of one price calculates the *expected* exchange rate between the German mark and U.S. dollar to be DM 1.5/$. However, suppose the *actual* mark/dollar exchange rate as witnessed on currency markets is DM 1.2/$. A kilogram of coal still costs $1 in the United States and DM 1.5 in Germany. But in order to pay for German coal *with dollars denominated after the exchange-rate change*, one must convert not just $1 into German marks, but $1.25 (the expected exchange rate ÷ the actual exchange rate, or 1.5 ÷ 1.2).

Thus the price of coal is higher in Germany than in the United States. Moreover, because the law of one price is being violated, an *arbitrage* opportunity arises—that is, an opportunity to buy a product in one country and sell it in another country where it has a higher value. For example, one could earn a profit by buying coal at $1 per kilogram in the United States and selling it at $1.25 (DM 1.5) per kilogram in Germany. Note, however, that as traders begin buying in the United States and selling in Germany, greater demand drives *up* the price of U.S. coal whereas greater supply drives *down* the price of German coal. Eventually, the price of coal in both countries will settle at a price somewhere between the previously low U.S. price and the previously high German price.

If it seems that the arbitrage opportunity would disappear for the same reason that it arose, that is essentially the case. According to William Louis Dreyfus, one of the world's leading commodities traders, companies like his are constantly seeking new opportunities as they themselves arbitrage old ones out of existence. In other words, it's the nature of arbitrage to even out excessive fluctuation by destroying its own profitability. An arbitrageur, says Dreyfus, is "like a microbe. While the microbe attacks your body, it has a wonderful time living, but it ends up killing your body and dies as a result. The arbitrageur is exactly the same. When he sees a market inefficiency, he goes to it and makes it efficient. As a consequence, his profit margin disappears."[6]

Big MacCurrencies   The usefulness of the law of one price is that it helps us determine whether a currency is overvalued or undervalued. Each year *The Economist* magazine publishes what it calls its "Big MacCurrencies" exchange-rate index (see Table 10.1). This index uses the law of one price to determine the exchange rate that should exist between the U.S. dollar and other major currencies. It employs the McDonald's Big Mac as its single product to test the law of one price. Why the Big Mac? Because

TABLE 10.1 Burgers and Exchange Rates

	Big Mac prices		Implied PPP* of the dollar	Actual $ exchange rate 6/4/98	Under (–)/ over (+) valuation against dollar, %
	in local currency	in dollars			
United States†	$2.56	2.56	—	—	—
Argentina	Peso2.50	2.50	0.98	1.00	−2
Australia	A$2.65	1.75	1.04	1.51	−32
Austria	Sch34.0	2.62	13.28	12.96	+2
Belgium	BFr109	2.87	42.58	38.00	+12
Brazil	Real3.10	2.72	1.21	1.14	+6
Britain	£1.84	3.05	1.39‡	1.66‡	+19
Canada	C$2.79	1.97	1.09	1.42	−23
Chile	Peso1,250	2.75	488	455	+7
China	Yuan9.90	1.20	3.87	8.28	−53
Czech Republic	CKr54.0	1.57	21.1	34.4	−39
Denmark	DKr23.8	3.39	9.28	7.02	+32
France	FFr17.5	2.84	6.84	6.17	+11
Germany	DM4.95	2.69	1.93	1.84	+5
Hong Kong	HK$10.2	1.32	3.98	7.75	−49
Hungary	Forint259	1.22	101	213	−52
Indonesia	Rupiah9,900	1.16	3,867	8,500	−55
Israel	Shekel12.50	3.38	4.88	3.70	+32
Italy	Lire4,500	2.47	1,758	1,818	−3
Japan	¥280	2.08	109	135	−19
Malaysia	M$4.30	1.16	1.68	3.72	−55
Mexico	Peso17.9	2.10	6.99	8.54	−18
Netherlands	Fl5.45	2.63	2.13	2.07	+3
New Zealand	NZ$3.45	1.90	1.35	1.82	−26
Poland	Zloty5.30	1.53	2.07	3.46	−40
Russia	Rouble12,000	2.00	4,688	5,999	−22
Singapore	S$3.00	1.85	1.17	1.62	−28
South Africa	Rand8.00	1.59	3.13	5.04	−38
South Korea	Won2,600	1.76	1,016	1,474	−31
Spain	Pta375	2.40	146	156	−6
Sweden	SKr24.0	3.00	9.38	8.00	+17
Switzerland	SFr5.90	3.87	2.30	1.52	+51
Taiwan	NT$68.0	2.06	26.6	33.0	−20
Thailand	Baht52.0	1.30	20.3	40.0	−49

*Purchasing-power parity: local price divided by price in United States
†Average of New York, Chicago, San Francisco and Atlanta
‡Dollars per pound
Source: McDonald's.

each one is fairly identical in quality and content across national markets and almost entirely produced within the nation in which it is sold. According to the Big Mac index, the average price of a Big Mac was $2.56 in the United States. The cheapest Big Macs were found in Indonesia and Malaysia at a dollar-equivalent price of $1.16, the most expensive in Switzerland at $3.87. According to the Big Mac index, therefore, the Indonesian rupiah and Malaysian ringgit are undervalued by 55 percent $\{[(((8,500 - 3,867) / 8,500) \times -100] = -55$ percent$\}$. On the other hand, the Swiss franc is overvalued by 51 percent $\{[(((1.52 - 2.30) / 1.52) \times -100] = 51$ percent$\}$.

Such large discrepancies between a currency's exchange rate on currency markets and the rate predicted by the Big Mac index are not surprising for several reasons. For one thing, the selling price of food is affected by subsidies for agricultural products in most countries. Also, a Big Mac is not a "traded" product in the sense that one can buy Big Macs in low-priced countries and sell them in high-priced countries. Prices can also be affected because Big Macs are subject to different marketing strategies in different countries. Finally, countries impose different levels of sales tax on restaurant meals.

The drawbacks of the Big Mac index reflect the fact that applying the law of one price to a single product is too simplistic a method for estimating exchange rates. Nonetheless, a recent study finds that currency values in eight out of twelve industrial countries do tend to change in the direction suggested by the Big Mac index. And for six out of seven currencies that changed more than 10 percent, the Big Mac index was as good a predictor as more sophisticated methods.[7]

PURCHASING POWER PARITY

We were introduced to the purchasing power parity concept in Chapter 4 when we discussed economic development. The purchasing power parity concept is also useful in determining what level an exchange rate should be. Recall that **purchasing power parity (PPP)** is the relative ability of two countries' currencies to buy the same "basket" of goods in those two countries. Thus although the law of one price holds for single products, PPP is meaningful only when applied to a *basket* of goods. Let's look at an example to see why this is so.

Suppose 650 baht in Thailand will buy a bag of groceries that costs $30 in the United States. What do these two numbers tell us about the economic conditions of people in Thailand as compared to people in the United States? First, they help us compare the *purchasing power* of a Thai consumer with that of a consumer in the United States. But the question is: Are Thai consumers better off or worse off than their counterparts in the United States? In order to address this question, we first need to know the *GNP per capita* of both countries:

Thai GNP/capita = 122,277 baht
U.S. GNP/capita = 26,980 U.S. $

Suppose the *exchange rate* between the two currencies is 41.45 baht = 1 U.S. $.[8] With this figure, we can translate 122,277 baht into U.S. dollars: 122,277/41.45 = 2,950 U.S. $. We can now restate our question: Do prices in Thailand enable a Thai consumer with $2,950 to buy more or less than a consumer in the United States with $26,980?

We already know that 650 baht will buy in Thailand what $30 will buy in the United States. Thus 650/$30 = 21.67 baht per 1 U.S. $. Note, then, that whereas the exchange rate on currency markets is 41.45 baht/$, the *purchasing power parity rate* of the baht is 21.67/$. Let's now use this figure to calculate a different comparative rate between the two currencies. We can now recalculate Thailand's GNP per capita at PPP as follows: 122,277/21.67 = $5,643. Clearly, Thai consumers, on average, are not nearly as affluent as their counterparts in the United States. But when we consider the *goods and services that they can purchase with their baht*—not the amount of U.S. dollars that they can buy—we see that a GNP per capita at PPP of $5,643 more accurately portrays the real purchasing power of Thai consumers.

Our new calculation, therefore, considers *price levels* in adjusting the relative values of the two currencies. Thus in the context of exchange rates, the principle of purchasing power parity can be interpreted as the exchange rate between two nations' currencies is equal to the ratio of their price levels (in our example, 21.67 instead of 41.45). In other words, in our example, PPP tells us how many units of Thai currency a consumer in Thailand needs in order to buy the same amount of products as a consumer in the United States can buy with 1 dollar.

As we can see in the above example, the exchange rate at PPP (21.67/$) is normally different from the actual exchange rate in financial markets (41.45/$). However, PPP states that economic forces will push the actual market exchange rate toward that determined by purchasing power parity. If not, arbitrage opportunities would arise. Purchasing power parity holds for internationally traded products that are not restricted by trade barriers and that entail few or no transportation costs. In order to earn a profit, arbitrageurs must be certain that the basket of goods purchased in the low-cost country would still be lower-priced in the high-cost country *after adding transportation costs, tariffs, taxes, and so forth.* Let's now see what impact inflation and interest rates have on exchange rates and purchasing power parity.

Role of Inflation   Inflation is the result of the supply and demand for a currency. Suppose additional money is injected into an economy that is not producing greater output. Thus people will have more money to spend on the same amount of products as before. As growing demand for products outstrips stagnant supply, prices will rise and devour any increase in the amount of money that consumers have to spend. Inflation, therefore, erodes people's purchasing power.

When the Soviet Union collapsed in 1991, the West hoped a new capitalist Russia would emerge. Six years later, the West was still hoping. By early 1997, Russia's economy was so troubled that even its strengths—low inflation and a stable currency—had begun to falter. In August 1997, Russia's economy was collapsing under fast-mounting foreign debt and an economic system that hadn't had adequate time to institute and solidify free-market reforms. In an emergency effort in late 1998, the Russian Central Bank printed more rubles and moved them into the economy—a measure some Russians supported but which critics said would raise inflation astronomically. To see how Russia says it fares today, go to its exchange site at ⟨**www.re.ru**⟩.

Impact of Money-Supply Decisions Because of the damaging effects of inflation, governments try to manage the supply of and demand for their currencies. They do this through the use of two types of policies designed to influence a nation's money supply. *Monetary policy* refers to activities that directly affect a nation's interest rates or money supply. Selling government securities reduces a nation's money supply because investors pay money to the government's treasury to acquire the securities. Conversely, when the government buys its own securities on the open market, cash is infused into the economy and the money supply increases.

Fiscal policy involves using taxes and government spending to influence the money supply indirectly. Increasing taxes, for instance, reduces the money supply because people pay money to the government coffers. But lowering taxes increases the money supply by leaving money in the hands of the people. Governments can also step up their own spending activities to increase the money supply or cut government spending to reduce it.

Impact of Unemployment and Interest Rates Many industrialized countries were very effective at controlling inflation throughout the middle and late 1990s (see Figure 10.3). Some economists claim that this was accomplished by these nations tightly controlling their money supplies. But others claim that international competition was responsible for keeping inflation under control. The logic (called "the new paradigm") runs as follows: Global competition and the mobility of companies to move anywhere that costs are lowest keeps a lid on wages. Because wages are kept under control, companies do not raise prices on their products, thus containing inflation. More research and time will be needed to see whether this is in fact the case.

Other key factors in the inflation equation are a country's unemployment and interest rates. When unemployment rates are low, there is a shortage of labor and employers pay higher wages to attract employees. Then, in order to maintain reasonable

FIGURE 10.3

HOW LOW CAN THEY GO?

The world's most developed economies maintained very low rates of inflation in the middle to late 1990s. Despite differing views on the cause for these low rates, their levels are quite astonishing. Inflation became so low that falling prices (called deflation) became a concern for some countries in this group—especially Japan. Compare these rates with those in Figure 10.4 for developing nations.

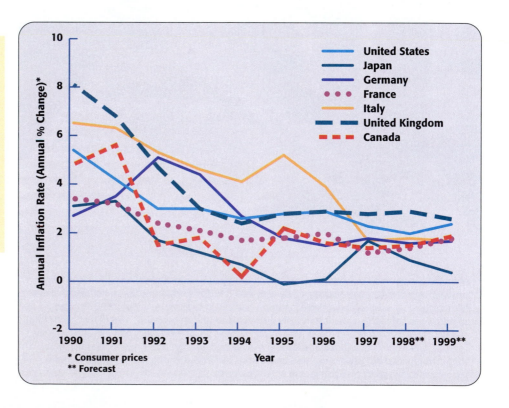

Japan's unemployment rate is rising. These jobless, homeless people sleep at a Tokyo train station. Economists hope that Japan, one of the most stable of the Asian nations, will correct its own problems soon so that it can help pull its neighbors—such as Korea, Thailand, and Indonesia—out of financial turmoil.

profit margins with higher labor costs, they usually raise the prices of their products, thus passing off the cost of higher wages to the consumer—thus causing inflation.

Interest rates (discussed shortly in detail) affect inflation because they affect the cost of borrowing money. Low interest rates encourage people to take out loans to buy such items as new homes and cars, and to run up debt on their credit cards. High interest rates prompt people to cut down on the amount of debt they carry because higher rates mean larger monthly payments on debt. Thus one way to cool off an inflationary economy is to raise interest rates because raising the cost of debt reduces consumer spending and makes it more costly for businesses to expand.

What problems does inflation create for business? For one, international companies often adjust cash management policies to avoid holding currencies of countries that are experiencing high inflation. Also, large international companies will likely choose to borrow money in those countries where inflation is low because the cost of borrowing is likely to be relatively low as well.

How Exchange Rates Adjust to Inflation An important component of the concept of purchasing power parity is that exchange rates adjust to different rates of inflation in different countries. Such adjustment is necessary to maintain purchasing power parity between nations. For example, suppose that at the beginning of the year the exchange rate between the Mexican peso and the U.S. dollar is 8 pesos/$ (or $.125/peso). Also suppose that inflation is pushing consumer prices higher in Mexico at an annual rate of 20 percent while prices are rising just 3 percent per year in the United States. To find the new exchange rate (E_e) at the end of the year, we use the following formula:

$$E_e = E_b (1 + i_1)/(1 + i_2)$$

where E_b is the exchange rate at the beginning of the period, i_1 is the inflation rate in country 1 and i_2 is the inflation rate in country 2. Plugging the numbers for this example into the formula, we get:

$$E_e = 8_{pesos/\$} [(1 + 0.20)/(1 + 0.03)] = 9.3_{pesos/\$}$$

It is important to remember that *because the numerator of the exchange rate is pesos, the inflation rate for Mexico must also be placed in the numerator for the ratio of inflation rates.* Thus we see that the exchange rate adjusts from 8 pesos/$ to 9.3 pesos/$ because of the higher inflation rate in Mexico and the corresponding change in currency values. Higher inflation in Mexico reduces the number of U.S. dollars that a peso will buy and increases the number of pesos that a dollar will buy. In other words, whereas it cost only 8 pesos to buy a dollar at the beginning of the year, it now costs 9.3 pesos.

In our example, while tourists from the United States can now take less expensive vacations in Mexico, Mexicans will find the cost of U.S. vacations more expensive. While companies based in Mexico must pay more in pesos for any supplies bought from the United States, U.S. companies will pay less, in dollar terms, for supplies bought from Mexico. For instance, the Mexico subsidiary of Levi-Strauss had a traumatic year in 1995 because of the sudden currency devaluation of the peso in the previous year. A key strategy for surviving during this period was finding local suppliers in Mexico to manufacture products that were suddenly too expensive to import from the United States. Ultimately, this push to consolidate a domestic supply chain had a positive result for Mexico: Fully 85 percent of the products that Levi's now sells in Mexico are manufactured by Mexican companies.[9]

This discussion illustrates at least one of the difficulties facing countries with high rates of inflation. Both consumers and companies in countries experiencing rapidly increasing prices see their purchasing power eroded. Figure 10.4 shows inflation rates in several developing countries and countries in transition—those most often plagued by rocketing prices. Notice the difference between these inflation rates and those in Figure 10.3 (p. 336) for developed nations.

Role of Interest Rates   In order to see how interest rates affect exchange rates between two currencies, we must first review the connection between inflation and interest rates within a single economy. We distinguish between two types of interest rates:

FIGURE 10.4

THE CURSE OF INFLATION
Developing countries and countries in transition toward free-market economies are often plagued by very high interest rates. Russia was especially hard hit by rising consumer prices in 1992–1993. Meanwhile, China has had much better luck at taming inflationary pressures in its economy. Compare these rates with those in Figure 10.3 for developed nations.

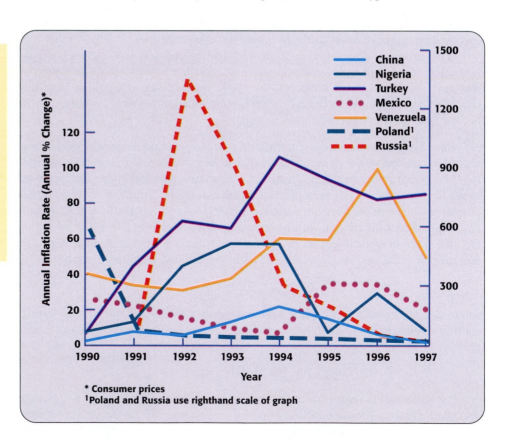

real interest rates and *nominal interest rates*. Let's say that your local banker quotes you an interest rate on a new-car loan. The quoted rate charged by the bank is the nominal interest rate, which consists of the real interest rate plus an additional charge for inflation. The reasoning behind this principle is simple. Recall from our earlier discussion that inflation erodes the purchasing power of currencies: The lender must be compensated for this erosion during the loan period. Table 10.2 shows interest rates charged by central banks in selected countries. These are interest rates charged to commercial banks: Businesses and consumers will pay higher rates than those shown here.

Fisher Effect   Now suppose instead that your bank lends you money to buy a delivery van for your home-based business. Let's say that, given your credit-risk rating, the bank would normally charge you 5 percent annual interest. But if inflation is expected to be 2 percent over the next year, your annual rate of interest will be 7 percent: 5 percent real interest plus 2 percent to cover inflation. This principle relating inflation to interest rates is called the **Fisher effect**: the principle that the nominal interest rate is the sum of the real interest rate and the expected rate of inflation over a specific time period. We write this relation between inflation and interest rates as:

Nominal Interest Rate = Real Interest Rate + Inflation Rate

If money were free from all controls when transferred internationally, the real rate of interest should be the same in all countries. To see why this is true, suppose that real interest rates are 4 percent in Canada and 6 percent in the United States. This situation creates an arbitrage opportunity: Investors could borrow money in Canada at 4 percent, lend it in the United States at 6 percent, and earn a profit on the 2 percent spread in interest rates. If enough people took advantage of this opportunity, interest rates would go up in Canada where demand for money would become heavier, and down in the United States where the money supply was growing. Again, the arbitrage opportunity would disappear because of the same activities that made it a reality. Thus theoretically, real interest rates remain equal across countries.

We demonstrated earlier the relation between inflation and exchange rates. The Fisher effect clarifies the relation between inflation and interest rates. Now, let's investigate the relation between exchange rates and interest rates. To illustrate this relation, we refer to the **international Fisher effect**—the principle that a difference in nominal

Fisher effect
Principle that the nominal interest rate is the sum of the real interest rate and the expected rate of inflation over a specific time period.

international Fisher effect
Principle that a difference in nominal interest rates supported by two countries' currencies will cause an equal but opposite change in their spot exchange rates.

TABLE 10.2   **Interest Rates around the World**

Country	Interest Rate*
Armenia	65.10%
Brazil	40.92
Canada	4.50
China	8.55
Germany	2.50
Japan	0.50
Kenya	32.27
Slovak Republic	8.80
South Africa	16.00
Switzerland	1.00
United States	5.00
Uruguay	95.50

*Central bank annual discount rate

interest rates supported by two countries' currencies will cause an equal but opposite change in their *spot exchange rates*. Recall from Chapter 9 that the spot rate is the rate quoted for delivery of the traded currency within two business days.

Because real interest rates are theoretically equal across countries, any difference in interest rates in two countries must be due to different expected rates of inflation. A country experiencing inflation higher than that of another country should see the value of its currency fall. If so, the exchange rate must be adjusted to reflect this change in value. For example, suppose nominal interest rates are 12 percent in France and 10 percent in Britain. Expected inflation in France, then, is 2 percent higher than in Britain. The international Fisher effect predicts that the future spot exchange rate between the French franc and British pound will adjust to a 2 percent drop in the value of the franc say, from Ffr 9.5/£, to Ffr 9.3/£.

Evaluating Purchasing Power Parity   Purchasing power parity is better at predicting long-term exchange rates (more than 10 years) than short-term rates. Unfortunately, accurate forecasts of short-term rates are most beneficial to international managers because most companies plan less than five years into the future. Even so, most short-term plans assume a great deal about future economic and political conditions in different countries. Among common considerations are added costs, trade barriers, and even investor psychology.

Impact of Added Costs   There are many possible reasons for the failure of PPP to accurately predict exchange rates. For one thing, PPP assumes no transportation costs. Suppose, for example, that the same basket of goods costs $100 in the United States and $150 in Norway. Seemingly, one could make a profit through arbitrage by purchasing these goods in the United States and selling them in Norway. However, if it costs another $60 to transport the goods to Norway, the total cost of the goods once they arrive in Norway will be $160. Obviously, no shipment will occur. Because no arbitrage opportunity exists after transportation costs are added, there will be no leveling of prices between the two markets and the price discrepancy will persist. Thus even if PPP predicts that the Norwegian krone is overvalued, the effect of transportation costs will keep the dollar/krone exchange rate from adjusting. In a world where transportation costs exist, PPP does not always correctly predict shifts in exchange rates.

Impact of Trade Barriers   PPP also assumes no barriers to international trade. However, such barriers certainly do exist. Governments establish trade barriers for many reasons including helping domestic companies remain competitive and preserving jobs for their citizens. Suppose the Norwegian government in our earlier example imposes a 60 percent tariff on the $100 basket of imported goods or makes its importation illegal. Because no leveling of prices or exchange-rate adjustment will occur, PPP will fail to predict accurate exchange rates.

Impact of Business Confidence and Psychology   Finally, PPP overlooks the human aspect of exchange rates: the role of people's confidence and beliefs about a nation's economy and its currency's value. Many countries gauge confidence in their economies by conducting a *business confidence survey*. The largest survey of its kind in Japan is called the tankan survey. It gauges business confidence four times each year among 10,000 companies! Figure 10.5 shows two decades of results for the tankan survey.

The confidence of investors in the value of a currency plays an important role in determining its exchange rate. Suppose several currency traders believe that the French franc will increase in value. They will buy French francs at the current price, sell them if the value increases, and earn a profit. Suppose, however, that all traders share the same belief and all follow the same course of action. The activity of the

In the years following the collapse of the Soviet Union, many Russians lost faith in the ruble, preferring to hold on to dollars. When the ruble collapsed in August 1998, Russian consumers panicked. As Russian banks closed their doors to citizens looking to exchange dollars for rubles before the rubles ran out—and to access their accounts—Russians rushed to sink their money into durable goods, such as cars and real estate.

traders themselves will be sufficient to push the value of the French franc higher. It doesn't matter why traders believed the price would increase. As long as enough people act on a similar belief regarding the future value of a currency, its value will change accordingly.

Thus nations try to maintain the confidence of investors, businesspeople, and consumers in their economies. The reason is that lost confidence causes companies to put

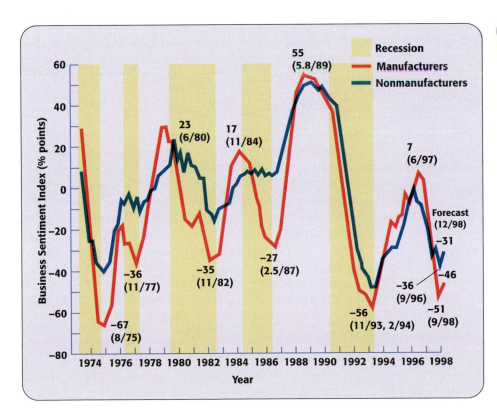

FIGURE 10.5
JAPAN'S TANKAN SURVEY

off investing in new products and technologies. They also tend not to hire additional employees but wait to see if the economy picks up. Consumers tend to increase their savings and not increase their debts if they've lost confidence in an economy. These kinds of behaviors definitely act to weaken a nation's currency.

FORECASTING EXCHANGE RATES

Before undertaking any international business activity, managers must consider the impact that currency values will have on financial results. They must, therefore, know how to obtain accurate exchange-rate forecasts. This section explores two distinct views regarding how accurately future exchange rates can be predicted by forward exchange rates—the rate agreed upon for foreign exchange payment at a future date. We also take a brief look at different techniques for forecasting exchange rates.

EFFICIENT MARKET VIEW

efficient market view
View that prices of financial instruments reflect all publicly available information at any given time.

A great deal of debate revolves around the issue of whether markets themselves are *efficient* or *inefficient* in forecasting exchange rates. A market is *efficient* if prices of financial instruments quickly reflect new public information made available to traders. The **efficient market view** thus holds that prices of financial instruments reflect all publicly available information at any given time. As applied to exchange rates, this means that forward exchange rates are accurate forecasts of future exchange rates.

Recall from Chapter 9 that a forward exchange rate reflects a market's expectations about the future values of two currencies. In an efficient currency market, forward exchange rates reflect all relevant, publicly available information at any given time. Therefore, they are considered the best possible predictors of exchange rates. Proponents of this view hold that there is no other publicly available information that could improve the forecast of exchange rates over that provided by forward rates. If one accepts this view, companies waste time and money collecting and examining information believed to affect future exchange rates. But there is always a certain amount of deviation between forward and actual exchange rates. The fact that forward exchange rates are less than perfect inspires companies to search for more accurate forecasting techniques.

INEFFICIENT MARKET VIEW

inefficient market view
View that prices of financial instruments do not reflect all publicly available information.

The **inefficient market view** holds that prices of financial instruments do not reflect all publicly available information. Proponents of this view believe that companies can search for new pieces of information to improve forecasting. However, the cost of searching for further information must not outweigh the benefits of its discovery.

Naturally, the inefficient market view is more compelling when the existence of *private* information is considered. Suppose a single currency trader holds privileged information regarding a future change in a nation's economic policy—information that she believes will affect its exchange rate. Because the market is unaware of this information, it is not reflected in forward exchange rates. Our trader will no doubt earn a profit by acting on her store of private information.

Now that we understand the two basic views related to market efficiency, let's look at some specific methods that companies use to forecast exchange rates.

FORECASTING TECHNIQUES

Spilling out of the debate about whether markets are efficient or inefficient forecasters of exchange rates, is the question of whether experts can improve upon the forecasts of forward exchange rates in *either* an efficient or inefficient market. As we've already seen, some analysts believe that exchange-rate forecasts can be improved by uncovering information not reflected in forward exchange rates. In fact, companies exist to provide exactly this type of service. There are two main forecasting techniques based on this belief in the value of added information—*fundamental analysis* and *technical analysis.*

Fundamental Analysis   **Fundamental analysis** employs statistical models based on fundamental economic indicators to forecast exchange rates. These models are often quite complex, with many variations reflecting different possible economic conditions. Economic variables used in these models include factors such as inflation, interest rates, money supply, tax rates, and government spending. Such analyses also often consider a country's balance-of-payments situation (see Chapter 7) and government intervention in foreign exchange markets to influence its currency's value.

fundamental analysis
Technique using statistical models based on fundamental economic indicators to forecast exchange rates.

Technical Analysis   Another method of forecasting exchange rates is **technical analysis**—a technique that employs charts of past trends in currency prices and other factors to forecast exchange rates. Using highly statistical models and charts of past data trends, analysts estimate the conditions prevailing during changes in exchange rates and try to estimate the timing, magnitude, and direction of future exchange-rate changes. Many forecasters combine the techniques of both fundamental and technical analyses to arrive at potentially more accurate forecasts.

technical analysis
Technique using charts of past trends in currency prices and other factors to forecast exchange rates.

DIFFICULTIES OF FORECASTING

The business of forecasting exchange rates is a rapidly growing industry. This trend seems to provide evidence that a growing number of people believe it is possible to improve on the forecasts of exchange rates embodied in forward rates. However, difficulties remain. Despite highly sophisticated statistical techniques in the hands of well-trained analysts, forecasting is not a pure science. Few forecasts are ever 100 percent accurate because of unexpected events that occur throughout the forecast period.

Over and above the problems associated with the data used by these techniques, failings can be traced to the human element involved in forecasting. People might, for example, miscalculate the importance of economic news becoming available to the market, placing too much emphasis on some elements and ignoring others.

So far in this chapter, we've discussed how companies are affected by exchange-rate changes and why managers prefer exchange rates to be stable and predictable. We saw how inflation and interest rates affect currency values, and in turn exchange rates, in different countries. We also learned that despite attempts to forecast exchange rates accurately, difficulties remain. For all these reasons, governments develop systems designed to manage exchange rates between their currencies. In this section, we examine international arrangements and institutions aimed at managing exchange rates. We also briefly trace the evolution of the current international monetary system.

For hundreds of years, governments have tried to manage movements in exchange rates. Groups of nations have created both formal and informal agreements to control exchange rates between their currencies. The present-day **international monetary system** is the collection of agreements and institutions that govern exchange rates.

EVOLUTION OF THE INTERNATIONAL MONETARY SYSTEM

international monetary system
Collection of agreements and institutions governing exchange rates.

EARLY YEARS: THE GOLD STANDARD

In the earliest days of international trade, gold was the internationally accepted currency for payment of goods and services. Using gold as a medium of exchange in international trade has several advantages. First, its limited supply made it a highly demanded commodity. Second, because gold is highly resistant to corrosion, it can be traded and stored for hundreds of years. Third, because it can be melted into either small coins or large bars, gold is a good medium of exchange for both small and large purchases.

But gold also has its disadvantages. First, its weight made transporting it expensive. Second, when a transport ship sank at sea, the gold sank to the ocean floor and was lost. Thus merchants wanted a new way to make their international payments without the need to haul large amounts of gold around the world. The solution was found in the **gold standard**—an international monetary system in which nations linked the value of their paper currencies to specific values of gold. Britain was the first nation to implement the gold standard in the early 1700s—it remained intact until the First World War.

gold standard
International monetary system in which nations linked the value of their paper currencies to specific values of gold.

Par Value   The gold standard required a nation to fix the value (price) of its currency to an ounce of gold (e.g., $35/oz.). The value of a currency expressed in terms of gold is called its *par value*. Each nation must then guarantee to convert its paper currency into gold for anyone demanding it at its par value. The calculation of each currency's par value was based on the concept of purchasing power parity. This provision made the purchasing power of gold the same everywhere and maintained the purchasing power of currencies across nations.

All nations fixing their currencies to gold also indirectly link their currencies to one another. Because the gold standard *fixed* nations' currencies to the value of gold, it is called a **fixed exchange-rate system**—one in which the exchange rate for converting one currency into another is fixed by international governmental agreement. This system and the use of par values made calculating exchange rates between any two currencies a very simple matter. For example, under the gold standard the U.S. dollar was originally fixed at $20.67/oz. of gold, the British pound at £ 4.2474/oz. To calculate the dollar/pound exchange rate, we simply divide the par value of the pound into the par value of the dollar as follows:

fixed exchange-rate system
System in which the exchange rate for converting one currency into another is fixed by international agreement.

$$(\$20.67/oz.)/(£\ 4.2474/oz.) = \$4.87/£$$

Advantages of the Gold Standard   The gold standard was quite successful in its early years of operation. In fact, this early record of success is causing some economists and policy makers to call for its rebirth today. Three main advantages of the gold standard underlie its early success.

Reducing Exchange-Rate Risk   First, the gold standard drastically reduces exchange-rate risk because it maintains highly fixed exchange rates between currencies. Deviations that do arise are much smaller than they would be under a system of freely floating currencies. The more stable exchange rates are, the less that companies are affected by actual or potential adverse changes in them. Because the gold standard significantly reduced exchange-rate risk and, therefore, the risks and costs of trade, international trade grew rapidly following its introduction.

Imposing Strict Monetary Policies   Second, the gold standard imposes strict monetary policies on all countries participating in the system. Recall that the gold standard requires governments to convert paper currency into gold if demanded by holders of the currency. If all holders of a nation's paper currency decided to trade it for gold, the government must have an equal amount of gold reserves to pay them. Thus a government cannot allow the volume of its paper currency to grow faster than the growth in its reserves of gold. Recall, too, that limiting the growth of a nation's money supply preserves purchasing power by keeping inflation low. Thus the gold standard was an effective tool in helping to control inflationary pressures.

What's wrong with just printing more money when your country is in debt? It causes inflation. Germany learned this lesson the hard way in 1923, when inflation rose 9,439 percent in one year as a result of the government's printing money for its Ruhr River Valley workers. At one point, the German mark had an exchange rate of DM 4.2 trillion to 1 dollar. Postage stamps carried prices in the billions. Banks had to conduct transactions by the cartful, and much daily commerce was conducted by bartering.

The classic case of inflation due to a government's free hand with the monetary printing press occurred in Germany in 1923. The German government began printing huge quantities of paper money to help support workers in the Ruhr River valley. This move triggered history's most horrendous inflationary spiral—9439 percent inflation in just one year! Any German citizen lucky enough to have 10,000 marks (about $2,500) in the bank in July 1922 found this nest egg at the end of 1923 to be worth about *one millionth of a penny!* Life savings were wiped out, and money became practically worthless.[10] With a gold standard in place, this scenario would not have been possible.

Correcting Trade Imbalances Third, the gold standard can help correct a nation's trade imbalance. Suppose Australia is importing more than it is exporting (experiencing a trade deficit). As gold flows out of Australia to pay for imports, its government must decrease the supply of paper currency in the domestic economy because it cannot have paper currency in excess of its gold reserves. As the money supply falls, so do prices of goods and services in Australia because demand is falling (consumers have less to spend) while supply is unchanged. Meanwhile, the falling prices of Australian-made goods makes Australian exports cheaper on world markets. Exports will rise until Australia's international trade is once again in balance.

The exact opposite occurs in the case of a trade surplus: The inflow of gold supports an increase in the supply of paper currency, which increases demand for, and, therefore, the cost of, goods and services. Thus exports will fall in reaction to their higher price until trade is once again in balance.

Collapse of the Gold Standard Nations involved in the First World War needed to finance their enormous war expenses, and they did so by printing more paper currency. Of course, this violated the fundamental principle of the gold standard and forced nations to abandon the standard. The aggressive printing of paper currency caused rapid inflation for these nations. When the United States returned to the gold standard in 1934, it adjusted its par value from $20.67/oz. of gold to $35.00/oz. to reflect the lower value of the dollar resulting from inflation. Thus the U.S. dollar had undergone a devaluation. However, Britain returned to the gold standard several years earlier at its previous level that did not reflect the effect inflation had on its currency.

Because the gold standard links each currency to one another, devaluation of one currency in terms of gold affects exchange rates between currencies. The decision of the United States to devalue its currency and Britain's decision not to do so, lowered the price of U.S. exports on world markets and increased the price of British goods imported into the United States. For example, whereas it had previously required $4.87 to purchase one British pound, it now required $8.24 {($35.00/oz.)/(£ 4.2474/oz.)}. This forced the cost of a £10 bottle of Scotch imported from Britain to the United States to go from $48.70 before devaluation to $82.40 after devaluation. This drastically increased the price of imports from Britain (and other countries), lowering its export earnings. As countries devalued their currencies in retaliation, a period of "competitive devaluation" resulted. To improve their trade balances, nations chose arbitrary par values to which they devalued their currencies. People quickly lost faith in the gold standard because it was no longer an accurate indicator of a currency's true value. In effect, the gold standard was dead.

BRETTON WOODS AGREEMENT

Bretton Woods Agreement
Agreement (1944) among nations to create a new international monetary system based on the value of the U.S. dollar.

In 1944, representatives from 44 nations met in the New Hampshire resort town of Bretton Woods to lay the foundation for a new international monetary system. The resulting **Bretton Woods Agreement** was an accord among nations to create a new international monetary system based on the value of the U.S. dollar.

The new system was designed to balance the strict discipline of the gold standard with the flexibility that countries needed to deal with temporary domestic monetary difficulties. It imposed discipline by creating a fixed exchange-rate system. But it also maintained flexibility by creating a short-term lending agency and would allow large currency devaluation only under extreme circumstances. Thus the most important features of the new system were *fixed exchange rates*, *built-in flexibility*, *funds for economic development*, and an *enforcement mechanism*. Let's now take a closer look at each one of these features.

Fixed Exchange Rates   The Bretton Woods Agreement incorporated fixed exchange rates by tying the value of the U.S. dollar directly to gold and the value of other currencies to the value of the dollar. The par value of the U.S. dollar was fixed at $35/oz. of gold. Other currencies were then given par values against the U.S. dollar instead of gold. For example, the par value of the British pound was established as $2.40/£. Member nations were expected to keep their currencies from deviating more than 1 percent above or below their par values. The Bretton Woods Agreement also improved on the gold standard by extending the right to exchange gold for dollars only to national governments, rather than anyone who demanded it.

fundamental disequilibrium
Economic condition in which a trade deficit causes a permanent negative shift in a country's balance of payments.

Built-In Flexibility   The new system also incorporated a degree of built-in flexibility. For example, although competitive currency devaluation was ruled out, large devaluation was allowed under the extreme set of circumstances called **fundamental disequilibrium**—an economic condition in which a trade deficit causes a permanent negative shift in a country's balance of payments. In this situation, a nation can devalue its currency more than 10 percent. Devaluation under these circumstances should accurately reflect a permanent economic change for the country in question, not temporary misalignments.

World Bank (International Bank for Reconstruction and Development, or IBRD)
Agency created by the Bretton Woods Agreement to provide funding for national economic development efforts.

World Bank   To provide funding for countries' efforts toward economic development, the Bretton Woods Agreement created the **World Bank**—officially called the **International Bank for Reconstruction and Development (IBRD)**. The immediate purpose of the World Bank was to finance European reconstruction following the Second

World War. It later shifted its focus to the general financial needs of developing countries. The Bank funds economic development projects in Africa, South America, and Southeast Asia.

The World Bank offers funds to countries unable to obtain capital from commercial sources for certain projects considered too risky. The Bank often undertakes projects to develop transportation networks, power facilities, and agricultural and educational programs. For example, World Bank funding is helping to increase attendance of girls at school in Pakistan's rural Balochistan Province. In two years alone, 198 new rural schools for girls were established. Moreover, enrollment of girls in areas with new schools increased to 87 percent, compared to 15 percent in the province as a whole.[11]

International Monetary Fund The Bretton Woods Agreement established the International Monetary Fund (IMF) as the agency to regulate the fixed exchange rates and enforce the rules of the international monetary system. At the time of its formation, the IMF had just 29 members—today 182 countries belong. Included among the main purposes of the IMF are:[12]

➡ Promoting international monetary cooperation

➡ Facilitating expansion and balanced growth of international trade

➡ Promoting exchange stability, maintaining orderly exchange arrangements, and avoiding competitive exchange devaluation

➡ Making the resources of the Fund temporarily available to members

➡ Shortening the duration and lessening the degree of disequilibrium in the international balance of payments of member nations

Special Drawing Right (SDR) World financial reserves of dollars and gold grew scarce in the 1960s at a time when the activities of the IMF demanded greater amounts of dollars and gold. The IMF reacted by creating what is called a **special drawing right (SDR)**—an IMF asset whose value is based on a "basket" of its five biggest members' currencies (France, Germany, Japan, the United Kingdom, and the United States). Figure 10.6 shows the "weight" each currency contributes to the overall value of the SDR. The value of the SDR changes with increases and declines in the values of its underlying currencies. In late 1998, there were more than 21 billion SDRs in existence worth about $29 billion (1 SDR equaled about $1.36 at that time).

> *International Monetary Fund (IMF)*
> *Agency created by the Bretton Woods Agreement to regulate fixed exchange rates and enforce the rules of the international monetary system.*

> *special drawing right (SDR)*
> *IMF asset whose value is based on a "weighted basket" of the currencies of five industrialized countries.*

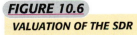

FIGURE 10.6

VALUATION OF THE SDR

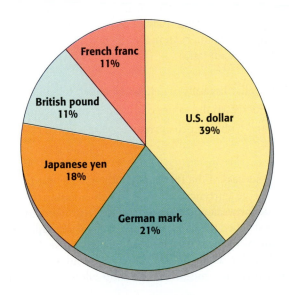

French franc
11%

British pound
11%

U.S. dollar
39%

Japanese yen
18%

German mark
21%

FIGURE 10.7

LARGEST IMF MEMBERS BY QUOTA

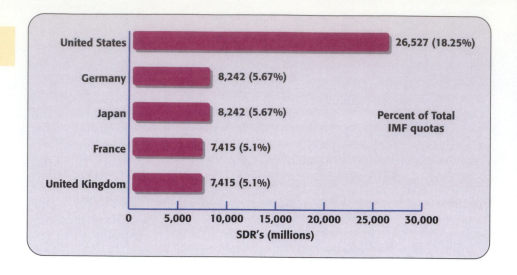

The significance of the SDR is that it is the unit of account for the IMF. Each nation is assigned a quota based on the size of its economy when it enters the IMF. Payment of this quota by each nation provides the IMF with the funds it needs to make short-term loans to members. Figure 10.7 shows the quotas for the five biggest members of the IMF.

Collapse of the Bretton Woods Agreement

The system developed at Bretton Woods worked quite well for about 20 years—an era boasting unparalleled exchange-rate stability. In the 1960s, however, the Bretton Woods system began to falter. The main problem was that the United States was experiencing a trade deficit (imports were exceeding exports) and a budget deficit (expenses were outstripping revenues). Governments that were holding dollars began to doubt that the U.S. government had an adequate amount of gold reserves to redeem all its paper currency held outside the country. When they began demanding gold in exchange for dollars, there followed a large sell-off of dollars on world financial markets.

Smithsonian Agreement In August 1971, the U.S. government held less than one-fourth the amount of gold needed to redeem all U.S. dollars in circulation. In late 1971 the United States and other countries reached the so-called **Smithsonian Agreement** to restructure and strengthen the international monetary system. The Smithsonian Agreement accomplished three main tasks:

1. The value of the dollar in terms of gold was lowered to $38/oz. of gold
2. Other countries increased the values of their currencies against the dollar
3. The 1 percent band within which currencies were allowed to float was increased to 2.25 percent

Final Days The success of the Bretton Woods system relied on the U.S. dollar remaining a strong reserve currency. However, high inflation and a persistent trade deficit had kept the dollar weak and so demonstrated a fundamental flaw in the system. The weak U.S. dollar strained the abilities of central banks in Japan and most European countries to maintain exchange rates with the dollar. Because these nations' currencies were tied to the U.S. dollar, as the dollar continued to fall, so too did their currencies. Britain left the system in the middle of 1972 and allowed the pound to float freely

Smithsonian Agreement
Agreement (1971) among IMF members to restructure and strengthen the international monetary system created at Bretton Woods.

against the dollar. The Swiss abandoned the system in early 1973. In January 1973, the dollar was again devalued, this time to around $42/oz. of gold. But even this move was not enough. As nations began dumping their reserves of the dollar on a massive scale, currency markets were temporarily closed to prevent further selling of the dollar. When markets reopened, the values of most major currencies were floating against the U.S. dollar. The era of an international monetary system based on *fixed* exchange rates was over once and for all.

MANAGED FLOAT SYSTEM

The Bretton Woods system collapsed because it depended so heavily on the stability of the dollar. As long as the dollar remained strong, it worked well. But when the dollar weakened, it failed to perform properly. Originally, the new system of *floating* exchange rates was viewed as a temporary solution to the shortcomings of the Bretton Woods and Smithsonian agreements. However, no new coordinated international monetary system was forthcoming. Rather, there emerged several independent efforts to manage exchange rates.

Jamaica Agreement By January 1976, returning to a system of fixed exchange rates seemed unlikely. World leaders thus met to draft the so-called **Jamaica Agreement**—an accord among members of the IMF to formalize the existing system of floating exchange rates as the new international monetary system. The Jamaica Agreement contained several main provisions. First, it endorsed a **managed float system** of exchange rates—that is, a system in which currencies float against one another, with governments intervening to stabilize their currencies at particular target exchange rates. This is in contrast to a **free float system**—a system in which currencies float freely against one another without governments intervening in currency markets.

Second, gold was no longer the primary reserve asset of the IMF. Member countries could retrieve their gold from the IMF if they so desired. Third, the mission of the IMF was augmented: Rather than being the manager of a fixed exchange-rate system only, it was now a "lender of last resort" for nations with balance-of-payments difficulties. Member contributions were increased to support the newly expanded activities of the IMF.

Plaza Accord Between 1980 and 1985, the U.S. dollar rose anywhere from 50 to 80 percent against most major world currencies. The rapidly rising dollar also pushed up prices of U.S. exports on world markets and so added once again to a U.S. trade deficit. In September 1985, representatives of the world's five largest industrialized economies, known as the "G5" (Britain, France, Germany, Japan, and the United States), met to discuss measures to force down the value of the dollar.

The meeting resulted in the **Plaza Accord**—a 1985 agreement among the G5 nations to act together on forcing down the value of the U.S. dollar. The Plaza Accord involved no detailed plan but was simply a signal to financial markets that the G5 were determined to intervene to force down the value of the dollar. When currency markets responded, the dollar fell most severely against the Japanese yen. Between 1985 and 1987, the dollar lost half its value against the yen, falling from about 250 ¥/$ to 125 ¥/$.

Louvre Accord By February 1987, the industrialized nations were concerned that the value of the U.S. dollar was now in danger of falling *too* low. Meeting in Paris, leaders of the "G7" nations (the G5 plus Italy and Canada) drew up the **Louvre Accord**—a 1987 agreement among the G7 nations that affirmed the U.S. dollar was appropriately valued and that they would intervene in currency markets to maintain its current market value. Once again, currency markets responded as hoped, and the dollar stabilized.

Jamaica Agreement
Agreement (1976) among IMF members to formalize the existing system of floating exchange rates as the new international monetary system.

managed float system
Exchange-rate system in which currencies float against one another, with governments intervening to stabilize their currencies at particular target exchange rates.

free float system
Exchange-rate system in which currencies float freely against one another, without governments intervening in currency markets.

Plaza Accord
Agreement (1985) among the G5 nations to act together in forcing down the value of the U.S. dollar.

Louvre Accord
Agreement (1987) among the G7 nations affirming that the U.S. dollar was appropriately valued and that they would intervene in currency markets to maintain its current market value.

Following the Louvre Accord, the leaders of the G8 (the G7 plus Russia) meet each year to discuss issues related to the international monetary system and trade. The European Union is also often represented.

Today's Exchange-Rate Arrangements   Today's international monetary system remains in large part a managed float system whereby most nations' currencies float against one another, and governments intervene to realign exchange rates. Within the larger monetary system, however, certain countries try to maintain more stable exchange rates by tying their currencies to another country's stronger currency. We can distinguish between three broad categories of exchange-rate arrangements that countries implement: *pegged*, *limited flexibility*, and *more flexible* (see Map 10.1).[13]

Pegged Exchange-Rate Arrangement   Think of one country as a small lifeboat tethered to a giant cruise ship as it navigates choppy monetary waters. Many economists argue that rather than let their currencies face the tides of global currency markets alone, developing economies should tie them to the U.S. dollar, French franc, or other more stable currency.

MAP 10.1

EXCHANGE-RATE ARRANGEMENTS

Pegged exchange-rate arrangements "peg" a country's currency to a more stable and widely used currency in international trade. As you can see in Map 10.1, many small countries peg their currencies to the U.S. dollar, French franc, the special drawing right (SDR) of the IMF, or other individual currency. Other nations peg their currencies to groups, or "baskets," of currencies. For example, Bangladesh and Burundi tie their currencies (the *taka* and *Burundi franc*, respectively) to those of its major trading partners.

Limited Flexibility Exchange-Rate Arrangement   Countries implementing this type of exchange-rate arrangement allow their currencies to float within a 2.25 percent band of the U.S. dollar. Four countries with this type of arrangement are Bahrain, Qatar, Saudi Arabia, and the United Arab Emirates (U.A.E.). Another group of countries operating under limited flexibility arrangements is the European Union (discussed in detail shortly). These countries link their currencies to float within a 2.25 percent band of a stated exchange rate.

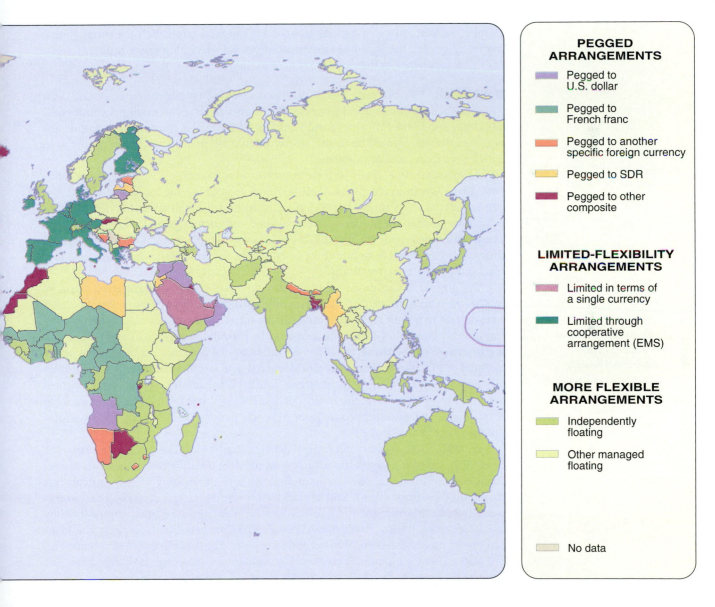

PEGGED ARRANGEMENTS

- Pegged to U.S. dollar
- Pegged to French franc
- Pegged to another specific foreign currency
- Pegged to SDR
- Pegged to other composite

LIMITED-FLEXIBILITY ARRANGEMENTS

- Limited in terms of a single currency
- Limited through cooperative arrangement (EMS)

MORE FLEXIBLE ARRANGEMENTS

- Independently floating
- Other managed floating

- No data

More Flexible Exchange-Rate Arrangement   Countries in the "other managed floating" group link their currencies to those of other nations but allow greater flexibility than countries with limited flexibility arrangements. For example, Israel links its currency (the *new sheqel*) to a currency basket comprising the German mark, French franc, Japanese yen, British pound, and U.S. dollar. Israel's currency then fluctuates within a margin of 7 percent around the group's central exchange rate. Another country in this group is Hungary. It allows its currency (the *forint*) to float against a currency basket comprising the German mark and U.S. dollar but resets the official exchange rate each day at 11 A.M.

Countries labeled in Map 10.1 as "independently floating" let their currencies float independently on global currency markets. These nations let their currencies' values be determined by the forces of supply and demand in the market. However, a government will intervene to influence the value of its nation's currency by buying or selling its own currency and those of other nations.

RECENT FINANCIAL CRISES

Despite the best efforts of nations to head off financial crises with the international monetary system, the world has experienced several wrenching crises in recent years. Let's now take a look at the most prominent of these.

Debt Crisis   By the early 1980s, certain developing countries (especially in Latin America) had amassed huge debts payable not only to large international commercial banks but also to the IMF and World Bank. In 1982, Mexico, Brazil, and Argentina announced that they would be unable to pay interest on their loans. Many countries in Africa were facing similar problems.

At the same time, many of these countries were also experiencing runaway inflation. The 1980s in Brazil, for example, are now recalled as "the lost decade." In 1988, annual inflation was running at 933 percent. Although Brazil spent heavily on social programs, much of the money went to a bloated and corrupt government bureaucracy. These conditions made for incredibly bleak years. The poor celebrated carnival with their usual fervor, but in honor of the collapsing economy, the theme for the 1988 carnival in Rio was "Bye, Bye, Brazil."[14]

To prevent a meltdown of the entire financial system, international agencies stepped in with a number of temporary solutions to the crisis. Repayment schedules were revised to put off repayment until further into the future. One international institution that played a key role in the debt crisis by providing temporary loans is the **Bank for International Settlements (BIS)**—an international banking institution that serves national central banks around the world and helps to stabilize the international monetary system. Traditionally, only the largest industrialized nations have been members of the BIS. But in 1996–1997, the bank added to its membership emerging markets from Asia, central and eastern Europe, Latin America, and the Middle East. Today, 45 nations are represented at the BIS.[15]

In 1989, U.S. Treasury Secretary Nicholas Brady unveiled the Brady Plan. The Brady Plan called for large-scale reduction of the debt owed by poorer nations, the exchange of old loans for new low-interest loans, and the making of debt instruments (based on these loans) that would be tradable on world financial markets. This last feature allowed a debtor country to receive a loan from an institution and then use it to buy special securities (called "Brady Bonds") on financial markets. Funds for these new loans came from private commercial banks and were backed by the IMF and World Bank. Figure 10.8 shows the amount of outstanding credit and loans of the IMF over time. The large increase during the 1980s (much of it going to Latin America) is apparent.

> **Bank for International Settlements (BIS)**
> *International banking institution serving national central banks around the world and helping to stabilize the international monetary system.*

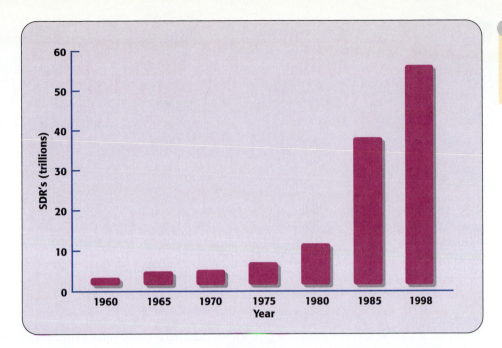

FIGURE 10.8

OUTSTANDING CREDIT AND LOANS FROM THE IMF, 1960–1998 (BILLIONS OF SDRs)

Mexico's Peso Crisis

Armed rebellion in the poor Mexican state of Chiapas and assassination of a presidential candidate shook investors' faith in Mexico's financial system in 1993 and 1994.[16] Capital flowing into Mexico was mostly in the form of stocks and bonds (portfolio investment) rather than factories and equipment (foreign direct investment). Portfolio investment fled Mexico for the United States as the Mexican peso grew weak and U.S. interest rates rose. A lending spree by Mexican banks, coupled with weak banking regulations, also played a role in delaying the government's response to the crisis.[17] In late 1994, the Mexican peso was devalued, forcing a loss of purchasing power on the Mexican people.

In response to the crisis, the IMF and private commercial banks in the United States stepped in with about $50 billion in loans to shore up the Mexican economy. Thus Mexico's peso crisis contributed to an additional boost in the level of IMF loans. Mexico repaid the loans ahead of schedule and once again has a sizable reserve of foreign exchange.

Southeast Asia's Currency Crisis

The roar of the "four tiger" economies and those of other high-growth Asian nations suddenly fell silent in the summer of 1997. For 25 years, the economies of five Southeast Asian countries—Indonesia, Malaysia, the Philippines, Singapore, and Thailand—had wowed the world with growth rates twice those of most other countries. Even though many analysts projected continued growth for the region, and even though billions of dollars in investment flooded in from the West, savvy speculators were pessimistic. They knew that banks in Thailand were linked to prominent politicians and were lending money for office towers with no occupants. They knew that Malaysia was building a Silicon Valley long before it had trained the high-tech personnel with which to staff it. In short, they privately knew that the values of these countries' currencies were higher than conditions warranted. What speculators already knew would come as a surprise to businesspeople such as Raul Concepcion and Jay Link, whom we met at the beginning of this chapter.

On July 11, 1997, the speculators struck, selling off Thailand's baht on world currency markets. The selling forced an 18 percent drop in the value of the baht before

TABLE 10.3 *Bailout of Asian Economies (in billions of U.S. dollars)*

	IMF	World Bank and Asian Development Bank	Other	Total
Indonesia	11.2	10.0	21.1	42.3
South Korea	20.9	14.0	23.3	58.2
Thailand	4.0	2.7	10.5	17.2
Total	**36.1**	**26.7**	**54.9**	**117.7**

speculators moved on to the Philippines and Malaysia. By November, the baht had plunged another 22 percent and every other economy in the region was in a slump. The shock waves of Asia's crisis could be felt throughout the global economy. In the United States, a drop in Hong Kong's Hang Seng stock market caused a flood of selling on Wall Street, and on October 27, 1997, the Dow dropped 522 points in a single day of trading.

Suddenly, countries thought to be strong emerging market economies—"tigers" even to be emulated by other developing countries—were in need of billions of dollars to keep their economies from crumbling. When the dust settled, the world's richest nations were nervous that the region couldn't recover on its own. In particular, Japan and the United States—the heaviest lenders to troubled Southeast Asian countries—feared that Southeast Asia's problems would carry over into their banking systems. In the end, Indonesia, South Korea, and Thailand all needed IMF and World Bank funding. Table 10.3 shows the commitments the IMF and other institutions have made to help these countries through this crisis. As incentives for these countries to begin the long process of economic restructuring, IMF loan packages came with a number of strings attached. The Indonesian loan package, for example, has three long-term goals to help put the Indonesian economy on a stronger footing: (1) to restore the confidence of international financial markets; (2) to restructure the domestic financial sector; and (3) to support domestic deregulation and trade reforms.

What caused the crisis in the first place? Well, it depends on whom you ask. Some believe it was caused by an Asian style of crony capitalism. They say that poor regulation, the practice of extending loans to friends and relatives who are poor credit risks, and a lack of transparency regarding the financial health of banks and companies are to blame. Others point to currency speculators and panicking investors as the main causes. Still others argue that persistent current account deficits in these countries are what caused the large dumping of these nations' currencies. What really caused the crisis is probably a combination of all these forces.[18]

FUTURE OF THE INTERNATIONAL MONETARY SYSTEM

Recurring crises in the international monetary system are raising calls for a new system that is designed to meet the challenges of a global economy. Many believe that the vestiges of the IMF created by the Bretton Woods Agreement are no longer adequate to insulate the world's economies from disruptions in a single country or small group of countries. In fact, some call for the elimination of the IMF and its replacement by institutions not yet clearly defined.

IMF Reform   More likely is substantial revision of the IMF. As of 1999, IMF reform to strengthen the international monetary system was underway. First, efforts were being taken to develop internationally accepted codes of good practice to allow com-

South Koreans protested the International Monetary Fund's bailout when their currency failed a few years ago. Koreans, like the people of most every nation, reject foreign influence as a general rule. But they especially resented the IMF because of its condition that Korea keep interest rates high to prevent foreign investors from fleeing. To read more about the IMF, go to its Web site at ⟨**www.imf.org**⟩.

parisons of countries' fiscal and monetary practices. Second, countries are being encouraged to be more open and clear regarding their financial policies. Transparency on the part of the IMF is also being increased to instill greater accountability on the part of its leadership. Third, the IMF is increasing its efforts at surveillance of member nations' macroeconomic policies and increasing its abilities in the area of financial sector analysis. Fourth, orderly ways must still be found to integrate international financial markets so that risks are better managed.

Finally, the private sector must become involved in the prevention and resolution of financial crises. Policy makers are concerned with the way money floods into developing economies when growth is strong, and then just as quickly heads for the exits at the first sign of trouble. Furthermore, some argue that because the IMF bails out debtor countries, private-sector banks do not exercise adequate caution when loaning money in risky situations: After all, the IMF will be there to pay off the loans of debtor countries. Greater cooperation and understanding between the IMF, private-sector banks, and debtor nations is needed.[19]

One World, Ready or Not   Despite these and future IMF reforms, leaders of many developing and newly industrialized countries are bemoaning what global capital has done to their economies. In a speech in late 1998, Indian Prime Minister Bihari Vajpayee said the "world is paying the price for the dogma of the invisible hand of market forces."[20] Malaysian Prime Minister Mahathir Mohamad echoed these sentiments: "The only system allowed is that of capitalist free markets, of globalization. That the unfettered, unregulated free market has destroyed the economies of whole regions and of many countries in the world does not matter," he wrote.[21]

Countries are even considering imposing controls on the flow of capital over their nations' borders to stem the tide of "hot money" that abandons economies at the first signs of weakness. Malaysia, for example, has already done so. It instituted currency and stock market controls in the wake of the financial crisis. These controls require that (1) non-Malaysians get central bank approval before converting ringgit into other currencies, (2) Malaysian ringgit held abroad must be repatriated back to Malaysia, and (3) non-Malaysians investing in Malaysian stocks must hold those stocks for at least one year.[22]

World Business Survey

Pessimism Over Capital Controls

How do you expect capital controls to affect Malaysia?

	Hurt the country	Help the country	Don't know
Singapore	72.7	20.5	6.8
Philippines	68.2	27.3	4.5
Taiwan	67.8	14.3	17.9
Australia	67.7	19.4	12.9
Hong Kong	67.2	23	9.8
Japan	53.9	25.6	20.5
Indonesia	52.9	32.4	14.7
South Korea	49.9	31.3	18.8
Thailand	50	33.3	16.7
Malaysia	27.5	67.5	5

Should other countries follow Malaysia institute capital controls of their own?

	No	Yes	Do...
Hong Kong	85.3		
Australia	83.8		
Philippines	81.8		
Indonesia	79.4		
South Korea	74.9		
Singapore	75		
Japan	71.8		
Taiwan	71.4		
Thailand	55.5		
Malaysia	32.5	42.5	

Malaysia's controls have received support from certain government leaders and some international organizations. But many economists and businesspeople fear that these types of capital controls scare off potential investors. The results of a poll shortly after Malaysia implemented its capital controls, revealed that executives across Asia did not believe that the controls would be effective at solving Malaysia's problems. The World Business Survey "Pessimism over Capital Controls" shows that these executives also overwhelmingly felt that other Asian nations should steer clear of such controls.

Moves such as Malaysia's may signal a return to a less interdependent international monetary system. However, this is highly unlikely because a pullback in globalization would be very costly to all nations in terms of trade and investment. Nevertheless, globalization makes it crucial that the system be improved to lessen the effects of financial crises. Old plans for a new global currency have even been given new life following the crisis.[23] Some argue that if the European Union's efforts at a single currency (discussed next) are successful, that the idea of a single, worldwide currency might be an option worth considering.[24] Let's now take a look at European efforts to stabilize currencies and exchange rates.

EUROPEAN MONETARY SYSTEM

Following the collapse of the Bretton Woods system, leaders of many European Union (EU) nations did not give up hope for a system that could stabilize currencies and reduce exchange-rate risk. Their efforts became increasingly important as trade between EU nations continued to expand.

In the early 1970s, the EU set up its own system of fixed exchange rates. Currencies of member nations could not rise more than 2.25 percent against the weakest currency in the system or fall more than 2.25 percent against the strongest currency. Governments were to intervene in financial markets in order to keep their currencies within this tight trading band. Failure to do so would cause the currency to be dropped from the system. However, volatility in the world economy in the early 1970s caused the system to falter, and it soon broke down.

HOW THE SYSTEM FUNCTIONS

Another attempt at a monetary system for the European Union was made in 1979. The new **European monetary system (EMS)** is a complex system designed to manage exchange rates among EU countries. It was established to stabilize exchange rates, promote trade among nations, and keep inflation low through monetary discipline.

The mechanism that limits the fluctuations of European Union members' currencies within a specified trading range is called the **exchange-rate mechanism (ERM)**. Of the 15 EU member nations, only Britain and Sweden are not members of the ERM. Under the new system, members are required to keep their currencies within 2.25 percent of the highest- and lowest-valued currencies. If keeping their currencies within the prescribed band means intervening in financial markets, nations are to do so. Weaker currencies (like the Italian lira) have been allowed to fluctuate in a wider band.

To illustrate, suppose that a weakening French franc were about to reach the 2.25 percent variation in its exchange rate with the German mark. The central banks of both France and Germany must drive the value of the French franc higher—forcing the exchange rate away from the 2.25 percent band limit. How can they do so? By buying up French francs on currency markets, thereby increasing demand for the franc and forcing its value higher. Thus the system rests on the shared responsibility of nations to operate effectively. Moreover, all ERM members must agree on any currency devaluation.

The new EMS also created a special agency called the European Monetary Cooperation Fund (EMCF). The assigned purpose of the EMCF is to help members keep their currencies within the prescribed trading band and is modeled after the IMF.

The EMS also created the European Currency Unit, or *ecu*. Similar to the International Monetary Fund's SDR, the ecu is an asset whose value is based on a "basket" of European currencies. Also similar to the SDR, each currency's contribution to the overall value of the ecu is based on the size of each member's economy. The popularity of the ecu grew dramatically in the early 1990s. The main reason is that international lending institutions increasingly denominated bonds in the ecu. Such bond issues appealed to European investors because the fact that their own currency was part of the ecu made the exchange rate between the ecu and their own currency more stable than against dollar- or yen-denominated bonds. For similar reasons, investors in countries that do a great deal of business with European Union members have also invested in ecu-denominated investments.

> **European monetary system (EMS)**
> *System designed to manage exchange rates among European Union countries.*

> **exchange-rate mechanism (ERM)**
> *Mechanism limiting the fluctuations of European Union members' currencies within a specified trading range.*

PERFORMANCE OF THE SYSTEM

The EMS was quite successful in its early years. Currency realignments were infrequent and occurred mostly before 1992. The system was also quite successful in controlling inflation. Although inflation and interest rates varied greatly among members in the 1970s, they are now much more in line with one another.

Effects of Currency Speculation   The early record of success ended abruptly in September 1992. In the early 1990s, Germany responded to inflationary pressures in its economy by raising interest rates. Higher interest rates, however, attracted investment capital from other countries. This trend pushed demand for German marks higher and decreased demand for other currencies—particularly the British pound and Italian lira.

By September 1992, both currencies had been on the lower fringe of the allowable 2.25 percent fluctuation band with the mark for some time. Believing that both currencies would be forced even lower, speculators frantically started selling pounds and lira. The central banks of neither Britain nor Italy had enough money to buy their currencies on the open market. As their currencies' values plummeted, they were forced to leave the ERM. The Italian lira returned to the ERM in November 1996 and is now allowed to fluctuate 15 percent up or down from the midpoint of the target zone.[25] The British pound remains outside the ERM.

Maastricht Treaty and European Monetary Union   Despite the speculative attacks in the 1990s, EU leaders remained determined to merge their currencies. The **European monetary union** is the European Union plan that established its own central bank and currency in January 1999.

European monetary union
European Union plan establishing its own central bank and currency as of January 1999.

Signed in 1991, the Maastricht Treaty stated the economic criteria with which member nations must comply if they want to partake in the single currency, called the *euro*. First, consumer price inflation must be below 3.2 percent and must not exceed that of the three best-performing countries by more than 1.5 percent. Second, the debt of government must be 60 percent of GDP or lower. An exception is made if the ratio is diminishing and approaching the 60 percent mark. Third, the general government deficit must be at or below 3 percent of GDP. An exception is made if the deficit is close to 3 percent, or if the deviation is temporary and unusual. Fourth, interest rates on long-term government securities must not exceed those of the three lowest-inflation-rate countries by more than 2 percent.

Meeting these criteria better aligns countries' economies and paves the way for smoother policy making under a single European Central Bank. Of the 15 EU members, the nations that are taking part in the single currency are Austria, Belgium, Finland, France, Germany, Ireland, Italy, Luxembourg, the Netherlands, Portugal, and Spain. The only countries opting out of transition to the euro (at least for now) are Britain, Denmark, Greece, and Sweden. Greece is the only one of these nations that cannot join the single currency until it is economically better prepared—it hopes to be ready by 2001.

Benefits of Monetary Union   The main benefit of a single currency is the complete elimination of exchange-rate risk for business deals between member nations using the euro. It will reduce transaction costs by eliminating the cost of converting from one currency to another. In fact, the EU leadership has estimated the financial gains to Europe at 0.5 percent of GDP.[26] The efficiency of trade between members will resemble that of interstate trade in the United States because only a single currency is involved. To see how the euro benefits small companies located outside the EU but that do business with EU customers, see the Entrepreneurial Focus "A Single Currency, Ready or Not."

The euro will also help end the need for shoppers in countries with strong currencies and high prices to flock to countries like Spain and Italy—which have weaker currencies and lower prices—to save on high-ticket items. For instance, shortly before monetary union a Mercedes-Benz S320 cost $72,614 in Germany but only $66,920 in Italy. A Renault Twingo that sold for $13,265 in France cost $11,120 in Spain. Car brokers and shopping agencies even sprang up specifically to help European consumers reap such savings.

Drawbacks of Monetary Union   Despite its potential advantages, monetary union does have potential drawbacks. Some argue that unlike the U.S. market, immobile labor and rigid wages characterize the EU. These factors do not allow specific re-

A Single Currency, Ready or Not

Introduction of a single currency, the euro, in the European Union (EU) is impacting businesses not just in the EU but around the world. Companies outside the European Union but whose customers belong to the EU can price their products in euros and thereby eliminate exchange-rate risk. Here are the benefits gained by one medium-size business in central Europe and one small business in Hong Kong that are embracing the euro:

➡ Companies in countries such as the Czech Republic, Hungary, and Poland, are preparing for the euro even though they will not join the EU until at least 2005. Twenty percent of the output of Hungary's home-textile maker Graboplast is sold to EU customers. The company's chief financial officer, Tibor Bori, relays the edge that pricing in euros now gives his company over its EU competitors. "We have a great price advantage, and [the euro] will make it easier for our marketing guys to make that clear," says Bori. Thus the euro makes prices more transparent, thereby giving the company a way of showing customers its advantage over EU competitors.

➡ "We are very conscious about the euro because our main market is Europe," says Willy Lin, garment maker in Hong Kong. His family-owned company, Milo's Manufacturing, does 70 percent of its business in Europe. His company priced its inventory in euros ever since its official introduction on January 1, 1999. Lin's company not only sells in Europe but also buys its yarn there—particularly Italian yarn. "We purchase a lot of European materials, so we can use a lot of our euro earnings to pay for our supplies. If we can now do without exchange risk we can be more competitive to our customers, and of course consumers will also get a better deal," says Lin. "This will be good for the whole world."

gions to deal as effectively with local economic slumps—for example, the defense cutbacks in California in the early 1990s.

The speculative currency sell-offs of 1992 and 1993 shook the confidence of some members and observers in eventual monetary union. Critics contend that expanding the ERM fluctuation band for currencies to 15 percent essentially means that currencies now float freely against one another. However, supporters of monetary union reply that because speculative crises are impossible under a single currency, EMU should move ahead even more quickly. They also point to the recovery and success of the system since the problems of 1993.

Management Implications of the Euro   The move to a single currency influences all the activities of companies within the European Union. First, the euro has marketing implications. Price differences are more obvious between markets when priced in a common currency. This makes it more difficult to charge different prices in different markets—especially in border regions. In addition, because many consumers initially find it difficult to estimate the value of their currency in euros, retailers need to create dual-pricing displays.

Second, staff must be trained in working with the euro. This is especially important for people in the company who must deal with suppliers and customers. They must feel comfortable negotiating contracts in terms of the euro and explaining new euro prices to customers. Third, because the euro creates a deeper and more liquid market for debt and equity, finance and treasury functions are affected. The amount of financing done in euros could become great if euro-denominated financial instruments become appealing to investors beyond the EU.

Fourth, many companies will need to maintain dual-currency ledgers because national currencies, though merely as a denomination of the euro, will continue to exist. It will not be until January 2002 that euro paper currency and coins will be introduced and replace national currencies. It must be determined whether companies should report their books to tax authorities and stock exchange commissions in euro, the home currency, or both. Any new accounting standards issued by the EU must be incorporated into a company's financial reporting system. The decision of which currency or currencies the company will use during the transition period determines the extent to which it will need to adjust its computer information systems. Many company databases containing financial information must be modified to include figures in euros.[28]

A FINAL WORD

Raul Concepcion and Jay Link, although half a world away from each other, both saw their businesses hurt by the Asian financial crisis. However, they were not the only ones caught off-guard, as many large companies around the world also had not seen it coming. The crisis underscores the need for managers to fully understand the complexities of the international financial system. In the last two chapters, we've discussed the international financial markets and international monetary system in detail. Understanding this material improves our knowledge of financial risks in international business. But this knowledge must be paired with vigilance of financial market conditions to manage businesses in the global economy effectively.

The next chapter begins our in-depth look at the main aspects of managing an international business. As we saw in this chapter, not only are a company's financial decisions impacted by events in international financial markets, but so too are production and marketing decisions. Our understanding of national business environments, international trade and investment, and the international financial system will serve us well as we embark on our tour of international business management.

There is a variety of additional material available on the companion Web site that accompanies this text. You can access this information by visiting the Web site at ⟨**www.prenhall.com/wild**⟩.

summary

① **Explain how *exchange rates* influence the activities of domestic and international companies.** Exchange rates influence two areas of a firm's activities. First, they influence *production and marketing decisions* because they affect demand for a company's products in the global marketplace. When a country's currency is *weak* (valued low relative to other currencies), the price of its exports on world markets declines and the price of imports increases. Lower prices make the country's exports more appealing on world markets. Furthermore, a company selling in a country with a *strong* currency (one that is valued high relative to other currencies) while paying workers at home in its own weak currency improves its profits.

The intentional lowering of the value of a currency by the nation's government is called *devaluation*. The reverse, the intentional raising of its value by the nation's government, is called *revaluation*. Devaluation lowers the price of a country's exports on world markets and increases the price of imports because the country's currency is now worth less on world markets. Revaluation has the opposite effects: It increases the price of exports and reduces the price of imports.

Second, exchange rates influence a firm's *financial decisions* because they affect how and when it pays its dividends. Finally, companies prefer that exchange rates be *stable* and *predictable* so that they are not caught off-guard by sudden and unexpected unfavorable changes in exchange rates.

② Identify the factors that help determine exchange rates and their impact on business. Two concepts are used to determine the level at which an exchange rate *should* be. The *law of one price* stipulates that when price is expressed in a common-denominator currency, an identical product must have an identical price in all countries. For this principle to apply, products must be identical in quality and content in all countries and must be entirely produced within each particular country. The *purchasing power parity* (*PPP*) concept helps determine the relative ability of two countries' currencies to buy the same "basket" of goods in those two countries. Thus although the law of one price holds for *single* products, PPP is meaningful only when applied to a *basket* of goods.

Two phenomena influence both exchange rates and PPP: inflation and interest rates. When additional money is injected into an economy that is not producing greater output, people will have more money to spend on the same amount of products. As growing demand for products outstrips stagnant supply, prices will rise and overtake any increase in the amount of money that consumers have to spend. *Inflation*, therefore, erodes purchasing power.

In turn, *interest rates* affect inflation because they affect the cost of borrowing money. Low rates encourage people and businesses to increase spending by taking on debt. On the other hand, high rates prompt them to reduce the debt because higher rates mean greater monthly debt payments. Because *real interest rates*—rates that do not account for inflation—are theoretically equal across countries, any difference in the rates of two countries must be due to different expected rates of inflation. A country experiencing inflation higher than that of another country should see the value of its currency fall. Exchange rates adjust to reflect such changes.

③ Describe the primary methods of *forecasting exchange rates.* There are two distinct views regarding how accurately future exchange rates can be predicted by *forward exchange rates*—that is, by the rate agreed upon for foreign exchange payment at a future date. The *efficient market view* holds that prices of financial instruments reflect all publicly available information at any given time. As applied to exchange rates, this means that forward exchange rates are accurate forecasts of future exchange rates.

The *inefficient market view* holds that prices of financial instruments do not reflect all publicly available information. Proponents of this view believe that companies can search for new pieces of information to improve forecasting. This view is held by analysts who believe that forecasts can be improved by information not reflected in forward exchange rates. Two main forecasting techniques are based on this belief in the value of added information. *Fundamental analysis* uses statistical models based on fundamental economic indicators to forecast exchange rates. Economic variables include such factors as inflation, interest rates, money supply, tax rates, and government spending.

The second method of forecasting exchange rates is *technical analysis*—a technique using charts of past trends in currency prices and other factors to forecast exchange rates. Many forecasters combine the techniques of both fundamental and technical analyses to arrive at potentially more accurate forecasts.

④ Discuss the evolution of the current *international monetary system* and explain how it operates. The *Bretton Woods Agreement* (1944) was an accord among nations to create an international monetary system based on the value of the U.S. dollar. The system was designed to balance the strict discipline of the *gold standard*, which linked paper currencies to specific values of gold, with the flexibility that countries needed to deal with temporary domestic monetary difficulties. The most important features of the system were *fixed exchange rates, built-in flexibility, funds for economic development*, and *an enforcement mechanism*.

To provide funding for countries' efforts toward economic development, Bretton Woods created the *World Bank*—officially called the *International Bank for Reconstruction and Development* (*IBRD*). The Bank funds poor nations' economic development projects such as the development of transportation networks, power facilities, and agricultural and educational programs.

Bretton Woods also established the *International Monetary Fund* (*IMF*) to regulate fixed exchange rates and enforce the rules of the international monetary system. A *special drawing right* (*SDR*) is an IMF asset whose value is based on a "basket" of its five biggest members' currencies (France, Germany, Japan, the United Kingdom, and the United States). The SDR is the unit of account for the IMF. Each nation is assigned a quota based on the size of its economy when it enters the IMF. Payment of this quota by each nation provides the IMF with the funds that it needs to make short-term loans to members.

Ultimately, Bretton Woods collapsed because it depended so heavily on the stability of the dollar. As long as the dollar remained strong, it worked well. But when the dollar weakened, it failed to perform properly. When no new coordinated international monetary system was forthcoming, there emerged several independent efforts to manage exchange rates. The *Jamaica Agreement* (1976) endorsed a *managed float system* of exchange rates—that is, a system in which currencies float against one another, with governments intervening to stabilize currencies at a particular target exchange rate. This system differs from a *free float system* in which currencies float freely against one another without governments intervening in currency markets.

The *Plaza Accord* (1985) was simply a signal to financial markets that governments were determined to intervene to force down the value of the dollar when it became too high. The *Louvre Accord* (1987) was a signal that governments would intervene in currency markets to maintain the current market value of the dollar when it fell to very low levels.

Today's international monetary system remains in large part a managed float system, with most currencies floating against one another and governments intervening to realign exchange rates. Within the larger monetary system, however, certain countries try to maintain more stable exchange rates by tying their currencies to another country's stronger currency.

⑤ Explain the *European monetary system* and assess its record of performance. Following collapse of the Bretton Woods system, leaders of many *European Union* (*EU*) nations continued to work toward a system that could stabilize currencies and reduce exchange-rate risk. In the early 1970s, an early attempt by the EU to set up its own system of fixed exchange rates failed because of great volatility in the world economy.

Devised for the EU in 1979, the *European monetary system* (*EMS*) is a complex system designed to manage exchange rates. It was established to stabilize exchange rates, promote trade, and control inflation through monetary discipline. An *exchange-rate mechanism* (*ERM*) requires members to keep their currencies within 2.25 percent of the highest- and lowest-valued currencies. If keeping their currencies within the prescribed band means intervening in financial markets, nations are to do so. Weaker currencies (like the Italian lira) have been allowed to fluctuate in a wider band.

The EMS also created a special agency called the *European Monetary Cooperation Fund* (*EMCF*), which is modeled after the International Monetary Fund. Its assigned purpose is to help members keep currencies within the prescribed trading band. In addition, the EMS created the *European Currency Unit*, or *ecu*. Much like the IMF's special drawing right (SDR), the ecu is an asset whose value is based on a "basket" of European currencies. Similarly, each currency's contribution to the overall value of the ecu is based on the size of each member's economy.

As of the 1990s, EU leaders also remained determined to merge their currencies. The EU established a single currency in January 1999 through a plan called *European monetary union*. Signed in 1991, the *Maastricht Treaty* states the economic criteria with which member nations must comply if they want to partake in the single currency, which is called the *euro*. The main benefit of a single currency is the complete elimination of exchange-rate risk in business deals between member nations using the euro. The single currency also reduces transaction costs by eliminating the cost of converting from one currency to another.

questions for review

1. How are *exchange rates* important to managers' decisions? Provide several examples.

2. Why is it desirable for exchange rates to be stable and predictable?

3. What is the *law of one price*? Explain briefly.

4. What are the limitations of the law of one price?

5. What is meant by *purchasing power parity* in the context of exchange rates? Explain briefly.

6. How does *inflation* influence exchange rates? Describe the impact of money-supply decisions and unemployment on inflation.

7. What is the impact of *interest rates* on exchange rates? Explain the *international Fisher effect*.

8. What are the limitations of purchasing power parity?

9. What is the relation between business confidence and psychology on the one hand, and exchange rates on the other?

10. What are the two market views regarding *exchange-rate forecasting*? Explain each briefly.

11. What are the two primary methods of forecasting exchange rates? Explain each briefly.

12. What was the *gold standard*? Briefly describe its evolution and collapse.

13. What is the *Bretton Woods Agreement*?

14. What factors led to the demise of the Bretton Woods monetary system?

15. Why did the world shift to a *managed float system* of exchange rates? Briefly describe the performance of this system.

16. How did the *World Bank* and *International Monetary Fund* assist countries during recent financial crises?

17. What is the purpose of the *European monetary system*? Briefly describe how it functions and its performance.

questions for discussion

1. There are benefits of both floating and fixed exchange-rate systems. Describe the advantages and disadvantages of each briefly. Do you think the world will move toward an international monetary system more characteristic of floating or fixed exchange rates in the future? Explain your answer.

2. Do you think that an international monetary system with currencies valued on the basis of gold would work today? Why or why not? Do you think implementing a system similar to the European monetary system on a global scale would work? Why or why not?

3. The activities of the IMF and World Bank largely overlap each other. Devise a plan to reduce the duplication of these institutions' services and to assign them responsibilities. Also, would you have them take a greater role on issues such as the environment and corruption? Describe your plan and justify your proposed solution.

in practice

The following article and accompanying graphs describe the havoc that the Asian financial crisis had on one economy in the region, that of South Korea. Read the short article below, look over the graphs on the next page, and answer the questions that follow.

It has been a miserable year for South Korea. The country's GDP, which grew by 5.5% in 1997, is expected to contract by 4.7% in 1998, according to the OECD's recent survey. Unemployment is soaring, from 2.6% in 1997 to a likely 7% in 1998. As domestic demand has collapsed, the current account has shifted from a deficit of $8.2 billion in 1997 to a surplus of $14.4 billion in 1998. But the OECD reckons that South Korea's economy could grow by 2.5% in 1999 if companies' balance sheets improve and government fiscal and monetary policy becomes less restrictive. That all depends on how quickly firms restructure in the face of high interest rates, a credit crunch, big falls in asset prices and increasing competition. It also depends on how Koreans react to greater uncertainty about their jobs and wages, and how investors respond now that the country has lifted barriers to foreign capital.

1. Briefly explain the relation between a nation's currency and both its balance of trade and balance of payments. Why do you think Korea was experiencing an increasing trade deficit from 1994 through 1997? Why was a fall in the value of Korea's currency forecast to a result in a trade surplus?

2. Update the progress of Korea's economy since the article above was written. What are current conditions in its GDP, inflation, unemployment, and trade balance? Did the government ease its fiscal and monetary policies as the article suggested?

3. Update how Korea's companies, investors, and people are faring since this article appeared. How did firms adapt to high interest rates, tight credit, and greater competition from abroad? How have investors reacted to the removal of barriers to capital? How have the Korean people adjusted to an era of higher unemployment and lower wages?

   Hint: Good sources of information to answer these questions include *The Economist*, the *Far Eastern Economic Review* (in print and free on the Web at ⟨**www.feer.com**⟩, and other national business magazines and newspapers. Also good to consult are publications by international agencies including the Organization for Economic Cooperation and Development (OECD), International Monetary Fund ⟨**www.imf.org**⟩, and World Bank ⟨**www.worldbank.org**⟩.

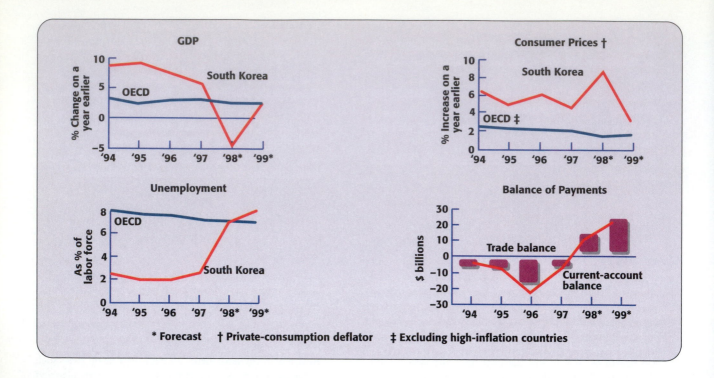

GDP

% Change on a year earlier

OECD
South Korea

'94 '95 '96 '97 '98* '99*

Consumer Prices †

% Increase on a year earlier

South Korea
OECD ‡

'94 '95 '96 '97 '98* '99*

Unemployment

As % of labor force

OECD
South Korea

'94 '95 '96 '97 '98* '99*

Balance of Payments

$ billions

Trade balance
Current-account balance

'94 '95 '96 '97 '98* '99*

* Forecast   † Private-consumption deflator   ‡ Excluding high-inflation countries

projects

1. You are the production manager for a manufacturing company based in Japan. You are forecasting the exchange rate between the Japanese yen and Indian rupee to decide whether to build a new factory in India. The current spot exchange rate is .32 rupee/¥. Inflation is 10 percent in India and 2 percent in Japan. What is your forecast of the rupee/yen exchange rate for one year from today?

2. With several of your classmates, select a country that interests you. Is the nation a member of the IMF? Does it participate in a regional monetary system to manage exchange rates, such as the European monetary system? How have inflation and interest rates affected the nation's exchange rate with other currencies? What impact has the country's exchange rate had on its imports and exports? How has the exchange rate recently impacted the activities of companies operating in the country? What is the forecasted exchange rate for the coming weeks, months, and year?

   Hint: Good sources to consult include *International Financial Statistics*, various issues (Washington, DC: International Monetary Fund); and *Exchange Arrangements and Exchange Restrictions, Annual Reports* (Washington, DC: International Monetary Fund).

3. Your company based in Finland wants to estimate demand for its newly developed product in the U.S. market. The market research firm you hired requires $150,000 to perform a thorough study. However, you are informed that your total research budget is 3 million Finnish markka and that no more than 20 percent of the budget can be spent on any one project.

   (a) If the current exchange rate is 5 markka/$, will you have the market study conducted? Why or why not?

   (b) If the exchange rate changes to 3 markka/$, will you have the study conducted? Why or why not?

   (c) At what exchange rate do you change your decision from rejecting the proposed research project to accepting the project?

business case 10
WORLD BANK SEES THE VALUE OF FORGIVENESS

When James Wolfensohn became head of the World Bank in 1996, he bluntly admitted that the Bank had "screwed up" in Africa. Decades of loans have erected a vast modern infrastruc- ture—dams, roads, and power plants—for Africa's poor, but the gap between rich and poor did not narrow. In fact, the policies of the Bank and global financial regulators have created a new crisis in sub-Saharan Africa: These nations are now mired in debt they cannot possibly repay. Africa's total debt almost equals the continent's annual gross national product. In Mozambique, for instance, where 25 percent of all children die before the age of five from infectious disease, the government spends twice as much paying off debt as it does on health care and education.

For years, nongovernmental organizations (NGOs), such as advocacy group Oxfam International, have lobbied the Bank and the International Monetary Fund (IMF) to write off loans to their poorest borrowers, calling for "debt forgiveness" or "debt relief." Fortunately for the African people and their advocates, the new head of the Bank has put debt forgiveness at the top of his agenda. In September 1996, Wolfenson announced a historic first for the Bank: a plan to write off some loans made to one borrower, Uganda, and subsequently to expand the program to 20 other nations in Africa and elsewhere. Burkina Faso, Mozambique, Guyana, and Bolivia are some of the countries next in line.

The decision to begin the program with Uganda was not an arbitrary one. While under the brutal dictatorship of Idi Amin, Uganda was treated as a pariah by creditors. But when Amin and his regime were toppled, new president Yoweri Musevini led the country through a decade-long process of economic reform. Uganda is now considered a model country, boasting a growth rate of 10 percent, with coffee as its main export. By offering debt relief to Uganda, the World Bank and IMF are rewarding Uganda's exemplary track record by reducing its debt to the lowest possible level—about twice the value of its exports. The international banking community is thus using debt as both a carrot and a stick: Whereas nations with good reform records will get relief, those who can point to little reform will not.

As for Uganda, its leaders have already determined where the money will go. According to Richard Kabonero, economic affairs counsel at the Ugandan Embassy in Washington, savings from the debt relief program are pledged to improve health care and make primary education available to all Ugandan families. In 1996 Uganda's total debt payment of $154 million was almost equal to the combined $175 million that it spent on education and health care. The World Bank program could not have come at a better time for Anna Asiimwe, a nine-year-old in Uganda's poorest district. "My deepest wish is to go back to school," says Anna. It looks like Anna just might get her wish.

thinking globally

1. In negotiating the debt forgiveness program, the World Bank and IMF worked closely together. At one point, however, the plan came to a standstill when the two organizations produced different figures for Uganda's coffee exports, with the IMF giving a more optimistic forecast and so arguing against the need for debt relief. Do you think there is any benefit to these organizations working together? Explain. Which organization do you think should play more of a role in aiding African development? Why?

2. The World Bank and IMF had once argued that the leniency of debt forgiveness would make it more difficult for the lenders themselves to borrow cheaply on the world's capital markets. If you were a World Bank donor, would you support the debt relief program or argue against it? Explain your answer.

3. Critics contend that the new, World Bank/IMF debt relief program falls short. For example, Harvard economist Jeffrey Sachs argues that the need for debt relief was obvious 10 years ago. The present carrot, says Sachs, is simply too little, too late, and he adds that for some countries, the situation is so grim that entire external indebtedness should be written off. Do you think the World Bank and IMF should write off the entire debt of countries? What are the pros and cons of this approach for debt relief?

a question of ethics

1. When currency speculators turned their backs on Malaysia and forced a devaluation of the ringgit in 1997, Prime Minister Mahathir Mohamad denounced currency speculators as "immoral" and argued that currency trading should take place only to facilitate deals between countries. Although most observers dismiss these comments as coming from a man known for his outspoken tirades against Western investors, others contend that the prime minister's rhetoric voices a genuine concern. Is it ethical for global currency speculators to bet against national currencies, perhaps sending whole economies into a tailspin while they profit? Or, do you feel that currency speculators perform a valuable service by correcting overvalued or undervalued currencies? What do you think would have happened to the economies of Southeast Asia if currency speculators had *not* forced devaluation? Support your answers with logical reasoning.[29]

2. In recent years, the governments of industrialized nations have stepped in to bail out emerging nations in the midst of financial crises. Consider the bailouts of Mexico, Indonesia, and Thailand. By early 1998, Japan and the IMF cobbled together $17.2 billion in credit to help Thailand and $23 billion for Indonesia. That's on top of billions in emergency loans to Mexico after the peso collapse of 1994. The IMF then announced a plan to boost its lending capital by $285 billion in

order to cope with the next crisis. Taxpayers in industrial countries would foot the bill.

In light of these developments, some critics have called this system a kind of "remnant socialism" that rescues financial institutions and investors from their own mistakes with money from taxpayers. For instance, the financial crisis in Thailand was largely a private-sector affair. Thai banks and insurance companies were heavily in debt, and the central bank had recklessly pledged its foreign exchange reserves to shore up the currency. Do you think it is ethical that losses are *socialized* (that is, subsidized through government-sponsored bailouts) while profits are *privatized*? Why or why not? Explain exactly who does benefit from bailouts like the one in Thailand. What might be a good alternative to an IMF bailout?[30]

integrative **video case**
PART FOUR: INTERNATIONAL FINANCIAL SYSTEM
yahoo! and the world bank

background

This video looks at Yahoo! as it deals with the international financial system through an on-line investment approach. Yahoo! Finance is a new system that people around the world can use to exchange stock and use credit cards. The World Bank, far larger than Yahoo!, is an international agency established in 1944, the same year as the International Monetary Fund (IMF). The World Bank provides loans for development to countries in need. The World Bank and the IMF together are major players in today's international monetary system.

The video discusses stock exchanges and how they operate through the Internet. It also illustrates the importance of the World Bank and the IMF in international financial markets and the role these two agencies play in the international monetary system. Furthermore, the video shows how the Bretton Woods Agreement of 1944 created a new era of international transactions.

yahoo!

For information on this company, please refer to the video case for Part I, page 30.

the world bank

The World Bank Group is made up of five organizations: the International Bank for Reconstruction and Development (IBRD), the International Development Association (IDA), the International Finance Corporation (IFC), the Multilateral Investment Guarantee Agency (MIGA), and the International Centre for the Settlement of Investment Disputes (ICSID). The term *World Bank* itself actually refers to only the IBRD and the IDA. The World Bank is the world's largest provider of development assistance to developing countries and countries in transition, committing about $20 billion in new loans each year. Its main focus is to help people in developing countries raise their standard of living through finance for agriculture, schools, health programs, transportation, and other essential needs. The IBRD was established in July 1944 at the United Nations Monetary and Financial Conference in Bretton Woods, New Hampshire. The World Bank opened for business on June 25, 1946. In 1947 it gave its first loan to France, $250 million to finance postwar construction. Today, the World Bank has a lending portfolio of $144 billion.

discussion questions

While you watch the video, keep the following questions in mind. You might want to take notes.

1. What contribution does Yahoo! make to the international financial markets?
2. How do consumers invest through the Internet?
3. How does Yahoo! overcome currency restrictions?
4. What is the role of the World Bank in the global financial markets?
5. What was the significance of the 1944 Bretton Woods Agreement?
6. What is the role of the IMF in the world economy today?
7. What role might Yahoo! play in the future of the world's financial markets?

student exercises

1. Break into groups of two or three people. Compare the World Bank and Yahoo! in terms of their contribution to the world's financial markets. Also consider what their future contributions might be.
2. What impact does the World Bank have on Europe? Keep the European Union and the European Bank of Reconstruction and Development in mind as you answer.
3. Assume that the United States, Canada, and Mexico adopt a fixed exchange rate system similar to the European Union's Exchange Rate Mechanism (ERM). What would be the likely consequences of the system to the rest of the world, in particular to international business transactions?

11 analyzing international opportunities

Beacons

A Look Back

CHAPTER 10 explored the operations of the international monetary system. We examined the factors affecting exchange-rate determination and forecasting and discussed international attempts to create a system of stable and predictable exchange rates.

A Look at This Chapter

This chapter begins our examination of the internal operations of companies engaged in international business activities. We learn how managers screen potential new markets and sites for operations and discuss the type of information required in the screening process. We also explore the ways in which companies evaluate proposed investment projects.

A Look Ahead

CHAPTER 12 explores the specific strategies and organizational structures that companies use in accomplishing their international business objectives. In later chapters, we show how companies enter new markets, acquire their needed resources, and manage day-to-day international business operations.

Learning Objectives

After studying this chapter, you should be able to

1. Explain each of the four steps in the *market- and site-screening process*.
2. Describe the three primary difficulties of conducting *international market research*.
3. Identify the main sources of *secondary international data* and explain their usefulness.
4. Describe the main methods used to conduct *primary international research*.
5. Explain how companies evaluate potential new investment projects.
6. Identify the issues important to countries when evaluating investment proposals.

"**P**er capita consumption of coffee in China is very small," admits Howard Behar, president of Starbucks Coffee International. "But what you have is a tremendous amount of people, so the market will grow." Thus in early 1999, Starbucks launched its first retail outlet in Beijing, China. But many observers ask: Is Starbucks making a mistake by trying to market coffee in a land of tea drinkers?

Long before its lively grand opening, complete with whirling lion dancers and the beating of Chinese drums, Starbucks was quietly but exhaustively researching the Chinese market. After careful study, the company was encouraged by the fact that one third of all Chinese households keep a jar of instant coffee on hand. But Starbucks does not expect to change the tea-drinking habits of the older generation: Its target is China's cash-flush youth. To establish its coffee as the drink of choice for the average 18- to 45-year-old Chinese consumer, Starbucks is setting its prices nearly 60 percent lower than a formidable homegrown rival in Beijing.

China's domestic companies, too, are discovering the value of market research in helping them fight off the invasion of their home market by multinational companies. Chen Yongming, manager of a Shanghai grocery store founded by a local fisherman in 1850, hired a Western consulting company called China Link to help him better understand his local market. China Link will supply Chen with six research reports on a variety of topics ranging from the market penetration of his own company's products to competitors' in-store promotions. Although Chinese companies that hire market research consultants remain the exception, Chen is sold on the idea. "Having good information is liking having good eyesight," says Chen. "If you don't have market research, you're blind."[1]

ompanies traditionally enter the international business arena by choosing familiar places—typically by entering nearby countries first. Managers feel comfortable about entering nearby markets because they likely have already interacted with the people of those cultures and have at least some understanding of them. Thus companies in Canada, Mexico, and the United States often gain their initial international experiences in one another's markets. Likewise, firms in Asian countries often seek out opportunities in one another's markets before pursuing investment opportunities outside the region.

But today companies find themselves bridging the gaps presented by space and culture far more often. For one thing, technological advances in communication and transportation continue to pry open national markets around the globe. Companies today can realistically consider nearly every location on earth as either a potential market or a site for business operations. In addition, the expansion of regional markets (such as the European Union) is causing companies to analyze opportunities farther from home. For example, companies are locating production facilities within regional markets because producing in one of a region's countries provides duty-free access to every consumer in the whole trade bloc.

Moreover, fast-paced change in the global marketplace is forcing companies to view business strategies from a global perspective. More than ever, they are formulating production, marketing, and other strategies as components of integrated plans. For instance, to provide a continuous flow of timely information into the production process, more and more firms are locating R&D facilities near their production sites abroad. Managers also more often find themselves simultaneously screening and analyzing locations as potential markets *and* as potential sites for operations. When Mercedes-Benz introduced its M-class sport utility vehicle to the U.S. market, it also decided to build the vehicle there. Thus managers were obliged not merely to estimate the size of the potential market for the vehicle, but to decide at the same time on a suitable production site.

The attraction of companies to distant markets and the integrated nature of location decisions demand that companies approach the location selection decision in a systematic manner. This chapter presents a systematic screening process for both markets and sites. After explaining the important cultural, political, legal, and economic forces affecting the screening process, we describe the difficulties of conducting international research. We then explore the main sources of existing data and the main methods for conducting international research firsthand. We close the chapter by presenting the ways in which both companies and governments evaluate proposed new investment projects.

SCREENING POTENTIAL MARKETS AND SITES

Two important issues concern managers during the market- and site-screening process. First, they want to keep the cost of the search as low as possible. Second, they want to examine every potential market and every possible location for facilities. To accomplish these two goals, managers typically approach the screening of markets and sites in a systematic way. We can break this *screening process* down into the following four steps:

1. Identify basic appeal
2. Assess the national business environment
3. Measure market or site potential
4. Select the market or site

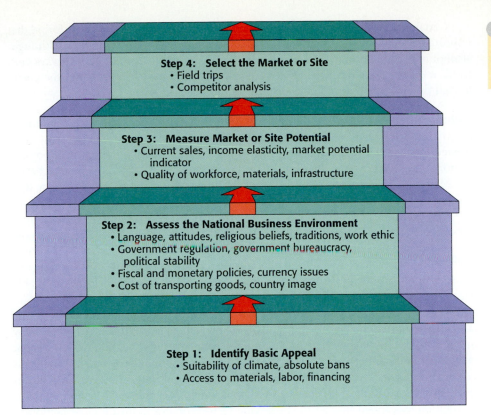

FIGURE 11.1

SCREENING PROCESS FOR POTENTIAL MARKETS AND SITES

Step 4: Select the Market or Site
• Field trips
• Competitor analysis

Step 3: Measure Market or Site Potential
• Current sales, income elasticity, market potential indicator
• Quality of workforce, materials, infrastructure

Step 2: Assess the National Business Environment
• Language, attitudes, religious beliefs, traditions, work ethic
• Government regulation, government bureaucracy, political stability
• Fiscal and monetary policies, currency issues
• Cost of transporting goods, country image

Step 1: Identify Basic Appeal
• Suitability of climate, absolute bans
• Access to materials, labor, financing

Figure 11.1 shows that this screening process involves spending more time, money, and effort on the markets and sites that remain in the later stages of screening. Thus expensive feasibility studies (conducted later in the process) are performed on a few markets and sites that hold the greatest promise. Therefore, this screening process is cost-effective yet does not overlook potential locations. Let's now discuss each of these four steps in detail.

STEP 1: IDENTIFY BASIC APPEAL

In Chapter 1, we saw that companies go international either to increase sales (and thus profits) or to access resources. Therefore, the first step in identifying potential markets is to assess the basic demand for a product. Similarly, the first step in selecting a site for a facility to undertake production, R&D, or some other activity is to explore the availability of required resources.

Determining Basic Demand   The first step in searching for potential markets means finding out whether there is a basic demand for a company's product. Important in determining this basic appeal is a country's climate. For example, no company would try to market snowboards in Indonesia, Sri Lanka, or Central America because they receive absolutely no snowfall. The same product, on the other hand, is well-suited for markets in the Canadian Rockies, northern Japan, and the Swiss Alps. This stage may seem quite simple, but it cannot be taken too lightly. During its initial forays into international business, Wal-Mart found itself stocked with ice-fishing huts in Puerto Rico and stocked out of snowshoes in Ontario, Canada.[2]

Certain countries also ban certain goods. Islamic countries, for instance, forbid the importation of alcoholic products, and penalties for smuggling are stiff. Also, although alcohol is available on the planes of international airlines such as British Airways and KLM, it cannot leave the airplane and consumption cannot take place until the plane has left the airspace of the country operating under Islamic law.

Determining Availability of Resources   Companies needing certain resources to carry out local business activities must be sure that they are available. Raw materials needed for manufacturing must be either found in the national market or imported. Imported inputs, however, may encounter tariffs, quotas, or other government barriers. Managers must therefore consider the additional costs of importing to ensure that total product cost does not rise to unacceptable levels.

The availability of labor is essential to production in any country. Many companies choose to relocate to countries where workers' wages are lower than they are in the home country. This practice is most common among makers of labor-intensive products—those for which labor accounts for a large portion of total cost. Companies considering local production must determine whether there is enough locally available labor for production operations.

Companies hoping to secure financing in a market abroad must determine the availability and cost of local capital. If local interest rates are too high, a company might be forced to obtain financing in its home country or in other markets in which it is active. On the other hand, access to low-cost financing may provide a powerful inducement to a company seeking international expansion. For example, British entrepreneur Richard Branson opened several of his Virgin Megastores in Japan despite its reputation as a tough market to crack. One reason for Branson's initial attraction to Japan was a cost of capital of only 2.5 percent—roughly one-third its cost in Britain. As the finance director for Virgin commented, "If resources are available locally, it would be silly for us not to utilize them."[3]

Markets and sites that fail to meet a company's requirements for basic demand or resource availability in step 1 are removed from further consideration. We describe how companies actually acquire the resources they need in Chapter 14.

STEP 2: ASSESS THE NATIONAL BUSINESS ENVIRONMENT

If the cultures, politics, laws, and economies of all countries were the same, deciding where to market or produce products would be rather straightforward. Managers could rely on data that report the performance of the local economy and analyze expected profits from proposed investments. But as we learned in Chapters 2, 3, and 4, national business environments differ greatly from one country to another. Thus international managers must work to understand these differences and to incorporate that understanding into market and site selection decisions. For a ranking of the top 30 nations according to their overall business climates, see the World Business Survey "Top Global Business Climates." Let's now examine how domestic forces in the business environment actually affect the location selection process.

Cultural Forces   Although some countries display cultural similarities, most differ in many ways, including language, attitudes towards business, religious beliefs, traditions, and customs. Some products can be sold in markets worldwide with little or no modification. Some of these products are industrial machinery such as packaging equipment, and consumer products including toothpaste and soft drinks. Other products, however, must undergo extensive adaptation to suit local preferences including certain types of ready-to-eat meals, and some books and magazines.

World Business Survey

Top Global Business Climates

Surveys of nations' business climates encompass their cultural, political, legal, and economic aspects. Such surveys can be very helpful to companies that are searching for new locations to sell their goods and services or conduct some other business operation. One international newsmagazine that specializes in supplying information useful to the location selection process is *Site Selection*. Below are the results of the magazine's most recent study of the best business climates around the world.

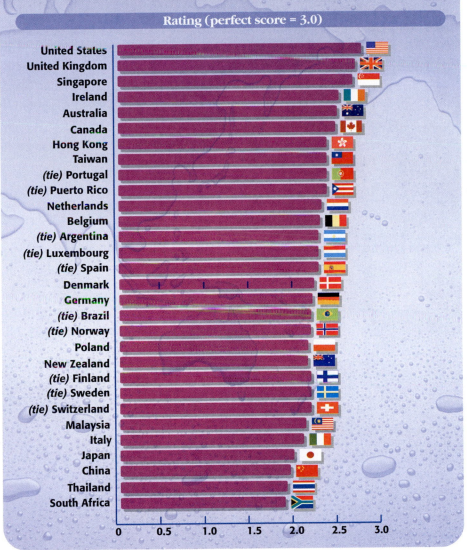

Rating (perfect score = 3.0)

- United States
- United Kingdom
- Singapore
- Ireland
- Australia
- Canada
- Hong Kong
- Taiwan
- (tie) Portugal
- (tie) Puerto Rico
- Netherlands
- Belgium
- (tie) Argentina
- (tie) Luxembourg
- (tie) Spain
- Denmark
- Germany
- (tie) Brazil
- (tie) Norway
- Poland
- New Zealand
- (tie) Finland
- (tie) Sweden
- (tie) Switzerland
- Malaysia
- Italy
- Japan
- China
- Thailand
- South Africa

0   0.5   1.0   1.5   2.0   2.5   3.0

Cultural elements can influence what kinds of products are sold and how they are sold. Managers must assess how local culture will affect the salability of its product if the location is a candidate as a market. For instance, consider the experience of Coca-Cola in China where many people take a traditional medicine to fight off flu and cold symptoms. As it turns out, the taste of this traditional medicine—which most people do not find appealing—is similar to that of Coke. Because of Coca-Cola's global marketing policy of one taste worldwide, the company had to overcome the aversion to the taste of Coke among Chinese consumers. It did so by creating a marketing campaign that associated buying Coke with experiencing a piece of America. Thus what initially looked like an unattractive market for Coke became very successful through a carefully tailored marketing campaign.

Cultural elements in the business environment can also affect site selection decisions. When substantial product modifications are needed for cultural reasons, a company might choose to establish production facilities in the target market itself. However, better serving customers' special needs in a target market must be offset against any potential loss of economies of scale due to producing in several locations rather than just one. But companies today can minimize such losses through the use of flexible manufacturing methods. For example, although cellular phone manufacturer Nokia produces in locations worldwide, it ensures that each one of its facilities can start producing any one of its mobile phones for its different markets within 24 hours.[4]

Having a qualified workforce is important for a company whatever activity it is to undertake at a particular site. Also, a strong work ethic among the local workforce is essential to having productive operations. Managers must assess whether an appropriate work ethic exists in each potential country for the purposes of production, service, or any other business activity. An adequate level of educational attainment among the local workforce for the planned business activity is also very important. Although product assembly operations may not require an advanced education, R&D, high-tech production, and certain services normally will require extensive higher education. If a potential site does not display an appropriate work ethic or educational attainment, it will be ruled out for further consideration.

Political and Legal Forces

Also influencing the market and site location decision are political and legal forces. Important factors include government regulation, government bureaucracy, and political stability. Let's take a brief look at each of these in turn.

Government Regulation As we saw in earlier chapters, nations differ in their attitudes toward trade and investment in their countries, which is rooted in culture, history, and current events. Some governments take a strongly nationalistic stance whereas others are quite receptive to international trade and investment. A government's attitude toward trade and investment is reflected in the quantity and types of restrictions it places on imports, exports, and investment in its country.

Government regulations can quickly eliminate a market or site from further consideration. First of all, they can create investment barriers to ensure domestic control of a company or industry. One way in which a government can accomplish this is by imposing investment rules on such matters as business ownership—for instance, forcing nondomestic companies into joint ventures. India's government originally forced PepsiCo to entrust 51 percent of its local ownership with Indian investors. PepsiCo was also required to give a certain portion of its revenue from sales in India to the Indian treasury.

Governments also can extend investment rules to bar international companies entirely from competing in certain sectors of the domestic economy. The practice is usually defended as a matter of national security. Economic sectors commonly declared off-limits include television and radio broadcasting, automobile manufacturing, aircraft manufacturing, energy exploration, military-equipment manufacturing, and iron and steel production. Such industries are protected either because they are culturally important, engines for economic growth, or essential to any potential war effort. Host governments often fear (rightly or wrongly) that losing control in these economic sectors means placing their fate in the hands of international companies.

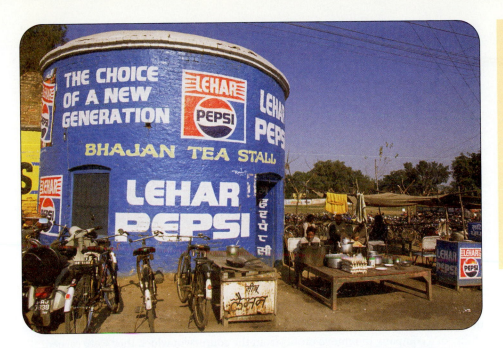

Governments can reduce competition and/or increase the cost of doing business within their borders by increasing the barriers of entry to their markets. Rather than give the Indian government its secret Coke formula, for instance, Coca-Cola actually gave up its attempt to battle Pepsi there until the government dropped its demand. How did Pepsi fare in India? The government at first required the firm to allow 51 percent of its local ownership to be in the hands of Indian investors and turn over a portion of its sales revenue to the Indian treasury.

Second, governments can restrict international companies from freely removing profits earned in the domestic market. This policy can force a company either to hold cash in the host country or to reinvest it in new projects there. Such policies are normally rooted in the inability of the host-country government to earn the foreign exchange needed to pay for badly needed imports. Motorola's Chinese subsidiary, for example, is required to convert the local currency (renminbi) to U.S. dollars before remitting profits back to the parent company in the United States. Motorola can satisfy this stipulation only as long as the Chinese government agrees to provide it with the needed U.S. dollars.

Third, governments can impose very strict environmental regulations. In most industrial countries, factories producing industrial chemicals as their main output or as by-products must adhere to strict pollution standards. Regulations typically demand the installation of expensive pollution-control devices and the close monitoring of nearby air, water, and soil quality. While protecting the environment, such regulations also increase short-run production costs. Many developing and emerging markets have far less strict environmental regulations. Regrettably, some companies are alleged to have moved production of toxic materials to emerging markets to take advantage of lax environmental regulations and, in turn, lower production costs. Although such behavior is roundly criticized as highly unethical, it will occur less often as nations continue cooperating to formulate common environmental protection policies.

Finally, governments also can require that companies divulge certain information. Coca-Cola actually left India when the government demanded that it disclose its secret Coke formula as a requirement for doing business there. Coca-Cola returned only after the Indian government dropped its demand.

Government Bureaucracy A lean and smoothly operating government bureaucracy can make a market or site more attractive, whereas a bloated and cumbersome system of obtaining approvals and licenses from government agencies can make it less appealing. In many developing countries, the relatively simple matter of obtaining a license to establish a retail outlet often means acquiring numerous documents from several agencies. The bureaucrats in charge of these agencies generally are little concerned with high-quality service. Managers must be prepared to deal with administrative delays and a maze of rules. For instance, in Tanzania managers of Milicom International Cellular, SA, must wait 90 days to get customs clearance on roughly $1 million in monthly cellular telephone equipment imports. But the size of the local market makes enduring such bureaucratic obstacles bearable: Several thousand cellular subscribers in Tanzania use their phones an average of 400 minutes per month.[5]

Thus companies will endure a cumbersome bureaucracy if the opportunity is sufficient to offset any potential delays and expenses. Companies entering China cite the patience needed to navigate a maze of government regulations that often contradict one another and complain about the large number of permissions required from different agencies. The trouble stems from the fact that China is continually revising and developing its system of business law as its economy develops. But an unclear legal framework and inefficient bureaucracy are not deterring investment in China—the opportunities in China for both marketers and manufacturers are simply too great to ignore.

Political Stability Every nation's business environment is affected to some degree by political risk. As we saw in Chapter 3, political risk is the likelihood that a nation will undergo political changes that negatively affect business activities. Political risk can threaten the market of an exporter, the production facilities of a manufacturer, or the ability of a company to remove profits from the country in which they were earned.

The key element of political risk that concerns companies is *unforeseen political change:* If a company cannot estimate the future political environment with a fair degree of accuracy, political risk is increased. Thus a negative-impact event expected to occur in the future is not, in itself, bad for companies because the event can be planned for and necessary precautions taken. Instead, unforeseen negative events are what create political risk for companies.

The perception of a market's political risk is often affected by managers' memories of past political unrest in a nation. Managers, however, cannot let past events blind them to future opportunities. International companies must try to monitor and predict political events that threaten operations and future earnings' potential. For example,

Political instability is an unpredictable factor in many markets, yet it remains one that companies must consider when they invest abroad. These Indonesian students clashed with police in Jakarta over the way the Indonesian government was handling the worst economic crisis in decades. The protests continued on and off for months as students called for the ouster of President Suharto. But even after Suharto resigned, social unrest rooted in economic hardship continued.

because Russia's future is so uncertain, doing business there today carries with it a fairly high level of political risk. After Boris Yeltsin, will Russia return to communist rule? Will civil disorder and chaos prevail? In asking such proactive questions, managers are focusing on political risk and developing action plans for dealing with it.

But where do managers get the information to answer such questions? They may assign company personnel to gather information on the level of political risk in a country, or they may obtain it from independent agencies that specialize in providing political-risk services. The advice of country and regional specialists who are knowledgeable about the current political climate of a market can be especially helpful. Such specialists can include international bankers, political consultants, reporters, country-risk specialists, international relations scholars, political leaders, union leaders, embassy officials, and other local businesspeople currently working and living in the country in question.

Economic and Financial Forces   Managers must carefully analyze a nation's economic policies before selecting it as a new market or site for operations. Poor fiscal and monetary policies of a nation's central bank can cause high rates of inflation, increasing budget deficits, a depreciating currency, falling productivity levels, and flagging innovation. Such consequences typically lower investor confidence and force international companies to scale back or cancel proposed investments. For example, restrictive trade and investment policies by the government of India finally gave way to more open policies in the early 1990s. Specifically, new investment policies encouraged investment in both production facilities and R&D centers, especially in the computer-software industry.

Currency and liquidity problems pose special challenges for international companies. Volatile currency values make it difficult for firms to predict future earnings accurately in terms of the home-country currency. Wildly fluctuating currency values also make it difficult to calculate how much capital a company needs for a planned investment. Unpredictable changes in currency values can also make liquidating assets more difficult because the greater uncertainty will likely reduce liquidity in capital markets—especially in countries with relatively small capital markets such as Bangladesh and Ecuador.

In addition to their home government's resources, managers can obtain information about economic and financial conditions from such institutions as the World Bank, International Monetary Fund, and Asian Development Bank. Other information sources include business and economic publications like the *Far Eastern Economic Review*, the annual country-risk guide published by *Euromoney*, and the series of reports called Economic Outlook published by *The Economist*.

Other Forces   The cost of transporting materials and goods and a country's image also play important roles in the assessment of national business environments. Let's now take a brief look at each of these forces.

Cost of Transporting Materials and Goods   The cost of transporting materials and finished goods affects any decision about where to locate manufacturing facilities. Some products cost very little to transport through the production and distribution process whereas others cost a great deal. **Logistics** refers to the management of the physical flow of products from point of origin as raw materials to end users as finished products. Logistics weds production activities to the activities needed to deliver products to buyers. It includes all modes of transportation, storage, and distribution.

To realize the importance of efficient logistics, consider that global logistics is a $400 billion industry. We often consider the United States an efficient logistics market because of its extensive interstate road system and rail lines that stretch from east to west. But because of overcrowded highways, 2 billion people-hours are lost to gridlock

logistics
Management of the physical flow of products from point of origin as raw materials to end users as finished products.

each year. That translates into $48 billion in lost productivity![6] Because of the financial cost to businesses of inefficient logistics, many transport companies and cargo ports strenuously advertise their services.

Country Image   Because *country image* embodies every facet of a nation's business environment, it is highly relevant to the selection of sites for production, R&D, or any other activity. For example, country image affects the location of manufacturing or assembly operations because products must typically be stamped with labels identifying where they were made or assembled—such as "Made in China" or "Assembled in Brazil." Although such labels do not affect all products to the same degree, they can present important positive or negative images and boost or dampen sales.

Products made in relatively more developed countries tend to be evaluated more positively than those from relatively less developed countries.[7] This relation can often be traced to the perception among consumers that the workforces of certain nations have superior skills in making particular products. For example, Procter & Gamble and Unilever, intense rivals in consumer products, both have manufacturing facilities in Vietnam. But Vietnamese consumers tend to shun locally made Close-Up toothpaste and Tide detergent and seek out the identical products produced in neighboring countries such as Thailand. As one young Vietnamese shopper explained, "Tide from Thailand smells nicer." A general perception among Vietnamese consumers is that goods from Japan or Singapore are the best, followed by Thai goods. Unfortunately for Procter & Gamble and Unilever in Vietnam, many goods from these other countries are smuggled in and sold on the black market, thereby denying the companies of sales revenue.[8]

A country's image also can be positive in one product class but negative in another. For example, consumers happily pay a premium for Corona beer imported from Mexico. Also, the fact that Volkswagen's new Beetle is made in Mexico for the U.S. market has not hurt the Beetle's sales one bit. But would affluent consumers buy a Rolls-Royce automobile if it were produced in Mexico? Because Rolls-Royce buyers buy the image of a brilliantly crafted luxury car, the Rolls-Royce image probably would not survive intact if the company moved its production facilities to Mexico.

Finally, note that country image can and does change over time. For example, "Made in India" has traditionally been associated with the production of low-technology products such as soccer balls and many types of textile products. But today world class computer-software companies increasingly rely on the software-development skills of engineers located in and around Madras and Bangalore in southern India.

Throughout our discussion of step 2 of the screening process (assessing the national business environment), we have discussed extensively many factors central to traditional business activities. However, there are many issues that are specific to successfully entering international markets through so-called "e-commerce"—selling exclusively or in part to customers over the Internet. The Global Manager "Global E-Commerce Issues" addresses some of the key infrastructure, legal, and financial aspects of national business environments that managers of Internet-based companies must consider.

STEP 3: MEASURE MARKET OR SITE POTENTIAL

Markets and sites passing the first two steps in the screening process undergo further analysis to arrive at a more manageable number of potential locations. Despite the presence of a basic need for a product and an adequately stable national business environment, potential customers might not be ready or able to buy a product for a variety of reasons. Despite the availability of resources, certain sites may be unable to supply a given company with the *level* of resources it needs. Let's now explore the factors further influencing the potential suitability of markets and sites for operations.

Global Manager

Global E-Commerce Issues

Generating sales in new geographic markets through the Internet (e-commerce) is an increasingly popular method of expansion for large multinationals and entrepreneurs alike. In fact, although estimates vary, the global value of e-commerce is expected to break the $1 trillion mark early in the twenty first century. Managers around the globe wishing to learn more about entering new markets through the Internet can access the U.S. Department of Commerce Web site devoted to e-commerce issues at ⟨**www.ecommerce.gov**⟩. In addition, here are some key issues managers should consider when entering new markets through the Internet:

➡ Infrastructure and Market Access Issues

• *Telecommunications infrastructure and information technology.* Before investing heavily in e-commerce, be sure to investigate whether your potential customers have easy access to the Internet. It should also be determined whether their government's telecommunications policies hinder development of advanced digital networks.

• *Content.* Issues of content include such topics as truth in advertising, fraud prevention, and violent, seditious, or pornographic materials. Companies must be informed about the different policies of each country through which their information travels to avoid liability.

• *Standards.* It is not yet clear which country has the power to establish standards of operations for e-commerce. Also, standards can be established to act as nontariff trade barriers to keep international companies out of a domestic market.

➡ Legal Issues

• *Privacy.* One of the strengths of e-commerce is that information on consumers can be easily collected and used to generate more sales. But consumer groups and others, particularly in the European Union, are concerned that collecting such data is an invasion of privacy. They are particularly vehement on this issue if consumers are not aware that this information is collected, how it is used, and if it is passed on to third parties.

• *Security.* Companies must ensure that their data communications are safe from unauthorized access or modification. While the technology exists to provide security—encryption, password controls, and firewalls, for example—it needs to be supported by a global infrastructure.

• *Intellectual property protection.* Protection of copyrights, databases, patents, and trademarks is governed by international agreements. But because a legal framework for the Internet has not yet been developed, these issues remain a global trade concern for managers of e-businesses.

➡ Financial Issues

• *Electronic payments.* Although secure encryption services in the credit card industry are well established, consumers remain concerned about security when it comes to their own credit card. Global electronic payment systems such as stored-value, smart cards, and other systems are still in various stages of development. Their increased use will alleviate many security issues for consumers.

• *Tariffs and taxation.* International policies regarding who should pay taxes on international e-commerce and to what nation they should be paid are not yet fully developed. Countries have widely different views on how these matters should be treated.

Measuring Market Potential   As barriers to trade continue to fall around the world, companies are looking to increase sales in industrialized and emerging markets worldwide. But companies can seldom create one marketing plan for every market in which they sell their products. Nations enjoy different levels of economic development, which affect what kinds of goods are sold, the manner in which they are sold, and the features they have. Likewise, the different levels of economic development require varying approaches to researching market potential. But how do managers estimate potential demand for particular products? Let's take a look at the factors managers consider when analyzing industrialized markets and then examine a special tool for analyzing emerging markets.

Industrialized Markets   Information needed to estimate market potential for a product in industrialized nations tends to be more readily available than in emerging markets. In fact, for the most developed markets, research agencies exist for the sole purpose of supplying market data to companies. Euromonitor is one such company with an extensive global reach in consumer goods. The company sells reports and does company-specific studies for many international corporations and entrepreneurs. Some of the information included in a typical industry analysis includes:

➠ Names, production volumes, and market shares of the largest competitors

➠ Volume of exports and imports of the product

➠ Structure of the wholesale and retail distribution networks

➠ Background on the market including population figures, important social trends, and a description of the kinds of marketing approaches used

➠ Total expenditure on the product (and similar products) in the market

➠ Retail sales volume and market prices of the product

➠ Future outlook for the market and potential opportunities

The value of such information supplied by specialist agencies is readily apparent—these reports provide a quick overview of the size and structure of a nation's market for a product. Reports vary in their cost (depending on the market and product) but many can be had for around $750 to $1,500. The company also allows online access to published reports through its World Wide Web site at ⟨**www.euromonitor.com**⟩. We discuss other sources for this type of market data later in this chapter.

e·biz

Thus companies entering industrialized countries often have a great deal of data available on a particular market. What becomes important then is the forecast for the growth or contraction of a potential market. One way of forecasting market demand is determining a product's **income elasticity**—the sensitivity of demand for a product relative to changes in income. The income-elasticity *coefficient* for a product is calculated by dividing a percentage change in the quantity of a product demanded by a percentage change in income. A coefficient greater than 1.0 conveys an *income-elastic* product, or one for which demand increases in a greater proportion to growth in income. These products tend to be discretionary purchases such as computers, video games, jewelry, or expensive furniture—generally not considered essential items. A coefficient less than 1.0 conveys an *income-inelastic* product, or one for which demand increases less relative to an increase in income. These products are considered essential and include food, utilities, and beverages. To illustrate, if the income-elasticity coefficient for carbonated beverages is 0.7, the demand for carbonated beverages will increase 0.7 percent for every 1.0 percent increase in income. Conversely, if the income-elasticity coefficient for DVD video players is 1.3, the demand for DVD video players will increase 1.3 percent for every 1.0 percent increase in income.

> **income elasticity**
> *Sensitivity of demand for a product relative to changes in income.*

Emerging Markets   Nearly every large company engaged in international business activities today is either in or considering entering the big emerging markets such as China, India, and Brazil. With their large consumer bases and rapid growth rates, they whet the appetite of marketers around the world. Although these markets are sure to experience speed bumps along their paths of economic development, in the long term they cannot be ignored. Table 11.1 shows the enormous consumption gap between China, India, and Brazil on the one hand, and the United States on the other, in several key industries.

Companies considering entry into emerging markets often face special problems related to a lack of information. Data on market size or potential may not be available, for example, due to undeveloped methods for collecting such data in a country. But there are ways companies can assess potential in emerging markets. One way is for companies to rank different locations by developing a so-called *market-potential indicator* for each. This method, however, is useful only to companies considering exporting. Companies considering investing in an emerging market must look at other factors

TABLE 11.1 Market Size: Emerging Markets versus the United States

Product	China	India	Brazil	United States
Televisions (million units)	13.6	5.2	7.8	23.0
Detergent (kilograms per person)	2.5	2.7	7.3	14.4
(million tons)	3.5	2.3	1.1	3.9
Shampoo (in billions of dollars)	1.0	0.8	1.0	1.5
Pharmaceuticals (in billions of dollars)	5.0	2.8	8.0	60.6
Automotive (million units)	1.6	0.7	2.1	15.5
Power (megawatt capacity)	236,542	81,736	59,950	810,964

that we examine next in the discussion of measuring site potential. Following are the main variables commonly included in market-potential analyses.[9]

➡ *Market size.* This variable provides a snapshot of the size of a market at any point in time. It does not estimate the size of a market for a particular product, but rather the *size of the overall economy.* Market-size data allow managers to rank countries from largest to smallest, regardless of a particular product. Market size is typically estimated from a nation's total population or the amount of energy it produces and consumes.

➡ *Market growth rate.* This variable reflects the fact that although overall size of the market (economy) is important, so too is its rate of growth. It helps managers avoid markets that are large but shrinking and target those that are small but rapidly expanding. It is generally obtained through estimates of growth in gross domestic product (GDP) and energy consumption.

➡ *Market intensity.* This variable estimates the wealth or buying power of a market from the expenditures of both individuals and businesses. It is estimated from per capita private consumption and/or per capita gross national product (GNP) at purchasing power parity (see Chapter 4).

➡ *Market consumption capacity.* The purpose of this variable is to estimate spending capacity. It is often estimated from the percentage of a market's population in the middle class, thereby concentrating on the core of an economy's buying power.

➡ *Commercial infrastructure.* This factor attempts to assess channels of distribution and communication. Variables may include the number of telephones, televisions, fax machines, or personal computers per capita; the density of paved roads or number of vehicles per capita; and the population per retail outlet. An increasingly important variable for businesses relying on the Internet for sales is the number of Internet hosts per capita. But because this data becomes quickly outdated, care must be taken to ensure accurate information from the most current sources.

➡ *Economic freedom.* This variable attempts to estimate the extent that free-market principles predominate. It is typically a summary of government trade policies, government involvement in business, the enforcement of property rights, and the strength of the black market. An index of political freedom, such as the annual report published by Freedom House called *Freedom in the World,* can be a useful resource.

➡ *Market receptivity.* This variable attempts to estimate market "openness." One way it can be estimated is by determining a nation's volume of international trade as a percent of gross domestic product (GDP). If a company wishes to see how receptive a market is to goods from its home country, it can ascertain the amount of per capita imports into the market from the home country. Managers can also examine the growth (or decline) in these imports.

➡ *Country risk.* This variable attempts to estimate the total risk of doing business, including political, economic, and financial risks. Some market-potential estimation techniques include this variable in the market-receptivity variable. This factor is typically obtained from one of the many services that rate the risk of different countries, such as Political Risk Services at ⟨**www.prsgroup.com**⟩.

After each of these factors is analyzed, they are assigned values according to their importance to the demand for a particular product. Then potential locations are ranked (assigned a market-potential indicator value) according to their appeal as a new market. As you may recall, we discussed several of these variables earlier under the topics of national and international business environments. For example, *country-risk* levels are shown in Map 3.3 (pages 90–91); *economic freedom* is shown in Map 4.1 (pages 122–123), and *market receptivity* (or openness) in Map 5.1 (pages 156–157). Map 11.1 captures one other variable, *commercial infrastructure*, by showing the telephone lines per 1,000 people of each nation. This variable is an important indicator of a nation's overall economic development. Other variables that are also good proxies for this vari-

MAP 11.1

COMMERCIAL
INFRASTRUCTURES OF
NATIONAL MARKETS

able include the portion of a nation's roads that are paved, or the number of personal computers, fax machines, and Internet hosts it has. However, one note of caution is important: Emerging markets often either lack such statistics, or in the case of paved roads, international comparison is difficult.

Measuring Site Potential   In this step of the site-screening process, managers must carefully assess the quality of the resources that they will employ locally. For many companies, the most important of these will be human resources—both labor and management. Wages are lower in certain markets because labor is abundant, relatively less skilled (though perhaps well-educated), or both. Employees may or may not be adequately trained to manufacture a given product or perform certain R&D activities. If workers are not adequately trained, the site selection process must consider the additional money and time needed to train them.

Training local managers also requires substantial investment of time and money. A lack of qualified local managers sometimes forces companies to send managers from the home market to the local market. This recourse adds to costs because home-coun-

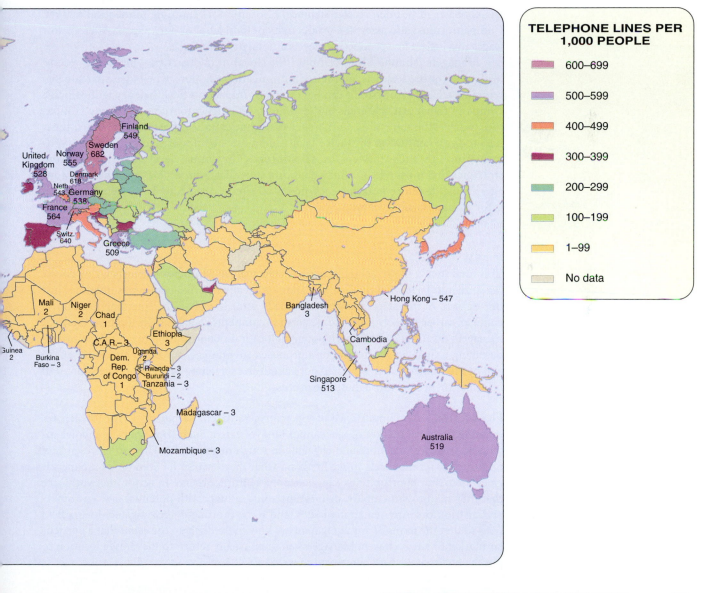

In gauging the amount of economic freedom in emerging markets such as China, for example, companies should consider government trade policies, government involvement in business, enforcement of property rights, and the strength of the black market. To learn more about China's trade policies, go to ⟨**www.chinatoday.com**⟩ and scroll down to the "international trade" link.

try managers must often receive significant bonuses for relocating to the local market. Companies must also assess the productivity of local labor and managers. After all, low wages may reflect low productivity levels among the workforce.

Managers should also examine the local infrastructure, including roads, bridges, airports, seaports, and telecommunications systems when assessing site potential. Each of these systems can have a major impact on the efficiency with which a company transports materials and products. Of chief importance to many companies today is the state of a country's telecommunications infrastructure. Much business today is conducted through e-mail, and many businesses electronically relay information on such matters as sales orders, inventory levels, and production strategies that must be coordinated among subsidiaries in different countries. Managers must therefore examine each potential site to determine how well prepared it is for contemporary communications.

STEP 4: SELECT THE MARKET OR SITE

This final step in the screening process involves the most intensive efforts yet of assessing remaining potential markets and sites—typically less than a dozen, sometimes just one or two. At this stage, managers normally want to visit each remaining location to confirm earlier expectations and perform a competitor analysis. In the final analysis, managers normally evaluate each potential location's contribution to cash flows by undertaking a financial evaluation of a proposed investment. We cover this topic at the end of this chapter, after we learn more about the screening process and the sources of information needed throughout the process.

Field Trips   The importance of top managers making a personal visit to each remaining potential market or site cannot be overstated. Such trips typically involve attending strings of meetings and engaging in tough negotiations. The trip represents an opportunity for managers to see firsthand what they have so far seen only on paper. It gives them an opportunity to experience the culture, observe in action the workforce that they might soon employ, or make personal contact with potential new customers and distributors. Any remaining issues tend to be thoroughly investigated during field trips so that the terms of any agreement are known precisely in the event that a particular market or site is chosen. Managers can then usually return to the chosen location to put the terms of the final agreement in writing.

Competitor Analysis   Because competitor analysis is covered in much greater detail in Chapter 12, we offer only a few comments here. Intensely competitive markets typically put downward pressure on the prices that firms can charge their customers. In addition, intensely competitive sites for production and R&D activities often increase the costs of doing business. Naturally, lower prices and higher costs due to competitive forces must be balanced against the potential benefits offered by each market and site under consideration. At the very least, then, competitor analysis should address the following issues:

➡ Number of competitors in each market (domestic and international)
➡ Market share of each competitor
➡ Whether each competitor's product appeals to a small market segment or has mass appeal
➡ Whether each competitor focuses on high quality or low price
➡ Whether competitors tightly control channels of distribution
➡ Customer loyalty commanded by competitors
➡ Potential threat from substitute products
➡ Potential entry of new competitors into the market
➡ Competitors' control of key production inputs (such as labor, capital, and raw materials)

So far we have examined a model that many companies follow when selecting new markets or sites for operations. We've seen what steps companies take in the screening process but have yet to learn how they undertake such a complex task. Let's now explore the types of situations companies encounter when conducting research in an international setting, and the specific tools used in their research.

CONDUCTING INTERNATIONAL RESEARCH

Today increased global competition forces companies to engage in high-quality research and analysis before selecting new markets and sites for operations. Companies are finding that such research helps them to better understand both buyer behavior and business environments abroad. **Market research** is the collection and analysis of information in order to assist managers in making informed decisions. We define market research here to apply to the assessment of both potential markets and sites for operations. International market research provides information on national business environments, including cultural practices, politics, regulations, and the economy. It also informs managers about a market's potential size, buyer behavior, logistics, and distribution systems.

> **market research**
> *Collection and analysis of information in order to assist managers in making informed decisions.*

Conducting market research on new markets is helpful in designing all aspects of marketing strategy and understanding buyer preferences and attitudes. What works in France, for example, might not work in Singapore. Market research also lets managers learn about aspects of local business environments such as employment levels, wage rates, and the state of the local infrastructure before committing to the new location. It supplies managers with timely and relevant market information to anticipate market shifts, changes in current regulations, and the potential entry of new competitors.

In this section, we first learn about several common problems confronting companies when conducting international research. Then we explore some actual sources that managers use to assess potential new locations. We then examine some methods commonly used for conducting international research firsthand in potential locations.

DIFFICULTIES OF CONDUCTING INTERNATIONAL RESEARCH

Market research serves essentially the same function in all nations. Unique conditions and circumstances, however, present certain difficulties that often force adjustments in the *way* research is performed in different nations. It is important for companies conducting market research themselves to be absolutely aware of such potential obstacles so that their results are reliable. Companies that hire outside research agencies must also be aware of such difficulties: After all, they must evaluate the research results and assess their relevance to the location selection decision. The three main difficulties associated with conducting international market research are:

1. Availability of data
2. Comparability of data
3. Cultural differences

Let's examine each of these items in turn.

Availability of Data   When trying to target specific population segments, marketing managers require highly detailed information. Fortunately, companies are often spared the time, money, and effort of collecting firsthand data for the simple reason that it has already been gathered. This is particularly true in the highly industrialized countries, including Australia, Canada, Japan, those in Western Europe, and the United States, where both government agencies and private research firms supply information. Information Resources Incorporated, Survey Research Group, and Nielsen Marketing Research are just three of these types of information suppliers.

In many emerging and developing countries, however, previously gathered quality information is hard to obtain. Even when market data are available, their reliability is questionable. For example, analysts sometimes charge the governments of certain emerging markets (particularly China) with trying to lure investors by overstating estimates of gross income and consumption levels. In addition to deliberate misrepresentation, tainted information can also result from improper local collection methods and analysis techniques. But research agencies in emerging and developing markets that specialize in gathering data for clients in industrialized countries are developing higher-quality techniques of collection and analysis. For example, information supplier and pollster Gallup is aggressively expanding its operations throughout Southeast Asia in response to the need for more accurate market research among Western companies.

Comparability of Data   Likewise, data obtained from other countries must be interpreted with great caution. Because terms such as *poverty*, *consumption*, and *literacy* differ greatly from one country to another, such data must be accompanied by precise definitions. In Canada, for example, a family of four is said to be below the poverty line if its annual income is less than CD$32,372.[10] The equivalent income for a Vietnamese family of four would place it in the high upper class.

The different ways in which countries measure data also affect its comparability across borders. Some countries, for instance, state the total quantity of foreign direct investment in their nations in terms of its *monetary value*. Others specify it in terms of the number of *investment projects* implemented during the year. But a single foreign direct investment into an industrialized nation can be worth many times what several or more projects are worth in a developing nation. Thus to gather a complete picture of a nation's investments, researchers will often need to obtain both figures. Moreover, reported statistics may not distinguish between foreign direct investment (accompanied by managerial control) and portfolio investment (which is not accompanied by managerial control). Misinterpreting data because one does not know how it is compiled or measured can sabotage even the best marketing plans and production strategies.

Cultural Problems   Marketers conducting research in unfamiliar markets must pay attention to the ways that cultural variables influence information. Perhaps the single most important variable is language. For example, if researchers are unfamiliar with a different spoken language in the market they are investigating, they might be forced to rely on interpreters. Interpreters might unintentionally misrepresent certain comments or be unable to convey the sentiment with which statements are made.

Researchers might also need to survey potential buyers through questionnaires written in the local language. To avoid any misstatement of questions or results, questionnaires must be translated into the language of the target market and the responses then translated back into the researcher's language. Written expressions must be highly accurate so that results do not become meaningless or, far worse, misleading. The potential to conduct written surveys is also affected by the illiteracy rates among the local population. A written survey is generally impossible to conduct in countries with high illiteracy rates such as Guatemala (44 percent), Egypt (49 percent), Haiti (59 percent), and Pakistan (62 percent).[11] Researchers would probably need to choose a different information-gathering technique such as personal interviews or observing retail purchases.

Companies having little experience in an unfamiliar market often hire local agencies to perform some or all of their market research. Local researchers know the cultural terrain; they understand which practices are acceptable and which types of questions can be asked. They also typically know whom to approach for certain types of information. Perhaps most importantly, they realize how to interpret the information they gather and are likely to know its reliability. But a company deciding to conduct its own market research must, if necessary, adapt its research techniques to the local market. Many cultural elements taken for granted in the home market must be reassessed in the host business environment.

SOURCES OF SECONDARY INTERNATIONAL DATA

Companies can consult a variety of sources to obtain information on a nation's business environment and markets. The particular source that managers should consult depends on the company's industry, the national markets it is considering, and how far along it is in its location screening process. The process of obtaining information that already exists within the company or that can be obtained from outside sources is called **secondary market research**. Managers often use information gathered from secondary research activities to broadly estimate market demand for a product or to form a general impression of a nation's business environment. Secondary data is relatively inexpensive because it has already been collected, analyzed, and summarized by another party. Let's now take a look at the main sources of secondary data that help managers make more informed location selection decisions. Table 11.2 provides the World Wide Web sites of many of the organizations and agencies discussed below as well as some others.

International Organizations   A variety of international organizations are excellent sources of much free and inexpensive information about product demand in particular countries. For example, the *International Trade Statistics Yearbook* published by the United Nations lists the export and import volumes of different products for each country. It also furnishes information on the value of exports and imports on an annual basis for the most recent five-year period. The International Trade Center, based in Geneva, Switzerland, also provides current import and export figures for more than 100 countries.

> **secondary market research**
> *Process of obtaining information that already exists within the company or that can be obtained from outside sources.*

e·biz

TABLE 11.2   *World Wide Web Sites of International Data Sources*

International Organizations

United Nations	⟨www.un.org⟩
World Bank	⟨www.worldbank.org⟩
International Monetary Fund	⟨www.imf.org⟩
World Trade Organization	⟨www.wto.org⟩
Asian Development Bank	⟨www.asiandevbank.org⟩
Association of Southeast Asian Nations	⟨www.asean.or.id⟩
Asia Pacific Economic Cooperation	⟨www.apecsec.org.sg⟩
Southern Common Market	⟨www.mercosurinvestment.com⟩
International Trade Center (Switzerland)	⟨www.intracen.org⟩

Government Agencies

Trade Information Center (U.S.)	⟨www.ita.doc.gov/tic⟩
STAT-USA	⟨www.stat-usa.gov⟩
World Factbook (CIA)	⟨www.odci.gov/cia/publications/nsolo/ wfb-all.htm⟩
Latin American Business	⟨www.lanic.utexas.edu/la/ region/business⟩
ProChile (Chile)	⟨www.chileinfo.com⟩
Japanese External Trade Organization	⟨www.jetro.go.jp⟩
Bank of Japan	⟨www.boj.or.jp⟩
Republic of Turkey	⟨www.turkey.org⟩

Industry and Trade Associations

PRISM International	⟨www.prismintl.org⟩
Federation of Malaysian Manufacturers	⟨www.fmm.org.my⟩
National Pasta Association (U.S.)	⟨www.ilovepasta.org⟩
National Onion Association (U.S.)	⟨www.onions-usa.org⟩

Service Organizations

Euromonitor	⟨www.euromonitor.com⟩
Janaky International Corporation	⟨www.indiaintl.com⟩
Export Today Online	⟨www.exporttoday.com⟩
Global Business Access	⟨www.globalltd.com⟩

International development agencies, such as the World Bank, International Monetary Fund, and Asian Development Bank, also provide valuable secondary data. For example, the World Bank publishes annual data on each member nation's population and economic growth rate. Most secondary sources today supply data on CD-ROM and through the Internet in addition to the traditional printed format.

Government Agencies   The commerce departments and international trade agencies of most countries typically supply information about import and export regulations, quality standards, and the sizes of various markets. These data are normally available directly from these departments, from agencies within each nation, and from the commercial attaché in each country's embassy abroad. In fact, visiting embassies and attending their social functions while visiting a potential location are excellent ways of making contact with potential future business partners.

Granted, the attractively packaged information supplied by host nations often ignores many potential hazards in a nation's commercial environment—governments typically try to present their country in the best possible light. By the same token, such sources are prone to paint incomplete or one-sided portraits of the home market. Thus it is important for managers to seek out additional sources that take a more objective view of a potential location.

One source that takes a fairly unbiased view of markets is the *World Factbook* published by the Central Intelligence Agency (CIA). This source can be a useful tool throughout the entire market- or site-screening process because of its wealth of facts on each nation's business environment. It identifies each nation's geography, climate, terrain, natural resources, land use, and important environmental issues in some detail. It also examines each nation's culture, system of government, and economic conditions, including government debt and exchange-rate conditions. It also provides an overview of the quality of each country's transportation and communications systems.

The Trade Information Center (TIC) operated by the U.S. Department of Commerce is a first stop for many importers and exporters. The TIC details product standards in other countries and offers advice on opportunities and best prospects for U.S. companies in individual markets. It also offers information on federal export-assistance programs that can be essential for first-time exporters. Other TIC information includes:

➡ National trade laws and other regulations
➡ Trade shows, trade missions, and special events
➡ Export counseling for specific countries
➡ Import tariffs and customs procedures
➡ The value of exports to other countries

The Chilean Trade Commission within Chile's Ministry of Foreign Affairs has been particularly aggressive in recent years in promoting Chile to the rest of the world. The commission is called ProChile and has 35 commercial offices worldwide. The organization assists in developing the export process, establishing international business relationships, fostering international trade, attracting investment, and forging strategic alliances. It offers a wealth of information on all of Chile's key industries and provides business environment information such as risk ratings. It also provides details on important trade regulations and standards of which exporters, importers, and investors must be aware.[12]

Commercial offices of the states and provinces of many countries also typically have offices in other countries to promote trade and investment. These offices usually encourage investment in the home market by companies from other countries and will sometimes even help companies in other countries export to the home market. For instance, the Lorraine Development Corporation in Atlanta is the investment-promotion office of the Lorraine region of France. The corporation helps U.S. companies evaluate location opportunities in the Lorraine region—a popular area for industrial investment. It supplies information on sites, buildings, financing options, conditions in the French business environment, and conducts 10 to 20 site selection studies per year for specific companies. "We've been in the U.S.A. since 1988," says director Frederic Mot. "Our main goal is to identify potential U.S. investors, and we contact about 2,000 American companies each year."[13] Figure 11.2 shows the U.S. states that have the most investment-promotion and trade offices abroad and the most popular locations for such offices.

Finally, many governments open their research libraries to businesspeople from all countries. For example, the Japanese External Trade Organization (JETRO) in central Tokyo has a large library full of trade data available to international companies already

FIGURE 11.2

U.S. STATES' GLOBAL
DEVELOPMENT OFFICES

Leading the Pack:
States with Five or More
Global Offices*

Favorite Destinations:
Top Countries for U.S.
Global Offices*

California   Mississippi
Connecticut Missouri
Florida   New York
Georgia   Ohio
Illinois   Utah
Indiana   Wisconsin
Michigan

Percentage of U.S. states with
offices in that country

* State offices outside the USA charged with foreign direct investment, export promotion, etc.

e·biz

in Japan. In addition, the JETRO Web site can be useful for companies screening the potential of the Japanese market for future business activities from any location. The organization is dedicated to serving companies interested in exporting to Japan or investing in Japan in addition to assisting Japanese companies go abroad.

Industry and Trade Associations   Companies often join associations composed of firms within their own industry or trade. In particular, companies trying to break into new markets join such associations in order to make contact with others in their field. Publications of these organizations keep members informed about current events and help managers to keep abreast of important issues and opportunities. Many associations publish special volumes of import and export data for domestic markets. Frequently they compile directories listing each member's top executives, geographic scope, and contact information such as phone numbers and addresses. Today, many associations also maintain informative Web sites. Two interesting examples are the sites of the National Pasta Association ⟨www.ilovepasta.org⟩ and the National Onion Association ⟨www.onions-usa.org⟩.

e·biz

Sometimes industry and trade associations will commission specialized studies of their industries and offer them to members at subsidized prices. Such studies typically address particularly important issues or explore new opportunities for international growth. For example, the Chocolate Manufacturers Association of the United States and the state of Washington's Washington Apple Commission hired the Gallup research firm to study the sweet tooth of Chinese consumers.[14] The findings of the study were then made available to each organization's members to act on as they saw fit.

Service Organizations   Many international service organizations in such fields as banking, insurance, management consulting, and accounting offer information to their clients on cultural, regulatory, and financial conditions in a market. For example, the accounting firm of Ernst & Young publishes a "Doing Business In" series for most countries. Each booklet contains information on a nation's business environment, regulations regarding foreign investment, legal forms of businesses, labor force, taxes, and culture.

Another service that provides information on world markets is MARKET: newsletters (see Figure 11.3). This company supplies specialized reports on market demographics, lifestyles, and consumer data and trends. Newsletters for each world region cover trends in such areas as population growth, consumer spending, purchase behavior, media, and advertising.

FIGURE 11.3

MARKET: NEWSLETTERS

Internet and World Wide Web   Companies engaged in international business are quickly realizing the wealth of secondary research information available on the Internet and World Wide Web. These electronic resources are usually user-friendly with vast amounts of information.

A leading online provider of market information is LEXIS-NEXIS ⟨**www.lexis-nexis.com**⟩. The LEXIS-NEXIS database of full-text news reports from around the world is updated continuously. It also offers special services such as profiles of executives and products, and information on the financial conditions, marketing strategies, and public relations of many international companies. Knight-Ridder, CompuServe, DIALOG, and Dow Jones are other popular on-line providers of global information. Internet search engines such as Alta Vista, Lycos, Yahoo!, and Infoseek can be quite helpful in narrowing down the plethora of electronically available information.

The Internet can be especially useful in seeking information about potential production sites. Because field trips to most likely candidates are expensive, on-line information can be enormously helpful in saving both time and money. You can, for instance, begin a search for information on a particular country or region on most large on-line information providers. Narrowing your search to a more manageable list of subjects—say, culture, economic conditions, or perhaps a specific industry—can yield clues about promising and unpromising sites.[15]

METHODS OF CONDUCTING PRIMARY INTERNATIONAL RESEARCH

Although secondary information is very informative and useful in the early stages of the screening process, sometimes more tailored data on a location are needed. Under such circumstances, it might be necessary to conduct **primary market research**—the process of collecting and analyzing original data and applying the results to current research needs. This type of research is very helpful in filling in the blanks left behind by secondary research. However, it is often more expensive to obtain than secondary research data because studies must be conducted in their entirety. Let's now explore some of the more common methods of primary research used by companies in the location screening process.

Trade Shows and Trade Missions An exhibition at which members of an industry or group of industries showcase their latest products, see what rivals are doing, and learn about recent trends and opportunities is called a **trade show**. They are held on a continuing basis in virtually all markets and normally attract companies from around the globe. They are typically held by national or global industry trade associations such as the "International Hardware Fair" in Cologne, Germany, in 1999. But they can also be organized by government agencies such as the "Tex-Styles India '99" textile show in New Delhi, India, sponsored by the India Trade Promotion Organization. An excellent source of trade shows and exhibitions worldwide is EXPOguide, Inc. which can be found on the World Wide Web at ⟨**www.expoguide.com**⟩.

Not surprisingly, the format and scope of trade shows differ from country to country. For example, because of its large domestic market, shows in the United States tend to be oriented toward business opportunities within the U.S. market. In line with U.S. culture, the atmosphere tends to be fairly informal and business cards are handed out to all the contacts one meets—no matter how briefly. Conversely, because of the relatively smaller market of Germany and its participation in the European Union, trade shows there are more international in focus, showcasing business opportunities in markets all across Europe. They also tend be quite formal and business cards are given to a contact only when a business relationship is highly desirable.[16]

On the other hand, a **trade mission** is an international trip by government officials and businesspeople that is organized by agencies of national or provincial governments for the purpose of exploring international business opportunities. Businesspeople who attend trade missions are typically introduced both to important business contacts and well-placed government officials.

Small and medium-size companies often find trade missions very appealing for two reasons. First, the support of government officials gives them additional clout in the target country as well as access to officials and executives whom they would otherwise have little opportunity to meet. Second, although such trips can sometimes be expensive for the smallest of businesses, they are generally worth the money because they almost always reap cost-effective rewards. Trade missions to faraway places sometimes involve visits to several countries to maximize the return for the time and money invested. For instance, a trade mission for European businesspeople to Latin America may include stops in Argentina, Brazil, Chile, and Mexico. A trade mission to Asia for North American or European companies might include stops in Hong Kong, Japan, South Korea, Thailand, and perhaps Vietnam.

Interviews and Focus Groups Although industry data are very useful to companies early in the screening process for potential markets, subsequent steps must assess buyers' emotions, attitudes, and cultural beliefs. Industry data cannot tell us how individuals feel about a company or its product. Deciding whether to enter a market and

---

primary market research
Process of collecting and analyzing original data and applying the results to current research needs.

trade show
Exhibition at which members of an industry or group of industries showcase their latest products, see what rivals are doing, and learn about recent trends and opportunities.

trade mission
International trip by government officials and businesspeople that is organized by agencies of national or provincial governments for the purpose of exploring international business opportunities.

subsequent development of an effective marketing plan require this type of buyer information. Many companies, therefore, supplement the large-scale collection of country data with other types of research, such as interviews with prospective customers. Interviews, of course, must be conducted carefully if they are to yield reliable and unbiased information. Respondents in some cultures might be unwilling to answer certain questions or may intentionally give vague or misleading answers to avoid getting too personal. For example, although individuals in the United States are renowned for their willingness to divulge all sorts of information about their shopping habits and even their personal lives, this is very much the exception as one goes around the world.

An unstructured but in-depth interview of a small group of individuals (8 to 12 people) by a moderator to learn the group's attitudes about a company or its product is called a **focus group**. Moderators guide a discussion on a topic but interfere as little as possible with the free flow of ideas. The interview is recorded for later evaluation to identify recurring or prominent themes among the participants. This type of research helps marketers to uncover negative perceptions among buyers and to design corrective marketing strategies. Because subtle differences in verbal and unspoken language could go unnoticed, focus group interviews tend to work best when moderators are natives of the countries in which the interview is held. Ironically, it is sometimes difficult to conduct focus groups in group-oriented cultures (see Chapter 2) because people have a tendency to agree with others in the group. In such instances, it might be advisable to use a **consumer panel**—research in which people record in personal diaries, information on their attitudes, behaviors, or purchasing habits.

Surveys   Research in which an interviewer has current or potential buyers answer written or verbal questions to obtain facts, opinions, or attitudes is called a **survey**. For example, if Reebok wants to learn about consumer attitudes toward its latest women's aerobics shoe in Britain, it could ask a sample of British women about their attitudes toward the shoe. Verbal questioning could be done in person or over the telephone, whereas written questioning could be done in person, through the mail, or through forms completed at Reebok's World Wide Web site. The results would then be tabulated, analyzed, and applied to the development of a marketing plan.

The single greatest advantage of survey research is the ability to collect vast amounts of data in a single sweep. But as a rule, survey methods must be adapted to local markets. For example, survey research can be conducted by any technological means in industrialized markets, such as over the telephone or World Wide Web. But telephone interviewing would yield poor results in Bangladesh because only a small percentage of the general population has telephones. Also, although a survey at a World Wide Web site is an easy way to gather data, it must be remembered that even in industrialized nations users still tend to represent the middle- to upper-income households.

Written surveys can also be hampered by other problems in some countries. Some countries' postal services are unreliable to the point that parcels are delivered weeks or months after arriving at post offices, or never arrive at all because they are stolen or simply lost. Naturally, written surveys are impractical to conduct in countries with high rates of illiteracy although this problem can perhaps be overcome by obtaining verbal responses to verbally asked questions.

Environmental Scanning   An ongoing process of gathering, analyzing, and dispensing information for tactical or strategic purposes is called **environmental scanning**. The environmental scanning process entails obtaining both factual and subjective information on the business environments in which a company is operating or considering entering. The continuous monitoring of events in other locations keeps managers aware of potential opportunities and threats to minimize financial losses and maximize

focus group
Unstructured but in-depth interview of a small group of individuals (8 to 12 people) by a moderator to learn the group's attitudes about a company or its product.

consumer panel
Research in which people record in personal diaries, information on their attitudes, behaviors, or purchasing habits.

survey
Research in which an interviewer has current or potential buyers answer written or verbal questions to obtain facts, opinions, or attitudes.

e·biz

environmental scanning
Ongoing process of gathering, analyzing, and dispensing information for tactical or strategic purposes.

returns. Environmental scanning contributes to making well-informed decisions and the development of effective strategies. It also helps companies develop contingency plans for a volatile environment in the event that an unfortunate scenario plays itself out rather than a more favorable one.

The falling cost of nearly all types of market research is opening doors for entrepreneurs and small businesses in international business. The Entrepreneurial Focus "Is the World Your Oyster?" details how entrepreneurs and small companies can make use of international market research and discusses the experiences of several small companies in exploring international opportunities.

Entrepreneurial Focus

Is the World Your Oyster?

How can an entrepreneur or small business succeed in international markets? How can they compete with the more competitive pricing and sales efforts of large multinationals? It isn't easy, but it can be done. First, small companies must do lots of homework before jumping into the global marketplace. Going international is a long-term investment and preparedness is a critical success factor. They also must plan on investing a good deal of cash. A typical small business can expect to pay anywhere from $10,000 to $20,000 to perform some basic market research, to attend a trade show, and to visit one or two countries. Furthermore, it can take up to three years to see a return on this investment. Consider the vastly different experiences of several small companies that are at various stages in their international dealings.

➤ Lucille Farms, Inc. of Montville, New Jersey, produces and markets cheese products. Alfonso Falivene, Lucille's chief executive, is taking a cautious approach to going international. He recently joined the U.S. Dairy Export Council that offers members, among other things, international trips to study new business opportunities and the competition. The Council also offers its members a great deal of free information on international markets. Notes Falivene, "I have stacks of information in my office. If I had to go out and get the information on my own, it would cost me thousands and thousands of dollars."

➤ Meter-Man, Inc. of Winnebago, Minnesota manufactures agricultural measuring devices. When Meter-Man decided to go international, it saw trade shows as a great way to gain market intelligence, establish contacts, and swap stories with other entrepreneurial firms. Over five days at an agricultural fair in Paris company executives held 21 meetings with potential customers and distributors. The result was an agreement with a major distributor that covers the Parisian market for Meter-Man's products. Besides hard work, Meter-Man has also benefited from plain old luck. James Neff, Meter-Man's sales and marketing director, was on a flight to a trade show in Barcelona, Spain, when he struck up a conversation with a man from Paraguay who was also attending the show. The man wound up ordering $200,000 of Meter-Man's products and is today a major South American distributor for the company. Says Neff, "All the classes in the world don't get you sitting next to a guy interested in your product." Meter-Man now has sales in 35 countries worldwide.

➤ But just as good luck operates across borders, so does its evil twin—bad luck. Anthony Bartarse, Jr. had four auto dealerships in California doing about $17 million in business each year. A native of El Salvador and the son of an exporter, Bartarse was not afraid of an international deal. When he heard that the government of Cameroon was looking to spend $24 million on 500 customized vehicles and a service center, he set about doing his homework. He painstakingly researched the market, even checking on Cameroon's human rights record. Bartarse decided to roll the dice. He took out his savings, got financing from the Ex-Im Bank and backed the loan up with mortgages on his home and a couple other buildings. After the State Department approved the deal, Bartarse sent engineers to Cameroon to start on the service center and ordered special cars from General Motors. Later, the State Department reversed its decision, citing the poor credit rating of Cameroon and human rights abuses. Bartarse was forced to sell two of his dealerships to pay off $750,000 he had already spent and is still in the red. "It almost put me out of business," laments Bartarse. Thus despite diligent fact-finding, uncontrollable events can destroy an international opportunity.

Up to this point, we have focused on how managers screen, analyze, and select new locations in which to do business. But engaging in a new project, such as marketing a company's product in another market, purchasing a distribution warehouse in another market, or building production facilities abroad, typically requires a sizeable financial investment. Most observers would agree that one (if not the main) purpose of a company is to make money for its owners. Thus it is important that managers evaluate the impact of any proposed investment on the company's financial condition. In other words, the final location selection decision is, by its nature, also an *investment* decision.

When it comes down to step 4 in the screening process (selecting the market or site), there often are two or more locations vying for the number-one spot. When companies evaluate competing investment proposals, they generally prefer to choose the project expected to generate the greatest return at any given level of risk. Thus the selection decision is also a *capital-budgeting decision* in which managers allocate a limited supply of capital to the best available investment opportunities. In making such decisions, managers analyze three factors:

➡ The cost of an investment
➡ The cash flows an investment is expected to generate
➡ The risk associated with the investment

But how do managers actually estimate the *value* of an investment project? In order to answer this question, we must look first at the issue of expected cash flows and then explore the concept of risk and return.

ESTIMATING FUTURE CASH FLOWS

Managers begin analyzing a proposed investment by estimating the total cash flows that the project is expected to generate. Bear in mind, however, that they are not considering cash flows generated by the investment in isolation from other company operations. Managers calculate not the cash flows of an investment project on its own, but rather *the cash flows a project generates in the context of all of a company's activities.* For instance, output from a new production facility in a market abroad might replace the company's prior exports to that market. Instead of importing from abroad, local buyers would now buy from the local operation in the host country. Therefore, the drop in exports must be offset against the gain in sales generated within the market by the new local production facility. Why then undertake the investment at all? Well, companies might invest in local production when countries charge tariffs that make the price of an import higher than the cost of locally produced goods. Companies might also locate inside a market to take advantage of lower-cost production resources such as labor or raw materials. Let's begin our discussion of how managers calculate future cash flows by exploring the concept of present value.

Present Value A concept at the core of future cash flow calculations is **present value**—the value today of an expected future cash flow. In other words, the *present value* of a given amount of currency received one year from now is worth less than the same amount of currency received today. The reason for this is that the currency can be invested to earn interest, resulting in a greater amount of money a year from now. For example, suppose you were given the choice of receiving 100 German marks today or 100 marks one year from today. You should choose to accept the 100 marks today and invest it a bank account or some other investment paying, say, 10 percent interest. After one year, you would have 110 rather than 100 marks. To put it another way, the present value of 110 marks to be received one year from now is equal to 100 marks.

present value
Value today of an expected future cash flow.

discount rate
Financial rate of return offered by comparable investment alternatives.

Managers apply the present value concept when they must estimate the value today of the cash flows that a project is expected to generate in the future. Thus we determine the value of an investment project launched today by (1) estimating expected cash flows in each future year and (2) estimating their value today by "discounting" them using a **discount rate**—a financial rate of return offered by comparable investment alternatives. The discount rate is usually equal to the interest rate at which the company normally borrows funds, plus a risk premium for the specific project. For instance, suppose a company must invest $50,000 to develop and implement an export promotion strategy. Suppose further that the export strategy is expected to generate income of $15,000 at the end of one year (computed after the $50,000 expenditure) and that the useful life of the expenditure is just one year. Suppose that the discount rate for the company is 8 percent. Thus the present value of the income is $10,185 {$15,000/ (1 + .08)}, not $15,000.

net present value
Present value of the future cash flows a project generates minus the amount of the initial investment.

The **net present value** of a project is equal to the present value of the future cash flows it generates minus the amount of the initial investment.[17] Thus the net present value of our export promotion example is $10,185 ($60,185 − $50,000). Companies should invest only in those projects that have positive net present values—projects that generate profits that exceed their cost.

return on investment (ROI)
Discounted income an investment generates divided by its cost.

Return on Investment   The **return on investment (ROI)** for a project is the discounted income an investment generates divided by its cost. In our example, the return of the project is $10,185 ($60,185 − $50,000) or 20.4 percent ($10,185/$50,000). For projects that have useful lives of more than one year, discounting must be performed on each year's financial returns. We must note that this discussion is a highly simplified example of how these concepts apply to an investment decision. The details involved in a real-life situation are more complex and go beyond our purposes in this discussion.

We should also note that companies sometimes invest in a project for other than financial reasons. For instance, a firm might invest in a *seemingly* unprofitable project because of hard-to-quantify strategic benefits that it generates. Perhaps it provides a good opportunity to learn about buyers in a new market with which a company is unfamiliar, for example.[18]

RISK AND RETURN

Every investment opportunity comes with a certain amount of risk. As we saw in earlier chapters, political, financial, and economic risks are not the same for all countries. Likewise, risk levels are not the same for all types of investment projects. The financial returns that an investment generates must compensate firms for accepting such risks.

We discussed the risks of international business environments in detail in Chapters 3 and 4. Domestic political instability or volatile relations with other countries can increase the risk level of a project in a market. Political tensions can result in social unrest and even open conflict. Such instability can result in physical damage to a company's assets or employees in a location or lead to impaired performance. Also, nationalistic sentiment could lead a government to confiscate key industries, such as public utilities, to ensure the provision of basic needs. There also are financial and economic risks of doing business across national borders. A government might suspend the exchange of local currency into the home-country's currency because of a shortage of hard currency. Or it could restrict the amount of profits that a company can take out of the host market and send back to headquarters. Managers must take into account every potential risk of a proposed investment.

How does risk affect the calculation of financial returns? One way to compensate for the increased risk of a project is to increase the discount rate, thus decreasing the present

Investing in conditions of uncertainty, which is the reality of business operations today, always carries some financial risk. The widespread destruction by Hurricane Mitch in Nicaragua, for instance, promised to hamper economic development for years while the country rebuilds itself.

value of expected future cash flows. Thus managers might increase the discount rate for investment in a very risky country from 8 percent to 11 percent. Likewise, they can reduce expected future cash flows by some amount that captures the greater probability of not receiving those flows. Companies can, for example, reduce the estimated cash flow from an investment from $300 million to $250 million. Either approach is acceptable as long as the estimate of financial returns is reduced for the greater risk of a business environment.

HOW COUNTRIES EVALUATE INVESTMENT PROJECTS

Nations apply different criteria than do companies when evaluating the benefits of an investment proposal. Whereas companies seek to maximize their financial returns by choosing investment projects with positive net present values, home and host governments are concerned with a project's impact on the nation as a whole. A nation is not necessarily concerned solely with the profits of an investment, but its impact on employment and wages, worker productivity, the environment, national security, and its balance of payments. Let's look at the most important factors that home and host countries consider when evaluating investment projects.

Home-Country Considerations   There are two main factors that home countries consider when evaluating the impact of an international investment project on their country. First, countries are concerned with the impact that a company's investment abroad will have on employment in the home market. For instance, negotiations surrounding the creation of free-trade areas (see Chapter 8) often cause labor groups to argue that such agreements allow companies to relocate to markets where wages are lower than at home.

Second, home countries are also concerned with the impact of an investment on their balance of payments. As we saw in Chapter 7, a nation's balance of payments is negatively affected by the outflow of capital. Thus countries sometimes restrict the value of the foreign direct investments it allows its domestic companies to make. Although the investment has an initial negative balance of payments effect, the nation's balance of payments is positively affected when companies repatriate profits earned abroad. Thus despite the initial negative impact, an international investment might contribute to the balance-of-payments position of the country in the long term.

Host-Country Considerations   One of the greatest concerns of a host country when considering the impact of a company's investment on its nation is the impact on wages and, in turn, its people's quality of life. This tends to be a greater concern for governments of developing and emerging markets because the size of investments there tends to be larger relative to the size of the economy. Wages tend to rise as new firms entering a market absorb unused labor. Higher wages allow citizens to afford more items and items of higher quality. Thus most nations welcome the investment projects of international companies.

Second, the impact of an investment on domestic companies is another important concern of governments. A major objective of many governments is to ensure that domestic companies are not suffocated by the entry of large multinational competitors. However, the greater competition that would ensue after their entry can prompt domestic competitors to become more productive and efficient—thus increasing their competitiveness. In addition, the local market will benefit if an international company invests in the training of local workers and the development of local managers. A well-trained workforce and local managerial talent are likely to attract even further investments by companies based in other countries.

Third, governments are often concerned with the impact of an investment project on the local cost of borrowing money. If international companies finance their investments with local money, the available pool of capital decreases and the cost of borrowing increases. Because the higher interest rates paid by international companies will appeal to local bankers, funding may also be diverted from public-works projects such as schools and hospitals toward the projects of private companies.

International flows of capital also affect the host country's balance-of-payments position. When companies repatriate profits back to their home countries, they deplete the foreign exchange reserves of their host countries. Alternatively, host countries conserve their foreign exchange reserves when international companies reinvest their earnings. Reinvesting in local manufacturing facilities can also improve the competitiveness of local producers and boost a host nation's exports—thus improving its balance-of-payments position.

Managers must remember the concerns of both host and home governments when evaluating their potential investment projects. They should try to relieve the types of concerns mentioned here by building trust and demonstrating commitment. Managers should convince officials of both countries of their desire to conduct business in a responsible and ethical manner that benefits all parties.

A FINAL WORD

In order to keep pace with an increasingly hectic and competitive global business environment, companies should follow a systematic screening process that incorporates high-quality research methods. This chapter provided a systematic way to screen potential locations as new markets or sites for business operations. We also explored how companies evaluate their investment proposals. These issues, however, constitute only the first step in the process of "going international."

The next step involves planning the actual entry into the targeted new location. In the next chapter, we explore how managers and companies actually accomplish this task. We examine corporate-, business-, and department-level strategies for entering selected markets and establishing operations abroad. In later chapters, we survey the types of entry modes available to companies, how they acquire the resources needed to carry out their activities, and how they manage their sometimes far-flung international business operations.

There is a variety of additional material available on the companion Web site that accompanies this text. You can access this information by visiting the Web site at ⟨**www.prenhall.com/wild**⟩.

summary

① Explain each of the four steps in the *market- and site-screening process*. Because managers want to keep the cost of searching markets and sites as low as possible but not overlook potentially attractive locations, they typically approach the *screening process* in a systematic four-step manner: (a) Identify basic appeal; (b) assess the national business environment; (c) measure market or site potential; and (d) select the market or site.

Identifying basic appeal for markets involves assessing a location's basic product demand. Companies must be certain that the product is suited to the local climate and not subject to an outright ban on its sale or use. The first step in selecting a site for business operations involves assessing the availability of required resources. Raw materials needed for manufacturing must be either found in the national market or imported. Companies considering local production must first determine whether there is enough locally available labor for production operations. Finally, companies hoping to secure financing in a new national market must also determine the availability and cost of local capital.

Step 2 of the screening process is to assess the national business environment of the location under consideration. This involves examining cultural, political, legal, and economic forces. Cultural forces, for instance, can influence what kinds of products are sold and how they are sold. Regarding sites for operations, a site not displaying an appropriate work ethic or educational attainment is likely to be ruled out for further consideration.

Important political and legal forces include government regulation, government bureaucracy, and political stability. Government regulations, for example, can create investment barriers to ensure domestic control of a company or extend investment rules to entire industries in order to bar foreign companies from selected economic sectors. A lean and smoothly operating government bureaucracy typically makes a market or site more attractive. Every nation's business environment is affected to some degree by *political risk*—the likelihood that the nation will undergo political changes that negatively affect business activities. Finally, poor fiscal and monetary policies of a nation's central bank can cause high rates of inflation, increasing budget deficits, a depreciating currency, falling productivity levels, and flagging innovation—factors reducing the appeal of a potential market or site.

Step 3 of the screening process is to measure the potential of each market or site for operations. Companies entering industrialized countries often have a great deal of market data available. What becomes important then is the forecast for the growth or contraction of a potential market. Companies considering entry into emerging markets often find that little or no market data exists. In such instances, companies can rank different locations by developing a so-called *market-potential indicator* for each. Main indicators include *market size, market growth rate, market intensity, market consumption capacity, commercial infrastructure, economic freedom, market receptivity,* and *country risk*. As a site for potential business operations, a location must be examined for availability of human resources (workers and managers), raw materials, and an adequate local infrastructure including roads, bridges, ports, and telecommunications systems.

In the fourth and final step in the screening process, managers normally visit each remaining location to confirm earlier expectations and perform a competitor analysis. In the final analysis, managers normally evaluate each potential location's contribution to overall company cash flows by undertaking a financial evaluation of a proposed investment.

② Describe the three primary difficulties of conducting *international market research*. Market research is the collection and analysis of information in order to assist managers in making informed decisions. International market research provides information on national business environments, including their cultural practices, politics, laws, and economic systems. It also informs managers about a market's potential size, buyer behavior, logistics, and distribution systems. Market research performs essentially the same function in all nations. Unique conditions and circumstances, however, present three main difficulties that often force adjustments in the *way* research is performed in different nations.

First, managers can face problems in the availability of data. Companies researching industrialized markets are often spared the time, money, and effort of collecting firsthand data for the simple reason that it has already been gathered. In many developing countries, however, previously gathered quality information is hard to obtain. Even when market data are available, their reliability is questionable. In addition to deliberate misrepresentation, tainted information can also result from improper local collection methods and analysis techniques.

Second, managers can face problems with the comparability of data across markets. Data obtained from different countries must be interpreted with great caution. Because terms such as *poverty, consumption,* and *literacy* differ greatly from one nation to another, such data must be accompanied by precise definitions. The different ways in which countries measure statistics also affect the comparability of data across borders.

Finally, managers can face problems rooted in cultural differences. Marketers conducting research in unfamiliar markets must pay attention to the ways that cultural variables influence information. Perhaps the single most important variable is language. Companies having little experience in an unfamiliar market often hire local agencies to perform some or all of their market research. Local researchers know the cultural terrain; they understand which practices are acceptable and which types of questions can be asked. They also typically know whom to approach for certain types of information. Perhaps most importantly, they realize how to interpret the information they gather and are likely to know its reliability.

❸ Identify the main sources of *secondary international data* and explain their usefulness. The process of obtaining information that already exists within the company or that can be obtained from outside sources is called *secondary market research.* Managers often use information from secondary research to broadly estimate market demand for a product or to form a general impression of a nation's business environment. Secondary research is relatively inexpensive because it has already been collected, analyzed, and summarized by another party.

International organizations are excellent sources of much free and inexpensive information about demand for a product in a particular country. For example, the *International Trade Statistics Yearbook* published by the United Nations lists the export and import volumes of different products for each country. International development agencies, such as the World Bank, International Monetary Fund, and Asian Development Bank, also provide valuable secondary data.

Government agencies—especially the commerce departments and international trade agencies of most countries—typically supply information about import and export regulations, quality standards, and the sizes of various markets. Commercial offices of the states and provinces of many countries also typically have offices in other countries to promote trade and investment. One source that includes objective information on markets is the *World Factbook* published by the Central Intelligence Agency (CIA). The Trade Information Center (TIC) operated by the U.S. Department of Commerce is a first stop for many importers and exporters. The TIC details product standards in other countries and offers advice on opportunities and best prospects for U.S. companies in individual markets.

Companies often join *industry and trade associations* composed of firms within their own industries or trades. Publications of these organizations keep members informed about current events and help managers to keep abreast of important issues and opportunities. Many international *service organizations* in such fields as banking, insurance, management consulting, and accounting offer information to their clients on cultural, regulatory, and financial conditions in a market. Finally, companies engaged in international business are quickly realizing the wealth of secondary research information available on the Internet and World Wide Web. Because field trips to most likely candidates are expensive, on-line information can be enormously helpful in saving both time and money.

❹ Describe the main methods used to conduct *primary international research.* Although secondary information is very informative and useful in the early stages of the screening process, sometimes more tailored data on a location are needed. Under such circumstances, it might be necessary to conduct *primary market research*—the process of collecting and analyzing original data and applying the results to current research needs. However, primary research data is often more expensive to obtain than secondary research data because studies must be conducted in their entirety.

Exhibitions at which members of an industry or group of industries showcase their latest products, see what rivals are doing, and learn about recent trends and opportunities are called *trade shows*. A *trade mission* is an international trip by government officials and businesspeople that is organized by agencies of national or provincial governments for the purpose of exploring international business opportunities. Businesspeople who attend trade missions are typically introduced to both important business contacts and well-placed government officials.

Although industry data are quite useful to companies early in the screening process, further stages of market selection must assess buyers' emotions, attitudes, and cultural beliefs. *Interviews*, of course, must be conducted carefully if they are to yield reliable and unbiased information. An unstructured but in-depth interview of a small group of individuals (8 to 12 people) by a moderator to learn the group's attitudes about a company or its product is called a *focus group*. The interview is recorded for later evaluation to uncover negative perceptions among buyers and to design corrective marketing strategies. In *surveys*, interviewers obtain facts, opinions, or attitudes by asking current or potential buyers to answer written or verbal questions. The single greatest advantage of survey research is the ability to collect vast amounts of data in a single sweep.

An ongoing process of gathering, analyzing, and dispensing information for tactical or strategic purposes is called *environmental scanning*. This process entails obtaining both factual and subjective information on the business environments in which a company is operating or considering entering.

5 **Explain how companies evaluate potential new investment projects.** When it comes down to step 4 in the screening process (selecting the market or site), there often are two or more locations vying for the number-one spot. When companies evaluate competing investment proposals, they generally prefer to choose the project expected to generate the greatest financial return at any given level of risk. Thus the selection decision is also a *capital-budgeting decision* in which managers allocate a limited supply of capital to the best available investment opportunities. In making such decisions, managers analyze three factors: (a) the cost of an investment, (b) the cash flows that it is expected to generate, and (c) the risk associated with it.

Managers begin analyzing a proposed investment by estimating the total cash flows that a project is expected to generate for the *overall company*. A concept at the core of such calculations is *present value*—the value today of an expected future cash flow. In other words, the present value of a given amount of currency received one year from now is worth less than the same amount of currency received today. Managers apply the present value concept when they estimate the value today of the cash flows that a project is expected to generate in the future. Thus we determine the value of an investment project launched today by first estimating expected cash flows in each future year and then estimating their value today by "discounting" them using a *discount rate*—a financial rate of return offered by comparable investment alternatives. The discount rate is usually equal to the interest rate at which the company normally borrows funds, plus a risk premium for the specific project. The *net present value* of a project is equal to the present value of the future cash flows it generates minus the amount of the initial investment.

The *return on investment* (*ROI*) for a project is the discounted income an investment generates divided by its cost. For projects that have useful lives of more than one year, discounting must be performed on each year's financial returns. Every investment opportunity comes with a certain amount of risk. Political, financial, and economic risks are not the same for all countries, and the financial returns that an investment generates must compensate firms for accepting such risks.

6 **Identify the issues important to countries when evaluating investment proposals.** Whereas companies seek to maximize their financial returns by choosing investment projects with positive net present values, home and host governments are concerned with a project's impact on the nation as a whole. A government tends to be more concerned with the impact of an investment on employment and wages, worker productivity, the environment, national security, and its balance of payments.

There are two main factors that *home* countries consider when evaluating the impact of an international investment project on their country. First, they are concerned with the impact that a company's investment abroad will have on employment in the home market. Second, they are concerned with the impact of an investment on their balance of payments, which is negatively affected by the outflow of capital. Thus countries sometimes restrict the amount of foreign direct investments that are allowed by its domestic companies.

One of the greatest concerns of *host* countries is the impact on wages and, in turn, its people's quality of life. This focus tends to be a greater concern for governments of developing and emerging markets because the size of investments there tends to be larger relative to the size of the economy. Second, the impact of an investment on domestic companies is another important concern of governments. A major objective is to ensure that domestic companies are not suffocated by the entry of large multinational competitors.

Third, governments are often concerned with the impact of an investment project on the local cost of borrowing money. If international companies finance their investments with local money, the available pool of capital decreases and the cost of borrowing increases. Finally, international flows of capital also affect the host country's balance-of-payments position. When companies repatriate profits back to their home countries, they deplete the foreign exchange reserves of their host countries. Alternatively, host countries conserve their foreign exchange reserves when international companies reinvest their earnings.

questions for review

1. What are the four steps in the *market-screening process*?

2. Identify the main factors to investigate when identifying the basic appeal of a market or site for operations.

3. What are the key *cultural, political, legal, economic,* and *financial forces* that should be taken into consideration when assessing a particular national business environment?

4. How do the cost of transport and country image affect the location decision?

5. Define *income elasticity* and explain how it is interpreted. What is its importance in measuring market potential?

6. Identify the main components of a *market-potential indicator*. Why is it often useful in assessing emerging markets?

7. What are the most important factors to consider in measuring site potential?

8. Describe the usefulness of undertaking a field trip and competitor analysis in the final stage of the screening process.

9. Define *market research*. What are some of the benefits associated with conducting international marketing research?

10. Identify the three main difficulties of conducting research in international markets. Explain each briefly.

11. Define *secondary market research*. When is secondary research data useful?

12. What are the main sources for secondary research data? Explain the value of the World Wide Web in conducting secondary market research.

13. Define *primary market research*. How does it differ from secondary market research?

14. What is the difference between a *trade show* and a *trade mission*?

15. What are some of the issues that arise when using *focus groups* in international marketing research?

16. How does a *consumer panel* differ from a *survey*? Explain why it is sometimes difficult to conduct a survey in international markets.

17. Explain the usefulness of *environmental scanning*.

18. What is meant by the term *present value*? Describe how it differs from the term *net present value*.

19. Define *discount rate*. What is its purpose in analyzing an investment project?

20. Define *return on investment*. Explain the *risk* and *return* relation for investment projects.

21. Identify the important concerns of home and host countries in evaluating an investment project.

questions for discussion

1. For many global companies, China represents a very attractive market in terms of size and growth rate. However, because China has a communist government, it ranks lower in terms of economic freedom and higher in political risk than other country markets. Despite these risks, Volkswagen, Isuzu, and Boeing are just a few of the hundreds of companies that have established manufacturing operations in China. In large part, this is because the Chinese government makes selling in China contingent on a company's willingness to locate production there. As an official from China's Ministry of Electronics Industry explained, the government "wants to allow Chinese companies to learn from foreign companies. We want them to bring their technology to the soil of the People's Republic of China."[19] Some observers believe that when Western companies agree to such conditions, they are bargaining away important industry know-how in exchange for sales today. Should Boeing and other companies go along with China's terms, or should they risk losing sales by refusing to transfer technology?

2. In 1996, Sony mounted its third official attempt to launch its MiniDisc recorder/player in the United States. Although the product has been a success in Japan, response to the Mini-Disc in the U.S. market has been lukewarm. A Sony executive noted, "This time around, we've done our homework, and we've found out what's in consumers' heads." What type of research do you think Sony used to "get inside the heads" of its target market? Do you think different cultures rely on different types of market research? Explain.

3. What are some of the benefits of "soft" market research data gathered using techniques such as focus groups and observation. What are the benefits of using "hard" data such as statistics on consumers buying habits and figures on market size? As a manager, which kind of data would you prefer to use? Why?

in practice

Read the following excerpt from the international business press and answer the questions that follow.

Sweden Struck by Company Exodus

Sweden's largest union movement, LO, representing blue-collar workers is pressuring Stockholm to stop the flow of companies out of the country, concerned about the jobs being lost through the exodus.

Volvo is seen as possibly the next Swedish company to relocate. Last year, Ericsson, the telecommunications group and Sweden's largest exporter, announced that it would move its headquarters to London, England. Pharmaceutical manufacturer Astra also announced a move to London in December after merging with Zeneca of the U.K.

Other companies that have moved headquarters out of Sweden in the recent past include Pharmacia, Nordbanken, Nobel Industries, ABB, Ikea, Tetra Laval, Electrolux, and SCA.

1. Using any available resources (such as the business press and statistical databases), explain why you think companies are leaving Sweden? List as many potential reasons for the moves as you can.

2. How do Sweden and the United Kingdom compare with regard to their appeal to companies relocating their headquarters to London? List as many direct and relevant comparisons as you can—you might want to use this chapter's screening process as a guide.

3. How do Sweden and the United Kingdom compare with regard to moving *manufacturing* from Sweden to London? Again, you might want to refer to this chapter's screening process.

projects

1. Visit the library at your college or university and consult the *Encyclopedia of Associations*. Select one or two associations that pertain to an industry that is of interest to you. Write or call the association and request an information packet. Compile a summary of the information you receive. Compare this information with that of your fellow students. Rank the trade associations in terms of the usefulness of their available information.

2. Select an emerging market that you would like to learn more about. Start by compiling fundamental country data; then do additional research to flesh out the nature of the market opportunity offered by this country or its suitability as a manufacturing site. Structure your report using the steps identified in this chapter. Make a list of the international companies that are pursuing market opportunities in the country, and identify the products or brands that the companies are mar-

keting. Are their reasons for doing business in the country consistent with the market opportunity as you have researched it? Determine whether these companies have established facilities for manufacturing, sales, or both.

3. A great deal of market information can be found in business-oriented magazines and journals. However, depending where the magazine is published, the editorial point of view or emphasis may vary. For a particular country market, find a recent feature article in magazines from at least two different countries. As a starting point, look for articles in *The Economist* (Europe), *Far Eastern Economic Review* (Asia), and *Business Week* (North America). Write a brief summary of each article in which you compare and contrast such issues as content coverage, point of view, and editorial tone in the different magazines. How might a manager's opinion of a market be shaped by the views expressed?

In 1990, Vietnam's communist government announced that non-Vietnamese manufacturers were welcome to set up shop in the Southeast Asian country. South Korea's Daewoo quickly established itself as the number-one investor in Vietnam. Other well-known companies, including Sony, Toshiba, Honda, Peugeot, and British Petroleum, also took Hanoi up on its invitation. However, the absence of trade and diplomatic relations between the United States and Vietnam meant that U.S. companies had to sit on the sidelines. Nearly four years later, the U.S. government lifted the trade embargo with Vietnam, paving the way for Carrier, Gillette, AT&T, Procter & Gamble, and a host of other U.S. companies to pursue opportunities in Vietnam.

Experts agree that the Vietnamese market holds tremendous potential over the long term. However, it may be two decades before Vietnam reaches the level of economic development found in Thailand today. Meanwhile, the country's location in the heart of Asia and the presence of a literate, low-wage workforce are powerful magnets for international companies. U.S. investment in Vietnam has lagged well behind that of other countries; by the end of 1996, Hong Kong ranked first among U.S. companies, with more than 270 projects valued at about $4 billion, followed by Taiwan and South Korea. The United States had some 60 investment projects in Vietnam valued at about $1.3 billion. One U.S. banker said, "The figures speak for themselves. They indicate that American companies start slowly. But I think they are picking up steam." Indeed, in 1998, the White House announced that it was exempting Vietnam from the Jackson-Vanik amendment. The exemption means that U.S. companies investing in Vietnam can get financial assistance from the Overseas Private Investment Corporation (OPIC) and the Export-Import Bank.

There are many challenges for investors in Vietnam. The population of 76 million is very poor, with annual per capita income of only about $200. The infrastructure is undeveloped: Only 10 percent of roads are paved, electricity sources are unreli-

able, there is less than 1 telephone per 100 people, and the banking system is undeveloped. Nevertheless, an emerging entrepreneurial class in Vietnam has developed a taste for expensive products such as Nikon cameras and Ray Ban sunglasses—both of which are available in stores. Says Do Duc Dinh of the Institute on the World Economy, "There is a huge unofficial economy. For most people, we can live only 5 days or 10 days a month on our salary. But people build houses. Where does the money come from? Even in government ministries, there are two sets of books—one for the official money and one for unofficial."

The Communist Party of Vietnam (CPV) is struggling to adapt to the principles of a market economy, and the layers of bureaucracy built up over decades of communist rule slow the pace of change. A key agency is the State Committee for Cooperation and Investment; as Vu Tien Phuc, a deputy director of the agency, explained, "Every authority would like to have the last say. We have to improve the investment climate." Despite such statements, the government continued to conduct itself in a way that left international investors scratching their heads. In January 1996, for example, Hanoi embarked on a "social evils crackdown" that included pulling down or painting over any sign or billboard printed in a language other than Vietnamese.

In the late 1990s, euphoria over Vietnam's potential showed signs of waning. Part of the problem was the "currency contagion" that had gripped Asia since mid-1997. Asian countries that had been major investors were scaling back their activities in Vietnam. More generally, many companies were finding it difficult to make a profit. Cross-border smuggling from Thailand depressed legitimate sales of products produced locally by Procter & Gamble, Unilever, American Standard, and other companies. It was also clear that the Hanoi bureaucracy was a major impediment. Laws concerning taxes and foreign exchange were in constant flux, and several companies were accused of violations such as tax evasion. As a Western investment lawyer in Ho Chi Minh City said, "People are tired of waiting for economic reforms that come too little, too late."

thinking globally

1. Assess Vietnam's potential both as a market and as a manufacturing site.

2. What, if anything, can Western countries do to help improve the political climate for doing business in Vietnam?

3. What problems might a company encounter while conducting market research in Vietnam?

4. What would be your perception of a product with the label "Made in Vietnam"? Do you think the type of product would play a role in forming your perception?

a question of ethics

1. In a recent book and several articles, editor and journalist William Greider argues that multinational corporations from wealthy countries are seriously endangering the global eco-

nomic system by investing capital in developing countries and laying off workers at home. In essence, Greider argues, globalization pits the interests of the older, more prosperous workers in wealthy countries against the interests of newly recruited, lower-paid workers in developing countries. Moreover, the disbursal of production and capital flight that Greider describes pit developing nations against one another as multinational companies move from one developing country to another in search of lower wages or bigger market opportunities. Greider believes that multinationals have an ethical obligation to try to preserve jobs for workers in their home-country markets. Do you agree?[20] Explain your answer.

2. As the CEO of a large international company, you are proud of the fact that you have built a profitable business by investing in a Latin American country. As a key catalyst in mobilizing the nation's low-cost labor force, your company has helped the nation achieve double-digit economic growth. Following a political upheaval, however, a military government takes control. Workers' rights are being violated, as are those of individual citizens. As CEO, it is up to you to decide on a course of action. Should you pull out of the country, effectively abandoning your employees? Should you publicly and directly confront the leaders of the new government and insist that they respect workers' rights? Should you proceed more discreetly and pursue diplomacy out of the public's eye? Or, would another course of action be advisable? Can you make an ethical decision that is also a good business decision?

3. Many marketing research organizations and associations have codes of ethics that promote high standards of integrity for researchers working in the field or with clients. For example, members of the Qualitative Research Consultants Association (QRCA) agree to abide by a nine-point code of ethics that forbids such practices as discriminating in respondent recruitment and offering kickbacks or other favors in exchange for business. The code also calls for research to be conducted for legitimate research purposes, and not as a front for product promotion. Why do you think the QRCA and other market research organizations create such codes? Do you believe they are helpful in reducing unethical research practices? Why or why not?

12 planning and organizing international operations

Beacons

A Look Back

CHAPTER 11 explained how companies analyze international business opportunities. We learned how managers screen and research potential markets and sites for operations. We also explored how companies evaluate proposed investment projects.

A Look at This Chapter

This chapter introduces us to planning and strategy in international companies. We explore the different types of strategies international companies employ and important factors in their selection. We also examine some organizational structures that companies devise to suit their international operations.

A Look Ahead

CHAPTER 13 describes the selection and management issues surrounding the different entry modes available to companies going international. We examine the importance of export strategy for exporters and the pros and cons of each entry mode.

Learning Objectives

After studying this chapter, you should be able to

1 Explain the stages of identification and analysis that precede strategy selection.

2 Identify the *strategies* that international companies employ at various levels in the organization.

3 Explain the important *production considerations* influencing strategy formulation.

4 Discuss the important *marketing considerations* influencing strategy formulation.

5 Describe each type of *international organizational structure* and identify the key issues in its selection.

Percy Barnevik is a revolutionary at ASEA Brown Boveri (ABB). The Swiss-Swedish electrical engineering firm does business worth $35 billion annually in 140 countries, with 219,000 employees working for 1,400 companies. For the past decade, Barnevik has been leading the company into uncharted territory.

Says Manfred de Vries, management professor at INSEAD in France, "As Alfred P. Sloan, Jr. of General Motors Corp. was the master architect of what used to be called the 'modern corporation,' a model that held up for many decades, Barnevik has become the designer of a prototype of organization more in line with the post-industrial age."

The organizational model of ABB is one with a truly global corporate culture, but with operations in each country adapted to local conditions. Although ABB is very decentralized, an iron-hard core at the center of the corporation maintains control. Diverse links between people at various levels in the company and in different countries assist in holding the corporation together. Although ABB's global operations benefit from scale economies, individual profit centers, some as small as five people, are as entrepreneurial as independent businesses. Technology is also important. "Without a very developed on-line communications system—teleconferences, videoconferences and all the modern communication techniques—it would be impossible to have a group of ABB's type," says Barnevik.

Barnevik sums up the key to the success of this revolutionary type of organization saying, "The world is changing around you but the basic idea [is] to have this decentralized structure, to be big and small, to be local and global, that continues to be the key." Although easy to say, it is hardly a simple accomplishment. One thing is for certain; Barnevik has earned his title of "revolutionary" in devising his company's strategies and structure.[1]

planning
Process of identifying and selecting an organization's objectives and deciding how the organization will achieve those objectives.

strategy
Set of planned actions taken by managers to help a company meet its objectives.

Planning is the process of identifying and selecting an organization's objectives and deciding how the organization will achieve those objectives. In turn, **strategy** is the set of planned actions taken by managers to help a company meet its objectives. The key to developing an effective strategy, then, is to clearly define a company's objectives (or goals) and carefully plan how it will achieve those goals. This requires a company to undertake an analysis of its own capabilities and strengths to identify what it can do better than the competition. It also means that a company must carefully assess the competitive environment and the national and international business environments in which it operates.

A well-defined strategy helps a company compete effectively in increasingly competitive international markets. It serves to coordinate a company's various divisions and departments so that it reaches its company-wide goals in the most effective and efficient manner possible. A clear, appropriate strategy focuses a company on the activities that it performs best and the industries for which it is best suited—helping to keep it away from a future characterized by mediocre performance or total failure. An inappropriate strategy can lead managers to take actions that cause internal tensions and pull a company in opposite directions, or take the firm into industries about which they know very little.

In this chapter, we learn about the different types of strategies companies employ to achieve their international business objectives. We begin by exploring important factors that managers consider when analyzing their companies' strengths and weaknesses. We examine the different international strategies and the corporate-, business-, and department-level strategies that companies employ. We then look at some important production and marketing considerations that influence companies' strategies. Finally, we explore the different types of organizational structures that companies use to coordinate their international activities.

INTERNATIONAL PLANNING AND STRATEGY

Many of the concerns facing managers when formulating strategy are the same for both domestic and international companies. Firms must determine what products to produce, where to produce them, and where and how to market them. The biggest difference lies in complexity. Companies considering international production need to select from perhaps many potential countries, each likely having more than one possible location. Depending on its product line, a company that wants to market internationally might have an equally large number of markets to consider. Whether being considered as a site for operations or as a potential market, each international location has a rich mixture of cultural, political, legal, and economic traditions and processes. All of these factors add to the complexity of planning and strategy for international managers.

STRATEGY FORMULATION

The strategy formulation process involves both planning and strategy. Strategy formulation permits managers to step back from day-to-day activities and get a fresh perspective on the current and future direction of the company and its industry. As you can see from Figure 12.1, this procedure can be regarded as a three-stage process. Let's now examine several important factors to consider in each stage of this process.

IDENTIFY COMPANY MISSION AND GOALS

mission statement
Written statement of why a company exists and what it plans to accomplish.

Most companies have a general purpose for why they exist that they express in a **mission statement**—a written statement of why a company exists and what it plans to accomplish. One company, for example, might set out to supply the highest level of ser-

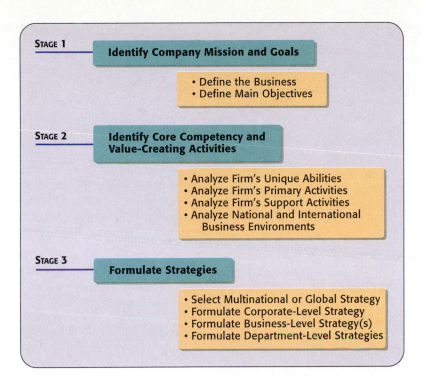

FIGURE 12.1
STRATEGY FORMULATION PROCESS

STAGE 1 Identify Company Mission and Goals
- Define the Business
- Define Main Objectives

STAGE 2 Identify Core Competency and Value-Creating Activities
- Analyze Firm's Unique Abilities
- Analyze Firm's Primary Activities
- Analyze Firm's Support Activities
- Analyze National and International Business Environments

STAGE 3 Formulate Strategies
- Select Multinational or Global Strategy
- Formulate Corporate-Level Strategy
- Formulate Business-Level Strategy(s)
- Formulate Department-Level Strategies

vice in a *market segment*—a clearly identifiable group of potential buyers. Another might determine to be the lowest-cost supplier in its segment worldwide. The mission statement often guides such decisions as which industries to enter or exit and how to compete in chosen segments.

Types of Mission Statements   Mission statements often spell out how a company's operations affect its **stakeholders**—all parties, ranging from suppliers and employees to stockholders and consumers, who are affected by a company's activities. For instance, some statements focus on the interests of consumers. Thus global eye-care company Bausch & Lomb includes the customer in its statement of its goals and activities:[2]

As a global eye care company, we will help consumers see, look and feel better through innovative technology and design.

Other companies issue very broad mission statements that recognize all their stakeholders. Britain's Cadbury Schweppes is a global company whose businesses in over 200 countries are beverages and confectionery (candies). Although most products in the confectionery group carry the Cadbury name, its beverage group includes such well-known brands as 7-Up, Dr. Pepper, Crush, and Mott's. The firm's mission statement reads as follows:[3]

Our task is to build on our traditions of quality and value to provide brands, products, financial results and management performance that meet the interests of our shareholders, consumers, employees, customers, suppliers and the communities in which we operate.

Thus the mission statement of an international business depends upon (among other things) the type of business it is in, the stakeholders it is most trying to satisfy, and the aspect of the business most important to achieving its goals. However, companies must be sensitive to the needs of its different stakeholders in different nations. For

stakeholders
All parties, ranging from suppliers and employees to stockholders and consumers, who are affected by a company's activities.

instance, the need of a company's stockholders in one nation for financial returns must be balanced against the needs of buyers in another country or the public at large where it has production facilities. For example, the company cannot be irresponsible in its duties for proper waste disposal activities or excessive noise levels near residential areas.

Managers must also define the *objectives* they wish to achieve in the global marketplace. Objectives at the highest level in a company tend to be stated in the most general terms. An example of this type of objective would be:

To be the largest global company in each industry in which we compete.

Objectives of individual business units in an organization tend to be more specific. They are normally stated in more concrete terms and sometimes even contain numerical targets. For example, such a mission statement could be stated as follows:

To mass-produce a zero-pollution emissions automobile by 2005.

Objectives usually become even more precise at the level of individual departments and almost always contain numerical targets of performance. For example, the following could be the objective of the marketing and sales department:

To increase market share by 5 percent in each of the next three years.

IDENTIFY CORE COMPETENCY AND VALUE-CREATING ACTIVITIES

Before managers formulate effective strategies, they must analyze the company, its industry (or industries), and the national business environments in which it is involved. Industries and countries being targeted for potential future entry should also be examined. In this section we address the company and its industries. We examine the business environment in the next section.

Unique Abilities of Companies   Although large multinational companies are often involved in multiple industries, most perform one activity (or a few activities) better than any competitor does. A **core competency** is a special company ability that

core competency
Special company ability that competitors find extremely difficult or impossible to equal.

After realizing in the 1980s that the emerging field of biotechnology offered enormous opportunity, Monsanto ⟨**www.monsanto.com**⟩ launched a major initiative to acquire a core competency in that field. The firm has since succeeded in transforming itself from a manufacturer of chemicals into a leader in the genetic engineering of crops and seeds, including cotton and soybean seeds that are resistant to common pests and herbicides.

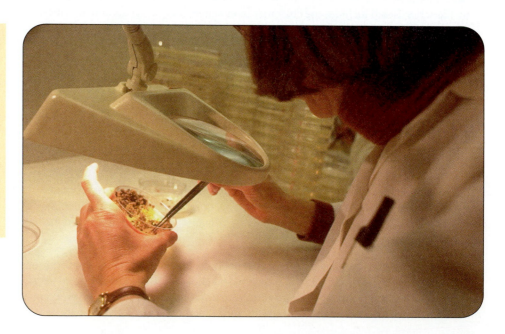

competitors find extremely difficult or impossible to equal.[4] It is not a *skill*; individuals possess skills. An architect's ability to design an office building in the Victorian style is a skill. A core competency refers to *multiple skills that are coordinated to form a single technological outcome.* Although skills can be learned through on-the-job training and personal experience, core competencies develop over longer periods of time and are difficult to teach.

At one point, for example, Canon of Japan invested money to acquire expertise in optic technology. Only later, however, did Canon succeed in developing a variety of products based on optic technology—cameras, copiers, and semiconductor lithographic equipment. When the firm possessed the ability to create such products, it had fully developed a legitimate core competency.[5] Likewise, Sony's core competency in miniaturizing electronic components fortifies its global leadership position in consumer electronics.

How do managers actually go about analyzing and identifying their unique abilities? Let's take a look at a tool commonly used by managers to analyze their companies—*value chain analysis*.

Value Chain Analysis   Managers must select strategies consistent with both their company's particular strengths and the market conditions the firm is facing. Managers should also select company strategies based on what the company does that customers find valuable. In identifying company activities that create value for customers, managers may conduct a **value chain analysis**.[6] As you can see from Figure 12.2, value chain analysis divides a company's activities into primary activities and support activities that are central to creating customer value. *Primary activities* include inbound and outbound logistics, manufacturing (or operations), marketing and sales, and customer service. Primary activities involve the physical creation of the product, its marketing and delivery to buyers, and its after-sales support and service. *Support activities* include firm infrastructure, human resource management, technology development, and procurement. Each of these activities provides the inputs and infrastructure required by the primary activities.

> **value chain analysis**
> *Process of dividing a company's activities into primary and support activities and identifying those that create value for customers.*

FIGURE 12.2

COMPONENTS OF A COMPANY'S VALUE CHAIN

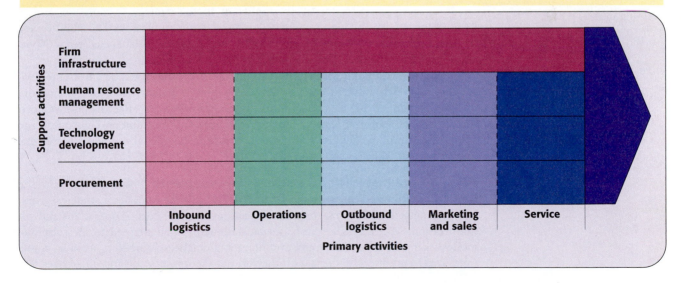

Each primary and support activity is a source of strength or weakness for a company. Managers determine whether each activity enhances or detracts from customer value and incorporate this knowledge into the strategy formulation process. Analysis of primary and support activities often involves finding activities in which improvements can be made with large benefits. Let's take a look at how managers determine whether an activity enhances customer value.

Primary Activities When analyzing primary activities, managers often look for areas in which the company can increase the value provided to customers. Managers might, for instance, examine production processes and discover new, more efficient manufacturing methods to reduce production costs and improve quality. Customer satisfaction might be increased by improving logistics management that shortens the time it takes to get a product to the buyer or by providing better customer service.

Companies might also lower costs by introducing greater automation into the production process.[7] For example, Stan Shih, founder of computer maker Acer (founded in Taiwan but based in Singapore), applied a fast-food production model to personal computer manufacturing. Rather than manufacture complete computers in Asia and ship them around the world, Acer builds components at plants scattered throughout the world. Those components are then shipped to assembly plants where computers are built according to customer specifications. Shih commented, "Today, there is no longer any value added in assembling computers—everyone can make a PC. To succeed, you have to gain a top position in component segments or else as a distribution leader in a country or region."[8] By altering its production and logistics processes, Acer created a business model that created value for customers.

Support Activities Support activities assist companies in performing their primary activities properly. The actions of any company's employees, for example, are crucial to its success. Manufacturing, logistics, marketing and sales, and customer service all benefit when employees are qualified and well trained. International companies can often improve product quality by investing in worker training and manager development. In turn, ensuring quality can increase the efficiency of a firm's manufacturing, marketing and sales, and customer service activities. Effective procurement can locate low-cost, high-quality raw materials or intermediate products and ensure on-time delivery to production facilities. Finally, a sophisticated infrastructure not only improves internal communication but also supports organizational culture and each primary activity.

Thus in-depth company analysis inherent in the strategy formulation process helps managers to discover a company's unique core competency and abilities and those activities that create customer value. See the Entrepreneurial Focus "Know Yourself, Know Your Product" for some self-analysis guidelines for small companies.

A company cannot identify its unique abilities in a vacuum separate from the environment in which it operates. As we saw in Chapter 1, the external business environment consists of all the elements outside a company that can affect its performance, such as cultural, political, legal, and economic forces, workers' unions, consumers, and financial institutions. Let's now explore some of the main environmental forces that impact strategy formulation.

National and International Business Environments   National differences in language, religious beliefs, customs, traditions, and climate complicate strategy formulation. Language differences, for example, can increase the cost of operations and administration. Manufacturing processes must sometimes be adapted to the supply of local workers and to local customs, traditions, and practices. Marketing activities sometimes can result in costly mistakes if they do not incorporate cultural differences. For

Know Yourself, Know Your Product

Going International. It's the most popular blueprint today for company growth. But if the blueprint is flawed, if the foundation isn't stable, if the materials aren't first class, international expansion could prove to be the tremor that takes down the temple. Here are some factors any small business should consider to be successful abroad.

➡ **Are you ready to go international?** Consider how long your company has been in business and whether it is stable enough to brave the rough international seas. Assess whether your product must be adapted for international markets and whether you can do it successfully. Determine whether the expected sales volume abroad is worth the effort. Are you a success at home? Potential international partners will be more eager to partner with a company that is doing very well in its domestic market.

➡ **Have a thorough understanding of your product.** You must know how to capitalize on your product's strengths, minimize its weaknesses, correct its flaws, and modify it for other markets—or not modify it as the case may be. Beverly Hills Polo Club (BHPC) licenses its trademark in more than 75 countries. "We export the concept of America," says Don Garrison, vice president of international marketing for BHPC. "That's difficult to define sometimes, but there's a certain identification with Beverly Hills and Southern California that people around the world find very appealing." The company understands that to modify its product or what it represents would gut it of its essence.

➡ **Examine your company's internal activities.** Does your company have the infrastructure to take the company international? The effort will require a great deal of managerial and financial resources to tackle the job. Check that each department—procurement, production, marketing and sales, credit and collections, and so on—can devote the resources needed to the new international activities. The financial investment will be great, but early profits will be slim to none. Be certain that international activities will not overly burden the company's domestic business in the near- to medium-term. Also, make sure that everyone—from the CEO to the shipping room clerk—appreciates the commitment needed and the role each will play.

➡ **Ask important questions of strategy.** Does your company have an overall strategy into which your international business will fit? Have you developed a separate international strategy? Is it one that can successfully complement your domestic strategy? The answers to these questions reflect what you want to gain from going international, how quickly you want to achieve profits, and how long-term your commitment is. The question of strategy development is also vital to building on your success.

➡ **Finally, create the strategic plan.** Create a written strategic plan for your international ambitions. Include the commitment in time and money that you are willing to make and the resources you have available. Be certain of what resources you *can* devote to your international effort and what resources you *should* devote to it. They may well not be the same. Determine what kind of international partners you *want* to attract and what kind of international partners you *will* attract. These also may not be the same.

instance, a company once decided to sell its laundry detergent in Japan but did not adjust the size of the box in which it was sold. The company spent millions of dollars developing a detailed marketing campaign and was shocked when it experienced disappointing sales. It turns out that the company should have packaged the detergent in smaller containers for the Japanese market. Japanese shoppers prefer smaller quantities because they tend to walk home from the store and have smaller storage areas in tight living quarters.[9]

Differences in political and legal systems also complicate international strategy. Legal and political processes often differ to such an extent in target countries that firms must hire outside consultants to teach them about the local system. Such knowledge is important to international companies because host-government approval is almost always necessary for making direct investments. Companies need to know which ministry or department has authority to grant approval for a big business deal—a process that can become extremely cumbersome. For example, non-Chinese companies in

China must often get approval from several agencies, and the process is further complicated by the tendency of local government officials to interpret laws differently than do bureaucrats in Beijing (the nation's capital).

Finally, different national economic systems further complicate strategy formulation. Negative attitudes of local people toward the impact of direct investment can generate political unrest. Economic philosophy affects the tax rates that governments impose. Whereas socialist economic systems normally levy high taxes on business profits, free-market economies tend to levy lighter taxes. The need to work in more than one currency also complicates international strategy. Finally, to minimize losses from currency fluctuations, companies must develop strategies to deal with exchange-rate risk.

FORMULATE STRATEGIES

As we've already seen, the strengths and special capabilities of international companies, along with the environmental forces they face, play a large role in the type of strategy that managers choose to employ. Let's now examine this final stage in the planning and strategy formulation process—formulating strategies.

Two International Strategies Companies engaged in international business activities can approach the market using either a *multinational* or a *global* strategy. It is important to note that these two strategies do not include companies that export. Exporters do not have foreign direct investments in other national markets and should instead devise an appropriate export strategy (see Chapter 11). Let's now examine what it means for a company to follow a multinational or a global strategy.

Multinational Strategy Some international companies choose to follow a **multinational (*multidomestic*) strategy**—a strategy of adapting products and their marketing strategies in each national market to suit local preferences. In other words, a multinational strategy is just what its name implies—a separate strategy for each of the multiple of nations in which a company markets its products. To implement a multinational strategy, companies often establish largely independent, self-contained units (or subsidiaries) in each national market. Each subsidiary typically undertakes its own

---

multinational (multidomestic) strategy
Adapting products and their marketing strategies in each national market to suit local preferences.

In assessing its strategy, Pepsico (**www.pepsico.com**) perceived its holdings in the declining fast-food restaurant business to be a weakness. Thus it spun off the Pizza Hut, KFC, and Taco Bell chains into a separate corporation. The plan was to see whether the businesses could survive on their own, which meant they must develop their own positioning, pricing, and product offering strategies, both at home and abroad.

product research and development, production, and marketing. In many ways, each unit functions largely as an independent company. Multinational strategies are often appropriate for companies in industries where buyer preferences do not converge across national borders, such as certain food products and some print media.

The main benefit of a multinational strategy is that it allows companies to closely monitor buyer preferences in each local market and respond quickly and effectively as new buyer preferences emerge. The result that companies hope for when offering a tailored product is that customers will perceive it as delivering greater value than do competitors' products, allowing a company using a multinational strategy to charge higher prices and/or gain market share.

The main drawback of a multinational strategy is that it does not allow companies to exploit scale economies in product development, manufacturing, or marketing. Thus a multinational strategy typically increases the cost structure for international companies and forces them to charge higher prices to recover such costs. As such, a multinational strategy is usually poorly suited to industries in which price competitiveness is a key success factor. Furthermore, the high degree of independence with which each unit operates can reduce opportunities for sharing knowledge between units within a company.

Global Strategy Other companies decide that what suits their operations is a **global strategy**—a strategy of offering the same products using the same marketing strategy in all national markets. Companies following a global strategy often take advantage of scale and location economies by producing entire inventories of products or components in a single, optimal location. They also perform product research and development in one location and typically design promotional campaigns and advertising strategies at headquarters. So-called "global products" are most common in industries characterized by price competition and, therefore, pressure to contain costs. They include certain electronic components, a wide variety of industrial goods such as steel, and some consumer goods such as paper and writing instruments.

global strategy
Offering the same products using the same marketing strategy in all national markets.

The main benefit of a global strategy is its cost savings due to product and marketing standardization. These cost savings can then be passed on to consumers to help the company gain market share in its market segment. A global strategy also allows managers to share lessons learned in one market with managers at other locations.

The main problem with a global strategy is that it may cause a company to overlook important differences in buyer preferences from one market to another. A global strategy does not allow a company to modify its products except for the most superficial features, such as the color of paint applied to a finished product or small add-on features. This can present an opportunity for a competitor to step in and satisfy the unmet needs of local buyers and create a niche market.

In addition to deciding whether the company will follow a multinational or a global strategy, managers must formulate strategies for the corporation, each business unit, and each department. Let's now explore the three different levels of company strategy shown in Figure 12.3: *corporate-*, *business-*, and *department-level* strategies.

Corporate-Level Strategies   Companies involved in more than one line of business must first formulate a *corporate-level strategy*. In part, this means identifying the national markets and industries in which the company will operate. It also involves laying out overall objectives for the company's different business units and specifying the role that each unit will play in reaching those objectives. The four key approaches to corporate strategy are *growth*, *retrenchment*, *stability*, and *combination*.

Growth Strategy A **growth strategy** is designed to increase the scale or scope of a corporation's operations. *Scale* refers to the *size* of a corporation's activities, *scope* to the *kinds* of activities it performs. Yardsticks commonly used to measure growth in-

growth strategy
Strategy designed to increase the scale (size of activities) or scope (kinds of activities) of a corporation's operations.

FIGURE 12.3

THREE LEVELS OF COMPANY STRATEGY

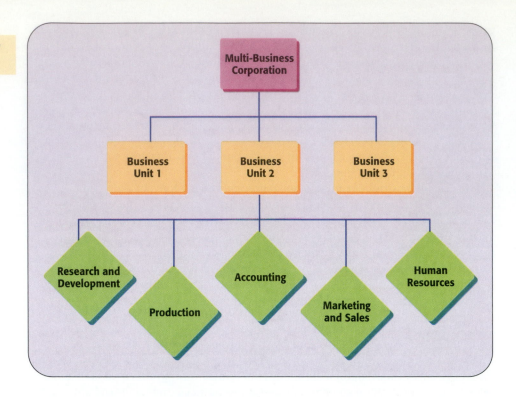

clude geographic coverage, number of business units, market share, sales revenue, and number of employees. *Organic growth* refers to a corporate strategy relying on internally generated growth. Management at 3M, for example, strongly encourages entrepreneurial activity, often spinning off business units to nurture the best ideas and carry them to completion. Microsoft, too, generates much of its growth organically, especially through the effective use of work teams.[10]

Other methods of growth include mergers and acquisitions, joint ventures, and strategic alliances (see Chapter 13). These tactics are used when companies do not wish to invest in developing certain skills internally or when other companies already do what managers are trying to achieve. Common partners in implementing these strategies include competitors, suppliers, and buyers. Corporations typically join forces with competitors to reduce competition, expand product lines, or expand geographically. A common motivation for joining forces with suppliers is to increase control over the quality, cost, and timing of inputs.

One corporation undertaking an aggressive global growth strategy is Intel. Intel's goal is "to be the preeminent building block supplier to the new computing industry worldwide." Intel manufactures computer components (the "building blocks" of computing systems), including microprocessors, chipsets, motherboards, memory units, and software. It provides these components to manufacturers in the computer, automobile, and mobile-phone industries. Intel's growth strategy focuses not only on delivering "the high-performance processors that drive today's connected PCs and related products," but working "with other industry leaders to expand the PC's role as a consumer and business communications device, driving future PC sales."[11] Central to Intel's accomplishing its growth strategy are the huge potential in large emerging markets such as China and Brazil, and the expected increasing access of these nations' citizens to the World Wide Web.

Retrenchment Strategy The exact opposite of a growth strategy is a **retrenchment strategy**—a strategy that is designed to reduce the scale or scope of a corporation's businesses. Corporations often cut back the *scale* of their operations when economic conditions worsen or competition increases. They may do so by closing factories with unused capacity and laying off workers. Corporations can also reduce the scale of their operations by laying off managers and salespeople in national markets that are not generating adequate sales revenue. Corporations reduce the *scope* of their activities by selling unprofitable business units or those no longer directly related to their overall aims. Weaker competitors often resort to retrenchment when national business environments grow more competitive.

> **retrenchment strategy**
> *Strategy designed to reduce the scale or scope of a corporation's businesses.*

Stability Strategy A **stability strategy** is designed to guard against change. It is often employed by corporations trying to avoid either growth or retrenchment. Such corporations have typically met their stated objectives or are satisfied with what they have already accomplished. They believe that their strengths are being fully exploited and their weaknesses fully protected against. They also see the business environment as posing neither profitable opportunities nor threats. They have no interest in expanding sales, increasing profits, increasing market share, or expanding the customer base; at present, they want simply to maintain their present positions. Stability is a relatively uncommon strategy among today's corporations. For one thing, few shareholders are content when management regards all objectives achieved and all opportunities seized.

> **stability strategy**
> *Strategy designed to guard against change and used by corporations to avoid either growth or retrenchment.*

Combination Strategy The purpose of a **combination strategy** is to mix growth, retrenchment, and stability strategies across a corporation's business units. For example, a corporation can invest in units showing promise, retrench in those where less exposure is desired, and stabilize others. In fact, corporate combination strategies are quite common because rarely do international corporations follow identical strategies in each of their business units.

> **combination strategy**
> *Strategy designed to mix growth, retrenchment, and stability strategies across a corporation's business units.*

> Retrenchment is often a painful strategy that can be met with considerable resistance, like that expressed by these protesting workers at Weirton Steel Corp. (**www.weirton.com**), which dominates the town of Weirton, West Virginia. Because demand for steel was weak in Asia and Russia in the late 1990s, inexpensive imports flooded the U.S. market and drove steel prices down by as much as 20 percent. Toward the end of 1998, Weirton laid off nearly one in 10 workers and gave another 13 percent temporary layoffs while it shut down part of the plant.

Business-Level Strategies   In addition to stipulating the overall corporate strategy, managers must also formulate separate *business-level strategies* for each business unit. For some companies, this means creating just one strategy. This is the case when the business-level strategy and the corporate-level strategy are one and the same because the corporation is involved in just one line of business.

For other companies, this means creating anywhere from two to dozens of strategies. For example, Cadbury Schweppes of Britain has two main business units—beverages and confectionery—each with its own strategy. The strategy of the beverages business unit is to "strengthen our soft drinks position worldwide and to be the largest and most successful non-cola brand owner." For the confectionery unit, strategy is "based on building viable positions in prioritised markets through organic growth and acquisitions."[12] Thus the beverages unit is focused on strengthening the position of its existing soft drink products. But the confectionery unit is attempting to create new products in promising markets through internal growth and by acquiring other firms.

The key to developing an effective business-level strategy is deciding on a *general competitive strategy in the marketplace.* Each business unit must decide whether to sell the lowest-price product in an industry or to integrate special attributes into its products. As you can see in Figure 12.4, a business unit can employ one of three generic business-level strategies for competing in its industry—*low-cost leadership, differentiation,* or *focus.*[13] Let's now explore each of these strategies in detail.

Low-Cost Leadership Strategy   A strategy in which a company exploits economies of scale to have the lowest cost structure of any competitor in its industry is called a **low-cost leadership strategy.** Companies pursuing the low-cost leadership position also try to contain administrative costs, and the costs of its various primary activities including marketing, advertising, and distribution. Although cutting costs is the mantra for firms pursuing a low-cost leadership position, other important competitive factors such as product quality and customer service cannot be ignored. Factors underlying the low-cost leadership position (efficient production in large quantities) help guard against attack by competitors because of the large up-front cost of getting started. Also, because

> **low-cost leadership strategy**
> *Strategy in which a company exploits economies of scale to have the lowest cost structure of any competitor in its industry.*

FIGURE 12.4

"THREE GENERIC BUSINESS-LEVEL STRATEGIES"

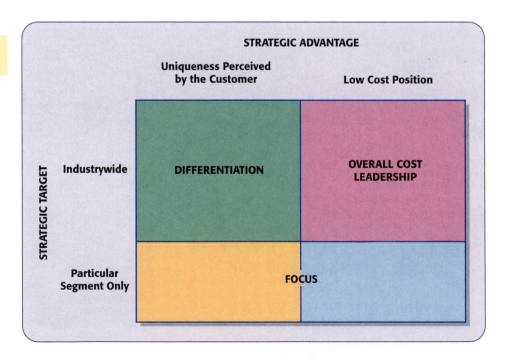

achieving low-cost leadership tends to rely on large-scale production to contain costs, the strategy typically requires the company to have a large market share. One negative aspect of the low-cost leadership strategy is low customer loyalty—all else equal, buyers will purchase from the low-cost leader regardless of who it is.

A low-cost leadership strategy works best with mass-marketed products aimed at price-sensitive buyers. This strategy is often well suited to companies with a standardized product and marketing promotions. Two global companies vying for the low-cost leadership position in their respective industries include Casio in sports watches and Texas Instruments in calculators and other electronic devices.

Differentiation Strategy A **differentiation strategy** is one in which a company designs its products to be perceived as unique by buyers throughout its industry. Because its buyers perceive the product as unique, a company following a differentiation strategy can charge a higher price and enjoys greater customer loyalty than does the low-cost leader. A differentiation strategy tends to force a company into a lower market share position because it generally involves the perception of exclusivity or as meeting the needs of only a certain group of buyers. Companies employing this type of strategy must develop loyal customer bases to offset smaller market shares and higher costs of producing and marketing a unique product.

One way products can be differentiated is by improving their reputation for *quality*. Ceramic tableware for everyday use is found at department stores in almost every country. However, the ceramic tableware made by Japanese producer Noritake differentiates itself from common tableware by emphasizing its superior quality. The perception of higher quality allows manufacturers to charge higher prices for their products worldwide.

Other products are differentiated by distinctive *brand images*. IZOD and Calvin Klein, for example, are relatively pricey global clothiers appealing to a young, fashionable clientele. Each is continually introducing new textures and colors that are at once stylish and functional. Another example is Italian carmaker Alfa Romeo. It does not compete in the fiercely competitive mass-consumer segment of the global automobile industry. To do so, it would have to be price-competitive and offer a wide selection of cars. Instead, Alfa Romeo offers a high-quality product with a brand image that rewards the Alfa Romeo owner with status and prestige.

differentiation strategy
Strategy in which a company designs its products to be perceived as unique by buyers throughout its industry.

Amazon.com has differentiated itself as a bookseller by eliminating retail outlets, taking orders only over the Internet, and filling requests with reliability and speed. The company's advantage may be short-lived, however, as well-armed traditional booksellers like Barnes & Noble and Borders try their hands at electronic commerce. Compare their Web sites to see which company makes the best use of the Web: (**www.amazon.com**, **www.barnesandnoble.com**, **www.borders.com**).

Another differentiating factor is *product design*—the sum of the features by which a product looks and functions according to customer requirements. For instance, the designs of Casio and other makers of mass-market sport watches stress functionality. On the other hand, TAG Heuer sports watches from Switzerland offer classy, stylish designs in addition to performance. Special features differentiate both goods and services in the minds of consumers who value those features. Manufacturers can also combine differentiation factors in formulating their strategies.

Focus Strategy A **focus strategy** is one in which a company focuses on serving the needs of a narrowly defined market segment by being the low-cost leader, by differentiating its product, or both. Increasing competition often means more products distinguished by price or differentiated by quality, design, and so forth. In turn, a greater product range leads to the continuous refinement of market segments. Many industries today consist of large numbers of market segments and even smaller subsegments. Some firms, for example, try to serve the needs of one ethnic or racial group whereas others, often entrepreneurs and small businesses, focus on a single geographic area.

For instance, we normally think of Johnson & Johnson as a consumer-products company. In fact, it is a conglomerate consisting of more than 160 separately chartered companies that market an enormous variety of products to a wide array of market segments. Many of these individual J&J companies try to dominate their segments by producing specialty goods and services. In so doing, they focus on narrow segments using either low-cost leadership or differentiation techniques.

A focus strategy often means designing products and promotions aimed at consumers who are either dissatisfied with existing choices or who want something distinctive. Consider the highly fragmented gourmet coffee market. One brand of coffee called Luwak sells for around *$300 per pound*! Certainly the coffee is made from distinctive beans. Apparently, luwaks (weasels on the Indonesian island of Java) eat coffee berries containing coffee beans. The beans "naturally ferment" as they pass through the luwaks and are recovered from the animals' waste. The beans are then washed, roasted, and sold around the world as a specialty coffee (certainly having a distinctive taste).[14]

The strategies we've discussed here can be applied to practically all firms in all markets worldwide. However, companies in emerging markets often face special problems. See the Global Manager "Competing with Giants" to see how domestic companies in emerging markets can survive the onslaught by the major multinational companies.

Department-Level Strategies Achieving corporate- and business-level objectives depends on effective departmental strategies that focus on the specific activities that transform resources into products. Formulation of *department-level strategies* brings us right back to where we began our analysis of a company's capabilities that support its strategy—to the primary and support activities that create value for customers. After managers analyze the primary and support activities of their companies that create value for customers, they must then develop strategies that exploit their firm's value-creating strengths.

Primary and Support Activities Each department is instrumental in creating customer value through lower costs or differentiated products. This is especially true of those departments conducting *primary activities*. Manufacturing strategies are obviously important in cutting production costs of both standardized and differentiated products. They are also crucial to improving product quality. Effective marketing strategies allow companies to promote the differences in their products. A strong sales force and good customer service contribute to favorable images among consumers or industrial buyers and generate loyal customers of both kinds. Efficient logistics in

---

focus strategy
Strategy in which a company focuses on serving the needs of a narrowly defined market segment by being the low-cost leader, by differentiating its product, or both.

Global Manager

Competing with Giants

Multinationals are rushing into emerging markets around the globe to find new opportunities for growth. For local companies, their arrival can appear to be a death sentence. Local companies suddenly face a rival who often has enormous financial resources, advanced technology, superior products, powerful brands, and seasoned marketing and management skills. Many local managers assume that they only can ask for government protection, become a subordinate partner to the multinational, or sell out.

Industries differ in the degree to which they are global—some, such as semiconductors or aircraft, are highly global, but others, such as retail banking, are not. Most industries, however, lie somewhere in between. Also, some emerging-market companies have a competitive edge that is germane to the local market, such as an extensive, strong distribution network. Others have a competitive advantage that is transferable to other markets, such as expertise in building efficient factories. By analyzing these two facets—industry globalization and asset transferability—emerging market companies can choose one of four strategies to combat multinational giants.

➡ **Defender.** If globalization pressures are weak, and a company's own assets are not transferable, the company needs to concentrate on defending its home turf. When India opened its automotive sector in the mid-1980s to international competitors, for instance, the country's largest domestic manufacturer of motor scooters, Bajaj Auto, was petrified. Honda soon burst onto the scene with superior technology, quality, and brand appeal. But Bajaj beefed up its distribution and service network and improved the design of its low-cost, rugged scooters. In the fall of 1998, Honda announced it was pulling out of its scooter-manufacturing venture in India.

➡ **Extender.** If globalization pressures are weak, but a company's assets can be transferred abroad, the company may be able to extend its success to a limited number of other markets. For example, when McDonald's entered the Philippines, local fast-food company Jollibee Foods upgraded its service and developed rival menus customized to local tastes. Using its battle-tested recipes from home, Jollibee established dozens of restaurants in markets with large Filipino populations including Hong Kong, the Middle East, and California.

➡ **Dodger.** If globalization pressures are strong, but a company's assets are not transferable, the company will need to dodge its larger rivals by restructuring itself around links in the value chain that buyers value. When Russia liberalized its economy, Russian personal computer maker Vist side-stepped oblivion by redefining its core business. When Compaq, IBM, and Hewlett-Packard came in with superior PCs, Vist focused on its strengths—distribution, service, and warranties. Although Vist's computers are unremarkable, all its manuals are in Russian and the company provides lengthy warranties—unlike its multinational rivals that charge a fee for an extended service contract. Vist is the leading brand of PCs in Russia with 20 percent of the market.

➡ **Contender.** If globalization pressures are strong, and a company's assets can be transferred abroad, the company may be able to compete head-to-head with its multinational rivals in world markets. For instance, when General Motors decided to purchase radiator caps for its North American autos rather than make them itself, Sundaram Fasteners of India bought an entire GM production line and shipped it home. One year later Sundaram was GM's sole North American supplier of 5 million radiator caps per year. What Sundaram learned as GM's supplier, benefited its core fastener business and allowed the company to target markets in Japan and Europe. Sundaram is now capable of supplying markets worldwide.

---

bringing into the factory raw materials and components and getting the finished product out the factory door can result in substantial cost savings.

Support activities also create customer value. Research and development, for example, identifies market segments with unsatisfied needs and designs products to meet them. Human resource managers can improve efficiency and cut costs by hiring well-trained employees and conducting worker training and management-development programs. Procurement tasks provide operations with quality resources at reasonable cost. Accounting and finance (elements of firm infrastructure) must develop efficient information systems to assist managers in making decisions and maintaining financial control, thus impacting costs and quality in general.

We now understand the different types of strategies employed by companies. But what important elements drive the decisions of world-class companies regarding strategy formulation? The important production issues to consider are the number and dispersion of production facilities, and whether to standardize production processes for all markets. The important marketing issue is whether to standardize either the physical features of products, or their marketing strategies, across markets. In the following two sections, we focus only on the strategic considerations of production and marketing activities. We discuss the tactical issues surrounding both production and marketing in the context of day-to-day international management in Chapter 15. Let's now take a closer look at the production and marketing aspects that influence strategy formulation.

PRODUCTION CONSIDERATIONS

Essential to successfully accomplishing business- and corporate-level strategies are good production techniques. During the 1970s and 1980s, a failure to focus on manufacturing processes contributed to the decline of U.S. producers in global markets in many product categories, including automobiles. Firms lost sight of their core competencies and competitive advantages in global markets and were beat out by the competition. Meanwhile, companies in Japan and Europe were implementing new computerized production technologies and seized greater market share at the expense of U.S. companies.

Production operations are important to achieving each of the strategies discussed earlier in this chapter. Careful planning of all aspects of production helps companies cut costs to become low-cost leaders and design new products or product features necessary for a differentiation strategy. Let's now examine the important issues that managers consider when planning for production capacity, facilities location, production processes, and facilities layout.

CAPACITY PLANNING

capacity planning
Process of assessing a company's ability to produce enough output to satisfy market demand.

The process of assessing a company's ability to produce enough output to satisfy market demand is called **capacity planning**. Companies must estimate global demand for their products as accurately as possible. If capacity is greater than the expected market demand, production must be scaled back. For example, the number of employees or work shifts can be reduced at certain locations. Countries, however, have different laws regulating the ability of employers to eliminate jobs. Depending on the country, a firm may or may not need to give advance notice of layoffs or plant closings. On the other hand, if market demand is growing, managers must determine in which facilities to expand production or whether additional facilities are needed to expand capacity. Rather than miss out on potential sales, a company might contract excess demand to other producers until new facilities are up and running.

Capacity planning is also extremely important for service companies. For example, a hotel chain moving into a new geographic market must estimate the number of rooms that its facilities should contain. It must also determine whether a facility will be used for conventions and the like and the number of meeting rooms that it must build. Videoconferencing facilities might be added if local firms require them to keep in touch with geographically dispersed operations.

FACILITIES LOCATION PLANNING

facilities location planning
Selecting the location for production facilities.

Selecting the location for production facilities is called **facilities location planning**. Companies often have many potential locations around the world from which to choose a site for production, research and development, or some other activity. Important environmental factors in facilities location planning include the cost and availability of labor and management, raw materials, component parts, and energy. Other key factors include political stability, the extent of regulation and bureaucracy, economic development, and the local culture, including beliefs about work and important traditions.

Reducing production costs by taking advantage of lower wages in another country is often essential to keeping a company's products competitive on price. This is especially important when labor accounts for a large portion of total production costs. However, the lower wages of a nation's workforce must be balanced against its potentially lower productivity. Worker productivity tends to be lower in most developing nations and some emerging markets as compared to developed nations.

Although service companies must locate near their customers, they must still consider a wide variety of customers' needs when locating facilities. Are convenience and being located in a high-traffic area important to customers? Such a location is clearly important for some companies including restaurants, banking facilities, and cinemas. For other service businesses, such as a consulting company or public utility, a convenient location is less important.

Supply issues are also important. For any one mode of transportation, the greater the distance between production facilities and target markets, the longer it takes for customers to receive shipments. In turn, marketing managers must compensate for delays by maintaining larger inventories in target markets—adding to storage and insurance costs. Shipping costs themselves are also greater when production is conducted away from target markets. Transportation costs are one of the driving forces behind the globalization of the steel industry. Shipping costs for steel can run $40 to $50 per ton— a significant amount when steel sells for $400 to $500 per ton. By building steel mills in those countries where their customers are located, steel producers significantly reduce their transportation costs.[15]

Carmakers from Japan and Germany invested in production facilities inside the United States for some of the reasons just identified. Honda, Toyota, Mitsubishi, and other Japanese companies manufacture cars in the United States to offset the risks from currency fluctuations, to defuse political concerns about the United States' trade deficit with Japan, and to be closer to their customers. Mercedes-Benz and BMW of Germany also built auto assembly plants in the United States for similar reasons. For one thing, the strength of the German mark in the 1990s made German products more expensive on world export markets. Another reason is that Germany is home to the world's highest paid workers—average hourly income is approximately $32. Finally, German companies are attracted by lower costs for wages, land, and tax breaks and other concessions offered by state governments eager to attract industry.

Location Economies   Selecting highly favorable locations often allows a company to achieve **location economies**—economic benefits derived from locating production activities in optimal locations. Location economies result from the right mix of the kinds of elements just described. To take advantage of location economies, companies either undertake business activities themselves in a particular location or obtain products and services from other companies located there. Location economies can involve practically any business activity that companies in a particular location do very well, including performing research and development or providing financial or advertising services.

The following examples illustrate the extent to which service and manufacturing companies exploit location economies. One company designed its precision ice hockey equipment in Sweden, obtained financing from Canada, assembled it in Cleveland and Denmark, and marketed it in North America and Europe. This equipment incorporated alloys whose molecular structure was researched and patented in Delaware and

location economies
Economic benefits derived from locating production activities in optimal locations.

fabricated in Japan. Airplane manufacturer Boeing designed an aircraft in the state of Washington and Japan. It was assembled in Seattle with tail cones made in Canada, special tail sections made in China and Italy, and engines from Britain. Finally, one company's advertising campaign was conceived in Britain, shot in Canada, dubbed back in Britain, and edited in New York.[16]

The key fact to remember here is that *each production activity generates more value in a particular location than could be generated anywhere else.* Productivity is a very important (though not the only) factor in determining the value that a location adds to a certain economic activity. The productivity of a location is heavily influenced by two resources—labor and capital. Take a look at the World Business Survey "By the Numbers" to see how several major industrialized nations compare in their productivity of labor and capital.

Granted, in order to take advantage of location economies, managers might need to familiarize themselves with vastly different customs and traditions. Political and legal differences, for example, can force firms to retain outside consultants or to train corporate lawyers in local traditions. Language differences might mean translating important documents on an ongoing basis. For these reasons, companies sometimes hire other companies in a location to perform an activity for them.

Centralization versus Decentralization   An important consideration for production managers is whether to centralize or decentralize production facilities. *Centralized production* refers to the concentration of production facilities in one location. With *decentralized production*, facilities are spread over several locations and could even

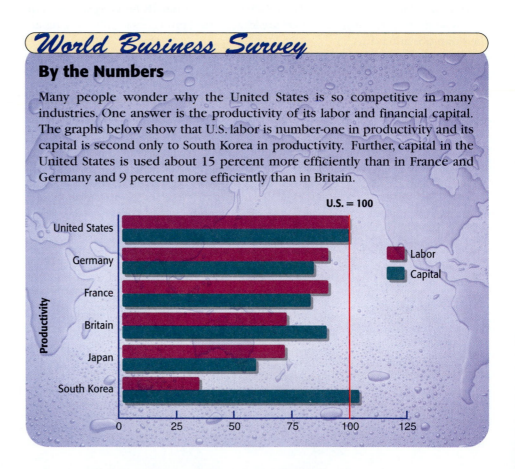

World Business Survey

By the Numbers

Many people wonder why the United States is so competitive in many industries. One answer is the productivity of its labor and financial capital. The graphs below show that U.S. labor is number-one in productivity and its capital is second only to South Korea in productivity. Further, capital in the United States is used about 15 percent more efficiently than in France and Germany and 9 percent more efficiently than in Britain.

mean having one facility for each national business environment in which the company markets its products—a common policy for companies following a multinational strategy. Companies often centralize production facilities in pursuit of low-cost strategies and to take advantage of economies of scale—typically, those companies following a global strategy. By producing large quantities of identical products in one location, they cut costs by reducing the per-unit cost of production.

Transportation costs and the physical landscape also affect the centralization versus decentralization decision. Recall, for example, that low-cost competitors generally do not need to locate near markets in order to stay on top of changes in buyer preferences: They usually sell undifferentiated products in all their markets. Low-cost producers, therefore, often choose locations with the lowest combined production and transportation costs. Even these firms, however, must balance the cost of getting inputs into the production process and the cost of getting products to markets. Thus, the local physical environment, including the availability of seaports, airports, or other transportation hubs, is an important factor in locating production facilities.

Conversely, companies selling differentiated products may find decentralized production the better option. By locating separate facilities near different markets, they remain in close contact with customers and can respond quickly to changing buyer preferences. Closer contact with customers also helps firms develop a deeper understanding of buyer behavior in local cultures.

When close cooperation between R&D and manufacturing is essential for effective differentiation, both activities are usually conducted in the same place. However, new technologies are giving companies more freedom to separate these activities. The speed with which information travels today allows the rapid relay of information between subsidiaries and the home office.

e·biz

PROCESS PLANNING

Deciding the process that a company will use to create its product is called **process planning**. In general, the particular process to be used is typically determined by a firm's business-level strategy. Low-cost strategies, for instance, normally require large-scale production because producers want the cost savings generated by economies of scale. A company mass-producing snowboards for average skiers will typically employ a highly automated production process integrating advanced computer technology. Differentiation strategies, however, demand that producers provide extra value by offering customers something unique, such as superior quality, added features, or special brand images. Companies that handcraft snowboards for professionals will rely not on automated production but skilled craftspeople. The company will design and produce each snowboard to suit the habits and special needs of each individual skier. For such a company, service is a major component of the production process.

Availability and cost of labor in the local market is crucial to process planning. If labor in the host country is relatively cheap, an international company will likely opt for less technology and more labor-intensive methods in the production process—depending on its particular product. However, the availability of labor and level of wages in the local market must be balanced against the productivity of the local workforce.

Standardization versus Adaptation   Another important production issue in strategic planning is deciding whether the production process will be standardized for all markets or adapted to manufacture products modified for different markets. Low-cost leadership, for example, often dictates automated, standardized production in large batches. Large production batches reduce the cost of producing each unit, thus offsetting the higher initial investment in automation. Costs are further reduced as em-

> **process planning**
> Deciding the process that a company will use to create its product.

ployees improve performance through repetition and a continual learning process that minimizes errors and waste.

But differentiation often demands decentralized facilities designed to improve local responsiveness. Because decentralized production facilities produce for one national market or for a regional market they tend to be smaller. This tends to eliminate the potential to take advantage of economies of scale and therefore increase per-unit production costs. Similarly, the smaller market share at which a differentiation strategy aims normally calls for smaller-scale production. Differentiating a product by incorporating certain customer-desired features requires more costly manufacturing processes. R&D costs also tend to be higher for products with special product designs, styles, and features.

FACILITIES LAYOUT PLANNING

facilities layout planning
Deciding the spatial arrangement of production processes within production facilities.

Deciding the spatial arrangement of production processes within production facilities is called **facilities layout planning**. Consider the fact that in Japan, Singapore, and Hong Kong, the supply of land is limited and its cost is high. Companies locating in these markets must use available space wisely by designing compact facilities. Conversely, in countries such as Canada, China, and the United States, an abundance of space reduces the cost of building facilities in many locations. Because land is cheaper, companies have more flexibility in designing facilities.

More importantly, facility layout depends on the type of production process a company employs. This process depends in turn on a company's business-level strategy. For instance, rather than produce mass quantities of computers to be stored in inventory, Compaq competes by manufacturing computers as it receives orders from individual customers. To implement this business strategy, Compaq executives decided to replace mass-assembly lines with three-person work cells. In production trials at a plant in Scotland, output increased 23 percent compared with the best assembly line. In addition, output per square foot went up 16 percent—a significant increase in the efficiency within the facility.

Here we've presented the major elements that managers must consider from a strategic point of view. In Chapter 15 we discuss the more tactical decisions managers make regarding production and operations planning.

MARKETING CONSIDERATIONS

Without considering its marketing needs, no company can develop sound corporate-, business-, and department-level strategies. As we already know, some companies implementing a global strategy use similar promotional messages and themes to market the same product around the world. Others, however, have found that their products require physical changes or changes in their promotional approaches to suit the tastes of consumers in different target markets. Yet other products need different marketing campaigns to reflect the unique cultures, politics, laws, or economies of different national markets. How do managers decide when a product or its promotional message needs modifying? To answer this question, we need a better understanding of marketing strategy. In this section, we explain when standardization and adaptation are appropriate for marketing activities.

STANDARDIZATION VERSUS ADAPTATION

In a well-known article, U.S. researcher Theodore Levitt argued that because the world is becoming standardized and homogeneous, companies should market the same products in the same way in all countries.[18] Technology, claimed Levitt, was already causing people's needs and preferences to converge throughout the world. He urged companies to reduce production and marketing costs by standardizing both the physical features of their products and their strategies for marketing them.

Some researchers have since countered that standardization is just one of a number of strategies with which firms have successfully entered the international marketplace.[19] Still others argue that standardization is not always the best strategy and advise smaller companies to adapt to local cultures while exploiting their unique international images to gain local market share.[20]

Influence of National Business Environments   Consumers in different national markets often demand products that reflect their unique tastes and preferences. Cultural, political, legal, and economic environments have a great deal to do with the preferences of both consumers and industrial buyers worldwide. Recall from Chapter 2 that a culture's aesthetics involves, among other things, preferences for certain colors. Ohio-based Rubbermaid discovered the role of aesthetics as it attempted to increase its international sales. Consumers in the United States prefer household products in neutral blues or almond; in southern Europe, red is the preferred color. The Dutch want white. In addition, many European cultures perceive plastic products as inferior and want tight lids on metal wastebaskets as opposed to U.S.-style plastic versions with open tops.[21]

But certain products do appeal to practically all cultures. Although it is not a traditional Asian drink, a passion for red wine is currently sweeping such Asian markets as Hong Kong, Singapore, Taiwan, and Thailand. Driving this demand are medical studies reporting the health benefits of red wine (the king of Thailand has publicly proclaimed its healthy properties). But other factors—including the fact that red is a good-luck color in many Asian cultures—are also at work. Many Asians choose red wine at restaurants because of its image as the beverage of choice for people who are sophisticated and successful. (The same is not true of white wine because from a distance it may resemble water.) Today in Beijing, fashionable young people often give red wine as a housewarming present instead of the traditional favorites of their parents and grandparents.[22]

Product standardization is more likely when producer and buyer nations share the same level of economic development. In the 1980s, consumers in India faced limited options when it came to purchasing automobiles. Most were made in India, expensive, and not fuel-efficient. Thanks to a fairly good record of economic progress over the past two decades, Indian consumers have a better standard of living and more discretionary income. Affording a brand-name automobile with a global reputation, such as Suzuki or Ford, is more commonplace in Indian cities than it was years ago. Much more will be said on the marketing aspects of managing an international business in Chapter 15 when we discuss tactical management issues.

INTERNATIONAL ORGANIZATIONAL STRUCTURE

Organizational structure is the way in which a company divides its activities among separate units and coordinates activities between those units. If a company's organizational structure is appropriate for its strategic plans, it will be more effective in working toward its goals. In this section, we explore several important issues related to organizational structures and examine several alternative forms that an organization's structure can take.

CENTRALIZATION VERSUS DECENTRALIZATION

In addition to deciding whether to centralize or decentralize production, managers must determine the degree to which decision making will be centralized or decentralized in the organization. *Centralized decision making* is the degree to which decision making is centralized at a high level in one location such as headquarters. *Decentralized*

> **organizational structure**
> *Way in which a company divides its activities among separate units and coordinates activities between those units.*

decision making is the degree to which decisions are made at lower levels, such as in international subsidiaries. Naturally, decentralized decision making gives subsidiaries greater autonomy in managing their activities.

Should managers at the parent company be actively involved in the decisions made by international subsidiaries? Or should they intervene relatively little, perhaps only in the most crucial decisions? Some decisions, of course, must be decentralized: If top managers involve themselves in the day-to-day decisions of every subsidiary, they are likely to be overwhelmed. They cannot, for example, get directly involved in every hiring decision or assignment of people to specific tasks at each facility. On the other hand, overall corporate strategy cannot be delegated to subsidiary managers. Only top management has the appropriate perspective to formulate corporate strategy.

In our discussion of centralization versus decentralization of decision making, it is important to remember two points:

1. Companies rarely centralize or decentralize all decision making. Rather, they seek the approach that will result in the greatest efficiency and effectiveness.
2. International companies may centralize decision making in certain geographic markets while decentralizing it in others. Numerous factors influence this decision, including the need for product modification and the abilities of managers at each location.

With these points in mind, let's take a look at some of the specific factors that determine whether centralized or decentralized decision making is most appropriate.

When to Centralize   Centralized decision making helps to coordinate the operations of international subsidiaries. This fact is important for companies operating in multiple lines of business or in many international markets. It is also important when one subsidiary's output is another's input. In such situations, coordinating operations from a single high-level vantage point is more efficient. Purchasing is often centralized if all subsidiaries use the same inputs in production. For example, a company that manufactures steel filing cabinets and desks will need a great deal of sheet steel. A central purchasing department will get a better bulk price on sheet steel than would subsidiaries negotiating their own agreements. Each subsidiary then benefits by being able to purchase sheet steel from central purchasing at lower cost than it would pay in the open market.

Some companies maintain strong central control over financial resources by channeling all subsidiary profits back to the parent for redistribution to subsidiaries based on their needs. This practice reduces the likelihood that certain subsidiaries will undertake investment projects when more promising projects go without funding at other locations. Other companies centrally design policies, procedures, and standards in order to stimulate a single global organizational culture. This policy makes it more likely that all subsidiaries will enforce company rules uniformly. It is also beneficial when companies transfer managers from one location to another: If policies are uniform, the transition proceeds more smoothly for both managers and subordinates.

When to Decentralize   Decentralized decision making is beneficial when fast-changing national business environments put a premium on local responsiveness. Because subsidiary managers are in closer contact with local culture, politics, laws, and economies, decentralized decisions can result in products that are better suited to the needs and preferences of local buyers. Local managers are more likely to perceive environmental changes that managers at headquarters would not even notice. Even if central managers did perceive such changes, they are likely to get a secondhand account of local events. Delayed response and misinterpreted events can result in lost orders, stalled production, and weakened competitiveness. Similarly, decentralized decision making can save money because informed decisions can be made without flying executives around the world on fact-finding missions.

Participative Management and Accountability Decentralization can also help foster participative management practices. Employee morale is likely to be higher if subsidiary managers and subordinates are involved in decision making. When delegated to subsidiaries, decisions related to national strategy—including production, promotion, distribution, and pricing decisions—can generate greater commitment from both managers and workers.

Decentralization often improves personal accountability for business decisions. When local managers are rewarded (or punished) for their decisions, they are likely to invest more effort in making and executing them. Conversely, if local managers must do nothing but implement policies dictated from above, they can attribute poor performance to decisions that were ill-suited to the local environment. When managers are held accountable for decision making and implementation, they typically delve more deeply into research and debate and consider all available options. The results are often better decisions and improved performance.

COORDINATION AND FLEXIBILITY

When designing organizational structure, managers seek answers to certain key questions. What, for example, is the most efficient method of linking divisions to one another? Who should coordinate the activities of different divisions in order to achieve overall strategies? How should information be processed and delivered to managers when and where it is required? What sorts of monitoring mechanisms and reward structures should be established? How should the company introduce corrective measures, and whose responsibility should it be to execute them? To answer these types of questions, we must look at the issues of coordination and flexibility.

Structure and Coordination As we have seen, some companies have a presence in several or more national business environments—they manufacture and market products practically everywhere. Others operate primarily in one country and export to, or import from, other markets. Each type of international company must design an appropriate organizational structure. Each needs a structure that clearly defines areas of responsibility and **chains of command**—the lines of authority that run from top management to individual employees and specify internal reporting relationships. Finally, every firm needs a structure that brings together those areas requiring close cooperation. For example, to avoid product designs that make manufacturing more difficult and costly than necessary, most firms ensure that R&D and manufacturing remain in close contact.

chains of command
Lines of authority that run from top management to individual employees and specify internal reporting relationships.

Structure and Flexibility Organizational structure is not permanent—it is often modified to suit changes both within a company and in its external environment. Because companies usually base organizational structures on strategies, changes in strategy usually require adjustments in structure. Similarly, because changes in national business environments can force changes in strategy, the same changes will influence company structure. Close monitoring of conditions in countries characterized by rapidly shifting cultural, political, and economic environments is especially important. Let's now explore four organizational structures that have been developed to improve the responsiveness and effectiveness of companies conducting international business activities.

TYPES OF ORGANIZATIONAL STRUCTURE

There are many different ways in which a company can organize itself to carry out its international business activities. But four organizational structures tend to be most common for the vast majority of international companies—*division structure, area structure, product structure,* and *matrix structure.*

International Division Structure   An **international division structure** is an organizational structure that separates domestic from international business activities by creating a separate international division with its own manager (see Figure 12.5). In turn, the international division is typically divided into units corresponding to the countries in which a company is active—say, China, Indonesia, and Thailand. Within each country, a general manager controls the manufacture and marketing of the firm's products. Each country unit typically carries out all of its own activities with its own departments such as marketing and sales, finance, and production.

Because the international division structure concentrates international expertise in one division, divisional managers become specialists in a wide variety of activities such as foreign exchange, export documentation, and host-government lobbying. By consigning international activities to a single division, a firm can reduce costs, increase efficiency, and prevent international activities from disrupting domestic operations. These are important criteria for firms that are new to international business and whose international operations account for a small percentage of their total business.

However, an international division structure can also create two problems for companies. First, international managers must often rely on home-country managers for the financial resources and technical know-how that give the company its international competitive edge. Poor coordination between managers can hurt the performance not only of the international division but also of the entire company. Second, the general manager of the international division typically is responsible for operations in all countries. Although this policy facilitates coordination across countries, it reduces the authority of each country manager. Rivalries and poor cooperation between the general manager and country managers can be damaging to overall company performance.

> **international division structure**
> *Organizational structure that separates domestic from international business activities by creating a separate international division with its own manager.*

FIGURE 12.5

INTERNATIONAL DIVISION STRUCTURE

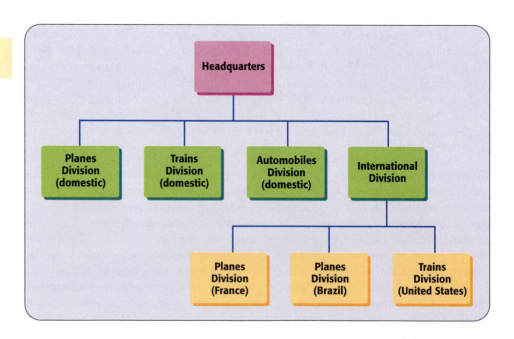

International Area Structure An **international area structure** is an organizational structure that organizes a company's entire global operations into countries or geographic regions (see Figure 12.6). The greater the number of countries in which a company operates, the greater the likelihood that it will organize into regions—say, Asia, Europe, and the Americas—instead of countries. Typically, a general manager is assigned to each country or region. Under this structure, each geographic division operates as a self-contained unit, with most decision making decentralized in the hands of the country or regional managers. Each unit has its own set of departments—purchasing, production, marketing and sales, R&D, and accounting. Each also tends to handle much of its own strategic planning. Parent-company headquarters makes decisions regarding overall corporate strategy and coordinates the activities of various units.

Area structure is best suited to companies that treat each national or regional market as unique. It is particularly useful when there are vast cultural, political, or economic differences between nations or regions. When they enjoy a great deal of control over activities in their own environments, general managers become experts on the unique needs of their buyers. On the other hand, because units act independently, allocated resources may overlap, and cross-fertilization of knowledge from one unit to another may be less than desirable.

Global Product Structure A **global product structure** is an organizational structure that divides worldwide operations according to a company's product areas (see Figure 12.7). For example, divisions in a computer company might be Internet and Communications, Software Development, and New Technologies. Each product division is then divided into domestic and international units. Each function—R&D, marketing, and so forth—is thus duplicated in both the domestic and international units of each product division.

Because it overcomes some of the coordination problems of the international division structure, the global product structure is suitable for companies offering diverse sets of products or services. Because primary focus is on the product, both domestic and international managers for each product division must coordinate their activities so that they do not conflict.

> **international area structure**
> *Organizational structure that organizes a company's entire global operations into countries or geographic regions.*

> **global product structure**
> *Organizational structure that divides worldwide operations according to a company's product areas.*

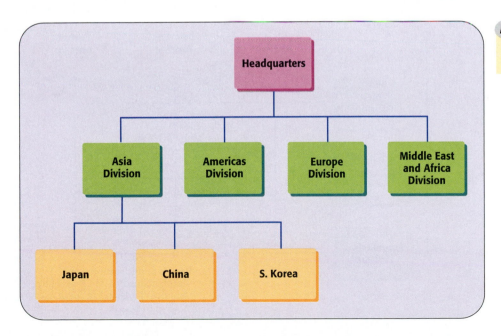

FIGURE 12.6

INTERNATIONAL AREA STRUCTURE

FIGURE 12.7

**GLOBAL PRODUCT
STRUCTURE**

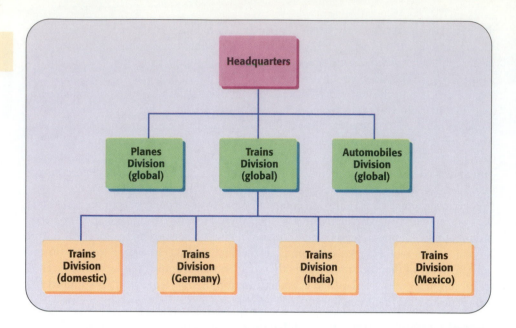

global matrix structure
*Organizational structure that
splits the chain of command
between product and area
divisions.*

Global Matrix Structure   A **global matrix structure** is an organizational structure that splits the chain of command between product and area divisions (see Figure
12.8). Each manager reports to two bosses—the president of the product division and
the president of the geographic area. A main goal of the matrix structure is to bring together *geographic* area managers and *product* area managers in joint decision making.
In fact, bringing together specialists from different parts of the organization creates a

FIGURE 12.8

**GLOBAL MATRIX
STRUCTURE**

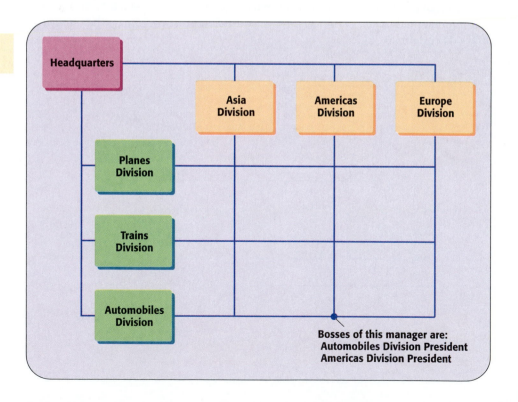

sort of team organization. The popularity of the matrix structure has grown among companies trying to increase local responsiveness, reduce costs, and coordinate worldwide operations.

The matrix structure resolves some of the shortcomings of other organization structures, especially by improving communication between divisions and increasing the efficiency of highly specialized employees. At its best, matrix structure can increase coordination while simultaneously improving agility and local responsiveness.

However, the global matrix structure suffers from two major shortcomings. First, the matrix form can be quite cumbersome. Numerous meetings are required simply to coordinate the actions of the various division heads, let alone activities within divisions. In turn, the need for complex coordination tends to make decision making time-consuming and slows organization reaction time. Second, individual responsibility and accountability can become foggy in the matrix organization structure. Because responsibility is shared, managers can attribute poor performance to the actions of the other manager. Moreover, the source of problems in the matrix structure can be hard to detect and corrective action equally difficult to take.

There are other ways international companies can improve responsiveness and effectiveness. An increasingly popular method among international companies is implementation of work teams to accomplish goals and solve problems. In the next section we explore the use of work teams in detail.

WORK TEAMS

Forces of globalization demand that companies respond quickly to changes in all their business environments. Formation of teams can be highly useful in improving responsiveness by cutting across functional boundaries (such as that between production and marketing) that slow decision making in an organization. Although a matrix organization accomplishes this by establishing cross-functional cooperation, companies do not always want to change their entire organizational structure to reap the benefits that cross-functional cooperation provides. In such cases, companies can implement several different types of teams without changing the overall company structure.

Work teams are assigned the tasks of coordinating their efforts to arrive at solutions and implementing corrective action. Today, international companies are turning to work teams on an unprecedented scale to increase direct contact between different operating units. Apple Computer, Federal Express, Motorola, and Volvo are just some of the thousands of companies making extensive use of teams. Companies are even forming teams to design and implement their competitive strategies. Let's take a look at several different types of teams—*self-managed teams*, *cross-functional teams*, and *global teams*.

Self-Managed Teams   A **self-managed team** is one in which employees from a single department take on responsibilities of their former supervisors. When used in production, such teams often reorganize the methods and flow of production processes. Because they are "self-managed," they reduce the need for managers to watch over their every activity. The benefits of self-managed teams typically include increased productivity, product quality, customer satisfaction, employee morale, and company loyalty. In fact, the most common self-managed teams in many manufacturing companies are *quality-improvement teams*, which help reduce waste in the production process and, therefore, costs.

The global trend in "downsizing" internal operations to make them more flexible and productive has increased the popularity of teams because they reduce the need for direct supervision. Companies around the world now employ self-managed teams in

self-managed team
Team in which employees from a single department take on responsibilities of their former supervisors.

international operations. Recent research, however, indicates that cultural differences can affect resistance to the concept of self-management and the practice of using teams. Among other things, experts suggest that international managers follow some basic guidelines:[23]

➡ Use selection tests to identify employees most likely to perform well in a team environment
➡ Adapt the self-managed work-team concept to the national culture of each subsidiary
➡ Adapt the process of integrating self-managed work teams to the national culture of each subsidiary
➡ Train local managers at the parent company and allow them to introduce teams when resistance is expected to be great

Similarly, the cultural differences discussed in Chapter 2 are important to managers designing teams in international operations. For example, certain cultures are less individual- and more group-oriented. Some harbor greater respect for differences in status. In others, people tend to believe that the future is largely beyond their personal control, and other cultures reflect a so-called "work to live" mentality. In these cases, say researchers, conventional management should retain fairly tight authority over teams. But in cultures in which people are very hard working, teams are likely to be productive if given greater autonomy.[24] Researchers stress, however, that much more study is needed into this aspect of work teams.

Cross-Functional Teams A **cross-functional team** is one that is composed of employees who work at similar levels in different functional departments. They work to develop changes in operations and are well-suited to projects requiring coordination across functions, such as reducing the time needed to get a product from idea stage to marketplace. International companies use cross-functional teams also to improve quality by having employees from purchasing, manufacturing, and distribution (among other functions) work together to address specific quality issues. For the same reason, cross-functional teams can help break down barriers between departments and reorganize operations around processes rather than functional departments.

> **cross-functional team**
> Team that is composed of employees who work at similar levels in different functional departments.

Global Teams Finally, some very large international corporations are moving toward so-called **global teams**—groups of top managers from both headquarters and international subsidiaries who meet to develop solutions to company-wide problems. For example, Northern Telecom of Canada created a global team of top executives from Britain, Canada, France, and the United States that traveled to Asia, Europe, and North America looking for ways to improve product-development practices.[25]

Depending on the issue at hand, team members can be drawn from a single business unit or assembled from several different units. While some teams are disbanded after resolving specific issues, others move on to new problems. The performance of global teams can be impaired by such matters as large distances between team members, lengthy travel times to meetings, and the inconvenience of working across time zones. Companies can sometimes overcome these difficulties, although doing so can be rather costly.

> **global team**
> Team of top managers from both headquarters and international subsidiaries who meet to develop solutions to company-wide problems.

A FINAL WORD

Managers have the important and complicated task of formulating international strategies at the levels of the corporation, business unit, and individual department. International managers must identify their companies' mission and the goals it is to achieve.

Managers often analyze their companies' operations by viewing them as a chain of activities that create customer value (value chain analysis). It is through this process that managers can identify and implement strategies suited to their companies' unique capabilities. The strategies that managers select then determine the firm's organizational structure. National business environments can affect managers' strategy and structure decisions: whether to alter their products (standardization versus adaptation), where to locate facilities (centralized versus decentralized production), and what type of decision making to implement (centralized versus decentralized decision making).

The role of managers in formulating strategies and creating the overall organizational structure cannot be overstated. The strategies they choose will determine the market segments in which the firm will compete and whether it will go for low-cost leadership in its industry or differentiate its product and charge a higher price. These decisions are crucial to all later activities of corporations that are going international. They impact how a company will enter international markets (Chapter 13), go about employing its human resources and acquiring its financial and physical resources (Chapter 14), and manage its day-to-day production, marketing, and other operations (Chapter 15).

There is a variety of additional material available on the companion Web site that accompanies this text. You can access this information by visiting the Web site at ⟨**www.prenhall.com/wild**⟩.

summary

① Explain the stages of identification and analysis that precede strategy selection. *Planning* is the process of identifying and selecting an organization's objectives and deciding how the organization will achieve those objectives. In turn, *strategy* is the set of planned actions taken by managers to help a company meet its objectives. The key to developing an effective strategy, then, is to clearly define a company's goals and carefully plan how it will achieve those goals.

As part of the strategy formulation process, managers must undertake two important steps of identification and analysis.

(a) *Identify company mission and goals.* Most companies have a general purpose that explains why they exist and is expressed in a *mission statement*—a written statement of why a company exists and what it plans to accomplish. The mission statement often guides such decisions as which industries to enter or exit and how to compete in chosen segments. Mission statements often spell out how a company's operations affect its *stakeholders*—all parties, ranging from suppliers and employees to stockholders and consumers, who are affected by a company's activities. Managers must also define the *goals* (or objectives) the firm is to achieve in the global marketplace.

(b) *Identify core competency and value-creating activities.* Before managers formulate effective strategies, they must analyze the company, its industry (or industries), and the national business environments in which it is involved. Although large multinational companies are often involved in multiple industries, most perform one activity (or a few activities) better than any competitor does. A *core competency* is a special company ability that competitors find extremely difficult or impossible to equal.

Managers can actually go about analyzing and identifying their unique abilities that create value for customers by conducting a *value chain analysis*—a procedure that divides a company's activities into primary activities and support activities that are central to creating value for customers. *Primary activities* include inbound and outbound logistics, manufacturing (or operations), marketing and sales, and customer service. *Support activities* include firm infrastructure, human resource management, technology development, and procurement. Managers determine whether each activity enhances or detracts from customer value and incorporate this knowledge into the strategy formulation process. Finally, managers must analyze national and international business environments to consider the cultural, political, legal, or economic factors that can complicate the firm's strategy.

2 **Identify the strategies that international companies employ at various levels in the organization.** Companies engaged in international business activities can approach the world market using one of two general international strategies. Some companies choose to follow a *multinational (or multidomestic) strategy*—a strategy of adapting products and their marketing strategies in each national market to suit local preferences. To implement a multinational strategy, companies often establish largely independent, self-contained units (or subsidiaries) in each national market. Other companies decide that what suits their operations is a *global strategy*—a strategy of offering the same products using the same marketing strategy in all national markets. Companies following a global strategy typically produce their entire inventories of products in a single location, perform product research and development in one location, and design promotional campaigns and advertising strategies at headquarters.

In addition to making the multinational versus global strategy decision, managers must formulate strategies for the corporation, each business unit, and each department. Companies involved in more than one line of business must first formulate a *corporate-level strategy* that lays out overall objectives for the company's different business units and specifies the role that each unit will play in reaching those objectives. The four key approaches to corporate strategy are *growth*, *retrenchment*, *stability*, and *combination*.

(a) A *growth strategy* is designed to increase the scale (*size* of activities) or scope (*kinds* of activities) of a corporation's operations. *Scale* refers to the *size* of a corporation's activities, *scope* to the *kinds* of activities it performs.

(b) The exact opposite of a growth strategy is a *retrenchment strategy*—a strategy that is designed to reduce the scale or scope of a corporation's businesses. Corporations often cut back the *scale* of their operations when economic conditions worsen, competition increases, or when a subsidiary or division is not generating adequate sales revenue. Corporations reduce the *scope* of their activities by selling or scaling down unprofitable business units or those no longer directly related to their overall aims.

(c) A *stability strategy* is designed to guard against change. It is often employed by corporations trying to avoid either growth or retrenchment. Stability is a relatively uncommon strategy among today's corporations.

(d) The purpose of a *combination strategy* is to mix growth, retrenchment, and stability strategies across a corporation's business units. For example, it will invest in units showing promise, retrench in those where less exposure is desired, and stabilize others.

In addition to stipulating the overall corporate strategy, managers must also formulate separate *business-level strategies* for each business unit. Most companies employ one of three generic business-level strategies for competing in an industry.

(a) A strategy in which a company exploits economies of scale to have the lowest cost structure of any competitor in its industry is called a *low-cost leadership strategy*. Although cutting costs is the mantra for firms pursuing a low-cost leadership position, important factors such as product quality and customer service cannot be ignored.

(b) A *differentiation strategy* is one in which a company designs its products to be perceived as unique by buyers throughout its industry. Although smaller segments mean smaller market share, buyers in such segments are usually willing to pay more for products with special value and tend to show the company greater brand loyalty.

(c) A *focus strategy* is one in which a company focuses on serving the needs of a narrowly defined market segment by being the low-cost leader, by differentiating its product or both. For instance, some firms serve the needs of one ethnic or racial group whereas others focus on serving a single geographic area.

Achieving corporate- and business-level objectives depends on effective *department-level strategies* that focus on the specific activities that transform resources into products. Each department is instrumental in creating customer value through lower costs or differentiated products. This is true of departments conducting either *primary activities* or *support activities*.

3 **Explain the important production considerations influencing strategy formulation.** Careful planning of all aspects of production helps companies cut costs to become low-cost leaders and design new products or product features necessary for a differentiation strategy.

The process of assessing a company's ability to produce enough output to satisfy market demand is called *capacity planning*. If capacity is greater than the expected market demand, production must be scaled back. If market demand is growing, managers must determine in which facilities to expand production or whether additional facilities are needed to expand capacity.

Selecting the location for production facilities is called *facilities location planning*. Important environmental factors in location planning include the cost and availability of labor and management, raw materials, component parts, and energy. Other key factors include political stability, the extent of regulation and bureaucracy, economic development, and the local culture.

Selecting highly favorable locations often allows a company to achieve *location economies*—economic benefits derived from locating production activities in optimal locations. Another important consideration for production managers is whether to centralize or decentralize production facilities. *Centralized production* refers to the concentration of production facilities in one location. With *decentralized production*, facilities are spread over several locations—possibly one for each national business environment in which the company markets its products.

Deciding the process that a company will use to create its product is called *process planning*. The particular process to be used is typically determined by a firm's business-level strategy. Another important production issue is deciding whether the production process will be standardized for all markets or adapted to manufacture products modified for different markets. Low-cost leadership, for example, often dictates automated, standardized production in large batches whereas differentiation often demands decentralized facilities to improve local responsiveness.

Deciding the spatial arrangement of production processes within production facilities is called *facilities layout planning*. Facility layout depends on the type of production process a company employs which in turn depends on a company's business-level strategy.

④ Discuss the important marketing considerations influencing strategy formulation. Without considering its marketing needs, no company can develop effective corporate-, business-, and department-level strategies. Some experts argue that because the world is becoming standardized and homogeneous, companies should market the same products in the same way in all countries. They claim that technology has already caused people's needs and preferences to converge throughout the world and urge companies to reduce production and marketing costs by standardizing both the physical features of their products and their strategies for marketing them. Other researchers, however, counter that standardization is just one of a number of strategies with which firms have successfully entered the international marketplace. Still others argue that standardization is not always the best strategy and emphasize instead the benefits of adapting products to different markets.

Consumers worldwide appear content with a standardized product in *certain* product categories. In others, however, they demand products that reflect their unique tastes and preferences. Cultural, political, legal, and economic environments have a great deal to do with the preferences of both consumers and industrial buyers worldwide. Product standardization is more likely when producer and buyer nations share the same level of economic development.

⑤ Describe each type of *international organizational structure* and identify the key issues in its selection. *Organizational structure* is the way in which a company divides its activities among separate units and coordinates activities between those units. Important to organizational structure is the degree to which decision making in an organization will be centralized (made at a high level) or decentralized (made at a low level such as international subsidiaries). Centralized decision making helps to coordinate the operations of international subsidiaries. Decentralized decision making is beneficial when fast-changing national business environments put a premium on local responsiveness. Decentralization can also help foster *participative management practices* and increase personal accountability for business decisions.

When designing organizational structure, managers must consider the issues of *coordination and flexibility*. Every international company must design an organizational structure that clearly defines areas of responsibility and *chains of command*—the lines of authority that run from top management to individual employees and specify internal reporting relationships. However, the organizational structure that is selected must be flexible enough to respond to changes in national business environments that can force changes in strategy. There are four different organizational structures that international companies can implement.

(a) An *international division structure* separates domestic from international business activities by creating a separate division with its own manager. In turn, the international division is typically divided into units corresponding to the countries in which a company is active. Within each country, a general manager controls the manufacture and marketing of the firm's products. By consigning international activities to a single division, a firm also reduces costs and increases efficiency.

(b) An *international area structure* organizes a company's entire global operations into countries or geographic regions. Under this structure, each geographic division operates as a self-contained unit, with most decision making decentralized in the hands of country or regional managers. Parent-company headquarters makes decisions regarding overall corporate strategy and coordinates the activities of various units. The international area structure is best suited to companies that treat each national market as unique.

(c) A *global product structure* divides worldwide operations according to a company's product areas. Each product division is then divided into domestic and international units. Each function—R&D, marketing, and so forth—is thus duplicated in both the domestic and international units of each product division. Because it overcomes some of the coordination problems of international division structure, the global product structure is suitable for companies offering diverse sets of products or services.

(d) A *global matrix structure* splits the chain of command between product and area divisions. Each manager and employee reports to two bosses—the general manager of the product division and the general manager of the geographic area. A main goal of the global matrix structure is to bring together *geographic* area managers and *product* area managers in joint decision making. The popularity of the global matrix structure has increased among companies trying to increase local responsiveness, reduce costs, and coordinate worldwide operations.

Finally, the formation of teams can be highly useful in improving responsiveness by cutting across functional boundaries (such as that between production and marketing) that slow decision making in an organization. *Work teams* are assigned the tasks of coordinating their efforts to arrive at solutions and implement corrective action. A *self-managed team* is one in which employees from a single department take on responsibilities of their former supervisors. A *cross-functional team* is composed of employees who work at similar levels in different functional departments. Finally, a *global team* is composed of top managers from both headquarters and international subsidiaries who meet to develop solutions to company-wide problems.

questions for review

1. Define the terms *planning* and *strategy*. What is the importance of strategy to company performance?

2. Identify the three stages of the *strategy formulation process*.

3. Define *mission statement*. How do companies incorporate *stakeholders* into the mission statement?

4. What is a *core competency*? Explain how it differs from a skill.

5. What is *value chain analysis*? Describe the difference between primary and secondary activities.

6. How are national and international business environments important to strategy formulation? Give several examples.

7. Define *multinational strategy*. Under what circumstances is it appropriate?

8. What is a *global strategy*? Explain its primary appeal and main drawback.

9. What are the four *corporate-level strategies*? Identify the main characteristics of each.

10. Identify the three *business-level strategies*. Explain how each strategy differs from the other two.

11. Explain the importance of *department-level strategies* in helping a company achieve its goals.

12. What is *capacity planning*? Explain why it is important to strategy formulation.

13. Define *facilities location planning*. How is it affected by *location economies*? Centralization versus decentralization of production?

14. What is *process planning*? Explain how it is affected by the standardization versus adaptation decision.

15. Define *facilities layout planning*. How is it relevant to the formulation of strategies?

16. What are the important marketing considerations in strategy formulation? Explain when standardization and adaptation are appropriate.

17. What are the four types of *organizational structure* international companies employ? For each one, supply its definition and describe its main characteristics.

18. Identify the three different types of *work teams*. How does each help a company improve its responsiveness and effectiveness?

questions for discussion

1. The elements affecting strategy formulation are the same whether a company is domestic or international. Do you agree or disagree with this statement? Why or why not? Support your argument with specific examples.

2. "Cultures around the world are becoming increasingly similar. Companies, therefore, should standardize both their products and global marketing efforts." Do you agree or disagree with this statement? Are there certain industries for which it might be more or less true? Provide specific examples.

3. Continuous advancements in technology are deeply affecting the way international businesses are managed. Do you think technology (the Internet, for example) will radically alter the fundamental strategies or organizational structures of international companies? Or do you think companies will simply graft new strategies and structures onto existing ones? Support your answers with specific examples.

in practice

Read the following brief article and answer the questions that follow.

Smoke-Free Snacks

RJR Nabisco announced yesterday that it was splitting its food and domestic tobacco businesses and selling its international tobacco company to government-contolled Japan Tobacco. "There's no reason for these businesses to be under the same roof. They are very different enterprises, with different problems, different challenges, and different investor groups," said RJR Nabisco's chairman and CEO, Steven F. Goldstone. People should have "the opportunity to choose whether they want to invest in a tobacco company or a food company," he added.

The deal vaults Japan Tobacco from fifth place to third in the global cigarette business and gives it a presence in Western Europe and Russia, among other markets. Japan Tobacco already owns Japan's biggest-selling cigarette brand, Mild Seven, and RJR's Winston and Camel brands will give the firm even greater market share. Japan Tobacco is also involved in pharmaceuticals and food, and controls Japan's largest vending-machine company—a key asset in a country where many products are sold that way.

RJR's domestic tobacco unit will become a separate company, which will be responsible for any smoking-related claims in the United States. Asked whether his company was concerned about liability from smokers' lawsuits, Yasushi Shingai, Japan Tobacco's chief strategist, replied, "We have three pending litigations, but the law system and the culture are very different here than in the United States."

1. What corporate-level strategy, or mix of strategies, do you think RJR is pursuing by undertaking the sale? What strategy or mix of strategies is Japan Tobacco pursuing?

2. Do you agree with RJR Nabisco's chairman when he says there is no reason for the company's two businesses—food and tobacco—to be owned by the same company? Why or why not? Support your answer by identifying as many strategic benefits or drawbacks as you can.

3. The article refers to one of RJR Nabisco's stakeholders—investors. Identify as many other stakeholders of the company as you can. Besides smoking-related lawsuits, what investment trends do you think encouraged the company to split its food and tobacco businesses?

4. The article mentions that Japan tobacco has other businesses, including food. Why do you think food and tobacco do not belong together in a U.S. company, but seems to be fine in a Japanese company? In your answer consider all the cultural, legal, and ownership factors you can think of.

projects

1. Select a recent business periodical, such as *Fortune* ⟨**www.fortune.com**⟩ or the *Wall Street Journal* ⟨**www.wsj.com**⟩, and identify several articles discussing changes taking place within a given industry over the past few months. Write a short summary of the articles. What changes are occurring, and how are companies responding? Are firms altering strategies, relocating production, or leaving or entering certain markets and/or lines of busi-

ness? Are they altering their organizational structures in some way?

2. Working with several of your classmates, select and research an international company that interests you. (Annual reports can be obtained from companies' investor relations departments or, perhaps, their World Wide Web sites.) What is the company's mission statement or overriding objective? What are its corporate- and business-level strategies? In which nations does it produce and market its products? Are its production facilities centralized or decentralized? Does it standardize products or adapt them for different markets? What

type of organizational structure does it have? Which of the two types of international strategy does it seem to follow? Does the company make use of work teams?

3. Make a list of five products that you used or consumed within the past 24 hours. Your list might include such goods as your toothpaste or your CD player and such services as an express mailing service, a cable/satellite TV program, and so forth. Which strategy does each product's or service's company employ—low-cost, differentiation, or focus? In one or two paragraphs, explain how you arrived at your answer for each company.

business case 12
THE IKEA KEY TO PRICING

IKEA is a $5.8 billion global furniture powerhouse based in Sweden. With 140 stores in 29 countries, the company's success reflects founder Ingvar Kamprad's "social ambition" of selling a wide range of stylish, functional home furnishings at prices so low that the majority of people can afford to buy them. In fact, the story of Kamprad's success is even the subject of a new book titled *IKEA: The Entrepreneur, the Business Concept, the Culture.* The store exteriors are painted with Sweden's national colors, bright blue and yellow. Shoppers view furniture on the main floor in scores of realistic settings arranged throughout the cavernous showrooms.

In a departure from standard industry practice, IKEA's furniture bears names such as "Ivar" and "Sten" instead of model numbers. At IKEA, shopping is very much a self-service activity; after browsing and writing down the names of desired items, shoppers can pick up their furniture on the lower level. There they find boxes containing the furniture in kit form; one of the cornerstones of IKEA's strategy is having customers take their purchases home in their vehicles and assemble the furniture themselves. The lower level of a typical IKEA store also contains a restaurant, a grocery store called the Swede Shop, a supervised play area for children, and a baby-care room.

IKEA's approach to the furniture business has enabled it to rack up impressive growth in a $30 billion industry where overall sales have been flat. Sourcing furniture from more than 2,300 suppliers in 70 countries helps the company maintain its low-cost position. During the 1990s, IKEA opened several stores in central and eastern Europe. Because many consumers in those regions have relatively low purchasing power, the stores offer a smaller selection of goods; some furniture was designed specifically for the cramped living styles typical in former Soviet bloc countries. Throughout Europe, IKEA benefits from the perception that Sweden is the source of high-quality products. In fact, one of the company's key selling points is its "Swedishness." The United Kingdom represents its fastest-growing market in Eu-

rope; IKEA's London store has achieved annual sales growth of 20 percent. Germany currently accounts for more than one quarter of Ikea's total revenues; store openings are planned in Berlin, Dresden, Leipzig, and other cities in the former East Germany.

Industry observers predict that the United States will eventually be IKEA's largest market. The company opened its first U.S. store in Philadelphia in 1985; today, IKEA has more than two dozen outlets—most on the East Coast—that generated $859 million in sales in 1996. In October 1995, the company opened a "flagship" store in New York City on 57th street. A $50 million superstore is slated for Schaumberg, Illinois. Many competitors are taking IKEA seriously. Jeff Young, chief operating officer of Lexington Furniture Industries, says, "IKEA is on the way to becoming the Wal-Mart Stores of the home-furnishing industry. If you're in this business, you'd better take a look." Some U.S. customers, however, are irked to find popular items sometimes out of stock. Another problem is the long lines resulting from the company's no-frills approach. Complained one shopper, "Great idea, poor execution. The quality of much of what they sell is good, but the hassles make you question whether it's worth it."

Goran Carstedt, president of IKEA North America, responds to such criticism by referring to the company's mission. "If we offered more services, our prices would go up," he explains. "Our customers understand our philosophy, which calls for each of us to do a little in order to save a lot. They value our low prices. And almost all of them say they will come back again." To keep them coming back, IKEA is spending between $25 million and $35 million on advertising to get its message across. Whereas common industry practice is to rely heavily on newspaper and radio advertising, two thirds of IKEA's North American advertising budget is allocated for TV. John Sitnik, an executive at IKEA's U.S. Inc., says, "We distanced ourselves from the other furniture stores. We decided TV is something we can own."

thinking globally

1. Has IKEA taken a standardization approach or an adaptation approach in the United States? Do you think the approach is the right one?

2. Which retailers do you think will be IKEA's biggest competitors in the United States?

3. Company founder Kamprad recently decided to expand into China. Kamprad's decision was not based on market research but, rather, on his own intuition. Find a recent article or check IKEA's Web site to update the company's China strategy. Did Kamprad's decision pay off?

a question of ethics

1. Julius Tahija is the 83-year-old president-commissioner of the Austindo Group in Indonesia. His diversified company (involved in such areas as financial services, mining, utilities, tobacco, and rubber) is an island of solidarity in an economy in turmoil since 1997. But unlike other companies and banks that got involved in corrupt business deals, Tahija steered clear. Tahija refused to compromise his principles in the face of political pressure when the youngest son of ex-President Suharto wanted financing from Tahija's bank to fund his national car project. "They wouldn't call us because they knew it wouldn't work," recalls Tahija. His son George adds, "We grew up believing in being independent. My father taught me that you never do things where you owe people favors." However, Tahija acknowledges that his company would have grown faster if he had made alliances with politically connected companies during the boom years. Do you think Tahija made the right decision by not doing business the way the majority of companies did in Indonesia? Would you give the same answer if you were an investor in his company and he refused to do what could earn you a greater financial return?[26]

2. An article in a recent issue of the *Journal of Business Ethics* noted the rapid rate of change in the international economy. Geographical and political borders continue to be redrawn especially in Europe. In addition, there is a growing interdependence of socially, politically, economically, and legally diverse countries. In response to these changes, a number of multinational corporations have begun revising their operating policies. These revisions are evident in revamped production and marketing strategies. Many international companies are also revising their approaches to ethics, with the result that all other strategies are impacted. The authors write, "The truly global company must come to grips with the legal and moral atmosphere in which it operates." Given the complexity of the issues involved, do you think it would be possible to create a uniform code of ethics that is applicable to any business operating in any culture? What issues should such a code address?[27]

3. Throughout 1999, the United States government pursued an antitrust lawsuit against Microsoft Corporation. One of the issues is whether Microsoft took unfair advantage of its powerful position in the computer industry by using "strong-arm tactics" on software customers throughout the world and by crushing weaker rivals. Regardless of whether or not Microsoft is guilty of anticompetitive acts in terms of the law, do you believe that Microsoft has conducted itself in an ethical manner in its business dealings? Has it abused its power in the industry, or is Microsoft simply a tough competitor?

13 selecting and managing entry modes

Beacons

A Look Back

CHAPTER 12 showed us how companies plan and organize themselves for international operations. We explored the different types of strategies and organizational structures that international companies employ to accomplish their strategic goals.

A Look at This Chapter

This chapter introduces the different entry modes companies use to "go international." We discuss the important issues surrounding the selection and management of the following: (1) exporting, importing, and countertrade; (2) contractual entry modes; and (3) investment entry modes.

A Look Ahead

CHAPTER 14 explains how companies acquire the business resources that they need to conduct their international operations. We identify and describe the key decision variables involved when employing human resources, and when acquiring financial and physical resources.

Learning Objectives

After studying this chapter, you should be able to

1 Explain why and how companies use *exporting*, *importing*, and *countertrade*.

2 Explain the various *means of financing* export and import activities.

3 Identify the different *contractual entry modes* and discuss the pros and cons of each.

4 Explain the various types of *investment entry modes*.

5 Discuss the important strategic factors in selecting an entry mode.

Sharon Doherty's company, Vellus Products, manufactures and markets pet-grooming products in Columbus, Ohio. One day a man in Bahrain (in the Middle East) was surfing the Internet for pet-related information and stumbled upon the Web site of a dog breeder in Spain that mentioned Doherty's dog shampoos.

That chance encounter led to two positive outcomes for Vellus Products: The puppy owner in Bahrain became a customer, and, more importantly, the dog breeder in Spain became Doherty's distributor in Western Europe. "The way this [business transaction] transpired just blew me away," says Doherty. But Doherty did not rest on her laurels once she had a satisfied customer in Bahrain and a distributor in Spain. She went after more international sales by developing her company's own Web site (check it out yourself at ⟨www.vellus.com⟩).

Although Vellus Products had been exporting for several years, the World Wide Web presents a new mode of entry into untapped markets abroad. "I think the Web site will help business tremendously. I have no doubt that it will pull in people from overseas," says Doherty.

This small company with annual revenues of only about $500,000 resembles a global company in at least one respect—it already earns more than half its revenues from international sales. It seems that in the dog-eat-dog world of international trade, Vellus Products is holding its own—and then some.[1]

S tories like the chance introduction of the puppy owner in Bahrain to Doherty through the company in Spain are not uncommon in international business. In fact, such encounters are how many small companies begin exporting their products to the world.

The decision of how to enter a new market abroad is influenced by many factors, including the local business environment and a company's own core competency. An **entry mode** is the institutional arrangement by which a firm gets its products, technologies, human skills, or other resources into a market.[2] Companies thus seek entry to new marketplaces for the purpose of manufacturing and/or selling products within them. Firms going international have many potential entry modes at their disposal, and their choice will depend on many factors, including experience in a market, amount of control that managers desire, and potential size of the market. Let's now explore each of the three categories of entry modes that are available to companies:

1. Exporting, importing, and countertrade
2. Contractual entry
3. Investment entry

> **entry mode**
> *Institutional arrangement by which a firm gets its products, technologies, human skills, or other resources into a market.*

EXPORTING, IMPORTING, AND COUNTERTRADE

The most common method of buying and selling goods internationally is exporting and importing. Recall from Chapter 1 that *exporting* is the act of sending goods and services from one nation to others and that *importing* is the act of bringing goods and services into a country from other countries. Companies export products when the international marketplace offers opportunities to increase sales and in turn profits. Companies worldwide often look to the United States as a great export opportunity because of the size of the market and the strong buying power of its citizens (see the World Business Survey "Land of Opportunity"). Companies often import products in order to obtain less expensive goods or those that are simply unavailable in the domestic market.

Because this chapter focuses on how companies take their goods and services to the global marketplace, the following discussion on exporting and importing concentrates on the exporting side of the transaction. The other end of the transaction, importing, is a sourcing decision for most firms and therefore is covered in Chapter 14, where we discuss how companies acquire the resources upon which their businesses depend. The subsequent section then explains how companies use countertrade to do business across borders when exporting and importing products in exchange for cash is not an option.

WHY COMPANIES EXPORT

In the global economy, companies increasingly sell goods and services to wholesalers, retailers, industrial buyers, and consumers in other nations. Generally speaking, there are three main reasons why companies begin exporting:

1. *Expand sales.* Most large companies use exporting as a means of expanding total sales when the domestic market has become saturated. Greater sales volume allows them to spread the fixed costs of production over a greater number of manufactured products, thereby lowering the cost of producing each unit of output. In short, going international is one way to achieve economies of scale.
2. *Diversify sales.* Exporting permits companies to diversify their sales. In other words, they can offset slow sales in one national market (perhaps due to recession) with increased sales in another. Diversified sales can level off a company's cash flow—making it easier to coordinate payments to creditors with receipts from customers.

World Business Survey

Land of Opportunity

Ask non-U.S. exporters what comes to mind when they think of international business and they'll likely tell you that consumers in the United States have an insatiable appetite for products from other countries. Many exporters truly see the U.S. market as a "land of opportunity" in which to sell their goods. In fact, the trade deficit in the United States hit record levels in 1999. Below are the top ten countries that are leading sources of exports to the United States. As you can see, the list includes both developing and industrialized countries.

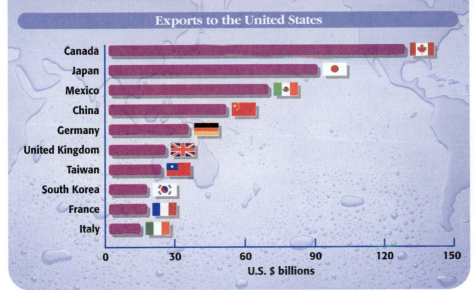

Exports to the United States

U.S. $ billions

3. *Gain experience.* Companies often use exporting as a low-cost, low-risk way of getting started in international business. For example, owners and managers of small companies, which typically have little or no knowledge of how to conduct business in other cultures, use exporting to gain valuable international experience.

DEVELOPING AN EXPORT STRATEGY: A FOUR-STEP MODEL

As we saw in this chapter's opening story about Vellus Products, companies are often drawn into exporting when customers in other countries solicit their goods. This is a fairly natural way for companies to become aware of their product's international potential. In the process, companies get their first taste of how international business differs from that in the domestic market. Unfortunately, it is also during these initial tentative steps outside the domestic market that companies commit their first international blunders.

Firms should not, however, fall into the habit of simply responding to random international requests for their products. A more logical approach is to research and analyze international opportunities and to develop a coherent export strategy. A firm with such a strategy actively pursues export markets rather than sitting back and waiting for international orders to come in by fax or e-mail. Let's now take a look at each of the four steps in developing a successful export strategy.

Step 1: Identify a Potential Market In order to identify clearly whether demand exists in a particular target market, market research should be performed and results interpreted (see Chapter 11). Novice exporters should focus on one or only a few markets. For example, a first-time Brazilian exporter might not want to export simultaneously to Argentina, Britain, and Greece. A better strategy would probably be to focus on Argentina because of its cultural similarities with Brazil (despite different, although related, languages). The company could then expand into more diverse markets after it gains some international experience in a nearby country. Also, the would-be exporter should seek the advice of experts on the regulations and the process of exporting in general, and to the selected target market in particular.

Step 2: Match Needs to Abilities The next step is to assess carefully whether the company has the ability to satisfy the needs of the market. For instance, suppose a market located in a region with a warm humid climate for much of the year displays the need for home air-conditioning equipment. If a company recognizes this need but makes only industrial-sized air-conditioning equipment, it might not be able to satisfy demand with its current product. However, if the company is able to use its smallest industrial air-conditioning unit to satisfy the needs of several homes, it might have a market opportunity. If there are no other options or if consumers want their own individual units, the company should probably rule out entry into the market.

Step 3: Initiate Meetings Having meetings early with potential local distributors, buyers, and others is a must. Initial contact should focus on building trust and developing a cooperative climate among all parties. The cultural differences between the parties will come into play already at this stage. Beyond building trust, successive meetings are designed to estimate the potential success of any agreement if interest is shown on both sides. At the most advanced stage, negotiations take place and details of agreements are finalized.

A group of companies from Arizona called the Environmental Technology Industry Cluster was searching for a market for its environmental products in Taiwan. When a delegation from Taiwan arrived in the Arizona desert to survey the group's products, it was not all formal meetings and negotiations. Although the schedule during the day was busy with company visits, evenings were designed to build relationships—important to businesspeople from Taiwan. There were outdoor barbecues, hayrides, line dancing, and visits to Mexican restaurants and frontier towns to give the visitors from Taiwan a feel for local culture and history. To make their counterparts from Taiwan feel more at ease in an environment in which they prefer getting to know business associates, nighttime schedules also included visits to karaoke spots and Chinese restaurants where a good deal of singing took place. Follow-up meetings resulted in several successful deals.[3]

Step 4: Commit Resources After all the meetings, negotiations, and contract signings, it is time to put the company's human, financial, and physical resources to work. First, the objectives of the export program must be clearly stated and should extend out at least three to five years. For small firms, it may be sufficient to assign one individual the responsibility for drawing up objectives and estimating resources. However, as companies expand their activities to include more products and/or markets, many firms discover the need for an export department or division. The head of this department usually has the responsibility (and authority) to formulate, implement, and evaluate the company's export strategy. See Chapter 12 for a detailed discussion of important organizational design issues to be considered at this stage.

DEGREE OF EXPORT INVOLVEMENT

Entrepreneurs, small and medium-size companies, and large multinational firms all engage in exporting. However, not all companies get involved in exporting activities to the same extent. Some companies (usually entrepreneurs and small and medium-size firms) perform few or none of the necessary activities to get their products in a market abroad. Instead they use intermediaries that specialize in getting products from one market into another. Other companies (usually only the largest of companies) perform all of their export activities themselves with an infrastructure that bridges the gap between two markets. Let's take a closer look at the two basic forms of export involvement—*direct exporting* and *indirect exporting*.

Direct Exporting   Some companies become deeply involved in the export of their products. **Direct exporting** occurs when a company sells its products directly to buyers in a target market. Direct exporters operate in such industries as aircraft (Boeing), industrial equipment (John Deere), apparel (Lands' End), and food and beverage products (Anheuser-Busch). Bear in mind that "direct exporters" need not sell directly to *end users*. Rather, they take full responsibility for getting their goods into the target market by selling directly to local buyers and not going through intermediary companies. Typically, they rely on either local sales representatives or distributors.

Sales Representatives   Whether an individual or an organization, a *sales representative* represents only its own company's products, not those of other companies. They promote those products in many ways, such as by attending trade fairs and making personal visits to local retailers and wholesalers. They do not take title to the merchandise. Rather, they are hired by a company and normally compensated with a fixed salary plus commissions based on the value of their sales.

Distributors   Alternatively, a direct exporter can sell in the target market through *distributors*, who take ownership of the merchandise when it enters their country. As owners of the products, they accept all the risks associated with generating local sales. They sell either to retailers and wholesalers or to end users through their own channels of distribution. Typically, they earn a profit equal to the difference between the price they pay and the price they receive for the exporter's goods. Although using a distributor reduces the exporter's risk, it also weakens the exporter's control over the prices actually charged to buyers. A distributor who charges unwarranted prices can stunt the growth of an exporter's market share. It is important, therefore, that exporters select reliable distributors. They should choose distributors who are willing to invest in the promotion of their products and who do not sell directly competing products. Despite the benefits of direct exporting, some companies implement a policy of *indirect exporting*.

Indirect Exporting   Some companies have few available resources to commit to exporting activities. Others simply find exporting a daunting experience because of a lack of contacts and experience. Fortunately, there is an option for such firms. **Indirect exporting** occurs when a company sells its products to intermediaries who then resell to buyers in a target market. The choice of intermediary depends on many factors, including the ratio of the exporter's international sales to its total sales, the company's available resources, and the growth rate of the target market. Let's take a closer look at several different types of intermediaries: *agents*, *export management companies*, and *export trading companies*.

Agents   Individuals or organizations that represent one or more indirect exporters in a target market are called **agents.** Agents typically receive compensation in the form of commissions on the value of sales. Because establishing a relationship with an agent

> **direct exporting**
> Practice by which a company sells its products directly to buyers in a target market.

> **indirect exporting**
> Practice by which a company sells its products to intermediaries who resell to buyers in a target market.

> **agents**
> Individuals or organizations that represent one or more indirect exporters in a target market.

is relatively easy and inexpensive, it is a fairly common approach to indirect exporting. Agents, however, should be chosen very carefully because terminating an agency relationship can be costly and difficult if problems arise. Careful selection is also necessary because agents often represent several indirect exporters simultaneously. They might focus their promotional efforts on the products of the company paying the highest commission rather than on the company with the better products.

export management company (EMC)
Company that exports products on behalf of indirect exporters.

Export Management Companies A company that exports products on behalf of an indirect exporter is called an **export management company (EMC)**. An EMC operates contractually, either as an agent (being paid in the form of commissions based on the value of sales) or as a distributor (taking ownership of the merchandise and earning a profit from its resale).

An EMC will usually provide additional services on a retainer basis, charging set fees against funds deposited on account. Typical EMC services include gathering market information, formulating promotional strategies, performing specific promotional duties (such as attending trade fairs), researching customer credit, making shipping arrangements, and coordinating export documents. It is common for an EMC to exploit contacts predominantly in one industry (say, agricultural goods or consumer products) or in one geographic area (such as Latin America or the Middle East). Indeed, the biggest advantage of an EMC is usually a deep understanding of the cultural, political, legal, and economic conditions of the target market. Its staff works comfortably and effectively in the cultures of both exporter and target nation. The average EMC tends to deploy a wide array of commercial and political contacts to facilitate business activities on behalf of clients.

Perhaps the only disadvantage to hiring an EMC is that the breadth and depth of its service can potentially hinder the development of the exporter's own international expertise. But an exporter and its EMC typically have such a close relationship that an exporter often considers its EMC as a virtual exporting division. When this is the case, exporters learn a great deal about the intricacies of exporting from their EMC. Then, after the EMC contract expires, it is common for a company to go it alone in exporting its products.

export trading company (ETC)
Company that provides services to indirect exporters in addition to those activities directly related to clients' exporting activities.

Export Trading Companies A company that provides services to indirect exporters in addition to those activities directly related to clients' exporting activities is called an **export trading company (ETC)**. Whereas an EMC is restricted to export-related activities, an ETC assists its clients by providing import, export, and countertrade services, developing and expanding distribution channels, providing storage facilities, financing trading and investment projects, and even manufacturing products.

European trading nations first developed the ETC concept centuries ago. More recently, the Japanese have refined the concept, which they call *sogo shosha*. The Japanese ETC can range in size from small, family-run businesses to enormous conglomerates such as C. Itoh, Mitsubishi, and Mitsui. The ETC in South Korea is called a *chaebol* and includes such well-known brands as Hyundai, Daewoo, and Samsung.

Because of their enormous success in gaining market share in global markets, Japanese and South Korean ETCs became formidable competitors. These Asian companies quickly came to rival the dominance of large multinationals based in the United States. The U.S. multinationals lobbied lawmakers in their home country for assistance in challenging the large ETCs from Asia in global markets. The result was the Export Trading Company Act passed in 1982. Despite this effort, the ETC concept never really caught on in the United States. Operations of the typical ETC in the United States remain small and are dwarfed by those of their Asian counterparts. One reason for lack of interest in the ETC concept in the United States relative to Asia is that governments, financial institutions, and companies have much closer working relationships in Asia. Thus the formation of huge conglomerates that engage in activities ranging from providing financing to manufacturing to distribution is easier to accomplish. In contrast, the regulatory environment in the United States is wary of such cozy business arrangements, and the lines between companies and industries are more clearly drawn.

AVOIDING EXPORT AND IMPORT BLUNDERS

Companies new to exporting often make several common errors. First, many fail to conduct adequate market research before exporting (see Chapter 11). In fact, many companies begin exporting by responding to unsolicited requests for their products. If a company enters a market in this manner, it should quickly devise an export strategy to manage its export activities effectively and not strain its resources.

Second, many companies fail to obtain adequate export advice. National and regional governments are often willing to assist firms that are new to exporting (again, see Chapter 11). Such sources can help managers and small-business owners understand and cope with the vast amounts of paperwork required by each country's exporting and importing laws. Naturally, more experienced exporters can be extremely helpful as well. They can help companies avoid embarrassing mistakes by guiding them through unfamiliar cultural, political, and economic environments.

To better ensure that it will not make embarrassing blunders, an inexperienced exporter might also wish to engage the services of a **freight forwarder**—a specialist in such export-related activities as customs clearing, tariff schedules, and shipping and insurance fees. Freight forwarders also can pack shipments for export and take responsibility for getting a shipment from the port of export to the port of import.

freight forwarder
Specialist in such export-related activities as customs clearing, tariff schedules, and shipping and insurance fees.

COUNTERTRADE

Companies are sometimes unable to import merchandise in exchange for financial payment. Two common reasons for this are that the government of the importer's nation lacks the hard currency to pay for imports, or because it restricts the convertibility of its currency. Fortunately, there is a way for firms to trade by using either a small amount of hard currency or even none at all. Selling goods or services that are paid for, in whole or part, with other goods or services is called **countertrade**. Although the effective use of countertrade often requires an extensive network of international contacts, even smaller companies can take advantage of its benefits.

Countertrade has been used extensively by formerly communist countries in eastern and central Europe since the 1960s. The governments of some nations in the Middle East and Africa also use countertrade. A lack of adequate hard currency has often forced those nations to employ countertrade to exchange oil for passenger aircraft and military equipment. Today, due to insufficient hard currency, developing and emerging markets frequently rely on countertrade to import goods. The greater involvement of firms from industrialized nations in those markets is causing the use of countertrade to increase.

countertrade
Practice of selling goods or services that are paid for, in whole or part, with other goods or services.

Types of Countertrade There are several different types of countertrade: *barter, counterpurchase, offset, switch trading,* and *buyback.* Let's take a brief look at each of these.

➡ **Barter** is the exchange of goods or services directly for other goods or services without the use of money. It is the oldest known form of countertrade.

➡ **Counterpurchase** is the sale of goods and services to a country by a company that promises to make a future purchase of a specific product from that country. The purpose of this type of agreement is to allow the country to earn back some of the currency that it paid out for the original imports.

barter
Exchange of goods or services directly for other goods or services without the use of money.

counterpurchase
Sale of goods and services to a country by a company that promises to make a future purchase of a specific product from the country.

offset
Agreement that a company will offset a hard-currency sale to a nation by making a hard-currency purchase of an unspecified product from that nation in the future.

switch trading
Practice in which one company sells to another its obligation to make a purchase in a given country.

buyback
Export of industrial equipment in return for products produced by that equipment.

➡ **Offset** is an agreement that a company will offset a hard-currency sale to a nation by making a hard-currency purchase of an unspecified product from that nation in the future. It differs from a counterpurchase in that this type of agreement does not specify the type of product that must be purchased, just the amount. Such an arrangement gives a firm greater freedom in fulfilling its end of a countertrade deal.

➡ **Switch trading** is countertrade whereby one company sells to another its obligation to make a purchase in a given country. For example, a firm wishing to enter a target market might promise to buy a product for which it has no use in return for market access. The company then sells this purchase obligation to a large trading company that may make the purchase itself because it has a use for the merchandise. Alternatively, if the trading company has no use for the merchandise, it can arrange for yet another buyer to make the purchase that has a use for the product.

➡ **Buyback** is the export of industrial equipment in return for products produced by that equipment. This practice usually typifies long-term relationships between the companies involved.

Thus countertrade can provide access to markets that are otherwise off-limits because of a lack of hard currency. But it can also cause a company a headache. The root cause is that much countertrade involves commodity and agricultural products such as oil, wheat, or corn—products whose prices on world markets tend to fluctuate a good deal. A problem arises when the price of a bartered product falls on world markets between the time that a deal is arranged and the time at which one party tries to sell the product. Thus fluctuating prices generate the same type of risk as encountered in currency markets. Managers might be able to hedge some of this risk on commodity futures markets in much the same way as they hedge against currency fluctuations in currency markets (see Chapter 9).

EXPORT/IMPORT FINANCING

International trade poses risks for both exporters and importers. Exporters run the risk of not receiving payment after their products are delivered. Importers fear that delivery might not occur once payment is made for a shipment. Accordingly, a number of export/import financing methods are designed to reduce the risk to which exporters and importers are exposed. These include *advance payment*, *documentary collection*, *letter of credit*, and *open account*. Let's take a closer look at each of these methods and the risk each holds for exporters and importers.

advance payment
Export/import financing in which an importer pays an exporter for merchandise before it is shipped.

Advance Payment   Export/import financing in which an importer pays an exporter for merchandise before it is shipped is called **advance payment.** This method of payment is common when two parties are unfamiliar with each other, the transaction is relatively small, or the buyer is unable to obtain credit due to a poor credit rating at banks. Payment normally takes the form of a wire transfer of money from the bank account of the importer directly to that of the exporter. Although prior payment eliminates the risk of nonpayment for exporters, it creates the complementary risk of nonshipment for importers—importers might pay for goods but never receive them. Thus advance payment is the most favorable method for exporters but the least favorable for importers (see Figure 13.1).

documentary collection
Export/import financing in which a bank acts as an intermediary without accepting financial risk.

Documentary Collection   Export/import financing in which a bank acts as an intermediary without accepting financial risk is called **documentary collection.** This payment method is commonly used when there is an ongoing business relationship be-

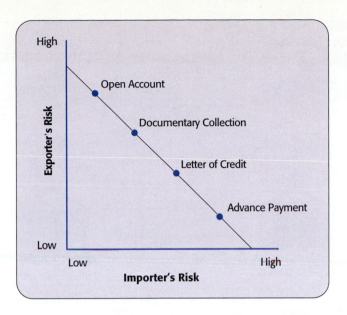

FIGURE 13.1

RISK OF ALTERNATIVE EXPORT/IMPORT FINANCING METHODS

tween two parties. The documentary-collection process can be broken into three main stages and nine smaller steps (see Figure 13.2 on page 452).

1. Before shipping merchandise, the exporter (with its banker's assistance) draws up a **draft** (or **bill of exchange**)—a document ordering the importer to pay the exporter a specified sum of money at a specified time. A *sight draft* requires the importer to pay when goods are delivered. A *time draft* extends the period of time (typically 30, 60, or 90 days) following delivery by which the importer must pay for the goods. (When inscribed "accepted" by an importer, a time draft becomes a negotiable instrument that can be traded among financial institutions.)

2. Following creation of the draft, the exporter delivers the merchandise to a transportation company for shipment to the importer. The exporter then delivers to its banker a set of documents that includes the draft, a *packing list* of items shipped, and a **bill of lading**—a contract between the exporter and shipper that specifies destination and shipping costs of the merchandise. The bill of lading is proof that the exporter has shipped the merchandise. An international ocean shipment requires an *inland bill of lading* to get the shipment to the exporter's border, and an *ocean bill of lading* for water transport to the importer nation. An international air shipment requires an *air way bill* that covers the entire international journey.

3. After receiving appropriate documents from the exporter, the exporter's bank sends the documents to the importer's bank. After the importer fulfills the terms stated on the draft and pays its own bank, the bank issues the bill of lading (which becomes title to the merchandise) to the importer.

Documentary collection reduces the importer's risk of nonshipment because the packing list details the contents of the shipment, and the bill of lading is proof that the merchandise was shipped. The exporter's risk of nonpayment is increased because although the exporter retains title to the goods until acceptance of the merchandise, the importer does not pay until he receives all necessary documents. Moreover, although importers have the option of refusing the draft (and, therefore, the merchandise), this action is unlikely. Refusing the draft—despite all terms of the agreement being fulfilled—would cause the importer's bank to be leery of doing business with the importer in the future.

> **draft** (or **bill of exchange**)
> *Document ordering an importer to pay an exporter a specified sum of money at a specified time.*

> **bill of lading**
> *Contract between an exporter and a shipper that specifies merchandise destination and shipping costs.*

FIGURE 13.2

DOCUMENTARY COLLECTION
PROCESS

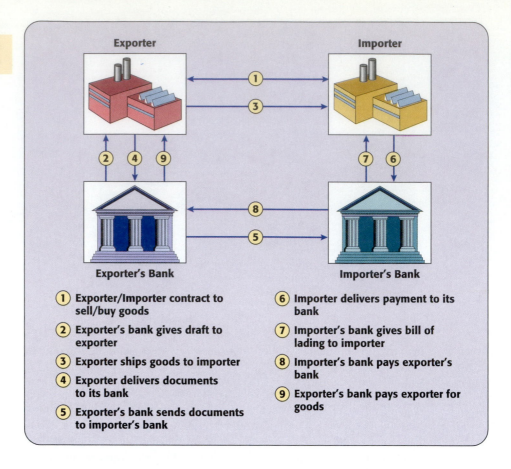

Exporter

Importer

Exporter's Bank

Importer's Bank

1. **Exporter/Importer contract to sell/buy goods**
2. **Exporter's bank gives draft to exporter**
3. **Exporter ships goods to importer**
4. **Exporter delivers documents to its bank**
5. **Exporter's bank sends documents to importer's bank**
6. **Importer delivers payment to its bank**
7. **Importer's bank gives bill of lading to importer**
8. **Importer's bank pays exporter's bank**
9. **Exporter's bank pays exporter for goods**

Letter of Credit   Export/import financing in which the importer's bank issues a document stating that the bank will pay the exporter when the exporter fulfills the terms of the document is called **letter of credit**. A letter of credit is typically used when an importer's credit rating is questionable, when the exporter needs a letter of credit to obtain financing, and when a market's regulations require it.

Before a bank issues a letter of credit, it checks on the importer's financial condition. Banks normally issue letters of credit only after an importer has deposited on account a sum equal in value to that of the imported merchandise. The bank is still required to pay the exporter, but the deposit protects the bank if the importer fails to pay for the merchandise. Banks will sometimes waive this requirement for their most reputable clients.

There are several types of letters of credit:

➡ An *irrevocable letter of credit* allows the bank issuing the letter to modify the terms of the letter only after obtaining the approval of both exporter and importer

➡ A *revocable letter of credit* can be modified by the issuing bank without obtaining approval from either the exporter or the importer

➡ A *confirmed letter of credit* is guaranteed by both the exporter's bank in the country of export and the importer's bank in the country of import

The letter of credit process for the payment of exports is shown in Figure 13.3. Following the issuance of a letter of credit, the importer's bank informs the exporter (through the exporter's bank) that a letter of credit exists and that it may now ship the

letter of credit

Export/import financing in which the importer's bank issues a document stating that the bank will pay the exporter when the exporter fulfills the terms of the document.

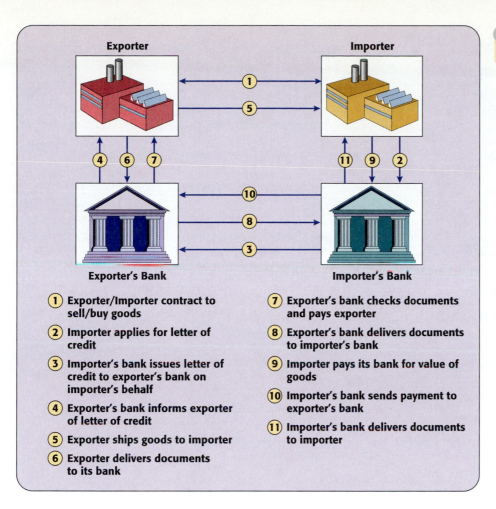

<figure>

FIGURE 13.3

LETTER OF CREDIT PROCESS

Exporter

Importer

Exporter's Bank

Importer's Bank

1. Exporter/Importer contract to sell/buy goods
2. Importer applies for letter of credit
3. Importer's bank issues letter of credit to exporter's bank on importer's behalf
4. Exporter's bank informs exporter of letter of credit
5. Exporter ships goods to importer
6. Exporter delivers documents to its bank
7. Exporter's bank checks documents and pays exporter
8. Exporter's bank delivers documents to importer's bank
9. Importer pays its bank for value of goods
10. Importer's bank sends payment to exporter's bank
11. Importer's bank delivers documents to importer

</figure>

merchandise. The exporter then delivers a set of documents (according to the terms of the letter) to its own bank. These documents typically include an invoice, customs forms, a packing list, and a bill of lading. The exporter's bank ensures that the documents are in order and pays the exporter.

When the importer's bank is satisfied that the terms of the letter have been met, it pays the exporter's bank. At that point, the importer's bank is responsible for collecting payment from the importer. Letters of credit are popular among traders because banks assume most of the risks. The letter of credit reduces the importer's risk of nonshipment (relative to advance payment) because the importer receives proof of shipment before making payment. Although the exporter's risk of nonpayment is slightly increased, it is a more secure form of payment for exporters because the nonpayment risk is accepted by the importer's bank when it issues payment to the exporter's bank.

Open Account Export/import financing in which an exporter ships merchandise and later bills the importer for its value is called **open account**. Because some receivables may not be collected, exporters should reserve shipping on open account only for their most trusted customers. This payment method is often used for sales between two subsidiaries within an international company and when the parties are very familiar with each other. The exporter simply invoices the importer (as in many domestic transactions), stating the amount and date due. This method reduces the risk of nonshipment that the importer faces under the advance payment method.

open account
Export/import financing in which an exporter ships merchandise and later bills the importer for its value.

Entrepreneurial Focus

Global Collection Guidelines

As Robbie Evans, president of Con-Tech International, says, "It doesn't do any good to make a sale if you don't get paid." Exporters should perform their due diligence in export deals and should always consider worst-case scenarios. They should also make sure that collection terms are clearly understood as an integral part of the sale. Below are several more pointers on how to arrange export deals to reduce the likelihood of not being paid.

➡ Know your market, its customary payment times for business debts, and its laws governing debt collections.

➡ Know which courts in that nation handle business debts. In some countries debt collections may take place in several different courts, depending upon the amounts involved.

➡ Have a clear understanding of payment terms built into your export sales agreements.

➡ Don't wait too long after shipment to begin collection efforts. Collection experts say they often see exporters wait a year or more to seek payment. Waiting too long may cause you to lose an opportunity to collect.

➡ If you find yourself with a bad debt on your hands, contact an international trade attorney, a global collection agency, or a collection agency in the debtor's country. If an arbitration process is available, be open to the idea. It could save time and money.

➡ If your customer wants to be cooperative but is having financial problems, consider stretching out the payment terms.

➡ Keep tabs on which parts of the globe are problem areas. Review journals, newsletters, and other news sources regularly so you can try to work around external events that may prevent a debtor from paying.

By the same token, the open account method increases the risk of nonpayment for the exporter. Thus, open account is the least favorable for exporters but the most favorable for importers. The Entrepreneurial Focus "Global Collection Guidelines" provides some insight on how small exporters can increase the probability of getting paid for a shipment.

CONTRACTUAL ENTRY MODES

The products of some companies simply cannot be traded in open markets because they are *intangible*. Thus a company can use neither importing, exporting, nor countertrade to exploit opportunities in a target market. Fortunately, there are other options for this type of company. A variety of contracts—*licensing, franchising, management contracts*, and *turnkey projects*—can be used to market highly specialized assets and skills in markets beyond its nations' borders. Let's examine each of these entry modes in detail.

LICENSING

licensing
Practice by which one company owning intangible property (the licensor*) grants another firm (the* licensee*) the right to use that property for a specified period of time.*

Companies sometimes grant other firms the right to use an asset that is essential to the production of a finished product. **Licensing** is a contractual entry mode in which a company owning intangible property (the *licensor*) grants another firm (the *licensee*) the right to use that property for a specified period of time. Licensors typically receive royalty payments based on a percentage of the licensee's sales revenue generated by the licensed property. The licensors might also receive a one-time fee to cover the cost of transferring the property to the licensee. Commonly licensed intangible property includes patents, copyrights, special formulas and designs, trademarks, and brand names. Thus licensing often involves granting companies the right to use *process technologies* inherent to the production of a particular good.

Here are a few examples of successful licensing agreements:

- Novell (United States) licenses its software to three Hong Kong universities that will install it as the campus-wide standard
- Hitachi (Japan) licenses from Duales System Deutschland (Germany) technology to be used in the recycling of plastics in Japan
- Hewlett-Packard (United States) licenses from Canon (Japan) a printer engine for use in its monochrome laser printers

An *exclusive* license grants a company exclusive rights to produce and market a property, or products made from that property, in a specific geographic region. The region can be the licensee's home country or may extend to worldwide markets. A *nonexclusive* license grants a company the right to use a property but does not grant it sole access to a market. Thus a licensor can grant several or more companies the right to use a property in the same region.

Cross licensing occurs when companies employ licensing agreements to swap intangible property with one another. In the early 1990s, for example, Fujitsu of Japan signed a five-year cross-licensing agreement with Texas Instruments of the United States. The agreement allowed each company to employ the other's technology in the production of its own goods—thus lowering R&D costs. It was a very extensive arrangement, covering all but a few semiconductor patents owned by each company.[4] Because asset values are seldom exactly equal, cross licensing also typically involves royalty payments from one party to the other.

cross licensing
Practice by which companies employ licensing agreements to exchange intangible property with one another.

Advantages of Licensing   There are several advantages to using licensing as an entry mode into new markets. First, licensors can use licensing to finance their international expansion. Most licensing agreements require licensees to contribute equipment and investment financing, whether by building special production facilities or by using existing excess capacity. Access to such resources can be a great advantage to a licensor who wants to expand but lacks the capital and managerial resources to do so. Moreover, because it need not spend time constructing and starting up its own new facilities, the licensor earns revenues sooner than it would otherwise.

Second, licensing can be a less risky method of international expansion for a licensor than other entry modes. For instance, whereas some markets are risky because of social or political unrest, others defy accurate market research for a variety of reasons (see Chapter 11). Licensing helps shield the licensor from the increased risk of operating its own local production facilities in unstable or hard-to-assess markets.

Third, licensing can help reduce the likelihood that a licensor's product will appear on the black market. The side streets of large cities in many emerging markets are dotted with tabletop vendors eager to sell bootleg versions of computer software, Hollywood films, and recordings of internationally popular musicians. Producers can, to some extent, foil black marketers by licensing local companies to market their products at locally competitive prices. Granted, royalties will be lower than profits generated by sales at higher international prices. But lower profits are obviously better than no profits at all—which is precisely what owners get from bootleg versions of their products.

Finally, licensees can also benefit from licensing by using it as a method of upgrading existing production technologies. For example, manufacturers of plastics and other synthetic materials in the Philippines are working to meet the high standards demanded by the local subsidiaries of Japanese electronics and office-equipment producers. Thus D&L Industries of the Philippines upgraded its manufacturing process by licensing materials technology from Nippon Pigment of Japan.[5]

Disadvantages of Licensing   There also are some important disadvantages to using licensing. First, it can restrict a licensor's future activities. Suppose, for example, that a licensee is granted the exclusive right to use an asset but fails to produce the sort of results that a licensor expected. Because the license agreement is exclusive, the licensor cannot simply begin selling directly in that particular market to meet demand itself or contract with another licensee. Thus a good product and lucrative market do not, in themselves, guarantee success for a producer trying to enter a market through the use of licensing.

Second, licensing might reduce the global consistency of the quality and marketing of a licensor's product in different national markets. A licensor might find the development of a coherent global brand image an elusive goal if each of its national licensees is allowed to operate in any manner it chooses. Promoting a global image might later require considerable amounts of time and money to change the misconceptions of buyers' in the various licensed markets.

Third, licensing might amount to a company "lending" strategically important property to its future competitors. This is an especially dangerous situation when a company licenses assets on which its competitive advantage is based. Licensing agreements are often made for several or more years (perhaps even a decade or more). During this time, licensees often become highly competent at producing and marketing the licensor's product. When the agreement expires, the licensor might find that its former licensee is capable of producing and marketing a better version of the product. Licensing contracts can (and should) restrict licensees from competing in the future with products based strictly on licensed property. Enforcement of such provisions, however, works only for identical or nearly identical products, not when substantial improvements are made.

FRANCHISING

A contractual entry mode in which one company (the *franchiser*) supplies another (the *franchisee*) with intangible property and other assistance over an extended period is called **franchising**. Franchisers typically receive compensation as flat fees, royalty payments, or both. The most popular franchises are those with widely recognized brand names such as Mercedes, McDonald's, and Holiday Inn. In fact, the brand name or trademark of a company is normally the single most important item desired by the franchisee. For this reason, smaller companies with lesser known brand names and trademarks have greater difficulty locating interested franchisees.

Franchising differs from licensing in several important ways. First, franchising gives a company greater control over the sale of its product in a target market. Franchisees must often meet strict guidelines on product quality, day-to-day management duties, and marketing promotions. Second, although licensing is fairly common in manufacturing industries, franchising is primarily used in service industries such as auto dealerships, entertainment, lodging, restaurants, and business services. Third, although licensing normally involves a one-time transfer of property, franchising requires ongoing assistance from the franchiser. In addition to the initial transfer of property, franchisers typically offer start-up capital, management training, location advice, and advertising assistance to their franchisees.

Some examples of the kinds of companies involved in international franchising include the following:

➡ Ozemail (Australia) awards Magictel (Hong Kong) a franchise to operate its Internet phone and fax service in Hong Kong

➡ Jean-Louis David (France) awards franchises to franchisees for more than 200 of its hairdressing salons in Italy

---

franchising
Practice by which one company (*the* franchiser) supplies another (the franchisee) *with intangible property and other assistance over an extended period.*

---

e·biz

➡ Brooks Brothers (U.S.) awards Dickson Concepts (Hong Kong) a franchise to operate Brooks Brothers stores across Southeast Asia.

Companies based in the United States dominate the world of international franchising. While U.S. companies were perfecting the practice of franchising (due to a large, homogeneous domestic market and low barriers to interstate trade and investment), most other markets remained small and dissimilar to one another. Franchising, however, is growing in the European Community with the advent of a unified currency and, as of 1999, a unified set of franchise laws. Many European managers with comfortable early-retirement packages have discovered franchising as an appealing second career. Franchising across much of Europe is expected to grow at between 10 percent and 15 percent per year through 2007.[6]

Despite projections for such robust growth, obstacles remain. For one thing, local European managers often misunderstand the franchising concept. For instance, Holiday Inn's Spanish franchise expansion is going more slowly than expected. According to the company's development director in Spain, Holiday Inn finds that it must convince local managers that the franchiser does not want to "take control" of their hotels.[7] In some eastern European countries, local managers do not understand why they must continue to pay royalties to brand and trademark owners. Franchise expansion in eastern European markets also suffers from a lack of local capital, high interest rates, high taxes, bureaucratic obstacles, restrictive laws, and corruption.[8]

Advantages of Franchising   There are several important advantages of franchising. First, franchisers can use franchising as a low-cost, low-risk mode of entry into new markets. In particular, companies following global strategies rely on consistent products and common themes in worldwide markets. Franchising allows them to maintain consistency by replicating the processes for standardized products in each target market. However, many franchisers make small modifications in products and promotional messages when marketing specifically to local buyers. But because franchisers exercise a high degree of control over operations, they do maintain consistency across national markets.

Second, franchising is an entry mode that allows for rapid geographic expansion. Firms often gain a competitive advantage by being first in seizing a market opportunity. For instance, Microtel Inns & Suites of Atlanta, Georgia, is using franchising to fuel its international expansion. Although it operates just 42 locations in the United States, Microtel is boldly entering Argentina and Uruguay and eyeing opportunities in Brazil and Western Europe. Rooms cost $50 to $60 per night and target business travelers who cannot afford $200.[9]

Finally, franchisers can profit from the cultural knowledge and know-how of local managers. This aspect of franchising is helpful both in lowering the risk of business failure in unfamiliar markets and in creating a competitive advantage.

Disadvantages of Franchising   Franchising can also pose problems for both franchisers and franchisees. First, franchisers may find it cumbersome to manage a large number of franchisees in a variety of national markets. A main concern is that product quality and promotional messages among franchisees will not be consistent from one market to another. One way to ensure greater control is by establishing in each market a so-called *master franchisee* that is responsible for monitoring the operations of individual franchisees.

Second, franchisees can experience a loss of organizational flexibility in franchising agreements. Franchise contracts can restrict their strategic and tactical options, and they may even be forced to promote products owned by the franchiser's other divisions. For example, for years PepsiCo owned the well-known restaurant chains Pizza

Hut, Taco Bell, and KFC. As part of their franchise agreements with PepsiCo, restaurant owners were required to sell only PepsiCo beverages to their customers. Many franchisees worldwide were displeased with such restrictions on their product offerings and were relieved when PepsiCo sold the restaurant chains.[10]

MANAGEMENT CONTRACTS

management contract
Practice by which one company supplies another with managerial expertise for a specific period of time.

Under the stipulations of a **management contract**, one company supplies another with managerial expertise for a specific period of time. The expertise supplier is normally compensated with either a lump-sum payment or a continuing fee based on sales volume. Such contracts are commonly found in the public utilities sectors of both developed and emerging markets.

Two types of knowledge can be transferred through management contracts—the specialized knowledge of technical managers and the business-management skills of general managers. BAA of Britain, for example, possesses general airport-management skills. In the United States, BAA operates the Indianapolis Airport under a 10-year management contract and provides retail management at the Air Mall in the Pittsburgh Airport.[11] Similarly, the Swedish-American drug manufacturer Pharmacia & Upjohn entered a 5-year, $55 million management contract for IBM Global Service expertise in making its computer systems "Year 2000" (or "Y2K") compliant.[12]

Other examples of management contracts include the following:

➡ DBS Asia (Thailand) awarded a management contract to Favorlangh Communication (Taiwan) to set up and run a company supplying digital television programming in Taiwan
➡ Lyonnaise de Eaux (France) and RWE Aqua (Germany) have agreed to manage drinking-water quality and client billing and to maintain the water infrastructure for the city of Budapest, Hungary, for 25 years

ADVANTAGES OF MANAGEMENT CONTRACTS Management contracts can benefit both organizations and countries. First, a firm can award a management contract to another company and thereby exploit an international business opportunity without having to place a great deal of its own physical assets at risk. Financial capital can then be reserved for other promising investment projects that would otherwise not be funded.

Second, governments can award companies management contracts to operate and upgrade public utilities, particularly when a nation is short of investment financing. Thus the government of the former Soviet republic Kazakhstan contracted with a group of international companies called ABB Power Grid Consortium to manage its national electricity-grid system for 25 years. Under the terms of the contract, the consortium paid past wages owed to workers by the government and is to invest more than $200 million in the first three years of the agreement. The Kazakhstan government had neither the cash flow to pay workers nor the funds to make badly needed improvements.[13]

Third, governments use management contracts to develop the skills of local workers and managers. ESB International of Ireland, for example, signed a three-year contract not only to manage and operate a power plant in Ghana, Africa, but also to train local personnel in the skills needed to manage it at some point in the future.[14]

Disadvantages of Management Contracts Unfortunately, management contracts also pose two important disadvantages for expertise suppliers. For one thing, although management contracts reduce the exposure of physical assets in another country, the same is not true for the supplier's personnel. International management contracts require that company managers relocate for given periods of time. In nations undergoing political or social turmoil, lives can be placed in significant danger.

Secondly, expertise suppliers may end up nurturing a formidable new competitor in the local market. After learning how to conduct certain operations, the party that had originally needed assistance may be in a position to compete with the providing firm. Obviously, firms must weigh the financial returns from a management contract against the potential future problems caused by a newly launched competitor.

TURNKEY PROJECTS

When one company designs, constructs, and tests a production facility for a client, the agreement is called a **turnkey** (or **build-operate-transfer**) **project**. The term *turnkey project* derives from the understanding that the client, who normally pays a flat fee for the project, is expected to do nothing more than simply "turn a key" to get the facility operating. The expression conveys the fact that the company awarded a turnkey project leaves absolutely nothing undone when preparing the facility for the client.

> **turnkey** (or **build-operate-transfer**) *project*
> *Practice by which one company designs, constructs, and tests a production facility for a client firm.*

Like management contracts, turnkey projects tend to be large-scale and often involve government agencies. Unlike management contracts, however, turnkey projects transfer special process technologies or production-facility designs to the client. They typically involve the construction of power plants, airports, seaports, telecommunication systems, and petrochemical facilities that are then turned over to the client. Under a management contract, the supplier of a service retains the asset—the managerial expertise.

Here are a few examples of international turnkey projects:

➡ Telecommunications Consultants India constructed telecom networks in both Madagascar and Ghana—two turnkey projects worth $28 million

➡ Webster Griffin (UK) installed $150,000 worth of cooking oil bagging machinery to fulfill its turnkey project with Palm-Oleo (Malaysia)

➡ Lubei Group (China) agreed with the government of Belarus to join in the construction of a facility for processing a fertilizer by-product into cement

e-biz

Advantages of Turnkey Projects   Turnkey projects provide benefits to both providers and recipients. First, turnkey projects permit firms to specialize in their core competencies and to exploit opportunities that they could not undertake alone. Mobil Exploration, for example, awarded a turnkey project to PT McDermott Indonesia and Toyo Engineering of Japan to build a liquid natural gas plant on the Indonesian island of Sumatra. The providers are responsible for constructing an offshore production platform, laying a 100-kilometer underwater pipeline, and building an on-land liquid natural gas refinery. The $316 million project is feasible only because each company will contribute unique expertise to the design, construction, and testing of the facilities.[15]

Second, turnkey projects allow governments to obtain designs for infrastructure projects from the world's leading companies. For instance, Turkey's government recently enlisted two separate consortiums of international firms to build four hydroelectric dams on its Coruh River. The dams combine the design and technological expertise of each company in the two consortiums.[16] The Turkish government has also awarded a turnkey project to Ericsson of Sweden to expand the country's mobile telecommunication system.[17]

e-biz

Disadvantages of Turnkey Projects   Among the disadvantages of turnkey projects is the fact that a company may be awarded a project for political reasons rather than for technological know-how. Because turnkey projects are often of high monetary

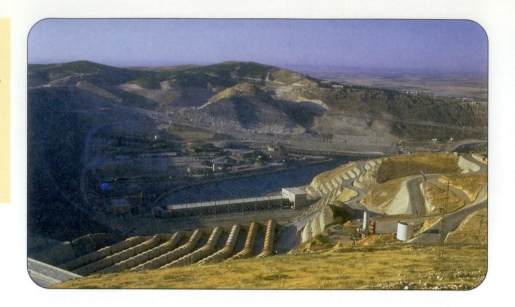

A turnkey project is a venture in which one organization designs, builds, and tests a production facility for another organization, which then merely "turns the key" to get the operation underway. This arrangement characterizes the building of four hydroelectric dams on Turkey's Çoruh River. The Turkish government benefited from the expertise of two international consortiums it hired to work on the project.

value and awarded by government agencies, the process of awarding them can be highly politicized. When the selection process is not entirely open, companies with the best political connections often win contracts, usually at inflated prices—the costs of which are typically passed on to local taxpayers.

Second, like management contracts, turnkey projects can create future competitors. A newly created local competitor could become a major supplier in its own domestic market and perhaps even in other markets in which the supplier operates. Companies therefore try to avoid projects in which they are in danger of transferring their core competencies to others.

INVESTMENT ENTRY MODES

The final category of entry modes is investment entry. Investment entry modes entail direct investment in plant and equipment in a country coupled with ongoing involvement in the local operation. Entry modes in this category take a company's commitment to a market to the next level. Let's now explore three common forms of investment entry: *wholly owned subsidiaries*, *joint ventures*, and *strategic alliances*.

WHOLLY OWNED SUBSIDIARIES

wholly owned subsidiary
Facility entirely owned and controlled by a single parent company.

As the term suggests, a **wholly owned subsidiary** is a facility entirely owned and controlled by a single parent company. Companies can establish a wholly owned subsidiary either by forming a new company from the ground up and constructing entirely new facilities (such as factories, offices, and equipment), or by purchasing an existing company and internalizing its existing facilities. Whether an international subsidiary is purchased or newly created depends to a large extent on its proposed operations. For example, when a parent company designs a subsidiary to manufacture the latest high-tech products, it typically must build new facilities because state-of-the-art operations are hard to locate. In other words, its easier to find companies in most target markets that make pots and pans rather than produce the most advanced computer chips. The major drawback of creation from the ground up is the time it takes to construct new facilities, hire and train employees, and launch production.

Conversely, finding an existing local company capable of performing marketing and sales will be easier because special technologies are typically not needed. By purchasing the existing marketing and sales operations of an existing firm in the target market, the parent can have the subsidiary operating relatively quickly. Buying an existing company's operations in the target market is a particularly good strategy when the company to be acquired has a valuable trademark, brand name, or process technology.

Advantages of Wholly Owned Subsidiaries   There are two main advantages to entering a market using a wholly owned subsidiary. First, managers have complete control over day-to-day operations in the target market and over access to valuable technologies, processes, and other intangible properties within the subsidiary. Complete control also decreases the chance for competitors to gain access to a company's competitive advantage—particularly important if it is technology-based. Managers also retain complete control over the subsidiary's output and prices. Unlike licensors and franchisers, the parent company also receives all profits generated by the subsidiary.

Second, a wholly owned subsidiary is a good mode of entry when a company wants to coordinate the activities of all its national subsidiaries. Companies employing global strategies (see Chapter 12) view each of their national markets as one part of an interconnected global market. Thus the ability to exercise complete control over a wholly owned subsidiary makes this entry mode attractive to companies pursuing global strategies.

Disadvantages of Wholly Owned Subsidiaries   Wholly owned subsidiaries also present two primary disadvantages. First, they can be expensive undertakings. Companies must finance investments internally or raise funds in financial markets. Obtaining the needed funding, therefore, can be difficult for small and medium-size companies. As a rule, only large companies are equipped to establish international wholly owned subsidiaries. However, citizens of one country living abroad in another country can find their unique knowledge and abilities an advantage.

Second, risk exposure is high because a wholly owned subsidiary requires substantial company resources. One source of risk is political or social uncertainty or outright instability in the target market. Such risks can place both physical assets and personnel in serious jeopardy. The sole owner of a wholly owned subsidiary also accepts all the risk that buyers will reject the company's product. Parent companies can reduce this risk by gaining a better understanding of target-market consumers prior to entry.

JOINT VENTURES

Under certain circumstances, companies prefer to share ownership of an operation rather than take complete ownership. A separate company that is created and jointly owned by two or more independent entities to achieve a common business objective is called a **joint venture**. Joint venture partners can be privately owned companies, government agencies, or government-owned companies. Each party may contribute anything valued by its partners, including managerial talent, marketing expertise, market access, production technologies, financial capital, and superior research and development knowledge or techniques.

Examples of joint ventures include:

➡ A joint venture between Suzuki Motor Corporation (Japan) and the government of India to manufacture a small-engine car specifically for the Indian market
➡ A joint venture between a group of Indian companies and a Russian partner to produce television sets in Russia for the local market

Wal-Mart is expanding into Germany by buying entire chains of stores that it will operate as wholly owned subsidiaries. In 1997, it bought the 21-store Wertkauf chain, which it will soon rename Wal-Mart, and in 1998 it purchased 74 Interspar "hypermarkets" with annual sales nearing $2 billion. Sales outside the United States accounted for close to 10 percent of Wal-Mart's revenues by the fall of 1998. Check out Wal-Mart's Web site at ⟨**www.wal-mart.com**⟩.

joint venture
Separate company that is created and jointly owned by two or more independent entities to achieve a common business objective.

➡ Biltrite Corporation (U.S.) and Shenzhen Petrochemical (China) created a shoe-soling factory as a joint venture in China to supply international shoe manufacturers located in China

Joint Venture Configurations   As you can see from Figure 13.4, there are four main joint venture configurations.[18] Although we illustrate each of these as consisting of just two partners, each configuration can also apply to ventures of several or more partners.

Forward Integration Joint Venture   Figure 13.4(a) outlines a joint venture characterized by *forward integration*. In this type of joint venture, the parties choose to invest together in *downstream* business activities—activities farther along within the "value system" that are normally performed by others. For instance, Hewlett-Packard and Apple Computer opening a retail outlet in a developing country would be a joint venture characterized by forward integration. The two companies now perform activities normally performed by retailers farther along in the product's journey to buyers.

Backward Integration Joint Venture   Figure 13.4(b) outlines a joint venture characterized by *backward integration*. In other words, the joint venture signals a move by each company into *upstream* business activities—activities earlier within the value sys-

FIGURE 13.4

ALTERNATIVE JOINT VENTURE CONFIGURATIONS

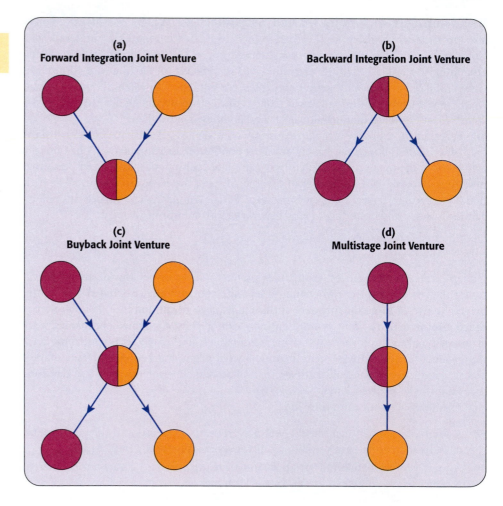

(a)
Forward Integration Joint Venture

(b)
Backward Integration Joint Venture

(c)
Buyback Joint Venture

(d)
Multistage Joint Venture

tem that are normally performed by others. Such a configuration would result if two steel manufacturers formed a joint venture to mine iron ore. The companies now engage in an activity that is normally performed by mining companies.

Buyback Joint Venture Figure 13.4(c) outlines a joint venture whose input is provided by, and whose output is absorbed by, each of its partners. A *buyback joint venture* is formed when each partner requires the same component in its production process. It might be formed when a production facility of a certain minimum size is needed to achieve economies of scale, but neither partner alone enjoys enough demand to warrant building it. By combining resources, however, the partners can construct a facility that serves their needs while achieving savings from economies of scale production. For instance, this is one reason behind the $500 million joint venture between Chrysler and BMW to build small-car engines in Latin America. Each party benefits from the economies of scale offered by the plant's annual production capacity of 400,000 engines—a volume that neither company could absorb alone.

Multistage Joint Venture Figure 13.4(d) outlines a joint venture that features downstream integration by one partner and upstream integration by another. A *multistage joint venture* often results when one company produces a good or service required by another. A sporting goods manufacturer, for example, might join with a sporting goods retailer to establish a distribution company designed to bypass inefficient local distributors in a developing country.

Advantages of Joint Ventures

Joint ventures offer several important advantages to companies going international. Above all, companies rely on joint ventures to reduce risk.[19] Generally, a joint venture exposes fewer of a partner's assets to risk than would a wholly owned subsidiary—each partner risks only its own contribution. Thus joint venture entry is particularly wise when market entry requires a large investment or when there is significant political or social instability in the target market. Similarly, a company can use a joint venture to learn about a local business environment prior to launching a wholly owned subsidiary.[20] In fact, many joint ventures are ultimately bought outright by one of the partners after it has gained sufficient expertise in the local market.

Second, companies can use joint ventures to penetrate international markets that are otherwise off-limits. For instance, some governments either require nonnative companies to share ownership with local companies, or provide incentives for them to do so.[21] Such requirements are most common among governments of developing countries. The goal is to improve the competitiveness of local companies by having them partner with, and learn from, their international partner(s).

Third, companies can gain access to another company's international distribution network through joint ventures. The joint venture between Caterpillar of the United States and Mitsubishi Heavy Industries of Japan was designed to improve the competitiveness of each against a common rival, Komatsu of Japan. While Caterpillar gained access to Mitsubishi's distribution system in Japan, Mitsubishi got access to Caterpillar's global distribution network—helping it compete more effectively internationally.[22]

Finally, companies form international joint ventures for defensive reasons. Entering a joint venture with a local government or government-controlled company gives the government a direct stake in the venture's success. In turn, the local government will be less likely to interfere if interference means that the venture's performance will suffer— thus sheltering the venture from government interference. This same strategy can also be used to create a more "local" image when feelings of nationalism are strong in a target country.

The ultimate joint venture is a *merger,* whereby two or more companies commit 100 percent of their assets to the formation of a new company. One of the biggest mergers of the century occurred in 1998, when Daimler-Benz chief executive Jürgen Schremp (left) and Chrysler Corp.'s CEO Robert Eaton announced the union of their two firms. The new German-U.S. company became the world's fifth-largest car maker, worth about $39 billion. Learn more about the merger at ⟨**www.daimler-benz.com**⟩.

Disadvantages of Joint Ventures   Among its disadvantages, joint venture ownership can result in conflict between partners. Conflict is perhaps most common when management is shared equally—that is, when each partner supplies top managers in what is commonly known as a "50–50 joint venture." Because neither partner's managers enjoy the final say on decisions, managerial paralysis can result, causing such problems as delays in responding to changing market conditions. Conflict can also arise from disagreements over how future investments and profits are to be shared. Parties can reduce the likelihood of conflict and indecision by establishing unequal ownership whereby one partner maintains 51 percent ownership of the voting stock and has the final say on decisions. A multiparty joint venture (commonly referred to as a *consortium*) can also feature unequal ownership. For example, ownership of a four-party joint venture could be distributed 20–20–20–40, with the 40 percent owner having the final say on corporate-wide decisions.

Second, loss of control over a joint venture's operations can also result when the local government is a partner in the joint venture. This situation occurs most often in industries considered culturally sensitive or important to national security such as broadcasting, infrastructure, and defense. Thus profitability of a joint venture could suffer because the local government would have motives that are based on cultural preservation or security.

STRATEGIC ALLIANCES

Sometimes companies who are willing to cooperate with one another do not wish to go so far as to create a separate jointly owned company. A relationship whereby two or more entities cooperate (but do not form a separate company) to achieve the strategic goals of each is called a **strategic alliance**. Like joint ventures, strategic alliances can be formed for relatively short periods or for many years, depending on the goals of the participants. Strategic alliances can be established between a company and its suppliers, its buyers, and even its competitors. In forming such alliances, it is common for each partner to purchase a portion of each of the others' stock. In this way, each company has a direct stake in the future performance of its partners. In turn, this stake decreases the likelihood that one partner will try to take advantage of the others.

strategic alliance
Relationship whereby two or more entities cooperate (but do not form a separate company) to achieve the strategic goals of each.

Examples of strategic alliances include:

- An alliance between Siemens (Germany) and Hewlett-Packard (United States) to create and market devices used to control telecommunications systems
- A strategic alliance between Nippon Life Group (Japan) and Putnam Investments (United States) to permit Putnam to develop investment products and manage assets for Nippon.

To see how aggressively companies are employing strategic alliances (along with joint ventures and wholly owned subsidiaries), we need only look at the global entertainment industry. Figure 13.5 on page 466 shows the myriad cross-holdings between the main global players in this industry. For instance, Bertelsmann, a Germany-based company, owns 50 percent of Barnesandnoble.com, the Internet sales company spun off from the well-known bookseller Barnes and Noble. Sony and Rupert Murdoch's News Corp each own a piece of SkyPerfecTV. We also see that global powerhouse Time Warner owns a small piece of Canal Satellite, of which French television company Canal+ (pronounced Canal "plus") owns 90 percent.

Advantages of Strategic Alliances   Strategic alliances offer several important advantages to companies. First, companies use strategic alliances to share the cost of an international investment project. Many firms, for example, are increasingly developing new products that not only integrate the latest technologies but also shorten the life spans of existing products. In turn, the shorter product life span is reducing the number of years during which a company can recoup its investment. Thus many companies are cooperating to share the costs of developing new products. For example, Toshiba of Japan, Siemens of Germany, and IBM of the United States shared the $1 billion cost of developing a facility near Nagoya, Japan, to manufacture small, efficient computer memory chips.[23]

Second, companies use strategic alliances to tap into competitors' specific strengths. A recently announced alliance between Microsoft and Liquid Audio is designed to do just that: Whereas Microsoft provides access to a large, global audience through its Web site, Liquid Audio supplies its know-how in delivering music over the Internet. Meeting the goals of the alliance—marketing music over the Web and developing industry standards for on-line previewing and purchasing of music—requires the competencies of both partners.[24]

Finally, companies turn to strategic alliances for many of the same reasons that they turn to joint ventures. Some use strategic alliances to gain access to a partner's channels of distribution in a target market. Others use them to reduce exposure to the same kinds of risks from which joint ventures provide protection.

Disadvantages of Strategic Alliances   Perhaps the most important disadvantage of a strategic alliance is that it can create a future local or even global competitor. One partner, for example, might be using the alliance to test a market and prepare the launch of a wholly owned subsidiary. By declining to cooperate with others in the area of its core competency, a company can reduce the likelihood of creating a competitor that would threaten its main area of business. Likewise, a company can insist on contractual clauses that constrain partners from competing against it in certain products or geographic regions. Firms are also careful to protect special research programs, production techniques, and marketing practices that are not committed to the alliance. Naturally, managers must weigh the potential for encouraging new competition against the benefits of international cooperation.

As in the case of joint ventures, conflict can arise and eventually undermine cooperation. As a rule, then, alliance contracts are drawn up to cover as many such contin-

FIGURE 13.5

CROSS-HOLDINGS IN THE GLOBAL ENTERTAINMENT INDUSTRY

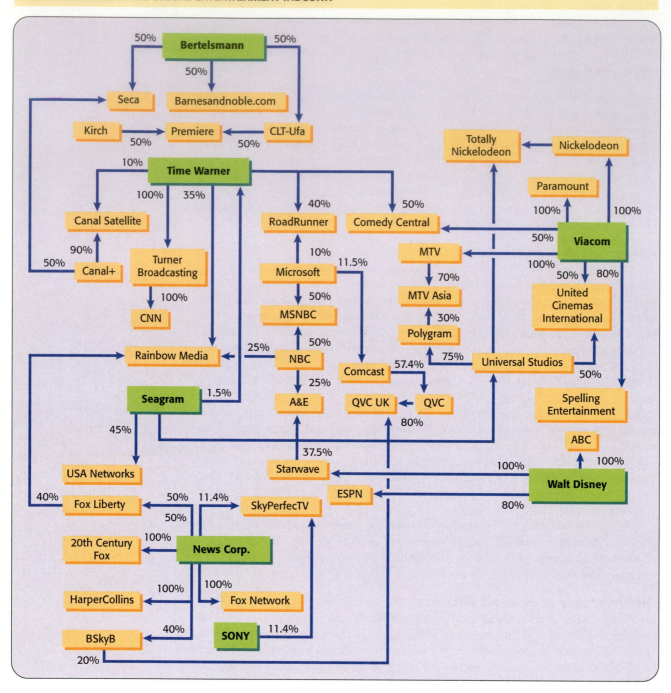

gencies as possible. Even so, communication and cultural differences can arise. As Tsuyoski Kawanishi, Toshiba director and senior executive vice president for partnerships and alliances, explains, "Each pact includes the equivalent of a prenuptial agreement, so both sides know who gets what if the partnership doesn't work out. During the honeymoon time, everything is great. But as you know, divorce is always a possibility, and that's when things can get bitter."[25]

SELECTING PARTNERS FOR COOPERATION

Every company's goals and strategies are influenced by both its competitive strengths and the challenges that it faces in the marketplace. Because the goals and strategies of any two companies are never exactly alike, cooperation can be difficult. Moreover, ventures and alliances often last many years, perhaps even indefinitely. Partner selection, therefore, is a crucial ingredient of success. The following discussion focuses on partner selection in joint ventures and strategic alliances. Many of the same points, however, also apply to such contractual entry modes as licensing and franchising, in which choosing the right partner is also important.

Every partner must be firmly committed to the goals of the cooperative arrangement. Many companies engage in cooperative forms of business, but the reasons behind each party's participation are never identical. Sometimes, a company stops contributing to a cooperative arrangement once it achieves its own objectives. Thus detailing the precise duties and contributions of each party to an international cooperative arrangement through prior negotiations can go a long way toward ensuring continued cooperation. See the Global Manager "Negotiating the Terms of Market Entry" for some important considerations in negotiating international agreements.

Global Manager

Negotiating the Terms of Market Entry

Exporters, importers, agents, distributors, freight forwarders, export management companies, and joint venture and strategic alliance partners must each negotiate the terms of their international business agreements. A cooperative atmosphere between partners to an international arrangement depends on both parties viewing contract negotiations as a success. The negotiation process normally occurs in four stages.

Stage 1: Preparation   Negotiators must develop a clear vision of what the company wants to achieve. For instance, is the proposed business arrangement a one-time technology transfer to a local company or the first phase of a long-term relationship?

Stage 2: Launch of Discussions   Discussions begin by each side stating its opening position—the most favorable terms for itself. Parties might state their positions immediately or make them known gradually so as to leave themselves room to modify their position.

Stage 3: Bargaining and Persuasion   The *bargaining power* of each party plays an important role in the final outcome of negotiations. Although this is the stage where direct conflict is most likely, cultures differ in their attitudes toward conflict. For instance, Chinese negotiators try to avoid conflict more than Canadians do. But if conflict erupts the Chinese are more likely to pursue negative strategies including calling off talks.

Stage 4: Agreement   Negotiations reaching this stage are a success. Negotiators from Western cultures view the signing of contracts as the end of negotiations. Yet in most Asian cultures it signals the beginning of a long-term working relationship; terms can be modified as the relationship matures and circumstances change.

Two key elements influence international business negotiations:

Cultural Elements   Negotiating styles differ from one culture to another. Negotiating in Asian cultures revolves around protecting the other party from *losing face* (being embarrassed or shamed). Thus "victory" normally means that each party gives equal ground and meets the other halfway. In most Western cultures negotiators typically hope to gain as many concessions as possible with little concern for whether the other party appears to have "lost" the negotiations.

Political and Legal Elements   Negotiators must be aware of any political motives underlying their counterparts' strategy. An inflexible public posture, for example, might simply be a ploy to show company or government officials back home that they are working first and foremost in the company's or nation's interest. Also, consumer groups, labor unions, and even stockholders can influence the outcome of a firm's negotiations. If consumer groups feel that a proposed arrangement will increase prices or restrict product choice, they might lobby government officials to kill the deal.

Although the importance of locating a trustworthy partner seems obvious, cooperation should be approached with caution. Companies can have hidden reasons for cooperating. Sometimes they try to acquire more from cooperation than their partners realize. If a hidden agenda is discovered during the course of cooperation, trust can break down—in which case the cooperative arrangement is virtually destroyed. Because trust is so important, firms naturally prefer partners with whom they have had a favorable working relationship in the past. Such arrangements, however, are much easier for large multinationals than for small and medium-size companies with little international experience and few international contacts.

Each party's managers must be comfortable working with people of other cultures and traveling to (even perhaps living in) other cultures. As a result, cooperation will go more smoothly and the transition—both in work life and personal life—will be easier for those managers who are sent to work for a joint venture. Each partner's managers should also be comfortable working with, and within, one another's corporate culture. For example, although some companies encourage the participation of subordinates in decision making, others do not. Such differences often reflect differences in national culture, and when managers possess cultural understanding, adjustment and cooperation is likely to run more smoothly.[26]

Above all, a suitable partner must have something valuable to offer. Firms should avoid cooperation simply because they are approached by another company. Rather, managers must be certain that they are getting a fair return on their cooperative efforts. In short, they must evaluate the benefits of a potential international cooperative arrangement just as they would any other investment opportunity.

STRATEGIC FACTORS IN SELECTING AN ENTRY MODE

The choice of entry mode has many important strategic implications for a company's future operations.[27] Because enormous investments in time and money can go into determining an entry mode, the choice must be made quite carefully. Several key factors that influence a company's international entry mode selection are the *cultural environment, political and legal environments, market size, production and shipping costs,* and *international experience.* Let's now explore each of these factors in-depth.

CULTURAL ENVIRONMENT

As we saw in Chapter 2, the dimensions of culture—values, beliefs, customs, languages, religions—can differ greatly from one nation to another. In such cases, managers are typically less confident in their ability to manage operations in the host country. Not surprisingly, they are concerned about the potential for not only communication problems but also interpersonal difficulties. As a result, they may avoid investment entry modes in favor of exporting or a contractual mode. On the other hand, cultural similarity encourages manager confidence and thus the likelihood of investment. Likewise, the importance of cultural differences diminishes when managers are knowledgeable about the culture of the target market.[28]

POLITICAL AND LEGAL ENVIRONMENTS

As mentioned earlier in this chapter, political instability in a target market increases the risk exposure of investments. Thus significant political differences and levels of instability cause companies to avoid large investments and favor entry modes that shelter assets.

Political considerations and a long-standing U.S. embargo on trade with Cuba are keeping U.S. businesses out of the Caribbean island. Meanwhile, European firms are making profitable investments there, such as the Spanish Sol Melia hotel chain, whose eleventh Cuban resort hotel has just opened. Some U.S. firms want to do business in Cuba because they hope to recover losses suffered in other markets such as Asia, because they are taking a stand against all trade sanctions worldwide, or because no other country has observed the more than 30-year-old embargo on Cuba.

A target market's legal system also influences the choice of entry mode. For example, certain import regulations such as high tariffs or low quota limits can encourage investment: A company producing locally avoids tariffs that increase product cost and does not have to worry about making it into the market below the quota (if there is one). But low tariffs and high quota limits discourage investment. Also, governments may enact laws that ban certain types of investment outright. For many years (though no longer), China banned wholly owned subsidiaries by non-Chinese companies and required that they form joint ventures with local partners. Finally, because investment entry often gives a company greater control over assets and marketing, firms tend to prefer investment when a market is lax in enforcing copyright and patent laws.

MARKET SIZE

The size of a potential market also influences the choice of entry mode. For example, rising incomes in a market encourage investment entry modes because investment allows a firm to prepare for expanding market demand and to increase its understanding of the target market. Thus high domestic demand in China is attracting investment in joint ventures, strategic alliances, and wholly owned subsidiaries. On the other hand, if investors believe that a market is likely to remain relatively small, better options might include exporting or contractual entry.

PRODUCTION AND SHIPPING COSTS

By helping to control total costs, low-cost production and shipping can give a company an advantage. Accordingly, setting up production in a market is desirable when the total cost of production there is lower than in the home market. Low-cost local production might also encourage contractual entry through licensing or franchising. If production costs are sufficiently low, the international production site might even begin supplying other markets, including the home country. An additional potential benefit of local production might be that managers observe buyer behavior and modify products to be better suited to the needs of the local market. Lower production costs at home makes exporting to international markets more appealing.

Naturally, companies producing products with high shipping costs typically prefer local production. Contractual and investment entry modes are viable options in this case. Alternatively, exporting is feasible when products have relatively lower shipping costs. Finally, because they are subject to less price competition, products for which there are fewer substitutes or those that are discretionary items can more easily absorb higher shipping and production costs. In this case exporting is a likely selection.

INTERNATIONAL EXPERIENCE

By way of summary, Figure 13.6 illustrates the control, risk, and experience relationships of each entry mode. Most companies enter the international marketplace through exporting. As companies gain international experience, they will tend to select entry modes that require deeper involvement. But this means that they must accept greater risk in return for greater control over operations and strategy. Eventually, they may explore the advantages of licensing, franchising, management contracts, and turnkey projects. Once they become comfortable in a particular market, joint ventures, strategic alliances, and wholly owned subsidiaries become viable options.

Bear in mind, however, that this evolutionary path of accepting greater risk and control with experience does not hold for every company. Whereas some firms remain fixed at one point, others skip several entry modes altogether. In particular, advances in technology and transportation are allowing more and more small companies to leapfrog several stages at once. These relationships will also vary for each company depending on its product and the relevant characteristics of the home and target markets.

FIGURE 13.6

EVOLUTION OF THE ENTRY MODE DECISION

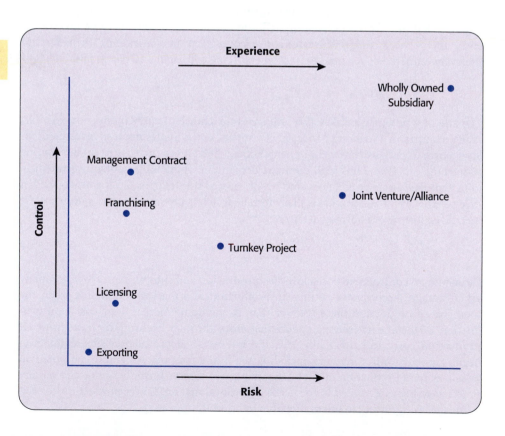

This chapter explained the important factors in selecting entry modes and key aspects in their management. We studied the circumstances under which each entry mode is most appropriate and the advantages and disadvantages that each provides. The choice of which entry mode(s) to use in entering international markets flows from a company's international strategy. Some companies will want entry modes that give them tight control over international activities because they are pursuing a global strategy, for example. Meanwhile, another company might not require an entry mode with central control because it is pursuing a multinational strategy. The entry mode must also be chosen to align well with an organization's structure.

As we progress through our study of international business management, we are beginning to see how the pieces of the puzzle fit together. Companies must identify and analyze their international opportunities, create strategies and organizational structures to help them reach their goals, and select entry modes that are best suited to their opportunities, strategies, and structures. In the next chapter, we continue our study of the process of "going international" by exploring how companies acquire the business resources they need to conduct their international operations.

There is a variety of additional material available on the companion Web site that accompanies this text. You can access this information by visiting the Web site at ⟨**www.prenhall.com/wild**⟩.

summary

1 **Explain why and how companies use *exporting, importing,* and *countertrade*.** *Exporting* is the act of sending goods and services from one nation to others, and *importing* is the act of bringing goods and services into a country from other countries.

Generally speaking, there are three main reasons why companies begin exporting: (a) *To expand sales:* Most large companies use exporting as a means of expanding total sales when the domestic market has become saturated. (b) *To diversify sales:* Exporting permits companies to offset slow sales in one national market with increased sales in another. (c) *To gain experience:* Companies often use exporting as a low-cost, low-risk way of getting started in international business.

A successful export strategy involves four steps: (a) *Identify a potential market:* In order to identify clearly whether demand exists in a particular target market, market research should be performed and results interpreted. (b) *Match needs to abilities:* The next step is to assess carefully whether the company has the ability to satisfy the needs of the market. (c) *Initiate meetings:* Having meetings early with potential local distributors, buyers, and others is a

must. Initial contact should focus on building trust and successive meetings are designed to estimate the potential success of any agreement if interest is shown on both sides. (d) *Commit resources:* After all the meetings, negotiations, and contract signings, it is time to put the company's human, financial, and physical resources to work.

Not all companies get involved in exporting activities to the same extent. There are two basic forms of export involvement. *Direct exporting* occurs when a company sells its products directly to buyers in a target market. Typically, they rely on either local *sales representatives* (who represent only their own company's products, not those of other companies) or *distributors* (who take ownership of merchandise when it enters their countries).

Indirect exporting occurs when a company sells its products to intermediaries who then resell to buyers in a target market. There are three general types of intermediaries: *agents* (individuals or organizations that represent one or more indirect exporters in a target market); *export management companies* (firms that export products on behalf of indirect exporters); and *export trading companies* (firms that provide services to indirect exporters in addition to those activities directly related to clients' exporting activities).

Companies are sometimes unable to import merchandise in exchange for financial payment. Selling goods or services that are paid for, in whole or part, with other goods or services is called *countertrade*. There are several different types of countertrade: (a) *barter*—the exchange of goods or services directly for other goods or services without the use of money; (b) *counterpurchase*—the sale of goods and services to a country by a company that promises to make a future purchase of a specific product from that country; (c) *offset*—an agreement that a company will offset a hard-currency sale to a nation by making a hard-currency purchase of an unspecified product from that nation in the future; (d) *switch trading*—countertrade whereby one company sells to another its obligation to make a purchase in a given country; (e) *buyback*—the export of industrial equipment in return for products produced by that equipment.

2 **Explain the various *means of financing* export and import activities.** A number of export/import financing methods are designed to reduce the risk to which exporters and importers are exposed. With *advance payment*, an importer pays an exporter for merchandise before it is shipped. *Documentary collection* calls for a bank to act as an intermediary without accepting financial risk. This process typically entails three steps: (a) Before shipping merchandise, the exporter (with its banker's assistance) draws up a *draft* (or *bill of exchange)*—a document ordering the importer to pay the exporter a specified sum of money at a specified time. (b) Following creation of the draft, the exporter delivers the merchandise to a transportation company for shipment to the importer. The exporter then delivers to its banker a set of documents that includes the draft, a *packing list* of items shipped, and a *bill of lading*—a contract between the exporter and shipper that specifies destination and shipping costs of the merchandise. (c) After receiving appropriate documents from the exporter, the exporter's bank sends the documents to the importer's bank. After the importer fulfills the terms stated on the draft and pays its own bank, the bank issues the bill of lading (which becomes title to the merchandise) to the importer.

Under a *letter of credit*, the importer's bank issues a document stating that the bank will pay the exporter when the exporter fulfills the terms of the document. There are several types of letters of credit. An *irrevocable letter of credit* allows the bank issuing the letter to modify the terms of the letter only after obtaining the approval of both exporter and importer. A *revocable letter of credit* can be modified by the issuing bank without obtaining approval from either the exporter or the importer. A *confirmed letter of credit* is guaranteed by both the exporter's bank in the country of export and the importer's bank in the country of import.

Finally, under *open account*, an exporter ships merchandise and later bills the importer for its value.

3 **Identify the different *contractual entry modes* and discuss the pros and cons of each.** The products of some companies simply cannot be traded in open markets because they are *intangible*. *Licensing* is a contractual entry mode in which a company owning intangible property (the *licensor*) grants another firm (the *licensee*) the right to use that property for a specified period of time. An *exclusive* license grants a company exclusive rights to produce and market a property, or products made from that property, in a specific geographic region. A *nonexclusive* license grants a company the right to use a property but does not grant it sole access to a market. *Cross licensing* occurs when companies employ licensing agreements to swap intangible property with one another.

There are several advantages to using licensing: (a) Licensors can use licensing to finance international expansion. (b) Licensing can be a less risky method of international expansion for a licensor than other entry modes. (c) Licensing can help reduce the likelihood that a licensor's product will appear on the black market. (d) Licensees can also benefit from licensing by using it as a method of upgrading existing production technologies. There also are some important disadvantages to using licensing: (a) It can restrict a licensor's future activities. (b) It might reduce the global consistency of the quality and marketing of a licensor's product in different national markets. (c) It might amount to "lending" strategically important property to one's future competitors.

A contractual entry mode in which one company (the *franchiser*) supplies another (the *franchisee*) with intangible property and other assistance over an extended period is called *franchising*.

There are several important advantages of franchising: (a) Franchisers can use franchising as a low-cost, low-risk mode of entry into new markets. (b) Franchising as an entry mode allows for rapid geographic expansion. (c) Franchisers can profit from the cultural knowledge and know-how of local managers. Franchising can also pose problems for both franchisers and franchisees: (a) Franchisers may find it cumbersome to manage a large number of franchisees in variety of national markets. (b) Franchisees can experience a loss of organizational flexibility in franchising agreements.

Under the stipulations of a *management contract*, one company supplies another with managerial expertise for a specific period of time. Two types of knowledge can be transferred through management contracts—the specialized knowledge of technical managers and the business-management skills of general managers. Management contracts can benefit both organizations and countries: (a) A firm can award a management contract to another company and thereby exploit an international business opportunity without having to place a great deal of its own physical assets at risk. (b) Governments can award companies with management contracts to operate and upgrade public utilities. (c) Governments use management contracts to develop the skills of local workers and managers. Unfortunately, management contracts also pose two important disadvantages for expertise suppliers: (a) Although management contracts reduce the exposure of physical assets in another country, the same is not true for the supplier's personnel. (b) Expertise suppliers may end up nurturing a formidable new competitor in the local market.

When one company designs, constructs, and tests a production facility for a client, the agreement is called a *turnkey* (or *build-operate-transfer*) *project.* Turnkey projects ordinarily benefit both providers and recipients. Turnkey projects permit firms to specialize in their core competencies and to exploit opportunities that they could not undertake alone. They allow governments to obtain designs for infrastructure projects from the world's leading companies. And of course, there are disadvantages: (a) A company may be awarded a project for political reasons rather than for technological know-how. Because turnkey projects are often of high monetary value and awarded by government agencies, the process of awarding them can be highly politicized. (b) Like management contracts, turnkey projects can create future competitors.

④ Explain the various types of *investment entry modes.* *Investment entry modes* entail the direct investment in plant and equipment in a country coupled with ongoing involvement in the local operation. A *wholly owned subsidiary* is a facility entirely owned and controlled by a single parent company.

There are two main advantages to entering a market using a wholly owned subsidiary: (a) Managers have complete control over day-to-day operations in the target market and over access to valuable technologies, processes, and other intangible properties within the subsidiary. (b) A wholly owned subsidiary is a good mode of entry when a company wants to coordinate the activities of all its national subsidiaries. Wholly owned subsidiaries also present two primary disadvantages: (a) They can be expensive undertakings; and (b) risk exposure is high because a wholly owned subsidiary requires substantial company resources.

Under certain circumstances, companies prefer to share ownership of an operation rather than take complete ownership. A separate company that is created and jointly owned by two or more independent entities to achieve a common business objective is called a *joint venture.* There are four main joint venture configurations. In a joint venture characterized by *forward integration*, the parties choose to invest together in *downstream* business activities—activities farther along within the value system that are normally performed by others. A joint venture characterized by *backward integration* signals a move by each company into *upstream* business activities—activities earlier within the value system that are normally performed by others. A *buyback joint venture* is one whose input is provided by, and whose output is absorbed by, each of its partners. A *multistage joint venture* features downstream integration by one partner and upstream integration by another.

Joint ventures offer several important advantages to companies going international: (a) Generally, a joint venture exposes fewer of a partner's assets to risk than would a wholly owned subsidiary—each partner risks only its own contribution. (b) Companies can use joint ventures to penetrate international markets that are otherwise off-limits. (c) Companies can gain access to another company's international distribution network through joint ventures. (d) Companies form international joint ventures for defensive reasons. Among its disadvantages, joint venture ownership can result in conflict between partners and a loss of control over the venture's operations.

A relationship whereby two or more entities cooperate (but do not form a separate company) to achieve the strategic goals of each is called a *strategic alliance.* Strategic alliances offer several important advantages to companies: (a) Companies use strategic alliances to share the cost of an international investment project. (b) Companies use strategic alliances to tap into competitors' specific strengths. (c) Companies use strategic alliances to gain access to a partner's channels of distribution in a target market. The most important disadvantage of a strategic alliance is that it can create a future local or even global competitor.

5 **Discuss the important strategic factors in selecting an entry mode.** The key factors that influence a company's international entry mode selection are the *cultural environment*, *political and legal environments*, *market size*, *production and shipping costs*, and *international experience*.

Dimensions of culture can differ greatly from one nation to another. In such cases, managers are typically less confident in their ability to manage operations in the host country and may avoid investment entry modes in favor of exporting or a contractual mode. On the other hand, cultural similarity encourages manager confidence and thus the likelihood of investment. Likewise, political differences and levels of instability cause companies to avoid large investments and favor entry modes that shelter assets.

The size of a potential market also influences the choice of entry mode. For example, rising incomes in

a market encourage investment entry modes because investment allows a firm to prepare for expanding market demand and to increase its understanding of the target market. If they help to control total costs, low-cost production and shipping can be a factor. Setting up production in a market is desirable when the total cost of production there is lower than in the home market. Naturally, companies producing products with high shipping costs typically prefer local production. Contractual and investment entry modes are viable options in this case. Alternatively, exporting is feasible when products have relatively lower shipping costs.

Finally, most companies make their initial foray into the international marketplace through exporting. As companies gain international experience, they will tend to select entry modes that require deeper involvement. But this means that they must accept greater risk in return for greater control over operations and strategy. Eventually, they may explore the advantages of licensing, franchising, management contracts, and turnkey projects—depending on their products. Once they become comfortable in a particular market, joint ventures, strategic alliances, and wholly owned subsidiaries become viable options.

questions for review

1. Identify the three categories of *entry mode* available to companies. Explain how they differ from one another.

2. What are the four steps of building an export strategy? Describe each briefly.

3. How does *direct exporting* differ from *indirect exporting*?

4. Explain how *export management companies* (*EMCs*) differ from *export trading companies* (*ETCs*).

5. What are the four primary methods of *export/import financing*? Discuss the risks each poses for exporters and importers.

6. Why do companies engage in *countertrade*? List the five kinds of countertrade.

7. What is *licensing*? Identify the advantages and disadvantages of licensing.

8. Define *franchising*. How does *franchising* differ from *licensing*?

9. What is a *management contract*? Identify the two types of knowledge transferred using management contracts.

10. Explain how *turnkey projects* differ from management contracts.

11. What is a *wholly owned subsidiary*? State its advantages and disadvantages.

12. What is a *joint venture*? Identify the four joint venture configurations.

13. Explain how *strategic alliances* differ from joint ventures.

14. List several points to consider when selecting a partner for cooperation.

15. What strategic factors should be considered when selecting an entry mode? Discuss each briefly.

questions for discussion

1. Not all companies "go international" by exporting, then using contracts, and then investing in other markets. How does a company's product influence the process of going international? How are the Internet and World Wide Web affecting the process of going international?

2. "Companies should use investment entry modes whenever possible because they offer the greatest control over business operations." Do you agree or disagree with this statement? Are there times when other types of market entry offer greater control? When is investment entry a poor option?

3. In earlier chapters, we learned how governments get involved in the international flow of trade and foreign direct investment. We also learned how regional economic integration is influencing international business. Identify two market entry modes and describe how each might be affected both by the actions of governments and by increasing regionalism.

in practice

Read the following brief article and answer the questions that follow.

Sharing the Pain

Chief executives from American Airlines, British Airways, Canadian Airlines, Cathay Pacific, and Qantas were in London to announce a new marketing alliance dubbed "oneworld." Says Anthony Tyler, director of corporate development for Cathay Pacific, "There's no future for an airline that's non-aligned."

Each airline in oneworld acknowledges the necessity of joining a network. Global alliances give members added marketing strengths. They can offer passengers a "seamless" route network that enables them to complete a journey on several airlines with a single ticket. As a group, the airlines can offer passengers flights to 632 destinations in 138 countries. Although the companies did not take equity ownership in one another, significant cross-holdings already exist: For instance, British Airways owns 25 percent of Qantas.

But the demands of the major European and American airlines for quality partners have as much to do about matching commercial culture as anything else. Because many Asian airlines are government controlled, they must keep operating whether or not they are making a profit. For this reason, such airlines are far less appealing partners than completely private ones. Says, David Sherman, a vice president with management consulting firm A.T. Kearney, "If your airline is not being operated for commercial purposes, its more difficult to join alliances."

1. Locate an article or two in the business press that discusses the economics of the airlines industry today. What is it that is encouraging cooperation among the major carriers? Are there any special reasons why airlines in Asia were interested in cooperating in the late 1990s?

2. The article states that the airlines are creating a marketing alliance. What marketing benefits do you think the airlines will obtain by cooperating? List as many possibilities as you can.

3. The article mentions the difficulty of government-controlled airlines in becoming part of an alliance. Why do you think this is so? Does the private airlines' hesitation have to do with organizational culture? Or is it something else?

4. What potential problems do you think the alliance could face in the future? Consider profitability, organizational culture, and national culture in your response.

projects

1. Make a list of five goods or services that you have consumed within the past week (this list might include a food product, an Internet service, a television program, etc.). For the company producing each product, which entry modes are possible options for entering new markets? Provide a one- to two-paragraph explanation of your answer for each good or service.

2. With several of your classmates, interview a manager of a company involved in international business. What method did the company use to go international initially? Which entry modes is the company currently using? Does the company export? If so, is it a direct or an indirect exporter? How does the company receive payment for its goods? Does the company use different entry modes in different markets? What factors influenced its choice of entry mode in each case? How do managers deal with cultural differences when negotiating across cultures? Provide any other information on the company that is relevant to the discussion of market entry.

3. The following project is designed to introduce you to the complexity of negotiations and help develop your negotiating skills.

    Background: A west European automobile manufacturer is considering entering markets in Southeast Asia. The company wants to construct an assembly plant outside Bangkok, Thailand, to assemble its lower-priced cars. Major components would flow in from manufacturing plants in Brazil, Poland, and China. The cars would then be sold in emerging markets throughout Southeast Asia and the Indian subcontinent. Managers are hoping to strike a $100 million joint venture deal with the Thai government. The company would supply technology and management for the venture, and the government would contribute a minority share of financing to the venture. The company considers the government's main contributions as providing tax breaks (and other financial incentives) and a stable business environment in which to operate.

Thailand is better off than some other countries following the economic crisis of the late 1990s. Financial capital is flowing back into the country, the currency is strengthening, and there is general political and social stability. However, inflation remains somewhat high and the government is experi-

encing some currency problems. The new auto assembly plant would help the economic recovery by reducing unemployment and increasing local wages. But local politicians fear the company might be interested only in exploiting the country's low-cost labor.

Activity: Break into an equal number of negotiating teams of 3 or 4 persons. Half the teams are to represent the company and the other half, the government. As a team, meet for 15 minutes to develop your opening position and negotiating strategy. Meet with a team from the other side and undertake 20 minutes of negotiations. Following the negotiating session, spend 15 minutes comparing the progress of your negotiations with that of the other groups.

business case 13
THE BRAVE NEW WORLD OF TELECOMMUNICATIONS JOINT VENTURES

The world of telecommunications is changing. The era of the global information superhighway is upon us, driven by new technologies such as cellular telephones, fax machines, and fiber optic cable that make possible video telephone connections and high-speed data transmission. Annual worldwide revenues for telecommunications services total $600 billion, with international companies accounting for 20 percent of the business. Market opportunities are opening around the world as post, telephone, and telegraph (PTT) monopolies are undergoing privatization. Effective January 1, 1998, telecom deregulation began in earnest in Europe. Meanwhile, governments in developing countries are boosting investments in infrastructure improvements to increase the number of available telephone lines. The demand for telephone service is growing at a sharp pace—international telephone call volume more than doubled between 1988 and 1994. The net result of these changes is the globalization of the telecommunications industry. As William Donovan, a vice president at Sea-Land Service, said recently, "I don't want to have to talk to a bunch of different PTTs around the world. I don't want to have to go to one carrier in one country and a second in another just because it doesn't have a presence there."

Several alliances and joint venture partnerships have been formed between companies hoping to capitalize on the changed market and business environment. France Telecom, Deutsche Telekom, and Sprint created Global One to bring international telecommunications services to Volvo, Samsung, SmithKline Beecham, and other businesses engaged in international commerce. As part of the deal, Sprint sold 10 percent of its stock to each of its French and German partners. One hurdle for the Brussels-based company has been to integrate the three partners' communication networks into a unified whole. Start-up costs have been high, and the need to communicate in three different languages has created some friction among personnel. Early on, lengthy negotiations were required to reach agreement about the value each partner brought to the venture. A former Global One executive noted, "There is no trust among the partners."

Other problems include equipment and billing incompatibilities resulting from distribution agreements with telephone monopolies in individual countries. The venture has yet to record its first profit and lost $280 million in 1997 on sales of about $800 million. The losses prompted Sprint chairman William T. Esrey to install Sprint executive Gary Forsee as CEO and president of Global One.

AT&T, America's largest telecommunications company, is also depending on various partnership strategies as entry modes. WorldPartners began in 1993 as an alliance of AT&T, Kokusai Denshin Daiwa (KDD) of Japan, and Telecom of Singapore. The goal was to provide improved telecommunications services for companies conducting business globally. Guaranteeing that virtually any call can be completed required better wiring as well as improved network transmissions systems. Today WorldPartners is comprised of 10 companies, including Telecom New Zealand, Telestra (Australia), Hong Kong Telecom, and Unisource.

Unisource, in turn, is itself a joint venture that originally included Sweden's Telia AB, Swiss Telecom PTT, and PTT Telecom Netherlands. In 1995, Telefonica de España became an equal equity partner in Unisource. Unisource and AT&T then agreed to form a 60–40 joint venture known as AT&T-Unisource Communications services to offer voice, data, and messaging services to businesses with European operations. AT&T would have preferred to form a joint venture with the French or German telephone companies. However, European regulators concerned about AT&T's strong brand name and enormous size refused to approve such a deal.

There was strong logic for the deal. As AT&T-Unisource CEO James Cosgrove explained recently from headquarters near Amsterdam in Hoofddorp, "You have to be European to play in Europe and yet you have to offer global solutions." Despite the fact that there are five corporate parents, a sense of equality and congeniality has developed. Notes CEO Cosgrove, "Working practices of two years have ironed out remarkably well. We have learned that you have to see this thing as a common operation. Otherwise too many bad compromises can be made." The presence of Telefonica de España in the alliance was especially significant for AT&T because the Spanish company has a strong influence in Latin America. Unfortunately, the alliance was weakened in 1997 when Telefonica decided to ally itself with Concert. To fill the void, AT&T and Italy's Stet announced a new alliance that would expand communication services to Latin American as well as Europe.

The third major telecommunications alliance, Concert Communications, was formed when British Telecommunications PLC bought a 20 percent stake in MCI Communications. Again, the goal of the alliance was to offer global voice and data network services to global corporations.

thinking globally

1. What strengths did AT&T bring to its joint venture with Unisource?

2. Can you think of any potential complications that could arise in the AT&T-Unisource joint venture?

3. Assess the formation of Global One, Unisource, and other partnerships discussed in this case in terms of the strategic factors for selecting entry modes identified in the chapter.

a question of ethics

1. U.S. firms doing business in Russia today are likely to have their guard up in the wake of the ruble's collapse, President Yeltsin's health problems, and a rash of murders of public figures. Beyond these headline-grabbing issues are the differences and similarities between the ways in which U.S. and Russian managers view business ethics. The following four categories of business behaviors and principles have been proposed:

   • Those considered ethical by both U.S. and Russian managers: keeping one's word, maintaining trust, fair competition, and rewards commensurate with performance.

   • Those considered unethical by both U.S. and Russian managers: gangsterism, racketeering, extortion, black marketeering, price gouging, failure to honor debts.

   • Those considered ethical by Russian managers but unethical by U.S. managers: personal favoritism, "grease" payments, price-fixing, data manipulation, ignoring nonsensical laws and regulations.

   • Those considered ethical by U.S. managers but unethical by Russian managers: maximizing profits, exorbitant differentials in salaries, layoffs, and whistle-blowing.[29]

   What can a U.S. businessperson do to minimize ethical friction when doing business in Russia?

2. A recent study investigated the differences between ethical perceptions of business managers from Australia and Hong Kong. The researchers determined that two factors had an impact on the perception of ethical problems: (a) culture and (b) the particular mode of market entry (e.g., exporting, contractual, investment in subsidiaries, or joint ventures). What ethical issues do you think might arise in conjunction with the market entry modes discussed in the chapter?

3. Special ethical concerns can arise when international companies consider a cooperative form of market entry (such as a joint venture) with local partners. This is especially true when each partner contributes personnel in addition to physical and financial assets. Perhaps the most important ethical concern is how to set the joint venture's ethical guidelines when the venture employs people from widely divergent cultural backgrounds. Cultural perspectives cause people to see right versus right (or ethical) decisions differently. Is there anything that two partners from diverse cultures can do to establish ethical principles in such a situation—either before or after formation of the cooperative arrangement? Can you think of a company that succeeded in the face of such difficulties?

14 acquiring business resources

Beacons

A Look Back

CHAPTER 13 explained the pros and cons of international entry modes and when each one is most appropriately used. We also described management issues regarding each entry mode and the important strategic factors in their selection.

A Look at This Chapter

This chapter explains how companies acquire the business resources they need for international operations. We identify and describe the key decision variables involved when employing human resources and when acquiring financial and physical resources.

A Look Ahead

CHAPTER 15 pulls together our knowledge of international business management. We discuss how companies manage their resources to accomplish international business objectives. We also explain how managers decide future courses of action.

Learning Objectives

After studying this chapter, you should be able to

1 Explain the three different *strategic staffing policies* used by international companies.

2 Describe the *recruitment* and *selection* issues facing international companies.

3 Discuss the importance of *training* and *development programs*, especially cultural training.

4 Explain how companies *compensate managers* and *workers* in international markets.

5 Describe the three potential *sources of financing* and the *main financial instruments* of each.

6 Identify key considerations in the *make-or-buy decision* when acquiring physical resources.

In 1997, John Bryan, CEO of Sara Lee Corporation, announced a major restructuring of his company. Bryan presides over an empire of well-known consumer brands, including Coach leather goods, L'Eggs hosiery, Jimmy Dean sausages, and Hanes clothing. He announced that the company would step up its outsourcing activities by selling many of its manufacturing units and subcontracting with the new owners.

The strategy, according to Bryan, would allow Sara Lee to focus on marketing and distribution. "This is a plan," he told reporters, "to 'de-verticalise' the company, in a world which has liberalized."

This new strategy would do more than simply shift the ownership of production facilities. It would provide Sara Lee with more cash to fund current operations and would reduce the need to make future capital investments in manufacturing. For example, sale of the company's thirteen textile plants in the southern United States should free up half a million dollars in cash flow over a three-year period.

Bryan anticipates that in the short term Sara Lee would continue buying knitted goods from U.S. subcontractors. But he did not rule out the possibility that the firm might someday shift to overseas sources. "Production," he explained, "moves around very fast to its lowest-cost point of manufacture."[1]

Whether an international company manufactures a product or provides a service, it must acquire many resources before beginning operations. How many employees will the company need and how will it select and train them? Where will it get the financial capital it needs to conduct its investment activities? Where will it get the raw materials or components it needs to perform its production activities? How much production capacity is needed? Will the company construct or buy new facilities? As the Sara Lee example shows, the answers to these questions are complex and interrelated.

This chapter explains how companies acquire the resources they need to accomplish company goals. We begin by discussing human resource staffing, recruitment, selection, training and development, and compensation policies. We then learn how a company acquires the financing that it needs to launch and maintain its international business operations. We close by explaining how firms acquire fixed (or tangible) assets such as production facilities, offices, equipment, and materials.

EMPLOYING HUMAN RESOURCES

human resource management (HRM)
Process of staffing a company and ensuring that employees are as productive as possible.

Perhaps the most important resource of any successful business is the people who comprise it. Highly trained and productive employees who are proficient in their duties allow a company to achieve its business goals both domestically and internationally. **Human resource management** (**HRM**) is the process of staffing a company and ensuring that employees are as productive as possible. It requires managers to be effective in recruiting, selecting, training, developing, evaluating, and compensating employees and in forming good relations with them. If viewed strategically, HRM can be seen to have a profound impact on performance.[2]

HRM must be in step with corporate-, business-, and department-level strategies. If, for example, a company chooses to pursue a low-cost position in the marketplace, human resource managers should select people with experience suited to the task. The same is true for differentiation and focus strategies (see Chapter 12). Development programs must help line managers—those directly responsible for generating results—acquire the skills needed to implement company strategies. Likewise, in preparing nonmanagerial workers for their tasks, training programs must be consistent with the company's strategic goals.

INTERNATIONAL HUMAN RESOURCE MANAGEMENT

International HRM differs considerably from HRM in a domestic setting. In particular, differences in national environmental forces (such as culture, politics, law, and economic systems) create special conditions. For one thing, recruiting and selecting practices must often be adapted to the host nation's hiring laws. For example, hiring practices regarding nondiscrimination among job candidates must be carefully monitored so that the company does not violate such laws.

Providing Training and Development   Likewise, training and development programs must often be tailored to local practices. Some countries, such as Germany and Japan, have extensive vocational-training schools that turn out graduates who are quite well prepared to perform their jobs proficiently. Finding well-qualified nonmanagerial workers in those markets is relatively easy. In contrast, developing a production facility in many emerging markets requires far more basic worker training. Workers in China, for example, work quite hard and tend to be well educated. But because China lacks a vocational training system like those in Germany and Japan, Chinese workers tend to require more intensive on-the-job training.

TABLE 14.1 — The Amount of Time It Takes to Earn a Big Mac

Longest Time		Shortest Time	
City	**Minutes**	**City**	**Minutes**
Nairobi	193	Chicago, Houston, Tokyo	9
Caracas	117	Los Angeles	10
Moscow	104	Hong Kong	11
Jakarta	103	Toronto, New York	12
Budapest	91	Luxembourg	13
Bombay	85	Montreal, Sydney, Zurich	14
Manila	77	Athens, Geneva	15
Shanghai	75	Frankfurt	16
Mexico City	71	Vienna	17
Prague	56	Berlin	18

Managing Compensation Compensation practices also differ in the international arena. Many companies go abroad in the first place to take advantage of a lower pay scale in another country. Then they adjust their pay scales and advancement criteria to suit local customs.

Union Bank of Switzerland in Zurich publishes an annual survey of earnings around the world. This survey has an interesting twist: It ranks earnings in terms of how long the average wage earner must work to be able to afford a McDonald's Big Mac (see Table 14.1). According to Union Bank's most recent survey of Big Mac buying power, employees in Chicago, Houston, Tokyo, Los Angeles, and Hong Kong enjoy the highest take-home pay. Workers in Nairobi, Caracas, Moscow, Jakarta, and Budapest rank at the bottom.

Accommodating Expatriates Finally, there is the issue of **expatriates**—citizens of one country who are living and working in another. Companies must determine how to compensate expatriate employees on job assignments that could last several years. For example, managers and other employees must be compensated for the inconvenience and stress of living in an unfamiliar culture and for relocating their families. This chapter discusses all these issues in detail.

expatriates
Citizens of one country who are living and working in another.

INTERNATIONAL STAFFING POLICY

The customary means by which a company staffs its offices is called its **staffing policy**. Staffing policy is greatly influenced by the extent of a firm's international involvement. There are three main approaches to the staffing of international business operations—*ethnocentric, polycentric,* and *geocentric.*

staffing policy
Customary means by which a company staffs its offices.

Ethnocentric Staffing In **ethnocentric staffing**, operations outside the home country are managed by individuals from the home country. This policy tends to appeal to companies that want to maintain tight control over the decision making of branch offices abroad. Accordingly, such companies work to formulate policies designed to work in every country in which they operate. Note, however, that firms generally pursue this policy only for the top managerial posts in their international operations. Implementing it at lower levels usually proves impractical.

ethnocentric staffing
Staffing policy in which operations outside the home country are managed by individuals from the home country.

Advantages of Ethnocentric Staffing Firms pursue this policy for several reasons. First, locally qualified people are not always available. In developing and newly industrialized countries, there is often a shortage of qualified personnel—resulting in a highly competitive local labor market.

Second, companies use ethnocentric staffing to re-create local operations in the image of home-country operations. Especially if they have climbed the corporate ladder in the home office, expatriate managers tend to infuse branch offices with the corporate culture. Naturally, this policy is important for companies needing a strong set of shared values among the people in each international office—such as global firms. For example, Mihir Doshi was born in Bombay but his family moved to the United States in 1978. Doshi graduated from New York University and became a naturalized U.S. citizen in 1988. In 1995, he became executive director of Morgan Stanley's operations in India. "Mentally," he reports, "I'm very American. Here, I can be Indian. What the firm gets is somebody to indoctrinate Morgan Stanley culture. I provide the link."[3]

By the same token, a system of shared values is important when a company's international units are highly interdependent. For instance, fashioning branch operations in the image of home-office operations can also ease the transfer of special know-how. This advantage is particularly valuable when that know-how is rooted in the expertise and experience of home-country managers.

Finally, some companies feel that managers sent from the home country will look out for the company's interests more earnestly than will host-country natives. Japanese companies are notorious for their reluctance to place non-Japanese managers at the helm of international offices, and when they do, they often place a Japanese manager in the office to monitor important decisions and report back to the home office. Companies operating in highly nationalistic markets and those worried about industrial espionage also typically find an ethnocentric approach appealing.

Disadvantages of Ethnocentric Staffing Despite its advantages, ethnocentric staffing has its negative aspects. First, relocating managers from the home country is expensive. The bonuses that managers often receive for relocating, plus relocation expenses for entire families, can increase the cost of a manager several times over. Likewise, the pressure of cultural differences and long periods away from relatives and friends can contribute to the failure of managers on international assignments.

Second, an ethnocentric policy can create barriers for the host-country office. The presence of home-country managers in the host country might encourage a "foreign"

According to Microsoft CEO Bill Gates, when you're opening an international office, "It sends the wrong message to have a foreigner come in to run things." So when Microsoft opened a branch in India, it hired native Indian Rajiv Nair to see that legitimate copies of Microsoft software went into the hundreds of thousands of PCs built in India each year. Five years later, Indian operations were promoted to a full-fledged subsidiary, with Nair as general manager. When operations were expanded to create a region consisting of India and several surrounding countries, Microsoft named as director an Indian-born computer scientist from its Redmond, Washington, headquarters.

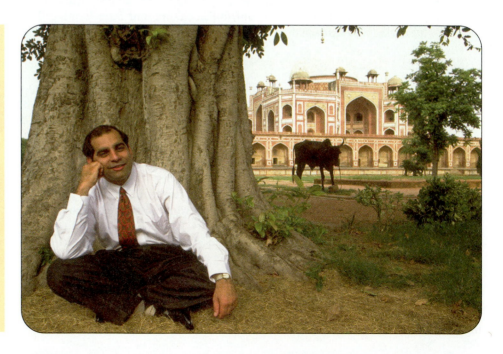

image of the business. Lower-level employees might feel that managers do not really understand their needs because they come from another culture. Occasionally they are right: Expatriate managers sometimes fail to integrate themselves into the local culture. As they fail to overcome cultural barriers, they fail to understand the needs not only of their local employees but those of their local customers.

Polycentric Staffing   In **polycentric staffing**, operations outside the home country are managed by individuals from the host country. Companies can implement a polycentric approach for top and mid-level managers, for lower-level staff, or for non-managerial workers. It is well suited to companies who want to give national units a degree of autonomy in decision making. This policy does not mean that host-country managers are left to run operations in any way they see fit. Large international companies usually conduct extensive training programs in which host-country managers visit home offices for extended periods. There they are exposed to the company's culture and specific business practices. Small and medium-size companies can find this policy expensive, but being able to depend on local managers who fully understand what is expected of them can far outweigh any costs.

<aside>
polycentric staffing
Staffing policy in which operations outside the home country are managed by individuals from the host country.
</aside>

Advantages and Disadvantages of Polycentric Staffing   An important advantage of polycentric staffing is elimination of the high cost of relocating expatriate managers and families. This advantage can be extremely helpful for small and medium-size businesses that cannot afford to hire expatriates.

Second, polycentric staffing places managerial responsibility in the hands of people intimately familiar with the local business environment. Managers with deep cultural understanding of the local market can be an enormous advantage. They are familiar with local business practices and can read the subtle cues of both verbal and nonverbal language. They need not overcome any cultural barriers created by an image of being an outsider, and they tend to have a better feel for the needs of employees, customers, and suppliers.

The major drawback to polycentric staffing is the potential for losing control of the host-country operation. When a company employs natives of each country to manage local operations, it runs the risk of becoming a collection of discrete national businesses. This situation might not be a problem when a firm's strategy calls for treating each national market differently. It is not a good policy, however, for companies following global strategies. If these companies lack integration, knowledge sharing, and a common image, performance will surely suffer.

Geocentric Staffing   In **geocentric staffing**, operations outside the home country are managed by the best-qualified individuals regardless of nationality. The local operation may choose managers from the host country, from the home country, or from a third country. The choice depends on the operation's specific needs. This policy is typically reserved for top-level managers.

<aside>
geocentric staffing
Staffing policy in which operations outside the home country are managed by the best-qualified individuals regardless of nationality.
</aside>

Advantages and Disadvantages of Geocentric Staffing   Geocentric staffing helps a company develop global managers who can adjust easily to any business environment—particularly to cultural differences. This advantage is especially useful for global companies trying to break down nationalistic barriers, whether between managers in a single office or between different offices. One hope of companies using this policy is that a global perspective among its managers will help them seize opportunities that may otherwise be overlooked.

The downside of geocentric staffing is expense. Understandably, top managers who are both capable of fitting into different cultures and effective at their jobs are highly prized among international companies. The combination of high demand for their skills and their short supply inflates their salaries. Moreover, there is the expense of relocating managers and their families—sometimes every year.

In practice, companies often blend different aspects of each staffing policy, which results in an almost infinite variety of international staffing policies.

RECRUITING AND SELECTING HUMAN RESOURCES

Naturally, companies try to recruit and select qualified managers and nonmanagerial workers who are well suited to their tasks and responsibilities. But how does a company know the number of managers and workers it needs? How does it recruit the best available individuals? How does it select from the pool of available candidates? In this section, we explore some answers to these and other important questions about recruiting and selecting employees.

Human Resource Planning   Recruiting and selecting managers and workers requires **human resource planning**—the process of forecasting both a company's human resource needs and supply. The first phase of HR planning involves taking an inventory of a company's current human resources—that is, collecting data on every employee, including educational background, special job skills, previous jobs, language skills, and experience living abroad.

The second phase of HR planning is estimating the company's future HR needs. Consider, for example, a firm that plans to sell its products directly to buyers in a new market abroad. Will it create a new operation abroad and staff it with managers from the home office or will it train local managers? Will it hire its own local sales force or will it hire a distributor? Likewise, manufacturing or assembling products in an international market requires factory workers. Companies must decide whether to hire these people themselves or to subcontract production to other producers—thus eliminating the need for it to hire factory workers itself.

As we have noted in previous chapters, this decision frequently raises ethical questions. The general public is becoming increasingly well informed about the fact that global companies such as Disney, Nike, Adidas-Salomon, and Reebok make extensive use of subcontractors in low-wage nations. Of particular concern is the question of whether subcontractors are taking advantage of "sweatshop labor." But publicity generated by allegations of workplace abuse are causing many firms to establish codes of conduct and step up efforts to ensure compliance. In 1997, for example, Nike severed ties with subcontractors in Indonesia that paid wages below the minimum levels set by the government.

In the third phase of HR planning, managers develop a plan for recruiting and selecting people to fill vacant and anticipated new positions, both managerial and nonmanagerial. Sometimes, a firm must also make plans for reducing its workforce—a process called *decruitment*—when current HR levels are greater than anticipated needs. Planning for decruitment normally occurs when a company decides to discontinue manufacturing or selling in a market. Unfortunately, the decision by global companies to shift the location of manufacturing from one country to another can also result in lost jobs.[4] Let's now take a closer look at the recruitment and selection processes.

Recruiting Human Resources   The process of identifying and attracting a qualified pool of applicants for vacant positions is called **recruitment**. Companies can recruit internally from among their current employees or look to external sources.

Current Employees Finding an international manager among current employees is easiest for a large company with an abundance of internal managers. Likely candidates within the company are those managers who were involved in previous stages of an international project—say, in identifying a new production site or potential market.

human resource planning
Process of forecasting both a company's human resource needs and supply.

recruitment
Process of identifying and attracting a qualified pool of applicants for vacant positions.

Perhaps these individuals have already made important contacts inside the host country and have already been exposed to its culture.

Recent College Graduates   Companies also recruit from among recent college graduates who have come from other countries to attend college in the firm's home country. This is a particularly common practice among companies in the United States. Over a one-year period, these new hires receive general and specialized training and then are given positions in their native countries. As a rule, they understand the organization's culture and the way in which it conducts business. Most important, perhaps, is their familiarity with the culture of the target market, including its customs, traditions, and language.

Local Managerial Talent   Companies can also recruit local managerial talent. Hiring local managers is common when cultural understanding is a key job requirement. Hiring local managers with government contacts can speed the process of getting approvals for local operations. In some cases, governments force companies to recruit local managers so that they can develop their own internal pools of managerial talent. Sometimes, for example, they restrict the number of international managers allowed to work in the host country.

Nonmanagerial Workers   Companies typically recruit locally for nonmanagerial positions because there is often little need for highly specialized skills or training. However, a specialist from the home country is typically brought in to train people chosen for more demanding positions.

Firms also turn to the local labor market when governments restrict the number of people allowed into the host country for work purposes. Such efforts are usually designed to reduce unemployment among the local population. On the other hand, countries sometimes permit the importation of nonmanagerial workers. Kuwait, a wealthy oil-producing country in the Middle East, has brought in large numbers of

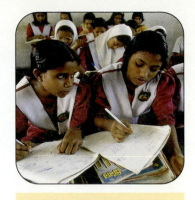

When contractors in Bangladesh admitted that they hired children, Levi Strauss demanded that they comply with local regulations. Unfortunately, it turned out that many of the underage workers were their families' sole sources of support. So Levi's struck a deal: While contractors agreed to continue paying wages and to rehire the young workers at age fourteen, Levi's would send them to school until they came of age. To find out why Levi's is doing business in Bangladesh, visit the following Web site: **⟨www.worldbiz.com/bizbang ladesh.html⟩**

"WHEN YOU CAME TO WORK WITH US, WALSH, YOU STRESSED THAT YOU HOPED TO GO FAR WITH THE COMPANY. WELL, WE'VE DECIDED TO OPEN AN OFFICE IN TIBET, AND..."

nonmanagerial workers for its blue-collar and technical jobs. Many of these workers come from Egypt, India, Lebanon, Pakistan, Palestinian territories, and the Philippines in search of jobs or higher wages.

Selecting Human Resources   The process of screening and hiring the best-qualified applicants with the greatest performance potential is called **selection**. The process for international assignments includes measuring a person's ability to bridge cultural differences. Expatriate managers must be able to adapt to a new way of life in the host country. Conversely, native host-country managers must be able to work effectively with superiors from different cultural backgrounds. The World Business Survey "No Common Thread in Expatriate Selection" suggests the diversity of programs that firms use to select managers for international job assignments.

In the case of expatriate managers, cultural differences between home country and host country are important factors in their potential success. Culturally sensitive managers increase the likelihood that a company will achieve its international business goals. Recruiters can assess cultural sensitivity by asking candidates questions about their receptiveness to new ways of doing things and questions about racial and ethnic issues.

It is also important to examine the cultural sensitivity of each family member who will be going to the host country. The inability of a family member (particularly a spouse) to adapt to a new culture is the most common reason for the failure of expatriate managers. In fact, in one recent survey of Canadian and U.S. companies, nearly 20 percent cited "lack of adaptability by the employee's spouse" as the number-one cause of failed relocation.[5]

> **selection**
> *Process of screening and hiring the best-qualified applicants with the greatest performance potential.*

World Business Survey

No Common Thread in Expatriate Selection

Only half of U.S. companies with expatriates overseas send their international assignees on a look-see trip prior to final selection. In addition, no one selection procedure is used by more than half of the survey participants. This is according to a "Survey of Human Resource Trends" published by Aon Consulting based in Chicago. The report shares the responses of 1,700 U.S. organizations representing 20 million employees and 165,000 HR professionals.

Companies use the following selection processes as part of their overall international assignment strategies:

Selection Procedures	Using	Considering
Pre-assignment visits	50%	13%
Language training	37%	20%
Health, drug, alcohol screening	34%	8%
Realistic job previews	33%	17%
Technical skills assessment	26%	18%
Family readiness evaluation	16%	21%
Psychological profile	11%	15%
Cultural proficiency assessment	10%	22%

Notice that although the *cultural proficiency assessment* method is currently the least used, it is also the one that most companies are considering for adoption. This study also finds that most U.S. based multinationals (49 percent) expect greater future growth in overseas markets than at home. Twenty percent expect more in the United States, and 19 percent expect equal growth.

Culture Shock   Successful international managers typically do not mind, and often enjoy, living and working outside their native lands. In extreme cases, they might even be required to relocate every year or so. These individuals are capable of adapting quickly to local conditions and business practices. Such managers are becoming increasingly valuable with the emergence of markets in Asia, central and eastern Europe, and Latin America. They are also helping to create a global pool of managers who are ready and willing to go practically anywhere on short notice. The size of this pool, however, remains limited because of the difficulties that many people experience in relocating to unfamiliar cultures.

Living in another culture can be a stressful experience. Therefore, selecting managers who are comfortable traveling to and living in unfamiliar cultures is an extremely important factor in recruitment for international posts. Set down in the midst of new cultures, many expatriates experience **culture shock**—a psychological process affecting people living abroad that is characterized by homesickness, irritability, confusion, aggravation, and depression. In other words, they have trouble adjusting to the new environment in which they find themselves. *Expatriate failure*—the early return by an employee from an international assignment because of inadequate job performance—often results from cultural stress. The higher cost of expatriate failure is convincing many companies to invest in cultural-training programs for employees sent abroad. For a detailed look at the culture-shock process and how to reduce its effects, see the Global Manager "This May Come as a Shock to You" on page 488.

culture shock
Psychological process affecting people living abroad that is characterized by homesickness, irritability, confusion, aggravation, and depression.

Reverse Culture Shock   Ironically, expatriates who successfully adapt to new cultures often undergo an experience called **reverse culture shock**—the psychological process of readapting to one's home culture. Because values and behavior that once seemed so natural now seem so strange, reverse culture shock may be even more disturbing than culture shock. In addition, returning managers often find that either no position or merely a "standby" position awaits them in the home office. Often, companies do not know how to take full advantage of the cross-cultural abilities developed by managers who have spent several potentially valuable years abroad. In fact, expatriates commonly leave their companies within a year of returning home because of difficulty blending back into the company culture.

reverse culture shock
Psychological process of readapting to one's home culture.

Moreover, spouses and children often have difficulty leaving the adopted culture and returning home. For many Japanese employees and their families, reentry into Japanese culture after a work assignment in the United States can be particularly difficult. The fast pace of business and social life in the United States, plus the relatively high degree of freedom and independence for women, contrasts sharply with conditions in Japan. Returning Japanese expatriates often find it difficult to adjust back to life in Japan after years of living in the United States.

Dealing with Reverse Culture Shock   The effects of reverse culture shock can be reduced. Home-culture reorientation programs and career-counseling sessions for returning managers and their families can be effective. The employer, for example, might bring the entire family home for a short stay several weeks before the official return. This kind of trip allows returnees to prepare for at least some of the reverse culture shock that may be waiting for them.

Likewise, good career development programs can help companies retain valuable managers. Ideally, the career development plan was worked out before the employee went abroad and revised before his or her return. Some companies work with employees before they go abroad to plan career paths of up to 20 years within the company. Mentors who have previously gone abroad and had to adjust to the return home can

This May Come as a Shock To You

Culture shock typically occurs during stays of a few months or longer in an unfamiliar culture. It begins upon arrival and normally occurs in four stages (although not all people go through every stage):

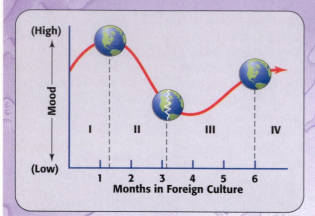

(High)

Mood

(Low)

I   II   III   IV

1   2   3   4   5   6
Months in Foreign Culture

Stage 1, the "honeymoon," typically lasts from a few days to a few weeks. New arrivals are fascinated by local sights, pleasant hospitality, and interesting habits. They are thrilled about their opportunity and optimistic about prospects for success. Often, however, this sense of security is false because, so far, interactions with locals are similar to those of a tourist.

Stage 2 lasts from a few weeks to a few months; in fact, some people never move on to stage 3. Unpredictable quirks of the culture become annoying, even maddening. Visitors begin mocking the locals and regarding the ways of their native cultures as superior. Relationships

with spouses and children suffer, and depression, perhaps even despair, sets in.

At **Stage 3**, emotions hit bottom—and recovery begins. As visitors begin to learn more about the local culture, interact more with locals, and form friendships, cynical remarks cease.

At **Stage 4**, visitors not only better understand local customs and behavior but actually appreciate many of them. They now treat differences as "unique" solutions to familiar problems in different cultural contexts. Reaching stage 4 is a sign that the expatriate has adapted well and that success in his or her international assignment is likely.

Here are some steps that prospective expatriates can take to reduce the burden of culture shock during an international assignment:

Undergo extensive psychological assessment to ensure that both you and your family members are emotionally able to handle the assignment.

Obtain knowledge of the local culture (especially the language) and critically examine your own culture biases before leaving home.

If possible, visit the assigned country, mingling with local people and getting a feel for your future assignment. Ask about local educational, financial, and health-care services.

Once you are inside a culture, meet with others—both natives and expatriates—to discuss your negative and positive experiences.

Most important: Relax, be adventurous, take a worldly perspective, and keep your sense of humor.

also be assigned to returning managers. The mentor becomes a confidant with whom the expatriate manager can discuss particular problems related to work, family, and readjusting to the home culture.

TRAINING AND DEVELOPMENT

After a company recruits and selects its managers and other employees, it normally identifies the skills and knowledge that employees have and those that they need to perform their duties. Employees lacking the necessary skills or knowledge can then be directed into specific training or development programs.

According to the National Foreign Trade Council (NFTC), 250,000 U.S. citizens live outside the United States on international assignment—in addition to hundreds of thousands more who travel abroad on business for stays of up to several weeks. According to the same study, it costs $60,000 to relocate an employee for a long-term international assignment. Moreover, this figure accounts for moving expenses only—it does not include ongoing costs for such things as housing, education, and cost-of-living adjustments. Thus many companies realize the need for in-depth training and development programs if they are to get the maximum productivity from managers posted abroad.

Methods of Cultural Training   Ideally, everyone involved in business should be culturally literate and prepared to go anywhere in the world on a moment's notice. Realistically, many employees and many companies do not need or cannot afford to be entirely literate in another culture. The extent of a company's international involvement demands a corresponding level of cultural knowledge from its employees. Companies whose activities are highly international need employees with language fluency and in-depth experience in other countries. Meanwhile, small companies or those new to international business can begin with some basic cultural training. As a company increases its international involvement and cross-cultural contact, employees' cultural knowledge must keep pace.

As you can see from Figure 14.1, companies use many methods to prepare managers for an international assignment. These methods tend to reflect a manager's level of international involvement. The goal of most programs is to create informed, open-minded, flexible managers with a level of cultural training appropriate to the duties required of them.

Environmental Briefings and Cultural Orientations   *Environmental* (or *area*) *briefings* constitute the most basic level of training—oftentimes the starting point for studying other cultures. Briefings include information on local housing, health care, transportation, schools, and climate. Such knowledge is normally obtained from books, films, and lectures. *Cultural orientations* offer insight into social, political, legal, and economic institutions. Their purpose is to add depth and substance to environmental briefings.

Cultural Assimilation and Sensitivity Training   *Cultural assimilation* teaches the culture's values, attitudes, manners, and customs. So-called "guerilla linguistics," which involves learning some phrases in the local language, is often used at this stage. It

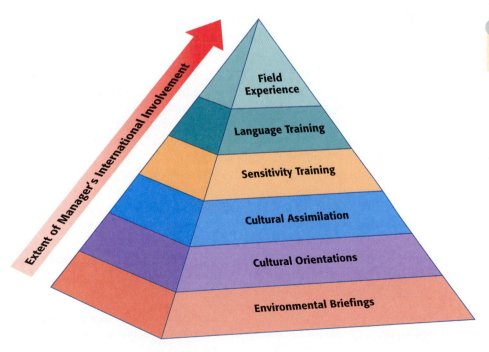

FIGURE 14.1

INTERNATIONAL ASSIGNMENT PREPARATION METHODS

Extent of Manager's International Involvement

Field Experience

Language Training

Sensitivity Training

Cultural Assimilation

Cultural Orientations

Environmental Briefings

also typically includes role playing: The trainee responds to a specific situation in order to be evaluated by a team of judges. This method is often used when someone is given little notice of a short stay abroad and wishes to take a crash course in social and business etiquette and communication. *Sensitivity training* teaches people to be considerate and understanding of other people's feelings and emotions; it gets the trainee "under the skin" of the local people.

Language Training   The need for more thorough cultural preparedness brings us to intensive *language training*. This level of training entails more than memorizing phrases for ordering dinner or asking directions. It gets a trainee "into the mind" of local people. The trainee learns more about why local people behave as they do. This is perhaps the most critical part of cultural training for long-term assignments.

A recent survey of top executives conducted by the Wats House for Select Appointments found that foreign-language skills topped the list of skills needed to maintain a competitive edge. According to the survey, 31 percent of male employees and 27 percent of female employees lacked foreign-language skills. To remedy this situation, many companies either employ outside agencies specializing in language training or develop their own programs. Employees at 3M Corporation developed a third way. They created an all-volunteer "Language Society" comprised of current and retired employees and family members. About 1,000 people are members, and the group offers classes in 17 languages taught by 70 volunteer employee teachers. The society meets 45 minutes per week and charges a nominal membership fee of $5. According to officials at 3M, the society nicely complements the company's formal language education program.[6]

Field Experience   *Field experience* means visiting the culture, walking the streets of its cities and villages, and becoming absorbed by it for a short period of time. The trainee gets to enjoy some of the unique cultural traits and feel some of the stresses inherent in living in the culture.

Finally, remember that spouses and children also need cultural training. Training for them is a good investment because the alternatives—an international "commuter marriage" or expatriate failure—are both psychologically and financially expensive options.[7]

Compiling a Cultural Profile   *Cultural profiles* can be quite helpful in deciding whether to accept an international assignment. Following are some excellent sources for constructing a cultural profile:

➡ *Culturgrams*   Published by the David M. Kennedy Center for International Studies at Brigham Young University, this guide can be found in the reference section of many libraries. Frequent updates make *Culturgrams* a timely source of information. Individual sections profile each culture's background and its people, customs and courtesies, lifestyle, and society. A section entitled "For the Traveler" covers such details as required entry visas and vaccinations.

➡ *Country Studies Area Handbooks*   This series explains how politics, economics, society, and national security issues are related to one another and shaped by culture in more than 70 countries. Handbooks tend to be politically oriented because they are designed for U.S. military personnel. They are available on the Web at ⟨lcweb2.loc.gov/frd/cs/cshome.html⟩.

➡ *Background Notes*   These notes contain much relevant factual information on human rights and related issues in various countries. However, because they are published by the U.S. Department of State, they take a U.S. political perspective.

Information can also be obtained by contacting embassies of other countries in your home country. People with firsthand knowledge and specific books and films are

In the wake of the North American Free Trade Agreement, computer maker Hewlett-Packard made a major commitment to the growing Mexican market. Through cultural training programs like this one in Mexico City, Mexican managers are trained in company operations and U.S. managers are trained in language as well as cultural attitudes and manners.

also good sources of information. Once you're inside a country, you'll find your home country's embassy a good source of further cultural advice. Embassies maintain networks of home-nation professionals who work in the local culture, some with many years of experience upon which to draw.

Nonmanagerial Worker Training   Nonmanagerial workers also have training and development needs. This is especially true in developing and newly industrialized countries where people have not even completed primary school. Even if the workforce is fairly well educated, workers may lack experience working in industry. In such cases, companies doing business abroad can train local workers in how to work on an assembly line or cultivate business leads to make sales. The need for such basic-skills training continues to grow as companies increasingly explore opportunities in emerging markets.

In many countries, national governments cooperate with businesses to train nonmanagerial workers. Japan and Germany lead the world in vocational training and apprenticeship programs for nonmanagerial workers. Students unable or unwilling to enter college can enter programs paid for by government and private industry. They undergo extensive practical training that exposes them to the cutting-edge technologies employed by the country's leading companies. For example, Germany's Mittelstand is a network of 3 million small and midsize companies that account for about two thirds of the country's jobs. Mittelstand companies provide 80 percent of Germany's apprenticeships. Although they typically employ fewer than 100 people, many Mittelstand companies are export powerhouses.

EMPLOYEE COMPENSATION

Essential to good HRM is a fair and effective compensation (reward) system. Such a system is designed to attract and retain the best and brightest employees and to reward them for their performance. Because a country's compensation practices are rooted in its culture and legal and economic systems, determining compensation can be complicated. In some countries, for example, base pay accounts for nearly all employee compensation. In others, bonuses and fringe benefits account for more than half.

Managerial Employees   Naturally, compensation packages for managers differ from company to company and from country to country. Good packages are fairly complicated to design for several reasons. First, consider the effect of *cost of living*, which includes such factors as the cost of groceries, dining out, clothing, housing, schooling, heath care, transportation, and utilities. Quite simply, it costs more to live in some countries than in others. Moreover, within a given country the cost of living typically varies from large cities to rural towns and villages. Most companies add a certain amount to an expatriate manager's pay to cover greater cost-of-living expenses. On the other hand, managers relocating to lower cost-of-living countries are typically paid the same amount that they were receiving at the home office. Otherwise, they would be financially penalized for accepting an international job assignment.

Even when the cost of living abroad is lower than at home, companies must cover other costs incurred by expatriate managers. One important concern for relocating managers is the quality of local education. In many cases, children cannot immediately enter local classes because they do not speak the local language. In such instances, most companies pay for private-school education.

Bonus and Tax Incentives   Companies commonly offer managers inducements to accept international postings. The most common is a financial bonus. This bonus can be in the form of a one-time payment or an add-on to regular pay—generally 15 to 20 percent. Bonuses for managers asked to go into a particularly unstable country or one with a very low standard of living often receive *hardship* or *combat pay*.

Managers can also be attracted by another income-related factor. For example, the U.S. government permits citizens working abroad to exclude "foreign-earned income" from their taxable income in the United States—even if it was earned in a country with no income tax.

Cultural and Social Contributors to Cost Culture also plays an important role in the compensation of expatriate managers. Some nations offer more paid holidays than others. Many offer free medical care to everyone living and working there. Granted, the quality of locally available medical care is not always good. Many companies, therefore, have plans for taking seriously ill expatriates and family members home or to nearby countries where medical care is equal to that available in the home country.

Companies that hire managers in the local market might encounter additional costs engendered by social attitudes. In some countries, for instance, employers are expected to provide free or subsidized housing. In others, the government obligates employers to provide paid maternity leaves of up to one and one-half years. Table 14.2 shows government-mandated maternity leaves for a sample of European countries. Although companies need not absorb all such costs, they tend to be reflected in a generally higher cost of doing business in a given country.

Managers recruited from within the host country generally receive the same pay as managers working for local companies. Often, however, they receive perks not offered by local firms. Some, for example, are required to visit the home office two or three

TABLE 14.2 *Parental Leave in Europe*

Country	Length of Leave	Pay	Limits
Austria	24 months	Flat rate	Up to fourth birthday
Denmark	10 weeks (plus six months extended leave)	Flat rate	Up to 36 months throughout career
Finland	Until child is 36 months	First six months linked to earnings, then flat rate	Up to third birthday
France	Until child is 36 months	Flat rate, but only for second and subsequent children	Up to third birthday
Germany	Until child is 36 months	Flat rate for 24 months, then means tested	Up to third birthday
Spain	Until child is 36 months	No benefit	Up to third birthday
Sweden	38 weeks per family, per child	80–90 percent of earnings	Up to eighth birthday
The Netherlands	Six months	No benefit	Up to fourth birthday, but only part-time

times per year. If time allows, many managers take along families, add on a few extra days, and fashion short vacations.

Nonmanagerial Workers   Two main factors influence the wages of nonmanagerial workers. First, their compensation is strongly influenced by increased cross-border business investment. Employers can relocate fairly easily to nations where wages are lower. In the home country, meanwhile, workers must often accept lower wages when an employer gives them a choice of accepting the reduction or watching their jobs move abroad. One result of this situation is a trend toward greater equality in workers' pay around the world. This equalizing effect, in turn, encourages economic development and improvement in workers' lives in some countries at the expense of those in others.

The freedom with which an employer can relocate, however, differs from country to country. Although firms in some countries are allowed to move with little notice, they are highly restricted in others. In fact, some countries force companies to compensate workers who lose their jobs because of relocation. This policy is common in European countries that have erected extensive social safety nets for unemployed workers.

Second, the fact that labor is more mobile today than ever before also affects wages. Although labor laws in Europe are still more stringent than in the United States, the countries of the European Union are abolishing the requirement that workers from one EU nation must obtain visas to work in another. If workers in Spain cannot find work at home, or if they feel that their current pay is inadequate, they are free to move to another EU country where unemployment is lower (say, Britain). Not surprisingly, employers in low-wage countries are finding that they must increase wages to retain their best employees.

ACQUIRING FINANCIAL RESOURCES

Companies need financial resources to pay for a variety of operating expenses and new investment projects. They must buy raw materials and component products for manufacturing and assembly activities. They must pay for training and development programs and reward workers and managers. They must pay advertising agencies for helping the company promote its goods and services. At certain times, they need large sums of capital, whether for expanding production capacity or entering new geographic markets. They also must make periodic interest payments to lenders and perhaps reward stockholders with dividends.

But where do companies obtain needed funds? Generally speaking, organizations obtain financial resources through one of three sources:

1. Borrowing (debt)
2. Issuing equity (stock ownership)
3. Internal funding

The first two are external sources, the third internal. With companies increasingly seeking capital in the international capital market, let's take a closer look at how they obtain financing from each of these sources.

BORROWING

International companies (like domestic companies) try to get the lowest interest rates possible on borrowed funds. This objective, however, is more complex on a global scale. Difficulties include exchange-rate risk, restrictions on currency convertibility, and restrictions on the international flow of capital. Sometimes, for example, governments refuse market entry to companies that do not obtain financing from local sources—usually so they can impose higher interest rates. If lower-cost capital exists elsewhere, such a restriction obviously increases the cost of capital for prospective companies.

Borrowing locally, however, can be advantageous, especially when the value of the local currency has fallen against that of the home-country currency. Suppose a Japanese company borrows from U.S. banks for investment in the United States. Let's say that one year later, the U.S. dollar has fallen against the Japanese yen; in other words, fewer yen are now needed to buy one dollar. In that case, the Japanese company can repay the loan with fewer yen than would have been required if the value of the dollar had not fallen.

Companies are not always able to borrow funds locally. Often they are forced to seek international sources of capital. This is sometimes the case when a subsidiary is new to the market and has not yet built a reputation with local lenders. In such cases, a parent firm can help a subsidiary acquire financing through a so-called **back-to-back loan**—loan in which a parent company deposits money with a host-country bank, which then lends it to a subsidiary located in the host country.

Suppose, for instance, that a Mexican company forms a new subsidiary in the United States but that this subsidiary cannot obtain a U.S. bank loan. The Mexican parent company can deposit Mexican pesos in the branch of a U.S. bank in Mexico (see Figure 14.2). The U.S. bank's home office then lends dollars to the subsidiary in the United States. The amount of money lent in dollars will be equivalent to the amount of pesos on deposit with the U.S. bank's Mexico branch. When the U.S. subsidiary repays the loan in full, the parent company withdraws its deposit (plus any interest earned) from the U.S. bank's Mexico branch.

back-to-back loan
Loan in which a parent company deposits money with a host-country bank, which then lends it to a subsidiary located in the host country.

FIGURE 14.2

MEXICO–UNITED STATES BACK-TO-BACK LOAN

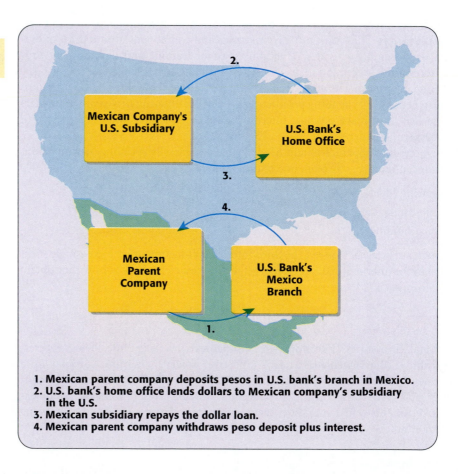

1. Mexican parent company deposits pesos in U.S. bank's branch in Mexico.
2. U.S. bank's home office lends dollars to Mexican company's subsidiary in the U.S.
3. Mexican subsidiary repays the dollar loan.
4. Mexican parent company withdraws peso deposit plus interest.

In Chapter 9, we defined the *international bond market* as consisting of all bonds sold by issuing companies, governments, or other organizations outside their own countries. Companies wanting access to a greater pool of investors or wanting to take advantage of lower interest rates can issue international bonds. For instance, Russian borrowers issuing bonds in Russia were paying interest rates of 15 to 20 percent in early 1997. But when issuing bonds internationally, they could pay interest rates as low as 9.5 to 11 percent. The resulting savings on large bond issues were enormous. At that time, Gazprom, a Russian natural gas company, made history when it issued a bond worth $429 million in the international bond market. It was the first Russian bond issued in the international bond market in nearly a century.[8]

Eurobonds   One instrument used by companies to access the international bond market is called a **Eurobond**—a bond issued outside the country in whose currency it is denominated. In other words, a bond issued by a Venezuelan company, denominated in U.S. dollars, and sold in Britain, France, Germany, and the Netherlands (but not available in the United States or to its residents) is a Eurobond. Because this Eurobond is denominated in U.S. dollars, the Venezuelan borrower both receives the loan and makes its interest payments in dollars. In 1997, for example, Siemens, the German electrical engineering and electronics giant, used the Eurobond market to raise 750 million German marks, 2.5 billion French francs, and 500 million Dutch guilders—a sum equal to about $1.1 billion.[9]

> **Eurobond**
> Bond issued outside the country in whose currency it is denominated.

Eurobonds account for approximately 75 to 80 percent of all international bonds. They are popular because they are not subject to regulation by the governments of the countries in which they are sold. The absence of regulation substantially reduces the cost of issuing a bond. Unfortunately, it increases its risk level—a fact that may discourage some potential investors.

The traditional markets for Eurobonds are Europe and North America. But strong economic growth across Asia through the mid-1990s led to large financial reserves in the central banks of many Asian countries. Low interest rates, small domestic bond markets, and increasing wealth across Asia encouraged investment in Eurobonds. Asian markets often meant the difference between a successful and an unsuccessful new Eurobond issue.[10] However, until Asia fully recovers from the currency crisis of the late 1990s, its importance to the Eurobond market will be diminished.

Ecubonds   A popular type of Eurobond, the Ecubond is denominated in the *ecu*—an artificial currency composed of a basket of European currencies. The weight of each nation's currency in the basket reflects the strength of its economy relative to those of the other EU nations. An Ecubond qualifies as a Eurobond in Europe because the ecu is not the currency of any one European country.

Governments and companies began issuing Ecubonds in Europe in the 1980s in anticipation of the European Monetary Union in 1999. The total volume of Ecubonds grew most rapidly in the 1980s and early 1990s. By 1997, the outstanding volume of Ecubonds was around $55 billion, down from $62 billion in December 1996 and nearly $79 billion in December 1995.[11] The decline in volume resulted from fears that monetary union would not go forward and that if it did proceed it may disrupt financial markets. Furthermore, the *euro* (the European Union's new single currency) will eventually replace the ecu.

Bearer versus Registered Bonds   Most Eurobonds are **bearer bonds**—bonds that come with coupons entitling the bearer of each coupon to collect each interest payment. To collect interest payments, the bearer presents the coupon to one of the financial institutions underwriting the bond. Anyone presenting a coupon is entitled to receive the payment. In contrast, **registered bonds** make scheduled interest payments only to individuals registered as owners. They are most common in the United States.

> **bearer bond**
> Bond that comes with coupons entitling the bearer of each coupon to collect each interest payment.

> **registered bond**
> Bond that makes scheduled interest payments only to the individual registered as its owner.

foreign bond
Bond sold outside the
borrower's country and
denominated in the currency
of the country in which it is
sold.

Foreign Bonds   Companies also obtain financial resources by issuing so-called **foreign bonds**—bonds sold outside the borrower's country and denominated in the currency of the country in which they are sold. For instance, a yen-denominated bond issued by the German carmaker BMW in Japan's domestic bond market is a foreign bond. Foreign bonds account for about 20 to 25 percent of all international bonds.

Foreign bonds are subject to the same rules and regulations as the domestic bonds of the country in which they are issued. Countries typically require issuers to meet certain regulatory requirements and to disclose details about company activities, owners, and upper management. Thus BMW's *samurai bonds* (the name for foreign bonds issued in Japan) would need to meet the same disclosure and other regulatory requirements that Toyota's bonds in Japan must meet. Foreign bonds in the United States are called *yankee bonds*, and those in the United Kingdom *bulldog bonds*. Foreign bonds issued and traded in Asia outside Japan (and normally denominated in dollars) are called *dragon bonds*.

"Roadshows": Increasing Competition in the International Bond Market

Companies issue their international bonds through investment banks. Low interest rates on debt and an increasing supply of bonds from newly industrialized and developing countries are generating greater competition among the banks that sell new bond issues. To counteract increasing competitive pressures, they have thus begun emphasizing so-called "roadshows": trips designed to elicit support for, and confidence in, bond issues before they reach the market.

The goal is to "sell" issues before they actually go on sale. The main reason being to ensure that banks are not left holding large amounts of unsold bonds. In the past, banks focused exclusively on the financial soundness of the company or government issuing the bond. Today, they also rely on elaborately orchestrated marketing events involving lavish dinners, free gifts, company videos, and professional presenters. A recent roadshow for U.S. toy maker Mattel gave away Barbie dolls. The Mexican satellite-television company Innova gave away baseball caps emblazoned with diagrams of its global connections. Such gimmicks were previously unheard of in the discreet world of investment banking.[12]

Interestingly, national culture is affecting the design of roadshows. London-based Imagination is in the business of designing roadshows for banks and their clients. Because most large new bond issues are now international, Imagination takes cultural differences into account. For instance, the company teaches bank officials how to present a client from one country to potential investors in others and coaches them in the all-important business of answering questions. Under Imagination's direction, the typical roadshow begins in continental Europe, where investors ask few, relatively simple questions. It then moves on to London, where the questions, though more numerous, are still polite. Finally, it is on to the U.S. market, where investors interrogate aggressively, often interrupting presenters with questions as they come to mind.[13]

ISSUING EQUITY

Recall from Chapter 9 that the *international equity market* consists of all stocks bought and sold outside the home country of the issuing company. Companies issue such stock primarily to access pools of investors with funds that are unavailable domestically. However, getting shares listed on another country's stock exchange can be a complex process. For one thing, complying with all the rules and regulations governing the operation of a particular stock exchange costs a great deal of time and money. Only large companies, therefore, tend to list shares on multiple exchanges.

To maximize international exposure (and access to funds), non-U.S. companies often list themselves on U.S. stock exchanges. The volume of shares traded on U.S. exchanges is by far the largest in the world, and new issues of stock tend to sell very quickly. In turn, U.S. exchanges actively seek new listings because they represent major sources of growth. As a result, the number of non-U.S. companies listed on U.S. exchanges continues to grow. Between 1990 and 1997, for instance, the number of non-U.S. companies listed on the computerized National Association of Securities Dealers Automated Quotation system (NASDAQ) increased from 256 to 428. The NASDAQ lists primarily the stocks of young high-technology companies. Meanwhile, non-U.S. listings on the New York Stock Exchange (NYSE) increased from 96 to 318 over the same period. The oldest and largest U.S. exchange, the NYSE lists many of the world's largest companies. Because they usually cannot meet stringent listing requirements, smaller firms typically list elsewhere.[14]

Issuing American Depository Receipts Non-U.S. companies can list shares directly in the United States by issuing **American Depository Receipts (ADRs)**—certificates that trade in the United States and represent a specific number of shares in a non-U.S. company. Large U.S. banks (including Citibank and Morgan Guaranty Trust) issue ADRs, which trade on the NYSE, NASDAQ, and over-the-counter (OTC) markets. In 1996, companies raised nearly $20 billion by issuing ADRs, and about 1,800 ADRs traded on U.S. exchanges in 1997.[15]

American Depository Receipt (ADR)
Certificate that trades in the United States and represents a specific number of shares in a non-U.S. company.

International companies also make use of Global Depository Receipts (GDRs). These are similar in principle to ADRs but are listed and traded in London and Luxembourg. Companies from India aggressively issue GDRs to circumvent stringent listing requirements in their home market.[16]

Advantages of ADRs Companies gain several important advantages through ADRs. First, investors who buy ADRs pay no currency-conversion fees. In contrast, if a U.S. investor were to purchase the shares of a non-U.S. company on another country's stock exchange, he or she would incur the expense of converting currencies. Avoiding such expenses, plus the added convenience of paying in dollars, encourages U.S. investors to buy ADRs. Second, there are no minimum purchase requirements for ADRs, as there sometimes are for shares of a company's stock.[17]

Third, companies offer ADRs in the United States to appeal to mutual funds. Investment laws in the United States limit the amount of money that a mutual fund can invest in the shares of companies not registered on U.S. exchanges. German software producer SAP (Systeme Anwendungen Produkte in der Datenverarbeitung) was recently approached by mutual fund managers. It appears they were forced to sell the company's shares because they were appreciating in price. Says Kevin McKay, chief operating officer of SAP America: "Some of these guys were telling us, 'We hate to sell, but we have to. Please get some ADRs.'" SAP complied. Listing ADRs in the United States also allowed the company to reward employees with discounted shares of company stock—something that it could not have done otherwise because companies are barred from awarding shares in unregistered companies to employees in the United States.[18]

Some firms, however, are unhappy with the performance of their ADRs. As stock markets globalize, modernize, and increase liquidity, major U.S. investors can buy stock directly on other nations' stock exchanges—a fact that decreases the attractiveness of ADRs. With fewer buyers, a company's ADRs will trade at lower prices in the United States than its stock in its home country. This predicament is particularly troublesome for lesser-known companies based in newly industrialized and developing countries. Roadshows then become quite important in keeping a company on the view screens of U.S. stock analysts and brokers.[19]

venture capital

Financing obtained from investors who believe that the borrower will experience rapid growth and who receive equity—part ownership—in return.

Venture Capital   Another source of equity financing for entrepreneurial start-ups and small businesses is **venture capital**—financing obtained from investors who believe that the borrower will experience rapid growth and who receive equity—part ownership—in return. Those supplying the venture with the capital it needs are called *venture capitalists*. Although there is often substantial risk associated with new, rapidly expanding enterprises, venture capitalists invest in them because they can also generate very large returns on investment.

In recent years, the venture capital industry has become global. Entrepreneur Ron Posner, for example, wanted to expand his $6 million CD-ROM publishing firm, Star Press Inc. based in San Francisco. "Most people," explains Posner, "don't realize that Europe is a hot market—more so than Asia—for software, and it's a ripe field for investors." He searched for a European firm that was desperate for his CD-ROM technology and ended up in a joint venture with Olivetti Group, Europe's number-two computer manufacturer. Because Olivetti needed Posner's CD-ROM technology as much as Posner needed Olivetti's European distribution, Olivetti's venture-capital arm swapped $1.5 million for a 10 percent equity stake in Star Press.[20] For some key strategies used by Star Press and other savvy entrepreneurs in finding international investors, see the Entrepreneurial Focus titled "Get Global Cash: Overseas Investors Await You."

Emerging Stock Markets   The total worldwide volume of outstanding stocks is enormous. In 1997, the world's publicly traded shares of stock were valued collectively at $23.5 trillion! Of this total, $21.3 trillion was located in countries with developed stock markets and about $2.2 trillion in countries with emerging stock markets (see Map 14.1 on pages 500–501). The value of stocks traded on emerging stock markets stood at 9.5 percent of total worldwide equity capital in 1997—up from 6.5 percent in 1990.[21]

Entrepreneurial Focus

Get Global Cash: Overseas Investors Await You

Small-business financing is becoming more global as the economies of different nations become interwoven and the phone, fax, and modem make it easy to communicate between nations. As we know, the international capital market offers entrepreneurs many advantages. For example, in order to gain a market or technology position in the United States, international investors may accept lower returns than their U.S. counterparts. Here are some tips from entrepreneurs who have succeeded in finding international capital for their companies:

➡ **Contact business schools with strong international programs** to build up contacts. Instructors of international business courses often have contacts in both education and industry abroad. To break into this network, you might visit your local college, take an executive education course there, or perhaps even join a program in which you can work closely with entrepreneurial advisers.

➡ **Consult your country's commerce department** about potential international markets in which your product might be appealing. Developing, newly industrialized, and highly developed countries all have needs in practi-

cally every economic sector. Your nation's commerce department can help in your preliminary scouting of opportunities, as can your country's embassies.

➡ **Leverage your contacts** and tap the professionals with whom you work—especially attorneys and accountants with international ties. Long before you start pursuing overseas investors, consider asking a respected executive with international experience to serve on your board of directors.

➡ **Attend industry events in other countries** to increase your contacts and exposure. Your specific trade association should be able to provide you with a schedule of shows taking place in other countries.

➡ **Consider hiring an intermediary** to help find capital. Companies like International Funding Inc. of Jersey City, New Jersey, can help locate funding from international venture-capital firms, banks, and other lending institutions. The company helps expanding businesses get capital from Canadian, European, and Asian financial institutions.

In some of the truly "emerging" nations of the world, "high tech" accoutrements in one-room stock exchanges include blackboards and telephones. In Bhutan (a tiny nation situated between India and China), the seven-year-old stock exchange now has a total value of more than $40 million. That figure represents substantial progress in a country that only switched from barter to hard currency in the 1960s. Numerous such exchanges have appeared in the last fifteen years, primarily to attract shares in the rapidly expanding fund of money available for global investing—a fund that has expanded from $2 billion in 1986 to about $150 billion today. To learn more about the kinds of opportunities that are attracting investors to Bhutan, visit the following Web site:
⟨**www.cgtd.com/global/asia/bhutan.htm**⟩

Naturally, companies from countries with emerging stock markets face certain problems. First, emerging stock markets commonly experience extreme volatility. An important contributing factor is the fact that investments into emerging stock markets are often so-called *hot money*—money that can be quickly withdrawn in times of crisis. In contrast, *patient money*—foreign direct investment in factories, equipment, and land—cannot be pulled out as readily.

Large and sudden sell-offs of equity are signs of market volatility in emerging stock markets. Table 14.3 shows that one year's top-performing stock market can easily become next year's worst performer. And vice versa—look at Nigeria in 1993 and 1994.[23] Over a one-week period in 1997, Brazil's stock market fell over 15 percent.[22] In just

TABLE 14.3   *The Rough and Tumble of Emerging Markets*

Year	Best Markets		Worst Markets	
	Country	Total Return %	Country	Total Return %
1987	Turkey	262	Brazil	−63
1988	Brazil	126	Turkey	−61
1989	Turkey	502	Venezuela	−33
1990	Venezuela	602	Brazil	−66
1991	Argentina	397	Zimbabwe	−52
1992	Thailand	40	Zimbabwe	−60
1993	Turkey	234	Nigeria	−12
1994	Nigeria	191	Poland	−42
1995	S. Africa	18	Sri Lanka	−38
1996	Venezuela	132	Korea	−39

MAP 14.1

WORLDWIDE STOCK MARKET CAPITALIZATION (U.S. $ MILLIONS)

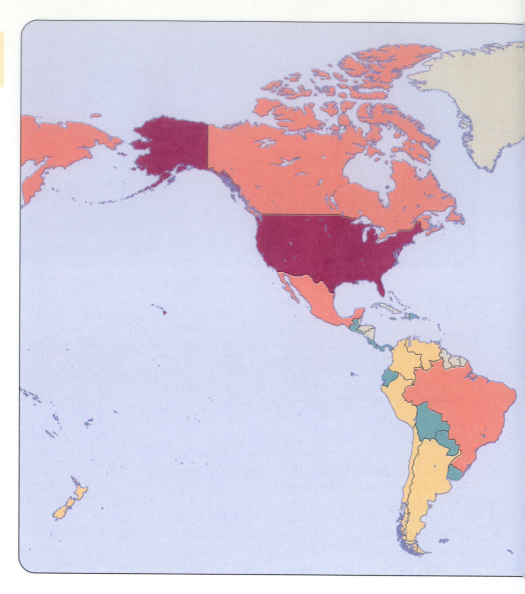

nine months from January to September 1998, the Russian stock market lost more than 80 percent of its value. Why do such large sell-offs occur? Usually because of uncertainty regarding future economic growth.

Second, companies that issue equity on their countries' emerging stock markets are often plagued by poor market regulation. The British brewer Bass, for example, increased its shareholding to 33 percent of the total shares of Czech Republic's number-two brewer, Pivovar Radegast. However, opposition from the banking group IPB, which held 34 percent of the brewery's stock, prevented Bass from dealing directly with a Czech investment company, KIS, which owned a 30 percent stake. The problem was rooted in an agreement, reached between IPB and KIS at the time of Radegast's privatization, that permitted KIS to talk to Bass only with IPB approval. As long as the Prague Stock Exchange is dominated by powerful domestic shareholders like IPB and KIS, international investors will likely stay away. The root of the problem lies in regulation that favors insiders over international investors who desire real shareholder influence.[24]

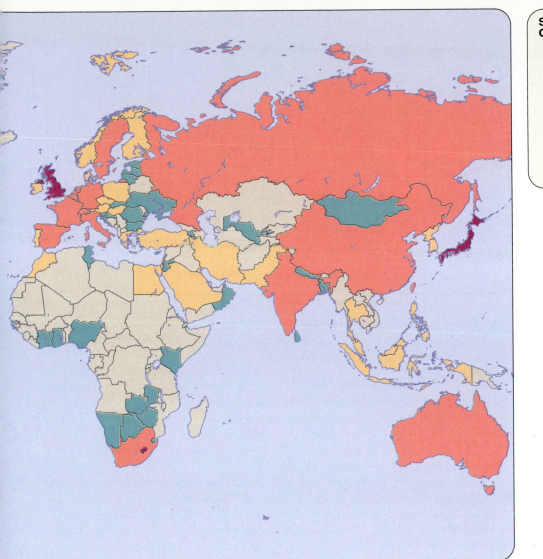

STOCK MARKET CAPITALIZATION (U.S. $ millions)

- 1,000,001 or more
- 100,001–1,000,000
- 10,001–100,000
- 10,000 or less

INTERNAL FUNDING

Ongoing international business activities and new investments can also be financed internally, whether with funds supplied by the parent company or by its international subsidiaries.

Internal Equity, Debt, and Fees   Spin-off companies and new subsidiaries typically require a period of time before they become financially independent. During this period, they often obtain internal financing from parent companies.

Many international subsidiaries obtain financial capital by issuing equity, which as a rule is not publicly traded. In fact, equity is often purchased solely by the parent, which obviously enjoys great influence over the subsidiary's decisions. If the subsidiary performs well, the parent earns a return from the appreciating share price, which reflects the increasing valuation of the company. If the subsidiary decides to pay stock dividends, the parent can also earn a return in this way. Parent companies commonly

FIGURE 14.3

INTERNAL SOURCES OF
CAPITAL FOR INTERNATIONAL
COMPANIES

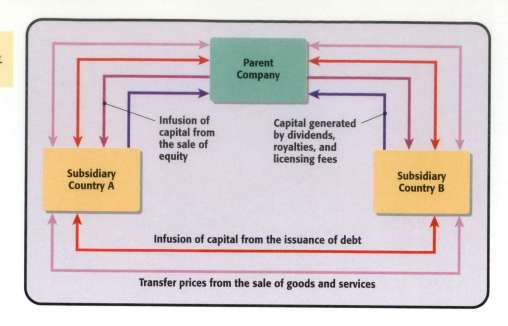

lend money to international subsidiaries during the start-up phase and when subsidiaries undertake large new investments. Conversely, subsidiaries with excess cash lend money to parent or sister companies when financial capital is needed.

Revenue from Operations   Monies earned from the sale of goods and services are called **revenue**. This source of capital is the lifeblood of international companies and their subsidiaries. If a company is to succeed in the long term, it must at some point generate sufficient internal revenue to sustain day-to-day operations. At that point, outside financing is required only to expand operations or to survive lean periods—say, during seasonal sales fluctuations.

International companies and their subsidiaries also generate revenues internally through so-called **transfer prices**—prices charged for goods or services transferred among a company and its subsidiaries. It is common for both parents and subsidiaries to buy from one another. Parents, for example, often license technologies to subsidiaries in return for royalties or licensing fees. Subsidiaries prefer this route to buying on the open market because they typically enjoy lower prices. Parents then buy finished products from subsidiaries at the stated transfer price.

Companies set subsidiaries' transfer prices high or low according to their own goals. Often, for instance, they pursue transfer pricing aggressively when they wish to minimize taxes in a high-taxation country. Transfer pricing can be used if there are no national restrictions on the use of foreign exchange or on the repatriation of profits to home countries. Figure 14.3 summarizes the internal sources of capital for international companies and their subsidiaries.

CAPITAL STRUCTURE

The **capital structure** of a company is the mix of equity, debt, and internally generated funds that it uses to finance its activities. Firms try to strike the right balance among financing methods in order to minimize the cost of capital and their risk.

Debt requires periodic interest payments to such creditors as banks and bondholders. If the company defaults on interest payments, creditors can take the company to court to force it to pay—even forcing it into bankruptcy. In the case of equity, however, only holders of certain types of preferred stock (which companies issue sparingly) can

revenue
Monies earned from the sale of goods and services.

transfer price
Price charged for a good or service transferred among a company and its subsidiaries.

capital structure
Mix of equity, debt, and internally generated funds used to finance a company's activities.

force bankruptcy due to default. As a rule, then, companies do not want to carry so much debt in relation to equity that it increases its risk of insolvency. Debt, however, appeals to companies in many countries because interest payments can be deducted from taxable earnings—thus lowering the amount of taxes the firm must pay.

The basic principles of capital structure do not vary from domestic to international companies. Recent research, however, indicates that multinational firms have lower ratios of debt to equity than domestic firms. Why is this so? Some observers cite increased political risk, exchange rate risk, and number of opportunities available to multinationals as possible explanations for the difference.[25] Others suggest that the debt-versus-equity option depends on a company's national culture.[26] This suggestion, however, has come under fire because companies from all cultures want to reduce capital costs. Moreover, many large international companies generate revenue from a large number of countries. How does one determine the "national culture" of these companies?

National restrictions, however, can influence the choice of capital structure. These restrictions include limits on the international flows of capital, the cost of local financing versus the cost of international financing, access to international financial markets, and controls imposed on currency exchange. The choice of capital structure for each of a company's international subsidiaries—and, therefore, its own capital structure—is a highly complex decision.

ACQUIRING PHYSICAL RESOURCES

International companies must also acquire a number of physical resources to begin operations. They must decide, for example, whether to make or buy the components they need in their production processes. They must determine the sources of needed raw materials. Finally, they must decide how they will acquire such fixed assets as facilities and production equipment. Let's begin by examining the ways firms decide whether to make or buy the components that go into their finished products.

MAKE-OR-BUY DECISION

The typical manufacturing company requires a wide range of inputs into its production process. These inputs typically enter the production line either as raw materials that require processing or as components needing only assembly. Bear in mind, too, that minor adjustments or other minor processing may be necessary before a component goes into production. Deciding whether to make a component or buy it from another company is called the **make-or-buy decision**. Each option has its own set of advantages and disadvantages.

Reasons to Make   The process by which a company extends its control over additional stages of production—either inputs or outputs—is called **vertical integration**. When a company decides to make a product rather than buy it, it engages in "upstream" activities: production activities that come before a company's current business operations. A carmaker, for example, who decides to manufacture its own window glass engages in a new upstream activity.

Lower Costs   Above all, companies make products rather than buy them in order to reduce total costs. Generally speaking, the manufacturer's profit is the difference between the product's selling price and its production cost. When a company buys a product, it rewards the manufacturer by contributing to the latter's profit margin. Therefore, companies often undertake in-house production when they can manufacture a product for less than they must pay someone else to produce it. Thus in-house production allows a company to reduce its own production costs.

make-or-buy decision
Deciding whether to make a component or buy it from another company.

vertical integration
Process by which a company extends its control over additional stages of production—either inputs or outputs.

At Compaq's Houston manufacturing facilities, for example, 13 production lines turn out a computer motherboard (the physical foundation of a PC to which the microprocessor, memory chips, and other components are attached). This critical component accounts for about 40 percent of a personal computer's total cost. In the mid-1990s, Greg Petsch, senior vice president of manufacturing, discovered that Compaq could produce motherboards for $25 less than its Asian suppliers (and save two weeks' shipping time in the process).[27]

Small companies are less likely than large ones to make rather than buy, especially when a product requires large financial investment in equipment and facilities. This rule of thumb, however, might not necessarily hold if the company possesses a proprietary technology or some other competitive advantage that is not easily copied.

Greater Control Companies that depend on others for key ingredients or components give up a degree of control. Making rather than buying can give managers greater control over raw materials, product design, and the production process itself—all of which are important factors in product quality. In turn, quality control is especially important when customers are highly sensitive to even slight declines in quality. For the same reason, greater quality control also gives a company greater control over its reputation among customers.

In addition, persuading an outside supplier to make significant modifications to quality or features can be difficult. This is especially true if modifications entail investment in costly equipment or promise to be time-consuming. If just one buyer requests costly product adaptations, or if there is reason to suspect that a buyer will eventually take its business elsewhere, a supplier may be reluctant to undertake a costly investment. Unless that buyer purchases in large volumes, the cost of the modifications may be too great for the supplier to absorb. In that case, the buyer simply could not obtain the product it wants without manufacturing it in-house. Thus, companies maintain greater control over product design and product features if they manufacture components themselves.

Finally, making a product is a good idea when buying from a supplier means providing the supplier with a firm's key technology. Through licensing agreements (see Chapter 13), companies often provide suppliers in low-wage countries with the technologies needed to make their products. If, however, a company's competitive advantage depends on that technology, the licenser could inadvertently be creating a future competitor. When controlling a key technology is paramount, it is often better to manufacture in-house.

Reasons to Buy The practice of buying from another company a good or service that is not central to a company's competitive advantage is called **outsourcing**. Outsourcing results from continuous specialization and technological advancement. For each successive specialization of its operations process, a manufacturer requires greater skill and knowledge than it did before. By outsourcing, a company can reduce the degree to which it is vertically integrated and thus the overall amount of specialized skill and knowledge that it must possess. As we saw in the chapter-opening vignette, Sara Lee has resorted to outsourcing for precisely this reason.

Outsourcing has become extremely popular in the business of computer manufacturing. Component makers, including Intel in microprocessors, Seagate in hard drives, U.S. Robotics in modems, and Mitsumi in CD-ROM drives, supply big and small manufacturers worldwide. Computer companies buy components from these manufacturers, assemble them in their own facilities, and sell completed systems to consumers and businesses. A related practice in the computer industry is known as "stealth manufacturing," which calls for outsourcing the actual assembly of the computers themselves,

outsourcing
Practice of buying from another company a good or service that is not central to a company's competitive advantage.

plus the job of shipping them to distributors and other intermediaries. For example, in addition to being the world's biggest computer wholesaler, Ingram Micro Inc. also builds PCs for Compaq, IBM, Apple, and other brand-name computer marketers.[28]

Phenomenal growth is also occurring in the outsourcing of information technology (IT)—the wide variety of items and abilities used by a firm to create, store, and disperse information. In 1997, over 60 percent of all organizations in the United Kingdom and the United States were outsourcing at least a portion of their IT activities. The world market for IT outsourcing is expected to exceed $121 billion in the year 2000.[29]

Clearly, companies buy when buying is the lower-cost option. When a firm cannot integrate vertically by manufacturing a product for less than a supplier can, it will continue to outsource. Let's explore some other reasons why companies prefer to buy rather than make.

Lower Risk In earlier chapters, we described the many types of risks faced by companies that construct and staff facilities in other countries. Recall, for example, that political risk is quite high in certain markets. The government of an intensely nationalistic nation might decide to expropriate businesses or nationalize industries without concern for the interests of an international company. In addition, social unrest or open conflict can threaten physical facilities, equipment, and employee safety.

One way a company can eliminate the exposure of assets to political risk in other countries is simply by refusing to invest in plants and equipment abroad. It can instead purchase products from international suppliers. This policy also eliminates the need to purchase expensive insurance coverage that is needed when a company undertakes production in an unstable country. It will not, however, completely eliminate all potential disruptions due to political instability in a given market. The buyer, for instance, may not receive timely shipments of needed parts. Indeed, even under normal circumstances, the longer delivery times involved in international outsourcing can increase the risk that the buyer will not meet its own production schedule.

Greater Flexibility Maintaining sufficient flexibility to respond to market conditions is increasingly important for companies everywhere. Making an in-house product that requires large investments in equipment and buildings often reduces flexibility. In contrast, companies that buy products from one or more outside suppliers gain flexibility. In fact, added flexibility is the key factor in a fundamental change in attitude toward outsourcing, which many managers now regard as a full-fledged strategy for change rather than a limited tactical tool for solving immediate problems.

Maintaining flexibility is important when the national business environments of suppliers are volatile. By buying from several suppliers, or by establishing production facilities in more than one country, a company can outsource products from one location if instability erupts in another. The same is true in periods of great exchange-rate volatility. Exchange-rate movements can increase or decrease the cost of importing a product from a given country. By buying from multiple suppliers located in several countries, a company can maintain the flexibility needed to change sources *and* reduce the risk associated with sudden swings in exchange rates.

Companies also maintain operational flexibility simply by not having to invest in production facilities. Unencumbered by investment in costly production equipment and facilities, a firm can alter its product line very quickly. This capability is especially important for products with small production runs or those with highly uncertain potential. Furthermore, a company can obtain financial flexibility if its capital is not locked up in plants and equipment. It can then use excess financial capital to pursue other domestic or international opportunities. Outsourcing can also free a company from having to recoup large research and development investments.

Maintaining flexibility to respond to market conditions was one factor in Nissan Motor Company's decision to build this truck-assembly plant in Smyrna, Tennessee. Obviously, Nissan wanted to locate in the vicinity of its customers in the U.S. market so that it could maintain tight inventories and schedules as market demand dictated. The Japanese firm also profits from favorable wage scales and a receptive local atmosphere. The principle of proximity also works both ways: by locating in the Tennessee Valley area, Nissan (along with Saturn) has attracted a circle of suppliers who can deliver parts and components within hours.

Market Power Companies can gain a great deal of power in their relationships with suppliers simply by becoming important customers. In fact, sometimes a supplier can become a sort of hostage to one particular customer. This situation occurs when a supplier becomes heavily dependent on a company that it serves with nearly all of its production capacity. If the main buyer suddenly begins outsourcing elsewhere, the supplier will have few other customers to whom it can turn. This situation gives the buyer significant control in dictating quality improvements, forcing cost reductions, and making special modifications.

Barriers to Buying For various reasons, companies sometimes face obstacles when buying products from international suppliers. First, the government of the buyer's country may impose import tariffs designed to improve the nation's balance of trade. Tariffs can add anywhere from 15 to 50 percent to the cost of a component that a manufacturer needs from abroad.

Second, the services provided by intermediaries increase the cost of buying abroad. Obtaining letters of credit, arranging physical transport, and obtaining insurance all add to the final cost that a manufacturer pays for a product supplied from abroad. Although these expenses are currently lower than they have ever been, they can significantly increase total product cost. If high enough, they can negate any advantage of buying from an international supplier.

RAW MATERIALS

Decisions about the selection and acquisition of raw materials are important to many different types of manufacturers. The twin issues of quantity and quality drive many decisions about raw material acquisition. First, some industries and companies rely almost exclusively on the quantity of locally available raw materials. This is most true for companies involved in mining, forestry, and fishing. There must be an adequate supply of iron ore, oil, lumber, or fish to justify the large financial investment required to build processing facilities.

Second, raw material quality has a huge influence on the quality of a company's end product. Food-processing companies, for instance, must examine the quality of the locally grown fruit, vegetables, grains, and any other ingredient. Beverage companies must assess the quality of the local water supply. Some markets may require large financial investments to build water-purifying facilities. Elsewhere (such as much of the Middle East), the only local water source may be seawater that must be desalinized. (Recall that Chapter 11 discusses the importance of raw materials in the site selection decision.)

FIXED ASSETS

fixed (or tangible) assets *Company assets, such as production facilities, inventory warehouses, retail outlets, and production and office equipment.*

Most companies must acquire **fixed** (or **tangible**) **assets**—such as production facilities, inventory warehouses, retail outlets, and production and office equipment—in the host country. They can, for instance, acquire and modify existing factories or build entirely new facilities. Considering either option involves many individuals within the company. Production managers, for example, must verify that an existing facility (or an empty lot) is large enough and will suit the company's facility layout needs. Site-acquisition experts and legal staff must guarantee that the proposed business activity abides by local laws. Public relations staff must work with community leaders to ensure that the company does not jeopardize the rights, values, and customs of the local population.

Finally, managers must make sure that the local infrastructure can support the firm's proposed on-site business operations. Also, factory and office equipment is likely to be available locally in most newly industrialized and developed markets. Little, if any, equipment, however, is likely to be available in developing markets. Thus, managers must assess both the cost in tariffs that will be imposed on imported equipment and the cost in time and effort that will be required to import it. (Again, Chapter 11 details the importance of fixed assets within the context of the site selection decision.)

A FINAL WORD

This chapter has presented the important factors that companies must consider when acquiring resources for international operations. As we saw in our opening example of Sara Lee Corporation, these factors are often complex and interrelated. The major categories of resources are human, financial, and physical. The resources that a company acquires reflect its particular resource needs which in turn depend on the future outlook for its industry. Once resources are acquired, they must be employed for the purpose of achieving the firm's international business goals. In the next chapter, we continue to build our understanding of the key issues involved in a company's determination to go international. The next chapter shows how companies make efficient use of their resources by managing them effectively.

There is a variety of additional material available on the companion Web site that accompanies this text. You can access this information by visiting the Web site at ⟨**www.prenhall.com/wild**⟩.

summary

1. **Explain the three different *strategic staffing policies* used by international companies.** In a company with an **ethnocentric staffing policy,** operations outside the home country are staffed and managed by home-country nationals. To provide headquarters with tight controls over the decision making of branch offices in other countries, policies are designed to work in each market in which the company operates. A *polycentric staffing policy* accomplishes just the opposite: International operations are staffed and managed by host-country natives who have usually participated in extensive training programs. Such policies are generally designed to give national units a certain level of autonomy in decision making. *Geocentric staffing* means staffing operations outside the home country with the best-qualified individuals regardless of nationality. This policy is typically reserved for top-level managers, who may be chosen from the home country, from the host country, or from a third country.

2. **Describe the *recruitment* and *selection* issues facing international companies.** Large companies often recruit international management from within the ranks of existing employees. Because small and midsize companies may not have qualified managers, managers for international assignments may have to be hired from other companies. Sometimes international students who have graduated from local colleges are hired, trained locally, and then posted in their home countries. Local managerial talent can also be recruited in the host country; such persons bring special capabilities, such as an understanding of the local culture and political system. In addition, local hires are often required when a company sets up manufacturing abroad or engages in extensive marketing activities. When selecting employees for international positions, companies look for an ability to adapt to cultural differences. When hiring in-country personnel, the employer's home-country bias may make it difficult to determine technical competence or leadership ability.

③ Discuss the importance of *training* and *development programs*, especially cultural training. *Culture shock* refers to the psychological difficulties experienced when living in an unfamiliar culture—it is often characterized by homesickness, irritability, confusion, aggravation, and depression. Many international managers return home early from an international job assignment because they or a family member cannot adapt to the new culture. Ironically, returning managers often experience *reverse culture shock*: the psychological process of readapting to one's home culture. For these reasons, cultural training is becoming increasingly important.

Cultural training is often effective in reducing the effects of both culture shock and reverse culture shock. Training ranges from reading books and seeing films about a culture to visiting it on a field trip, and there are various methods for preparing people for international assignment. All, however, share a basic purpose: creating informed, open-minded, flexible employees with a level of cultural training appropriate to the task required of them. *Environmental briefings* and *cultural orientations* provide insight on matters such as local housing and health care and describe political, economic, and social institutions. *Cultural assimilation* and *sensitivity training* explain the local values, attitudes, and customs and stress the importance of understanding local feelings and emotions. *Language training* provides specific, practical skills that allow employees to communicate in the local language. *Field experience* means visiting the culture for a brief period to begin growing accustomed to it.

④ Explain how companies *compensate managers* and *workers* in international markets. An effective compensation policy takes into account local cultures, laws, and practices. Issues include base pay as a percentage of total compensation, bonuses, and fringe benefits. Managerial compensation packages may have to be adjusted to reflect *cost of living*, and the cost of education for family members may also be a consideration. *Bonus* payments or hardship pay may be required as an incentive for managers to accept international assignments. Nonmanagerial compensation levels can be influenced by wage rates in other countries. Investment capital tends to flow to nations with low-cost labor, resulting in increased equality in worker pay from country to country.

⑤ Describe the three potential *sources of financing* and the *main financial instruments* of each. One source is *borrowing*, and international companies generally scan the world financial scene for the lowest interest rates. In some instances, fluctuations in currency exchange rates can make cross-border borrowing an attractive alternative. In *back-to-back loans*, parent firms loan money to subsidiaries by depositing money in host-country banks. Companies wanting access to a greater pool of investors or wanting to take advantage of lower interest rates can issue *international bonds*.

A second source is *equity financing*, wherein a company sells stock to raise capital. *Venture capital* is a source of equity for entrepreneurial start-ups and small businesses. Third, revenue from ongoing operations can be used to finance company growth and expansion. In addition to debt and equity, international companies and their subsidiaries can obtain funds from *transfer prices* and dividends, royalties, and licencing fees.

⑥ Identify key considerations in the *make-or-buy decision* when acquiring physical resources. In essence, the *make-or-buy* decision represents the decision for or against greater *vertical integration*—the process whereby a company extends control over additional stages of production. A firm that chooses to *make* a particular product or component often does so to take advantage of lower costs or to achieve greater control. On the other hand, *outsourcing*—buying from another company a good or service that is not central to a firm's competitive advantage—can provide greater flexibility while reducing the exposure to exchange-rate fluctuations and other forms of risk.

questions for review

1. List some of the ways in which *international HRM* differs from HRM in the domestic environment.

2. Identify the three different types of *international staffing policies* that companies can implement. What are the advantages and disadvantages of each?

3. What are the main sources from which companies *recruit* their international managers?

4. What is *culture shock*? Explain its importance in the *selection* of international managers.

5. What is *reverse culture shock*?

6. Identify the types of *training and development* used for international managers and nonmanagerial workers.

7. What are the main variables involved in decisions regarding employee *compensation* for managers and nonmanagerial workers?

8. What is *hardship* or *combat pay*? Under what circumstances do companies provide such compensation?

9. What are the three means by which international companies can acquire *financial resources*?

10. What is the difference between a *Eurobond* and a *foreign bond*?

11. Why might a company list its stock in the *international capital market*? Explain the advantages of issuing an *American Depository Receipt (ADR)*.

12. Why is *revenue* from operations so important to a company's future success?

13. What is meant by a company's *capital structure*?

14. What are some of the difficulties facing companies that issue equity on *emerging stock markets*?

15. What is meant by the phrase *make-or-buy decision*? List the reasons why a company might decide to make or buy a component.

16. What are the main factors involved in acquiring *raw materials*? *Fixed assets*?

questions for discussion

1. Many Japanese companies utilize ethnocentric staffing policies, both at home and in international operations. For example, at Mitsubishi Motor Manufacturing of America, the chief executive and president are both Japanese. Why do you think Japanese companies prefer to have Japanese in top management positions? Would you recommend a change in this policy?

2. Internet commerce (*e-commerce*, as it is commonly called) is increasingly popular. What resources does an Internet retailer need other than merely a storefront on the Internet? Does it require fewer human, financial, and physical resources than a traditional retailer or just as many? Explain.

3. What do you think a country with an emerging stock market can do to create a more stable capital market? How important are the political-, legal-, and economic-development factors discussed earlier in this text? Support your answers with examples.

4. Have you ever experienced culture shock? If so, in which country did it occur? What, if anything, did you do to overcome it? Did your methods work? Did you experience reverse culture shock upon returning home?

in practice

Read the brief article below and answer the questions that follow.

Xerox to Invest in Irish Facilities

The Xerox Corp. has said it will invest $270 million in new production and support facilities in Dublin and Dundalk, Ireland. The company plans to locate a large portion of its European shared services and customer support operations, as well as some of its customer financing and management, in the Dublin suburb of Blanchardstown. In addition, Xerox has acquired more than 100 acres in Dundalk—near the border with Northern Ireland—as the site of several facilities for color toner cartridge manufacturing, logistics, technical support, and other nonmanufacturing activities.

1. Why might Xerox have decided to build a facility in Ireland to produce toner cartridges itself rather than contract with a supplier for their production? List some benefits Xerox might expect to gain by making instead of buying.

2. Why do you think Xerox chose Ireland for expansion? How might relative unrest or stability in Northern Ireland affect the performance of its facilities so near the border between Ireland and Northern Ireland?

3. What sort of fixed assets might Xerox need for each type of activity it is proposing to carry out in Ireland?

projects

1. Suppose that you are vice president of operations for a major automobile manufacturer. Among your company's worldwide operations are plants in Spain and Germany. Your company is considering closing these two plants and moving production to Poland in order to take advantage of lower wages. Write a short report explaining how easy (or how difficult) it will be for your company to close the plant and lay off workers in each of Spain and Germany.

2. Suppose that you are the chief financial officer of a consumer-goods company based in Mexico. Your company wishes to expand internationally but lacks the necessary financial capital. Describe all the financing options that you think are available to your company. Explain why you think each option is feasible, taking into account the prevailing situation in the Mexican and international capital markets. Develop a short presentation to be delivered to your board of directors (your classmates).

3. The United States is home to some of the world's leading computer software companies, most of which commonly outsource software development to other countries, including Egypt, India, Ireland, Israel, Malaysia, Hungary, and the Philippines. Select one of these countries and explain why it has become a supplier to the computer software industry. Do you think that development of the industry in your chosen country will threaten companies in the United States?

THE FINE LINE BETWEEN EXPATRIATION AND DISCRIMINATION

One issue faced by companies with international operations is determining the right time to bring expatriate managers home. Promoting host-country personnel into key managerial positions can boost morale and provide a sense of equal opportunity. Also, local managers often have keen insights into local business conditions and, therefore, a potential advantage when it comes to decision making. Moreover, by bringing expatriate managers home, firms can often save considerable amounts of money. In China, for example, compensation for an expat can cost between $200,000 and $300,000 per year; the total package includes cost-of-living and hardship allowances of 15 to 20 percent each. By comparison, total compensation for a top-notch Chinese manager would be only about $50,000 per year.

Despite the benefits to be gained from turning over control to local managers, some industry experts warn that "localizing" too quickly can be a mistake. For example, as one expat manager in China put it, "Doing business the Chinese way is much less well-documented and can be dangerous. There is a serious risk when you give up financial control." Another problem is the fact that many expatriate managers are evaluated according to operating results rather than their efforts to train local managers.

The issue of expatriate assignments is not limited to such emerging markets as China. In developed countries, laying off employees or replacing local managers with persons from the home country can be controversial moves. Japanese-owned Ricoh Corporation, for example, put a Japanese manager in charge of optical computer-disk sales at its California File Products Division (FPD). After being laid off as a result of the move, American Chet Mackentire sued his former employer for discrimination under Title VII of the Civil Rights Act of 1964. Ricoh argued that Mackentire had been laid off for business reasons, not because he was a Caucasian-American.

Mackentire's case was dismissed by summary judgment in the United States District Court for the Northern District of California. The court found "no evidence to support Mackentire's theory that the layoff was discriminatory" and ruled that there was "substantial evidence that it was due to business necessity." Mackentire appealed to the Ninth Circuit Court of Appeals, but the appellate court upheld the lower court's summary judgment. Ricoh, wrote the judges, "offered affidavits stating that FPD was losing money, running into the millions of dollars annually. It also offered evidence that it reorganized the division to de-emphasize the product for which Mackentire was most responsible."

thinking globally

1. What are some key reasons for keeping expatriate managers in top positions?

2. Suppose a company decides that it has made a mistake by hiring local personnel in a key Asian country. What are some potential problems that it will face if it decides to install or reinstate expatriate managers in these positions?

3. In addition to those mentioned in the case, what are some other advantages associated with the hiring of local managers in emerging markets?

4. What steps should a company take to ensure that, if taken to court, it can demonstrate that staffing cuts have not been discriminatory?

a question of ethics

1. Imagine yourself on your first assignment abroad as a manager at a manufacturing facility in Asia. You are aware of increasing concern among your employees (mostly young women) about wages that barely permit them to live at subsistence level. The plant is not unionized, and you know that your superiors in your home country are not particularly supportive of efforts to organize workers. You also know that if workers vote to form a union and then demand higher wages, headquarters is likely to shift production to a lower-wage country. The plant could possibly be shut down, your employees could lose their jobs, and you could be transferred. Should you encourage or discourage your workers in their efforts to unionize?

2. You work in the office of the governor in a southeastern U.S. state. Unemployment rates in your state, especially in rural areas, is above the national average and the governor was elected on a pledge to attract industry and create jobs. A European automaker has put your state on its short list of potential sites for a new manufacturing facility. The facility is expected to employ about 1,500 people. Your boss (the governor) knows

that the automaker expects a significant package of incentives and concessions. The governor, who is planning to offer some $300 million in tax breaks and subsidies in an effort to bring the new plant to the state, wants your insight and recommendation. Do such outlays represent proper use of taxpayer money?

3. After graduating from college, you were hired by a financial-services company that is expanding operations in Latin America. You got the job in part because you double-majored in Spanish and finance and spent one semester studying in Mexico. Your company's policy is to provide employees working abroad with hardship pay, a generous housing allowance, a company car, and a fund of several thousand dollars to be used at your discretion. You are actually quite comfortable living abroad, but you have some expat friends who haven't adjusted so well. Every two months or so, they want to fly back home to visit friends and get a change of scenery. You aren't homesick at all, but your friends want you to go with them. Should you dip into your discretionary funds and go along or remain in the community doing volunteer work with local charities?

15 managing the international business

Beacons

A Look Back

CHAPTER 14 explained how companies acquire the resources they need to carry out their international operations. We examined how companies employ human resources and acquire their financial and physical resources.

A Look at This Chapter

This chapter completes our study of international business management. We examine how companies manage their resources to accomplish their international marketing and manufacturing objectives. We also examine how managers decide future courses of action.

Learning Objectives

After studying this chapter, you should be able to

1. Describe the factors influencing international *product policies*.
2. Discuss the elements influencing international *promotional policies* and how companies blend product and promotional policies.
3. Describe the factors influencing international *distribution policies*.
4. Discuss the elements influencing international *pricing policies*.
5. Explain the important aspects of *quality*, *logistics*, and *workforce* management.
6. Identify the managerial considerations in the *reinvest* and *divest decisions*.

The top brass from New York were attending the quarterly meeting of Avon's China operations. In fact, dinner was doubling as a birthday celebration for one regional executive. But the festive party mood ended abruptly when the phone call came. China's evening news had just announced a government ban on all direct selling, or *chuanxiao*—Avon's signature marketing approach for 112 years and now in 135 countries.

"It was a little hard to believe. Certainly it became a topic of conversation," says William Pryor, head of Avon's operations in China who took the call that evening. The next day, Avon was closing operations across China to comply with the government crackdown that was effective immediately.

The ban could not have come at a worse time for Avon. The company had already sunk $70 million into China, and its 100,000 sales reps were fanning out across the country's vast territory. It also had just begun work on a $40 million factory to churn out enough cosmetics to meet growing demand.

But Avon did not stand still. It couldn't afford to—it was losing $100,000 per day. Avon transformed 70 supply and training centers into stores and

began retailing. Across China, 12,000 resellers started hawking Avon products at street kiosks. Avon also struck an agreement with a drugstore chain to carry its products. Selling through TV home shopping channels and the Internet were also being explored.

But the company is hopeful the ban will be overturned. As Avon's Asia-Pacific president, José Ferreira, says about China's government, "They have bigger things to worry about than if we can sell lipstick person-to-person."[1]

As Avon and other companies using the direct-selling approach in China discovered, vigilance when doing business abroad may not be enough. Unpredictable events can devastate a business overnight. Many times such events have little to do with grand strategies but much to do with the day-to-day management of operations.

In earlier chapters, we continually emphasized the greater complexity of managing an international business as compared to a purely domestic one. Myriad differences in all aspects of a nation's business environment complicate matters. Managing business activities that span time zones and cultures can strain the resources of the largest company and can overwhelm a smaller one. Thus to wrap up our study of international business, we must examine the important issues that confront managers on a daily basis. These issues include how to promote and advertise a product, the price that a product should sell for, how to design distribution channels, how to ensure quality production processes, and how to manage the workforce.

We begin this chapter by discussing the most important aspects of managing international marketing activities. We then consider production issues, including international logistics, total quality management, and managing workers. We then explain the important factors influencing managers' decisions of whether to expand or reduce operations abroad.

MANAGING MARKETING ACTIVITIES

In Chapter 12, we discussed the *strategic* marketing issues that managers must consider when formulating their corporate, business, and departmental strategies. Now we turn our attention to the *tactical* issues managers deal with in their day-to-day management decisions. In this section we present the important elements that influence a company's *product*, *promotional*, *distribution*, and *pricing policies*.

PRODUCT POLICIES

Companies can standardize or adapt their products in many alternative ways when they decide to "go international." Let's take a look at some of the factors that influence the standardize-versus-adapt decision as well as several other international product policy issues.

Laws and Regulations   Companies often must adapt their products to satisfy the laws and regulations in a target market. Consider the dilemma facing chocolate makers in a unified European Union (EU). People's tastes, of course, vary across markets, and taste in chocolate is no exception to the rule. A so-called "Chocolate War" has erupted in the EU as it tries to standardize member countries' product content regulations. On one side stand the so-called "cocoa purists," including Belgium, France, Germany, Spain, Italy, the Netherlands, Luxembourg, and Greece. Opposite stand Britain, Denmark, Portugal, Austria, Finland, and Sweden—nations who permit manufacturers to add vegetable fats to chocolate products. The purists argue not only that European advertising should restrict the word *chocolate* to 100 percent cocoa products, but that the term *milk chocolate* be outlawed altogether. They want nonpure products labeled something like "chocolate with milk and noncocoa vegetable fats."[2]

The fact that many developing countries have fewer consumer-protection laws creates an ethical issue for some companies. Ironically, lower levels of education and less buying experience mean that consumers in developing countries are more likely to need protection. Many governments, however, impose less regulation in order to hold down production costs and consumer prices. Unfortunately, this can be an invitation for international distributors to withhold full information about products and their potential dangers.

Cultural Differences   Companies also adapt their products to suit local buyers' product preferences that are rooted in culture. Häagen-Dazs is an international company that prides itself in its ability to identify taste preferences of consumers in a target market. It then modifies its base product with just the right flavor to produce a product that satisfies consumers' needs. Following years of trial and error developing secret formulas and conducting taste tests, Häagen-Dazs finally launched its green-tea flavor ice cream throughout Japan. The taste is that of *macha* tea—an elite strain of green tea that's been used in elaborate Japanese ceremonies for centuries. Green-tea ice cream was a hit instantly and one day may even surpass Häagen-Dazs' perennial flavor champion in Japan—vanilla.[3]

Not all companies need to modify their product to the culture but instead identify a different cultural need that it satisfies. Altoids, for example, is a British product that has been used for 200 years to soothe upset stomachs. But the company identified a different use for its product in the United States. Because of its strong flavor, Altoids also acts as a breath mint. Altoids breath mints have pushed aside weaker-flavored candies including Certs to command 17 percent of the $281 million U.S. market.[4]

Brand and Product Names   Several issues related to a company's brand name are important concerns for the day-to-day activities of international managers. A **brand name** is the name of one or more items in a product line that identifies the source or character of the items. For example, when we see a product labeled BMW, Bic, Evian, Nike, Sony, or Starbucks, we assign to that product a certain value based on our past experiences with that particular brand. Thus a brand name is central to a product's personality and the image that it presents to buyers. It informs buyers about a product's source and protects both customer and producer from copycat products. Brand names help consumers to select, recommend, or reject products and function as legal property that owners can protect from trespass by competitors.

> **brand name**
> *Name of one or more items in a product line that identifies the source or character of the items.*

Indeed, a strong brand can become a company's most valuable asset and primary source of competitive advantage.[5] A consistent worldwide brand image is important, as more consumers and businesspeople travel internationally than ever before. Any inconsistency in brand name is sure to confuse existing and potential customers. Although companies keep their brand names consistent across markets, they often do create new product names or modify existing ones to suit local preferences.

Selecting International Brand and Product Names   Whether they are standardized or locally adapted, products in international markets need carefully selected names. All company and product brand names (like all nouns) are made up of *morphemes*—semantic elements, or language building blocks, such as the *van* in *advantage*.

NameLab is an identity-consultant firm that uses over 6,000 morphemes to develop new product names. Namelab points out that because most Western languages stem from the same linguistic source—Indo-European—companies can create brand names having similar meanings in these nations. *Accu*, for example, connotes *accuracy* among Western cultures and Japan. Thus Honda named its up-market car division *Acura*. Other names that are constructed to have similar connotations in many languages or embody no cultural bias include Compaq, Kodak, Lumina, and Sony.[6] Once a name is chosen, companies can survey local native speakers as to their reactions to it. These techniques help companies reduce the likelihood of committing potential marketing blunders.

Brand names seldom offend people in international markets, but product names can be highly offensive if they are not carefully researched and selected. Clarks Shoes, a British shoe company, once gave a name to a line of shoes that was offensive to the Hindu religious community in Britain. Consequently, the company had to issue the following apology in the British press:[7]

> *Clarks Shoes are concerned that the naming of some of their products with the names of Hindu Gods Vishnu and Krishna has caused hurt and offence to the British Hindu Community. The Company apologises for this mistake and is withholding the products before resuming sales with new names. In the future the company will carry out more detailed research before naming products.*

Other times, product names must be changed not because they're offensive, but because they mislead consumers. Consider the problem faced by the British beverage and chocolate producer Cadbury Schweppes. When Swiss chocolate manufacturers sued on the grounds that the public was being misled into thinking that Cadbury's Swiss Chalet bar was genuine Swiss chocolate, the company was forced to withdraw the product from the marketplace. A British court confirmed that the name and packaging of the product—the "Swiss" part of the name and the image of a snow-capped Swiss Alp—were likely to mislead consumers.[8]

National Image The value that customers obtain from a product is heavily influenced by the image of the country in which it is designed, manufactured, or assembled. We consider the influence of a country's name when thinking of Italian shoes, German luxury cars, and Japanese electronics. However, this image can be positive for some products but negative for others. For example, the best Russian caviar and vodkas have reputations of quality around the world. But what about Russian televisions, VCRs, automobiles, or computers? Thus attaching "Russia" to certain products is beneficial whereas attaching it to others is clearly a detriment.

Because it affects buyers' perceptions of quality and reliability, national image is an important element of product policy. However, national image can and does change over time—although slowly. Decades ago, Japanese products were considered to be of poor quality and rather unreliable. But a national effort toward quality improvement and the installation of quality control procedures by companies earned Japan a national image for precision and quality products.[9] Japanese cars, which were once vehicles for the budget-conscious consumer, now have luxury models that rival the quality and technological advancement of German autos.

Likewise, years ago Taiwan was known for basic, no-frills items such as toys and industrial products of all sorts. But today many of Taiwan's industries possess a reputation for innovation—designing products that reflect decades of investing in people's research and engineering skills. One company that benefited from an intense devotion to R&D is Giant Manufacturing, Taiwan's leading bicycle manufacturer. The company began in Taichung, Taiwan, nearly three decades ago producing bikes under the brand names of other companies. But in 1980 the company began to manufacture under its own brand name and today has a solid niche in the mountain bike market. Giant's innovation in using lightweight materials and creating groundbreaking designs recently earned it sponsorship of Spain's world-champion racing team. Today, high-tech products, and even those not traditionally thought of as high tech (such as bikes), stamped "Made in Taiwan" command respect in global markets.[10]

Counterfeit Goods and Black Markets   We discussed how companies are trying to protect their intellectual property and trademarks from counterfeit goods in Chapter 3. Recall that *counterfeit goods* are imitation products passed off as legitimate trademarks, patents, or copyrighted works—products that normally enjoy legal protection. Because developing nations often are weakest in enforcing such legal protections, they normally have the most active counterfeiting markets. Countries topping the list for the portion of their markets comprised of counterfeits include Bulgaria, China, India, Russia, and Turkey. Currently representing between 5 and 10 percent of international trade, counterfeiting is worth as much as $50 billion to $80 billion worldwide.[11]

Counterfeiting is common among highly visible brand-name consumer goods, including watches, perfumes, clothing, movies, music, and computer software. Counterfeit products are typically sold to consumers on what is called the *black market*—a marketplace of underground transactions that typically appears because a product is either illegal (such as counterfeits) or tightly regulated. Tabletop vendors working the back streets of the world's largest cities represent the retail side of the black market. For instance, in Sofia, capital of Bulgaria, you can buy one CD-ROM that contains 50 software applications for $10—buying all the official versions of these products would cost about $5,000![12] In Estonia's Kadaka flea market you can find the full Microsoft Office software bundle for around $18—about one fiftieth of its official selling price.[13] Increasingly, engineered industrial components such as aircraft parts, medicines, and other pharmaceutical products are also becoming targets of counterfeiters.

Counterfeit goods can damage buyers' image of a brand when the counterfeits are of inferior quality—which is nearly always the case. Buyers purchase an item bearing a company's brand name, expecting a certain level of craftsmanship and, therefore, satisfaction. But when the product fails to deliver up to expectations, the buyer is dissatisfied and the company's reputation is tarnished. The negative effects of counterfeits on brand image can be especially hard on small companies. Whereas large companies have deep pockets that help them to fight counterfeiters and to survive lost sales, small companies do not. Consider the case of WildeWood Creative Products of Sonora, California. When the company hit it big with its clear-plastic kaleidoscopes, Chinese copycats moved in with a similar product costing one-third as much. Sales went from $4 million to $1 million in just three years. "They really took the wind out of our sails," says founder Mark Eilrich. "I'm proud that we've survived."[14]

Shortened Product Life Cycles   Companies have historically managed to extend a product's life by introducing it into different markets consecutively. This was accomplished by introducing products in industrialized countries, and only afterward marketing them in developing and emerging markets. Thus while a product's sales are declining in one market, they might be growing in another.

However, advances in telecommunications have alerted consumers around the world to the latest product introductions. Consequently, consumers in developing and emerging markets also demand the latest products instead of being satisfied with yesterday's fad in highly developed nations. Also, the rapid pace with which technological innovation occurs today is shortening the life cycles of products. The actions of inter-

Bangkok officials rake over seized pirated videotapes to demonstrate their government's resolve against piracy, which has become a major area of dispute in trade between Thailand and the United States. The effect of such staged demonstrations in combating the flow of stolen and counterfeited goods remains to be seen.

national companies themselves actually helped create this situation. Companies are undertaking new-product development at an increasingly rapid pace and thus shortening the life cycles of their products.

PROMOTIONAL POLICIES

promotion mix
Efforts by a company to reach distribution channels and target customers through communications such as personal selling, advertising, public relations, and direct marketing.

Efforts by a company to reach distribution channels and target customers through communications such as personal selling, advertising, public relations, and direct marketing are called its **promotion mix**. Not surprisingly, promotional activities often receive the greatest attention among marketers because many people, even professionals, tend to equate "marketing" with "promotion." After we examine two general promotion strategies, we discuss the complications that can arise in international advertising and communications.

Push and Pull Strategies   There are two general promotional strategies that companies can employ in getting their marketing message across to buyers. They can rely completely on only one of these or use them in any combination they desire. A promotional strategy designed to create buyer demand that will encourage channel members to stock a company's product is called a **pull strategy**. In other words, buyer demand is generated in order to "pull" products through distribution channels to end users. Creating consumer demand through direct marketing techniques is a common example of a pull strategy. For instance, when Procter & Gamble encountered distribution difficulties in trying to introduce Rejoice hair-care products into Asia, the company opted to generate grassroots consumer demand. The company hired a fleet of trucks to drive through village squares and hand out loads of free trial packages to potential end users.

pull strategy
Promotional strategy designed to create buyer demand that will encourage channel members to stock a company's product.

In contrast, a **push strategy** is a promotional strategy designed to pressure channel members to carry a product and promote it to final users. A push strategy is often used by manufacturers of all sorts of products commonly sold through department and grocery stores. For example, manufacturer's sales representatives call on purchasing agents of Wal-Mart to try and encourage them to sell the manufacturer's product in their store and give it good visibility. Push strategies are also employed for office products including computers and office furniture. Key to successfully implementing a push strategy abroad is a company's international sales force. See the Global Manager "Managing an International Sales Force" for some insight into how global managers can successfully manage their salespeople in other cultures.

push strategy
Promotional strategy designed to pressure channel members to carry a product and promote it to final users of the product.

Whether the push or pull strategy is most appropriate in a given marketing environment depends on several factors:

➡ *Distribution system.* Implementing a push strategy can be difficult when channel members (such as distributors) wield a great deal of power relative to that of producers. It can also be ineffective when distribution channels are lengthy: the more levels of intermediaries, the more channel members who must be convinced to carry a product. In such cases, it might be easier to create buyer demand using a pull strategy than to persuade distributors to stock a product.

➡ *Access to mass media.* Developing and emerging economies typically have fewer available forms of mass media for use in implementing a pull strategy. Accordingly, it is difficult to increase consumer awareness of a product and generate product demand. This problem, however, is becoming less pervasive as broadcast and print media become increasingly global in their reach. Even so, many consumers in these markets cannot afford cable or satellite television, or perhaps even glossy magazines. In such cases, advertisers might turn to billboards and radio. At

Global Manager

Managing an International Sales Force

Today, even small companies with fewer than 25 employees stationed abroad are reaping up to 35 percent of their revenues from international sales. How can you get into the action? How can you become a better global manager of your company's international sales force? Managing and motivating an international sales force is no small task. The following guidelines provide some helpful hints on improving the effectiveness of your company's reps abroad.

➡ **Know the sales scene.** Your company probably does not wander into uncharted territory to produce or market its product. Likewise, it should conduct research before hiring and managing an international sales force. The information obtained from such research should help you formulate a targeted sales strategy and then empower your sales force to meet their performance targets. Compensation packages—the amount of financial remuneration as well as the way in which it is delivered—varies from country to country, culture to culture, and industry to industry. In the United States, for instance, a greater portion of salary is based on commission than it is in mainland Europe. Know the salary structure and incentive plans that salespeople with similar jobs have at local companies.

➡ **Research the customer.** Don't assume that customers abroad have the same needs and preferences as customers at home. Investigate everything you can about potential buyers to know what they want to purchase and how much they are willing and able to pay. ECA International sells memberships in its company that allow members to participate in the gathering and receipt of cost-of-living data and other marketing information worldwide. When ECA expanded into Asia, its sales force was unsuccessful time and again. The company found out through its sales force that its potential customers in Asia wanted to buy research piece-by-piece rather than buying a membership. Only after ECA adapted its methods to suit local buyers, was it able to sell its memberships in Asia. Thus the sales force is also a valuable source of information on what will and will not sell in the local market.

➡ **Work with the culture.** "Many companies fall short because they don't provide for their sales teams, whether it is in cultural training, language, brochures, or having enough staff members who speak the language and can support them," says John Wada, sales and marketing director for IOR, a cross-cultural management company. "In order to motivate individuals, you need to set realistic objectives for salespeople, and much of that is culturally bound," he adds. Your company should seek answers to a host of questions. Do people in the local culture feel differently about work teams and competition than your sales force at home? How about schedules and deadlines? Are you moving into a culture where "time is of the essence" or one where time is far less important? Make sure your company and the local sales force fully understand what is expected of one another.

➡ **Learn from your reps.** Although monetary compensation is important to your sales force in the local market, they must feel connected to the larger organization. If they do not, they can quickly lose their motivation. Many will also want to contribute to product development. If your salespeople believe they are pushing products that bear no relationship to the local market, their performance will suffer. "I'd do a great job," so the story goes, "but the product just won't sell here." Salespeople can begin focusing on critiquing products rather than selling them. Instead, involve them in the R&D process. Your reps will have a better sense of what's going on with the product. You might also bring your sales force to the home office each year to learn about your business so that they understand their vital link in your company's chain of business activities. Top managers should also visit the local office to better comprehend the needs of local customers. Finally, encourage cooperation between reps in different markets to increase the cross-fertilization of ideas.

➡ **Invest and profit.** Making a move abroad is a challenge but the potential for profit is huge. Your company's senior management will need to honestly examine all of the resources it will take to get into a market abroad and decide if the market is worth the investment. But once your company makes the decision—and does what's necessary to support and manage your international staff—it can make it work.

other times, gaining wide exposure can be difficult because existing media have only local, as opposed to national, reach. Indonesia, for example, did not launch its first nationwide television station until 1994. In yet other situations, advertising certain products on certain media is unlawful. Companies entering Canada or the United States, for example, cannot use television or radio to advertise tobacco products.

➡ *Type of product.* A pull strategy is most appropriate when buyers display a great deal of brand loyalty toward one particular brand name. In other words, brand-loyal buyers know what brand of a product they want before they go out to buy it. On the other hand, push strategies tend to be appropriate for inexpensive consumer goods characterized by buyers who are not brand loyal. Low brand loyalty means that a buyer will go shopping for a product, not knowing which brand is best, and will buy one of those carried by the retailer or wholesaler. A push strategy is also suited to industrial products because potential buyers usually need to be informed about a product's special features and benefits.

International Advertising   Money spent on advertising continues to grow in many markets around the world. In fact, it is in some developing nations and the big emerging markets that advertising spending is expected to grow at the quickest pace. For instance, as you can see in Figure 15.1, China, Portugal, and the Czech Republic are expected to experience the most growth in advertising spending. These figures represent advertising spending by both domestic companies and international companies active in those markets.

International advertising differs a great deal from advertising in domestic markets. Managers must rely on their knowledge of a market to decide whether an ad is suitable for the company's international promotion efforts. Cultural differences, for instance, can mean that ads must be only slightly modified for use in different nations or that entirely new ads must be created.

Coca-Cola's experience in creating an ad to appeal to Chinese in China, and throughout the world, illustrates the problems that can arise when developing highly specialized ads. Coca-Cola's desire to create a Coke ad that looked authentically Chi-

FIGURE 15.1

WHERE ADVERTISING WILL GROW

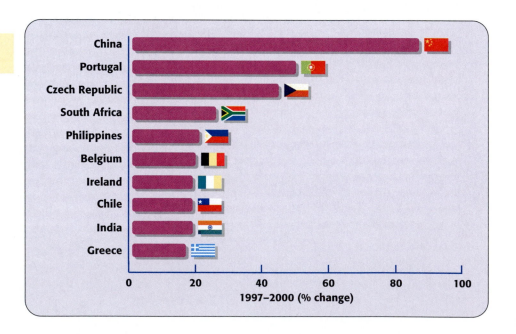

nese drew it to Harbin, a city in northeast China. But along the way, the bus in which the crew that was to shoot the commercial was traveling stalled. When the driver lit a fire under the gas tank to thaw the fuel, the horrified crew scrambled off the bus thinking it might explode. The crew stood in biting, subzero temperatures until the bus was once again running—the director's frostbitten nose bears the scars of the adventure. Then when a local older man hired to be in the ad had trouble following the director's instructions, local villagers pointed out why—he was deaf. Finally the crew had to trudge around in knee-deep snow first to get a field of frozen red pinwheels to spin and then to reorient the whole set so that the wind (which was blowing in an unfavorable direction) could spin the pinwheels. But it appears that Coke's efforts at creating an ad depicting people celebrating Chinese New Year in the traditional manner in a picturesque village paid off—"It made me feel very emotional," said Fang Chuanbao, an office worker in Shanghai who saw the ad.[15] Let's now explore some of the factors involved in the decision of whether to standardize or adapt avertisements.

Standardizing or Adapting Advertisements The vast majority of advertising that occurs in any one nation is produced solely for that domestic audience. But companies that advertise in multiple markets must determine those aspects of the advertising campaign that can be standardized across markets and those that cannot. Companies that do market their products across national boundaries try to contain costs by standardizing as many aspects of their campaigns as possible. However, companies seldom standardize all aspects of their international promotions for a variety of reasons, including differences in culture and laws.[16]

Firms that standardize their advertising usually control campaigns from the home office.[17] This policy helps them to project consistent brand images and promotional messages across all markets—the aim of a global strategy (Chapter 12). Companies can achieve consistency by standardizing their basic promotional message, creative concepts, graphics, and information content.

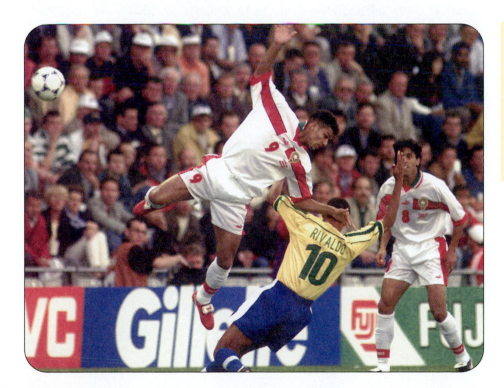

The 1998 World Cup broadcast offered advertisers a chance to put their messages before an enormous worldwide audience, not by buying air time but simply by putting up signs around the playing fields in France. Although signs may contain no more than the brand name, for most marketers even this benefit outweighs any drawback.

e·biz

Once a company decides to pursue a global marketing strategy, it naturally tries to get the most for its advertising expenditure. An increasingly popular method companies are using to reach a global audience is marketing over the World Wide Web. Companies that use direct marketing (such as telemarketing or leaflets through the mail) have benefited a great deal from this new form of marketing. Consumers have found it very convenient to shop for such items as clothing, music, movies, and books over the Web. See the World Business Survey "Primed for Online" for some additional information on the profitability of direct marketers' efforts on the Web.

Another way in which companies can reach a global audience is by sponsoring global sports events, such as the Olympics, World Cup Soccer, and Formula One automobile racing. These types of events receive heavy media coverage and are often telecast simultaneously in multiple nations. Even posting banners around the venues of such events can boost recognition of a company's brand name by exposing it to perhaps millions of viewers around the world. In fact, the banners of sponsors of Formula One auto racing are seen by viewers in 102 countries.[18]

Case: The Elusive Euro-Consumer The continuing integration of markets among nations belonging to the European Union is causing many marketers to dream of a day when they can standardize their advertising to appeal to a so-called "Euro-consumer." But the Euro-consumer remains a rare, almost mythical beast, managing to elude even the world's most clever advertisers.

World Business Survey

Primed for On-line

The World Wide Web is an increasingly appealing method for direct marketers to sell their products to consumers worldwide. In fact, 73 percent of direct marketers polled in a recent survey were conducting transactions on the Internet and 43 percent of those on-line efforts were profitable. Moreover, 69 percent of marketers offer their complete print catalogs on-line. As Karen Burka of Gruppo, Levey & Company put it, "The Web really taps into the same type of direct-to-end-user marketing that direct marketers have always known how to do." The survey also found the following results:

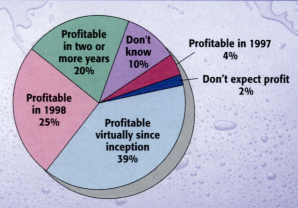

Profitability of the Web for Direct Marketers

- Profitable in two or more years 20%
- Don't know 10%
- Profitable in 1997 4%
- Don't expect profit 2%
- Profitable virtually since inception 39%
- Profitable in 1998 25%

Some well-known international advertising agencies have tried a pan-European advertising approach only to fail due to national differences. Consider the experience of the acclaimed Leo Burnett ad agency when it took on the goal of creating a single European campaign for United Distillers' Johnnie Walker whiskey. It took many painful tests and revisions before the ad could be rolled out. In the original ad, the tag line read "The Water of Life" and showed a man attending "the running of the bulls" in Pamplona, Spain. After narrowly escaping being trampled by the bull, the man celebrates with a glass of Johnnie Walker Red Label. But in many countries, the Pamplona setting raised hackles because people said, "The Spanish don't know anything about making good whiskey." Tests of the ad in Germany showed it would not work because to Germans it seemed simply reckless—not a widely admired trait there. Says Jenny Vaughn, worldwide brand director for Johnnie Walker, "Also, because of the German animal rights campaigners, you can't show a goldfish in a goldfish bowl on German television, so a bull run was just not [acceptable]." The tag line "The Water of Life" was baffling in many languages. "People thought it meant watered-down whiskey," said Vaughn, so the line was changed to "Taste Life." Then a voice-over in the ad was incorrectly translated in one language as "when your life flashes in front of you, make sure it's worth watching." In every market the words didn't make sense or the meaning was lost. In Italy the line was totally discarded. In Germany attempts at translation proved so maddening that the line was replaced with "Live every day as if it were your last."

Europe's many languages certainly create thorny translation issues for marketers. Thus the most successful pan-European ads are those that contain a great deal of visuals, have few written or spoken words, and focus on the product and consumer. One such ad is one for TAG Heuer watches, which positions the company's product as competitive and a winner. In the ad, a swimmer is shown racing a shark and a hurdler is shown leaping an oversized razor blade. The highly visual ad gets across the company's message that it is a winner.[19]

Blending Product and Promotional Policies   When companies extend their marketing to international markets, they develop communication strategies that blend product and promotional policies.[20] Thus their communication strategy for a particular market takes into account the nature of the product being marketed and the promotion mix to be used in marketing it. After we discuss the marketing communication process, we examine five product/promotional methods that companies use and the appropriate situation for each.

Communicating Promotional Messages The process of sending promotional messages about products to target markets is called **marketing communication**.[21] Communicating the benefits of a product can be more difficult in international business than in domestic business for at least several reasons. Marketing internationally usually means translating promotional messages from one language into another. Marketers must also be knowledgeable of many cultural nuances that can affect how buyers interpret a promotional message. A nation's laws that govern the promotion of products in another country can also force changes in marketing communication.

Marketing communication is typically considered as a circular process (see Figure 15.2). The company that has an idea it wishes to communicate is the *source* of the communication. The idea is *encoded* (translated into images, words, and symbols) into a *promotional message* that the company is trying to get across. The promotional message is then sent to the *audience* (potential buyers) through various *media*. Media commonly used by companies to communicate their promotional messages include radio, television, newspapers, magazines, billboards, and direct mailings. Once the audience receives the message, they *decode* the message and interpret its meaning. Information in

> **marketing communication**
> *Process of sending promotional messages about products to target markets.*

FIGURE 15.2

**MARKETING
COMMUNICATION PROCESS**

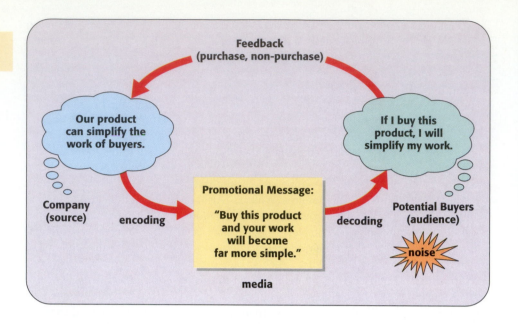

the form of *feedback* (purchase or nonpurchase) then flows back to the source of the message. The decoding process by the audience can be disrupted by the presence of *noise*—anything disrupting the audience's ability to receive and interpret the promotional message. By ignoring important cultural nuances, companies can inadvertently increase the potential for noise that can cloud the audience's understanding of their promotional message. Language barriers between the company and potential buyers, for instance, can create noise if a company' promotional message is incorrectly translated into the local language.

*Product/Communications Extension (**Dual Extension**)* This method extends the same home-market product and marketing promotion into target markets. Under certain conditions, it can be the simplest and most profitable strategy. For example, because of a common language and other cultural similarities, companies based in English-speaking Canadian provinces can sell the same product with identical packaging and advertising in the U.S. market—provided the product is not required by the U.S. government to carry any special statements or warnings. The Canadian companies thus contain costs by developing a single product and one promotional campaign for both markets. However, it is important that Canadian companies not ignore any subtle cultural differences that could cause confusion in interpreting the promotional message.

As the information age continues to knit the world more tightly together, this method will probably grow more popular. Today, consumers in seemingly remote parts of the world are rapidly becoming aware of the latest worldwide fads and fashions. But it appears that this strategy is better-suited for certain groups of buyers including brand-conscious teenagers, business executives, and wealthy individuals. The strategy also tends to be better-suited for companies employing a global strategy with their products, such as upscale personal items with global brand names—examples include Rolex watches, Hermes scarves and ties, and Coco Chanel perfumes. It can also be appropriate for global brands that have mass appeal and cut across all age groups and social classes—such as Sony, Levi's, Coca-Cola, Mars candies, and McDonald's. The strategy also is useful to companies that are the low-cost leaders in their industries. One product and one promotional message keeps costs down.

Product Extension, Communications Adaptation Under this method, a company extends the same product into new target markets but alters its promotion. Communications require adaptation because the product satisfies a different need, serves a different function, or appeals to a different type of buyer. Companies adjust their marketing communication to inform potential buyers that the product either satisfies their needs or serves a distinct function. This approach helps companies contain costs because the good itself does not need to undergo any alteration whatsoever. However, altering communications can be expensive—especially if there are significant cultural differences among target markets. Filming altered ads with local actors and on location can significantly add to promotional costs.

One company that changes its promotional message for international markets is the Japanese retailer Muji. Muji offers a wide variety of goods including writing materials, clothing, and home furnishings. Everything, however, is inspired by a central theme rooted in centuries of Japanese culture—the simplicity of everyday life. Muji's philosophy is one of selling unbranded quality goods and company promotions boast the motto "Functional Japanese minimalism for everyone." Its target market in Japan is the average school-age child and young adult. However, Muji has a different promotional message for its four stores in London—one in the upscale Kensington High Street district. Muji's British customers tend to be older and see themselves as sophisticated and stylish buyers of the company's products. Thus Muji's promotional message in London is to shop at a business that has a very respectable brand name—clearly different from its message in Japan. Also, the company's British customers are not buying simply a product (as do its Japanese customers) but are buying into the traditional Japanese concept of simplicity.[22]

Low economic development also can demand that communications be adapted to suit local conditions. For instance, companies in Europe, North America, and certain Asian countries can rely on a modern telecommunications system to reach millions of consumers through television, radio, and even the World Wide Web. But in developing countries (such as Sri Lanka, rural parts of India and China, and those in Africa), television and radio coverage are limited and development of the Web is years behind developed nations. Marketers in those markets must use alternative techniques including door-to-door personal selling and regional product shows or fairs.

e·biz

Product Adaptation, Communications Extension Using this method, a company adapts its product to the requirements of the international market while retaining the product's original marketing communication. There are many reasons why companies need to adapt their products; one might be to meet legal requirements in the local market, for example. Moreover, governments can require firms to use a certain amount of local materials, labor, or some other resource in their local production process. If the exact same materials or components are not available locally, the result can be a modified product.

This method can be costly because appropriately modifying a product to suit the needs of local buyers often means that the company must invest in production facilities in the local market. If each national market requires its own production facility, cost savings provided by economies of scale in production can be elusive. However, a company can implement this strategy successfully if it sells a differentiated product for which it can charge a higher price to offset greater production costs.[23]

Product/Communications Adaptation (Dual Adaptation) This method adapts both the product and its marketing communication to suit the target market. The product itself is adapted to match the needs or preferences of local buyers. The promotional message is adapted to explain how the product meets those needs and prefer-

A good example of line extension, in which a new product is introduced in an existing product line, is the disposable camera. Fuji's disposable camera takes stop-action photos in which several frames are reproduced in a single image. Learn more about Fuji at ⟨**www.fujifilm.co.jp**⟩.

ences. Because both production and marketing efforts must be altered, this strategy can be expensive and therefore is not very common. However, it can be implemented successfully if a sufficiently large and profitable market segment exists.

Product Invention This method requires that an entirely new product be developed for the target market. Product invention is often necessary when many important differences exist between the home and target markets. One reason for product invention is that local buyers cannot afford a company's current product because of low purchasing power. In Thailand, for example, Honda produces a car called the "City" that is designed for budget-conscious buyers in Southeast Asian and European markets.

Product inventions can also arise due to a lack of adequate infrastructure needed to operate certain products. One day, London inventor Trevor Baylis was watching a television documentary on the difficulty of educating Africans about AIDS because much of the continent did not have the electricity infrastructure nor batteries to operate radios. Baylis set to work and developed the Freeplay windup radio—30 seconds of cranking keeps it going for 40 minutes. Baylis and several South African businessmen then formed a company called Bay-Gen Power Corporation in Cape Town, South Africa. The radio was first sold only to relief agencies working in developing nations. However, due mostly to word of mouth, it is now popular worldwide among hikers, environmentalists, and even hip shoppers looking for "retro" appliances.[24]

DISTRIBUTION POLICIES

distribution

Planning, implementing, and controlling the physical flow of a product from its point of origin to its point of consumption.

Planning, implementing, and controlling the physical flow of a product from its point of origin to its point of consumption is called **distribution**. The physical path that a product follows on its way to customers is called a *distribution channel*. Companies along this channel that work together in delivering products to customers are called *channel members* or *intermediaries*. Bear in mind that manufacturers of goods are not the only producers who need distribution channels. Service providers, such as consulting companies, health-care organizations, and news services, also need distribution (or delivery) systems to reach their customers. For instance, delivering news services through the World Wide Web is a burgeoning business. Channel members involved in getting news

e·biz

from the newsroom to the Web surfer include, among others, Internet service providers (such as America Online) and search engine providers (such as Excite).

Companies develop their international distribution policies based on two related decisions: (1) how to get the goods *into* a country and (2) how to distribute goods *within* a country. We presented the different ways companies get their products into countries in Chapter 13. Thus here we focus on distribution strategies within countries.

Designing Distribution Channels Managers consider two overriding concerns when establishing distribution policies: (1) the amount of *market exposure* that a product needs and (2) the *cost* of distributing a product. Let's now take a look at each of these concerns.

Degree of Exposure In promoting its product to the greatest number of potential customers, a marketer must determine the right amount of exposure needed. An **exclusive channel** is one in which a manufacturer grants the right to sell its product to only one or a limited number of resellers. Thus an exclusive channel gives producers a great deal of control over the sale of their product by channel members such as wholesalers and retailers. It also helps a producer constrain distributors from selling competing brands. In this way, an exclusive channel creates a barrier that makes it difficult or impossible for outsiders to penetrate the channel. New car dealerships, for example, in most countries reflect exclusive distribution. Thus Honda dealerships cannot normally sell Toyotas and Chrysler dealers cannot sell Fords.

When a producer wants its product to be made available through as many distribution outlets as possible, it prefers to use an **intensive channel**—one in which a producer grants the right to sell its product to many resellers. An intensive channel provides buyers with location convenience because of the large number of outlets through which a product is sold. However, it does not create strong barriers to channel entry for producers nor give them much control over such reseller decisions as what competing brands to sell. Large companies whose products are sold through grocery stores and department stores typically take an intensive channel approach to distribution. The obstacle faced by small companies that choose an intensive channel approach is gaining shelf space—especially small companies with lesser-known brands. This problem is exacerbated by the increasing global trend toward retailers developing their own *private-label brands*—brands created by retailers themselves. Manufacturers produce the good for the retailer and label it with the retailer's brand name instead of their own. Thus retailers give their own products the best shelf space close to the best brands, and small, lesser-known brands end up getting the poorest shelf location—up high or near the floor.

Channel Length and Cost *Channel length* refers to the number of intermediaries between the producer and the buyer. In a *zero-level channel*—which is also called *direct marketing*—producers sell directly to final buyers. A *one-level channel* places only one intermediary between producer and buyer. Two intermediaries make up a *two-level channel* and so forth. Generally, the more intermediaries in a channel, the more costly it becomes because each additional player tacks on to the product a charge for its services. This is an important consideration for companies selling price-sensitive consumer products such as candy, food, and small household items that usually compete on price. As we saw in Chapter 12, companies selling highly differentiated products can charge higher prices because of their products' distinctiveness and therefore have fewer problems employing a channel of several levels.

Influence of Product Characteristics The value of a product relative to its weight and volume is called its **value density**. Value density is an important variable in formulating distribution policies. As a rule, *the lower a product's value density, the more*

exclusive channel
Distribution channel in which a manufacturer grants the right to sell its product to only one or a limited number of resellers.

intensive channel
Distribution channel in which a producer grants the right to sell its product to many resellers.

value density
Value of a product relative to its weight and volume.

localized the distribution system. Most commodities, including cement, iron ore, and crude oil, have low value-density ratios—they're heavy but not particularly "valuable" if gauged in, say, shipping weight per cubic meter. Relative to their values, therefore, the cost of transporting them is high. Consequently, such products are processed or integrated into the manufacturing process at points close to their original locations. Products with high value-density ratios include emeralds, semiconductors, and premium perfumes. Because the cost of transporting these products is small relative to their values, they can be processed or manufactured in the most optimal location of the producer's choice, then shipped to market. Health-care provider Johnson & Johnson manufactures Vistakon contact lenses. Because contact lenses have high value density, the company produces and inventories its products in one U.S. location and serves the world market from there.

When products need to be modified for local markets, companies can design their distribution systems accordingly. Caterpillar moved the manufacture of its lift trucks (forklifts) out of the United States to reduce labor costs. The company then redesigned its distribution system so that it doubles as the final component in the company's production system. Each national market carries a range of optional product components for Caterpillar's lift trucks. Caterpillar ships partially completed lift trucks, along with optional parts, to distribution warehouses in each target market. After a buyer decides what options it desires, final assembly takes place. Thus Caterpillar's distribution warehouses now extend the company's assembly line—allowing the company to maintain or improve service at little cost.

Special Distribution Problems   A nation's distribution system develops over time and reflects its unique cultural, political, legal, and economic traditions. Thus the distribution system of each nation has its own unique pros and cons. However, it is the negative aspects of distribution that pose the greatest threat to the business activities of international companies. In some countries risks arise mostly from the potential for theft and property damage. In others it is simply the lack of understanding that creates uncertainty and risk. Let's take a look at a few special problems that can affect a company's international distribution operations.

Lack of Market Understanding   Companies can experience a great deal of frustration and financial loss simply by not understanding fully the local market in which they operate. Amway Asia Pacific Ltd. (the Asian arm of Amway of the United States) learned the hard way the pitfalls of overestimating the knowledge of distributors in emerging markets. The company has a worldwide policy of giving distributors a full refund on its soaps and cosmetics if the distributor's customers are dissatisfied—even if the returned containers are empty. But the policy had some bizarre results shortly after Amway entered China. Word of the guarantee spread quickly. Some distributors repackaged the products in other containers, sold them, and took the empty containers back to Amway for a refund. Others scoured garbage bins, gathering bags full of discarded bottles. In Shanghai returns were beginning to total $100,000 a day. Amway's Shanghai chief Percy Chin said, "Perhaps we were too lenient." Amway changed its refund policy to allow a refund only for bottles at least half full. Amway's distributors were furious. Grumbled one unhappy distributor, "Don't open a company if you can't afford losses."[25]

Theft and Corruption   A high incidence of theft and corruption can present obstacles to distribution. The distribution system in Russia, for instance, reflects its roughly 75-year experiment with communism. When Acer Computers (a Taiwan-founded but Singapore-based firm) recently decided to sell its computers in Russia, it built production facilities in Russia's stable neighbor Finland—the company was too leery of investing directly in Russia. Acer also considered it too risky to navigate Russia's archaic distribution system on its own. In three years' time, a highway that serves as a main route to get goods overland from Finland to Russia saw 50 Finnish truckers hijacked, 2 drivers killed, and another 2 missing. Acer solved its distribution problem by selling its computers to Russian distributors outside its factory in Finland. The Russian distributors, who understood how to negotiate their way through Russia's distribution system, would deal with headaches in Russia.[26]

PRICING POLICIES

The pricing policy that a company adopts must match its overall international strategy. For instance, the product of a company that is the low-cost leader in its industry cannot generally be sold at a premium price because it likely has few special features and stresses functionality rather than uniqueness. On the other hand, a company following a differentiation strategy usually can charge a premium price for its product because buyers value the product's uniqueness. Let's now examine two pricing policies (*worldwide pricing* and *dual pricing*) that companies use in international markets and then explore the important factors influencing managers' pricing decisions.

Worldwide Pricing   A pricing policy in which one selling price is established for all international markets is called **worldwide pricing**. In practice, a worldwide pricing policy is very difficult to achieve. First, production costs differ from one nation to another. Keeping production costs the same is not possible for a company that has production bases within each market it serves. Thus selling prices often reflect these different costs of production.

Second, a company producing in just one location (to maintain an equivalent cost of production for every product) cannot guarantee that selling prices will be the same in every target market. The cost of exporting to certain markets will likely be higher than exporting costs to other markets. In addition, distribution costs differ across markets. Where distribution is efficient, selling prices might well be lower than in locations where distribution systems are archaic and inefficient. Third, the purchasing power of local buyers must be taken into account. Managers might decide to lower the sales price in a market so that buyers can afford the product and the company can gain market share. Finally, fluctuating currency values also must be taken into account. When the value of a country's currency where production takes place rises against a target market's currency, the product will become more expensive in the target market.

Dual Pricing   Because of the problems associated with worldwide pricing, another pricing policy is often used in international markets. A pricing policy in which a product has a different selling price in export markets than it has in the home market is called **dual pricing**. When a product has a higher selling price in the target market than it does in the home market (or the country where production takes place), it is called *price escalation*. It is commonly the result of the reasons just discussed—exporting costs and currency fluctuations.

But sometimes a product's export price is lower than the price in the home market. Under what circumstances does this occur? Some companies determine that domestic market sales are to cover all product costs (such as expenses related to R&D, administration, and overhead). Thus exports must cover only the *additional* costs associated with exporting and selling in a target market (such as tariffs). In this sense, exports are considered a sort of "bonus."

To apply dual pricing in international marketing successfully, a company must be able to keep its domestic buyers and international buyers separate. Buyers in one market might retaliate by not purchasing the product if they discover they are paying a higher

worldwide pricing
Policy in which one selling price is established for all international markets.

dual pricing
Policy in which a product has a different selling price (typically higher) in export markets than it has in the home market.

price than are buyers in another market. If a company cannot keep its buyers separate when employing dual pricing, buyers could potentially undermine the policy through *arbitrage*—buying products where they are sold at lower prices and reselling them where they command higher prices. However (as is often the case), the higher selling price of a product in an export market often reflects the additional costs of transportation to the local market and any trade barriers of the target market, such as tariffs. For arbitrageurs to be successful, the profits they earn must be enough to outweigh these additional costs.

Factors Affecting Pricing Decisions Many factors have an important influence on managers' pricing decisions. We devote the following discussion to four of the most important—*transfer prices, arm's length pricing, price controls,* and *dumping*.

Transfer Prices Recall from Chapter 14 that a transfer price is the price charged for a good or service transferred among a company and its subsidiaries. At one time, companies enjoyed a great deal of freedom in setting their transfer prices. Subsidiaries in countries with high corporate tax rates would reduce their tax burdens by charging a low price for their output to other subsidiaries. By charging a lower price, the subsidiary lowered the taxes that the parent company must pay by reducing its profits in the high-tax country. Likewise, subsidiaries in countries with low tax rates would charge relatively high prices for their output to other subsidiaries of the parent company.

Transfer prices followed a similar pattern based on the tariffs that different nations charged imports. Subsidiaries in countries that charged relatively high tariffs were charged lower prices by other subsidiaries to lower the cost of the good in the local market. This pattern of transfer prices helped large corporations with many subsidiaries to better manage their global tax burden and become more price-competitive in certain markets.

Arm's-Length Pricing Today, increasing regulation of transfer pricing practices is causing reduced freedom in manipulating transfer prices. In fact, many governments now regulate internal company pricing practices by assigning products approximate transfer prices based on their free-market price. Thus most international transfers between subsidiaries now occur at a so-called **arm's-length price**—the free-market price that unrelated parties charge one another for a specific product.

arm's-length price
Free-market price that unrelated parties charge one another for a specific product.

Another factor that is increasing the use of arm's-length pricing is pressure on companies to be good corporate citizens in each of their target markets. Developing and emerging markets are hurt most by lost revenue when international companies manipulate prices to reduce tariffs and corporate taxes. They depend on the revenue for building such things as schools, hospitals, and infrastructure including telecommunications systems and shipping ports. These items in turn benefit international companies by improving the productivity and efficiency of the local business environment. Indeed, some international companies have even developed codes of conduct specifying that transfer prices will follow the principle of arm's-length pricing.

Price Controls Pricing policies must also consider the potential for government **price controls**—upper or lower limits placed on the prices of products sold within a country. Upper-limit price controls are designed to provide price stability in an inflationary economy (one in which prices are rising). Companies wanting to raise prices in a price-controlled economy must often apply to government authorities to request permission to do so. Those companies with good contacts in the government of the target market might be more likely to get a price-control exemption. Those unable to obtain an exemption will typically try to lessen the impact of upper-limit price controls by reducing production costs.

price controls
Upper or lower limits placed on the prices of products sold within a country.

In contrast, lower-limit price controls prohibit the lowering of prices below a certain level. Governments sometimes impose lower-limit prices to help local companies compete against less expensive imports of international companies. Other times, lower-limit price controls are designed to ward off price wars that could eliminate the competition and thereby give one company a monopoly in the domestic market.

Dumping We detailed the practice of dumping in Chapter 6 when discussing government involvement in international trade. Recall that dumping occurs when the price of a good is lower in export markets than it is in the domestic market. Accusations of dumping are often made against competitors from other countries when inexpensive imports flood a nation's domestic market. Although charges of dumping normally result from deliberate efforts to undercut the prices of competitors in the domestic market, changes in exchange rates can cause unintentional dumping. When a country's government charges another nation's producers of dumping a good on its market, antidumping tariffs are typically imposed. Such tariffs are designed to punish producers in the offending nation by increasing the price of their products to a fairer level.

MANAGING PRODUCTION ACTIVITIES

Most of the important manufacturing and logistics issues that concern international managers were discussed in previous chapters. In Chapter 12 we covered the issues surrounding the number and location of manufacturing facilities because of their important influence on company strategy and organizational structure. In that chapter we also explored logistics because of its influence on strategy. In Chapter 14 we examined how international mangers select particular locations for their facilities in the context of acquiring business resources. Therefore, at this point, there remain only a few—although important—issues to discuss related to manufacturing operations. First, we examine how companies maintain and improve quality in their international production facilities. Then we take a look at logistics, workforce management, and issues related to reinvestment and divestment.

QUALITY IMPROVEMENT EFFORTS

Why are companies concerned with the quality of output in their international production facilities? Companies strive toward quality improvement for two reasons: costs and customer value. First, quality products help keep production costs low because they reduce waste in valuable inputs, reduce the cost of retrieving defective products from buyers, and reduce disposal costs due to defective products. Second, some minimum level of acceptable quality is an aspect of nearly every product today. Even companies producing low-cost products try to maintain or improve quality so long as it does not erode their position in what is typically a price-competitive market or market segment. Companies that succeed in combining a low-cost position with a high-quality product can gain a tremendous competitive advantage in their market.

Improving quality is also important for a company that provides services—whether as its only product or in conjunction with goods it manufactures and markets. Managing quality in services is complicated by the fact that a service is created and, at the same time, consumed. Important to service quality, therefore, is the human interaction between an employee delivering a service and the buyer. At the same time, however, activities that must be conducted prior to the actual delivery of a service are also important. For example, it is important that a restaurant be clean and have an inventory of the ingredients it needs to prepare the meals on its menu. Likewise, a bank can provide high-quality service only if employees arrive for work on time and interact professionally with customers.

Let's now take a brief look at two movements that inspire the drive toward quality: *total quality management* and *International Standards Organization (ISO) 9000 certification*.

total quality management (TQM)
Emphasis on continuous quality improvement to meet or exceed customer expectations involving a company-wide commitment to quality-enhancing processes.

Total Quality Management   An emphasis on continuous quality improvement to meet or exceed customer expectations is called **total quality management (TQM)**. Total quality management stresses a company-wide commitment to quality-enhancing processes. It also places a great deal of responsibility on each individual to be focused on the quality of his or her own output—regardless of whether the employee's activities are based in the factory, in administration, or in management.

By continuously improving the quality of its products, a company can differentiate itself from rivals and attract loyal customers. The TQM philosophy initially took hold in 1960s and 1970s Japan, where electronics and automobile firms applied TQM techniques to reduce costs and thereby gain significant market share around the world through price competitiveness and a reputation for quality. It was not until U.S. and European companies lost a great deal of market share to their Japanese rivals, that they embraced TQM principles.

ISO 9000   The International Standards Organization (ISO) 9000 is an international certification that companies get when they meet the highest quality standards in their industries. Firms in the European Union are leading the way in quality certification. Thus both European and non-European companies alike are working toward certification in order to ensure their products' access to the European marketplace. To become certified, companies must demonstrate the reliability and soundness of all business processes affecting the quality of their products. Many companies also seek ISO 9000 certification because of the message of quality that certification sends to prospective customers. To see how companies can blend together TQM principles and the drive toward ISO 9000 certification, see the Entrepreneurial Focus titled "Linking TQM and ISO 9000 Standards."

Entrepreneurial Focus

Linking TQM and ISO 9000 Standards

In today's competitive environment, many small-business owners and entrepreneurs are applying TQM principles in their companies. When doing business internationally, ISO 9000 certification is becoming increasingly important. However, the ISO 9000 standards do not specify *how* a company should develop its quality processes. Rather, ISO requires each company to define and document its own quality processes and show evidence of implementing them. The following is a framework describing how TQM and ISO 9000 principles can be linked to enhance a company's capability of delivering quality products or services.

The main principles of TQM include:

➡ *Delight the customer.* Companies must strive to be the best at what customers consider most important. This can change over time, so business owners must be in close touch with customers.

➡ *Utilize people-based management.* Systems, standards, and technology cannot, in and of themselves, guarantee quality. The key is to provide employees with the knowledge of what to do and how to do it and to provide feedback on performance.

➡ *Continuous improvement.* TQM is not a short-term quick fix. Major breakthroughs are less important than incremental improvement.

➡ *Management by fact.* Quality management and improvement are based on clear understanding of consumer perceptions of the performance of a company's goods and services. Rather than trusting "gut feelings," obtain factual information and share it with employees.

Companies can link these TQM principles to ISO 9000 standards in three ways:

➡ *Process definition.* The existing business process must be defined. Once defined, it must be satisfying to key stakeholders—in other words, it must "delight the customer."

➡ *Process improvement.* The defined process must be used properly by everyone within the organization. If this is not the case, then "people-based management" is lacking in the company.

➡ *Process management.* Management and employees must possess factual knowledge about process details in order to manage them properly.

INTERNATIONAL LOGISTICS

As we saw in Chapter 12, *logistics* involves activities ranging from managing the physical flow of raw materials to delivery of the finished product to end users. Likewise, *distribution* is that segment of logistics concerned with getting finished products from the company to end users. In this section, we discuss the segment of logistics concerned with moving materials and components into and through the company itself.

Shipping and Inventory Costs   As we saw earlier in this chapter, the value density of a finished product affects its shipping costs. Likewise, shipping costs can have a dramatic effect on the cost of getting materials and components to the location of production facilities. When the cost of getting inputs into the production process is a large portion of the product's total cost, producers tend to locate close to the source of those inputs. Shipping costs are affected by many elements of a nation's business environment such as its general level of economic development including the condition of seaports, airports, roads, and rail networks.

It used to be the practice that producers bought large quantities of materials or components and stored them in large warehouses until they were needed in the production process. However, storing great amounts of inventory for production is costly in terms of insuring them against damage or theft, and the rent or purchase price of the warehouse needed to store them.

Because companies have far better uses for the money tied up in such inventory, they developed better inventory management techniques. A production technique in which inventory is kept to a minimum and inputs to the production process arrive exactly when they are needed (or *just in time*) is called **just-in-time (JIT) manufacturing**. Although the technique was originally developed in Japan, it quickly spread throughout manufacturing operations worldwide. JIT drastically reduces the costs associated with large inventories. It also helped reduce wasteful expenses because defective materials and components are spotted quickly during production. Under traditional systems, defective materials or components were sometimes discovered only after being built into finished products.

> **just-in-time** (JIT) **manufacturing**
> *Production technique in which inventory is kept to a minimum and inputs to the production process arrive exactly when they are needed (or just in time).*

MANAGING THE WORKFORCE

The positive or negative condition of relations between company management and its workers (labor) is referred to as **labor-management relations**. Cooperative relations between labor and management can give a firm a tremendous competitive advantage. When management and workers realize they depend on one another, the company is often better prepared to meet its goals and surmount unexpected obstacles that may crop up. Giving workers a greater stake in the company—say, through profit-sharing plans—is one way to increase morale and generate commitment to improved quality and customer service.

> **labor-management relations**
> *Positive or negative condition of relations between company management and its workers.*

Because relations between labor and managers are human relations, they are rooted in culture and are often affected by political movements in a market. Large international companies tend to make high-level labor decisions at the home office because it gives them greater control over their network of production operations around the world. Lower-level decisions, however, are often left to managers in each country. In effect, this policy places decisions having a direct impact on workers' lives in the hands of experts in the local market. Such decisions might include the number of annual paid holidays, the length of maternity leave, and the provision of day-care facilities. Localizing such management decisions tends to contribute to better labor-management relations because managers familiar with local practices are better equipped to handle matters that affect workers personally.

Importance of Labor Unions   The strength of labor unions in a country where a company has operations is important to its performance and can even affect the selection of a location. Developing and emerging markets in Asia are a popular location for international companies. Some Asian governments appeal to international companies to locate facilities in their nations by promising to keep labor unions in check. But companies also find developed nations attractive if, for whatever reason, a cooperative atmosphere exists between company management and labor unions. In some Asian countries, especially Japan, a cultural emphasis on harmony and balanced interests discourages confrontation between labor and management.

Meanwhile, Britain and Ireland are becoming favorite locations for toeholds in the European Union (EU). The main attractions are productive labor, lower wages, and a reduced likelihood of disruptive strikes. Labor unions are not as strong in these countries as they are on the continent, particularly in France and Germany. Nevertheless, Germany has not been immune to the trend of falling union membership. Union membership has dropped off in Germany over the past decade. Membership has fallen from about 12 million workers in 1991 to about 8 million in 1997. The main reason for the decline is the lack of interest in union membership in the former East German territories. By contrast, labor unions comprise only about 9 percent of the labor force in the United States today, compared with 36 percent 50 years ago.

Despite declines in union membership, labor in Germany exercises a good deal of power in management decisions. In fact, under a plan called *codetermination*, German workers enjoy a direct say in the strategies and policies of their employers. This plan allows labor representatives to participate in high-level company meetings by actually voting on proposed actions.

International Labor Movements The global activities of unions are making progress in such areas as improving the treatment of workers and reducing incidences of child labor. However, the efforts of separate national unions to increase their cooperation are somewhat less successful. Although unions in one nation might wish to support their counterparts in another country, generating grassroots support is difficult for two reasons. First, events taking place in another country are difficult for many

Workers in Germany and France are often protected by strong unions that take part in management decisions. Here German autoworkers take to the streets to demand action on their request for a pay raise.

people to comprehend. Distance and cultural difference make it hard for people to understand others who live and work elsewhere.

Second, whether they realize it or not, workers in different countries sometimes compete against one another. Today, for example, firms can relocate internationally rather easily. Thus labor unions in one country might offer concessions in order to attract the jobs that will be created by a new production facility. In this way, unions in different nations can wind up competing against one another. Some observers argue that this phenomenon creates downward pressure on both wages and union power worldwide.[28]

REINVEST AND DIVEST DECISIONS

The last issue to discuss is the managerial decision of whether to invest further in operations abroad or to reduce or divest international operations. Maintaining the current level of operations is another option and one that is acceptable when a firm foresees no new opportunities in the international marketplace. Let's take a closer look at the other two possibilities: *reinvestment* and *divestment*.

Reinvesting in Business Operations   If new and potentially profitable opportunities present themselves in the market, managers might decide to expand operations. As such they typically *reinvest* profits from current activities to expand operations. In general, the reinvestment decision is based on four considerations.

1. Companies must decide whether to continue investing in markets that require long payback periods, as is often the case in developing countries and large emerging markets. For example, corruption, red tape, distribution problems, and a vague legal system present challenges for non-Chinese companies. But because long-term returns on their investments are expected, companies such as General Motors, Gillette, and J. Walter Thompson continue to invest heavily in China despite uncertain short-term profits.[29]

2. Firms must decide whether increasing local investment is necessary merely to maintain market share and its competitive position. Maintaining market share is a defensive posture and is common when a market shows little potential for future growth. In such cases, competition promises to intensify because a company can gain market share only by taking business away from its rivals.

3. Companies usually decide to reinvest when a market is experiencing rapid growth. Reinvestment can mean either expanding in the market itself, or expanding in a location that serves the growing market. Investing in expanding markets is often an attractive option because potential new customers usually have not yet become loyal to the products of any one company or brand. It can be easier and less costly to attract customers in such markets than it is to gain market share in markets that are stagnant or contracting.

4. Companies may try to reduce international competition by investing in the home markets of international competitors. In this way, the competitor is forced to defend its home market, often at the expense of market share elsewhere. Firms with little competition in their home markets, and thus able to focus many resources on increasing international market share, often employ this approach.

Reducing and Divesting Operations   All companies have a limited supply of resources at their disposal to invest in current operations or new endeavors. Thus companies must often reduce investments in certain markets so as to fund investments in more promising ones. There are three main reasons why companies decide either to scale back or to eliminate operations abroad.

1. Companies scale back their international investments when it becomes apparent that making operations profitable will take longer than expected. Again, China serves as a good example. Lured by the possibilities for growth offered by 1.2 billion consumers, companies flooded into the Chinese marketplace over the past two decades. Many of those firms, however, scaled back their ambitious plans once they realized that profitability would require continuous investment for five years or more.

2. Problems in the political, social, or economic sphere can force companies either to reduce investment or eliminate operations altogether. Such problems are usually intertwined with one another. In 1998, for example, Western companies pulled personnel out of Indonesia because of intense social unrest stemming directly from a combination of political problems (discontent with the nation's political leadership) and economic upheaval (the collapse of the Indonesian economy).

3. Naturally, companies invest in those operations offering the best return on their investments. That policy often means reducing investments or divesting operations in some markets even though they may be profitable, in order to invest in more profitable opportunities elsewhere. However, in such instances, managers must be confident that their forecasts for the new market are reliable.

A FINAL WORD

This chapter concludes our survey of international business. We began by understanding how cultural blinders restrict our view of business and the importance of taking a global perspective on business activities. We also saw the importance of political, legal, and economic environments in influencing business operations around the world. International companies must understand such nuances of diverse business environments if they are to be successful. This laid the foundation for our look at the international business environment. We saw how and why companies get involved in international trade and investment and how and why national governments and supranational organizations interfere in the free flow of trade and investment. We then went on to survey the main components of the international financial system and how it operates.

We completed our study of international business by seeing how all types of firms—entrepreneurs, small- and medium-size businesses, and large global companies—actually "go international." We learned the importance of careful research and analysis in identifying international opportunities and how to evaluate them. We saw how companies decide on their international business goals and create strategies and organizational structures to achieve those goals. We then went on to learn how companies select entry modes that are suited to their strategies and structures and when different entry modes are appropriate. Once this groundwork for international operations is laid, companies must acquire the business resources—human, physical, and financial—they need to perform their activities. Finally, we learned important issues managers deal with on a day-to-day basis when managing an international business.

We have covered a great deal of territory in our "tour" of international business. We hope we have piqued your interest in the goings-on of the global marketplace and in the activities of international companies of all types and sizes. Nevertheless, our learning does not end here. Each of us will continue to be exposed to international business in our daily lives—whether as consumers or as current or future business managers. Thus our knowledge of other national cultures, the international business environment, and how companies manage their international operations will continue to expand. We wish you well on your continued journey through this fascinating and dynamic subject.

There is a variety of additional material available on the companion Web site that accompanies this text. You can access this information by visiting the Web site at ⟨**www.prenhall.com/wild**⟩.

summary

① Describe the factors influencing international _product policies._ Many elements influence a company's decision of whether to standardize or adapt its product when it decides to "go international." First, companies undertake mandatory product adaptation in response to a target market's _laws and regulations._ Ethical issues can arise in the decision to adapt a product to local laws in developing nations because they often have weaker consumer-protection laws. Ironically, this makes these markets more likely to need protection. Companies also adapt their products to suit _cultural differences._ Sometimes companies do not need to modify their product if they can identify a different need that the product serves in the culture.

Although companies keep their _brand names_ consistent across markets, they often create new _product names_ or modify existing ones to suit local preferences. Giving a product a name that offends local buyers or is misleading can be a costly mistake. Also, the _image of a nation_ where a company is located that designs, manufactures, or assembles a product influences buyers' perceptions of quality and reliability. _Counterfeit goods_ can damage buyers' image of a brand when the counterfeits are of inferior quality— which is nearly always the case. Buyers expect a certain level of craftsmanship from any given brand but are disappointed with the counterfeited product's performance—tarnishing the company's reputation. Finally, _shortened product life cycles_ are affecting the timing of when to market internationally.

② Discuss the elements influencing international _promotional policies_ and how companies blend product and promotional policies. Efforts by a company to reach distribution channels and target customers through communications such as personal selling, advertising, public relations, and direct marketing are called its _promotion mix._ There are two general promotional strategies that companies can employ in getting their marketing message across to buyers. They can rely completely on only one of these or use them in any combination they desire. (a) A promotional strategy designed to create buyer demand that will encourage channel members to stock a company's product is called a _pull strategy._ In other words, buyer demand is generated in order to "pull" products through distribution channels to end users. (b) In contrast, a promotional strategy designed to pressure channel members to carry a product and promote it to final users of the product is called a _push strategy._

The process of sending promotional messages about products to target markets is called _marketing communication._ Marketing communication can be thought of as a circular process. The company that has an idea it wishes to communicate is the _source_ of the communication. The idea or _promotional message_ that the company is trying to get across to potential buyers is _encoded_—translated into images, words, and symbols that are understood by the _audience._ The promotional message is then sent to the audience through various _media._ Once the audience receives the message, they _decode_ the message and interpret its meaning. Information in the form of _feedback_ (purchase or nonpurchase) then flows back to the source of the message.

Companies blend their international product and promotional policies to create five generic promotional methods. _Product/communications extension (dual extension)_ extends the same home-market product and marketing promotion into target markets. *Product extension, communications adaptation* extends the same product into new target markets but alters its promotion. Communications are adapted because the same product satisfies a different need, serves a different function, or appeals to a different type of buyer. *Product adaptation, communications extension* adapts a product to the requirements of the international market while retaining the product's original marketing communication. *Product/communications adaptation (dual adaptation)* adapts both the product and its marketing communication to suit the target market. The product itself is adapted to match the needs or preferences of local buyers. The promotional message is adapted to explain how the product meets those needs and preferences. *Product invention* requires that an entirely new product be developed for the target market.

③ Describe the factors influencing international *distribution policies.* Planning, implementing, and controlling the physical flow of a product from its point of origin to its point of consumption is called *distribution*. The physical path that a product follows on its way to customers is called a *distribution channel*. An *exclusive channel* is one in which a manufacturer grants the right to sell its product to only one or a limited number of resellers. An exclusive channel gives producers a great deal of control over the sale of their product by channel members such as wholesalers and retailers. An *intensive channel* is one in which a producer grants the right to sell its product to many resellers. This type of channel does not create strong barriers to channel entry for producers nor give them much control over such reseller decisions as what competing brands to sell.

Channel length refers to the number of intermediaries between the producer and the buyer. In a *zero-level channel*—which is also called *direct marketing*—producers sell directly to final buyers. A *one-level channel* places only one intermediary between producer and buyer, two intermediaries make up a *two-level channel*, and so forth. Generally, the more intermediaries in a channel, the more costly it becomes because a greater number of players must tack on to the product a charge for their services. The value of a product relative to its weight and volume is called its *value density*. As a rule, *the lower a product's value density, the more localized the distribution system.*

A nation's distribution system develops over time and reflects its unique cultural, political, legal, and economic traditions. Companies can experience a great deal of frustration and financial loss simply by not understanding fully the local market in which they operate. A high incidence of theft and corruption can present obstacles to distribution. The distribution system in Russia, for instance, reflects its roughly 75-year experiment with communism.

④ Discuss the elements influencing international *pricing policies.* *Worldwide pricing* is a pricing policy in which one selling price is established for all international markets. A worldwide pricing policy is very difficult to achieve because nations have different levels of production, exporting, and distribution costs, purchasing power among buyers, and currency values. A pricing policy in which a product has a different selling price in export markets than it has in the home market is called *dual pricing*. When a product has a higher selling price in the target market than it does in the home market (or the country where production takes place) it is called *price escalation*.

Several factors have an important influence on managers' pricing decisions. A *transfer price* is the price charged for products sold between a company's divisions or subsidiaries. In the past, companies enjoyed a great deal of freedom in setting their transfer prices and did so to reduce their tax burden and tariffs. But today many governments regulate internal company pricing practices by assigning products approximate transfer prices based on a so-called *arm's-length price*—the free-market price that unrelated parties charge one another for a specific product.

Price controls are upper or lower limits placed on the prices of products sold within a country. Upper-limit price controls are designed to provide price stability in an inflationary economy. Lower-limit price controls prohibit the lowering of prices below a certain level. *Dumping* occurs when the price of a good is lower in export markets than it is in the domestic market. When a country's government charges another nation's producers of dumping a good on its market, antidumping tariffs are typically imposed to punish producers in the offending nation.

⑤ Explain the important aspects of *quality, logistics,* and *workforce* management. Companies strive toward quality improvement for two reasons: costs and customer value. First, quality products help keep production costs low because they reduce waste in valuable inputs, reduce the cost of retrieving defective products from buyers, and reduce disposal costs due to defective products. Second, some minimum level of acceptable quality is an aspect of every product.

An emphasis on continuous quality improvement to meet or exceed customer expectations is called *total quality management (TQM)*. Total quality management stresses a company-wide commitment to quality-enhancing processes. The *International Standards Organization (ISO) 9000* is an international certification that companies get when they meet the highest quality standards in their industries. Many companies seek ISO 9000 certification because of the message of quality that certification sends to prospective customers.

Logistics involves activities ranging from managing the physical flow of raw materials to delivery of the finished product to end users. Shipping costs can have a dramatic effect on the cost of getting materials and components to production facilities. A production technique in which inventory is kept to a minimum and inputs to the production process arrive exactly when they are needed is called *just-in-time (JIT) manufacturing*. JIT drastically reduces the costs associated with large inventories.

The positive or negative condition of relations between company management and its workers is referred to as *labor-management relations*. When management and workers realize they depend on one another, the company is often better prepared to meet its goals and surmount unexpected obstacles that may crop up. Because relations between labor and managers are human relations, they are rooted in culture and are often affected by political movements in the local market. Finally, the strength of labor unions in a country where a company has operations is important to its performance and can even affect the selection of a location.

6 **Identify the managerial considerations in the *reinvest* and *divest decisions*.** If new and potentially profitable opportunities present themselves in the market, managers might decide to expand operations. As such they typically *reinvest* profits from current activities to expand operations. Companies often choose to reinvest (a) when they believe a market will provide a large return over time, (b) when investment is necessary to maintain market share and competitive position, (c) when a market is experiencing rapid growth, and (d) to force international competitors to defend their home markets.

Companies also reduce investments in certain markets so as to fund investments in more promising ones. Companies decide either to scale back or to eliminate local operations when (a) making operations profitable will take longer than expected; (b) problems in the political, social, or economic sphere arise; and (c) more profitable opportunities arise in other markets.

questions **for review**

1. Identify at least four factors that influence a company's product policies in international markets.

2. Define the term *promotion mix*.

3. Briefly describe the difference between a *push strategy* and a *pull strategy*. What are some factors that affect the choice of an appropriate strategy?

4. What are some of the factors that affect the standardize versus adapt decision as it pertains to international advertising?

5. What is *marketing communication*? Describe each element in the marketing communications process and how they interact.

6. What are the *five generic strategies* for blending product and promotional policies for international markets? Describe each briefly.

7. What is *distribution*?

8. What is the difference between *exclusive* and *intensive* channels of distribution? Give an example of a product sold through each type of channel.

9. What is *value density*? Explain its importance to distribution policies.

10. Briefly explain the difference between *worldwide pricing* and *dual pricing*.

11. Explain the influence of *transfer prices, arm's length pricing, price controls,* and *dumping* on the pricing decisions of international companies.

12. How do *total quality management (TQM)* and *ISO 9000* help companies improve quality and control costs?

13. Define *just-in-time (JIT) manufacturing*. How do shipping and inventory costs influence a company's international logistics decision?

14. What does *labor-management relations* mean? Describe the influence of labor unions and international labor movements on managing a workforce.

15. Compare and contrast the considerations underlying the decision to *reinvest* in business operations with the considerations underlying the decision to *reduce and divest* operations.

questions for discussion

1. During the next few years, the Internet will become an increasingly important communication and selling tool for companies of all types and sizes. List five companies in different industries and tell what impact you think the Internet will have on how the companies market their products? Will the Internet's impact be greater in certain industries than in others? Explain why or why not.

2. Suppose that cultures and people's product preferences around the world continue to converge. Identify two products that will likely be affected and two products that will likely not be affected by such a convergence. For each prod-

uct that is affected, how will the changes influence the marketing manager's job? The production manager's job?

3. Companies around the world are increasingly committing themselves to attaining International Standards Organization (ISO) certification in a variety of areas including quality and pollution minimization. Do you think this is just the beginning of a trend toward worldwide homogenization of product and process standards? Do you think that some day all companies and their products will need certification in order to conduct international business? Why or why not?

in practice

Read the following brief article and answer the questions that follow.

Ad with Hitler Causes Furor in Thailand

The Thai television ad depicts Adolf Hitler eating brand "X" potato chips and then being transformed by a voodoo spell into a good person. The ad closes with Hitler stripping off his Nazi uniform and dancing, a Nazi swastika morphing into the logo for the Thai potato chip brand "X."

This week, after days of outcry from critics including the Israeli Embassy in Bangkok, the agency that created the campaign, Leo Burnett, recalled it. The agency said in a statement that the ad "was never intended to cause ill feelings." The agency also promised to remove print versions of the ad from all tuk-tuks, or three wheeled taxis.

The situation sheds light not only on how far some ad agencies will go to create striking images, but also how a lack of internal controls at agencies can cause problems, some ad-industry insiders say. That's because the local units of international ad agencies aren't typically required to consult with parent companies when creating ads for the domestic audience.

Leo Burnett says the ad was not intended as a publicity stunt for the potato chip brand. "The brand already has 10 percent market share," says spokeswoman Simone Wheeler. Asked if her agency will introduce new review steps to avoid similar problems, Ms. Wheeler says, "We haven't talked about it at this stage, but it's not to say that they will be or they won't be."

1. The international subsidiaries of advertising agencies tend to have a great deal of freedom in developing ads for the local market. Do you think this is a wise decision? Why or why not?

2. If you were the CEO of a large agency based in London, what could you do to tighten controls in your international offices? What impact, if any, would tighter controls have on the creative talent in local offices?

3. The Hitler ad was successfully market-tested with teenagers (who likely knew who Hitler was) before it was aired. Do you think that Thai teens are just insensitive or do you think that the cultural distance between Thailand and Germany plays a role? Why or why not?

4. Despite any potential cultural influence, do you think the fact that Hitler's reign was more than 50 years ago played a role in the successful testing of the ad? How do you think teens in your own country would react to such an ad? Would they think it humorous or insensitive? Explain.

projects

1. Choose a company that you are interested in. Consult recent annual reports or other sources to find out what new products that company has brought to market in the past year or two. Are those products truly new innovations, or are they simply extensions of existing products? What considerations guided the company in its product development efforts?

2. Gather several magazines from different parts of the world. Look through each of them for ads from one company or for advertisements featuring a particular product or brand. After you have identified three or four such ads, determine which of the five types of product and promotion policies is being used: dual extension, product extension/communications adaptation, product adaptation/communications extension, dual adaptation, or product invention. What explanation do you have for the particular method being used?

3. With several classmates, contact a manager at a local company that does business internationally. Talk to the manager about total quality management and ISO standards. Find out whether the company has a formal TQM program and whether it has obtained any type of ISO certification. Compile your findings and present them to the class in a short talk. Compare and contrast the findings obtained for each company the class studied.

business case 15
TPS: THE BENCHMARK IN PRODUCTION EFFICIENCY

At the end of 1998, the *Financial Times* published its annual report on the world's most respected companies based on a survey of industry leaders. The five top-ranked companies were General Electric, Microsoft, Coca-Cola, IBM, and Toyota. In a separate company ranking by area, Toyota was ranked number one among companies located in the Asia-Pacific region. One reason for Toyota's strong showing in both rankings is the fact that the company has managed to maintain profitability in the face of the Asian currency crisis and slack demand in Japan, where the company commands a 40 percent market share. Another reason is that leaders in a wide range of industries have high regard for Toyota's management and production practices.

Toyota first began producing cars in 1937. In the mid-1950s, a machinist named Taiichi Ohno began developing a new concept of auto production. Today, the approach known as the Toyota Production System has been intently studied and widely copied throughout the auto industry. Ohno, who was addressed by fellow employees as *sensei* ("teacher and master"), followed the lead of the family that founded Toyota (spelled Toyoda) by exhibiting high regard for workers. Ohno also believed that mass production of automobiles was obsolete and that a flexible production system that produced cars according to specific customer requests would be superior.

It was at Toyota that the well-known just-in-time approach to inventory management was developed and perfected.

Implementing just-in-time required *kanban*, a simple system of colored paper cards that accompanied the parts as they progressed down the assembly line. *Kanban* eliminates inventory buildup by quickly telling the production personnel which parts are being used and which are not. The third pillar of the Toyota Production System was quality circles, groups of workers that discuss ways of improving the work process and making better cars. Finally, the entire system was based on *jidoka*, which literally means "automation." However, as used at Toyota, the word expresses management's faith in the worker as a human being and thinker.

Nearly 50 years after the groundwork for the Toyota Production System was first laid, the results speak for themselves. Toyota's superior approach to manufacturing has been estimated to yield a cost advantage of $600 to $700 per car due to more efficient production, plus another $300 savings per car because fewer defects mean less warranty repair work. Ohno's belief in flexible production can also be seen in the fact that Toyota's new Sienna minivan is produced on the same assembly line in Georgetown, Kentucky, as the company's Camry models. The Sienna and Camry share the same basic chassis and 50 percent of their parts. Out of 300 different stations on the assembly line, Sienna models require different parts at only 26 stations. Toyota expects to build one Sienna for every three Camrys that come off the assembly line.

thinking globally

1. Chrysler engineers helped Toyota develop its new Sienna minivan. In return, Toyota provided input on auto production techniques to Chrysler. Why do you think Chrysler was willing to share its minivan know-how with a key competitor?

2. Many companies seek to cut costs and improve quality by introducing techniques such as just-in-time and quality circles. However, the results often fall short of those achieved at Toyota. Why is this?

3. Chrysler minivans are the market leaders in the United States. Why would Toyota want to offer a minivan of its own?

a question of ethics

1. The International Chamber of Commerce in Paris recently issued a set of voluntary guidelines on tactics for interactive marketing and advertising on the Internet. It is hoped that the guidelines will both reduce consumer resistance to online ads and quiet calls for restrictive legislation. The document contains, among other things, "users rights" guidelines stating that advertisers should disclose their reasons for collecting personal information on Web users and not sell such information to others without permission. Do you think that all the companies that sign on to such guidelines actually follow them? Do you think it is more difficult for small companies to resist the temptation to sell data on their users—particularly because such data can fetch a fairly high selling price? Do you think selling such data is ethical?

2. At some companies, "reengineering" is synonymous with "downsizing"; that is, laying off employees or reducing employment ranks through early retirement or other approaches. Ironically, however, some companies are hiring back "downsized" employees as contract workers with lower pay and fewer benefits. Is it ethical for companies to behave in this manner?[30]

3. The practices ascribed to global tobacco companies such as Philip Morris put the "standardization versus adaptation" issue in an unusual perspective. Competitors allege that in important developing markets such as Turkey, Philip Morris created special blends containing additives that give brands such as Marlboro an extra "kick." If cigarette companies do, in fact, adapt their products to attract local smokers, do you believe such policies are ethical?

background

This video focuses on a variety of international business management issues. MTV faced the strategic challenge of how to penetrate overseas markets. One of the first questions it faced was whether it would be better to go after developed or developing countries. The company decided to look first to developed countries, specifically in Europe. Having chosen this market, the company had to select from three plans of attack: (a) Go after all of Europe with a pan-European strategy; (b) create regional channels; or (c) regionalize certain aspects of the channels. MTV selected the third option, customizing its services not only for each specific country but also for specific localities within each country. Ultimately, MTV Europe successfully penetrated the European market by following company president Peter Einstein's lead in listening to viewers' preferences from the various European countries.

The video looks at the strategic approach MTV Europe undertook in penetrating the European market and the way it adapted its operations to European consumer preferences by country and by region.

mtv europe

For additional information on this company, please refer to the video case for Part Two, page 153.

discussion questions

While you watch the video, keep the following questions in mind. You might want to take notes.

1. How would you describe MTV Europe's international efforts? How did the company screen potential markets in Europe?

2. Consider again the three options MTV faced: (a) go after all of Europe; (b) create regional channels; or (c) regionalize parts of the channels. Why did MTV choose the third option? Would you have chosen the same one? Why or why not?

3. Why did MTV decide to penetrate the European market and not the African or the Asian market?

4. How did MTV succeed in Europe? To what does the company owe its success? If it used the same approach in penetrating an Asian or an African country, would it be as successful? Why or why not?

5. Why was a careful consideration of the cultural, social, and political environment so important in MTV's entry into the European market?

6. In terms of international business, what impressed you the most about MTV Europe? Why? Base your answers on the material covered in Part V.

7. "Be there, giving them what they want, in whatever form." What do these words mean in terms of international business? In terms of MTV's strategic approach?

8. What is the Unique Selling Proposition (USP) that MTV implemented in Europe? Was it a successful approach in penetrating the European market?

student exercises

1. Break into groups of two or three people. Use the material covered in Part V to analyze the video case. Put together a 15- to 20-minute oral presentation of your findings.

2. From different regions of the world, pick the countries that are most appropriate for MTV to operate in, and explain the reasons for your opinion.

3. Analyze every approach and strategy MTV has taken in adapting to each country in Europe.

NOTES

Chapter 1

[1] Rebecca A. Fannin, "Counter Threat: PT Matahari, Indonesia's Top Retailer, Aims to Repel a Wave of Foreign Invaders," *Asia, Inc.*, December 1996–January 1997, pp. 36–37.

[2] Kevin Maney, "Companies Cast Worldwide Net: Technology Is 'Demolishing' Time, Distance," *USA Today*, April 24, 1997, p. B1.

[3] Timothy D. Schellhardt, "Star Search: Talent Pool Is Shallow as Corporations Seek Executives for Top Jobs," *Wall Street Journal*, June 26, 1997, p. A1.

[4] William Greider, *One World, Ready or Not: The Manic Logic of Global Capitalism* (New York: Simon & Schuster, 1997), p. 15.

[5] Adrian Wooldridge, "Insider Trading," *The Economist*, June 24, 1996, pp. SS6–12.

[6] Cyndee Miller, "Chasing Global Dreams," *Marketing News*, December 2, 1996, p. 1.

[7] Lester C. Thurow, *The Future of Capitalism* (New York: William Morrow, 1996), p. 115.

[8] Pete Engardio, "Why Multinationals Are So Gung Ho," *Business Week*, June 9, 1997, p. 54; Neal McGrath, "Express Carriers Gather in Subic Bay," *Asian Business*, June 1996, pp. 18, 20.

[9] For a more thorough discussion of the 1994 GATT agreement, see the following Web sites:
⟨www.ljextra.com/practice/internat/history⟩;
⟨www.ljextra.com/practice/internat/gattgood⟩;
⟨www.ljextra.som/practice/internat/GATTserv⟩; and ⟨www.wto.org/2_8_0_wpf⟩.

[10] *The World in 1997* (London: The Economist Newspaper Limited, 1996), p. 95.

[11] "Internet Literacy: New Key to Career Advancement," *Canadian Accounting Education and Research News*, November 1996, p. 20.

[12] Bill Gates, "The Internet Grows Out of Nappies," *The World in 1997* (London: The Economist Newspaper Limited, 1996), p. 103.

[13] Lawrence M. Fisher, "The Wired Enterprise: Here Come the Intranets," *Strategy & Business*, First Quarter 1997, pp. 84–90.

[14] Fred Hapgood, "Foreign Exchange," *Inc. Technology 1997*, No. 2, pp. 85–86, 88.

[15] "The Internet in the News." *Simon & Schuster College NewsLink*. Accessed March 14, 1997. Available World Wide Web: ⟨**cnluser@ssnewslink.com**⟩.

[16] J. William Gurley, "The Soaring Cost of E-Commerce," *Fortune*, August 3, 1998, pp. 226–228.

[17] Lori A. Phlamm, "Business on the Internet," *Checkers Simon & Rosner Newsletter*, Summer 1996.

[18] Greider, *One World, Ready or Not*, p. 14.

[19] Lotte Chow, "Drunk on Lemonade: Australian Brews Up a Best Seller," *Far Eastern Economic Review*, February 13, 1997, p. 54.

[20] As reported in "It's a Small World," *Entrepreneur Magazine*, February 1997, p. 39.

[21] John A. Quelch and Lisa R. Klein, "The Internet and International Marketing," *Sloan Management Review*, Spring 1996, pp. 60–75.

[22] Richard Cross, "Weekend in Florence Web Site: Is It Better Than the Real Thing?" *Direct Marketing*, August 1996, pp. 14–17.

[23] "The Fortune *Global 500*: The World's Largest Corporations," *Fortune*, August 3, 1998, pp. 130–134, F1–F29.

[24] Data in Tables 1.2, 1.3, and 1.4 come from the following sources: "The Fortune *Global 500*: The World's Largest Corporations," pp. 130–134, F1–F29; World Bank, *World Development Indicators 1998* (Washington, DC: International Bank for Reconstruction and Development, March 1998), pp. 180–183, Table 4-2.

[25] "Going to the Chapel," *Business Week*, January 11, 1999, p. 8.

[26] Wayne, "Wave of Mergers Is Recasting Face of U.S. Business," p. A1.

[27] Yutaka Yanagisawa, "Global Goal Spurs Sony's Shift," *The Nikkei Weekly*, February 17, 1997, p. 9.

[28] "Group: Abuse in Nike Factories in Vietnam," *Top Business Stories from Reuters*. Accessed March 28, 1997. Available World Wide Web: ⟨**aol://4344:3167.RTR_TOP.21037358.534202558**⟩.

[29] Ken Cottrill, "Global Codes of Conduct," *Journal of Business Strategy*, May–June 1996, pp. 55–59.

[30] Sam Dillon, "After Four Years of Nafta, Labor Is Forging Cross-Border Ties," *New York Times*, December 20, 1997, pp. A1, A7.

[31] Patricia Digh, "Shades of Gray in the Global Marketplace," *HRMagazine*, April 1997, pp. 91–98.

[32] Dana Canedy, "Nike's Asian Factories Pass Young's Muster," *New York Times*, June 25, 1997, p. D2.

[33] Guillermo Perez Diaz, "Clean Getaway," *Harper's Magazine*, July 1997, p. 86.

Chapter 2

[1] Martin Du Bois, "Euro-Disney's Dress Code Faces Challenge by French Prosecutors," *Wall Street Journal*, December 28, 1994, p. B5; "Lands' End Caters to Asian Market," *Asian Wall Street Journal Weekly*, September 16, 1996, p. 10; Chen May Yee, "Malaysia's New Islamic Visa Card Answers to a Higher Authority," *Asian Wall Street Journal Weekly*, September 23, 1996, p. 20.

[2] For a more detailed definition of *culture*, see Geert Hofstede, *Culture and Organizations: Software of the Mind* (New York: McGraw-Hill, 1997), pp. 3–19.

[3] Anne-Michele Morice, "New French Law Strikes Sour Note for Radio Stations," *Wall Street Journal*, January 22, 1996, p. A8.

[4] Carlos Tejada, "Here's the One Beer to Have When You're Facing Communist Rule," *Wall Street Journal*, April 30, 1997, p. B1.

[5] Namju Cho, "Korean Men Take a Drag on Virginia Slims," *Wall Street Journal*, January 14, 1997, p. B10.

[6] For a more in-depth discussion of cultural effects on the perception of time, see Lalita A. Manrai and Ajay K. Manrai, "Effects of Cultural-Context, Gender, and Acculturation on Perceptions of Work versus Social/Leisure Time Usage," *Journal of Business Research 32* (1995): 115–128.

[7] "America's Success, Europe's Shame," *The World in 1997* (London: The Economist Newspaper Limited, 1996), p. 102.

[8] Youssef M. Ibrahim, "In Old England, a Silicon Fen," *New York Times*, January 4, 1998, Sec. 3, pp. 1, 11.

[9] Esmond D. Smith, Jr. and Cuong Pham, "Doing Business in Vietnam: A Cultural Guide," *Business Horizons*, May–June 1996, pp. 47–51.

[10]Kenichi Ohmae, *The End of the Nation State* (New York: Free Press, 1995), pp. 28–30.

[11]Valeria Frazee, "Getting Started in Mexico," *Global Workforce*, January 1997, pp. 16–17.

[12]Jeffrey E. Garten, "Is America Abandoning Multilateral Trade?", *Foreign Affairs*, November–December 1995, pp. 50–62.

[13]Marlise Simons, "Did VW Mock the Gospel? French Bishops Sue," *New York Times*, February 7, 1998, p. A4.

[14]Yee, "Malaysia's New Islamic Visa Card Answers to a Higher Authority," p. 20.

[15]Elaine Sciolino, "Explain It Again, Please: Who Says I Can't Wear a Hat?", *New York Times*, February 8, 1998, p. WK7.

[16]Manjeet Kripalani, "A Traffic Jam of Auto Makers," *Business Week*, August 5, 1996, pp. 46–47.

[17]Erik Eckholm, "A Look at Religion in China by Three U.S. Clerics," *New York Times*, February 9, 1998, p. A3.

[18]Don Kirk, "Confucian Discipline at Core of Korean Management," *Asian Wall Street Journal Weekly*, September 9, 1996, p. 18.

[19]For more details on this debate, see Mark Lewis, Robert Fitzgerald, and Charles Harvey, *The Growth of Nations: Culture, Competitiveness, and the Problem of Globalization* (Bristol, UK: Bristol Academic Press, 1996); Francis Fukuyama, *Trust: The Social Virtues and the Creation of Prosperity* (New York: Free Press, 1995); Ryh-Song Yeh and John J. Lawrence, "Individualism and Confucian Dynamism: A Note on Hofstede's Cultural Root to Economic Growth," *Journal of International Business Studies*, Third Quarter 1995, pp. 655–669.

[20]Peter Kwong, "The Chinese Diaspora," *World Business*, May–June 1996, pp. 26–31.

[21]Serge Schmemann, "If It's a Hard Sell, Let's Try Beards and Yarmulkes," *New York Times*, February 4, 1998, p. A4.

[22]"A Modern Vogue for More Than a Brogue," *The Economist*, November 2, 1996, p. 52.

[23]Gary P. Ferraro, "The Need for Linguistic Proficiency in Global Business," *Business Horizons*, May–June 1996, pp. 39–46.

[24]"MTV Goes Local Again with Creation of a Third Asian Channel, for India," *Asian Wall Street Journal Weekly*, September 30, 1996, p. 12.

[25]"Hey, #!@*% Amigo, Can You Translate the Word 'Gaffe'?" *Wall Street Journal*, July 8, 1996, p. B6.

[26]Mariah E. de Forest, "Insulation from Mexican Culture Shock," *Wall Street Journal*, October 17, 1994, p. A14.

[27]For a more detailed discussion of this issue, see Paul Krugman, *Pop Internationalism* (Cambridge, MA: MIT Press, 1996); Michael E. Porter, *The Competitive Advantage of Nations* (New York: Free Press, 1990); Robert B.
Reich, *The Work of Nations* (New York: Vintage Books, 1992); Lester Thurow, *The Future of Capitalism* (New York: William Morrow, 1996).

[28]Trish Saywell and Yu Wong, "Brains for Sale: China's Professors—and Universities—Go into Business," *Far Eastern Economic Review*, January 23, 1997, pp. 23–24.

[29]Stephen Baker with Gary McWilliams and Majeet Kruipalani, "Forget the Huddled Masses: Send Nerds," *Business Week*, July 21, 1997, pp. 110–112+.

[30]Raymond Scupin, *Cultural Anthropology: A Global Perspective*, 3rd ed. (Upper Saddle River, NJ: Prentice Hall, 1998), p. 47.

[31]"DSC Wiring Nigeria," *World Trade*, October 1998, pp. 26–28.

[32]William McGurn, "City Limits," *Far Eastern Economic Review*, February 6, 1997, pp. 34–37.

[33]McGurn, "City Limits," pp. 34–37.

[34]Florence Kluckhohn and F. L. Strodtbeck, *Variations in Value Orientations* (Evanston, IL: Harper & Row, 1961).

[35]Geert Hofstede, "The Cultural Relativity of Organizational Practices and Theories," *Journal of International Business Studies*, Fall 1983, pp. 75–89.

[36]Hofstede's study, from which this method was developed, has been criticized on a number of grounds. First, it suffers from a "Western" bias in design and analysis, querying employees in just one firm in one industry. Second, it treats culture as "national" only and, therefore, ignores subcultures. Finally, it now appears old—it was conducted in the 1960s and 1970s. See R. Mead, *International Management: Cross-Cultural Dimensions* (Oxford: Basil Blackwell, 1994), pp. 73–75.

[37]For further details, see Randall S. Schuler et al., "Managing Human Resources in Mexico: A Cultural Understanding," *Business Horizons*, May–June 1996, pp. 55–61; Rosemary Stewart, "German Management: A Challenge to Anglo-American Managerial Assumptions," *Business Horizons*, May–June 1996, pp. 52–54.

[38]Richard J. Schmidt, "Japanese Management, Recession Style," *Business Horizons*, March–April 1996, pp. 70–76.

[39]Jennifer Cody, "Headhunting in Japan Gains Respectability," *Wall Street Journal*, July 6, 1994, p. B1.

Chapter 3

[1]Steve Barth, "In Dangerous Places," World Trade, October 1998, pp. 64–67; Peter Schweizer, "The Growth of Economic Espionage: America Is Target Number One," *Foreign Affairs*, January–February 1996, pp. 9–14; John R. Engen, "Corporate Terrorism and How to Avoid It," *Training*, October 1995, p. 84.

[2]Edmund L. Andrews, "Twenty-Nine Nations Agree to Outlaw Bribing Foreign Officials," *New York Times*, November 21, 1997, pp. A1, D2.

[3]Sam Dillon, "Union Vote in Mexico Illustrates Abuses," *New York Times*, October 13, 1997, p. A8.

[4]*Freedom in the World 1997–1998* (New York: Freedom House, 1998), pp. 3–6.

[5]For a discussion of changes occurring in Iran since the days of the revolution, see "Children of the Islamic Revolution" ("A Survey of Iran" Insert), *The Economist*, January 18, 1997; and "Those Behind Cried Forward," *The Economist*, May 30, 1998, p. 47.

[6]"Quote of the Day," *Far Eastern Economic Review*. Accessed August 4, 1997. Available World Wide Web: ⟨www.db.webhk.com:3268/feer/owa/industry.contents⟩.

[7]Mark Landler, "Reversing Course, Levi Strauss Will Expand Its Output in China," *New York Times*, April 9, 1998, pp. D1, D5.

[8]Karen Lowry Miller, "Central Europe's Best Companies," *Business Week* (International Edition), June 30, 1997; Jenny C. McCune, "Stormy Weather," *Management Review*, February 1997, pp. 12–17.

[9]Donald G. McNeil, Jr., "Black Pioneer Answers the Call," *New York Times*, July 7, 1998, pp. D1, D6.

[10]Constance L. Hays and Donald G. McNeil, Jr., "Putting Africa on Coke's Map," *New York Times*, May 26, 1998, pp. D1, D4.

[11]Terri Morrison, Wayne A. Conaway, and Joseph J. Douress, *Dun and Bradstreet's Guide to Doing Business Around the World* (Upper Saddle River, NJ: Prentice Hall, 1997), pp. 86, 244.

[12]*Patterns of Global Terrorism: 1997* (Washington, DC: U.S. Department of State, 1998), p. iii.

[13]"Kidnapping: Big Business," *The Economist*, October 19, 1996, p. 50.

[14]Kate Murphy, "Security Risk," *Working Woman*, March 1997, pp. 47–48.

[15]Joseph Kahn, "In a Reversal, China Will Allow a Resumption of Amway Sales," *New York Times*, July 21, 1998, p. D20.

[16]Agis Salpukas, "Burmese Project Tests Unocal Resolve," *New York Times*, May 22, 1997, pp. D1, D2.

[17]Ryuzaburo Kaku, "The Path of *Kyosei*," *Harvard Business Review*, July–August 1997, pp. 55–63.

[18]"Managing Challenges of Going Global: Executive Checklist," *Crossborder Monitor*, February 22, 1995, pp. 1, 9.

[19]Kozo Mizoguchi, "Executive Arrests Rock Japan Bank," *Wisconsin State Journal*, June 11, 1997, p. 5B; Brian Bremner, "A Big Stink Speeds Up the Big Bang," *Business Week*, July 7, 1997, p. 118.

[20]David E. Sanger, "Bad Debt Now Held by Japan's Banks Now Estimated Near $1 Trillion," *New York Times*, July 30, 1998, pp. A1, A8.

[21]Ray August, *International Business Law: Text, Cases, and Readings* (Upper Saddle River, NJ: Prentice Hall, 1993), p. 51.

[22]John Tagliabue, "Fakes Blot a Nation's Good Names," *New York Times*, July 3, 1997, pp. D1, D2.

[23]"Who Dares, in China, Can Still Win," *The Economist*, June 7, 1997, p. 62.

[24]Claudia H. Deutsch, "As Much Time in Court as in the Laboratory," *New York Times*, July 12, 1997, pp. 33, 34.

[25]Tagliabue, "Fakes Blot a Nation's Good Names," pp. D1, D2.

[26]Christopher Wagner, "Safe Products and Global Trade," *The OECD Observer*, October–November 1996, pp. 13–15.

[27]Jane Perlez, "Fenced In at Home, Marlboro Man Looks Abroad," *New York Times*, June 24, 1997, pp. A1, A16.

[28]Melody Peterson, "Antitrust Scrutiny Ends Plans to Merge Accounting Firms," *New York Times*, February 14, 1998, pp. A1, D2.

[29]Catherine Yang, "When Protectionism Wears Camouflage," *Business Week*, June 2, 1997, p. 60; Edmund L. Andrews, "Boeing Concession Averts Trade War with Europe," *New York Times*, July 24, 1997, pp. A1, D5.

[30]Linda Greenhouse, "Justices Reject Challenge of Patent for AIDS Drug," *New York Times*, January 17, 1996, p. A14; Jon Cohen, "Bringing AZT to Poor Countries," *Science*, August 4, 1995, pp. 624–626.

[31]Richard Rapaport, "Singapore Sting," *Forbes ASAP*, April 7, 1997, pp. 85–89.

[32]Salpukas, "Burmese Project Tests Unocal Resolve," pp. D1, D2.

Chapter 4

[1]Jeffrey E. Garten, "Troubles Ahead in Emerging Markets," *Harvard Business Review*, May–June 1997, pp. 38–50; "Nothing Is Really Private in Vietnam," *The Economist*, May 17, 1997, pp. 45–46.

[2]"Disappearing Taxes," *The Economist*, May 31, 1996, pp. 21–23.

[3]Steven V. Brull, "North Korea's Bitter Choice: Famine or Foreign Aid," *Business Week*, March 3, 1997, p. 53.

[4]Robert Kuttner, "Everything for Sale," *Business Week*, March 17, 1997, pp. 92–96.

[5]"The French Election: Chirac and Juppé Hope for Change," *The Economist*, May 24, 1997, pp. 21–23.

[6]Gail Edmondson, "A Continent at the Breaking Point," *Business Week*, February 24, 1997, pp. 50–51; Craig R. Whitney, "French Jobless Find the World Is Harsher," *New York Times*, March 19, 1998, pp. A1, A6.

[7]Carol Kaesuk Yoon, "Chocoholics Take Note: Beloved Bean Is in Peril," *New York Times*, May 4, 1998, pp. A1, A15.

[8]Stan Crock, Catherine Yang, and Gary McWilliams, "More Antitrust Woes for Gates?" *Business Week*, April 28, 1997, p. 4; Joel Brinkley, "Microsoft Winner in Appeal to Keep Software Intact," *New York Times*, June 24, 1998, pp. A1, D3.

[9]Maria Atanasov, "Nike's Lead: Just Follow It?" *Fortune*, September 8, 1997, p. 188.

[10]James Jones, "The Golden Land of Opportunity," *World Trade*, July 1996, pp. 14–15.

[11]Jones, "The Golden Land of Opportunity," pp. 14–15.

[12]Matthew Brzezinski, "For Ukraine, the Economic Statistic Lie," *Wall Street Journal*, May 13, 1996, p. A16.

[13]Daniel S. Levine, "Got a Spare Destroyer Lying Around? Make a Trade: Embracing Countertrade as a Viable Option," *World Trade*, June 1997, pp. 34–35.

[14]"Central Russian Teachers to Get Paid in Vodka." Accessed September 22, 1998. Available World Wide Web: ⟨**www.cnn.com/WORLD/europe/9809/22/fringe/russia.vodka.ap/index.html**⟩.

[15]Justin Fox, "The Great Emerging Markets Rip-Off," *Fortune*, May 11, 1998, pp. 98–100+.

[16]Tarun Khanna and Krishna Palepu, "Why Focused Strategies May Be Wrong for Emerging Markets," *Harvard Business Review*, July–August 1997, pp. 41–51.

[17]Stephen Parker, Gavin Tritt, and Wing Thye Woo, "Some Lessons Learned from the Comparison of Transitions in Asia and Eastern Europe," in *Economies in Transition: Comparing Asia and Europe*, eds. Wing Thye Woo, Stephen Parker, and Jeffrey D. Sachs (Cambridge, MA: MIT Press, 1997), pp. 3–5; *World Development Report 1996*, "From Plan to Market: Executive Summary," (Washington, D.C.: World Bank, 1996), p. 2.

[18]*World Development Report*, p. 139.

[19]David E. Sanger and Richard W. Stevenson, "Second-Guessing the Economic Doctor: I.M.F.'s Bitter Medicine under Siege on Many Fronts," *New York Times*, February 1, 1998, Sec. 3, pp. 1, 8–9; Michael Lewis, "The World's Biggest Going-Out-of-Business Sale," *New York Times Magazine*, May 31, 1998, pp. 34–41+.

[20]Joe Cook, "Worlds Apart?" *Business Central Europe*, May 1997, p. 48.

[21]Susan Moffat, "Asia Stinks," *Fortune*, December 9, 1996, pp. 120–132.

[22]Y. Fan, N. Chen, and D. A. Kirby, "Chinese Peasant Entrepreneurs: An Examination of Township and Village Enterprises in Rural China," *Journal of Small Business Management*, October 1996, pp. 72–76.

[23]Mark L. Clifford, Dexter Roberts, and Pete Engardio, "How You Can Win in China," *Business Week*, May 26, 1997, pp. 66–68.

[24]David Phinney, "China's Capitalist Army." Accessed October 17, 1997. Available World Wide Web: ⟨**www.abcnews.aol.com**⟩.

[25]Clifford J. Shultz II, "Marketing in the 'Land of the Moving Goal Posts,'" *Marketing News*, April 22, 1996, pp. 14, 18; Cyndee Miller, "U.S. Firms Rush to Claim Share of Newly Opened Vietnam Market," *Marketing News*, March 14, 1994, p. 11; Michael Paterniti, "The Laptop Colonialists," *New York Times Magazine*, January 12, 1997, p. 24; Lee Paul Dana, "A Marxist Mini-Dragon? Entrepreneurship in Today's Vietnam," *Journal of Small Business Management*, April 1994, pp. 95–102.

[26]Drew Robb, "Central and Eastern Europe: The Highway to Success (Under Construction)," *World Trade*, February 1998, pp. 68–72.

[27]Gene Koretz, "Paths toward a Free Market," *Business Week* January 27, 1997, p. 20; Andrew Kozlowski, "Poland: The Next Big Thing," *Director*, April 1997, p. 21.

[28]Howard W. French, "Oil Profits Trickle Up or Out of Africa's Forgotten Land," *New York Times*, February 15, 1998, Sec. 1, p. 10.

[29]James C. McKinley, Jr., "Almost All the News on Kenya Is Turning Out Bad," *New York Times*, February 15, 1998, Sec. 1, p. 3.

[30]Edmund L. Andrews, "Germans Cut Labor Costs with a Harsh Export: Jobs," *New York Times*, March 21, 1998, pp. A1, A3.

[31]Craig R. Whitney, "Gallic Smiles Have Erased Gallic Gloom, for Now," *New York Times*, July 11, 1998, p. A3.

[32]Andrews, "Germans Cut Labor Costs with a Harsh Export: Jobs," pp. A1, A3.

[33]William Safire, "Absurdity Increases as Europe Staggers toward Single Currency," *Wisconsin State Journal*, June 22, 1997, p. 2B.

[34]Kuttner, "Everything for Sale," pp. 92–96.

[35]Andrew Tanzer, "The People's Liberation Army, Inc.," *Forbes*, March 24, 1997, pp. 44–46.

Chapter 5

[1]Drew Robb, "Out of Africa: Rediscovering a Misplaced Market," *World Trade*, November 1998, pp. 32–36; Constance L. Hays and Donald G. McNeil, Jr., "Putting Africa on Coke's Map," *New York Times*, May 26, 1998, pp. C1, C4; James Srodes, "America's Marshall Plan for Africa?" *World Trade*, September 1997, pp. 30–31, 49.

[2]"Getting on the Fast Track: Small Business and International Trade," Small Business Survival Committee, Trade Brochure. Accessed October 13, 1998. Available World Wide Web: ⟨**www.sbsc.org/fasttrack/tradebroch.html**⟩.

[3] This discussion is based on "World Trade Growth Accelerated in 1997, Despite Turmoil in Some Asian Financial Markets," World Trade Organizations, March 1998. Accessed November 3, 1998. Available World Wide Web: ⟨**www.wto.org/wto/intltrad/internat.htm**⟩.

[4] 1998 World Development Indicators (Washington, DC: World Bank, 1998), p. 317.

[5] Karen Lowry Miller and John Templeman, "Germany's New East Bloc," Business Week, February 3, 1997, pp. 50–52.

[6] William J. Zeile, "U.S. Intrafirm Trade in Goods," Survey of Current Business, February 1997, pp. 23–38.

[7] "S. Africa's Quiet Revolution," World Trade, May 1997, pp. 66–71.

[8] Adam Smith, The Wealth of Nations (Chicago: University of Chicago Press, 1976).

[9] David Ricardo, The Principles of Political Economy and Taxation, first published in 1817.

[10] Paul R. Krugman and Maurice Obstfeld, International Economics: Theory and Policy (Reading, MA: Addison-Wesley, 1997), pp. 32–34.

[11] Bertil Ohlin, Interregional and International Trade (Cambridge, MA: Harvard University Press, 1933).

[12] Wassily Leontief, "Domestic Production and Foreign Trade: The American Capital Position Re-Examined," Economia Internationale, February, 1954, pp. 3–32.

[13] Raymond Vernon and Louis T. Wells, Jr., Economic Environment of International Business, 7th ed. (Upper Saddle River, NJ: Prentice Hall, 1991).

[14] Rosabeth Moss Kanter, World Class (New York: Simon & Schuster, 1995), p. 95.

[15] Gary A. Knight and S. Tamer Cavusgil, "The Global Firm: A Challenge to Traditional Internationalization Theory," Advances in International Marketing, Vol. 8 (1996): 11–26.

[16] Elhanan Helpman and Paul Krugman, Market Structure and Foreign Trade (Cambridge, MA: MIT Press, 1985).

[17] For a detailed discussion of the first-mover advantage and its process, see Alfred D. Chandler, Scale and Scope (New York: Free Press, 1990).

[18] Michael E. Porter, The Competitive Advantage of Nations (New York: Free Press, 1990).

[19] Michael E. Porter, "Clusters and The New Economics of Competition," Harvard Business Review, November–December, 1998, pp. 77–90.

[20] Thomas Fullerton and Richard Sprinkle, "Latin American Progress under Structural Reform," Texas Centers Technical Report TX97-5 (El Paso, TX: Texas Centers for Border Economic Development, 1997).

[21] Kyle Pope and Mark Robichaux, "Waiting for HDTV? Don't Go Turning in Your Old Set Just Yet," Wall Street Journal, September 12, 1997, pp. A1, A10.

[22] Joe Rogaly, "Another Finger in the Banana Pie," Financial Times, March 1–2, 1997, p. iii.

Chapter 6

[1] Fred Coleman, "A Great Lost Cause: France vs. the Internet," U.S. News & World Report, April 21, 1997, pp. 57–58; "Ado Cherche Appart," The Economist, May 11, 1996, pp. 80–82; Anne-Michele Morice, "New French Law Strikes Sour Note for Radio Stations," Wall Street Journal, January 22, 1996, p. A8; Marlise Simone, "Ban English? French Bicker on Barricades," New York Times, March 15, 1994, p. A1.

[2] Joseph Weber, "Does Canadian Culture Need This Much Protection?" Business Week, June 18, 1998. Available World Wide Web: ⟨**bwarchive.businessweek.com**⟩.

[3] Jeffrey E. Garten, "Cultural Imperialism Is No Joke," Business Week, November 30, 1998. Available World Wide Web: ⟨**bwarchive.businessweek.com**⟩.

[4] "Guyanans Urged to Be 'Patriotic' and Spurn Imports," World Trade, January 1999, p. 20.

[5] Dexter Roberts, "Will Kodak Get Lucky in Japan?" Business Week, July 28, 1997, p. 48.

[6] Stephen Blakely, "Seeds of Change for Farmers," Nation's Business, December 1996, pp. 42–44.

[7] "Technology Deals with China Harmed U.S. Security, House Committee Says," CNN Interactive, December 30, 1998. Accessed December 30, 1998. Available World Wide Web: ⟨**www.cnn.com/US9812/30/china.satellites.02**⟩.

[8] Brian Bremner, "This Is Going to Happen: MITI's Yosano Pledges Reform," Business Week, December 7, 1998, pp. 106–107.

[9] Brian Bremmer, "Two Japans," Business Week, January 27, 1997, pp. 24–28.

[10] "U.S. Congress Considers Stiff Restraints against Korea's Firms," Business Korea, December 1995–January 1996, p. 79.

[11] Steven V. Brull and Catherine Keumhyun Lee, "Why Seoul Is Seething," Business Week, January 27, 1997, pp. 44–46.

[12] Jackie Calmes, "Despite Buoyant Economic Times Americans Don't Buy Free Trade," Wall Street Journal, December 10, 1998, p. A10.

[13] Deborah Baldwin, "The Proof Will Be in the 'Europudding,'" Los Angeles Times, April 24, 1997, p. D4.

[14] Gareth Porter, "Natural Resource Substitutes and International Policy: A Role for APEC," Journal of Environment and Development, September 1997, pp. 276–291.

[15] Daniel S. Levine, "Ex-Im Bank Year in Review," World Trade, January 1999, p. 30.

[16] Ellie Winninghof, "Derailing Critics," International Business, May 1996, pp. 20–25; Daniel S. Levine, "Little Big Shots," World Trade, December–January 1997, pp. 42–47.

[17] Winninghof, "Derailing Critics," pp. 20–25.

[18] Anne Stevenson-Yang, "Quiet Incursions," The China Business Review, September–October 1996, pp. 36–42.

[19] "The Border," Business Week, May 12, 1997, pp. 64–74.

[20] Kenneth E. Grubbs, Jr., "The Opening of Japan," World Trade, June 1997, pp. 28–32.

[21] Lily Tung, "Behind-the-Scenes Obstacles for Film-Makers," Asian Business, February 1996, p. 11.

[22] Emily Thornton, "The Japan That Can Say No to Cold Pills," Business Week, May 19, 1997, p. 54.

[23] "Saudi Arabia Simplifies Import Clearance," World Trade, January 1999, p. 24.

[24] Many of the facts included in the following discussion concerning the General Agreement on Tariffs and Trade (GATT) and the World Trade Organization (WTO) are drawn from the extensive database located at the WTO Web site: ⟨**www.wto.org**⟩.

[25] Sean Milmo, "PE Processors May Seek Duties on Asia Imports," Chemical Market Reporter, March 10, 1997, pp. 9, 39.

[26] Robert S. Greenberger, "U.S. Current-Account Deficit Widens to Record," Wall Street Journal, December 10, 1998, p. A2.

[27] "Clinton Urges Fast-Track Economic Repair Package for Japan," CNN Interactive, November 20, 1998. Accessed December 30, 1998. Available World Wide Web: ⟨**cnn.com/WORLD/asiapcf/9811/20/japan.us.02/index.html**⟩.

[28] "Unfair Protection," The Economist, November 7, 1998, pp. 75–76.

[29] Michael D. White, "Pile on the Fertilizer and Keep 'Em in the Dark," World Trade, January 1999, pp. 14–16.

[30] Michael D. White, "Let's Meet and Talk about It," World Trade, December 1998, p. 14.

[31] "Big U.S. Industries Launch Attack on Warming Treaty," Wall Street Journal, December 12, 1997, p. A3.

[32] World Development Indicators (Washington, DC: The World Bank, 1998), p. 117.

[33] Laurie Lande, "Pariahs Forever?" World Trade, August 1997, pp. 18–20; Paul Magnusson, "A Troubling Barrage of Trade Sanctions from All across America," Business Week, February 24, 1997, p. 59.

[34] "Massachusetts Sanctions Called Unconstitutional," World Trade, December 1998, pp. 17–18.

[35] "China Levels Ancient Mosque to Assist Urban Redevelopment," International Herald Tribune, December 18, 1998, p. 6.

Chapter 7

[1] William Greider, *One World, Ready or Not: The Manic Logic of Global Capitalism* (New York: Simon & Schuster, 1997), p. 15.

[2] United Nations Conference on Trade and Development, *World Investment Report 1996* (New York: United Nations, 1996).

[3] "Acer: A Global Powerhouse," *Business Week*, July 1, 1996, pp. 94–95.

[4] "How To Merge: After the Deal," *Economist*, January 9, 1999, pp. 21–23.

[5] Bill Vlasic, et al, "Daimler and Chrysler: What the Deal Would Mean," *Business Week: International Edition*, May 18, 1998, pp. 20–23.

[6] Janet Guyon, "Cellular Start-Up: Some Good Old Boys Make Lots of Money Phoning Up Tashkent," *Wall Street Journal*, June 21, 1996, p. A1.

[7] U.N. Conference on Trade and Development, *World Investment Report 1996*, p. 4.

[8] U.N. Conference on Trade and Development, *World Investment Report 1996*, p. 52.

[9] Keith Bradsher, "In South America, Auto Makers See One Big Showroom," *New York Times*, April 25, 1997, p. D1; Rebecca Blumenstein, "GM Is Building Plants in Developing Nations to Woo New Markets," *Wall Street Journal*, August 4, 1997, p. A1.

[10] Raymond Vernon and Louis T. Wells, Jr., *Economic Environment of International Business*, 7th ed. (Upper Saddle River, NJ: Prentice Hall, 1991).

[11] John H. Dunning, "Toward an Eclectic Theory of International Production," *Journal of International Business Studies*, Spring–Summer, 1980, pp. 9–31.

[12] For an excellent discussion of the economic benefits particular geographic locations can provide, see Paul Krugman, "Increasing Returns and Economic Geography," *Journal of Political Economy*, June 1991, pp. 483–499.

[13] "India Shakes Off Its Shackles," *Business Week*, January 30, 1995, pp. 48–49.

[14] Bernard Hanon, "The Path to Competitiveness: Strategies for Investment in Central Europe," *The Columbia Journal of World Business*, Summer 1996, pp. 76–85.

[15] Daniel Michaels, "Auto Makers Beat a Path to Poland for Production, Sales, and EU Backdoor," *Wall Street Journal*, December 19, 1996, p. A11.

[16] Daniel Dombey, "Well-Built Success," *Industry Week*, May 5, 1997, pp. 32–38; David R. Francis, "Welcome Mat Now Offered Foreign Firms," *Christian Science Monitor*, February 28, 1996, p. 4.

[17] Geri Smith, "The Border (A Special Report)," *Business Week*, May 12, 1997, pp. 64–74.

[18] Naomi Freundlich, "Finding a Cure in DNA?" *Business Week*, March 10, 1997, pp. 90–91.

[19] Richard Florida, "The Globalization of R&D: Results of a Survey of Foreign-Affiliated R&D Laboratories in the USA," *Research Policy*, March 1997, pp. 85–103.

[20] Bill Vlasic, "In Alabama, the Soul of a New Mercedes?" *Business Week*, March 31, 1997, pp. 70–71.

[21] Johnnie L. Roberts, "Farewell Pretoria," *Newsweek*, June 23, 1997, p. 58.

[22] Craig Torres and Diane Solis, "Mexican Election Results Aid Stocks, Peso," *Wall Street Journal*, July 7, 1997, p. A11.

[23] Michael R. Pakko, "Interpreting the U.S. Current Account Deficit," *International Economic Trends*, April 1997, p. 1.

[24] Aid Astbury, "Struggling to Acquire Expertise," *Asian Business*, July 1996, pp. 58–62.

[25] Marcus W. Brauchli, "Indonesia Fights for Foreign Investment," *Wall Street Journal*, September 22, 1994, p. A5; Astbury, "Struggling to Acquire Expertise," pp. 58–62.

[26] Melanie Treviño, *The Decision-Making Process for Technology Transfer Policy in Latin America: Focus on Mexico*. Doctoral dissertation, The George Washington University, 1986.

[27] "Uncommercial Travellers," *The Economist*, February 1, 1997, p. 25.

[28] "Virtually Fantastic," *The Economist*, March 1, 1997, pp. 83–86.

[29] Joan E. Rigdon, "Technology and Health: Silicon Graphics Plans to Unveil Pact with NTT," *Wall Street Journal*, June 8, 1994, p. B6.

[30] David L. Aaron, "After GATT, U.S. Pushes Direct Investment," *Wall Street Journal*, February 2, 1995, p. A18; George Monbiot, "A Charter to Let Loose the Multinationals," *Guardian*, April 15, 1997, pp. 1, 19.

[31] William Greider, *One World, Ready or Not: The Manic Logic Global Capitalism* (New York: Simon & Schuster, 1997), p. 2.

Chapter 8

[1] Judith Warner, John Parry, and Stefan Theil, "A Race Won by the Swift and the Strong," *Newsweek*, Euroland Special Issue, Winter 1998, pp. 42–46; Michael Forbes, "Exponential Exporting," *Business Mexico* 6, no. 12, (1997): 58–62.

[2] Dan McCosh, "Korea Moves Quickly to Grab NAFTA Advantages," *El Financiero International Edition*, May 26–June 1, 1997, p. 15.

[3] Emeric Lepoutre, "Europe's Challenge to the U.S. in South America's Biggest Market," *Christian Science Monitor*, April 8, 1997, p. 19.

[4] Richard Stevenson, "U.S. to Report to Congress NAFTA Benefits Are Modest," *New York Times*, July 11, 1997, pp. C1, C4.

[5] "Farm Policy: Snout Slimmed, Not for Long," *The Economist*, July 8, 1995, p. 46.

[6] James T. Little, "Business Restructuring in Response to the Single Market," in *Europe after Maastricht*, ed. Paul M. Lutzeler (Providence, RI: Berghahn Books, 1994), pp. 53–67.

[7] Russ Banham, "Getting on Tract," *International Business*, March 1997, pp. 14–19.

[8] Timothy Aeppel, "Europe's 'Unity' Undoes a U.S. Exporter," *Wall Street Journal*, April 1, 1996, p. B1.

[9] Murray Weidenbaum, "The U.S./EC Relationship?" in Lutzeler, ed., *Europe after Maastricht*, pp. 27–40.

[10] "EMU Vulnerable but Still on Course," *Euromoney Treasury Manager*, July 11, 1997, pp. 4–5; Elke Thiel, "The European Economic and Monetary Union," in Lutzeler, ed., *Europe after Maastricht*, pp. 125–138.

[11] William Echikson, "Belgians Fall Out of Love with Europe as Resentment of Eurocrats Grows," *Business Week*, International Edition, August 11, 1997.

[12] "Zigzag Path to the Euro," *Euromoney*, July 1997, p. 5.

[13] Holman W. Jenkins, Jr., "Monetary Union? Sure, Just Don't Mention the War," *Wall Street Journal*, June 17, 1997, p. A19.

[14] Sayed Tariq Anwar, "How NAFTA Provisions Will Affect Marketers," *Marketing News*, May 24, 1993, pp. 14, 18.

[15] "Doing Business in NAFTA Country," *Industrial Distribution* (Supplement), May 1995, pp. S10–S12.

[16] "NAFTA's Three-Year Report Card," *Backgrounder*, May 16, 1997.

[17] "Aaron Robertson, "North America: Trade is Brisk Despite Bumps in the Road," *World Trade*, May 1999, pp. 28–32.

[18] Drew Robb, "Keeping Track of U.S. Trade Agreements," *World Trade*, June 1998, pp. 92–96; James Srodes, "Barshefsky on Trade," *World Trade*, August 1998, pp. 38–41.

[19] "Canada's Trade Policy," Canadian Department of Foreign Affairs and International Trade, July 1998. Accessed December 4, 1998. Available World Wide Web: (**www.dfait-maeci.gc.ca/english/trade/ftaa-e.htm**).

[20] William Holstein and Linda Robinson, "Economic NAFTA Thoughts," *U.S. News & World Report*, July 7, 1997, pp. 59–60.

[21] Richard Stevenson, "U.S. to Report to Congress NAFTA Benefits are Modest," *New York Times*, July 11, 1997, pp. C1, C4.

[22] Richard Bruner, "Delphi Gets into Gear Now for the Year 2000," *El Financiero International Edition*, June 30–July 6, 1997, p. 16.

[23] Brian Feagans, "Polluters Beware," *Business Mexico*, November 1996, pp. 44–46.

[24] Roberta Maynard, "At a Crossroads in Latin America," *Nation's Business*, April 1996, pp. 38–43.

[25] Inaugural Remarks by Cesar Gaviria, Secretary General of the Organization of American States, Conference on U.S.-Andean Trade and Investment Relations: The Policy

Issues and Choices, The Brookings Institution, September 3, 1997. Accessed December 4, 1998. Available World Wide Web: ⟨**www.oas.org/en/pinfo/sg/caf%2Diad.htm**⟩.

[26]Drew Robb, "A Hot Market's Hottest Trading Bloc," *World Trade*, June 1998, pp. 34–38.

[27]"Murky Mercosur," *The Economist*, July 26, 1997, pp. 66–67.

[28]Ian Katz, "Is Europe Elbowing the U.S. Out of South America?" *Business Week*, August 4, 1997, p. 56.

[29]Christopher Lion, "Regional Trade Agreements in the Western Hemisphere," *Business America*, December 1994, pp. 19–21.

[30]"Central America Opens for Business," *The Economist*, June 21, 1997, pp. 35–36.

[31]Carrie Meyer, "Public-Nonprofit Partnerships and North-South Finance," *Journal of Environment and Development*, June 1997, pp. 123–146.

[32]Howard LaFranchi, "Summit Shows 'Maturing' of US-Latin America Ties," *Christian Science Monitor*, April 21, 1998. Accessed December 4, 1998. Available World Wide Web: ⟨**www.csmonitor.com/durable/1998/04/21/p7s1.htm**⟩.

[33]James Srodes, "Barshefsky on Trade," *World Trade*, August 1998, pp. 38–41.

[34]Howard LaFranchi, "Summit Shows 'Maturing' of US-Latin America Ties."

[35]"Large Delegation of Canadians Will Participate in Santiago Summit," *Canadian Newswire*, March 1998. Accessed December 4, 1998. Available World Wide Web: ⟨**www.newswire.ca/releases/March1998/11/c2589.html**⟩.

[36]"The Roots of Music Piracy," *World Trade*, December 1998, p. 12.

[37]Douglass Stinson, "Hard Sell," *Latin Trade*, December 1998, p. 88–90.

[38]Juergen E. Schrempp, "Neighbors Across the Pond," *The World in 1999* (London: The Economist Newspaper Limited, 1998), p. 28.

[39]Drew Robb, "Western Europe: The Transatlantic Economic Partnership," *World Trade*, December 1998, pp. 30–33.

[40]"Burma and Laos Admitted to ASEAN," *Wall Street Journal*, July 24, 1997, p. A1.

[41]John S. McClenahen with Tanya Clark, "ASEAN at Work," *Industry Week*, May 19, 1997, pp. 42–48.

[42]Susan Porjes, "Strengthening Diversity," *International Business*, November 1996, pp. 22–23.

[43]"APEC's Family Feud," *The Economist*, November 21, 1998, p. 41.

[44]"The Gulf: Turbulent Waves," *The Economist*, February 24, 1996, pp. 45–50.

[45]Frederic J. Gaynor, "West-Africa—The Newest of the Emerging Markets," *Business America*, January 1997, pp. 12–15; Philip Michelini, "Côte d'Ivoire," *Business America*, January 1997, pp. 16–18.

[46]Jagdish Bhagwati, "Preferential Trade Agreements: The Wrong Road," *Law & Policy in International Business*, Summer 1996, pp. 865–871; Larry Rohter, "Blows from Nafta Batter the Caribbean Economy," *New York Times*, January 30, 1997, p. A1; Peter Passell, "Trade Pacts by Regions: Not the Elixir as Advertised," *New York Times*, February 4, 1997, p. D1.

[47]Paul Meller, "European Ad Rules Pulling Union in Many Directions," *Advertising Age*, October 1996, p. 117.

[48]Statistics from "Snapshot of the Emerging Border Economy," *Business Week*, May 12, 1997, p. 67.

Chapter 9

[1]Dermot Tatlow and Aaron Sheldrick, "Frontier Wheeler-Dealers," *Asia, Inc.*, December 1996–January 1997, pp. 14–16.

[2]Thomas Easton, "A Cosmopolitan Bond Portfolio," *Forbes*, June 16, 1997, pp. 228–230.

[3]James Leung and Helen Johnstone, "Asia's Banks Harness Latest Technology to Outclass Rivals," *Asian Business*, August 1996, pp. 16–23.

[4]Jim Kharouf and Ken Masunaga, "Cannon or BB Gun? How Japan's Big Bang Will Affect Traders," *Futures*, April 1997, pp. 74–78.

[5]See Frank J. Fabozzi, Franco Modigliani, and Michael G. Ferri, *Foundations of Financial Markets and Institutions*, 2nd ed. (Upper Saddle River, NJ: Prentice Hall, 1998), p. 18; J. Kimball Dietrich, *Financial Services and Financial Institutions: Value Creation in Theory and Practice* (Upper Saddle River, NJ: Prentice Hall, 1996), p. 97.

[6]"Another Hectic Year," *Euromoney*, February 1997, pp. 14–20.

[7]Sara Calian, "World Business: Eyes on the Prize," *Wall Street Journal*, September 18, 1997, p. R18; Stanley Reed, "Bigger, Faster, Cheaper: Revolution in the Bourses," *Business Week*, September 29, 1997, p. 134.

[8]See Alan C. Shapiro, *Foundations of Multinational Financial Management*, 3rd ed. (Upper Saddle River, NJ: Prentice Hall, 1998), pp. 424–425.

[9]Charles Platt, "Plotting Away in Margaritaville," *Wired*, July 1997, pp. 140–144, 175–179.

[10]Bank for International Settlements, *International Banking and Financial Market Developments* (Basel, Switzerland: BIS, May 1997), p. 3.

[11]Nicholas Evans, "Are the Good Times Here to Stay?" *Euroweek*, January 1997 (Supplement: Review of the Year, 1996); C. Pavel and D. McElravey, *Globalization in the Financial Services Industry* (Chicago: Federal Reserve Bank of Chicago, 1990), pp. 3–18; ⟨**www.euromoney.com/contents/data/bondware/bw.97/bw.97.4/bw.97.debt.volcur.html**⟩.

[12]"Year of the Borrower," *Euromoney*, February 1997, pp. 33–41.

[13]Nannette Hechler, "Economic Report: Declining Bond Rates," *UBS International Finance* (Zurich, Switzerland: Union Bank of Switzerland, Autumn 1996), pp. 9–12.

[14]Pamela Druckerman, "Bond Traders Hunt for Yields in the Nicaraguan Hinterlands," *Wall Street Journal*, September 16, 1997, p. A14.

[15]Appell, "World Business: Desperate for Debt," p. R20.

[16]Peter Lee, "Equity Boom or Bust?" *Euromoney*, February 1997, pp. 4–8.

[17]Michael Lindeman, "Survey—International Capital Markets," *Financial Times*, May 23, 1997.

[18]This value was obtained August 30, 1998, from ⟨**www.euromoney.com/contents/data/bondware/bw.97/bw.97.4/bw.97.equity.volcur-qtr4.html**⟩.

[19]"Deals of 1996," *Euromoney*, February 1997, pp. 23–26.

[20]Lee, "Equity Boom or Bust?" pp. 4–8.

[21]Paula Dwyer, Andrew Osterland, Kerry Capell, and Sharon Reier, "The 21st Century Stock Market," *Business Week*, August 10, 1998, pp. 66–72.

[22]Bank for International Settlements, *63rd Annual Report* (Basel, Switzerland: BIS, June 1993), p. 99.

[23]Signet Banking Corp., "Welcome to Signet Bank Online: Foreign Exchange." Accessed July 22, 1997. Available World Wide Web: ⟨**www.signet.com/fx**⟩.

[24]"Assessing the Damage," *Euromoney* Web site. Available World Wide Web: ⟨**www.euromey.com**⟩. Accessed August 30, 1998.

[25]Bank for International Settlements, *Central Bank Survey of Foreign Exchange and Derivatives Market Activity*, April 1995 (Basel, Switzerland: BIS, May 1996), p. 5.

[26]Bank for International Settlements, *Central Bank Survey*, Table F2, p. 6.

[27]"Business This Week," *The Economist*, June 7, 1997.

[28]Bank for International Settlements, *Real-Time Gross Settlement Systems* (Basel, Switzerland: BIS, March 1997), No. 22.

[29]Bank for International Settlements, *Central Bank Survey*, p. 15.

[30]Bank for International Settlements, *Central Bank Survey*, p. 7 and Table F3, p. 8.

[31]Information obtained from London International Financial Futures Exchange, "LIFFE net." Accessed June 22, 1997. Available World Wide Web: ⟨**http://www.liffe.com**⟩.

[32]Information obtained from "Philadelphia Stock Exchange." Accessed June 22, 1997. Available World Wide Web: ⟨**http://www.phlx.com**⟩.

[33]David E. Sanger, "The Global Search for an Economic Parachute," *New York Times*, September 2, 1998, pp. A1, A11.

[34]"Cuba Barters Its Sugar," *Financial Times*, April 23, 1994, p. 22.

[35]"Saudis Agree to Trade Oil for Aircraft and Missiles," *Aviation Week and Space Technology*, September 20, 1985, p. 19.

[36]Marcus Brauchli, "World Business: Free to Choose," *Wall Street Journal*, September 18, 1997, p. R12.

[37]Mark P. Hampton, *The Offshore Interface* (London: Macmillan Press Ltd., 1996), pp. 1–36.

[38]Stephen L. Harris and Charles A. Pigott, "A Changed Landscape for Financial Services," *The OECD Observer*, June–July 1997, pp. 28–31.

Chapter 10

[1]Sheryl Nance-Nash, "Many Big Businesses Are Suffering from the Downturn Abroad." Accessed December 16, 1997. Available World Wide Web: ⟨**www.pathfinder.com/money/yourco/weekly.html**⟩; Bruce Einhorn, "The Currency Crisis Is Sweeping Southeast Asia," *Business Week*, July 28, 1997, pp. 66–70; Ronald Henkoff, "Asia: Why Business Is Still Bullish," *Fortune*, October 27, 1997, pp. 139–140; John Ridding, "Caught in the Asian Smog," *Financial Times*, October 25–26, 1997, p. 8.

[2]"Exporters in Germany: The Subtle Curse of a Cheap Mark," *The Economist*, August 16, 1997, pp. 50–51.

[3]Keith Naughton, "Who's Afraid of the Dollar?" *Business Week*, February 24, 1997, pp. 34–36.

[4]Naughton, "Who's Afraid of the Dollar?" pp. 34–36: Ed Brown, "Do You Really Need to Worry about the Dollar?" *Fortune*, May 26, 1997, pp. 22–23.

[5]Albert C. Bersticker, "A Guide to Global Competitiveness," *Vital Speeches of the Day*, June 15, 1997, pp. 519–523.

[6]Joshua Levine and Graham Button, " 'A' Is for Arbitrage," *Forbes*, July 15, 1996, pp. 116–121.

[7]"Big MacCurrencies," *The Economist*, April 12, 1997, p. 71; "Big MacCurrencies," *The Economist*, April 11, 1998, p. 58.

[8]The numbers used in this section are available online. Accessed December 3, 1997. Available World Wide Web: ⟨**www.asiaspirit.com/a-th.htm**⟩ *and* ⟨**www.xe.net/cgi-bin/ucc/convert**⟩.

[9]Jose Antonio Hernandez, "Cursing the 501 Blues," *Business Mexico* 6/7, no. 12 (1997): 22–24.

[10]Roland N. Stromberg, *Europe in the Twentieth Century* (Upper Saddle River, NJ: Prentice Hall, 1997), p. 151.

[11]"What Does the World Bank Do?" Accessed October 7, 1998. Available World Wide Web: ⟨**www.worldbank.org/html/extdr/whatdoes.htm**⟩.

[12]Stanley Fischer, "The Asian Crisis and the Changing Role of the IMF," *Finance & Development*, June 1998, pp. 2–5.

[13]The material contained in the following descriptions of these three arrangements is contained in *International Financial Statistics* 51, no. 10, 1998 (Washington, DC: International Monetary Fund, 1998); *Exchange Arrangements and Exchange Restrictions, Annual Report 1998* (Washington, DC: International Monetary Fund, 1998).

[14]Eugene Robinson, "Brazil's Malaise Extends beyond Economic Crisis," *Washington Post*, January 23, 1989, p. A11; Alma Guillermoprieto, *Samba* (New York: Knopf, 1990), p. 87.

[15]"About the BIS." Accessed October 7, 1998. Available World Wide Web: ⟨**www.bis.org/about/index.htm**⟩.

[16]Lawrence H. Summers, "The Mexican Financial Crisis, One Year After: Two Contrasting Opinions," *EDI Forum* 1, no. 1 (Fall 1996): 9, 15; Marco Espanosa and Steven Russell, "The Mexican Economic Crisis: Alternative Views," *Economic Review*, Federal Reserve Bank of Atlanta, January–February 1996, pp. 21–43.

[17]Ricardo Hausmann, "The Mexican Financial Crisis, One Year After: Two Contrasting Opinions," *EDI Forum* 1, no. 1 (Fall 1996): 8, 14.

[18]"The Asian Crisis: Causes and Cures," *Finance & Development*, June 1998, pp. 18–21; "The Perils of Global Capital," *The Economist*, April 11, 1998, pp. 52–54.

[19]"Strengthening the Architecture of the International Monetary System." Accessed October 7, 1998. Available World Wide Web: ⟨**www.imf.org/external/np/exr/facts/arch.htm**⟩.

[20]Pete Engardio, "Crisis of Faith for the Free Market," *Business Week*, Octrober 19, 1998, pp. 38–39.

[21]Steve Barth, "The New Asia?" *World Trade*, November, 1998, pp. 38–42.

[22]Mel Mandel, "Trade Winds, Asia Pacific: Opportunities in Malaysia," *World Trade*, November 1998, p. 28.

[23]For one particularly insightful and articulate account of what a one-currency global financial system would look like, see Richard N. Cooper, "A Monetary System for the Future," *Foreign Affairs* 63, no. 1 (1984): 166–184.

[24]Faith Keenan and Henry Sender, "Little Help in Sight," *Far Eastern Economic Review*, October 15, 1998. Accessed October 13, 1998. Available World Wide Web: ⟨**www.feer.com**⟩; "One World, One Money," *The Economist*, September 26, 1998, p. 80.

[25]Christopher J. Neely, "The Lira: Back in the Zone," *The Federal Reserve Bank of St. Louis*, February 1997, p. 1.

[26]"An Awfully Big Adventure," EMU Survey, *The Economist*, April 11, 1998, p. 5.

[28]"EMU and the Single Currency," Information Programme for the European Citizen. Accessed October 7, 1998. Available World Wide Web: ⟨**europa.eu.int/euro/html/page-dossier5.html**⟩.

[29]Michael Switow, "Malaysia's Mahathir vs. 'Immoral' Markets," *Christian Science Monitor*, September 24, 1997, p. 8; David Wessel and Darren McDermott, "Soros & Malaysia's Mahathir Cross Swords," *Wall Street Journal*, September 22, 1997, p. A16.

[30]"The Risk of a Rescue Too Far," *The Economist*, October 25, 1997, pp.80–81; Mark Clifford and Leah Nathans Spiro, "Let the Markets Do the Rescuing," *Business Week*, October 6, 1997, p. 152.

Chapter 11

[1]"Starbucks Brings Coffee Culture to China," *CNN Interactive*, January 11, 1999. Accessed January 13, 1999. Available World Wide Web: ⟨**www.cnn.com/FOOD/news/9901/11/china.starbucks.reut**⟩; "Starbucks Sets Sights on Converting China to Coffee," *CNN Interactive*, January 11, 1999. Accessed January 13, 1999. Available World Wide Web: ⟨**www.cnn.com/WORLD/asiapcf/9901/11/PM-China-Starbucks.ap/index.html**⟩; Trish Saywell, "Research and Rescue: China's State Firms Tap Western Specialists for Help," *Far Eastern Economic Review*, Marketing section, August 13, 1998. Accessed January 13, 1999. Available World Wide Web: ⟨**www.feer.com**⟩.

[2]Wendy Zellner, Louisa Shepard, Ian Katz, and David Lindorff, "Wal-Mart Spoken Here," *Business Week*, June 23, 1997. Accessed: March 7, 1999. Available World Wide Web: ⟨**www.bwarchive.businessweek.com**⟩.

[3]Tim Jackson, *Virgin King: Inside Richard Branson's Business Empire* (Rocklin, CA: Putnam, 1996), p. 316.

[4]Jack Lyne, "Nokia Wirelessly Takes On the World," *Site Selection*, December 1997–January 1998, pp. 1124–1128.

[5]Robert S. Greenberger, "Africa Ascendant: New Leaders Replace Yesteryears' 'Big Men,' and Tanzania Benefits," *Wall Street Journal*, December 10, 1996, pp. A1, A6.

[6]Laurie Joan Aron, "Global Logistics Boosts Competitive Advantage," *Site Selection*, August 1997. Accessed January 16, 1999. Available World Wide Web: ⟨**www.conway.com/sshighlites/0897/695.htm**⟩.

[7]Johny K. Johansson, Ilkka A. Ronkainen, and Michael R. Czinkota, "Negative Country-of-Origin Effects: The Case of The New Russia,"

Journal of International Business Studies 25, no. 1 (1994): 157–176.

8 Samantha Marshall, "Soap Smugglers Cleaning Up in Vietnam," *Wall Street Journal*, April 1, 1998, pp. B1, B15.

9 This discussion is based on S. Tamer Cavusgil, "Measuring the Potential of Emerging Markets: An Indexing Approach," *Business Horizons*, January–February 1997, pp. 87–91; "Market Potential Indicators for Emerging Markets," Michigan State University CIBER. Accessed March 27, 1998. Available World Wide Web: ⟨ciber.bus.msu.edu/publicat/mktptind.htm⟩.

10 Chris Sarlo, "The Problems with LICO," The Fraser Institute. Accessed January 14, 1999. Available World Wide Web: ⟨www.fraserinstitute.ca/forum/1998/june/welfare.html⟩.

11 World Development Report 1997: The State in a Changing World (New York: World Bank, 1997), Table 1, pp. 214–215.

12 This information is taken from the ProChile World Wide Web site at: ⟨www.chileinfo.com⟩.

13 Tim Venable, "Searching the World for Facility Investments: U.S. States' Global Development Offices," *Site Selection*, December 1997–January 1998, p. 1122.

14 Jennifer Cody, "They Hired Someone to Find Out if People Really Like Chocolate?" *Wall Street Journal*, November 26, 1993, p. B1.

15 Reva Basch, "Business Site Location: Think Global, Search Local," *Online User*, January–February 1997, pp. 48–49.

16 Perry A. Trunick, "Trade Shows: Where Culture Meets Commerce," *Transportation & Distribution*, December 1996, pp. 66–67.

17 Richard A. Brealey and Stewart C. Myers, *Principles of Corporate Finance*, 3rd ed. (New York: McGraw-Hill, 1988), pp. 13–23.

18 John Stopford, Susan Strange, and John S. Henley, *Rival States, Rival Firms* (Cambridge, UK: Cambridge University Press, 1991), p. 150.

19 David P. Hamilton, "China, with Foreign Partners' Help, Becomes a Budding Technology Giant," *Wall Street Journal*, December 7, 1995, p. A10.

20 William Greider, "One World, Ready or Not," *Rolling Stone*, February 6, 1997, pp. 37–41; Greider, "Who Governs Globalism?" *The American Prospect*, January 1997, pp. 73–80.

Chapter 12

1 Steve Barth, "World Trade's Executive of the Decade," *World Trade*, December 1998, pp. 42–45.

2 *Bausch & Lomb 1996 Annual Report*, Rochester, NY, p. 2.

3 *Cadbury Schweppes 1996 Annual Report*, London, England, p. 1.

4 Gary Hamel and C. K. Prahalad, *Competing for the Future* (Boston, MA: Harvard Business School Press, 1994).

5 Helen Deresky, *International Management: Managing across Borders and Cultures* (New York: HarperCollins, 1997), p. 156.

6 Michael E. Porter, *On Competition* (Boston, MA: Harvard Business School Press, 1998).

7 See Gene Bylinsky, "Five Heroes of U.S. Manufacturing," *Fortune*, May 26, 1997, pp. 104B–104C.

8 Richard Halloran, "Parallel Lives," *World Business*, November–December 1996, p. 25.

9 Sherrie E. Zhan, "Marketing Across Cultures: To Minimize *Faux Pas*, Don't Assume Anything," *World Trade*, February 1999, pp. 80–81.

10 Michael A. Cusumano, "How Microsoft Makes Large Teams Work Like Small Teams," *Sloan Management Review*, Fall 1997, pp. 9–20; Randall E. Stross, "Mr. Gates Builds His Brain Trust," *Fortune*, December 8, 1997, pp. 84–88+.

11 *Intel 1996 Annual Report*, Santa Clara, CA, inside cover; Alicia Hills Moore, "Killer Chip," *Fortune*, November 10, 1977, pp. 70–72+.

12 *Cadbury Schweppes 1996 Annual Report*, pp. 11, 19.

13 The discussion of these strategies is based on Michael E. Porter, *Competitive Strategy* (New York, NY: Free Press, 1980), pp. 34–46.

14 Dave Barry, "Poopacino Pick-Me-Up Not So Swell Afterall," *Wisconsin State Journal*, November 9, 1997, p. 3G.

15 Chris Adams, "Hot Metal: Steelmakers Scramble in a Race to Become Global Powerhouses," *Wall Street Journal*, August 26, 1997, p. A10.

16 Robert B. Reich, *The Work of Nations* (New York: Vintage Books, 1992), p. 112.

17 Theodore Levitt, "The Globalization of Markets," *Harvard Business Review*, May–June 1983, pp. 92–102.

18 Susan Douglas and Yoram Wind, "The Myth of Globalization," *Columbia Journal of World Business*, Winter 1987, pp. 19–29.

20 Vern Terpstra, *International Dimensions of Marketing*, 3rd ed. (Belmont, CA: Wadsworth, 1993), p. 9.

21 Raju Narisetti, "Can Rubbermaid Crack Foreign Markets?" *Wall Street Journal*, June 20, 1996, p. B1.

22 Antony Thorncroft, "Do You Drink Lots?" *Financial Times* (How to Spend It Magazine Issue), October 18, 1997, pp. 24–32; Janis Robinson, "The Genie Is Uncorked," *Financial Times* (Weekend), September 27–28, 1997, p. 1.

23 Bradley L. Kirkman and Debra L. Shapiro, "The Impact of Cultural Values on Employee Resistance to Teams: Toward a Model of Globalized Self-Managing Work Team Effectiveness," *Academy of Management Review*, 22, no. 3 (1997): 730–757.

24 Kirkman and Shapiro, "The Impact of Cultural Values on Employee Resistance to Teams," pp. 730–757.

25 Helen Axel, "Company Experiences with Global Teams," *HR Executive Review*, 4, no. 2 (1966): 3–18.

26 John McBeth and Salil Tripathi, "Ethics at Work," *Far Eastern Economic Review*, October 29, 1998, pp. 72–74.

27 Dinah Payne, Cecily Raiborn, and Jorn Askvik, "A Global Code of Business Ethics," *Journal of Business Ethics* Vol. 16 (December 1997): 1727–1735.

Chapter 13

1 Roberta Maynard, "Trade Links via the Internet," *Nation's Business*, December 1997, pp. 51–53.

2 Franklin R. Root, *Entry Strategies for International Markets* (Lexington, MA: Lexington Books, 1987), p. 5.

3 Arthur Jones, "The 10 Steps of Global Trade," *World Trade*, Supplement, 1997.

4 Martyn Williams, "Fujitsu Wins Texas Instruments Japan Lawsuit," *Newsbytes News Network*, September 10, 1997.

5 "Philippines: Nippon Pigment Provides Compounding Technology," *Japan Chemical Week*, September 11, 1997.

6 Julie Bennett, "Europe Finally Right for U.S. Franchises," *Franchise Times*, 3, no. 9 p. 13.

7 David Ing, "Spain Proves Tough to Crack," *Hotel & Motel Management*, 212, no. 15 p. 8.

8 Laura Gatland, "Eastern Europe Eagerly Accepts U.S. Franchisors," *Franchise Times*, 3, no. 9 p. 17.

9 Frank H. Andorka, Jr., "Microtel Introduces New-Construction Plan," *Hotel & Motel Management*, 212, no. 13 p. 1.

10 Ian Jones, "She's Leaving Home . . . Bye-Bye," *World Trade*, May 1997, pp. 90–92.

11 "BAA Takes Majority Stake in Naples," *Airports International*, March 1997, p. 3.

12 Owen Hughes, "Road Show Ahead for Asian DTH Platform," *Multichannel News*, March 10, 1997, p. 107.

13 "ABB Snatches Grid Management Contract from National Grid," *Modern Power Systems*, June 1997, p. 7.

14 "Power Plant Management Contract," *Power in Europe*, June 6, 1997, p. 30.

15 "$316m LNG Refining Deal," *Power in Asia*, April 7, 1997, p. 21.

16 "Projects," *Power in Europe*, August 29, 1997, p. 25–26.

17 "Telecom Roundup—Ericsson Inks Turkish Contract," *Newsbytes News Network*, July 28, 1997.

18 This classification is made in Peter Buckley and Mark Casson, *A Theory of Cooperation in International Business*, in Farok J. Contractor and Peter Lorange (eds.), *Cooperative Strate-*

gies in International Business (Lexington, MA: Lexington Books, 1988) pp. 31–53.

[19]Kathryn R. Harrigan, "Joint Ventures and Competitive Strategy," *Strategic Management Journal*, 9 (1988), pp. 141–58.

[20]See for example Sanjeev Agarwal, "Socio-Cultural Distance and the Choice of Joint Ventures: A Contingency Perspective," *Journal of International Marketing*, 2, no. 2, 1994, pp. 63–80.

[21]Stephen B. Tallman and Oded Shenkar, "A Managerial Decision Model of International Cooperative Venture Formation," *Journal of International Business Studies*, 25, no. 1, 1994, pp. 91–113.

[22]Brian Bremner et al., "Cozying Up to Keiretsu," *Business Week-International Edition*, July 22, 1996. Accessed January 2, 1998. Available World Wide Web: 〈**www.bwarchive. businessweek.com**〉.

[23]Bremner et al., "Cozying Up To Keiretsu," *Business Week-International Edition*, July 22, 1996, Online. Internet.

[24]Mike Tanner, "AT&T and Microsoft Tune into Music on the Net," *Wired News*, November 4, 1997. Accessed January 2, 1998. Available World Wide Web: 〈**www.wired. com/news/news/culture/story/8245.html**〉.

[25]Brenton R. Schlender, "How Toshiba Makes Alliances Work," *Fortune*, October 4, 1993, pp. 116–118.

[26]Geert Hofstede, *Cultures and Organizations: Software of the Mind* (New York: McGraw-Hill, 1997), p. 228.

[27]This section is based in part on Franklin R. Root, *Entry Strategies for International Markets* (Lexington, MA: Lexington Books, 1987), pp. 8–21.

[28]See for example Sanjit Sengupta and Monica Perry, "Some Antecedents of Global Strategic Alliances," *Journal of International Marketing*, 5, no. 1, 1997, pp. 31–50.

[29]Sheila M. Puffer and Daniel J. McCarthy, "Finding the Common Ground in Russian and American Business Ethics," *California Management Review*, Winter 1995, pp. 29–46.

Chapter 14

[1]David Leonhardt, "Sara Lee: Playing with the Recipe," *Business Week*, April 27, 1998, pp. 114+; Nikki Tait, "The Focus Narrows," *Financial Times*, September 19, 1997, p. 13; Roger Lowenstein, "Remember When Companies Made Things?" *Wall Street Journal*, September 18, 1997, p. C1.

[2]Dave Ulrich, "A New Mandate for Human Resources," *Harvard Business Review*, January–February 1998, pp. 124–134.

[3]Barry Newman, "Expat Archipelago: The New Yank Abroad Is the 'Can-Do' Player in the

Global Village," *Wall Street Journal*, December 12, 1995, p. A12.

[4]Carl Quintanilla, "Huffy to Close Its Largest U.S. Factory, Idle 950, to Combat Asian Production," *Wall Street Journal*, May 29, 1998, p. A4.

[5]Valeria Frazee, "An Unhappy Spouse Is the #1 Deal Breaker," *Global Workforce*, July 1998, p. 8.

[6]Stephen Dolainski, "Are Expats Getting Lost in the Translation?" *Workforce*, February 1997, pp. 32–39.

[7]Valeria Frazee, "Special Preparation When Relocating with Children," *Global Workforce*, January 1997, p. 10.

[8]"The Year of the Bond," *Euromoney*, April 1997, pp. 90–92.

[9]Michael R. Sesit, "World Business: A Common Bond," *Wall Street Journal*, September 18, 1997, p. R16.

[10]Garry Evans, "Growing Appetite," *Euromoney*, February 1997, pp. 71–73.

[11]Bank for International Settlements, *International Banking and Financial Market Developments* (Basel, Switzerland: BIS, May 1997), Statistical Annex, Table 11B, p. 41.

[12]Michelle Celarier, "It's the Roadshow, Stupid!" *Euromoney*, June 1997, pp. 60–62.

[13]Celarier, "It's the Roadshow, Stupid!" pp. 60–62.

[14]Jonathan Karp, "U.S. Markets Battle to List Foreign Firms," *Wall Street Journal*, July 8, 1997, p. C1.

[15]Robert J. Sherwood, "The World of ADRs," *Forbes*, July 28, 1997, pp. 230–232.

[16]Kenneth M. Morris, Alan M. Siegel, and Beverly Larson, *Guide to Understanding Money and Investing in Asia* (New York: Lightbulb Press, 1998), p. 37.

[17]Sherwood, "The World of ADRs," p. 231.

[18]Sandy Serwer, "It's Big. It's German. It's . . . SAP," *Fortune*, September 7, 1998, p. 191.

[19]Cherie Marriott, "Why Depositary Receipts Perform Differently for Asians," *Global Finance*, May 1997, pp. 11–12.

[20]Jenny C. McCune, "Get Global Cash," *Success*, December 1995, p. 16.

[21]International Finance Corporation, *Emerging Stock Markets Factbook 1998* (Washington, DC: IFC, April 1998), pp. 16–18.

[22]Karen Damato, "Emerging-Market Investors Get Warning," *Wall Street Journal*, July 24, 1997, p. C1.

[23]Vikas Nath, "Equity Markets: Emerging Equities Investment Myths," *UBS International Finance* (Zurich, Switzerland: Union Bank of Switzerland, Winter–Spring 1997), pp. 13–16.

[24]Conor De Lion, "Turned Off by the Czechs," *Global Finance*, February 1997, pp. 56–58.

[25]Charles J.P. Chen et al. "An Investigation of the Relationship between International Ac-

tivities and Capital Structure," *Journal of International Business Studies* 28, no. 3 (1997): 563–577; Todd A. Burgman, "An Empirical Examination of Multinational Corporate Capital Structure," *Journal of International Business Studies* 27, no. 3 (1996): 553–570.

[26]Williams S. Sekely and J. Markham Collins, "Cultural Influences on International Capital Structure," *Journal of International Business Studies* 19, no. 1 (1988): 87–100.

[27]Doron P. Levin, "Compaq Storms the PC Heights from Its Factory Floor," *New York Times*, November 13, 1994, Sec. 3, p. 5.

[28]Saul Hansell, "Is This the Factory of the Future?" *New York Times*, July 26, 1998, Sec. 3, pp. 1, 12. See also Scott Thurm, "Solectron Becomes a Force in 'Stealth Manufacturing,'" *Wall Street Journal*, August 18, 1998, p. B4.

[29]Leslie P. Willcocks, "Reducing the Risks of Outsourced IT," *Financial Times*, Mastering Global Business Series—Week Four, 1997, pp. 10–12.

Chapter 15

[1]Joanna Slater, "Cosmetic Surgery," *Far Eastern Economic Review*, October 22, 1998, pp. 64–65.

[2]Charles Bremner, "All Because the Belgians Do Not Like Milk Tray," *London Times*, October 24, 1997, p. 5.

[3]Bill Spindle, "Are Sushi Sundaes Next? Tokyo Screams for Green-Tea Ice Cream," *Wall Street Journal*, August 27, 1997, p. B1.

[4]David Leonhardt, "It Was a Hit in Buenos Aires—So Why Not Boise?" *Business Week*, September 7, 1998, pp. 56, 58.

[5]David Aaker, *Building Strong Brands* (New York: Free Press, 1996).

[6]This information was obtained from the World Wide Web site of Namelab, Inc. at: 〈**www.namelab.com**〉. Accessed January 29, 1999.

[7]This one-quarter-page apology appeared in *The Independent* (London), November 8, 1997.

[8]Robin Young, "Cadbury Loses Swiss Chocolate Bar Wars," *Time*, October 30, 1997, p. 11.

[9]Johny K. Johansson, Ilkka A. Ronkainen, and Michael R. Czinkota, "Negative Country-of-Origin Effects: The Case of the New Russia," *Journal of International Business Studies* 25, no. 1 (1994): 157–176.

[10]Julian Baum, "Riding High: A Taiwanese Bicycle Maker Races to Success in the West," *Far Eastern Economic Review*, May 7, 1998. Accessed June 9, 1998. Available World Wide Web: 〈**www.feer.com**〉.

[11]Dan Atkinson, "Fakes the Real Thing on Hooky Street," *The Guardian* (London), Jobs and Money Supplement, October 25, 1997, p. 2.

[12]Harry Maurer and Justin Keay, "'We Have

Nowhere to Go but Up' . . . but CD Pirates Are Raking It In," *Business Week*, International Edition, April 28, 1997. Accessed February 1, 1999. Available World Wide Web: ⟨**www.bwarchive.businessweek.com**⟩.

[13]William Echikson, "Finnish Cash Helps a Baltic Tiger . . . and Buys Some Useful Lessons, Too," *Business Week*, International Edition, March 23, 1998. Accessed February 1, 1999. Available World Wide Web: ⟨**www.bwarchive.businessweek.com**⟩.

[14]Mike France and Sana Siwolop, "How to Skin a Copycat," *Business Week*, October 21, 1996. Accessed February 1, 1999. Available World Wide Web: ⟨**www.bwarchive.businessweek.com**⟩.

[15]Pamela Yatsko, "Coke on Ice," *Far Eastern Economic Review*, February 27, 1997, p. 54.

[16]See for example, Robert Hite and Cynthia Fraser, "International Advertising Strategies of Multinational Corporations," in Michael Czinkota and Ilkka Ronkainen, eds., *Readings in Global Marketing* (Fort Worth, TX: Dryden Press, 1995), pp. 206–218.

[17]Ursula Gruber, "The Role of Multilingual Copy Adaptation in International Advertising," in Stanley Paliwoda and John Ryans, eds., *International Marketing Reader* (London: Routledge, 1995), pp. 202–213.

[18]Alan Henry and Ewen MacAskill, "Analysis: Tobacco Sponsorship," *The Guardian* (London), November 6, 1997, p. 21.

[19]John Helemann, "All Europeans Are Not Alike," *The New Yorker*, April 28–May 5, 1997, pp. 174–181.

[20]This section draws upon Warren J. Keegan, *Global Marketing Management*, 5th ed. (Upper Saddle River, NJ: Prentice Hall, 1995), pp. 489–494.

[21]John Burnett and Sandra Moriarty, *Introduction to Marketing Communication: An Integrated Approach* (Upper Saddle River, NJ: Prentice Hall, 1998), p. 3.

[22]Michael Horsham, "Is High Tech Making Way for an Earthy Orientalism in Japan? Or Is It Just a Case of Smart Marketing?" *The Guardian* (London), October 21, 1994, pp. 4–5.

[23]This comparison is made in Tatsuo Ohbora, Andrew Parsons, and Hajo Riesenbeck, "Alternative Routes to Global Marketing," *McKinsey Quarterly* no. 3 (1992): 52–74.

[24]Kimberly A. Strassel, "Low-Tech, Windup Radio Makes Waves," *Wall Street Journal*, July 15, 1997, p. B1.

[25]Craig S. Smith, "In China, Some Distributors Have Really Cleaned Up with Amway," *Wall Street Journal*, August 4, 1997, p. B1.

[26]"Laptops from Lapland," *The Economist*, September 6, 1997, pp. 67–68.

[27]"Unhappy German Peace," The Economist, February 20, 1999, p. 62.

[28]William Greider, *One World, Ready or Not: The Manic Logic of Global Capitalism* (New York: Simon & Schuster, 1997).

[29]Richard Tomlinson, "Why So Many Western Companies Are Coming Down with China Fatigue," *Fortune*, May 25, 1998, pp. 60–64.

[30]Louis Uchitelle, "More Downsized Workers Are Returning as Rentals," *New York Times*, December 8, 1996, pp. 1, 22.

[31]Seuin L. Hwang, "Sucked In: How Philip Morris Got Turkey Hooked on American Tobacco," *Wall Street Journal*, September 11, 1998, pp. A1, A8.

SOURCE NOTES

Chapter 1

Map 1.1 Data obtained from *World Development Indicators 1998* (Washington, D.C.: World Bank, March 1998), Tables 4.4, 4.5, 4.6, and 4.7, pp. 188–203. **World Business Survey: *The International Top Fifteen*** "The United Kingdom Remains the Top Location," *Global Workforce*, May 1998, p. 6. **Figure 1.1** Forrester Research. **The Global Manager: *The Keys to Success*** Adapted from John Davies, "That Elusive Success," *International Business*, October 1996, p. 35. **Entrepreneurial Focus: *Untapped Potential: Four Myths That Keep Small Businesses from Export Success*** "Is Business Really Going International?" *Inc.*, The State of Small Business, 1997, p. 121; **Table 1.1** "The Fortune Global 500," *Fortune*, August 3, 1998, pp. 130–34 & F1–F14; *World Development Indicators 1998* (Washington, D.C.: World Bank, March 1998), Table 4.2, pp. 180–82. **Table 1.2** "The Fortune Global 500," *Fortune*, August 3, 1998, pp. 130–34 & F1–F14. **Table 1.3** "The Fortune Global 500, *Fortune*, August 3, 1998, pp. 130–34 & F1–F14. Kelly Adams-Smith, "Export 'Myths': The Four Myths That Are Most Likely to Hold Your Company Back from Export Success," *Business America*, May 1996, pp. 16–17. **In Practice** "BMW, VW Expand in Russia," *World Trade*, January 1999, p. 28. **Business Case 1: *Coffee, Anyone?*** Anne Stevenson-Yang, "All the Coffee in China," *The China Business Review*, November–December 1996, pp. 47–49. **Business Case 2: *MTV: Going Global with a Local Beat*** "Pan-European Idea Is Dead, Says Three-Way MTV," *New Media Markets*, April 4, 1996, pp. 6–7; Horst Stipp, "MTV German-Style," *American Demographics*, May 1996, p. 49; Peter Hund, "High Tech Helps MTV Evolve," *World Trade*, June 1996, p. 10; "MTV Europe Is Rocking to a Local Beat," *New York Times*, February 6, 1994, Sec. 3, p. 6; Gail Russell Chaddock, "Europe: Clones of MTV Compete for Viewers," *Christian Science Monitor*, March 22, 1995, p. 8; Bernard Wysocki, Jr., "The Global Mall: in Developing Nations," *Wall Street Journal*, June 26, 1997, p. A1.

Chapter 2

Entrepreneurial Focus: *Entrepreneurs Respect Culture* Greg Steinmetz, "Hi, You're Hired: Workers of the World Who Need a Job Fast Might Look in Prague," *Wall Street Journal*, December 2, 1996, p. A1; William McGurn, "How to Lose Your Shirt: Competition Pushes Garment Maker into Wine Trade," *Far Eastern Economic Review*, November 21, 1996, p. 76; and Trish Saywell, "Frozen Assets: TCBY Takes a Scoop Out of the China Market," *Far Eastern Economic Review*, November 14, 1996, p. 68. **World Business Survey: *Listen Up, Employers*** Adapted from Bodil Jones "What European Recruits Want," *Management Review*, January 1998, p. 6. Poll conducted by Universum AB. **Figure 2.1** © The National Foundation for Women Business Owners. **Map 2.1** Mapping © Bartholomew, 1990. Extract taken from Plate 5 of *The Comprehensive Atlas of the World*, 8th ed. Reprinted with permission. **Figure 2.3** Louis E. Boone, David L. Kurtz, and Judy R. Block, *Contemporary Business Communication*, 2 ed. (Upper Saddle River, NJ: Prentice Hall, 1997), p. 71. **Table 2.1** *World Development Report 1997: The State in a Changing World* (New York: World Bank, 1997), Table 1, pp. 214–215. **Cartoon 2.1** Bizzaro, Wisconsin State Journal, November 6, 1996. **Figure 2.4** Geert Hofstede, "The Cultural Relativity of Organizational Practices and Theories," *Journal of International Business Studies*, Fall 1983, pp. 82, 84. **Map 2.2** Simcha Ronen and Oded Shenkar, "Clustering Countries on Attitudinal Dimensions: A Review and Synthesis," *Academy of Management Review* 10, 3 (1985): 449. **Business Case 2: *Asian Values under Fire*** Steve Barth, "The New Asia?" *World Trade*, November 1998, pp. 38–42; Bruce Einhorn and Ron Corben, "Asia's Social Backlash," *Business Week*, August 17, 1998, pp. 46–51; "What Would Confucius Say Now?" *The Economist*, July 25, 1998, pp. 23–28; Simon Elegant and Margot Cohen, "Rock Solid," *Far Eastern Economic Review*, December 5, 1996, pp. 50–52; Michael Vatikiotis, "Children of Plenty: Parents Spoil Their Kids—To Show Off New-Found Wealth," *Far Eastern Economic Review,* December 5, 1996, pp. 54–55. **In Practice** "Nike Building Playground at Virginia Mosque," *Antigo Daily Journal,* November 23, 1998, p. 5.

Chapter 3

Map 3.1 Data obtained from *Freedom in the World 1997–1998* (New York: Freedom House, 1998), pp. 605–606. **World Business Survey: To What Extent Western-Style Democratic Freedoms Foster Economic Stability** *Far Eastern Economic Review,* February 19, 1998, p. 38. **Map 3.3** Data obtained form *International Country Risk Guide* (East Syracuse, NY: PRS Group, 1998), October 1998, V. 19, N. 1, Table 2B, pp. 167–69. **The Global Manager:** *Your Global Security Checklist* Kate Murphy, "Security Risk," *Working Woman,* March 1997, pp. 47–48; John R. Engen, "Corporate Terrorism and How to Avoid It," *Training,* October 1995, pp. 84–88; and Charlene Marmer Solomon, "Global Business under Siege," *Global Workforce,* pp. 18–23. **Table 3.1** Information adapted from "1998 Corruption Perceptions Index," Transparency International. Accessed February 9, 1999. Available World Wide Web: www.transparency.de.documents/cpi/index. **Table 3.2** *USTR 1998 'Special 301' Decisions,* International Intellectual Property Alliance, September 3, 1998; *1997 Global Software Piracy Report,* Business Software Alliance. Accessed October 24, 1998. Available World Wide Web: ⟨**www.bsa.org/statistics/97ipr.pd**⟩ **Table 3.2** *USTR 1998 'Special 301' Decisions,* International Intellectual Property Alliance, September 3, 1998. **Table 3.4** *USTR 1998 'Special 301' Decisions,* International Intellectual Property Alliance, September 3, 1998. **Table 3.2** Business Software Alliance. **Table 3.3** International Federation of the Phonographic Industry. **Table 3.4** Motion Picture Association of America. **Figure 3.1** "Total Tax Revenues," *Economist,* September 5, 1998, p. 101. © 1998. The Economist Newspaper Group, Inc. Reprinted with permission. Further reproduction prohibited. **Table 3.5** "Effect of Value-Added Taxes," *Economist,* May 13, 1997, p. 23. **Figure 3.2** "The United Nations System," courtesy of the United Nations. **In Practice** "India Clears Insurance Reforms," *Wall Street Journal,* November 24, 1998, p. A14. **Busines Case 3:** *Intellectual Property Rights in Asia* "Now These Copycats Have to Discover New Drugs," *The Economist* (Science & Technology), March 24, 1997; "Second Thoughts on Going Global," *The Economist* (International Business), March 13, 1995; "Chart: Annual Trade Losses to U.S. Firms Due to Copyright Violations in Asia," *Far Eastern Economic Review,* May 19, 1994, p. 55; "Trade Friction with China Looms despite MFN Sta-

tus," *Wall Street Journal,* May 27, 1994, p. A6; "Trademark Piracy at Home and Abroad," *Wall Street Journal,* May 7, 1991, p. 1B; and "China Inches along Copyright Path," *Financial Times,* June 20, 1991, p. 6.

Chapter 4

Figure 4.2 "Chocoholics Take Note." *New York Times,* May 4, 1998, pp. A1, A15. Copyright © 1998 by The New York Times. Reprinted by permission. **Map 4.1** Data obtained from *1998 Index of Economic Freedom,* The Heritage Foundation. Accessed October 4, 1998. Available World Wide Web: ⟨www.heritage.org⟩. **Figure 4.3** Brzezinski, "For Ukraine the Economic Statistics Lie," Wall Street Journal, May 13, 1996, p. A16. **Table 4.1** *World Development Report* (New York: Oxford University Press for the World Bank, 1997), pp. 214–15. **Table 4.2** *Human Development Report* (New York: Oxford University Press for the United Nations, 1997), pp. 44–45. **Map 4.3** Data obtained from *1998 Human Development Index,* United Nations. Accessed September 10, 1998. Available World Wide Web: ⟨**www.undp.org/undp/hdro/98hdi.htm**⟩. **Figure 4.3** Justin Fox, "The Great Emerging Markets Rip-Off," *Fortune,* May 11, 1998, pp. 98–100+. **Map 4.2** Data obtained from *World Development Report 1997: The State in A Changing World,* (New York: World Bank, 1997), pp. 264–265. **Global Manager:** *Guidelines for Good* **Guanxi** Steve Barth, "Bridge over Troubled (Cultural) Water," *World Trade,* August 1997, pp. 32–33; Michele Marchetti, "Selling in China? Go Slowly," *Sales & Marketing Management,* January 1997, pp. 35–36; Charlene Marmer Solomon, "The Big Question," *Global Workforce,* July 1997, pp. 10–16. **Entrepreneurial Focus:** *Vietnam, Inc.: America's Youth Seek Their Fortunes* Bonnie Rochman, "American Twentysomethings Land in Vietnam," *Fortune,* June 24, 1996, pp. 114–128; Alessandra Bianchi, "Good Morning, Vietnam," *Inc.,* November 1994, p. 37; Michael Paterniti, "The Laptop Colonialists," *The New York Times Magazine,* January 12, 1997, 6, 24:1. **World Business Survey:** *The Pain of Being Set Free,* "Self-Destruction," *The Economist,* August 29, 1998, p. 50. © 1998 The Economist Newspaper Group, Inc. Reprinted with permission. Further reproduction prohibited. **Figures 4.4 and 4.5** Edmund L. Andrews, "German Cut Labor Costs with a Harsh Export: Jobs," *New York Times,* March 21, 1998, pp. A1, A3. **Video Case 4:** *Business Administration, Havana Style* Wall Street Journal Report #701. Gail DeGeorge, "A Touch of Capitalism," *Business Week,* March 17, 1997, pp. 50, 52; William C. Symonds and DeGeorge, "Castro's Capitalist," *Business Week,* March 17, 1997, pp. 48–49; Deroy Murdock, "Cuba: This Island of Lost Potential," *World Trade,* August 1997, pp. 28–31.

Chapter 5

Map 5.1 *World Development Indicators 1998* (Washington, DC: World Bank, March 1998), Table 6.1, pp. 310–312. **Figure 5.1** World Trade Organization, "World Trade Growth Accelerated in 1997, Despite Turmoil in Some Financial Markets" (March 1998). Available World Wide Web: ⟨www.wto/org⟩. **Figure 5.2** *World Development Indicators 1998* (Washington, DC: World Bank, March 1998), p. 191. **Global Manager:** *Five Rules for Building Good Relations in the "Rim" and Beyond* Reprinted from Bradford W. Ketchum, Jr., "Five Rules for Building Good Relations in the 'Rim' and Beyond, *Inc.* [Advertising Supplement], May 20, 1997. **Table 5.1** Adapted from *World Development Indicators 1998* (Washington, DC: World Bank, March 1998), Table 6.3, p. 318. **Figure 5.3** World Trade Organization Web site: ⟨www.wto.org⟩. **Figure 5.4** Adapted from *World Development Indicators 1998* (Washington, DC: World Bank, March 1998), Table 6.3, p. 318. **Figure 5.8** Raymond Vernon and Louis T. Wells, Jr., *The Economic Environment of International Business,* 5e (Upper Saddle River, NJ: Prentice Hall, 1991), p. 85. **Entrepreneurial Focus** *Teaming Up: Prospering from Alliances with Other Entrepreneurs* Adapted from David Carnoy, "Teaming Up: Prospering from Alliances with Other Entrepreneurs," *Success,* April 1997, p. 20. **Figure 5.9** Michael E. Porter, "The Competitive Advantage of Nations," *Harvard Business Review* (March–April 1990), p. 77. Reprinted by permission of Harvard Business Review (Determinants of National Competitive Advantage) for *The Competitive Advantage of Nations* by Michael E. Porter, March-April 1990, Copyright © 1990 by the President and Fellows of Harvard College, all rights reserved. **World Business Survey:** *On Top of the World* "Survey Taiwan: In Praise of Paranoia," *The Economist* (November 7, 1998), p. 6. © 1998 The Economist Newspaper Group, Inc. Reprinted with permission. Further reproduction prohibited. **Map 5.2** *Harvard Business Review* (November–December 1998), p. 82. **In Practice** Adapted from "France Opens Genetic Valley," *World Trade,* March 1999, p. 22. **Business Case 5:** *DHL Express Worldwide: First in Asia and the World* Josephine Bow, "The Fast-Paced World of Asian Express," *Distribution,* February 1996, pp. 44–47; Nagami Kishi and David Russell, *Successful Gaijin in Japan: How Foreign Companies Are Making It in Japan* (Lincolnwood, IL: NTC Business Books, 1996), pp. 315–335; Geoffrey Lee Martin, "Air Cargo Carriers Fight for Global Dominance," *Business Marketing,* August 1995, p. 10; "DHL Scoops Asia's Leading Freight Awards Again." Available World Wide Web: ⟨**www.dhl.com/dhlnews/press_rel_031497.html**⟩.

Chapter 6

Figure 6.1 "Liberalism Lives," *The Economist*, January 2, 1999, p. 59. © 1998 The Economist Newspaper Group, Inc. Reprinted with permission. Further reproduction prohibited. **World Business Survey: To Trade Freely, Or Not to Trade Freely** Adapted from Jackie Calmes, "Despite Buoyant Economic Times Americans Don't Buy Free Trade," *Wall Street Journal*, December 10, 1998, p. A10. Reprinted by permission of the Wall Street Journal, © 1998, Dow Jones & Company, Inc. All rights reserved. **Entrepreneurial Focus: Ex-Im Bank: Experts in Export Financing** Leslie A. Richards and Stephen F. Borde, "International Trade Financing: An Exposition and Update," *Business Credit*, November/December 1996, pp. 19–22. **Global Manager: Surfing the Regulatory Seas** Adapted from Eric J. Adams "Navigating the Regulatory Seas," *World Trade*, September 1996, pp. 44–46; Adams, "More Web Galore: There's No End to Trade-Dedicated Web Sites," *World Trade*, August 1997, pp. 40–42. **Map 6.1** *World Development Indicators 1998* (Washington, DC: The World Bank, 1998), pp. 226–228. **Figure 6.4** World Trade Organization Web site. Available World Wide Web: ⟨**www.wto.org/wto/about/agmnts3.htm**⟩. **Table 6.1** World Trade Organization, "About the WTO." Available World Wide Web: ⟨**www.wto.org**⟩. **Table 6.2** The Economist, November 7, 1998, p. 76. © 1998 the Economist Newspaper Group, Inc. Reprinted with permission. Further reproduction prohibited. **Map 6.3** *World Development Indicators 1998* (Washington, DC: The World Bank, 1998), pp. 146–148. **Figure 6.5** *World Development Indicators 1998* (Washington, DC: The World Bank, 1998), p. 117. **In Practice** Excerpted from "Japan Slammed on Agricultural Trade," *World Trade*, January 1999, p. 26. **Business Case 6: Unfair Protection or Valid Defense?** "Steel at the Core of U.S.- Japan Trade Tensions," World Trade, March 1999, p. 14; "Mexico Widens Anti-dumping Measure, "World Trade, February, 1999, p. 14; "Against Anti-Dumping," the Economist, November 7, 1998, p. 18; "Unfair Protection," the Economist, November 7, 1998, pp. 75–76.

Chapter 7

World Business Survey: Critical M&A Considerations Tim Galpin, "A Meeting of Minds," *Asia Business*, January 1999, pp. 32–34. **Entrepreneurial Focus: Cowboy Candy Rides into Manchuria** Reprinted from Marcus W. Brauchli, "Global Investing: Pick an Instrument: Sweet Dreams," *Wall Street Journal*, June 27, 1996, R, 10:1. **Figure 7.1** "Worldwide Flows of Foreign Direct Investment" 1998 World Development Indicators (Washington D.C.: World Bank, 1998), p. 308. **Map 7.1** 1998 World Development Indicators, (Washington D.C.: World Bank, 1998) Table 6.8, pp.

334–337. **Global Manager: Investing Abroad? Be Prepared for Surprises** Adapted from: Jim Schriner, "Be Prepared for Surprises," *Industry Week*, December 2, 1996, p. 22. **Table 7.1** Survey of Current Business, January 1999 (Washington, D.C.: U.S. Department of Commerce, 1999), p. 12. **Figure 7.2** 1998 World Development Indicators (Washington D.C.: World Bank, 1998), Figure 4–16a, p. 237. **Map 7.2** 1998 World Development Indicators, (Washington, D.C.: World Bank 1998), Table 4.16, pp. 234–236. **In Practice** "Lebanon to Encourage Foreign Investment," *World Trade*, April 1999, pp. 20–22. **Business Case 7: Mercedes Benz: Foot-Loose in Tuscaloosa** Based in part on "Real People, Real Choices," #2, *Custom Videos for Marketing*, Part II. Robert Baxter, Mercedes Benz of North America; Justin Martin, "Mercedes: Made in Alabama," *Fortune*, July 7, 1997, pp. 150–158; Bill Vlasic, "In Alabama, the Soul of a New Mercedes?" *Business Week*, March 31, 1997, pp. 70–71; Brian S. Moskal, "Not the Same Old Mercedes," *Industry Week*, October 7, 1996, pp. 12–21; and "The New Generation," *Industry Week*, October 7, 1996, p. 21.

Chapter 8

Global Manager: The Central American Market: Staying Ahead of the Curve Adapted from Peter Hudson, "Ahead of the Curve," *Business Latin America*, December 2, 1996, pp. 4–5. **World Business Survey: Corruption Perceptions in the FTAA** Adapted from "The Corruption Perceptions Index," *Transparency International*. Available World Wide Web: ⟨**www.transparency.de/documents/cpi/index.html**⟩. **Table 8.1** "European Union Facts and Figures." Available World Wide Web: ⟨**www.eurunion.org/profile/facts.htm**⟩. **Entrepreneurial Focus: The West Africa Enterprise Network: Small Businesses with a Large Mission** Adapted from Michel Courcelle and Anne de Lattre, "The Enterprise Impulse in West Africa," *The OECD Observer*, December 1996/January 1997, pp. 32–34. **In Practice** Douglas Stinson, "Building Blocks," *Latin Trade*, January, 1999, pp. 44–45. **Business Case 8: Tainted Trade: Increasing Imports Brings Increase in Illness** Paul Magnusson, John Carey, and Elisabeth Malkin, "Eating Scared," *Business Week*, September 8, 1997, pp. 30–32; Jeff Gerth and Tim Weiner, "Imports Swamp U.S. Food-Safety Efforts," *New York Times*, September 29, 1997, p. A1; James Bennet, "President Wants F.D.A. to Regulate Foreign Produce," *New York Times*, October 3, 1997, p. A1; Richard A Ryan, "Mom Says NAFTA Is a 'Safety Issue,'" *Detroit News*, September 10, 1997, p. B3; Lawrence K. Altman, "153 Hepatitis Cases Are Traced to Frozen Imported Strawberries," *New York Times*, April 3, 1997, p. A1.

Chapter 9

Entrepreneurial Focus: Where Microcredit Is Due Adapted from Skip Kaltenheuser, "Spearing Loan Sharks," *World Trade*, May 1997, pp. 32–34. **Figure 9.1** Data are for 1997 and were obtained August 30, 1998, from ⟨**www.euromoney.com/contents/data/bondware/bw.97/bw.97.4/bw.97.debt.volcur-qtr4.html**⟩ and ⟨**www.euromoney.com/contents/data/bondware/bw.97/bw.97.4/bw.97.debt.volnat-qtr4.html**⟩. **Figure 9.2** International Finance Corporation, *Emerging Stock Markets Factbook 1998* (Washington, DC: IFC, April 1998), p. 8. **Figure 9.3** Data are for the first three quarters of 1997 and were obtained August 30, 1998, from ⟨**www.euromoney.com/contents/data/bondware/bw.97/bw.97.4/bw.97.equity.volcur-qtr4.html**⟩ and ⟨**www.euromoney.com/contents/data/bondware/bw.97/bw.97.4/bw.97equity.volnat-qtr4.html**⟩. **Figure 9.4** International Finance Corporation, *Emerging Stock Markets Factbook 1998* (Washington, DC: IFC, April 1998), p. 8. **World Business Survey: Ranking the Top Investment Banks** Euromoney, September 1998, p. 225. **Table 9.1** *Wall Street Journal*, October 23, 1998. **Table 9.2** *Wall Street Journal*, October 23, 1998. **World Business Survey: Choosing a Foreign Bank** "Taken Aback by a Leap Forward," *Euromoney*, May 1997, pp. 61–77. **Global Manager: Five Strategies for More Effective Foreign Exchange** Adapted from David Spiselman, *Five Strategies for Saving Money and Improving Control over Foreign Exchange* (San Mateo, CA: Sonnet Financial Inc., 1995), pp. 8–10. **In Practice** Excerpted from Marianne Sullivan, "Further Weakness in Dollar Is Forecast amid Volatility in Currency Markets, *Wall Street Journal* (Foreign Exchange), October 12, 1998, p. C18. **Business Case 9: Hong Kong Handover: "One Country, Two Systems"** ABC Word News Tonight, #970627. John Flinn, "Changeover in Full Flower," *San Francisco Chronicle*, June 29, 1997, p. T5; Mark L. Clifford, "Can China Reform Its Economy?" *Business Week*, September 29, 1997, pp. 116–124; Sara Webb, "World Business: Still on Top," *Wall Street Journal*, September 18, 1997, p. R18; Clifford, "Red Chips Rising," *Business Week*, June 9, 1997, pp. 50–51; "The Hong Kong Handover," *The Economist*, June 28th 1997, pp. 24.

Chapter 10

Figure 10.1 "Exchange Rates of Major World Currencies," Economic Report of the President, 1998. **Global Manager: Exporting Against the Odds: Key Strategies for Success** Louis Uchitelle, "Reconsidering a Trade Equation," *New York Times*, October 31, 1997, pp. D1, D2. **Entrepreneurial Focus: A Single Currency, Ready or Not** Alkman Granitsas and Shada Islam, "Ready or Not," *Far Eastern Economic Review*, October 15, 1998. Internet: Accessed October 13, 1998. Available World Wide Web:

⟨www.feer.com/Restricted/index_air.html⟩; Karen Lowry Miller, "Why Central Europe Loves the Euro," *Business Week*, September 7, 1998, p. 50. **Figure 10.2** "Exchange Rates of Major World Currencies," Economic Report of the President, 1998. **Table 10.1** © 1998 The Economist Newspaper Group, Inc. Reprinted with permission. Further reproduction prohibited. **Figure 10.3** "How Low Can They Go," *World Economic Outlook*, International Monetary Fund, Washington DC, May 1998, p.157. **Figure 10.4** "The Curse of Inflation," *World Economic Outlook*, International Monetary Fund, May 1998, p. 157. **Table 10.2** "Interest Rates Around the World," *International Financial Statistics*, September 1998, (Washington DC: IMF, 1998) pp. 45–46. **Figure 10.5** "Japan Tanken Survey," *The Japan Times Weekly International Edition*, October 12–18, 1998, p. 1. **Figure 10.6** David R. Driscoll, "What Is the International Monetary Fund?" Accessed on-line October 2, 1998, ⟨www.imf.org/external/pubs/ft.what.htm⟩. **Figure 10.7** ibid. **Figure 10.8** Ibid. **Map 10.1** *International Financial Statistics* (Washington, D.C.: International Monetary Fund, August 1998), August 1998), p. 8. **World Business Survey: Pessimism Over Capital Controls** Asian Executives Poll, *Far Eastern Economic Review*, October 1, 1998, p. 39. **In Practice** "The Crisis in South Korea, *The Economist*, August 15, 1998, p. 86 © 1998. The Economist Newspaper Group, Inc. Reprinted with permission. Further reproduction prohibited. **Business Case 10: *World Bank Sees the Value of Forgiveness*** "The World Bank: the Great Experiment," Part 2 of 2, *Films for the Humanities and Sciences* (FFH 6799), Richard W. Stevenson, "Global Banks Offer a First: Forgiveness on Some Debt," *New York Times*, March 12, 1997, p. A5; "When Forgiving Debt Pays Off," *Christian Science Monitor*, April 2, 1997, p. 20; "Debt Relief for Model Countries," *New York Times*, May 1, 1997, p. A26; David Francis, "Rich Nations Look to Ease Debt Burden for Poor," *Christian Science Monitor*, April 30, 1997, p. 8.

Chapter 11

World Business Survey: *Top Global Business Climates* Jack Lyne, "1998's Business Climate Rankings: The Playing Field Levels," *Site Selection*, October/November, 1998. Online. Internet. Accessed 16 January 1999. Available World Wide Web: ⟨www.conway.com/sshighlites/current/9810p884.htm⟩. **Table 11.1** Adapted from C.K. Prahald and Kenneth Lieberthal, "The End of Corporate Imperialism," *Harvard Business Review*, July–August 1998, p. 70. **Map 11.1** Data from *World Development Indicators 1998* (Washington, DC: World Bank, 1998), Table 5.10, pp. 290–292. **Figure 11.2** *Site Selection*, December 1997/January 1998, p. 1122. **In Practice** Excerpted and adapted from "Sweden Concerned at Company Exodus," *World Trade*,

March 1999, pp. 22–23. **Business Case 11: *Revisiting Vietnam*** Samantha Marshall, "Vietnam Pullout: This Time, Investors Pack Up Gear, Stymied by Bureaucracy, Lack of Reforms," *Wall Street Journal*, June 30, 1998, p. A18; Marshall, "P&G Squabbles with Vietnamese Partner," *Wall Street Journal*, February 27, 1998, p. A10; Reginald Chua, "Vietnam Frustrates Foreign Investors as Leaders Waffle on Market Economy," *Wall Street Journal*, November 25, 1996, p. A10; "Vietnam," *The Economist*, July 8, 1995, pp. 1–18 (survey); William J. Ardrey, Anthony Pecotich, and Clifford J. Schultz, "American Involvement in Vietnam, Part II: Prospects for U.S. Business in a New Era," *Business Horizons*, 38 (March/April 1995), pp. 21–27; Edward A. Gargan, "For U.S. Business, a Hard Road to Vietnam," *New York Times*, July 14, 1995, p. C1.

Chapter 12

Figure 12.2 Michael E. Porter, *On Competition* (Boston: Harvard Business School Press, 1998), p. 77. **Entrepreneurial Focus: *Know Yourself, Know Your Product*** Adapted from Davis P. Goodman, "The First Pillar: Assess Your Capabilities," *World Trade*, March 1999, pp. 48–53. **Figure 12.4** Michael E. Porter, *Competitive Strategy* (New York: Free Press, 1980), p. 39. **Global Manager: *Competing with Giants*** Adapted from Niraj Dawar and Tony Frost, "Competing with Giants: Survival Strategies for Local Companies in Emerging Markets," *Harvard Business Review*, March–April 1999, pp. 119–129. **World Business Survey: *By the Numbers*** Adapted from "America vs. The New Europe: By the Numbers" *Fortune*, December 21, 1998, pp. 151–154. **In Practice** Excerpted and adapted from Constance L. Hays, "RJR Nabisco Splits Tobacco Ventures and Food Business," *New York Times*, March 10, 1999, p. A1, C8. **Business Case 12: *The Ikea Key to Pricing*** Julia Flynn and Lori Bongiorno, "Ikea's New Game Plan," *Business Week*, October 6, 1997, pp. 99, 102; Loretta Roach, "Ikea: Furnishing the World," *Discount Merchandiser*, October 1994, pp. 46, 48; "Furnishing the World," *The Economist*, Nov. 19, 1994, pp. 79–80; Jeffrey A. Trachtenberg, "Home Economics: Ikea furniture Chain Pleases with Its Prices, Not with Its Service," *Wall Street Journal*, September 17, 1991, pp. A1, A5; Jack Burton, "Rearranging the Furniture," *International Management*, September 1991, pp. 58–61; Ela Schwartz, "The Swedish Invasion," *Discount Merchandiser*, July 1990, pp. 52, 56; Lisa Marie Petersen, "The 1992 Client Media All-Stars: John Sitnik, "Ikea," *Mediaweek*, December 12, 1992, pp. 25+.

Chapter 13

World Business Survey: Land of Opportunity Martha L. Celestino, "Imports: Selling in the U.S.," *World Trade*, February 1999, pp. 30–32.

Entrepreneurial Focus: *Global Collection Guidelines* Adapted from James Welsh, "Covering Your Bets on Credit and Collections," *World Trade*, February 1999, pp. 28–29. **Figure 13.4** Adapted from Peter J. Buckley and Mark Casson, "A Theory of Cooperation in International Business," in Farok J. Contractor and Peter Lorange (eds.), *Cooperative Strategies in International Business* (Lexington, MA: Lexington Books, 1988), pp. 31–53. **Figure 13.5** *The Economist*, December 21, 1998, Technology and Entertainment Survey, p. 9. © 1998 The Economist Newspaper Group, Inc. Reprinted with permission. Further reproduction prohibited. **Global Manager: *Negotiating the Terms of Market Entry*** Andrew C. Inkpen and Paul W. Beamish, "Knowledge, Bargaining Power, and the Instability of International Joint Ventures," *Academy of Management Review*, vol. 22, no. 1 (1997), pp. 177–202; Arvind V. Phatak and Mohammed M. Habib, "The Dynamics of International Business Negotiations," *Business Horizons*, May–June 1996, pp. 30–38; David K. Tse, June Francis, and Jan Walls, "Cultural Differences in Conducting Intra- and Inter-Cultural Negotiations: A Sino-Canadian Comparison," *Journal of International Business Studies*, vol. 25, no. 3 (1994), pp. 537–555. **Figure 13.6** Franklin R. Root *Entry Strategies for International Markets*, (Lexington, MA: Lexington Books, 1997), p. 18. **In Practice** Excerpted and adapted from Charles Bickers, "Sharing the Pain: Asian Downturn Creates New Partnership," *Far Eastern Economic Review*, October 1. 1998, pp. 79–80. **Business Case 13: *The Brave New World of Telecommunications Joint Ventures*** Barbara Martinez, "Sprint Names Its Long-Distance Chief to Run Loss-Beset Global One Venture," *Wall Street Journal*, February 17, 1998, p. B20; Jennifer L. Schenker and James Pressley, "European Telecom Venture with Sprint Hasn't Become the Bully Some Feared," *Wall Street Journal*, December 23, 1997, p. A11; Alan Cane, "Unisource Partners to Strengthen Ties," *Financial Times*, June 4, 1997, p. 13; Gautam Naik, "Unisource Expected to Merge Operations," *Wall Street Journal*, June 4, 1997, p. B6; Clay Harris, "Complexity Starts at Home," *Financial Times Survey*, October 29, 1996, p. vi.

Chapter 14

Table 14.1 Union Bank of Switzerland. **World Business Survey: *No Common Thread in Expariate Selection*** Global Workforce, July 1998, p. 9. **Global Manager: *This May Come as a Shock to You*** Adrian Furnham and Stephen Bochner, *Culture Shock* (London: Methuen, 1986); Kalervo Oberg, "Culture Shock: Adjustments to New Cultural Environments," *Practical Anthropology*, July–August 1960, pp. 177–82; J.T. Gullahorn and J.E. Gullahorn, "An Extension of the U-Curve Hypothesis," *Journal of Social Sciences*,

January 1963, pp. 34–47; David Stamps, "Welcome to America: Watch Out for Culture Shock," *Training*, November 1996, pp. 22–30; John R. Engen, "Coming Home," *Training*, March 1995, pp. 37–40; and Gary P. Ferraro, *The Cultural Dimension of International Business* (Upper Saddle River, NJ: Prentice Hall, 1994), pp. 145–156. **Box Figure** Stephen P. Robbins, *Organizational Behavior: Concepts, Controversies, Applications*, 7e (Upper Saddle River, NJ: Prentice Hall, 1996), p. 60. **Table 14.2** *Global Workforce*, July 1998, p. 26. **Entrepreneurial Focus:** *Get Global Cash: Overseas Investors Await You* Adapted from Jenny C. McCune, "Get Global Cash," *Success*, December 1995, p. 16. **Map 14.1** International Finance Corporation, *Emerging Stock Markets Factbook 1998* (Washington, DC: IFC, April 1998), pp. 16–17. **Table 14.3** Vikas Nath, "Equity Markets: Emerging Equities Investment Myths," *UBS International Finance* (Zurich: Union Bank of Switzerland, Winter/Spring 1997), pp. 13–16. **In Practice**

"Xerox to Invest in Irish Facilities, World Wide, November 1998, p. 24. **Business Case 14:** *The Fine Line between Expatriation and Discrimination* James Harding, "When Expats Should Pack Their Bags," *Financial Times* September 1, 1998, p. 10; C.K. Prahalad and Kenneth Lieberthal, "The End of Corporate Imperialism," *Harvard Business Review*, July–August 1998, pp. 68–79.

Chapter 15

Global Manager: *Managing an International Sales Force* Adapted from Charlene Marmer Solomon, "Managing an Overseas Sales Force," *World Trade*, Global Sales and Technology Special Section, pp. S4–S6. **Figure 15.1** Adapted from "The World in Figures: Industries, The World in 1999," *The Economist*, 1998 p. 81 **World Business Survey:** *Primed for Online* Adapted from Carol Krol, "Primed for Online," *Advertising Age*, January 4, 1999, pp. 20–21. **Figure 15.2** Adapted from Courtland L. Bovée,

John V. Thill, George P. Dovel, and Marian Burk Wood, *Advertising Excellence* (New York: McGraw-Hill, 1995), p. 14. **Entrepreneurial Focus:** *Linking TQM and ISO 9000 Standards* Adapted from G.K. Kanji, "An Innovative Approach to Make ISO 9000 Standards More Effective," *Total Quality Management*, February 1998, pp. 67–79. **Business Case 15:** *TPS: The Benchmark in Production Efficiency* Ranganath Nayak and John M. Ketteringham, *Breakthroughs!* (San Diego, CA: Pfeiffer & Company, 1994), Chap. 9; Micheline Maynard, "Camry Assembly Line Delivers New Minivan," *USA Today* (August 11, 1997), p. 3B; William Greider, *One World, Ready or Not: The Manic Logic of Global Capitalism* (New York, NY: Simon & Schuster, 1997), Chapter 6 "*Jidoka.*" **In Practice** Excerpted and adapted from Pichayaporn Utumporn, "Ad with Hitler Causes Furor in Thailand," *Wall Street Journal*, June 5, 1998, p. B8.

PHOTO CREDITS

Chapter 1
Page 3 Poriaman Sitanggang/Poriaman Photography Page 8 Maria Dumla/Impact Visuals Photo & Graphics, Inc. Page 12 John Maier Jr./The Image Works

Chapter 2
Page 41 Emmanuel Dunand/AFP/Agence France-Presse Page 47 Fritz Hoffmann/Network Photographers Page 49 Grochiowiak/Sygma Page 56 Chris Brown/SABA Press Photos, Inc. Page 62 Alan O'Connor

Chapter 3
Page 77 Michel Lipchitz/AP/Wide World Photos Page 80 James McGoon/James McGoon Photography Page 88 SABA Press Photos, Inc. Page 89 Chris Brown/SABA Press Photos, Inc. Page 96 Andy Johnstone/Impact Photos Page 97 Ki Ho Park/Kistone Photography

Chapter 4
Page 115 G. Paul Burnett/New York Pictures Page 115 Xinhua News Agency Page 121 Francois Mori/AP/Wide World Photos Page 135 Paul Hu/Assignment Asia Ltd. Page 135 Fritz Hoffmann Page 137 Greg Girard/Contact Press Images Inc. Page 139 Fritz Hoffmann

Chapter 5
Page 155 Ron Haviv/SABA Press Photos, Inc. Page 160 Archive Photos Page 174 Fuji Fotos/Impact Visuals Photo & Graphics, Inc.

Chapter 6
Page 185 James Leynse/Rea/SABA Press Photos, Inc. Page 188 Alex Quesada/Matrix International, Inc. Page 199 Horacio Paone/Horacio Paone Page 202 Jeffrey Aaronson/Network Aspen

Chapter 7
Page 221 Boeing Commercial Airplane Group Page 236 Richard Nowitz Photograph Page 237 Aslan/Barthelemy/Niviere/Roussier/SIPA Press Page 243 David Portnoy/AP/Wide World Photos

Chapter 8
Page 255 Alro Exportaciones S. A. De C. V. Page 259 AP/Wide World Photos Page 266 Chamussy/SIPA Press Page 269 Jose Luis Magana/AP/Wide World Photos Page 280 Peter Charlesworth/SABA Press Photos, Inc.

Chapter 9
Page 293 John Giordano/SABA Press Photos, Inc. Page 297 Tom Wagner/SABA Press Photos, Inc. Page 307 Patrick de Noirmont/Archive Photos Page 317 Tom Wagner/SABA Press Photos, Inc. Page 319 Kistone Photography

Chapter 10
Page 327 Jack Link's Snack Foods Page 330 Dario Lopez-Mills/AP/Wide World Photos Page 335 Laski Diffusion/Liaison Agency, Inc. Page 337 Wolf/Visum/SABA Press Photos, Inc. Page 341 Peter Blakely/SABA Press Photos, Inc. Page 345 AP/Wide World Photos/ Page 355 Youn-Kong/Agence France-Presse

Chapter 11
Page 369 Greg Baker/AP/Wide World Photos Page 382 Jeffrey Aaronson/Network Aspen Page 375 Earl Kowall/Corbis Page 377 Charles Dharapak/AP/Wide World Photos Page 397 Ilkka Uimonen/Sygma

Chapter 12
Page 407 Peter Korniss/Black Star Page 410 Michael L. Abramson Photography Page 414 Vincent Yu/AP/Wide World Photos Page 417 AP/Wide World Photos Page 419 Larry Davis/New York Times Pictures

Chapter 13
Page 442 Vellus Products, Inc. Page 460 Dreieich/Sprendlingen/Ulrike Welsch Photography Page 461 Aral/SIPA Press Page 464 Reuters/Kevin Lamarque/Archive Photos Page 469 Alex Quesada/Matrix International, Inc.

Chapter 14
Page 479 James Schneph/Liaison Agency, Inc. Page 482 Dilip Mehta/Contact Press Images Inc. Page 485 Pablo Bartholomew/Liaison Agency, Inc. Page 490 Hewlett-Packard Company Page 499 Dilip Mehta/Contact Press Images Inc. Page 505 William Strode/Woodfin Camp & Associates

Chapter 15
Page 513 Adrian Bradshaw/SABA Press Photos, Inc. Page 517 REUTERS/Will Burgess/Archive Photos Page 521 Tsugufumi Matsumoto/AP/Wide World Photos Page 526 Luca Bruno/AP/Wide World Photos Page 534 Heinz Ducklau/AP/Wide World Photos

Cover
Kan/Watson & Spierman Productions, Inc.

GLOSSARY

absolute advantage Ability of a nation to produce a good more efficiently than any other nation.

ad valorem tariff Tariff levied as a percentage of the stated price of an imported product.

administrative delays Regulatory controls or bureaucratic rules designed to impair the rapid flow of imports into a country.

advance payment Export/import financing in which an importer pays an exporter for merchandise before it is shipped.

aesthetics What a culture considers to be in "good taste" in the arts, the imagery evoked by certain expressions, and the symbolism of certain colors.

agents Individuals or organizations that represent one or more indirect exporters in a target market.

American Depository Receipt (ADR) Certificate that trades in the United States and represents a specific number of shares in a non-U.S. company.

antidumping duty Additional tariff placed on an imported product that a nation believes is being dumped on its market.

antitrust laws Laws designed to prevent companies from fixing prices, sharing markets, and gaining unfair monopoly advantages.

arm's-length price Free-market price that unrelated parties charge one another for a specific product.

attitudes Positive or negative evaluations, feelings, and tendencies that individuals harbor toward objects or concepts.

back-to-back loan Loan in which a parent company deposits money with a host-country bank, which then lends it to a subsidiary located in the host country.

balance of payments A national accounting system that records all payments to entities in other countries and all receipts coming into the nation.

Bank for International Settlements (BIS) International banking institution serving national central banks around the world and helping to stabilize the international monetary system.

barter Exchange of goods or services directly for other goods or services without the use of money.

base currency In a quoted exchange rate, the currency that is to be purchased with another currency.

bearer bond Bond that comes with coupons entitling the bearer of each coupon to collect each interest payment.

Berne Convention International treaty protecting copyrights.

bill of lading Contract between an exporter and a shipper that specifies merchandise destination and shipping costs.

bond Debt instrument specifying the timing of principal and interest payments.

brain drain Departure of highly educated people from one profession, geographic region, or nation to another.

brand name Name of one or more items in a product line that identifies the source or character of the items.

Bretton Woods Agreement Agreement (1944) among nations to create a new international monetary system based on the value of the U.S. dollar.

buyback Export of industrial equipment in return for products produced by that equipment.

capacity planning Process of assessing a company's ability to produce enough output to satisfy market demand.

capital account A national account that records transactions involving the purchase or sale of assets.

capital market System that allocates financial resources in the form of debt and equity according to their most efficient uses.

capital structure Mix of equity, debt, and internally generated funds used to finance a company's activities.

capitalism The belief that ownership of the means of production belongs in the hands of individuals and private businesses.

caste system System of social stratification in which people are born into a social ranking, or *caste*, with no opportunity for social mobility.

centrally planned economy Economic system in which a nation's land, factories, and other economic resources are owned by the government which plans nearly all economic activity.

chains of command Lines of authority that run from top management to individual employees and specify internal reporting relationships.

civil law Legal system based on a detailed set of written rules and statutes that constitute a legal code.

class system System of social stratification in which personal ability and actions decide social status and mobility.

clearing Process of aggregating the currencies that one bank owes another and then carrying out the transaction.

climate Weather conditions of a geographic region.

combination strategy Strategy designed to mix growth, retrenchment, and stability strategies across a corporation's business units.

common market Economic integration whereby countries remove all barriers to trade *and* the movement of labor and capital between themselves but erect a common trade policy against nonmembers.

commonn law Legal system based on a country's legal history (tradition), past cases that have come before its courts (precedent), and the ways in which laws are applied in specific situations (usage).

communication System of conveying thoughts, feelings, knowledge, and information to others through speech, actions, and writing.

communism The belief that social and economic equality can be obtained only by establishing an all-powerful Communist Party and by granting the government ownership and control over all types of economic activity.

comparative advantage Inability of a nation to produce a good more efficiently than other nations, but an ability to produce that good more efficiently than it does any other good.

compound tariff Tariff levied on an imported product and calculated partly as a percentage of its stated price, and partly as a specific fee for each unit.

confiscation Forced transfer of assets from a company to the government without compensation.

consumer panel Research in which people record in personal diaries, information on their attitudes, behaviors, or purchasing habits.

convertible currency (or **hard currency**) Currency that trades freely in the foreign exchange market, with its price determined by the forces of supply and demand.

copyright Property right giving creators of original works the freedom to publish or dispose of them as they choose.

core competency Special company ability that competitors find extremely difficult or impossible to equal.

counterpurchase Sale of goods and services to a country by a company that promises to make a future purchase of a specific product from the country.

countertrade Practice of selling goods or services that are paid for, in whole or part, with other goods or services.

countervailing duty Additional tariff placed on an imported product that a nation believes is receiving an unfair subsidy.

cross licensing Practice by which companies employ licensing agreements to exchange intangible property with one another.

cross rate Exchange rate calculated using two other exchange rates.

cross-functional team Team that is composed of employees who work at similar levels in different functional departments.

cultural diffusion Process whereby cultural traits spread from one culture to another.

cultural imperialism Replacement of one culture's traditions, folk heroes, and artifacts with substitutes from another.

cultural literacy Detailed knowledge about a culture that enables people to live and work within it.

cultural trait Anything that represents a culture's way of life, including gestures, material objects, traditions, and concepts.

culture shock Psychological process affecting people living abroad that is characterized by homesickness, irritability, confusion, aggravation, and depression.

culture Set of values, beliefs, rules, and institutions held by a specific group of people.

currency arbitrage Instantaneous purchase and sale of a currency in different markets for profit.

currency controls Restrictions on the convertibility of a currency into other currencies.

currency futures contract Contract requiring the exchange of a specific amount of currency on a specific date at a specific exchange rate, with all conditions fixed and not adjustable.

currency hedging Practice of insuring against potential losses that result from adverse changes in exchange rates.

currency option Right, or option, to exchange a specific amount of a currency on a specific date at a specific rate.

currency speculation Purchase or sale of a currency with the expectation that its value will change and generate a profit.

currency swap Simultaneous purchase and sale of foreign exchange for two different dates.

current account deficit When a country imports more goods, services, and income than it exports (also called a trade deficit).

current account surplus When a country exports more goods, services, and income than it imports (also called a trade surplus).

current account A national account that records transactions involving the import and export of goods and services, income receipts on assets abroad, and income payments on foreign assets inside the country.

customs union Economic integration whereby countries remove all barriers to trade between themselves but erect a common trade policy against nonmembers.

customs Habits or ways of behaving in specific circumstances that are passed down through generations in a culture.

debt Loans in which the borrower promises to repay the borrowed amount (the principal) plus a predetermined rate of interest.

demand Quantity of a good or service that buyers are willing to purchase at a specific selling price.

democracy Political system in which government leaders are elected directly by the wide participation of the people or by their representatives.

derivative Financial instrument whose value derives from other commodities or financial instruments.

devaluation Intentional lowering of the value of a nation's currency.

developed country Country that is highly industrialized, highly efficient, and whose people enjoy a high quality of life.

developing country (also called *less developed country*) Nation that has a poor infrastructure and extremely low personal incomes.

differentiation strategy Strategy in which a company designs its products to be perceived as unique by buyers throughout its industry.

direct exporting Practice by which a company sells its products directly to buyers in a target market.

discount rate Financial rate of return offered by comparable investment alternatives.

distribution Planning, implementing, and controlling the physical flow of a product from its point of origin to its point of consumption.

documentary collection Export/import financing in which a bank acts as an intermediary without accepting financial risk.

draft (or **bill of exchange**) Document ordering an importer to pay an exporter a specified sum of money at a specified time.

dual pricing Policy in which a product has a different selling price (typically higher) in export markets than it has in the home market.

dumping Practice of exporting a product at a price lower than the price that the product normally commands in the domestic market.

eclectic theory Theory stating that firms undertake foreign direct investment when the features of a particular location combine with ownership and internalization advantages to make a location appealing for investment.

economic development Measure for gauging the economic well-being of one nation's people, as compared to that of another nation's people.

economic system Structure and processes that a country uses to allocate its resources and conduct its commercial activities.

economic transition Process by which a nation changes its fundamental economic organization and creates new free-market institutions.

economic union Economic integration whereby countries remove barriers to trade and the movement of labor and capital, erect a common trade policy against nonmembers, *and* coordinate their economic policies.

efficient market view View that prices of financial instruments reflect all publicly available information at any given time.

embargo Complete ban on trade (imports and exports) in one or more products with a particular country.

emerging markets Newly industrialized countries plus those with the potential to become newly industrialized.

entry mode Institutional arrangement by which a firm gets its products, technologies, human skills, or other resources into a market.

environmental scanning Ongoing process of gathering, analyzing, and dispensing information for tactical or strategic purposes.

equity Part ownership of a company in which the equity holder participates with other part owners in the company's financial gains and losses.

ethical behavior Personal behavior that is in accordance with rules or standards for right conduct or morality.

ethnocentric staffing Staffing policy in which operations outside the home country are managed by individuals from the home country.

ethnocentricity Belief that one's own ethnic group or culture is superior to that of others.

Eurobond Bond issued outside the country in whose currency it is denominated.

Eurocurrency market Market consisting of all the world's currencies (referred to as *Eurocurrency*) that are banked outside their countries of origin.

European monetary system (EMS) System designed to manage exchange rates among European Union countries.

European monetary union European Union plan establishing its own central bank and currency as of January 1999.

exchange rate risk (or **foreign exchange risk**) Risk of adverse changes in exchange rates.

exchange rate Rate at which one currency is exchanged for another.

exchange-rate mechanism (ERM) Mechanism limiting the fluctuations of European Union members' currencies within a specified trading range.

exclusive channel Distribution channel in which a manufacturer grants the right to sell its product to only one or a limited number of resellers.

expatriates Citizens of one country who are living and working in another.

export management company (EMC) Company that exports products on behalf of indirect exporters.

export trading company (ETC) Company that provides services to indirect exporters in addition to those activities directly related to clients' exporting activities.

exports All goods and services sent from one country to other nations.

expropriation Forced transfer of assets from a company to the government with compensation.

facilities layout planning Deciding the spatial arrangement of production processes within production facilities.

facilities location planning Selecting the location for production facilities.

factor proportions theory Trade theory holding that countries produce and export goods that require resources (factors) that are abundant and import goods that require resources in short supply.

first-mover advantage Economic and strategic advantage gained by being the first company to enter an industry.

Fisher effect Principle that the nominal interest rate is the sum of the real interest rate and the expected rate of inflation over a specific time period.

fixed (or **tangible**) **assets** Company assets, such as production facilities, inventory warehouses, retail outlets, and production and office equipment.

fixed exchange-rate system System in which the exchange rate for converting one currency into another is fixed by international agreement.

focus group Unstructured but in-depth interview of a small group of individuals (8 to 12 people) by a moderator to learn the group's attitudes about a company or its product.

focus strategy Strategy in which a company focuses on serving the needs of a narrowly defined market segment by being the low-cost leader, by differentiating its product, or both.

folk custom Behavior, often dating back several generations, that is practiced within a homogeneous group of people.

foreign bond Bond sold outside the borrower's country and denominated in the currency of the country in which it is sold.

Foreign Corrupt Practices Act (FCPA) 1977 statute forbidding U.S. companies from bribing government officials or political candidates in other nations.

foreign exchange market Market in which currencies are bought and sold and in which currency prices are determined.

foreign trade zone (FTZ) Designated geographic region in which merchandise is allowed to pass through with lower customs duties (taxes) and/or fewer customs procedures.

forward contract Contract requiring the exchange of an agreed-upon amount of a currency on an agreed-upon date at a specific exchange rate.

forward market Market for currency transactions at forward rates.

forward rate Exchange rate at which two parties agree to exchange currencies on a specified future date.

franchising Practice by which one company (the *franchiser*) supplies another (the *franchisee*) with intangible property and other assistance over an extended period.

free float system Exchange-rate system in which currencies float freely against one another, without governments intervening in currency markets.

free trade area Economic integration whereby countries remove all barriers to trade between themselves but each country determines its own barriers against nonmembers.

free trade Pattern of imports and exports that would result in the absence of trade barriers.

freight forwarder Specialist in such export-related activities as customs clearing, tariff schedules, and shipping and insurance fees.

fundamental analysis Technique using statistical models based on fundamental economic indicators to forecast exchange rates.

fundamental disequilibrium Economic condition in which a trade deficit causes a permanent negative shift in a country's balance of payments.

General Agreement on Tariffs and Trade (GATT) Treaty that was designed to promote free trade by reducing both tariff and nontariff barriers to international trade.

geocentric staffing Staffing policy in which operations outside the home country are managed by the best-qualified individuals regardless of nationality.

global matrix structure Organizational structure that splits the chain of command between product and area divisions.

global product structure Organizational structure that divides worldwide operations according to a company's product areas.

global strategy Offering the same products using the same marketing strategy in all national markets.

global team Team of top managers from both headquarters and international subsidiaries who meet to develop solutions to company-wide problems.

globalization Process involving the integration of national economies.

GNP or GDP per capita Nation's GNP or GDP divided by its population.

gold standard International monetary system in which nations linked the value of their paper currencies to specific values of gold.

gross domestic product (GDP) Value of all goods and services produced by a country's domestic economy over a one-year period.

gross national product (GNP) Value of all goods and services produced by a country during a one-year period, including income generated by both domestic and international activities.

group-oriented culture Culture in which the group shares responsibility for the well-being of each member.

growth strategy Strategy designed to increase the scale (*size* of activities) or scope (*kinds* of activities) of a corporation's operations.

Hofstede framework Framework for studying cultural differences along four dimensions, such as individualism versus collectivism and power distance.

human development index (HDI) Measure of the extent to which a government satisfies its people's needs and the extent to which these needs are addressed equally across a nation's entire population.

human resource management (HRM) Process of staffing a company and ensuring that employees are as productive as possible.

human resource planning Process of forecasting both a company's human resource needs and supply.

imports All goods and services brought into a country that were purchased from organizations located in other countries.

income elasticity Sensitivity of demand for a product relative to changes in income.

indirect exporting Practice by which a company sells its products to intermediaries who resell to buyers in a target market.

individual-oriented culture Culture in which each individual tends to be responsible for his or her own well-being.

industrial property Patents and trademarks.

inefficient market view View that prices of financial instruments do not reflect all publicly available information.

intellectual property Property that results from people's intellectual talent and abilities.

intensive channel Distribution channel in which a producer grants the right to sell its product to many resellers.

interbank interest rates Interest rates that the world's largest banks charge one another for loans.

interbank market Market in which the world's largest banks exchange currencies at spot and forward rates.

interest arbitrage Profit-motivated purchase and sale of interest-paying securities denominated in different currencies.

international area structure Organizational structure that organizes a company's entire global operations into countries or geographic regions.

international bond market Market consisting of all bonds sold by issuing companies, governments, or other organizations outside their own countries.

international business Total of all business transactions that cross the borders of two or more nations.

international capital market Network of individuals, companies, financial institutions, and governments that invest and borrow across national boundaries.

international company Business that engages directly in any form of international business activity.

international division structure Organizational structure that separates domestic from international business activities by creating a separate international division with its own manager.

international equity market Market consisting of all stocks bought and sold outside the issuer's home country.

international Fisher effect Principle that a difference in nominal interest rates supported by two countries' currencies will cause an equal but opposite change in their spot exchange rates.

International Monetary Fund (IMF) Agency created by the Bretton Woods Agreement to regulate fixed exchange rates and enforce the rules of the international monetary system.

international monetary system Collection of agreements and institutions governing exchange rates.

international trade Purchase, sale, or exchange of goods and services across national borders.

Jamaica Agreement Agreement (1976) among IMF members to formalize the existing system of floating exchange rates as the new international monetary system.

joint venture Separate company that is created and jointly owned by two or more independent entities to achieve a common business objective.

just-in-time (JIT) manufacturing Production technique in which inventory is kept to a minimum and inputs to the production process arrive exactly when they are needed (or *just in time*).

Kluckhohn-Strodtbeck framework Framework for studying cultural differences along six dimensions, such as focus on past or future events and belief in individual or group responsibility for personal well-being.

labor-management relations Positive or negative condition of relations between company management and its workers.

law of one price Principle that an identical item must have an identical price in all countries when price is expressed in the same currency.

legal system Set of laws and regulations, including the processes by which a country's laws are enacted and enforced and the ways in which its courts hold parties accountable for their actions.

letter of credit Export/import financing in which the importer's bank issues a document stating that the bank will pay the exporter when the exporter fulfills the terms of the document.

licensing Practice by which one company owning intangible property (the *licensor*) grants another firm (the *licensee*) the right to use that property for a specified period of time.

lingua franca Third or "link" language that is understood by two parties who speak different languages.

liquidity Ease with which bondholders and shareholders may convert their investments into cash.

lobbying Policy of hiring people to represent a company's views on political matters.

location economies Economic benefits derived from locating production activities in optimal locations.

logistics Management of the physical flow of products from point of origin as raw materials to end users as finished products.

Louvre Accord Agreement (1987) among the G7 nations affirming that the U.S. dollar was appropriately valued and that they would intervene in currency markets to maintain its current market value.

low-cost leadership strategy Strategy in which a company exploits economies of scale to have the lowest cost structure of any competitor in its industry.

make-or-buy decision Deciding whether to make a component or buy it from another company.

managed float system Exchange-rate system in which currencies float against one another, with governments intervening to stabilize their currencies at particular target exchange rates.

management contract Practice by which one company supplies another with managerial expertise for a specific period of time.

manners Appropriate ways of behaving, speaking, and dressing in a culture.

market economy Economic system in which the majority of a nation's land, factories, and other economic resources are privately owned, whether by individuals or businesses.

market imperfections Theory stating that when an imperfection in the market makes a transaction less efficient than it could be, a company will undertake foreign direct investment to internalize the transaction and thereby remove the imperfection.

market power Theory stating that a firm tries to establish a dominant market presence in an industry by undertaking foreign direct investment.

market research Collection and analysis of information in order to assist managers in making informed decisions.

marketing communication Process of sending promotional messages about products to target markets.

material culture All the technology employed in a culture to manufacture goods and provide services.

mercantilism Trade theory holding that nations should accumulate financial wealth, usually in the form of gold, by encouraging exports and discouraging imports.

mission statement Written statement of why a company exists and what it plans to accomplish.

mixed economy Economic system in which land, factories, and other economic resources are more equally split between private and government ownership.

multinational (*multidomestic*) strategy Adapting products and their marketing strategies in each national market to suit local preferences.

multinational corporation (MNC) Business that has direct investments abroad in several or more countries.

national competitive advantage theory Trade theory holding that a nation's competitiveness in an industry depends on the capacity of the industry to innovate and upgrade.

nationalism Devotion of a people to their nation's interests and advancement.

nationalization Government takeover of an entire industry.

natural resources Products from nature that are economically or technologically useful.

net present value   Present value of the future cash flows a project generates minus the amount of the initial investment.

new trade theory   Trade theory holding that (1) there are gains to be had from specialization and increasing economies of scale, (2) those companies first to market can create barriers to entry, and (3) government may have a role to play in assisting its home companies.

newly industrialized country (NIC)   Country that has recently increased the portion of its national production and exports derived from industrial operations.

normal trade relations   (formerly **most-favored nation status**)   Requirement that GATT (and WTO) members extend the same favorable terms of trade to all members that they extend to any single member.

offset   Agreement that a company will offset a hard-currency sale to a nation by making a hard-currency purchase of an unspecified product from that nation in the future.

offshore financial center   Country or territory whose financial sector features very few regulations and few, if any, taxes.

open account   Export/import financing in which an exporter ships merchandise and later bills the importer for its value.

organizational structure   Way in which a company divides its activities among separate units and coordinates activities between those units.

outsourcing   Practice of buying from another company a good or service that is not central to a company's competitive advantage.

over-the-counter (OTC) market   Exchange consisting of a global computer network of foreign exchange traders and other market participants.

patent   Property right granted to the inventor of a product or process that excludes others from making, using, or selling the invention.

planning   Process of identifying and selecting an organization's objectives and deciding how the organization will achieve those objectives.

Plaza Accord   Agreement (1985) among the G5 nations to act together in forcing down the value of the U.S. dollar.

political risk   Likelihood that a government or society will undergo political changes that negatively affect local business activity.

political system   Structures, processes, and activities by which a nation governs itself.

political union   Economic and political integration whereby countries coordinate aspects of their economic *and* political systems.

polycentric staffing   Staffing policy in which operations outside the home country are managed by individuals from the host country.

popular custom   Behavior shared by a heterogeneous group or by several groups.

portfolio investment   Investment that does not involve obtaining a degree of control in a company.

present value   Value today of an expected future cash flow.

price controls   Upper or lower limits placed on the prices of products sold within a country.

primary market research   Process of collecting and analyzing original data and applying the results to current research needs.

private sector   Segment of the economic environment comprised of independently owned firms that exist to make a profit.

privatization   Policy of selling government-owned economic resources to private companies and individuals.

process planning   Deciding the process that a company will use to create its product.

product liability   Responsibility of manufacturers, sellers, and others for damage, injury, or death caused by defective products.

promotion mix   Efforts by a company to reach distribution channels and target customers through communications such as personal selling, advertising, public relations, and direct marketing.

property rights   Legal rights to resources and any income they generate.

pull strategy   Promotional strategy designed to create buyer demand that will encourage channel members to stock a company's product.

purchasing power parity (PPP)   Relative ability of two countries' currencies to buy the same ``basket'' of goods in those two countries.

purchasing power   Value of goods and services that can be purchased with one unit of a country's currency.

push strategy   Promotional strategy designed to pressure channel members to carry a product and promote it to final users of the product.

quota   Restriction on the amount (measured in units or weight) of a good that can enter or leave a country during a certain period of time.

quoted currency   In a quoted exchange rate, the currency with which another currency is to be purchased.

rationalized production   System of production in which each of a product's components are produced where the cost of producing that component is lowest.

recruitment   Process of identifying and attracting a qualified pool of applicants for vacant positions.

regional economic integration   Process whereby countries in a geographic region cooperate with one another to reduce or eliminate barriers to the international flow of products, people, or capital.

regional trading bloc   Group of nations in a geographic region undergoing economic integration.

registered bond   Bond that makes scheduled interest payments only to the individual registered as its owner.

representative democracy   Democracy in which citizens nominate individuals from their groups to represent their political needs and views.

retrenchment strategy   Strategy designed to reduce the scale or scope of a corporation's businesses.

return on investment (ROI)   Discounted income an investment generates divided by its cost.

revaluation   Intentional raising of the value of a nation's currency.

revenue   Monies earned from the sale of goods and services.

reverse culture shock   Psychological process of readapting to one's home culture.

secondary market research   Process of obtaining information that already exists within the company or that can be obtained from outside sources.

secular totalitarianism   Political system in which leaders rely on military and bureaucratic power.

securities exchange   Exchange specializing in currency futures and options transactions.

securitization   Unbundling and repackaging of hard-to-trade financial assets into more liquid, negotiable, and marketable financial instruments (or *securities*).

selection   Process of screening and hiring the best-qualified applicants with the greatest performance potential.

self-managed team   Team in which employees from a single department take on responsibilities of their former supervisors.

Smithsonian Agreement   Agreement (1971) among IMF members to restructure and strengthen the international monetary system created at Bretton Woods.

social group   Collection of two or more people who identify and interact with one another.

social mobility   Ease with which individuals can move up or down a culture's social ladder.

social responsibility   Practice of companies going beyond legal obligations to actively balance commitments to investors, customers, other companies, and communities.

social stratification   Process of ranking people into social layers or classes.

social structure   A culture's fundamental organization, including its groups and institutions, its system of social positions and their relationships, and the process by which its resources are distributed.

socialism The belief that social and economic equality is obtained through government ownership and regulation of the means of production.

special drawing right (SDR) IMF asset whose value is based on a "weighted basket" of the currencies of five industrialized countries.

specific tariff Tariff levied as a specific fee for each unit (measured by number, weight, etc.) of an imported product.

spot market Market for currency transactions at spot rates.

spot rate Exchange rate requiring delivery of the traded currency within two business days.

stability strategy Strategy designed to guard against change and used by corporations to avoid either growth or retrenchment.

staffing policy Customary means by which a company staffs its offices.

stakeholders All parties, ranging from suppliers and employees to stockholders and consumers, who are affected by a company's activities.

stock Shares of ownership in a company's assets that give shareholders a claim on the company's future cash flows.

strategic alliance Relationship whereby two or more entities cooperate (but do not form a separate company) to achieve the strategic goals of each.

strategy Set of planned actions taken by managers to help a company meet its objectives.

subculture Group of people who share a unique way of life within a larger, dominant culture.

subsidy Financial assistance to domestic producers in the form of cash payments, low-interest loans, tax breaks, product price supports, or some other form.

supply Quantity of a good or service that producers are willing to provide at a specific selling price.

survey Research in which an interviewer has current or potential buyers answer written or verbal questions to obtain facts, opinions, or attitudes.

switch trading Practice in which one company sells to another its obligation to make a purchase in a given country.

tariff-quota Lower tariff rate for a certain quantity of imports and a higher rate for quantities that exceed the quota.

tariff Government tax levied on a product as it enters or leaves a country.

technical analysis Technique using charts of past trends in currency prices and other factors to forecast exchange rates.

technological dualism Use of the latest technologies in some sectors of the economy coupled with the use of outdated technologies in other sectors.

theocracy Political system in which a country's political leaders are religious leaders who enforce laws and regulations based on religious beliefs.

theocratic law Legal system based on religious teachings.

theocratic totalitarianism Political system in which religious leaders govern without the support of the people and do not tolerate opposing viewpoints.

topography All the physical features that characterize the surface of a geographic region.

total quality management (TQM) Emphasis on continuous quality improvement to meet or exceed customer expectations involving a company-wide commitment to quality-enhancing processes.

totalitarian system Political system in which individuals govern without the support of the people, government maintains control over many aspects of people's lives, and lenders do not tolerate opposing viewpoints.

trade creation Increase in level of trade between nations that results from regional economic integration.

trade deficit Condition that results when the value of a country's imports is greater than the value of its exports.

trade diversion Diversion of trade away from nations not belonging to a trading bloc and toward member nations.

trade mission International trip by government officials and businesspeople that is organized by agencies of national or provincial governments for the purpose of exploring international business opportunities.

trade show Exhibition at which members of an industry or group of industries showcase their latest products, see what rivals are doing, and learn about recent trends and opportunities.

trade surplus Condition that results when the value of a nation's exports is greater than the value of its imports.

trademark Property right in the form of words or symbols distinguishing a product and its manufacturer.

transfer price Price charged for a good or service transferred among a company and its subsidiaries.

turnkey (or *build-operate-transfer*) project Practice by which one company designs, constructs, and tests a production facility for a client firm.

United Nations (U.N.) International organization formed after World War II to provide leadership in fostering peace and stability around the world.

unspoken language Language communicated through unspoken cues, including hand gestures, facial expressions, physical greetings, eye contact, and the manipulation of personal space.

value added tax (VAT) Tax levied on each party that adds value to a product throughout its production and distribution.

value chain analysis Process of dividing a company's activities into primary and support activities and identifying those that create value for customers.

value density Value of a product relative to its weight and volume.

values Ideas, beliefs, and customs to which people are emotionally attached.

vehicle currency Currency used as an intermediary to convert funds between two other currencies.

venture capital Financing obtained from investors who believe that the borrower will experience rapid growth and who receive equity—part ownership—in return.

vertical integration Extension of company activities into stages of production that provide a firm's inputs (*backward integration*) or absorb its output (*forward integration*).

voluntary export restraint (VER) Unique version of export quota that a nation imposes on its exports usually at the request of an importing nation.

wholly owned subsidiary Facility entirely owned and controlled by a single parent company.

World Bank (International Bank for Reconstruction and Development, or IBRD) Agency created by the Bretton Woods Agreement to provide funding for national economic development efforts.

World Trade Organization (WTO) Only international organization regulating trade between nations.

worldwide pricing Policy in which one selling price is established for all international markets.

List of Maps